TRIUMPH OVER ODDS

TRIUMPH OVER ODDS

An Anthology of Man's Unconquerable Spirit

Edited with a Foreword and Introductory Notes

By J. DONALD ADAMS

DUELL, SLOAN AND PEARCE

New York

First Edition

LIBRARY OF CONGRESS CATALOG CARD NUMBER: 57-7568

MANUFACTURED IN THE UNITED STATES OF AMERICA

VAN REES PRESS • NEW YORK

For Jaqueline

Acknowledgments

For permission to use the following copyright material, acknowledgment is gratefully made:

APPLETON-CENTURY-CROFTS, INC. for a passage from *And How to Live* by Betsey Barton, copyright 1944 by Betsey Barton;

IULIA DE BEAUSOBRE for a passage from *The Woman Who Could Not Die* by Iulia de Beausobre, published by the Viking Press, copyright 1948;

JONATHAN CAPE, LTD. and the TRUSTEES OF THE T. E. LAWRENCE ESTATE for passages from *Seven Pillars of Wisdom* by T. E. Lawrence, copyright 1926, 1935, by Doubleday, Doran and Company;

DODD, MEAD AND COMPANY for passages from *Scott's Last Expedition,* copyright 1913, 1941, by Dodd, Mead and Company;

DOUBLEDAY AND COMPANY for a passage from *Anne Frank: Diary of a Young Girl,* copyright 1952 by Otto H. Frank, copyright 1952 by the American Jewish Committee;

DUELL, SLOAN & PEARCE, INC. for a passage from *Rescue!* by Elliott Arnold, copyright 1956 by Elliott Arnold; and for passages from *The Power Within Us* by Haniel Long, copyright 1936-1939, 1944, by Haniel Long;

E. P. DUTTON AND COMPANY for a passage from *Days of the Phoenix* by Van Wyck Brooks, copyright 1957 by Van Wyck Brooks; for a selection from *New England: Indian Summer,* copyright 1940, 1950, by Van Wyck Brooks; and for passages from *Annapurna* by Maurice Herzog, copyright 1952 by E. P. Dutton and Company;

MAX EASTMAN and *The Vineyard Gazette* for permission to reprint a letter by Eliena Krylenko;

THE FOLIO SOCIETY, LONDON, for passages from *The Trial of Joan of Arc (the Orleans Manuscript):*

HARCOURT, BRACE AND COMPANY for a passage from *Wind, Sand and Stars* by Antoine de Saint-Exupéry, copyright 1939 by Antoine de Saint-Exupéry;

HARPER AND BROTHERS for a passage from *Death Be Not Proud* by John Gunther, copyright 1949 by John Gunther;

BURTON HARRIS for a selection from *John Colter* by Burton Harris, published by Charles Scribner's Sons, copyright 1952 by Charles Scribner's Sons;

HOUGHTON MIFFLIN COMPANY for a selection from *Beyond the 100th Meridian* by Wallace Stegner, copyright 1953, 1954, by Wallace Stegner;

ALFRED A. KNOPF, INC. and NAVIN SULLIVAN for passages from *Beethoven* by J. W. N. Sullivan, copyright 1927 by J. W. N. Sullivan;

LITTLE, BROWN AND COMPANY for a passage from *As I Remember Him* by Hans Zinsser, copyright 1939, 1940, by Hans Zinsser;

McGRAW-HILL BOOK COMPANY for a selection from *George Rogers Clark* by Walter Havighurst, copyright 1952 by McGraw-Hill Book Company;

EARL SCHENCK MIERS for passages from his introduction to *American Keepsake No. 2, Trial by Wilderness*, published by the Kingsport Press, copyright 1957 by Earl Schenck Miers;

WILLIAM MORROW AND COMPANY for a selection from *Daniel Boone, Master of the Wilderness* by John Bakeless, copyright 1939 by John Bakeless; and THE HOGARTH PRESS, London, for a passage from *Venture to the Interior* by Laurens van der Post, copyright 1951 by Laurens van der Post;

W. W. NORTON AND COMPANY for a passage from *Give Us This Day* by Sidney Stewart, copyright 1956 by Sidney Stewart;

OXFORD UNIVERSITY PRESS for selections from *The Reader's Bible*, copyright 1951;

PENGUIN BOOKS, Baltimore, Maryland, for a selection from *Herodotus: The Histories*, translated by Aubrey de Selincourt, copyright 1954;

PRENTICE-HALL, INC. for a passage from *Sea of Glory* by Francis B. Thornton, copyright 1953;

G. P. PUTNAM'S SONS for passages from *Alone* by Richard E. Byrd, copyright 1938 by G. P. Putnam's Sons;

THE READER'S DIGEST ASSOCIATION, INC. for *Miracle at Dunkirk* by Arthur D. Divine, copyright 1940 by The Reader's Digest Association, Inc.; and for *Unforgettable Character* by Anne Morrow Lindbergh, copyright 1946 by The Reader's Digest Association, Inc.;

CHARLES SCRIBNER'S SONS for a selection from *Of Flight and Life* by Charles A. Lindbergh, copyright 1948 by Charles A. Lindbergh; and for passages from *The Spirit of St. Louis* by Charles A. Lindbergh, copyright 1953 by Charles Scribner's Sons;

SIMON AND SCHUSTER, INC. for passages from *Charles Dickens* by Edgar Johnson, copyright 1952 by Edgar Johnson;

WILLIAM SLOANE ASSOCIATES and RUPERT HART-DAVIS, LONDON, for a passage from *The Moving Waters* by John Stewart Collis, copyright 1955;

J. VAN GOGH-BONGER, for part of the Introduction to *Letters to Theo*;

THE VIKING PRESS, INC. for a passage from John Mason Brown's Introduction to *The Portable Charles Lamb*, copyright 1948, 1949, by The Viking Press.

Foreword

MY PURPOSE in compiling this anthology was to bring together in a single volume some of the outstanding records in literature of what the subtitle refers to as "Man's unconquerable spirit." He is, as we all know, a creature of strange and often startling duality. He is capable now, as he was at the dawn of history, of shocking brutality and selfishness, of behavior indistinguishable from that of the most savage beast. Indeed, he stands alone in the animal kingdom, with the exception of the ants, as the only creature given to massed warfare upon his own kind or another, the only one that enslaves his fellows, and, unlike the ants, the only one that kills for the sheer lust of killing.

He can act as he did in Hungary recently, both in depravity and splendor. He can prostitute the imagination which has helped to lift him into dominion over all other living things, to the end of inflicting fiendish tortures upon his brother men—practices which make the mauling by a lion of his prey seem like the innocent antics of a child. He can, in short, be the most despicable of living things.

We of this century are painfully aware that man's capacity for abominable conduct is fully as great today—with one possible exception—as it was when he first came down from the trees and set about his butchery. The sole exception I have in mind is his modern urge to effect the alleviation of pain under certain circumstances, an urge which does not as yet extend to his refusal to inflict it. I believe one may say that this constitutes the only over-all ethical advance which man has made since he evolved from the lower orders. He was amused by lunacy as late as the eighteenth century, and has come to regard chronic alcoholism as a disease only in the course of the present century. But he is still ready to induce lunacy to advance his purpose. He is, in short, a living paradox.

One can say with full justice that by the subtle machinations of his brain he has even succeeded in increasing his capacity for doing evil. He can conceive now, and does, of more dreadful ways of treating his enemies than could occur to him when he was a far less "civilized" being. One can say of him, as we used to say, "Scratch a Russian and you find a Tartar," that if you peel away the veneer with which he has covered himself you will find under the surface a creature no whit closer to God than the insect he crushes beneath his heel, a creature no further advanced in moral stature, with the one exception I have noted, than when he wore only the skins of other animals and tore at his food in the same fashion as they.

All this would be true—and yet he can, and still does, rise to heights which are little less than sublime. He can act with the justice and mercy which he attributes to God himself. His courage has been, and is, of a nearly incredible quality. His selflessness can pass understanding. He can lay down his life for a friend with a smile and a jest. He can face terrors which the wildest nightmare could not surpass. He can give of himself until he has nothing left to give. We can say of him, as did the Psalmist, "What is man, that thou art mindful of him?" but we can also say with Shakespeare, "What a piece of work is a man! How noble in reason! how infinite in faculty! in form and moving how express and admirable! in action how like an angel! in apprehension how like a god! the beauty of the world! the paragon of animals!" But Shakespeare found fit to add, in Hamlet's words, "And yet, to me, what is this quintessence of dust? man delights not me; no, nor woman neither, though by your smiling, you seem to say so."

It is infinitely more important for us today, when we are all aware that man, in technological cunning, has far outstripped his day-to-day moral stature, to remember the spiritual peaks he has reached at many moments in his history than it is to dwell upon our knowledge of his repeated descents into bestiality. It is not only more important, it is essential to his continuance on this planet. Only by such remembering, only by his fervent conviction that what he has once done he can do again, will it be possible for him to keep on with his spiraling climb, to mount as well as to slip back, as he always will. Only by such means can he hope to save himself and to realize the vast potentialities within him.

For these reasons, as well as for the pleasure and profit of the labor (are we not dual creatures?) I have made these selections and talked a little about each one of them and their individual qualities. They are all, in one form or another, stories of ordeal, outer or inner, stories of man's unending struggle against the outer world, and stories of equally unending conflict within himself. Though I have made these two divisions of the outer and inner worlds, it is true that they sometimes overlap. Some of the conflicts here described, although primarily physical in nature, had their spiritual element also, and some of my protagonists whose inner being was racked by conflict within themselves were faced by outer stress as well. This was true, for example, of Joan of Arc.

Not all the battles of this world are fought with guns and bombs, or by men massed in great armies. Some of the greatest have been lonely battles, fought by men or women standing alone. Sometimes they were fighting a visible foe—another person, an animal, a mountain, the sea, the air, a raging river, or some other force of nature. Sometimes the fight was with an enemy they could not see—something without material form—an idea, a weakness within themselves, a physical handicap, like blindness, or an illness to be faced and overcome. These lonely battles, these singlehanded triumphs over odds, have given us some of the greatest stories in man's history.

There are many such I could have taken from the great works of fiction, many poems which would fall within the scope of this book's purpose. I have preferred to limit myself to the factual records of things that actually took place, of deeds that were actually done, of ordeals that were actually endured. I think that such records have a great fascination for us today. We read countless books about them, and I have a suspicion that one of the chief reasons why current literature about the Civil War has mounted to such impressive proportions is that the War between the States was the greatest single ordeal that we as a people have yet lived through, not even excepting the War for Independence.

It was George Santayana who said, some forty years ago, that the world would not know whether the Americans were basically a materially or a spiritually minded people until they had endured the trials of Job. This, by comparison with other peoples who are our contemporaries in this distraught world, we have not yet done.

It is well, I think, that we *are* fascinated by such records, for we need, in the years ahead, all the courage and all the force of example that we can draw from these accounts of man's enormous capacity for greatness. These records speak, largely, for themselves, and there is little I need add in placing them before you. They are among the proudest pages in the heritage we have to leave to those who may come after us.

J. Donald Adams

New York City

Contents

Part I: MAN AGAINST THE OUTER WORLD

Part II: MAN AGAINST THE INNER WORLD

PART I

Man Against the Outer World

THE OLD TESTAMENT

(King James Version)

I have chosen as the opening entry in this record of man's struggle against the outer world, the story, cherished by countless generations, of young David's battle with the giant Goliath. It is one of the best told of the Bible tales, and it typifies a particular aspect of man's unconquerable spirit: the audacity of youth. Also, the story takes first place here in point of time; David, one of the greatest of Hebrew heroes, is believed to have lived between 1012 and 972 B.C.

David and Goliath

NOW the Philistines gathered together their armies to battle, and were gathered together at Shochoh, which belonged to Judah, and pitched between Shochoh and Azekah, in Ephes-dammim. And Saul and the men of Israel were gathered together, and pitched by the valley of Elah, and set the battle in array against the Philistines. And the Philistines stood on a mountain on the one side, and Israel stood on a mountain on the other side: and there was a valley between them. And there went out a champion out of the camp of the Philistines, named Goliath, of Gath, whose height was six cubits and a span. And he had an helmet of brass upon his head, and he was armed with a coat of mail; and the weight of the coat was five thousand shekels of brass. And he had greaves of brass upon his legs, and a target of brass between his shoulders. And the staff of his spear was like a weaver's beam; and his spear's head weighed six hundred shekels of iron: and one bearing a shield went before him. And he stood and cried unto the armies of Israel, and said unto them, "Why are ye come out to set your battle in array? am not I a Philistine, and ye servants to Saul? choose you a man for you, and let him come down to me. If he be able to fight with me, and to kill me, then will we be your servants: but if I prevail

against him, and kill him, then shall ye be our servants, and serve us."
And the Philistine said, "I defy the armies of Israel this day; give me a
man, that we may fight together." When Saul and all Israel heard those
words of the Philistine, they were dismayed, and greatly afraid.

Now David was the son of that Ephrathite of Beth-lehem-judah,
whose name was Jesse; and he had eight sons: and the man went
among men for an old man in the days of Saul. And the three eldest
sons of Jesse went and followed Saul to the battle: and the names of
his three sons that went to the battle were Eliab the firstborn, and next
unto him Abinadab, and the third Shammah. And David was the
youngest: and the three eldest followed Saul. But David went and returned from Saul to feed his father's sheep at Beth-lehem. And the
Philistine drew near morning and evening, and presented himself
forty days.

And Jesse said unto David his son, "Take now for thy brethren an
ephah of this parched corn, and these ten loaves, and run to the camp
to thy brethren; and carry these ten cheeses unto the captain of their
thousand, and look how thy brethren fare, and take their pledge." Now
Saul, and they, and all the men of Israel, were in the valley of Elah,
fighting with the Philistines. And David rose up early in the morning,
and left the sheep with a keeper, and took, and went, as Jesse had
commanded him; and he came to the trench, as the host was going
forth to the fight, and shouted for the battle. For Israel and the Philistines had put the battle in array, army against army. And David left
his carriage in the hand of the keeper of the carriage, and ran into the
army, and came and saluted his brethren. And as he talked with them,
behold, there came up the champion, the Philistine of Gath, Goliath
by name, out of the armies of the Philistines, and spake according to
the same words: and David heard them. And all the men of Israel,
when they saw the man, fled from him, and were sore afraid. And the
men of Israel said, "Have ye seen this man that is come up? surely to
defy Israel is he come up: and it shall be, that the man who killeth him,
the king will enrich him with great riches, and will give him his daughter, and make his father's house free in Israel!" And David spake to
the men that stood by him, saying, "What shall be done to the man
that killeth this Philistine, and taketh away the reproach from Israel?
for who is this uncircumcised Philistine, that he should defy the armies
of the living God?" And the people answered him after this manner,
saying, "So shall it be done to the man that killeth him." And Eliab
his eldest brother heard when he spake unto the men; and Eliab's anger
was kindled against David, and he said, "Why camest thou down
hither? and with whom hast thou left those few sheep in the wilderness? I know thy pride, and the naughtiness of thine heart; for thou

art come down that thou mightest see the battle." And David said, "What have I now done? Is there not a cause?" And he turned from him toward another, and spake after the same manner: and the people answered him again after the former manner. And when the words were heard which David spake, they rehearsed them before Saul: and he sent for him. And David said to Saul, "Let no man's heart fail because of him; thy servant will go and fight with this Philistine." And Saul said to David, "Thou art not able to go against this Philistine to fight with him: for thou art but a youth, and he a man of war from his youth." And David said unto Saul, "Thy servant kept his father's sheep, and there came a lion, and a bear, and took a lamb out of the flock: and I went out after him, and smote him, and delivered it out of his mouth: and when he arose against me, I caught him by his beard, and smote him, and slew him. Thy servant slew both the lion and the bear: and this uncircumcised Philistine shall be as one of them, seeing he hath defied the armies of the living God." David said, moreover, "The Lord that delivered me out of the paw of the lion, and out of the paw of the bear, he will deliver me out of the hand of this Philistine." And Saul said unto David, "Go, and the Lord be with thee." And Saul armed David with his armour, and he put an helmet of grass upon his head; also he armed him with a coat of mail. And David girded his sword upon his armour, and he assayed to go; for he had not proved it. And David said unto Saul, "I cannot go with these; for I have not proved them." And David put them off him. And he took his staff in his hand, and chose him five smooth stones out of the brook, and put them in a shepherd's bag which he had, even in a scrip; and his sling was in his hand: and he drew near to the Philistine. And the Philistine came on and drew near unto David; and the man that bare the shield went before him. And when the Philistine looked about, and saw David, he disdained him: for he was but a youth, and ruddy, and of a fair countenance. And the Philistine said unto David, "Am I a dog, that thou comest to me with staves?" And the Philistine cursed David by his gods. And the Philistine said to David, "Come to me, and I will give thy flesh unto the fowls of the air, and to the beasts of the field." Then said David to the Philistine, "Thou comest to me with a sword, and with a spear, and with a shield: but I come to thee in the name of the Lord of hosts, the God of the armies of Israel, whom thou hast defied. This day will the Lord deliver thee into mine hand; and I will smite thee, and take thine head from thee; and I will give the carcases of the host of the Philistines this day unto the fowls of the air, and to the wild beasts of the earth; that all the earth may know that there is a God in Israel. And all this assembly shall know that the Lord saveth not with sword and spear: for the battle is the Lord's, and he will give you into our hands." And it came to pass, when the Philistine arose, and came and drew nigh to meet David, that David hasted, and ran toward the army to meet the Philistine. And David put his hand in his bag, and took thence a stone, and slang it, and smote the Philistine in his forehead, that the stone sunk into his forehead; and he fell upon his face to the earth. So David prevailed over the Philistine with a sling and with a stone, and smote the Philistine, and slew him; but there was no sword in the hand of David. Therefore David ran, and stood upon the Philistine, and took his sword, and drew it out of the sheath thereof, and slew him, and cut off his head therewith. And when the Philistines saw their champion was dead, they fled. And the men of Israel and of Judah arose, and shouted, and pursued the Philistines, until thou come to the valley, and to the gates of Ekron. And the wounded of the Philistines fell down by the way to Shaaraim, even unto Gath, and unto Ekron. And the children of Israel returned from chasing after the Philistines, and they spoiled their tents. And David took the head of the Philistine, and brought it to Jerusalem; but he put his armour in his tent.

XENOPHON

The Greek historian Xenophon was born about 430 B.C. and died about seventy-five years later. He was one of the comfortably placed young men who hung upon the words of Socrates, and was in his late twenties when he left Athens to join the Greek army (the famous Ten Thousand) which was in the service of Cyrus the Younger of Persia. He was one of the leaders of the heroic retreat which followed the ill-fated battle of Cunaxa, and told its story in his best-known work, the *Anabasis,* bane of many a schoolboy's life for centuries past. The passages I have chosen describe the battle and the death of Cyrus, followed by the high points of the retreat, to its joyous close.

March of the Ten Thousand

IT WAS already about full market time and the halting-place at which the army was to take up quarters was nearly reached, when Pategyas, a Persian, a trusty member of Cyrus's personal staff, came galloping up at full speed on his horse, which was bathed in sweat, and to every one he met he shouted in Greek and Persian, as fast as he could ejaculate the words: "The king is advancing with a large army ready for battle." Then ensued a scene of wild confusion. The Hellenes and all alike were expecting to be attacked on the instant, and before they could form their lines. Cyrus sprang from his carriage and donned his corselet; then leaping on to his charger's back, with the javelins firmly clutched, he passed the order to the rest, to arm themselves and fall into their several ranks.

The orders were carried out with alacrity; the ranks shaped themselves. Clearchus held the right of the wing resting on the Euphrates, Proxenus was next, and after him the rest, while Menon with his troops held the Hellenic left. Of the Asiatics, a body of Paphlagonian cavalry, one thousand strong, were posted beside Clearchus on the right, and with them stood the Hellenic peltasts. On the left was Ariaeus, Cyrus's second in command, and the rest of the barbarian host. Cyrus was with his bodyguard of cavalry about six hundred strong, all armed with corselets like Cyrus, and cuisses and helmets; but not so Cyrus: he went into battle with head unhelmeted. So too all the horses with Cyrus wore forehead-pieces and breast-pieces, and the troopers carried short Hellenic swords.

It was now mid-day, and the enemy was not yet in sight; but with the approach of afternoon was seen dust like a white cloud, and after a considerable interval a black pall as it were spread far and high over the plain. As they came nearer, very soon was seen here and there a glint of bronze and spear-points; and the ranks could plainly be distinguished. On the left were troopers wearing white cuirasses. That is Tissaphernes in command, they said, and next to these a body of men bearing wicker-shields, and next again heavy-armed infantry, with long wooden shields reaching to the feet. These were the Egyptians, they said, and then other cavalry, other bowmen; all were in national divisions, each nation marching in densely-crowded squares. And all along their front was a line of chariots at considerable intervals from one another,—the famous scythe-chariots, as they were named,—having their scythes fitted to the axle-trees and stretching out slantwise, while others protruded under the chariot-seats, facing the ground, so as to cut through all they encountered. The design was to let them dash full speed into the ranks of the Hellenes and cut them through.

Curiously enough the anticipation of Cyrus, when at the council of war he admonished the Hellenes not to mind the shouting of the Asiatics, was not justified. Instead of shouting, they came on in deep silence, softly and slowly, with even tread. At this instant, Cyrus, riding past in person, accompanied by Pigres, his interpreter, and three or four others, called aloud to Clearchus to advance against the enemy's centre; for there the king was to be found: "And if we strike home at this point," he added, "our work is finished." Clearchus, though he could see the compact body at the centre, and had been told by Cyrus that the king lay outside the Hellenic left (for, owing to numerical superiority, the king, while holding his own centre, could well overlap Cyrus's extreme left), still hesitated to draw off his right wing from the river, for fear of being turned on both flanks; and he simply replied, assuring Cyrus that he would take care all went well.

At this time the barbarian army was evenly advancing, and the Hellenic division was still riveted to the spot, completing its formation as the various contingents came up. Cyrus, riding past at some distance from the lines, glanced his eye first in one direction and then in the other, so as to take a complete survey of friends and foes; when Xenophon the Athenian, seeing him, rode up from the Hellenic quarter to meet him, asking whether he had any orders to give. Cyrus, pulling up his horse, begged him to make the announcement generally known that the omens from the victims, internal and external alike, were good. While he was still speaking, he heard a confused murmur passing through the ranks, and asked what it meant. The other replied that it was the watchword being passed down for the second time. Cyrus wondered who had given the order, and asked what the watchword was. On being told it was "Zeus our Saviour and Victory," he replied, "I accept it; so let it be," and with that remark rode away to his own position. And now the two battle lines were no more than three or four furlongs apart, when the Hellenes began chanting the paean, and at the same time advanced against the enemy.

With the forward movement a certain portion of the line curved onwards in advance, with wave-like sinuosity, and the portion left behind quickened to a run; and simultaneously a thrilling cry burst from all lips, like that in honour of the war-god—eleleu! eleleu! and the running became general. Some say they clashed their shields and spears, thereby causing terror to the horses; and before they had got within arrowshot the barbarians swerved and took to flight. And now the Hellenes gave chase with might and main, checked only by shouts to one another not to race, but to keep their ranks. The enemy's chariots, reft of their charioteers, swept onwards, some through the enemy themselves, other past the Hellenes. They, as they saw them coming, opened a gap and let them pass. One fellow, like some dumbfoundered mortal on a race-course, was caught by the heels, but even he, they said, received no hurt; nor indeed, with the single exception of some one on the left wing who was said to have been wounded by an arrow, did any Hellene in this battle suffer a single hurt.

Cyrus, seeing the Hellenes conquering, as far as they at any rate were concerned, and in hot pursuit, was well content; but in spite of his joy and the salutations offered him at that moment by those about him, as though he were already king, he was not led away to join in the pursuit, but keeping his squadron of six hundred horsemen in close order, waited and watched to see what the king himself would do. The king, he knew, held the centre of the Persian army. Indeed it is the fashion for the Asiatic monarch to occupy that position during action, for this twofold reason: he holds the safest place, with his troops on either side of him, while, if he has occasion to despatch any necessary order along the lines, his troops will receive the message in half the time. The king accordingly on this occasion held the centre of his army, but for all that, he was outside Cyrus's left wing; and seeing that no one offered him battle in front, nor yet the troops in front of him, he wheeled as if to encircle the enemy. It was then that Cyrus, in apprehension lest the king might get round to the rear and cut to pieces the Hellenic body, charged to meet him. Attacking with his six hundred, he mastered the line of troops in front of the king, and put to flight the six thousand, cutting down, as is said, with his own hand their general, Artagerses.

But as soon as the rout commenced, Cyrus's own six hundred themselves, in the ardour of pursuit, were scattered, with the exception of a handful who were left with Cyrus himself—chiefly his table companions, so-called. Left alone with these, he caught sight of the king and the close throng about him. Unable longer to contain himself, with a cry, "I see the man," he rushed at him and dealt a blow at his chest, wounding him through the corselet. This, according to the statement of Ctesias the surgeon, who further states that he himself healed the wound. As Cyrus delivered the blow, some one struck him with a javelin under the eye severely; and in the struggle which then ensued between the king and Cyrus and those about them to protect one or other, we have the statement of Ctesias as to the number slain on the king's side, for he was by his side. On the other, Cyrus himself fell, and eight of his bravest companions lay on the top of him. The story says that Artapates, the trustiest esquire among his wand-bearers, when he saw that Cyrus had fallen to the ground, leapt from his horse and threw his arms about him. Then, as one account says, the king bade one slay him as a worthy victim to his brother: others say that Artapates drew his scimitar and slew himself by his own hand. A golden scimitar it is true, he had; he wore also a collar and bracelets and the other ornaments such as the noblest Persians wear; for his kindliness and fidelity had won him honours at the hands of Cyrus.

So died Cyrus; a man the kingliest and most worthy to rule of all the Persians who have lived since the elder Cyrus. . . .

The next day it was resolved that they should set off with all possible speed, before the enemy had time to collect and occupy the defile. Having got their kit and baggage together, they at once began their march through deep snow with several guides, and, crossing the high pass the same day on which Tiribazus was to have attacked them, got safely into cantonments. From this point they marched three desert stages—fifteen parasangs—to the river Euphrates, and crossed it in water up to the waist. The sources of the river were reported to be at no great distance. From this place they marched through deep snow over a flat country three stages—fifteen parasangs. The last of these marches was trying, with the north wind blowing in their teeth, drying up everything and benumbing the men. Here one of the seers suggested to them to do sacrifice to Boreas, and sacrifice was done. The effect was obvious to all in the diminished fierceness of the blast. But there was six feet of snow, so that many of the baggage animals and slaves were lost, and about thirty of the men themselves.

They spent the whole night in kindling fire; for there was fortunately no dearth of wood at the halting-place; only those who came late into camp had no wood. Accordingly those who had arrived a good while and had kindled fires were not for allowing these late-comers near their fires, unless they would in return give a share of their corn or of any other victuals they might have. Here then a general exchange of goods was set up. Where the fire was kindled the snow melted, and great trenches formed themselves down to the bare earth, and here it was possible to measure the depth of the snow.

Leaving these quarters, they marched the whole of the next day over snow, and many of the men were afflicted with "boulimia" (or hunger-faintness). Xenophon, who was guarding the rear, came upon some men who had dropt down, and he did not know what ailed them; but some one who was experienced in such matters suggested to him that they had evidently got boulimia; and if they got something to eat, they would revive. Then he went the round of the baggage train, and laying an embargo on any eatables he could see, doled out with his own hands, or sent off other able-bodied agents to distribute to the sufferers, who as soon as they had taken a mouthful got on their legs again and continued the march.

On and on they marched, and about dusk Cheirisophus reached a village, and surprised some women and girls who had come from the village to fetch water at the fountain outside the stockade. These asked them who they were. The interpreters answered for them in Persian: "They were on their way from the king to the satrap"; in reply to which the women gave them to understand that the satrap was not at home, but was away a parasang farther on. As it was late they entered with the water-carriers within the stockade to visit the headman of the village. Accordingly Cheirisophus and as many of the troops as were able got into cantonments there, while the rest of the soldiers—those namely who were unable to complete the march—had to spend the night out, without food and without fire; under the circumstances some of the men perished.

On the heels of the army hung perpetually bands of the enemy, snatching away disabled baggage animals and fighting with each other over the carcases. And in its track not seldom were left to their fate disabled soldiers, struck down with snow-blindness or with toes mortified by frostbite. As to the eyes, it was some alleviation against the snow to march with something black before them; for the feet, the only remedy was to keep in motion without stopping for an instant, and to loose the sandal at night. If they went to sleep with the sandals

on, the thong worked into the feet, and the sandals were frozen fast
to them. This was partly due to the fact that, since their old sandals
had failed, they wore untanned brogues made of newly-flayed ox-hides.
It was owing to some such dire necessity that a party of men fell out
and were left behind, and seeing a black-looking patch of ground
where the snow had evidently disappeared, they conjectured it must
have been melted; and this was actually so, owing to a spring of some
sort which was to be seen steaming up in a dell close by. To this they
had turned aside and sat down, and were loth to go a step further.
But Xenophon, with his rearguard, perceived them, and begged and
implored them by all manner of means not to be left behind, telling
them that the enemy were after them in large packs pursuing; and he
ended by growing angry. They merely bade him put a knife to their
throats; not one step farther would they stir. Then it seemed best to
frighten the pursuing enemy if possible, and prevent their falling upon
the invalids. It was already dusk, and the pursuers were advancing with
much noise and hubbub, wrangling and disputing over their spoils.
Then all of a sudden the rearguard, in the plenitude of health and
strength, sprang up out of their lair and ran upon the enemy, whilst
those weary wights bawled out as loud as their sick throats could sound,
and clashed their spears against their shields; and the enemy in terror
hurled themselves through the snow into the dell, and not one of them
ever uttered a sound again.

The Taochians lived in strong places, into which they had carried
up all their stores. Now when the army arrived before one of these
strong places—a mere fortress, without city or houses, into which a
motley crowd of men and women and numerous flocks and herds were
gathered—Cheirisophus attacked at once. When the first regiment fell
back tired, a second advanced, and again a third, for it was impossible
to surround the place in full force, as it was encircled by a river. Presently Xenophon came up with the rearguard, consisting of both light
and heavy infantry, whereupon Cheirisophus hailed him with the
words: "In the nick of time you have come; we must take this place, for
the troops have no provisions, unless we take it." Thereupon they consulted together, and to Xenophon's inquiry, "What it was which
hindered their simply walking in?" Cheirisophus replied, "There is
just this one narrow approach which you see; but when we attempt to
pass by it they roll down volleys of stones from yonder overhanging
crag," pointing up, "and this is the state in which you find yourself, if
you chance to be caught"; and he pointed to some poor fellows with
their legs or ribs crushed to bits. "But when they have expended their
ammunition," said Xenophon, "there is nothing else, is there, to hinder

our passing? Certainly, except yonder handful of fellows, there is no one in front of us that we can see; and of them, only two or three apparently are armed, and the distance to be traversed under fire is, as your eyes will tell you, about one hundred and fifty feet as near as can be, and of this space the first hundred is thickly covered with great pines at intervals; under cover of these, what harm can come to our men from a pelt of stones, flying or rolling? So then, there is only fifty feet left to cross, during a lull of stones." "Ay," said Cheirisophus, "but with our first attempt to approach the bush a galling fire of stones commences." "The very thing we want," said the other, "for they will use up their ammunition all the quicker; but let us select a point from which we shall have only a brief space to run across, if we can, and from which it will be easier to get back, if we wish."

Thereupon Cheirisophus and Xenophon set out with Callimachus the Parrhasian, the captain in command of the officers of the rearguard that day; the rest of the captains remained out of danger. That done, the next step was for a party of about seventy men to get away under the trees, not in a body, but one by one, every one using his best precaution; and Agasias the Stymphalian, and Aristonymus the Methydrian, who were also officers of the rearguard, were posted as supports outside the trees; for it was not possible for more than a single company to stand safely within the trees. Here Callimachus hit upon a pretty contrivance—he ran forward from the tree under which he was posted two or three paces, and as soon as the stones came whizzing, he retired easily, but at each excursion more than ten wagon-loads of rocks were expended. Agasias, seeing how Callimachus was amusing himself, and the whole army looking on as spectators, was seized with the fear that he might miss his chance of being first to run the gauntlet of the enemy's fire and get into the place. So, without a word of summons to his next neighbour, Aristonymus, or to Eurylochus of Lusia, both comrades of his, or to any one else, off he set on his own account, and passed the whole detachment. But Callimachus, seeing him tearing past, caught hold of his shield by the rim and in the meantime Aristonymus the Methydrian ran past both, and after him Eurylochus of Lusia; for they were one and all aspirants to valour, and in that high pursuit, each was the eager rival of the rest. So in this strife of honour, the four of them took the fortress, and when they had once rushed in, not a stone more was hurled from overhead.

And here a terrible spectacle displayed itself: the women first cast their infants down the cliff, and then they cast themselves after their fallen little ones, and the men likewise. In such a scene, Aeneas the Stymphalian, an officer, caught sight of a man with a fine dress about to throw himself over, and seized hold of him to stop him; but the other caught him to his arms, and both were gone in an instant headlong down the crags, and were killed. Out of this place the merest handful of human beings were taken prisoners, but cattle and asses in abundance and flocks of sheep.

On the fifth day they reached the mountain, the name of which was Theches. No sooner had the men in front ascended it and caught sight of the sea than a great cry arose, and Xenophon, with the rearguard, catching the sound of it, conjectured that another set of enemies must surely be attacking in front; for they were followed by the inhabitants of the country, which was all aflame; indeed the rearguard had killed some and captured others alive by laying an ambuscade; they had taken also about twenty wicker shields, covered with the raw hides of shaggy oxen.

But as the shout became louder and nearer, and those who from time to time came up, began racing at the top of their speed towards the shouters, and the shouting continually recommenced with yet greater volume as the numbers increased, Xenophon settled in his mind that something extraordinary must have happened, so he mounted his horse, and taking with him Lycius and the cavalry, he galloped to the rescue. Presently they could hear the soldiers shouting and passing on the joyful word, *The sea! the sea!*

HERODOTUS

One of the most engaging writers in the whole range of world literature, Herodotus (484–425 B.C.), has long been named the "Father of
History." He left us little record of himself, but we do know, among
other things, that he was one of the most traveled men of his time. It
is believed that he spent about the last twenty years of his life in southern Italy, where he helped to found an Athenian colony and where
the writing of his history was completed.

Its nine books, named after the Nine Muses, made the first comprehensive attempt at secular history. Though it is primarily concerned
with the story of the Persian wars, the earlier books give us a great
deal of information (not all of it, perhaps, gospel truth) and much
vivid writing about the world as it was known to him. He was one
of the best of storytellers, and by means of lively anecdote he was
able to point up for us many aspects of the early cultures which he
knew and appraised at firsthand. For, like our own Parkman, he was a
man who wanted to see with his own eyes, and, like his American
successor twenty-three centuries later, he was able to make us see as
well.

I have chosen that portion of Book Seven which tells the deathless
story of the fighting in the pass at Thermopylae.

In the Pass at Thermopylae

THE Persian army was now close to the pass, and the Greeks,
suddenly doubting their power to resist, held a conference to
consider the advisability of retreat. It was proposed by the Pelopon-
nesians generally that the army should fall back upon the Peloponnese
and hold the Isthmus; but when the Phocians and Locrians expressed
their indignation at this suggestion, Leonidas gave his voice for staying
where they were and sending, at the same time, an appeal for rein-
forcements to the various states of the confederacy, as their numbers
were inadequate to cope with the Persians.

During the conference Xerxes sent a man on horseback to ascertain the strength of the Greek force and to observe what the troops were doing. He had heard before he left Thessaly that a small force was concentrated here, led by the Lacedaemonians under Leonidas of the house of Heracles. The Persian rider approached the camp and took a thorough survey of all he could see—which was not, however, the whole Greek army; for the men on the farther side of the wall which, after its reconstruction, was now guarded, were out of sight. He did, nonetheless, carefully observe the troops who were stationed on the outside of the wall. At that moment these happened to be the Spartans, and some of them were stripped for exercise, while others were combing their hair. The Persian spy watched them in astonishment; nevertheless he made sure of their numbers, and of everything else he needed to know, as accurately as he could, and then rode quietly off. No one attempted to catch him, or took the least notice of him.

Back in his own camp he told Xerxes what he had seen. Xerxes was bewildered; the truth, namely that the Spartans were preparing themselves to kill and to be killed according to their strength, was beyond his comprehension, and what they were doing seemed to him merely absurd. Accordingly he sent for Demaratus, the son of Ariston, who had come with the army, and questioned him about the spy's report, in the hope of finding out what the unaccountable behaviour of the Spartans might mean. "Once before," Demaratus said, "when we began our march against Greece, you heard me speak of these men. I told you then how I saw this enterprise would turn out, and you laughed at me. I strive for nothing, my lord, more earnestly than to observe the truth in your presence; so hear me once more. These men have come to fight us for possession of the pass, and for that struggle they are preparing. It is the common practice of the Spartans to pay careful attention to their hair when they are about to risk their lives. But I assure you that if you can defeat these men and the rest of the Spartans who are still at home, there is no other people in the world who will dare to stand firm or lift a hand against you. You have now to deal with the finest kingdom in Greece, and with the bravest men."

Xerxes, unable to believe what Demaratus said, asked further how it was possible that so small a force could fight with his army. "My lord," Demaratus replied, "treat me as a liar, if what I have foretold does not take place." But still Xerxes was unconvinced.

For four days Xerxes waited, in constant expectation that the Greeks would make good their escape; then, on the fifth, when still they had made no move and their continued presence seemed mere impudent and reckless folly, he was seized with rage and sent forward the Medes and Cissians with orders to take them alive and bring them into his presence. The Medes charged, and in the struggle which ensued many fell; but others took their places, and in spite of terrible losses refused to be beaten off. They made it plain enough to anyone, and not least to the king himself, that he had in his army many men, indeed, but few soldiers. All day the battle continued; the Medes, after their rough handling, were at length withdrawn and their place was taken by Hydarnes and his picked Persian troops—the king's Immortals—who advanced to the attack in full confidence of bringing the business to a quick and easy end. But, once engaged, they were no more successful than the Medes had been; all went as before, the two armies fighting in a confined space, the Persians using shorter spears than the Greeks and having no advantage from their numbers.

On the Spartan side it was a memorable fight; they were men who understood war pitted against an inexperienced enemy, and amongst the feints they employed was to turn their backs in a body and pretend to be retreating in confusion, whereupon the enemy would come on with a great clatter and roar, supposing the battle won; but the Spartans, just as the Persians were on them, would wheel and face them and inflict in the new struggle innumerable casualties. The Spartans had their losses too, but not many. At last the Persians, finding that their assaults upon the pass, whether by divisions or by any other way they could think of, were all useless, broke off the engagement and withdrew. Xerxes was watching the battle from where he sat; and it is said that in the course of the attacks three times, in terror for his army, he leapt to his feet.

Next day the fighting began again, but with no better success for the Persians, who renewed their onslaught in the hope that the Greeks, being so few in number, might be badly enough disabled by wounds to prevent further resistance. But the Greeks never slackened; their troops were ordered in divisions corresponding to the states from which they came, and each division took its turn in the line except the Phocian, which had been posted to guard the track over the mountains. So when the Persians found that things were no better for them than on the previous day, they once more withdrew.

How to deal with the situation Xerxes had no idea; but while he was still wondering what his next move should be, a man from Malis got himself admitted to his presence. This was Ephialtes, the son of Eurydemus, and he had come, in hope of a rich reward, to tell the king about the track which led over the hills to Thermopylae—and the information he gave was to prove the death of the Greeks who held the pass. . . .

Xerxes found Ephialtes' offer most satisfactory. He was delighted with it, and promptly gave orders to Hydarnes to carry out the movement with the troops under his command. They left camp about the time the lamps are lit.

The track was originally discovered by the Malians of the neighbourhood; they afterwards used it to help the Thessalians, taking them over it to attack Phocis at the time when the Phocians were protected from invasion by the wall which they had built across the pass. That was a long time ago, and no good ever came of it since. The track begins at the Asopus, the stream which flows through the narrow gorge, and, running along the ridge of the mountain—which, like the track itself, is called Anopaea—ends at Alpenus, the first Locrian settlement as one comes from Malis, near the rock known as Black-Buttocks' Stone and the seats of the Cercopes. Just here is the narrowest part of the pass.

This, then, was the mountain track which the Persians took, after crossing the Asopus. They marched throughout the night, with the mountains of Oeta on their right hand and those of Trachis on their left. By early dawn they were at the summit of the ridge, near the spot where the Phocians, as I mentioned before, stood on guard with a thousand men, to watch the track and protect their country. The Phocians were ready enough to undertake this service, and had, indeed, volunteered for it to Leonidas, knowing that the pass at Thermopylae was held as I have already described.

The ascent of the Persians had been concealed by the oak-woods which cover this part of the mountain range, and it was only when they reached the top that the Phocians became aware of their approach; for there was not a breath of wind, and the marching feet made a loud swishing and rustling in the fallen leaves. Leaping to their feet, the Phocians were in the act of arming themselves when the enemy was upon them. The Persians were surprised at the sight of troops preparing to resist; they had not expected any opposition—yet here was a body of men barring their way. Hydarnes asked Ephialtes who they were, for his first uncomfortable thought was that they might be Spartans; but on learning the truth he prepared to engage them. The Persian arrows flew thick and fast, and the Phocians, supposing themselves to be the main object of the attack, hurriedly withdrew to the highest point of the mountain, where they made ready to face destruction. The Persians, however, with Ephialtes and Hydarnes paid no further attention to them, but passed on along the descending track with all possible speed.

The Greeks at Thermopylae had their first warning of the death that was coming with the dawn from the seer Megistias, who read their doom in the victims of sacrifice; deserters, too, had begun to come in during the night with news of the Persian movement to take them in the rear, and, just as day was breaking, the look-out men had come running from the hills. At once a conference was held, and opinions were divided, some urging that they must on no account abandon their post, others taking the opposite view. The result was that the army split: some dispersed, the men returning to their various homes, and others made ready to stand by Leonidas.

There is another account which says that Leonidas himself dismissed a part of his force, to spare their lives, but thought it unbecoming for the Spartans under his command to desert the post which they had originally come to guard. I myself am inclined to think that he dismissed them when he realized that they had no heart for the fight and were unwilling to take their share of the danger; at the same time honour forbade that he himself should go. And indeed by remaining at his post he left a great name behind him, and Sparta did not lose her prosperity, as might otherwise have happened; for right at the outset of the war the Spartans had been told by the oracle, when they asked for advice, that either their city must be laid waste by the foreigner or one of their kings be killed. The prophecy was in hexameter verse and ran as follows:

> Hear your fate, O dwellers in Sparta of the wide spaces;
> Either your famed, great town must be sacked by Perseus' sons,
> Or, if that be not, the whole land of Lacedaemon
> Shall mourn the death of a king of the house of Heracles,
> For not the strength of lions or of bulls shall hold him,
> Strength against strength; for he has the power of Zeus,
> And will not be checked till one of these two he has consumed.

I believe it was the thought of this oracle, combined with his wish to lay up for the Spartans a treasure of fame in which no other city should share, that made Leonidas dismiss those troops; I do not think that they deserted, or went off without orders, because of a difference of opinion. Moreover, I am strongly supported in this view by the case of Megistias, the seer from Acarnania who foretold the coming doom by his inspection of the sacrificial victims: this man—he was said to be descended from Melampus—was with the army, and quite plainly received orders from Leonidas to quit Thermopylae, to save him from sharing the army's fate. But he refused to go, sending away instead an only son of his, who was serving with the forces.

Thus it was that the confederate troops, by Leonidas' orders, abandoned their posts and left the pass, all except the Thespians and the Thebans who remained with the Spartans. The Thebans were detained by Leonidas as hostages very much against their will—unlike the loyal Thespians, who refused to desert Leonidas and his men, but stayed, and died with them. They were under the command of Demophilus the son of Diadromes.

In the morning Xerxes poured a libation to the rising sun, and then waited till about the time of the filling of the market-place, when he began to move forward. This was according to Ephialtes' instructions, for the way down from the ridge is much shorter and more direct than the long and circuitous ascent. As the Persian army advanced to the assault, the Greeks under Leonidas, knowing that the fight would be their last, pressed forward into the wider part of the pass much farther than they had done before; in the previous days' fighting they had been holding the wall and making sorties from behind it into the narrow neck, but now they left the confined space and battle was joined on more open ground. Many of the invaders fell; behind them the company commanders plied their whips, driving the men remorselessly on. Many fell into the sea and were drowned, and still more were trampled to death by their friends. No one could count the number of the dead. The Greeks, who knew that the enemy were on their way round by the mountain track and that death was inevitable, fought with reckless desperation, exerting every ounce of strength that was in them against the invader. By this time most of their spears were broken, and they were killing Persians with their swords.

In the course of that fight Leonidas fell, having fought like a man indeed. Many distinguished Spartans were killed at his side—their names, like the names of all the three hundred, I have made myself acquainted with, because they deserve to be remembered. Amongst the Persian dead, too, were many men of high distinction—for instance, two brothers of Xerxes, Habrocomes and Hyperanthes, both of them sons of Darius by Artanes' daughter Phratagune.

There was a bitter struggle over the body of Leonidas; four times the Greeks drove the enemy off, and at last by their valour succeeded in dragging it away. So it went on, until the fresh troops with Ephialtes were close at hand; and then, when the Greeks knew that they had come, the character of the fighting changed. They withdrew again into the narrow neck of the pass, behind the walls, and took up a position in a single compact body—all except the Thebans—on the little hill at the entrance to the pass, where the stone lion in memory of Leonidas stands to-day. Here they resisted to the last, with their swords, if they had them, and, if not, with their hands and teeth, until the Persians, coming on from the front over the ruins of the wall and closing in from behind, finally overwhelmed them.

Of all the Spartans and Thespians who fought so valiantly on that day, the most signal proof of courage was given by the Spartan Dieneces. It is said that before the battle he was told by a native of Trachis that, when the Persians shot their arrows, there were so many of them that they hid the sun. Dieneces, however, quite unmoved by the thought of the terrible strength of the Persian army, merely remarked: "This is pleasant news that the stranger from Trachis brings us: for if the Persians hide the sun, we shall have our battle in the shade." He is said to have left on record other sayings, too, of a similar kind, by which he will be remembered. After Dieneces the greatest distinction was won by the two Spartan brothers, Alpheus and Maron, the sons of Orsiphantus; and of the Thespians the man to gain the highest glory was a certain Dithyrambus, the son of Harmatides.

The dead were buried where they fell, and with them the men who had been killed before those dismissed by Leonidas left the pass. Over them is this inscription, in honour of the whole force:

> *Four thousand here from Pelops' land*
> *Against three million once did stand.*

The Spartans have a special epitaph; it runs:

> *Go tell the Spartans, you who read:*
> *We took their orders, and are dead.*

For the seer Megistias there is the following:

> *I was Megistias once, who died*
> *When the Mede passed Spercheius' tide.*
> *I knew death near, yet would not save*
> *Myself, but share the Spartan's grave.*

LIVY (TITUS LIVIUS)

Generally regarded as the greatest prose writer of the Augustan age, the Roman historian Livy (59 B.C.–A.D. 17) might also be called Latin literature's opposite number to Herodotus in the Greek. Like Herodotus, he has not been commonly esteemed for his accuracy or his critical judgment, but like that father of historians also he had a sharp eye for the telling detail, an unerring sense of what is interesting, and a flair for the dramatic.

The pages that follow have been selected from Book XXI of his *Annals of the Roman People* (translated by Church and Broadribb, revised and amended by Duffield Osborne). They tell in stirring fashion the story of Hannibal's remarkable crossing of the Alps, complete with elephants. In the space of five months he moved his army from Spain, across the Pyrenees, over the Rhone, across the Alps, and down into the Italian peninsula, circled around the Roman army, took time out for much-needed rest, re-equipped his men, and then attacked, catching the Roman legions unprepared. It was one of the most spectacular feats in history.

Hannibal Crosses the Alps

FROM the Druentia Hannibal marched through a country generally flat to the Alps, wholly unmolested by the Gauls in those parts. And then, though rumor which usually magnifies the unknown far beyond truth had given some anticipation of the facts, still the near sight of the mountain heights with their snows almost mingling with the sky, the rude huts perched on the rocks, cattle and beasts of burden shrivelled with cold, human beings unkempt and wild, and all things animate and inanimate stiffened with frost, with other scenes more horrible to behold than to describe, revived the terror of the soldiers.

As the vanguard was struggling up the first slopes, the mountain tribes showed themselves on the overhanging hills. Had they lain hid in some of the obscurer valleys and suddenly rushed out to the attack, they must have caused terrible panic and loss. Hannibal ordered a halt, and the Gauls were sent on to reconnoitre. When he ascertained that here there was no passage for his troops, he pitched his camp in the broadest valley he could find, where the country all around was rugged and precipitous. Then from those same Gauls, mingling and conversing with the mountaineers, whom indeed in language and manners they resembled, he learned that it was only by day that the pass was barred, and that at night all dispersed to their various dwellings. With early dawn he advanced to the foot of the hills, as if he meant to push his way by force in open day through the defiles. In this feint, preparing a movement not really intended, the day was spent, and the camp was fortified on the spot on which it had been pitched. But the moment Hannibal saw the mountaineers coming down from the hills and the outpost weakly manned, he had a multitude of fires lit for show, greater than would correspond with the number of troops in camp, and then leaving behind him the baggage with the cavalry as well as the greater part of the infantry, and taking with him some lightly armed men, the bravest he could pick, he rapidly mounted the passes and established himself on the very hills which the enemy had occupied.

At daybreak the camp was broken up and the rest of the army began to move. The mountaineers on a signal given were now gathering in force from their fortresses to one of their regular positions, when suddenly they saw the enemy, some on the heights over their heads and in possession of their own stronghold, the remainder marching through the pass. The double impression thus made on their sight and imagination held them for a brief while rooted to the earth. Soon, when they saw the hurry in the defiles, and how the army was in utter confusion from its own disorder, the horses especially being wild with fright, they thought that, could they in any way increase the panic, it would insure the enemy's destruction, and rushed down the face of the rocks they knew so well, whether along pathless steeps or obscure tracks. Then indeed both the foe and the perils of the place fought against the Carthaginians, and while every man strove for himself to get soonest out of danger, there was more struggling among the soldiers themselves than between them and the enemy. The horses were the most dangerous hindrance to the army. They were terrified and scared by the confused cries which the woods and echoing valleys further multiplied, and if they chanced to be struck and wounded, in the wildness of their terror they made fearful havoc alike among the men and the baggage of every description. The pressure, too, in the defile each side of which was a sheer precipice, hurled numbers down to an

immense depth, and among them were soldiers with their accoutre-
ments; but it was more particularly the beasts with their burdens,
which rolled down with just such a crash as a falling house.

Horrible as all this was to behold, Hannibal halted a while and kept
his men in their ranks, so as not to aggravate the disorder and panic,
and then, as soon as he saw a break in the line, and the danger that
the army might accomplish the passage safely indeed but to no purpose, because stripped of all their baggage, he hurried down from his
position on the heights and routed the enemy, but at the same time
increased the confusion of his own troops. This confusion, however,
was quieted in a moment when the flight of the mountaineers left the
roads clear, and all soon marched through the pass not merely in peace
but almost in silence. Next he took a fortress, the capital of the district,
and some villages in the neighbourhood, and fed his troops for three
days on the corn and cattle he had seized. In those three days he accomplished a considerable march, as there was not much hindrance
from the ground or from the mountaineers, whom they had cowed
at the outset.

Then they reached a canton, which, for a mountain district, was
densely peopled. Here Hannibal was all but cut off, not by open fighting, but by his own peculiar arts, treachery and ambuscade. Some old
men, governors of the fortresses, came to him as envoys, with assurances
that warned by the salutary examples of the misfortunes of others, they
preferred to make trial of the friendship rather than of the might of
the Carthaginians; that thereupon they would obediently do his bidding; and they begged him to accept supplies, guides for his march,
and hostages as a guarantee of their promises. Hannibal, feeling that
he must not either rashly trust or slight them, lest refusal might make
them open enemies, gave them a gracious answer. He accepted the
offered hostages, and used the supplies which they had themselves
brought to the road, but he followed the guides with his army in fighting order, not as if he was among a friendly people. His van was
formed of the elephants and cavalry, while he marched himself in the
rear with the main strength of the infantry anxiously reconnoitring at
every step. The moment they entered a narrow pass, dominated on one
side by an overhanging height, the barbarians sprang out of their ambuscades in every direction, attacking in front and rear, discharging
missiles and coming to close quarters and rolling down huge stones
upon the army. It was on the rear that the enemy pressed in greatest
force. The infantry column wheeled and faced him; but it was proved
beyond a doubt that, had not the rear been well strengthened, a terrible
disaster would have been sustained in that pass. Even as it was, they
were brought to the extremest jeopardy, and were within a hair's

breadth of destruction. For while Hannibal was hesitating about sending his men into the defile because, though he himself could support the cavalry, he had no reserve in his rear for the infantry, the mountaineers rushed on his flanks, and having cut his line in half barred his advance. One night he had to pass without his cavalry and his baggage.

Next day, as the barbarians were less active in their attacks, the army was again united, and fought its way through the pass, but not without loss, which, however, fell more heavily on the beasts of burden than on the men. From this point the mountaineers became less numerous; hovering round more like brigands than soldiers, they threatened now the van, now the rear, whenever the ground gave them a chance, or stragglers in advance or behind offered an opportunity. The elephants, though it was a tedious business to drive them along the narrow precipitous passes, at least protected the troops from the enemy wherever they went, inspiring, as they did, a peculiar fear in all who were unused to approach them.

On the ninth day they reached the top of the Alps, passing for the most part over trackless steeps, and by devious ways, into which they were led by the treachery of their guides. Two days they encamped on the height, and the men, worn out with hardships and fighting, were allowed to rest. Some beasts of burden too, which had fallen down among the crags, found their way to the camp by following the army's tracks. The men were already worn out and wearied with their many miseries, when a fall of snow coming with the setting of the Pleiades added to their sufferings a terrible fear. At daybreak, the march was resumed, and as the army moved wearily over ground all buried in snow, languor and despair were visibly written on every face, when Hannibal stepped to the front, and having ordered a halt on a peak which commanded a wide and distant prospect, pointed to Italy and to the plains round the Po, as they lay beneath the heights of the Alps, telling his men, " 'Tis the walls not of Italy only but of Rome itself that you are now scaling. What remains," he added, "will be a smooth descent; in one, or at the most, in two battles we shall have the citadel and capital of Italy in our grasp and power."

The army then began to advance, and now even the enemy attempted nothing but some stealthy ambuscades, as opportunity offered. The remainder, however, of the march proved far more difficult than the ascent, as the Alps for the most part on the Italian side have a shorter and therefore a steeper slope. In fact the whole way was precipitous, narrow, and slippery, so much so that they could not keep themselves from falling, nor could those who had once stumbled maintain their foothold. Thus they tumbled one over another and the beasts of burden over the men.

Next they came to a much narrower pass with walls of rock so perpendicular that a light-armed soldier could hardly let himself down by feeling his way, and grasping with his hands the bushes and roots sticking out around him. The place of old was naturally precipitous, and now by a recent landslip it had broken away sheer to a depth of a thousand feet. Here the cavalry halted, as if it must be the end of their route, and Hannibal, wondering what delayed the march, was told that the rock was impassable. Then he went himself to examine the spot. There seemed to be no doubt that he must lead his army round by pathless and hitherto untrodden slopes, however tedious might be the circuit. This route, however, was impracticable, for while on last season's still unmelted snow lay a fresh layer of moderate depth, where the foot of the first newcomer found a good hold on the soft and not very deep drift as soon as it had been once trampled down under the march of such a host of men and beasts, they had to walk on the bare ice beneath, and the liquid mud from the melting snow. Here there was a horrible struggle. The slippery ice allowed no firm foothold, and indeed betrayed the foot all the more quickly on the slope, so that whether a man helped himself to rise by his hands or knees, his supports gave way, and he fell again. And here there were no stalks or roots to which hand or foot could cling. Thus there was incessant rolling on nothing but smooth ice or slush of snow. The beasts broke through, occasionally treading down even to the very lowest layer of snow, and when they fell, as they wildly struck out with their hoofs in their efforts to rise, they cut clean to the bottom, still many of them stuck fast in the hard and deep frozen ice, as if caught in a trap.

At last, when both men and beasts were worn out with fruitless exertion, they encamped on a height, in a spot which with the utmost difficulty they had cleared; so much snow had to be dug out and removed. The soldiers were then marched off to the work of making a road through the rock, as there only was a passage possible. Having to cut into the stone, they heaped up a huge pile of wood from great trees in the neighbourhood, which they had felled and lopped. As soon as there was strength enough in the wind to create a blaze they lighted the pile, and melted the rocks, as they heated, by pouring vinegar on them. The burning stone was cleft open with iron implements, and then they relieved the steepness of the slopes by gradual winding tracks, so that even the elephants as well as the other beasts could be let down. Four days were spent in this rocky pass, and the beasts almost perished of hunger, as the heights generally are quite bare, and such herbage as grows is buried in snow. Amid the lower slopes were valleys, sunny hills too, and streams, and woods beside them, and spots now at last more worthy to be the habitations of man. Here they sent the beasts to feed, and the men, worn out with the toil or road-making, were allowed to rest. In the next three days they reached level ground, and now the country was less wild, as was also the character of the inhabitants.

Such on the whole was the march which brought them to Italy, in the fifth month, according to some authors, after leaving New Carthage, the passage of the Alps having occupied fifteen days. As to the numbers of Hannibal's army on his arrival in Italy, historians are not agreed. The highest reckoning is a hundred thousand infantry and twenty thousand infantry and twenty thousand cavalry; the lowest twenty thousand infantry and six thousand cavalry. Cincius Alimentus, who tells us that he was taken prisoner by Hannibal, would have the greatest weight with me, did he not confuse the numbers by adding the Gauls and Ligurians. Including these there arrived eighty thousand infantry and ten thousand cavalry, though it is more probable that they flocked to his standard in Italy; and so some writers state. Cincius says that Hannibal himself told him that, after crossing the Rhone, he lost thirty-six thousand men, and a vast number of horses and beasts of burden.

SIR CHARLES OMAN

Sir Charles Oman, British historian, was born in India in 1860 and died in England in 1946. He was for many years a professor of history at Oxford University. His books were numerous, and wide-ranging in their scope, but his special interest was in military history, and the selection from his work which follows is taken from his *History of the Art of War in the Middle Ages*.

This account of the battle of Hastings, which secured the Norman Conquest of England, is, I think, one of the most vivid and dramatic stories of a great and decisive encounter ever written. It was a case of both sides battling against heavy odds: the Normans against the strength of the English position; the English against the irresistible combination of archers and horsemen. No other men ever made a more gallant stand, none a more furious and unrelenting attack.

The Battle of Hastings, A.D. 1066

AS THE last great example of an endeavour to use the old infantry tactics of the Teutonic races against the now fully-developed cavalry of feudalism, we have to describe the battle of Hastings, a field which has been fought over by modern critics almost as fiercely as by the armies of Harold Godwineson and William the Bastard.

About the political and military antecedents of the engagement we have no need to speak at length. Suffice it to say that the final defeat of the old English thegnhood was immediately preceded by its most striking victory. In the summer of 1066 the newly-chosen King Harold was forced to watch two enemies at once. The Norman Duke William had openly protested against the election that had taken place in January, and was known to be gathering a great army and fleet at St. Valery. Harold knew him well, and judged him a most formidable enemy; he had called out the available naval strength of his realm, and a strong squadron was waiting all through June, July, and August, ranging between the Isle of Wight and Dover, ready to dispute the passage of the Channel. At the same time the earls and sheriffs had been warned to have the land forces of the realm ready for mobilisation, and the king with his housecarles lay by the coast in Sussex waiting for news. Duke William came not, for many a week; his host took long to gather, and when his ships were ready, August turned out a month of persistent storm and northerly winds, unsuited for the sailing of a great armament.

Meanwhile there was danger from the North also. King Harold's rebel brother, Earl Tostig, had been hovering off the coast with a small squadron, and had made a descent on the Humber in May, only to be driven away by the Northumbrian Earl Edwin. But Tostig had leagued himself with Harold Hardrada, the warlike and greedy King of Norway, and a Norse invasion was a possibility, though it seemed a less immediate danger than the Norman threat to the South Coast. September had arrived before either of the perils materialised.

By a most unlucky chance the crisis came just when the English fleet had run out of provisions, after keeping the sea for three months. On September 8, Harold ordered it round to London to revictual, and to refit, for it had suffered in the hard weather. It was to resume its cruising as soon as possible. Seven days later came the news that a Norwegian fleet of three hundred sail had appeared off the Yorkshire coast, and had ravaged Cleveland and taken Scarborough. Harold was compelled to commit the guard of the Channel to the winds, which had hitherto served him well, and to fly north with his housecarles to face Hardrada's invasion. On his way he got the disastrous message that the two Earls Edwin of Northumbria and Morkar of Mercia had been beaten in a pitched battle at Fulford, in front of York (September 20), and that the city was treating for surrender. Pressing on with all possible speed, the English king arrived at York in time to prevent this disaster, and the same afternoon he brought the Norsemen to action at Stamford Bridge on the Derwent, seven miles from the city. Here he inflicted on them an absolutely crushing defeat—Hardrada was slain, so was the rebel Earl Tostig, and the invading host was so nearly exterminated that the survivors fled on only twenty-four ships, though they had brought three hundred into the Humber.

The details of the fight are absolutely lost—we cannot unfortunately accept one word of the spirited narrative of the *Heimskringla,* for all the statements in it that can be tested are obviously incorrect. Harold *may* have offered his rebel brother pardon and an earldom, and have promised his Norse ally no more than the famous "seven feet of English earth, since his stature is greater than that of other men." The Vikings *may* have fought for long hours in their shieldring, and have failed at evening only, when their king had been slain by a chance arrow. But we cannot trust a saga which says that Morkar was King Harold Godwineson's brother, and fell at Fulford; that Earl Waltheof (then a child) took part in the fight, and that the English army was mostly composed of cavalry and archers. The whole tale of the *Heimskringla* reads like a version of the battle of Hastings transported to Stamford Bridge by some incredible error. The one detail about it recorded in the Anglo-Saxon Chronicle, namely, that the fighting included a desperate defence of a bridge against the pursuing English, does *not* appear in the Norse narrative at all. We can only be sure that both sides must have fought on foot in the old fashion of Viking and Englishman, "hewing at each other across the war-linden" till the beaten army was well-nigh annihilated.

Meanwhile, on September 28—two days after Stamford Bridge— William of Normandy had landed at Pevensey, unhindered either by the English fleet, which was refitting at London, or by the king's army, which had gone north to repel the Norwegians. The invaders began to waste the land, and met with little resistance, since the king and his chosen warriors were absent. Only at Romney, as we are told, did the landsfolk stand to their arms and beat off the raiders.

Meanwhile, the news of William's landing was rapidly brought to Harold at York, and reached him—as we are told—at the very moment when he was celebrating by a banquet his victory over the Northmen. The king received the message on October 1 or October 2: he immediately hurried southward to London with all the speed that he could make. The victorious army of Stamford Bridge was with him, and the North Country levies of Edwin and Morkar were directed to follow as fast as they were able. Harold reached London on the 7th or 8th of October, and stayed there a few days to gather in the fyrd of the neighbouring shires of the South Midlands. On the 11th he marched forth from the city to face Duke William, though his army was still incomplete. The slack or treacherous earls of the North had not yet brought up their contingents, and the men of the western shires had not been granted time enough to reach the mustering place. But Harold's heart had been stirred by the reports of the cruel ravaging of Kent and Sussex by the Normans, and he was resolved to put his cause to the arbitrament of battle as quickly as possible, though the delay of a few days would perhaps have doubled his army. A rapid march of two days brought him to the outskirts of the Andredsweald, within touch of the district on which William had for the last fortnight been exercising his cruelty.

Harold took up his position at the point where the road from London to Hastings first leaves the woods, and comes forth into the open land of the coast. The chosen ground was the lonely hill above the marshy bottom of Senlac, on which the ruins of Battle Abbey stand, but then marked to the chronicler only by "the hoar apple tree" on its ridge, just as Ashdown had been marked two centuries before by its aged thorn.

The Senlac position consists of a hill some 1,100 yards long and 150 yards broad, joined to the main bulk of the Wealden Hills by a sort of narrow isthmus with steep descents on either side. The road from London to Hastings crosses the isthmus, bisects the hill at its highest point, and then sinks down into the valley, to climb again the opposite ridge of Telham Hill. The latter is considerably the higher of the two, reaching 441 feet above the sea-level, while Harold's hill is but 275 at its summit. The English hill has a fairly gentle slope towards the south, the side which looked towards the enemy, but on the north the fall on either side of the isthmus is so steep as to be almost precipitous. The summit of the position, where it is crossed by the road, is the highest point. Here it was that King Harold fixed his two banners, the Dragon of Wessex, and his own standard of the Fighting Man.

The position was very probably one that had served before for some army of an older century, for we learn from the best authorities that there lay about it, especially on its rear, ancient banks and ditches, in some places scarped to a precipitous slope. Perhaps it may have been the camp of some part of Alfred's army in 893–894, when, posted in the east end of the Andredsweald, between the Danish fleet which had come ashore at Lymne and the other host which had camped at Middleton, he endeavoured from his central position to restrain their ravages in Kent and Sussex. No place indeed could have been more suited for a force observing newly-landed foes. It covers the only road from London which then pierced the Andredsweald, and was so close to its edge that the defenders could seek shelter in the impenetrable woods if they wished to avoid a battle.

The hill above the Senlac bottom, therefore, being the obvious position to take, for an army whose tactics compelled it to stand upon the defensive, Harold determined to offer battle there. We need not believe the authorities who tell us that the King had been thinking of delivering a night attack upon the Normans, if he should chance to find them scattered abroad on their plundering, or keeping an inefficient lookout. It was most unlikely that he should dream of groping in the dark through eight miles of rolling ground, to assault a camp whose position and arrangements must have been unknown. His army had marched hard from London, had apparently only reached Senlac at nightfall, and must have been tired out. Moreover, Harold knew William's capacities as a general, and could not have thought it likely that he would be caught unprepared. It must have seemed to him a much more possible event that the Norman might refuse to attack the strong Senlac position, and offer battle in the open and nearer the sea. It was probably in anticipation of some such chance that Harold ordered his fleet, which had run back into the mouth of the Thames in very poor order some four weeks back, to refit itself and sail round the North Foreland, to threaten the Norman vessels now drawn ashore under the cover of a wooden castle at Hastings. He can scarcely have thought it likely that William would retire over seas on the news of his approach, so the bringing up of the fleet must have been intended either to cut off the Norman retreat in the event of a great English victory on land, or to so molest the invader's stranded vessels that he would be forced to return to the shore in order to defend them.

The English position is said by one narrator of the battle to have been entrenched. According to Wace, the latest and the most diffuse of our authorities, Harold ordered his men to rear a fence of plaited wood-work from the timber of the forest which lay close at their backs. But the earlier chroniclers, without exception, speak only of the shield-wall of the English, of their dense mass covering the crest of the hill, and of relics of ancient fortifications, the *antiquas agger* and *frequentia fossarum,* and *fovea magna* mentioned above. There is nothing inconceivable in the idea of Harold's having used the old Danish device of palisading a camp, save that he had arrived only on the preceding night, and that his army was weary. In the morning hours of October 14 little could have been done, though between daybreak and the arrival of the Norman host there were certainly three long hours. But it is difficult to suppose that if any serious entrenching had been carried out, the earlier Norman narrators of the fight would have refrained from mentioning it, since the more formidable the obstacles opposed to him, the more notable and creditable would have been the triumph of their duke. And the Bayeux Tapestry, which (despite all destructive criticism) remains a primary authority for the battle, appears to show no traces of any breastwork covering the English front. Probably Wace, writing from oral tradition ninety years after the battle, had heard something of the *frequentia fossarum* mentioned by William of Poictiers, and the *agger* described by Orderic, and translated them into new entrenchments, which he described as works of the best military type of his day.

From end to end of the crest of the hill the English host was ranged in one great solid mass. Probably its line extended from the high road, which crosses the summit nearer to its eastern than to its western side, for some 200 yards to the left, as far as the head of the small steep combe (with a rivulet at its bottom) which lies 200 yards to the due

east of the modern parish church; while on the other, or western, side
of the high road, the battle-front was much longer, running from the
road as far as the upper banks of the other ravine (with a forked brook
flowing out of it from two sources) which forms the western flank of
the hill. From the road to this ravine there must have been a front of
800 or 850 yards. Harold's two standards were, as we know, set up on
the spot which was afterwards marked by the high altar of Battle Abbey.
His standing-place must therefore have been in the left-centre rather
than in the absolute middle-front of the line. But the spot was dictated
by the lie of the ground—here is the actual highest point of the hill,
275 feet above sea-level, while the greater part of the position is along
the 250 feet contour. It was the obvious place for the planting of standards to be visible all around, and a commander standing by them could
look down from a slight vantage-ground on the whole front of his host.

In this array, the English centre being slightly curved forward, its
flank slightly curved back, the army looked to the Normans more like
a circular mass than a deployed line. Although the Northumbrian and
West-country levies were still missing, the army must have numbered
many thousands, for the fyrd of south and central England was present
in full force, and stirred to great wrath by the ravages of the Normans.
It is impossible to guess at the strength of the host: the figures of the
chroniclers, which sometimes swell up to hundreds of thousands, are
wholly useless. As the position was about 1,100 yards long, and the
space required by a single warrior swinging his axe or hurling his
javelin was some three feet, the front rank must have been at least some
eleven hundred or twelve hundred strong. The hilltop was completely
covered by the English, whose spear-shafts appeared to the Normans
like a wood, so that they cannot have been a mere thin line: if they were
some eight or ten deep, the total must have reached ten or eleven thousand men. Of these the smaller part must have been composed of the
fully-armed warriors, the king's housecarles, the thegnhood, and the
wealthier and better-equipped freemen, the class owning some five
hides of land. The rudely-armed levies of the fyrd must have consti-
tuted the great bulk of the army: they bore, as the Bayeux Tapestry
shows, the most miscellaneous arms—swords, javelins, clubs, axes, a
few bows, and probably even rude instruments of husbandry turned to
warlike uses. Their only defensive armour was the round or kite-
shaped shield: body and head were clothed only in the tunic and cap
of everyday wear.

In their battle array we know that the well-armed housecarles—
perhaps two thousand chosen and veteran troops—were grouped in the
centre around the king and the royal standards. The fyrd, divided no
doubt according to its shires, was ranged on either flank. Presumably

the thegns and other fully-armed men formed its front ranks, while the peasantry stood behind and backed them up, though at first only able to hurl their weapons at the advancing foe over the heads of their more fully-equipped fellows.

We must now turn to the Normans. Duke William had undertaken his expedition not as the mere feudal head of the barons of Normandy, but rather as the managing director of a great joint-stock company for the conquest of England, in which not only his own subjects, but hundreds of adventurers, poor and rich, from all parts of western Europe had taken shares. At the assembly of Lillebonne the Norman baronage had refused in their corporate capacity to undertake the vindication of their duke's claims on England. But all, or nearly all, of them had consented to serve under him as volunteers, bringing not merely their usual feudal contingent, but as many men as they could get together. In return they were to receive the spoils of the island kingdom if the enterprise went well. On similar terms William had accepted offers of help from all quarters: knights and sergeants flocked in, ready, "some for land and some for pence," to back his claim. It seems that, though the native Normans were the core of the invading army, yet the strangers considerably outnumbered them on the muster-rolls. Great nobles like Eustace Count of Boulogne, the Breton Count Alan Fergant, and Haimar of Thouars were ready to risk their lives and resources on the chance of an ample profit. French, Bretons, Flemings, Angevins, knights from the more distant regions of Aquitaine and Lotharingia, even—if Guy of Amiens speaks truly—stray fighting men from among the Norman conquerors of Naples and Sicily, joined the host.

Many months had been spent in the building of a fleet at the mouth of the Dive. Its numbers, exaggerated to absurd figures by many chroniclers, may possibly have reached the six hundred and ninety-six vessels given to the duke by the most moderate estimate. What was the total of the warriors which it carried is as uncertain as its own numbers. If any analogies may be drawn from contemporary hosts, the cavalry must have formed a very heavy proportion of the whole. In continental armies the foot-soldiery were so despised that an experienced general devoted all his attention to increasing the numbers of his horse. If we guess that there may have been three thousand or even four thousand mounted men, and eight thousand or nine thousand foot-soldiers, we are going as far as probability carries us, and must confess that our estimate is wholly arbitrary. The most modest figure given by the chroniclers is sixty thousand fighting men; but, considering their utter inability to realise the meaning of high numbers, we are dealing liberally with them if we allow a fifth of that estimate.

After landing at Pevensey on September 28, William had moved to Hastings and built a wooden castle there for the protection of his fleet. It was then in his power to have moved on London unopposed, for Harold was only starting on his march from York. But the duke had resolved to fight near his base, and spent the fortnight which was at his disposal in the systematic harrying of Kent and Sussex. When his scouts told him that Harold was at hand, and had pitched his camp by Senlac hill, he saw that his purpose was attained; he would be able to fight at his own chosen moment, and at only a few miles' distance from his ships. At daybreak on the morning of October 14, William bade his host get in array, and marched over the eight miles of rolling ground which separate Hastings and Senlac. When they reached the summit of the hill at Telham, the English position came in sight, on the opposite hill, not much more than a mile away.

On seeing the hour of conflict at hand, the duke and his knights drew on their mail-shirts, which, to avoid fatigue, they had not yet assumed, and the host was arrayed in battle order. The form which William had chosen was that of three parallel corps, each containing infantry and cavalry. The centre was composed of the native contingents of Normandy; the left mainly of Bretons and men from Maine and Anjou; the right, of French and Flemings. But there seem to have been some Normans in the flanking divisions also. The duke himself, as was natural, took command in the centre, the wings fell respectively to the Breton Count Alan Fergant and to Eustace of Boulogne: with the latter was associated Roger of Montgomery, a great Norman baron.

In each division there were three lines: the first was composed of bowmen mixed with arbalesters: the second was composed of foot-soldiery armed not with missile weapons but with pike and sword. Most of them seem to have worn mail-shirts, unlike the infantry of the English fyrd. In the rear was the really important section of the army, the mailed knights. We may presume that William intended to harass and thin the English masses with his archery, to attack them seriously with his heavy infantry, who might perhaps succeed in getting to close quarters and engaging the enemy hand to hand; but evidently the crushing blow was to be given by the great force of horsemen who formed the third line of each division.

The Normans deployed on the slopes of Telham, and then began their advance over the rough valley which separated them from the English position.

When they came within range, the archery opened upon the English, and not without effect; at first there must have been little reply to the showers of arrows, since Harold had but very few bowmen in his ranks. The shield-wall, moreover, can have given but a partial protection, though it no doubt served its purpose to some extent. When, however, the Normans advanced farther up the slope, they were received with a furious discharge of missiles of every kind, javelins, lances, taper-axes, and even—if William of Poictiers is to be trusted— rude weapons more appropriate to the neolithic age than to the eleventh century, great stones bound to wooden handles and launched in the same manner that was used for the casting-axe. The archers were apparently swept back by the storm of missiles, but the heavy armed foot pushed up to the front of the English line and got to hand-to-hand fighting with Harold's men. They could, however, make not the least impression on the defenders, and were perhaps already recoiling when William ordered up his cavalry. The horsemen rode up the slope already strewn with corpses, and dashed into the fight. Foremost among them was a minstrel named Taillefer, who galloped forward cheering on his comrades, and playing like a *jongleur* with his sword, which he kept casting into the air and then catching again. He burst right through the shield-wall and into the English line, where he was slain after cutting down several opponents. Behind him came the whole Norman knighthood, chanting their battle-song, and pressing their horses up the slope as hard as they could ride. The foot-soldiery dropped back—through the intervals between the three divisions, as we may suppose—and the duke's cavalry dashed against the long front of the shield-wall, whose front rank men they may have swept down by their mere impetus. Into the English mass, however, they could not break: there was a fearful crash, and a wild interchange of blows, but the line did not yield at any point. Nay, more, the assailants were ere long abashed by the fierce resistance that they met; the English axes cut through shield and mail, lopping off limbs and felling even horses to the ground. Never had the continental horsemen met such infantry before. After a space the Bretons and Angevins of the left wing felt their hearts fail, and recoiled down the hill in wild disorder, many men unhorsed and overthrown in the marshy bottom at the foot of the slope. All along the line the onset wavered, and the greater part of the host gave back, though the centre and right did not fly in wild disorder like the Bretons. A rumour ran along the front that the duke had fallen, and William had to bare his head and to ride down the ranks, crying that he lived, and would yet win the day, before he could check the retreat of his warriors. His brother Odo aided him to rally the waverers, and the greater part of the host was soon restored to order.

As it chanced, the rout of the Norman left wing was destined to bring nothing but profit to William. A great mass of the shire-levies on the English right, when they saw the Bretons flying, came pouring after them down the hill. They had forgotten that their sole chance of victory lay in keeping their front firm till the whole strength of the assailant should be exhausted. It was mad to pursue when two-thirds of the hostile army was intact, and its spirit still unbroken. Seeing the tumultuous crowd rushing after the flying Bretons, William wheeled his centre and threw it upon the flank of the pursuers. Caught in disorder, with their ranks broken and scattered, the rash peasantry were ridden down in a few moments. Their light shields, swords, and javelins availed them nothing against the rush of the Norman horse, and the whole horde, to the number of several thousands, were cut to pieces. The great bulk of the English host, however, had not followed the routed Bretons, and the duke saw that his day's work was but begun. Forming up his disordered squadrons, he ordered a second general attack on the line. Then followed an encounter even more fierce than the first. It would appear that the fortune of the Normans was somewhat better in this than in the earlier struggle: one or two temporary breaches were made in the English mass, probably in the places where it had been weakened by the rash onset of the shire-levies an hour before. Gyrth and Leofwine, Harold's two brothers, fell in the forefront of the fight, the former by William's own hand, if we may trust one good contemporary authority. Yet, on the whole, the duke had got little profit by his assault: the English had suffered severe loss, but their long line of shields and axes still crowned the slope, and their cries of "Out! out!" and "Holy Cross!" still rang forth in undaunted tones.

A sudden inspiration then came to William, suggested by the disaster which had befallen the English right in the first conflict. He determined to try the expedient of a feigned flight, a stratagem not unknown to Bretons and Normans of earlier ages. By his orders a considerable portion of the assailants suddenly wheeled about and retired in seeming disorder. The English thought, with more excuse on this occasion than on the last, that the enemy was indeed routed, and for the second time a great body of them broke the line and rushed after the retreating squadrons. When they were well on their way down the slope, William repeated his former procedure. The intact portion of his host fell upon the flanks of the pursuers, while those who had simulated flight faced about and attacked them in front. The result was again a foregone conclusion: the disordered men of the fyrd were hewn to pieces, and few or none of them escaped back to their comrades on the height. But the slaughter in this period of the fight did not fall wholly on the English; a part of the Norman troops who had carried out the false flight suffered some loss by falling into a deep ditch,—perhaps the remains of old entrenchments, perhaps the "rhine" which drained the Senlac bottom,—and were there smothered or trodden down by the comrades who rode over them. But the loss at this point must have been insignificant compared with that of the English.

Harold's host was now much thinned and somewhat shaken, but, in spite of the disasters which had befallen them, they drew together their thinned ranks, and continued the fight. The struggle was still destined to endure for many hours, for the most daring onsets of the Norman chivalry could not yet burst into the serried mass around the standards. The bands which had been cut to pieces were mere shire-levies, and the well-armed housecarles had refused to break their ranks, and still formed a solid core for the remainder of the host.

The fourth act of the battle consisted of a series of vigorous assaults by the duke's horsemen, alternating with volleys of arrows poured in during the intervals between the charges. The Saxon mass was subjected to exactly the same trial which befell the British squares in the battle of Waterloo—incessant charges by a gallant cavalry mixed with a destructive hail of missiles. Nothing could be more maddening than such an ordeal to the infantry-soldier, rooted to the spot by the necessities of his formation. The situation was frightful: the ranks were filled with wounded men unable to retire to the rear through the dense mass of their comrades, unable even to sink to the ground for the hideous press. The enemy was now attacking on both flanks: shields and mail had been riven: the supply of missile spears had given out: the English could but stand passive, waiting for the night or for the utter exhaustion of the enemy. The cavalry onsets must have been almost a relief compared with the desperate waiting between the acts, while the arrow-shower kept beating in on the thinning host. We have indications that, in spite of the disasters of the noon, some of the English made yet a third sally to beat off the archery. Individuals worked to frenzy by the weary standing still, seem to have occasionally burst out of the line to swing axe or sword freely in the open and meet a certain death. But the mass held firm—"a strange manner of battle," says William of Poictiers, "where the one side works by constant motion and ceaseless charges, while the other can but endure passively as it stands fixed to the sod. The Norman arrow and sword worked on: in the English ranks the only movement was the dropping of the dead: the living stood motionless." Desperate as was their plight, the English still held out till evening; though William himself led charge after charge against them, and had three horses killed beneath him, they could not be scattered while their king still survived and their standards still stood upright. It was finally the arrow rather than the sword that settled the day: the duke is said to have bade his archers shoot not point-blank, but with a high trajectory, so that the shafts fell all over the English host, and not merely on its front ranks. One of these chance shafts struck Harold in the eye and gave him a mortal wound. The arrow-shower, combined with the news of the king's fall, at last broke up the English host: after a hundred ineffective charges, a band of Norman knights burst into the midst of the mass, hewed Harold to pieces as he lay wounded at the foot of his banners, and cut down both the Dragon of Wessex and the Fighting Man.

The remnant of the English were now at last constrained to give ground: the few thousands—it may rather have been the few hundreds —who still clung to the crest of the bloodstained hill turned their backs to the foe and sought shelter in the friendly forest in their rear. Some fled on foot through the trees, some seized the horses of the thegns and housecarles from the camp and rode off upon them. But even in retreat they took some vengeance on the conquerors. The Normans, following in disorder, swept down the steep slope at the back of the hill, scarped like a glacis and impossible for horsemen,—the back defence, as we have conjectured, of some ancient camp of other days. Many of the knights, in the confused evening light, plunged down this trap, lost their footing, and lay floundering, man and horse, in the ravine at the bottom. Turning back, the last of the English swept down on them and cut them to pieces before resuming their flight. The Normans thought for a moment that succours had arrived to join the English—and, indeed, Edwin and Morkar's Northern levies were long overdue. The duke himself had to rally them, and to silence the fainthearted counsels of Eustace of Boulogne, who bade him draw back when the victory was won. When the Normans came on more cautiously, following, no doubt, the line of the isthmus and not plunging down the slopes, the last of the English melted away into the forest and disappeared. The hard day's work was done.

The stationary tactics of the phalanx of axemen had failed decisively before William's combination of archers and cavalry, in spite of the fact that the ground had been favourable to the defensive. The exhibition of desperate courage on the part of the English had only served to increase the number of the slain. Of all the chiefs of the army, only Esegar the Staller and Leofric, Abbot of Bourne, are recorded to have escaped, and both of them were dangerously wounded. The king and his brothers, the stubborn housecarles, and the whole thegnhood of Southern England had perished on the field. The English loss was never calculated; practically it amounted to the entire army. Nor is it possible to guess that of the Normans: one chronicle gives twelve thousand,—the figure is absurd, and the authority is not a good or a trustworthy one for English history. But whatever was the relative slaughter on the two sides, the lesson of the battle was unmistakable. The best of infantry, armed only with weapons for close fight and destitute of cavalry support, were absolutely helpless before a capable general who knew how to combine the horseman and the archer. The knights, if unsupported by the bowmen, might have surged for ever against the impregnable shield-wall. The archers, unsupported by the knights, could easily have been driven off the field by a general charge. United by the skilful hand of William, they were invincible.

HANIEL LONG

Haniel Long, who died in 1956, was one of those writers whose quality was never widely and fully perceived in their lifetime. This is more often true, I believe, in the case of those whose gift is delicate in texture, subtle in effect, and lingering in its flavor. The writers of coarser grain and vehement tone—the Menckens and James Joneses—make an immediate and crushing impact, but much of what they wrote withers away.

Haniel Long, who lived for many years in the enchanted and history-drenched region of Santa Fe, was not a prolific writer. Men of his temperament and cast of mind rarely are. Born in Rangoon, Burma, in 1888, he spent his early life as a teacher in Pittsburgh's Carnegie Institute of Technology. His first book was a volume of poems published in 1920. It was to be followed by *Notes for a New Mythology, Atlantides, Pittsburgh Memoranda, Malinche, Walt Whitman and the Springs of Courage, Piñon Country, A Letter to St. Augustine,* and the book by which he is represented here, *The Power Within Us.* Most of these, but not, fortunately, the last, are now out of print.

The Power Within Us should alone suffice, at least among discriminating readers, to preserve his reputation. It is a remarkable little book. It reconstructs, with careful documentation, the account which Cabeza de Vaca might have sent to the Spanish king, of the astounding journey made by him and three others, the human vestiges of a Conquistadorial expedition, across the North American continent. It is a book which, once read, will never be forgot.

Cabeza de Vaca

ALONG in late November, 1528, a handful of Spaniards, survivors of an ill-starred expedition to Florida, were washed ashore in the Gulf of Mexico, some think near the present site of Galveston. One of these men was Nuñez Cabeza de Vaca, thirty-eight years old, the lieutenant of the expedition, an adaptable man with some secret of growth in him. Despite the privations he had endured, this Nuñez led two other Spaniards and a Moor on a journey across the entire continent, barefoot and naked, which occupied them eight years.

After he reached Mexico City, Nuñez wrote a letter to his King, relating what had befallen him. It begins as the usual story of a European adventurer who leaves home to exploit people. But Nuñez little by little finds out that people are his brothers and sisters, and feels genuine concern for them. Stories require the right audience, and he seems afraid that His Majesty might not be interested in what he has to say, for it is the story of a disaster in Spanish colonial history and in the King's personal finances. In the world of the individual, nonetheless, it is a story of triumph, however lackadaisical the manner of its telling.

My account of Nuñez is not the account he sent the King, apart of course from the actual facts. But I believe it to be the account he wished to send the King. I preserve the core of his narrative, as translated by Fanny Bandelier, and I try to show what, quite plainly, was happening to the spirit of the man. That is, I allow him to speak as though unafraid of his King and his times. I wish him to address us four hundred years later, in this world of ours where human relation is still the difficult problem, and exploitation the cancer.

Nuñez found the limitless within the narrowly limited. He helped when he had no means of helping, and gave when he had nothing to give. So, what is interesting is that at a certain point he ceases to be a historical personage and becomes a symbol. If he were alive today, he would be free to bring into the open the inwardness of his adventure. Thus he would greatly concern the present western world and our entire human world, for we are his proper audience.

In his emergency Nuñez slides out of theories and prejudices which unfit one to live on. Possibly the capacity to survive depends upon courage of spirit to accept one's fate. Possibly also, danger can be a real benefit to the physical man. Nuñez was remarkably flexible; he had what seems unlimited courage, unlimited strength. To him life itself was not different from hardship and danger, life *was* these things, and they are what make life good. His plight was hopeless, but he set in motion a train of thought and action which saved him. My attention wanders from the perfunctory narrative to the thing he refrains from confiding to the royal ear. That thing is a mystical feeling about the increase of life in a man from effort and from taking thought of his fellows. The weather-beaten explorer of the XVIth century, lost in a thorny land among copper-colored savages and facing a blank future, discovered religion to be a reality of which he had never dreamt. His effort, his feeling for others, take novel paths; but underneath, quite apparently, lies an ageless and universal experience.—H. L.

Your Majesty is at liberty to picture *us* under this aging, adipose, credulous commander. Across that steaming land we marched with our armor glittering and our horses covered with gaudy trappings, 578 of us, towards utter ruin. Believing that on the page of history we would share the glory of Cortés and his murderous band. . . .

Pámfilo would summon the copper-colored natives and tell them with gestures that he was searching for a city of the size and value of Tenochtitlan. The Indians had never heard of Tenochtitlan nor of Montezuma. But they had heard of a big town and pointed northward exclaiming, "Apaláchee!"

We marched and we marched, and had fevers and fevers. Yes, your Majesty is at liberty to picture us.

Apaláchee was no Tenochtitlan. . . . We found it. It was in an immense swamp, a large impoverished settlement of thatched huts, a place of unbearable squalor.

There was nothing for it but seek the sea again and sail back to Cuba. Our arms and armor made us feel like dolts, and we wished we had pierced the jungle carrying carpenter's tools. For now, without axe, adze, or hammer, we had to build ourselves boats.

This is the tale of what men can and cannot do when they must do something or die. We built nine open boats. During the weeks it required, some of us went with scant food, and those whose palates allowed it devoured the horses.

Our 580 men had become 400 when at last we set sail and left behind us the Indian marksmen and the snakes, neither of which in Florida err when they strike.

Day after day tide and wind washed us out to sea and then washed us in to land, along a dazzling and uncertain coast. From thirst, and from the exposure to the frightful sun, our 400 became 40.

Who knows what was lost in these boats? Another Magellan, another Camoëns, another Cervantes, another St. John of the Cross . . .

No one has so sympathetic an imagination as your Majesty. You will understand what I am not telling you; that I saw men jump overboard, mad from thirst and sun. That I saw them swell and die slowly in delirium, heard their words and songs pour out the pitiful contents of their minds. That I saw men gnaw at corpses. And that these were Spanish gentlemen.

It is curious to have so graphic a lesson in what life may become. We had been a proud band, relying on our united strength, our armor, and our horses. Slowly our strength disunited, until nothing that we had in common remained to help any of us.

As I say, it is curious when one has nobody and nothing to rely upon outside of oneself.

Yet again that music, that fitful run and flash of brightness I first heard on the battlefield of Ravenna. Your Majesty is renowned as a patron of music; here was a music it is possible you may never have heard.

Somewhere on that coast a handful of us crawled ashore, and were fed and tended by kindly Indians till we regathered nervous vitality for the hopeless voyage to Cuba. We stript and launched the boat, first putting our clothes aboard her. But a great comber capsized the rotten heavy hulk, imprisoning and drowning three of us. The others emerged mother-naked on the beach, shivering in the November wind of that overcast afternoon.

The Indians came back and found us as naked as they were, and our barge gone, and in tears. They sat down beside us and cried, too. I cried all the harder, to think people so miserable had pity for us. I have informed your Majesty of their tears and mine. These simple Indians were the first relenting of nature to us in months and months. That evening, for fear we might die on the way, the Indians made fires at intervals along the path to their village, warming us at each fire. That night and many nights after we slept beside them on the oyster shells which floor their huts, wrapt in hides against the cold winds from the sea.

While we were subjects of your Majesty, we had everything life offers, and now we had nothing. To understand what it means to have nothing one must have nothing. No clothing against the weather might appear the worst. But for us poor skeletons who survived it, it was not.

The worst lay in parting little by little with the thoughts that clothe the soul of a European, and most of all of the idea that a man attains strength through dirk and dagger, and serving in your Majesty's guard. We had to surrender such fantasies till our inward nakedness was the nakedness of an unborn babe, starting life anew in a womb of sensations which in themselves can mysteriously nourish. Several years went by before I could relax in that living plexus for which even now I have no name; but only when at last I relaxed, could I see the possibilities of a life in which to be deprived of Europe was not to be deprived of too much.

Tempests came, we could pull no more roots from the sea-channels, the canebrake yielded no more fish. People died in the flimsy lodges. News came that five Spaniards further down the coast, men from another barge, had eaten one another up till but one remained. This deed startled the innocence of our Indians. They debated whether to kill us, to be rid of us. Instead, they made us their beasts of burden.

In April the Indians went down to the sea taking us with them; for a whole month we ate the blackberries of the sand dunes. The Indians danced incessantly. They asked us to cure their sick. When we said we did not know how to cure, they withheld our food from us. We began to watch the procedure of their medicine men. It seemed to us both irreligious and uninstructed. Besides, we found the notion of healing Indians somewhat repellent, as your Majesty will understand. But we had to heal them or die. So we prayed for strength. We prayed on bended knees and in an agony of hunger. Then over each ailing Indian we made the sign of the Cross, and recited the Ave María and a Pater noster. To our amazement the ailing said they were well. And not only they but the whole tribe went without food so that we might have it. Yet so great was the lack of food for us all, it seemed impossible that life could last.

Truly, it was to our amazement that the ailing said they were well. Being Europeans, we thought we had given away to doctors and priests our ability to heal. But here it was, still in our possession, even if we had only Indians to exercise it upon. It was ours after all, we were more than we had thought we were.

I am putting my words together for whatever intelligence there may be in the world. There is no other reality among men than this intelligence; Sire, it is greatly to your glory that you can incarnate it.

To be more than I thought I was—a sensation utterly new to me. . . .

Starvation, nakedness, slavery: sensations utterly new to me, also. . . . The last of my fellow Spaniards on the island dies. . . . Nothing to eat after the sea-roots sprouted but the blackberries of the sand dunes. Nothing to protect me from the attack of the terrible frost, or the terrible sun. No one who knew my language. . . . And it endured for months, for years maybe. . . . Everyone I saw as starved as I was. The human body emaciated, the lean cheek, the burning eye—the ribs showing, each rib distinct—the taut skin, the weak loins, the shrunken haunch and pap. In the whole world there can be no poverty like the poverty of these people. I could not stand it. I ran away. . . .

At this time, as I remember it, I began to think of Indians as fellow human beings. If I introduce this idea it is to prepare your Majesty for other ideas which came to me later, in consequence.

These were days when I reassorted the pictures of my childhood, as a child turns his kaleidoscope. I saw the Gaunche slaves anew, and as though I were one of them. I saw my grandfather through the eyes of his slaves. I remembered, now without laughing, how he had tricked the Gaunches into slavery. He pretended to enlist them to sail from the Grand Canary to conquer Teneriffe, and when he had them below decks he battened down the hatches and set sail for Cádiz . . .

My grandfather's brutality earned him the public denunciation of Bishop Juan de Frías. This too I remembered.

In this wilderness I became a trader, and went to and fro on the coast and a little inland. I went inland with seashells and cockles, and a certain shell used to cut beans, which the natives value. I came out with hides, and red ochre for the face and hair, flint for arrow points, and tassels of deerhide. I came to be well known among the tribes, and found out the lay of the land.

One day I heard someone calling me by name, "Alvar Nuñez, Alvar Nuñez!" It was Alonso del Castillo, one of the captains of the expedition. He said that Pámfilo's barge had drifted ashore among unfriendly Indians, and left of its occupants were only himself and Captain Andrés Dorantes, and Dorantes' blackamoor, Estevanico. We hid ourselves in a thicket and laid our plans.

That summer, when the coast tribes came together for the summer orgies, we four made good our escape westward.

Thus our 580 had become 400, our 400, forty, and our forty, four.

Certain natives came to Castillo. From ribs to cleft they were having spasms, and they begged him to cure them. He prayed, and required us anxiously to pray with him. When he had done praying he made the sign of the Cross over the Indians, and their spasms left off. We knelt down to give thanks for this new amazement.

Through this region there are no trails, and I lost my way. I found a burning tree to spend that very cold night beside. In the morning I loaded myself with dry wood, and took two burning sticks. Thus with fuel and fire, I went on for five days, seeing nobody, but having the sun with me by day and Mazzaroth and Arcturus by night. These five days I felt a numbness of those organs which keep one aware of the misery of existence. When curing sick Indians, I have struggled to shut out the thought of Andrés and Alonso (for we are self-conscious, knowing one another's sins); and in the effort of praying I have felt as though something in me had broken, to give me the power of healing. But alone in this wilderness no tissue of the body hindered the mysterious power. . . .

Months went by as in a dream. The nerve of vision no longer rendered plausible that European world of which we had been a part. That world grew fantastic, and fantastic our countrymen there. We ourselves were only too real. From lack of clothing we had big sores and deep skin fissures on our backs and shoulders, and it hurt us to carry the hides we slept in. And it hurt us to find firewood among the cactus. My thighs and arms bled so much I stood it only by remembering—and yet whom or what did I remember? Was it a Person—was it a quality of life—was it an emotion? Was it even a remembering, was it not perhaps a listening?

Often for a time it rained gently at dusk, soothing our thighs and arms. In one such dusk we encountered squinting women in an opening. They were afraid to run away from the three pale figures and the shadowy blackamoor, for they took us to be gods floating about in the mist and rain. They led us to a village of fifty huts. Here we cured, and cured. . . .

Our journey westward was but a long series of encounters. Your Majesty, encounters have become my meditation. The moment one accosts a stranger or is accosted by him is above all in this life the moment of drama. The eyes of Indians who crossed my trail have searched me to the very depths to estimate my *power*. It is true the world over. It is true of a Spaniard meeting another on the road between Toledo and Salamanca. Whoever we meet watches us intently at the quick strange moment of meeting, to see whether we are disposed to be friendly.

Seeing our bodies, seeing my own, and Alonso's, and Andrés', and the black Moor's, sometimes I think how once I was different, and we all were. What would Doña Alonza Maldonado and her husband Dr. Castillo of Salamanca think, if they could see their little boy Alonso today, striding here ahead of me, lashed by starvation, scorched and baked by the sun, his hair and beard unkempt, small about the flanks, his body shrivelled like a mummy? . . .

To clarify the same occurrences, words can be arranged differently, as no one knows better than your Majesty. It was a drunkenness, this feeling I began to have of power to render life and happiness to others. Yet I was concerned about it. The concern was the important thing— not the wondering about the nature of the power, how widespread it might be, how deep, whether Andrés or Alonso or Estevanico had it in equal measure with me. What occupied me was whether I myself knew how to use it, whether I could master it, whether indeed it was for me to master—perhaps being a self-directing power that came through me. But after one accustoms oneself to the idea, it is good to be able to give out health and joy whether one man have it, or whether we all have it. Had this thought occurred to your Majesty? Never before had it occurred to me. . . .

At first I did not notice other ways in which our ancient civilisation was affecting me. Yet soon I observed a certain reluctance in me to do good to others. I would say to myself, Need I exert what is left of me, I who have undergone tortures in an open boat and every privation and humiliation among the Indians, when there are strong healthy men about me, fresh from Holy Church and from school, who know their Christian duty? We Europeans all talk this way to ourselves. It has become second nature to us. Each nobleman and alcalde and villager is an avenue that leads us to this way of talking; we can admit it privately, your Majesty, can we not? If a man need a cloak, we do not give it to him if we have our wits about us; nor are we to be caught stretching out our finger in aid of a miserable woman. Someone else will do it, we say. Our communal life dries up our milk: we are barren as the fields of Castile. We regard our native land as a power which acts of itself, and relieves us each of exertion. While with them I thought only about doing the Indians good. But back among my fellow countrymen, I had to be on my guard not to do them positive harm. If one lives where all suffer and starve, one acts on one's own impulse to help. But where plenty abounds, we surrender our generosity, believing that our country replaces us each and several. This is not so, and indeed a delusion. On the contrary the power of maintaining life in others, lives within each of us, and from each of us does it recede when unused. It is a concentrated power. If you are not acquainted with it, your Majesty can have no inkling of what it is like, what it portends, or the ways in which it slips from one. In the name of God, your Majesty,

FAREWELL.

FRANCIS PARKMAN

The greatest, in my estimation, of American historians, Francis Parkman, was one of the most remarkable and fascinating men in our literary history. He was born in Boston in 1823, and lived on into what Van Wyck Brooks has called the Indian summer of New England's flowering period. He died at the age of seventy.

As a historian, Parkman was not cut from the ordinary pattern. Although meticulous in matters of research, he was no library-bounded writer. From first to last, as much as he was physically able, he was determined to see for himself at firsthand the settings in which his histories were placed. While still an undergraduate at Harvard he had conceived the idea of his life's work, a conception which he was to carry through indefatigably to the end. He would, he told himself, write what he liked to think of as the history of the American forest. In actual scope, it was the story of the long battles waged for the possession of the North American continent, and in his sensitive imagination he saw the struggle as meaning the inevitable disappearance of the wilderness which had fired his thoughts from boyhood on.

He accomplished his task at terrific cost to his own health and well-being. With more than a touch of masochism, he inured himself to physical hardship and pursued his object with relentless zeal, to the point of repeated breakdown, near blindness, and psychic disorder. And between times he found leisure to make himself a famous horticulturist, a world-known authority on roses.

Much in his writing would serve the purposes of this book; I have chosen a section from *The Jesuits in North America in the Seventeenth Century,* which tells the story of one of those remarkable missionaries, in the life and death of Father Jogues. I have also selected some pages from *The Discovery of the Great West: La Salle.* The French explorer was a man to whom Parkman found himself irresistibly drawn; their characters, particularly in the determination and dedication which they shared, were in high degree similar. The portrait of La Salle is one of his greatest, one of the most deeply perceived.

The Oregon Trail, although an American classic, and the best known of Parkman's works, is by no means one of his best books, although a remarkable achievement for a man of twenty-five. The two books represented here reveal Parkman in the maturity of his powers.

Father Jogues

THE waters of the St. Lawrence rolled through a virgin wilderness, where, in the vastness of the lonely woodlands, civilized man found a precarious harborage at three points only,—at Quebec, at Montreal, and at Three Rivers. Here and in the scattered missions was the whole of New France,—a population of some 300 souls in all. And now, over these miserable settlements, rose a war-cloud of frightful portent.

It was thirty-two years since Champlain had first attacked the Iroquois. They had nursed their wrath for more than a generation, and at length their hour was come. The Dutch traders at Fort Orange, now Albany, had supplied them with firearms. The Mohawks, the most easterly of the Iroquois nations, had, among their seven or eight hundred warriors, no less than 300 armed with the arquebuse, a weapon somewhat like the modern carbine. They were masters of the thunderbolts which, in the hands of Champlain, had struck terror into their hearts.

We have surveyed in the introductory chapter the character and organization of this ferocious people,—their confederacy of five nations, bound together by a peculiar tie of clanship; their chiefs, half hereditary, half elective; their government, an oligarchy in form and a democracy in spirit; their minds, thoroughly savage, yet marked here and there with traits of a vigorous development. The war which they had long waged with the Hurons was carried on by the Senecas and the other Western nations of their league; while the conduct of hostilities against the French and their Indian allies in lower Canada was left to the Mohawks. In parties of from ten to a hundred or more, they would leave their towns on the river Mohawk, descend Lake Champlain and the river Richelieu, lie in ambush on the banks of the St. Lawrence, and attack the passing boats or canoes. Sometimes they hovered about the fortifications of Quebec and Three Rivers, killing stragglers, or luring armed parties into ambuscades. They followed like hounds on the trail of travellers and hunters; broke in upon unguarded camps at midnight; and lay in wait, for days and weeks, to intercept the Huron traders on their yearly descent to Quebec. Had they joined to their ferocious courage the discipline and the military knowledge that belong to civilization, they could easily have blotted out New France from the map, and made the banks of the St. Lawrence once more a solitude; but though the most formidable of savages, they were savages only.

In the early morning of the 2nd of August, 1642, twelve Huron canoes were moving slowly along the northern shore of the expansion of the St. Lawrence known as the Lake of St. Peter. There were on board about forty persons, including four Frenchmen, one of them being the Jesuit, Isaac Jogues, whom we have already followed on his missionary journey to the towns of the Tobacco Nation. In the interval he had not been idle. During the last autumn (1641) he, with Father Charles Raymbault, had passed along the shore of Lake Huron northward, entered the strait through which Lake Superior discharges itself, pushed on as far as the Sault Sainte Marie, and preached the Faith to two thousand Ojibwas and other Algonquins there assembled. He was now on his return from a far more perilous errand. The Huron mission was in a state of destitution. There was need of clothing for the priests, of vessels for the altars, of bread and wine for the eucharist, of writing materials,—in short, of everything; and early in the summer of the present year Jogues had descended to Three Rivers and Quebec, with the Huron traders, to procure the necessary supplies. He had accomplished his task, and was on his way back to the mission. With him were a few Huron converts and among them a noted Christian chief, Eustache Ahatsistari. Others of the party were in course of instruction for baptism; but the greater part were heathen, whose canoes were deeply laden with the proceeds of their bargains with the French fur-traders.

Jogues sat in one of the leading canoes. He was born at Orleans in 1607, and was thirty-five years of age. His oval face and the delicate mould of his features indicated a modest, thoughtful, and refined nature. He was constitutionally timid, with a sensitive conscience and great religious susceptibilities. He was a finished scholar, and might have gained a literary reputation; but he had chosen another career, and one for which he seemed but ill fitted. Physically, however, he was well matched with his work; for, though his frame was slight, he was so active that none of the Indians could surpass him in running.

With him were two young men, René Goupil and Guillaume Couture, *donnés* of the mission,—that is to say, laymen who, from a religious motive and without pay, had attached themselves to the service of the Jesuits. Goupil had formerly entered upon the Jesuit novitiate at Paris, but failing health had obliged him to leave it. As soon as he was able, he came to Canada, offered his services to the Superior of the mission, was employed for a time in the humblest offices, and afterwards became an attendant at the hospital. At length, to his delight, he received permission to go up to the Hurons, where the surgical skill which he had acquired was greatly needed; and he was now on his way thither. His companion, Couture, was a man of intelligence and vigor, and of character equally disinterested. Both were, like Jogues, in the foremost canoes; while the fourth Frenchman was with the unconverted Hurons, in the rear.

The twelve canoes had reached the western end of the Lake of St. Peter, where it is filled with innumerable islands. The forest was close on their right; they kept near the shore to avoid the current, and the shallow water before them was covered with a dense growth of tall bulrushes. Suddenly the silence was frightfully broken. The war-whoop rose from among the rushes, mingled with the reports of guns and the whistling of bullets; and several Iroquois canoes, filled with warriors, pushed out from their concealment, and bore down upon Jogues and his companions. The Hurons in the rear were seized with a shameful panic. They leaped ashore; left canoes, baggage, and weapons, and fled into the woods. The French and the Christian Hurons made fight for a time; but when they saw another fleet of canoes approaching from the opposite shores or islands, they lost heart, and those escaped who could. Goupil was seized amid triumphant yells, as were also several of the Huron converts. Jogues sprang into the bulrushes, and might have escaped; but when he saw Goupil and the neophytes in the clutches of the Iroquois, he had no heart to abandon them, but came out from his hiding-place, and gave himself up to the astonished victors. A few of them had remained to guard the prisoners; the rest were chasing the fugitives. Jogues mastered his agony, and began to baptize those of the captive converts who needed baptism.

Couture had eluded pursuit; but when he thought of Jogues and of what perhaps awaited him, he resolved to share his fate, and, turning, retraced his steps. As he approached, five Iroquois ran forward to meet him; and one of them snapped his gun at his breast, but it missed fire. In his confusion and excitement, Couture fired his own piece, and laid the savage dead. The remaining four sprang upon him, stripped off all his clothing, tore away his finger-nails with their teeth, gnawed his fingers with the fury of famished dogs, and thrust a sword through one of his hands. Jogues broke from his guards, and, rushing to his friend, threw his arms about his neck. The Iroquois dragged him away, beat him with their fists and war-clubs till he was senseless, and, when he revived, lacerated his fingers with their teeth, as they had done those of Couture. Then they turned upon Goupil, and treated him with the same ferocity. The Huron prisoners were left for the present unharmed. More of them were brought in every moment, till at length the number of captives amounted in all to twenty-two, while three Hurons had been killed in the fight and pursuit. The Iroquois, about seventy in number, now embarked with their prey; but not until they had knocked on the head an old Huron, whom Jogues, with his mangled hands, had just baptized, and who refused to leave the place. Then, under a burning sun, they crossed to the spot on which the town of Sorel now stands, at the mouth of the river Richelieu, where they encamped.

Their course was southward, up the river Richelieu and Lake Champlain; thence, by way of Lake George, to the Mohawk towns. The pain and fever of their wounds, and the clouds of mosquitoes, which they could not drive off, left the prisoners no peace by day nor sleep by night. On the eighth day, they learned that a large Iroquois war-party, on their way to Canada, were near at hand; and they soon approached their camp, on a small island near the southern end of Lake Champlain. The warriors, two hundred in number, saluted their victorious countrymen with volleys from their guns; then, armed with clubs and thorny sticks, ranged themselves in two lines, between which the captives were compelled to pass up the side of a rocky hill. On the way, they were beaten with such fury that Jogues, who was last in the line, fell powerless, drenched in blood and half dead. As the chief man among the French captives, he fared the worst. His hands were again mangled, and fire applied to his body; while the Huron chief, Eustache, was subjected to tortures even more atrocious. When, at night, the exhausted sufferers tried to rest, the young warriors came to lacerate their wounds and pull out their hair and beards.

In the morning they resumed their journey. And now the lake narrowed to the semblance of a tranquil river. Before them was a woody mountain, close on their right a rocky promontory, and between these flowed a stream, the outlet of Lake George. On those rocks, more than a hundred years after, rose the ramparts of Ticonderoga. They landed, shouldered their canoes and baggage, took their way through the woods, passed the spot where the fierce Highlanders and the dauntless regiments of England breasted in vain the storm and lead and fire, and soon reached the shore where Abercrombie landed and Lord Howe fell. First of white men, Jogues and his companions gazed on the romantic lake that bears the name, not of its gentle discoverer, but of the dull Hanoverian king. Like a fair Naiad of the wilderness, it slumbered between the guardian mountains that breathe from crag and forest the stern poetry of war. But all then was solitude; and the clang of trumpets, the roar of cannon, and the deadly crack of the rifle had never as yet awakened their angry echoes.

The Iroquois landed at or near the future site of Fort William Henry, left their canoes, and, with their prisoners, began their march for the nearest Mohawk town. Each bore his share of the plunder. Even Jogues, though his lacerated hands were in a frightful condition and his body covered with bruises, was forced to stagger on with the rest under a heavy load. He with his fellow-prisoners, and indeed the whole party, were half starved, subsisting chiefly on wild berries. They crossed the upper Hudson, and in thirteen days after leaving the St. Lawrence neared the wretched goal of their pilgrimage,—a palisaded town, standing on a hill by the banks of the river Mohawk.

The whoops of the victors announced their approach, and the savage hive sent forth its swarms. They thronged the side of the hill, the old and the young, each with a stick, or a slender iron rod, bought from the Dutchmen on the Hudson. They ranged themselves in a double line, reaching upward to the entrance of the town; and through this "narrow road of Paradise," as Jogues calls it, the captives were led in single file, —Couture in front, after him a half-score of Hurons, then Goupil, then the remaining Hurons, and at last Jogues. As they passed, they were saluted with yells, screeches, and a tempest of blows. One, heavier than the others, knocked Jogues's breath from his body, and stretched him on the ground; but it was death to lie there, and, regaining his feet, he staggered on with the rest. When they reached the town, the blows ceased, and they were all placed on a scaffold, or high platform, in the middle of the place. The three Frenchmen had fared the worst, and were frightfully disfigured. Goupil, especially, was streaming with blood, and livid with bruises from head to foot.

They were allowed a few minutes to recover their breath, undisturbed, except by the hootings and gibes of the mob below. Then a chief called out, "Come, let us caress these Frenchmen!"—and the crowd, knife in hand, began to mount the scaffold. They ordered a Christian Algonquin woman, a prisoner among them, to cut off Jogues's left thumb, which she did; and a thumb of Goupil was also severed, a clam-shell being used as the instrument, in order to increase the pain. It is needless to specify further the tortures to which they were subjected, all designed to cause the greatest possible suffering without endangering life. At night, they were removed from the scaffold and placed in one of the houses, each stretched on his back, with his limbs extended, and his ankles and wrists bound fast to stakes driven into the earthen floor. The children now profited by the examples of their parents, and amused themselves by placing live coals and red-hot ashes on the naked bodies of the prisoners, who, bound fast, and covered with wounds and bruises which made every movement a torture, were sometimes unable to shake them off.

In the morning, they were again placed on the scaffold, where, during this and the two following days, they remained exposed to the taunts of the crowd. Then they were led in triumph to the second Mohawk town, and afterwards to the third, suffering at each a repetition of cruelties, the detail of which would be as monotonous as revolting.

In a house in the town of Teonontogen, Jogues was hung by the wrists between two of the upright poles which supported the structure, in such a manner that he remained for some fifteen minutes, in extreme torture, until, as he was on the point of swooning, an Indian, with an impulse for pity, cut the cords and released him. While they were in this town, four fresh Huron prisoners, just taken, were brought in, and placed on the scaffold with the rest. Jogues, in the midst of his pain and exhaustion, took the opportunity to convert them. An ear of green corn was thrown to him for food, and he discovered a few raindrops clinging to the husks. With these he baptized two of the Hurons. The remaining two received baptism soon after from a brook which the prisoners crossed on the way to another town.

Couture, though he had incensed the Indians by killing one of their warriors, had gained their admiration by his bravery; and, after torturing him most savagely, they adopted him into one of their families, in place of a dead relative. Thenceforth he was comparatively safe. Jogues and Goupil were less fortunate. Three of the Hurons had been burned to death, and they expected to share their fate. A council was held to pronounce their doom; but dissensions arose, and no result was reached. They were led back to the first village, where they remained, racked with suspense and half dead with exhaustion. Jogues, however, lost no opportunity to baptize dying infants, while Goupil taught children to make the sign of the cross. On one occasion, he made the sign on the forehead of a child, grandson of an Indian in whose lodge they lived. The superstition of the old savage was aroused. Some Dutchmen had told him that the sign of the cross came from the Devil, and would cause mischief. He thought that Goupil was bewitching the child; and, resolving to rid himself of so dangerous a guest, applied for aid to two young braves. Jogues and Goupil, clad in their squalid garb of tattered skins, were soon after walking together in the forest that adjoined the town, consoling themselves with prayer, and mutually exhorting each other to suffer patiently for the sake of Christ and the Virgin, when, as they were returning, reciting their rosaries, they met the two young Indians, and read in their sullen visages an augury of ill. The Indians joined them, and accompanied them to the entrance of the town, where one of the two, suddenly drawing a hatchet from beneath his blanket, struck it into the head of Goupil, who fell, murmuring the name of Christ. Jogues dropped on his knees, and, bowing his head in prayer, awaited the blow, when the murderer ordered him to get up and go home. He obeyed, but not until he had given absolution to his still breathing friend, and presently saw the lifeless body dragged through the town amid hootings and rejoicings.

Jogues passed a night of anguish and desolation, and in the morning, reckless of life, set forth in search of Goupil's remains. "Where are you going so fast?" demanded the old Indian, his master. "Do you not see those fierce young braves, who are watching to kill you?" Jogues persisted, and the old man asked another Indian to go with him as a protector. The corpse had been flung into a neighboring ravine, at the bottom of which ran a torrent; and here, with the Indian's help, Jogues found it, stripped naked, and gnawed by dogs. He dragged it into the water, and covered it with stones to save it from further mutilation, resolving to return alone on the following day and secretly bury it. But with the night there came a storm; and when, in the gray of the morning, Jogues descended to the brink of the stream, he found it a rolling, turbid flood, and the body was nowhere to be seen. Had the Indians or the torrent borne it away? Jogues waded into the cold current: it was the first of October; he sounded it with his feet and with his stick; he searched the rocks, the thicket, the forest; but all in vain. Then, crouched by the pitiless stream, he mingled his tears with its waters, and, in a voice broken with groans, chanted the service of the dead.

The Indians, it proved, and not the flood, had robbed him of the remains of his friend. Early in the spring, when the snows were melting in the woods, he was told by Mohawk children that the body was lying, where it had been flung, in a lonely spot lower down the stream. He went to seek it; found the scattered bones, stripped by the foxes and the birds; and, tenderly gathering them up, hid them in a hollow tree, hoping that a day might come when he could give them a Christian burial in consecrated ground.

After the murder of Goupil, Jogues's life hung by a hair. He lived in hourly expectation of the tomahawk, and would have welcomed it as a boon. By signs and words, he was warned that his hour was near; but, as he never shunned his fate, it fled from him, and each day, with renewed astonishment, he found himself still among the living.

Late in the autumn, a party of the Indians set forth on their yearly deer-hunt, and Jogues was ordered to go with them. Shivering and half-famished, he followed them through the chill November forest, and shared their wild bivouac in the depths of the wintry desolation. The game they took was devoted to Areskoui, their god, and eaten in his honor. Jogues would not taste the meat offered to a demon; and thus he starved in the midst of plenty. At night, when the kettle was slung, and the savage crew made merry around their fire, he crouched in a corner of the hut, gnawed by hunger, and pierced to the bone with cold. They thought his presence unpropitious to their hunting, and the women especially hated him. His demeanor at once astonished and incensed his masters. He brought them firewood, like a squaw; he did their bidding without a murmur, and patiently bore their abuse; but when they mocked at his God, and laughed at his devotions, their slave assumed an air and tone of authority, and sternly rebuked them.

He would sometimes escape from "this Babylon," as he calls the hut, and wander in the forest, telling his beads and repeating passages of Scripture. In a remote and lonely spot, he cut the bark in the form of a cross from the trunk of a great tree; and here he made his prayers. This living martyr, half clad in shaggy furs, kneeling on the snow among the icicled rocks and beneath the gloomy pines, bowing in adoration before the emblem of the faith in which was his only consolation and his only hope, is alike a theme for the pen and a subject for the pencil.

The Indians at last grew tired of him, and sent him back to the village. Here he remained till the middle of March, baptizing infants and trying to convert adults. He told them of the sun, moon, planets, and stars. They listened with interest; but when from astronomy he passed to theology, he spent his breath in vain. In March, the old man with whom he lived set forth for his spring fishing, taking with him his squaw and several children. Jogues also was of the party. They repaired to a lake, perhaps Lake Saratoga, four days distant. Here they subsisted for some time on frogs, the entrails of fish, and other garbage. Jogues passed his days in the forest, repeating his prayers, and carving the name of Jesus on trees, as a terror to the demons of the wilderness. A messenger at length arrived from the town; and on the following day, under the pretence that signs of an enemy had been seen, the party broke up their camp, and returned home in hot haste. The messenger had brought tidings that a war-party, which had gone out against the French, had been defeated and destroyed, and that the whole population were clamoring to appease their grief by torturing Jogues to death. This was the true cause of the sudden and mysterious return; but when they reached the town, other tidings had arrived. The missing warriors were safe, and on their way home in triumph with a large number of prisoners. Again Jogues's life was spared; but he was forced to witness the torture and butchery of the converts and allies of the French. Existence became unendurable to him, and he longed to die. War-parties were continually going out. Should they be defeated and cut off, he would pay the forfeit at the stake; and if they came back, as they usually did, with booty and prisoners, he was doomed to see his countrymen and their Indian friends mangled, burned, and devoured.

Jogues had shown no disposition to escape, and great liberty was therefore allowed him. He went from town to town, giving absolution to the Christian captives, and converting and baptizing the heathen. On one occasion, he baptized a woman in the midst of the fire, under pretence of lifting a cup of water to her parched lips. There was no lack of objects for his zeal. A single war-party returned from the Huron country with nearly a hundred prisoners, who were distributed among the Iroquois towns, and the greater part burned. Of the children of the Mohawks and their neighbors, he had baptized, before August, about seventy; insomuch that he began to regard his captivity as a Providential interposition for the saving of souls.

At the end of July, he went with a party of Indians to a fishing-place on the Hudson, about twenty miles below Fort Orange. While here, he learned that another war-party had lately returned with prisoners, two of whom had been burned to death at Osseruenon. On this, his conscience smote him that he had not remained in the town to give the sufferers absolution or baptism; and he begged leave of the old woman who had him in charge to return at the first opportunity. A canoe soon after went up the river with some of the Iroquois, and he was allowed to go in it. When they reached Rensselaerswyck, the Indians landed to trade with the Dutch, and took Jogues with them.

The centre of this rude little settlement was Fort Orange, a miserable structure of logs, standing on a spot now within the limits of the city of Albany. It contained several houses and other buildings; and behind it was a small church, recently erected, and serving as the abode of the pastor, Dominie Megapolensis, known in our day as the writer of an interesting though short account of the Mohawks. Some twenty-five or thirty houses, roughly built of boards and roofed with thatch, were scattered at intervals on or near the borders of the Hudson, above and below the fort. Their inhabitants, about a hundred in number, were for the most part rude Dutch farmers, tenants of Van Rensselaer, the patroon, or lord of the manor. They raised wheat, of which they made beer, and oats, with which they fed their numerous horses. They traded, too, with the Indians, who profited greatly by the competition among them, receiving guns, knives, axes, kettles, cloth, and beads, at moderate rates, in exchange for their furs. The Dutch were on excellent terms with their red neighbors, met them in the forest without the least fear, and sometimes intermarried with them. They had known of Jogues's captivity, and, to their great honor, had made efforts for his release, offering for that purpose goods to a considerable value, but without effect.

At Fort Orange, Jogues heard startling news. The Indians of the village where he lived were, he was told, enraged against him, and determined to burn him. About the first of July, a war-party had set out for Canada, and one of the warriors had offered to Jogues to be the bearer of a letter from him to the French commander at Three Rivers, thinking probably to gain some advantage under cover of a parley. Jogues knew that the French would be on their guard; and he felt it his duty to lose no opportunity of informing them as to the state of affairs among the Iroquois. A Dutchman gave him a piece of paper; and he wrote a letter, in a jargon of Latin, French, and Huron, warning his countrymen to be on their guard, as war-parties were constantly going out, and they could hope for no respite from attack until late in the autumn. When the Iroquois reached the mouth of the river Richelieu, where a small fort had been built by the French the preceding summer, the messenger asked for a parley, and gave Jogues's letter to the commander of the post, who, after reading it, turned his cannon on the savages. They fled in dismay, leaving behind them their baggage and some of their guns; and returning home in a fury, charged Jogues with having caused their discomfiture. Jogues had expected this result, and was prepared to meet it; but several of the principal Dutch settlers, and among them Van Curler, who had made the previous attempt to rescue him, urged that his death was certain if he returned to the Indian town, and advised him to make his escape. In the Hudson, opposite the settlement, lay a small Dutch vessel nearly ready to sail. Van Curler offered him a passage in her to Bordeaux or Rochelle,— representing that the opportunity was too good to be lost, and making light of the prisoner's objection that a connivance in his escape on the part of the Dutch would excite the resentment of the Indians against them. Jogues thanked him warmly; but, to his amazement, asked for a night to consider the matter, and take counsel of God in prayer.

He spent the night in great agitation, tossed by doubt, and full of anxiety lest his self-love should beguile him from his duty. Was it not possible that the Indians might spare his life, and that, by a timely drop of water, he might still rescue souls from torturing devils and eternal fires of perdition? On the other hand, would he not, by remaining to meet a fate almost inevitable, incur the guilt of suicide? And even should he escape torture and death, could he hope that the Indians would again permit him to instruct and baptize their prisoners? Of his French companions, one, Goupil, was dead; while Couture had urged Jogues to flight, saying, that he would then follow his example, but that, so long as the Father remained a prisoner, he, Couture, would share his fate. Before morning, Jogues had made his decision. God, he thought, would be better pleased should he embrace the opportunity given him. He went to find his Dutch friends, and, with a profusion of thanks, accepted their offer. They told him that a boat should be left for him on the shore, and that he must watch his time, and escape in it to the vessel, where he would be safe.

He and his Indian masters were lodged together in a large building, like a barn, belonging to a Dutch farmer. It was a hundred feet long, and had no partition of any kind. At one end the farmer kept his cattle; at the other he slept with his wife, a Mohawk squaw, and his children, while his Indian guests lay on the floor in the middle. As he is described as one of the principal persons of the colony, it is clear that the civilization of Rensselaerswyck was not high.

In the evening, Jogues, in such a manner as not to excite the suspicion of the Indians, went out to reconnoitre. There was a fence around the house, and, as he was passing it, a large dog belonging to the farmer flew at him, and bit him very severely in the leg. The Dutchman, hearing the noise, came out with a light, led Jogues back into the building, and bandaged his wound. He seemed to have some suspicion of the prisoner's design; for, fearful perhaps that his escape might exasperate the Indians, he made fast the door in such a manner that it could not readily be opened. Jogues now lay down among the Indians, who, rolled in their blankets, were stretched around him. He was fevered with excitement; and the agitation of his mind, joined to the pain of his wound, kept him awake all night. About dawn, while the Indians were still asleep, a laborer in the employ of the farmer came in with a lantern, and Jogues, who spoke no Dutch, gave him to understand by signs that he needed his help and guidance. The man was disposed to aid him, silently led the way out, quieted the dogs, and showed him the path to the river. It was more than half a mile distant, and the way was rough and broken. Jogues was greatly exhausted, and his wounded limb gave him such pain that he walked with the utmost difficulty. When he reached the shore, the day was breaking, and he found, to his dismay, that the ebb of the tide had left the boat high and dry. He shouted to the vessel, but no one heard him. His desperation gave him strength; and, by working the boat to and fro, he pushed it at length, little by little, into the water, entered it, and rowed to the vessel. The Dutch sailors received him kindly, and hid him in the bottom of the hold, placing a large box over the hatchway.

He remained two days, half stifled, in this foul lurking-place, while the Indians, furious at his escape, ransacked the settlement in vain to find him. They came off to the vessel, and so terrified the officers that Jogues was sent on shore at night, and led to the fort. Here he was hidden in the garret of a house occupied by a miserly old man, to whose charge he was consigned. Food was sent to him; but, as his host appropriated the larger part to himself, Jogues was nearly starved. There was a compartment of his garret, separated from the rest by a partition of boards. Here the old Dutchman, who, like many others of the settlers, carried on a trade with the Mohawks, kept a quantity of goods for that purpose; and hither he often brought his customers. The boards of the partition had shrunk, leaving wide crevices; and Jogues could plainly see the Indians, as they passed between him and the light. They, on their part, might as easily have seen him, if he had not, when he heard them entering the house, hidden himself behind some barrels in the corner; where he would sometimes remain crouched for hours, in a constrained and painful posture, half suffocated with heat, and afraid to move a limb. His wounded leg began to show dangerous symptoms; but he was relieved by the care of a Dutch surgeon of the fort. The minister, Megapolensis, also visited him, and did all in his power for the comfort of his Catholic brother, with whom he seems to have been well pleased, and whom he calls "a very learned scholar."

When Jogues had remained for six weeks in this hiding-place, his Dutch friends succeeded in satisfying his Indian masters by the payment of a large ransom. A vessel from Manhattan, now New York, soon after brought up an order from the Director-General, Kieft, that he should be sent to him. Accordingly he was placed in a small vessel, which carried him down the Hudson. The Dutch on board treated him with great kindness; and, to do him honor, they named after him one of the islands in the river. At Manhattan he found a dilapidated fort, garrisoned by sixty soldiers, and containing a stone church and the Director-General's house, together with storehouses and barracks. Near it were ranges of small houses, occupied chiefly by mechanics and laborers; while the dwellings of the remaining colonists, numbering in all four or five hundred, were scattered here and there on the island and the neighboring shores. The settlers were different sects and nations, but chiefly Dutch Calvinists. Kieft told his guest that eighteen different languages were spoken at Manhattan. The colonists were in the midst of a bloody Indian war, brought on by their own besotted cruelty; and while Jogues was at the fort, some forty of the Dutchmen were killed on the neighboring farms, and many barns and houses burned.

The Director-General, with a humanity that was far from usual with him, exchanged Jogues's squalid and savage dress for a suit of Dutch cloth, and gave him passage in a small vessel which was then about to sail. The voyage was rough and tedious; and the passenger slept on deck or on a coil of ropes, suffering greatly from cold, and often drenched by the waves that broke over the vessel's side. At length she reached Falmouth, on the southern coast of England, when all the crew went ashore for a carouse, leaving Jogues alone on board. A boat presently came alongside with a gang of desperadoes, who boarded her, and rifled her of everything valuable, threatened Jogues with a pistol, and robbed him of his hat and coat. He obtained some assistance from the crew of a French ship in the harbor, and, on the day before Christmas, took passage in a small coal vessel for the neighboring coast of Brittany. In the following afternoon he was set on shore a little to the north of Brest, and, seeing a peasant's cottage not far off, he approached it, and asked the way to the nearest church. The peasant and his wife, as the narrative gravely tells us, mistook him, by reason of his modest deportment, for some poor but pious Irishman, and asked him to share their supper, after finishing his devotions,—an invitation which Jogues, half famished as he was, gladly accepted. He reached the church in time for the early mass, and with an unutterable joy knelt before the altar, and renewed the communion of which he had been deprived so long. When he returned to the cottage, the attention of his hosts was at once attracted to his mutilated and distorted hands. They asked with amazement how he could have received such injuries; and when they heard the story of his tortures, their surprise and veneration knew no bounds. Two young girls, their daughters, begged him to accept all they had to give,—a handful of sous; while the peasant made known the character of his new guest to his neighbors. A trader from Rennes brought a horse to the door, and offered the use of it to Jogues, to carry him to the Jesuit College in that town. He gratefully accepted it; and, on the morning of the 5th of January, 1644, reached his destination.

He dismounted, and knocked at the door of the college. The porter opened it, and saw a man wearing on his head an old woolen nightcap, and in an attire little better than that of a beggar. Jogues asked to see the Rector; but the porter answered, coldly, that the Rector was busied in the Sacristy. Jogues begged him to say that a man was at the door with news from Canada. The missions of Canada were at this time an object of primal interest to the Jesuits, and above all to the Jesuits of France. A letter from Jogues, written during his captivity, had already reached France, as had also the Jesuit *Relation* of 1643, which contained a long account of his capture; and he had no doubt been an engrossing theme of conversation in every house of the French Jesuits. The Father Rector was putting on his vestments to say mass; but when he heard that a poor man from Canada had asked for him at the door, he postponed the service, and went to meet him. Jogues, without discovering himself, gave him a letter from the Dutch Director-General attesting his character. The Rector, without reading it, began to question him as to the affairs of Canada, and at length asked him if he knew Father Jogues.

"I knew him very well," was the reply.

"The Iroquois have taken him," pursued the Rector. "Is he dead? Have they murdered him?"

"No," answered Jogues; "he is alive and at liberty, and I am he." And he fell on his knees to ask his Superior's blessing.

That night was a night of jubilation and thanksgiving in the college of Rennes.

Jogues became a centre of curiosity and reverence. He was summoned to Paris. The Queen, Anne of Austria, wished to see him; and when the persecuted slave of the Mohawks was conducted into her presence, she kissed his mutilated hands, while the ladies of the Court thronged around to do him homage. We are told, and no doubt with truth, that these honors were unwelcome to the modest and single-hearted missionary, who thought only of returning to his work of converting the Indians. A priest with any deformity of body is debarred from saying mass. The teeth and knives of the Iroquois had inflicted an injury worse than the torturers imagined, for they had robbed Jogues of the privilege which was the chief consolation of his life; but the Pope, by a special dispensation, restored it to him, and with the opening spring he sailed again for Canada.

It was the Mohawks who had made war on the French and their Indian allies on the lower St. Lawrence. They claimed, as against the other Iroquois, a certain right of domain to all this region; and though the warriors of the four upper nations had sometimes poached on the Mohawk preserve, by murdering both French and Indians at Montreal, they employed their energies for the most part in attacks on the Hurons, the Upper Algonquins, and other tribes of the interior. These attacks still continued, unaffected by the peace with the Mohawks. Imperfect, however, as the treaty was, it was invaluable, could it but be kept inviolate; and to this end Montmagny, the Jesuits, and all the colony anxiously turned their thoughts.

It was to hold the Mohawks to their faith that Couture had bravely gone back to winter among them; but an agent of more acknowledged weight was needed, and Father Isaac Jogues was chosen. No white man, Couture excepted, knew their language and their character so well. His errand was half political, half religious; for not only was he to be the bearer of gifts, wampum belts, and messages from the Governor, but he was also to found a new mission, christened in advance with a prophetic name,—the Mission of the Martyrs.

For two years past, Jogues had been at Montreal; and it was here that he received the order of his Superior to proceed to the Mohawk towns. At first, nature asserted itself, and he recoiled involuntarily at the thought of the horrors of which his scarred body and his mutilated hands were a living memento. It was a transient weakness; and he prepared to depart with more than willingness, giving thanks to

Heaven that he had been found worthy to suffer and to die for the saving of souls and the greater glory of God.

He felt a presentiment that his death was near, and wrote to a friend, "I shall go, and shall not return." An Algonquin convert gave him sage advice. "Say nothing about the Faith at first, for there is nothing so repulsive, in the beginning, as our doctrine, which seems to destroy everything that men hold dear; and as your long cassock preaches, as well as your lips, you had better put on a short coat." Jogues, therefore, exchanged the uniform of Loyola for a civilian's doublet and hose; "for," observes his Superior, "one should be all things to all men, that he may gain them all to Jesus Christ." It would be well if the application of the maxim had always been as harmless.

Jogues left Three Rivers about the middle of May, with the Sieur Bourdon, engineer to the Governor, two Algonquins with gifts to confirm the peace, and four Mohawks as guides and escort. He passed the Richelieu and Lake Champlain, well-remembered scenes of former miseries, and reached the foot of Lake George on the eve of Corpus Christi. Hence he called the lake "Lac St. Sacrement"; and this name is preserved, until, a century after, an ambitious Irishman, in compliment to the sovereign from whom he sought advancement, gave it the name it bears.

From Lake George they crossed on foot to the Hudson, where, being greatly fatigued by their heavy loads of gifts, they borrowed canoes at an Iroquois fishing-station, and descended to Fort Orange. Here Jogues met the Dutch friends to whom he owed his life, and who now kindly welcomed and entertained him. After a few days he left them, and ascended the river Mohawk to the first Mohawk town. Crowds gathered from the neighboring towns to gaze on the man whom they had known as a scorned and abused slave, and who now appeared among them as the ambassador of a power which hitherto, indeed, they had despised, but which in their present mood they were willing to propitiate.

There was a council in one of the lodges; and while his crowded auditory smoked their pipes, Jogues stood in the midst, and harangued them. He offered in due form the gifts of the Governor, with the wampum belts and their messages of peace, while at every pause his words were echoed by a unanimous grunt of applause from the attentive concourse. Peace speeches were made in return; and all was harmony. When, however, the Algonquin deputies stood before the council, they and their gifts were coldly received. The old hate, maintained by traditions of mutual atrocity, burned fiercely under a thin semblance of peace; and though no outbreak took place, the prospect of the future was very ominous.

The business of the embassy was scarcely finished, when the Mohawks counselled Jogues and his companions to go home with all despatch, saying that if they waited longer, they might meet on the way warriors of the four upper nations, who would inevitably kill the two Algonquin deputies, if not the French also. Jogues, therefore, set out on his return; but not until, despite the advice of the Indian convert, he had made the round of the houses, confessed and instructed a few Christian prisoners still remaining here, and baptized several dying Mohawks. Then he and his party crossed through the forest to the southern extremity of Lake George, made bark canoes, and descended to Fort Richelieu, where they arrived on the twenty-seventh of June.

His political errand was accomplished. Now, should he return to the Mohawks, or should the Mission of the Martyrs be for a time abandoned? Lalemont, who had succeeded Vimont as Superior of the missions, held a council at Quebec with three other Jesuits, of whom Jogues was one, and it was determined, that, unless some new contingency should arise, he should remain for the winter at Montreal. This was in July. Soon after, the plan was changed, for reasons which do not appear, and Jogues received orders to repair to his dangerous post. He set out on the 24th of August, accompanied by a young Frenchman named Lalande, and three or four Hurons. On the way they met Indians who warned them of a change of feeling in the Mohawk towns, and the Hurons, alarmed, refused to go farther. Jogues, naturally perhaps the most timid man of the party, had no thought of drawing back, and pursued his journey with his young companion, who, like other *donnés* of the missions, was scarcely behind the Jesuits themselves in devoted enthusiasm.

The reported change of feeling had indeed taken place; and the occasion of it was characteristic. On his previous visit to the Mohawks, Jogues, meaning to return, had left in their charge a small chest or box. From the first they were distrustful, suspecting that it contained some secret mischief. He therefore opened it, and showed them the contents, which were a few personal necessaries; and having thus, as he thought, reassured them, locked the box, and left it in their keeping. The Huron prisoners in the town attempted to make favor with their Iroquois enemies by abusing their French friends,—declaring them to be sorcerers, who had bewitched, by their charms and mummeries, the whole Huron nation, and caused drought, famine, pestilence, and a host of insupportable miseries. Thereupon, the suspicions of the Mohawks against the box revived with double force; and they were convinced that famine, the pest, or some malignant spirit was shut up in it, waiting the moment to issue forth and destroy them. There was sickness in the town, and caterpillars were eating their corn: this was ascribed to the sorceries of the Jesuit. Still they were divided in opinion. Some stood firm for the French; others were furious against them. Among the Mohawks, three clans or families were predominant, if indeed they did not compose the entire nation,—the clans of the Bear, the Tortoise, and the Wolf. Though, by the nature of their constitution, it was scarcely possible that these clans should come to blows, so intimately were they bound together by ties of blood, yet they were often divided on points of interest or policy and on this occasion the Bear raged against the French, and howled for war, while the Tortoise and the Wolf still clung to the treaty. Among savages, with no government except the intermittent one of councils, the party of action and violence must always prevail. The Bear chiefs sang their war-songs, and, followed by the young men of their own clan, and by such others as they had infected with their frenzy, set forth, in two bands, on the war-path.

The warriors of one of these bands were making their way through the forests between the Mohawk and Lake George, when they met Jogues and Lalade. They seized them, stripped them, and led them in triumph to their town. Here a savage crowd surrounded them, beating them with sticks and with their fists. One of them cut thin strips of flesh from the back and arms of Jogues, saying, as he did so, "Let us see if this white flesh is the flesh of an oki."—"I am a man like yourselves," replied Jogues; "but I do not fear death or torture. I do not know why you would kill me. I come here to confirm the peace and show you the way to heaven, and you treat me like a dog."—"You shall die to-morrow," cried the rabble. "Take courage, we shall not burn you. We shall strike you both with a hatchet, and place your heads on the palisade, that your brothers may see you when we take them prisoners." The clans of the Wolf and the Tortoise still raised their voices in behalf of the captive Frenchmen; but the fury of the minority swept all before it.

In the evening,—it was the 18th of October—Jogues, smarting with his wounds and bruises, was sitting in one of the lodges, when an Indian entered, and asked him to a feast. To refuse would have been an offense. He arose and followed the savage, who led him to the lodge of the Bear chief. Jogues bent his head to enter, when another Indian, standing concealed within, at the side of the doorway, struck at him with a hatchet. An Iroquois, called by the French Le Berger, who seems to have followed in order to defend him, bravely held out his arm to ward off the blow; but the hatchet cut through it, and sank into the missionary's brain. He fell at the feet of his murderer, who at once finished the work by hacking off his head. Lalade was left in suspense all night, and in the morning was killed in a similar manner. The bodies of the two Frenchmen were then thrown into the Mohawk, and their heads displayed on the points of the palisade which enclosed the town.

Thus died Isaac Jogues, one of the purest examples of Roman Catholic virtue which this Western continent has seen. The priests, his associates, praise his humility, and tell us that it reached the point of self-contempt,—a crowning virtue in their eyes; that he regarded himself as nothing, and lived solely to do the will of God as uttered by the lips of his Superiors. They add that, when left to the guidance of his own judgment, his self-distrust made him very slow of decision, but that when acting under orders he knew neither hesitation nor fear. With all his gentleness, he had a certain warmth of vivacity of temperament; and we have seen how, during his first captivity, while humbly submitting to every caprice of his tyrants and appearing to rejoice in abasement, a derisive word against his faith would change the lamb into the lion, and the lips that seemed so tame would speak in sharp, bold tones of menace and reproof.

The Death of La Salle

THE travellers were crossing a marshy prairie towards a distant belt of woods, that followed the course of a little river. They led with them their five horses, laden with their scanty baggage, and, with what was of no less importance, their stock of presents for Indians. Some wore the remains of the clothing they had worn from France, eked out with deer-skins, dressed in the Indian manner; and some had coats of old sail-cloth. Here was La Salle, in whom one would have known, at a glance, the chief of the party; and the priest, Cavelier, who seems to have shared not one of the high traits of his younger brother. Here too, were their nephews, Moranget and the boy Cavelier, now about seventeen years old; the trusty soldier Joutel; and the friar Anastase Douay. Duhaut followed, a man of respectable birth and education; and Liotot, the surgeon of the party. At home, they might perhaps have lived and died with a fair repute; but the wilderness is a rude touchstone, which often reveals traits that would have lain buried and unsuspected in civilized life. The German Hiens, the ex-buccaneer, was also of the number. He had probably sailed with an English crew, for he was sometimes known as *Gemme Anglais,* or "English Jem." The Sieur de Marle; Teissier, a pilot; L'Archevêque, a servant of Duhaut; and others, to the number in all of seventeen,— made up the party; to which is to be added Nika, La Salle's Shawnee hunter, who, as well as another Indian, had twice crossed the ocean with him, and still followed his fortunes with an admiring though undemonstrative fidelity.

They passed the prairie, and neared the forest. Here they saw buffalo; and the hunters approached, and killed several of them. Then they traversed the woods; found and forded the shallow and rushy stream, and pushed through the forest beyond, till they again reached the open prairie. Heavy clouds gathered over them, and it rained all night; but they sheltered themselves under the fresh hides of the buffalo they had killed.

It is impossible, as it would be needless, to follow the detail of their daily march. It was such an one, though with unwonted hardship, as is familiar to the memory of many a prairie traveller of our own time. They suffered greatly from the want of shoes, and found for a while no better substitute than a casing of raw buffalo-hide, which they were forced to keep always wet, as, when dry, it hardened about the foot like iron. At length they bought dressed deer-skin from the Indians, of which they made tolerable moccasins. The rivers, streams, and gullies filled with water were without number; and to cross them they made a boat of bull-hide, like the "bull boat" still used on the Upper Missouri. This did good service, as, with the help of their horses, they could carry it with them. Two or three men could cross in it at once, and the horses swam after them like dogs. Sometimes they traversed the sunny prairie; sometimes dived into the dark recesses of forest, where the buffalo, descending daily from their pastures in long files to drink at the river, often made a broad and easy path for the travellers. When foul weather arrested them, they built huts of bark and long meadow-grass; and safely sheltered lounged away the day, while their horses, picketed near by, stood steaming in the rain. At night, they usually set a rude stockade about their camp; and here, by the grassy border of a brook, or at the edge of a grove where a spring bubbled up through the sands, they lay asleep around the embers of their fire, while the man on guard listened to the deep breathing of the slumbering horses, and the howling of the wolves that saluted the rising moon as it flooded the waste of prairie with pale mystic radiance.

They met Indians almost daily,—sometimes a band of hunters, mounted or on foot, chasing buffalo on the plains; sometimes a party of fishermen; sometimes a winter camp, on the slope of a hill or under the sheltering border of a forest. They held intercourse with them in the distance by signs; often they disarmed their distrust, and attracted them into their camp; and often they visited them in their lodges, where, seated on buffalo-robes, they smoked with their entertainers, passing the pipe from hand to hand, after the custom still in use among the prairie tribes. Cavelier says that they once saw a band of 150 mounted Indians attacking a herd of buffalo with lances pointed with sharpened bone. The old priest was delighted with the sport, which he pronounces "the most diverting thing in the world." On another occasion, when the party were encamped near the village of a tribe which Cavelier calls Sassory, he saw them catch an alligator about twelve feet long, which they proceeded to torture as if he were a human enemy,—first putting out his eyes, and then leading him to the neighboring prairie, where, having confined him by a number of stakes, they spent the entire day in tormenting him.

Holding a northerly course, the travellers crossed the Brazos, and reached the waters of the Trinity. The weather was unfavorable, and on one occasion they encamped in the rain during four or five days together. It was not an harmonious company. La Salle's cold and haughty reserve had returned, at least for those of his followers to whom he was not partial. Duhaut and the surgeon Liotot, both of whom were men of some property, had a large pecuniary stake in the enterprise, and

were disappointed and incensed at its ruinous result. They had a
quarrel with young Moranget, whose hot and hasty temper was as
little fitted to conciliate as was the harsh reserve of his uncle. Already
at Fort St. Louis, Duhaut had intrigued among the men; and the mild
admonition of Joutel had not, it seems, sufficed to divert him from his
sinister purposes. Liotot, it is said, had secretly sworn vengeance against
La Salle, whom he charged with having caused the death of his
brother, or, as some will have it, his nephew. On one of the former
journeys this young man's strength had failed; and, La Salle having
ordered him to return to the fort, he had been killed by Indians on
the way.

The party moved again as the weather improved, and on the 15th
of March encamped within a few miles of a spot which La Salle had
passed on his preceding journey, and where he had left a quantity of
Indian corn and beans in *cache;* that is to say, hidden in the ground or
in a hollow tree. As provisions were falling short, he sent a party from
the camp to find it. These men were Duhaut, Liotot, Hiens the buc-
caneer, Teissier, L'Archevêque, Nika the hunter, and La Salle's servant
Saget. They opened the *cache,* and found the contents spoiled; but as
they returned from their bootless errand they saw buffalo, and Nika
shot two of them. They now encamped on the spot, and sent the
servant to inform La Salle, in order that he might send horses to bring
in the meat. Accordingly, on the next day, he directed Moranget and
De Marle, with the necessary horses, to go with Saget to the hunters'
camp. When they arrived, they found that Duhaut and his companions
had already cut up the meat, and laid it upon scaffolds for smoking,
though it was not yet so dry as, it seems, this process required. Duhaut
and the others had also put by, for themselves, the marrow-bones and
certain portions of the meat, to which, by woodland custom, they had
a perfect right. Moranget, whose rashness and violence had once before
caused a fatal catastrophe, fell into a most unreasonable fit of rage,
berated and menaced Duhaut and his party, and ended by seizing upon
the whole of the meat, including the reserved portions. This added fuel
to the fire of Duhaut's old grudge against Moranget and his uncle.
There is reason to think that he had harbored deadly designs, the
execution of which was only hastened by the present outbreak. The
surgeon also bore hatred against Moranget, whom he had nursed with
constant attention when wounded by an Indian arrow, and who had
since repaid him with abuse. These two now took counsel apart with
Hiens, Teissier, and L'Archevêque; and it was resolved to kill
Moranget that night. Nika, La Salle's devoted follower, and Saget,
his faithful servant, must die with him. All of the five were of one mind
except the pilot Teissier, who neither aided nor opposed the plot.

Night came; the woods grew dark; the evening meal was finished, and the evening pipes were smoked. The order of the guard was arranged; and, doubtless by design, the first hour of the night was assigned to Moranget, the second to Saget, and the third to Nika. Gun in hand, each stood watch in turn over the silent but not sleeping forms around him, till, his time expiring, he called the man who was to relieve him, wrapped himself in his blanket, and was soon buried in a slumber that was to be his last. Now the assassins rose. Duhaut and Hiens stood with their guns cocked, ready to shoot down any one of the destined victims who should resist or fly. The surgeon, with an axe, stole towards the three sleepers, and struck a rapid blow at each in turn. Saget and Nika died with little movement; but Moranget started spasmodically into a sitting posture, gasping and unable to speak; and the murderers compelled De Marle, who was not in their plot, to compromise himself by despatching him.

The floodgates of murder were open, and the torrent must have its way. Vengeance and safety alike demanded the death of La Salle. Hiens, or "English Jem," alone seems to have hesitated; for he was one of those to whom that stern commander had always been partial. Meanwhile, the intended victim was still at his camp, about six miles distant. It is easy to picture, with sufficient accuracy, the features of the scene,—the sheds of bark and branches, beneath which, among blankets and buffalo-robes, camp-utensils, pack-saddles, rude harness, guns, powder-horns, and bullet-pouches, the men lounged away the hour, sleeping or smoking, or talking among themselves; the blackened kettles that hung from tripods of poles over the fires; the Indians strolling about the place or lying, like dogs in the sun, with eyes half-shut, yet all observant; and, in the neighboring meadow, the horses grazing under the eye of a watchman.

It was the 18th of March. Moranget and his companions had been expected to return the night before; but the whole day passed, and they did not appear. La Salle became very anxious. He resolved to go and look for them; but not well knowing the way, he told the Indians who were about the camp that he would give them a hatchet if they would guide him. One of them accepted the offer; and La Salle prepared to set out in the morning, at the same time directing Joutel to be ready to go with him. Joutel says: "That evening, while we were talking about what could have happened to the absent men, he seemed to have a presentiment of what was to take place. He asked me if I had heard of any machinations against them, or if I had noticed any bad design on the part of Duhaut and the rest. I answered that I had heard nothing, except that they sometimes complained of being found fault with so often; and that this was all I knew; besides which, as they were persuaded that I was in his interest, they would not have told me of any bad design they might have. We were very uneasy all the rest of the evening."

In the morning, La Salle set out with his Indian guide. He had changed his mind with regard to Joutel, whom he now directed to remain in charge of the camp and to keep a careful watch. He told the friar Anastase Douay to come with him instead of Joutel, whose gun, which was the best in the party, he borrowed for the occasion, as well as his pistol. The three proceeded on their way,—La Salle, the friar, and the Indian. "All the way," writes the friar, "he spoke to me of nothing but matters of piety, grace, and predestination; enlarging on the debt he owed to God, who had saved him from so many perils during more than twenty years of travel in America. Suddenly, I saw him overwhelmed with a profound sadness, for which he himself could not account. He was so much moved that I scarcely knew him." He soon recovered his usual calmness; and they walked on till they approached the camp of Duhaut, which was on the farther side of a small river. Looking about him with the eye of a woodsman, La Salle saw two eagles circling in the air nearly over him, as if attracted by carcasses of beasts or men. He fired his gun and his pistol, as a summons to any of his followers who might be within hearing. The shots reached the ears of the conspirators. Rightly conjecturing by whom they were fired, several of them, led by Duhaut, crossed the river at a little distance above, where trees or other intervening objects hid them from sight. Duhaut and the surgeon crouched like Indians in the long, dry, reed-like grass of the last summer's growth, while L'Archevêque stood in sight near the bank. La Salle, continuing to advance, soon saw him, and, calling to him, demanded where was Moranget. The man, without lifting his hat, or any show of respect, replied in an agitated and broken voice, but with a tone of studied insolence, that Moranget was strolling about somewhere. La Salle rebuked and menaced him. He rejoined with increased insolence, drawing back, as he spoke, towards the ambuscade, while the incensed commander advanced to chastise him. At that moment a shot was fired from the grass, instantly followed by another; and, pierced through the brain, La Salle dropped dead.

The friar at his side stood terror-stricken, unable to advance or to fly; when Duhaut, rising from the ambuscade, called out to him to take courage, for he had nothing to fear. The murderers now came forward, and with wild looks gathered about their victim. "There thou liest, great Bashaw! There thou liest!" exclaimed the surgeon Liotot, in base exultation over the unconscious corpse. With mockery and insult, they stripped it naked, dragged it into the bushes, and left it there, a prey to the buzzards and the wolves.

Thus in the vigor of his manhood, at the age of forty-three, died Robert Cavelier de la Salle, "one of the greatest men," writes Tonty, "of this age"; without question one of the most remarkable explorers whose names live in history. His faithful officer Joutel thus sketches his portrait: "His firmness, his courage, his great knowledge of the arts and sciences, which made him equal to every undertaking, and his untiring energy, which enabled him to surmount every obstacle, would have won at last a glorious success for his grand enterprise, had not all his fine qualities been counterbalanced by a haughtiness of manner which often made him insupportable, and by a harshness towards those under his command which drew upon him an implacable hatred, and was at last the cause of his death."

The enthusiasm of the disinterested and chivalrous Champlain was not the enthusiasm of La Salle; nor had he any part in the self-devoted zeal of the early Jesuit explorers. He belonged not to the age of the knight-errant and the saint, but to the modern world of practical study and practical action. He was the hero not of a principle nor of a faith, but simply of a fixed idea and a determined purpose. As often happens with concentred and energetic natures, his purpose was to him a passion and an inspiration; and he clung to it with a certain fanaticism of devotion. It was the offspring of an ambition vast and comprehensive, yet acting in the interest both of France and of civilization.

Serious in all things, incapable of the lighter pleasures, incapable of repose, finding no joy but in the pursuit of great designs, too shy for society and too reserved for popularity, often unsympathetic and always seeming so, smothering emotions which he could not utter, schooled to universal distrust, stern to his followers and pitiless to himself, bearing the brunt of every hardship and every danger, demanding of others an equal constancy joined to an implicit deference, heeding no counsel but his own, attempting the impossible and grasping at what was too vast to hold,—he contained in his own complex and painful nature the chief springs of his triumphs, his failures, and his death.

It is easy to reckon up his defects, but it is not easy to hide from sight the Roman virtues that redeemed them. Beset by a throng of enemies, he stands, like the King of Israel, head and shoulders above them all. He was a tower of adamant, against whose impregnable front hardship and danger, the rage of man and of the elements, the southern sun, the northern blast, fatigue, famine, disease, delay, disappointment, and deferred hope emptied their quivers in vain. That very pride which, Coriolanus-like, declared itself most sternly in the thickest press of foes, has in it something to challenge admiration. Never, under the impenetrable mail of paladin or crusader, beat a heart of more intrepid mettle than within the stoic panoply that armed the breast of La Salle. To estimate aright the marvels of his patient fortitude, one must follow on his track through the vast scene of his interminable journeyings,—those thousands of weary miles of forest, marsh, and river, where, again and again, in the bitterness of baffled striving, the untiring pilgrim pushed onward towards the goal which he was never to attain. America owes him an enduring memory; for in this masculine figure she sees the pioneer who guided her to the possession of her richest heritage.

JOHN BAKELESS

John Bakeless, born in 1894, has to his credit an already imposing list of books in the fields of biography and history. They include a two-volume life of Christopher Marlowe (the product of some twenty years of research), a combined biography of Lewis and Clark, a life of Daniel Boone, *Eyes of Discovery,* a book which undertook to present America as it appeared to the first white men who came here, and, most recently, a biography of George Rogers Clark, whose greatest exploit, the march on and capture of Vincennes, is related elsewhere in this volume.

From Mr. Bakeless' work I have selected the greater part of a chapter from *Daniel Boone: Master of the Wilderness.* This is the best life we have to date of that fabulous frontiersman, the man I like to think of as the American Ulysses. At the age of ninety, ending his days in shameful yet unembittered poverty (shameful on the part of Kentucky, the state he had opened up to settlement), he was asked by the artist who came to do his portrait (while Boone cooked himself a strip of venison wound about his ramrod) if, traveling through the wilderness without a compass, as was his custom, he had ever been lost. "No," said Boone, "I can't say as ever I was lost, but I was bewildered once for three days."

As I have written elsewhere (*Literary Frontiers*), "Of all our folk heroes he is, it seems to me, the one in whom the stuff of epic poetry and of epic narrative in general is most abundantly present. He is all of a piece, and never out of character, and he is so completely, so unmixedly, our own. The story of American life is in one sense the story of American rivers, as the late Constance Lindsay Skinner so wisely perceived when she launched the Rivers of America series, and like the Kanawha and the Ohio that he knew, the life of Daniel Boone has the flow of destiny and that mysterious beckoning toward what lies beyond that is not only the appeal of rivers, but the essence of our American life that took its rise from them."

The episodes in Boone's life which are recounted here concern his capture by the Shawnees, his remarkably cool-headed behavior in the face of probable torture and death, and his eventual escape. It may be

75

interesting to note that Boone once told his son Nathan that "in his whole life he was sure of having killed only one Indian and that was at the Blue Licks battle." Sometimes he raised the score to three—never any more. Few frontiersmen of his or later periods could say the same.

Daniel Boone, Prisoner of the Shawnee King

IN January of 1778, Boonesborough's salt supply began to run short. Salt was one of the most pressing needs of the pioneers. They had to have it for curing meat and hides, and they enjoyed it as one of the few condiments that added flavor to their monotonous diet. To be left in the wilderness without bread or salt was one of the few hardships of which they ever complained, and Boonesborough at the moment had eastern militia wintering there who were probably complaining very loudly indeed.

Daniel Boone took a party of some thirty men, lashed the station's salt-kettles, which had been especially sent out as a gift from the Virginia government, on pack-horses, and set out for the Blue Licks. These salt springs were a central point on the forest traces on the Licking River, a tributary flowing north into the Ohio River in north-eastern Kentucky.

Boone's salt-makers were to camp at the Licks for about a month and were then to be relieved by a new party. These reliefs were to continue until a year's supply of salt had been sent to the station on pack-horses, which were the only kind of transport that could negotiate the narrow wilderness paths. But Captain Boone did not keep his fellow-settlers at Boonesborough waiting till a pack train could get through. A special messenger rushed back with the first small sack of salt his men could make.

Fortunately they were living in a country where nature provided salt in abundance. Far below their feet, imprisoned in rock and sand, lingered the waters of prehistoric seas. Rainwater, seeping down through many strata, forced the salt waters to the surface, where they bubbled out in those salt and sulphur springs common in all limestone country. There were innumerable springs of this sort, large and small, throughout Kentucky, scattered ten to thirty miles apart.

These were the "licks"—so called because the deer and buffalo, eager for salt, licked up the impregnated earth. These animals, like the mammoth and the mastodon before them, had found the springs long before the white man came, perhaps even before the red man. Mammoth and mastodon had crowded around the salt licks, where even the earth was full of the mineral they craved. "Big Bone Lick" took its name from the disjointed skeletons of the huge beasts which millennia before had died there, caught in the marshes into which their gigantic bulks sank easily and fatally. They had perished in such numbers that a man could walk for several hundred yards without touching ground, stepping from one huge bone to another.

The pioneers gazed upon the remnants of these enormous carcasses with wonder but accepted their presence without much speculation. The huge vertebrae made comfortable camp seats. They were neatly rounded to accommodate the appropriate portion of the human frame weary with much hunting. They were also a convenient rest for the poles from which camp kettles swung above the fire. The big bones were just one of the benefits the wilderness provided, and the hunters accepted them without troubling their heads over fossil lore. A few were sent back to Virginia for the edification of the philosophic Mr. Jefferson, and others to France for the great Cuvier to study.

It was fairly simple for Daniel Boone to make salt. The settlers merely had to go to the springs, fill their kettles with salt water, and boil it down. The mineral mixture that resulted contained a good many things besides sodium chloride, but salt predominated and the iodine mixed with it was very good for them, though nobody suspected it. Iodized salt is a modern invention, but sea water is full of iodine, and the settlers, willy-nilly, ate iodine with their home-boiled product.

The labor of salt-making was prodigious. It took 840 gallons of this weak brine to yield a single bushel, though very fine springs were said to give a bushel for every eighty gallons or even less. But the work was worth doing. A bushel of salt was worth a cow and a half.

Salt-making was not merely laborious, it was also dangerous. The Indians knew quite as much about the salt licks as the white men. Red man-hunters watched the licks for scalps as eagerly as white pot-hunters watched them for game. Salt-making parties like Boone's had to go out in force, ready to defend themselves at any time.

At first there was no trouble. Boone's salt-kettles bubbled merrily for some weeks, and several horse-loads of salt had already been sent back to the station, in charge of three men. It was about time for the relief to arrive, and the thoughts of the salt-makers in the lonely little camp began to turn to their homes and families in Boonesborough. They had been undisturbed for some time and had begun to feel entirely secure. The Indians usually kept close to their villages in Ohio during the bitter weather. That was why winter was the best time for salt-making —warm work, anyhow. Furthermore, the Indians had been very badly beaten only a few months before, and it did not seem likely that they would be returning to Kentucky before spring at the earliest.

Early in February Daniel Boone went out to scout, hunt, and follow his trapline for beaver. The camp had to be supplied with meat; there was beaver sign in the Licking River and Hinkston's Creek. Pelts were valuable, and Daniel Boone was never one to scorn an honest dollar. The salt party kept three scouts in the woods at all times. Boone was to reconnoiter in one direction, while his son-in-law Flanders Callaway and a companion were operating in the other.

In winter the buffalo left the licks and sought areas where plenty of cane had grown. As there were no canebrakes near the salt camp, Boone made a wide swing of five or six miles to find game and to make sure his reconnaissance included country well out to the flank. Toward evening he loaded his pack-horse with buffalo meat and headed home for camp through a blinding snowstorm, hardly able to see or hear anything in the forest on one side or along the river on the other.

He had been leading his burdened horse slowly along the riverbank and had just passed a narrow place where the upturned roots of a fallen tree left barely room to squeeze through. The Shawnees were on him before he was aware. Boone noticed that his horse seemed nervous. He glanced back quickly. The Indians were right behind, thirty paces away, having hidden behind the fallen tree to let him pass. The best accounts say that he was attacked by four braves at once. All accounts agree there were too many Indians for comfort. The warriors were scouts from a Shawnee war party, sent toward the Blue Licks to see if anyone was there. They had stumbled upon Boone by accident.

Daniel snatched at his knife, hoping to slash the thongs of green hide—"buffalo tugs"—that held the load of buffalo meat on the horse, scramble up, and ride for his life. But after using the knife to skin and clean a buffalo, he had thrust it back into the sheath covered with blood and grease. It had frozen fast, and its greasy hilt was so slippery that his hands, also greasy, could not get grip enough to pull it out.

He dropped the bridle and ran, leaving the horse to shift for itself. One Shawnee stayed with the game. Two more opened out, one on either side, to flank the fugitive. A fourth slashed off the load, mounted Boone's own horse, and proceeded to ride him down.

It was no use trying to hide. His trail in the snow was plain to follow. There was a lively chase for half a mile and then, as Boone dodged through the wintry forest, the Indians drew closer and bullets began to sing about his ears. Indians were notoriously poor shots, but the range was now getting very short. Spurts of snow and bits of flying bark warned him. Then, at a few yards' range, a bullet cut the thongs of his powder-horn. Boone had a charge in his rifle, but he would never get a chance to reload if he fired it.

Daniel knew Indians, and he also knew when he had had enough. He did not believe the bullets so far had been meant to kill, but only to warn him. The next shots would be aimed to kill. He halted in his tracks. No chance of escape was left. He prepared to surrender to his red brothers.

Slipping behind a tree, he placed his rifle in front of it as evidence that he would not resist. The braves came up, laughing, disarmed him, shook hands warmly, and marched him off.

The Indians were naïvely delighted with their capture. This was no ordinary white man, but the great hunter himself, long known to them by reputation. They all set off together for the Indian camp on Hinkston's Creek, not far from the Blue Licks.

As they came into camp, Boone stared in amazement and horror at what he saw. In a sheltered part of the valley blazed a fire thirty or forty feet long, and around it sat a party of more than a hundred Shawnee warriors, fully armed. Boone looked quickly at their faces. All were painted for war. The chief approached, a short and sturdy warrior, past middle age. It was Blackfish. The war chief himself had taken command of the party. This, Boone must have realized instantly, was no ordinary raid.

As he looked around, he saw that not all were Indians. With the warriors about the fire were several white men, hardly distinguishable from redskins in their rough woods dress. Worse and worse. White brains were directing red savagery. There was Charles Beaubien, a French-Canadian whom the British employed as Indian agent. There was Louis Lorimier, French-Canadian trader, whose post in Ohio was a center for the Shawnees and who had enormous influence in the tribe. Worst of all, here were the "white Indians," George and James Girty, brothers of the notorious Simon whose mere name spread terror along the American frontier.

There was even a negro slave named Pompey, who later in the year was to fight with the Indians at the long siege of Boonesborough. According to one account, the negro had escaped from the Kentucky settlements and joined the tribe voluntarily. More probably, he had been captured in some raid and held as slave by the Indians, who often kept negroes and sometimes traded in them.

Boone must at first have supposed he had been captured by an isolated raiding party of a few adventurous warriors. As he looked at the savage group stretched out by the fire or rising curiously to see the prisoner, he knew the full extent of the danger.

The presence of white men showed that the attack had been carefully planned and encouraged by the British. The band was strong enough to overwhelm Boonesborough in a few hours. It might even be able to capture the other settlements, surprising them one by one. Boone was calm as usual as the painted warriors led him up to Chief Blackfish, but behind the quiet blue eyes his brain was working furiously.

"King" Cornstalk, the great chief of the Shawnees, had been treacherously murdered by irresponsible American soldiery while in an American fort on a mission of peace only three months before. The Shawnee war party was now out to take revenge on the nearest and weakest of the Big Knives' settlements. Indian justice demanded revenge—it did not matter on which individuals vengeance fell so long as somebody belonging to the offending tribe of the Big Knives suffered. The British had astutely taken advantage of Shawnee indignation to spur the Indians on. Hence the unusual venture on the warpath in midwinter, contrary to all custom.

The distinguished prisoner received a hearty, if somewhat sardonic, welcome. The Indians shook hands, uttered the usual[1] greeting, "How d' do," or "How d'y," patted him on the back, made much of him, and laughed mightily over his capture.

Among the chiefs who gathered about him Boone recognized the leader of the band who had captured him nine years before, and boldly greeted him by name:

"How d' do, Captain Will?"

Captain Will was greatly surprised, but when reminded of his earlier captures showed no resentment at Boone's previous escape. Instead, he shook hands once more, with increased cordiality. Thereupon all the warriors who had already shaken hands did it all over again with the utmost gravity.

This friendly reception meant nothing in particular. Sometimes it was merely an ironic prelude to torture and death at the stake. In this case it may have been entirely sincere, for there was always a faintly chivalrous note in Daniel Boone's warfare with the Indians. He hated killing. He was never cruel himself (there is no record that he ever took a scalp), and he was never the victim of cruelty. The Indians admired him, were invariably pleased on the rare occasions when they outwitted him, were delighted to have caught him this time, and later obstinately refused to give him up, even for cash. Daniel Boone was as good a woodsman as any of them, and a far better shot. Such men were

---

[1] All the early documents give this form of the greeting. Later, the Plains Indians made it simply, "How." In Minnesota and Ontario the modern Ojibway still use the greeting, "B'joo," an obvious adaptation from the French of the early explorers.

valuable in any camp. The Shawnees regarded him as a prospective ornament to the tribe and made no secret of their plans.

With the negro Pompey as interpreter, Blackfish explained that his band was going to attack Boonesborough, and then inquired who the men at the salt springs were. His scouts had by this time discovered them. Seeing that his first attempts at evasion did no good, Boone admitted the salt-makers were his own men. Blackfish blandly announced that he would go down and kill them right away.

Daniel Boone did some quick thinking. The fortifications at Boonesborough, he knew, were in their usual bad condition. According to one story, a whole side of the stockade was still missing and there were only two blockhouses. With nearly thirty men at the salt camp and the relief already outside the fort on the way thither, the almost empty settlement would hardly be able to resist assault. The settlers, entirely off guard, could be taken by surprise and easily killed. Even if the Indians spared their lives, the very best that could be expected was a long march with helpless women and children through bitter weather, with prolonged captivity at the end for those who did not die of hardships, torture, or the tomahawk.

The salt-making party were now some distance away, and the Indians were not at the moment heading in their direction, but Blackfish's scouts had seen them. Boone's little party would probably also be taken by surprise, just as he had been himself.

On the other hand, there was still a chance to save Boonesborough. The Shawnee was an intrepid daredevil, but Indian nature is rarely persevering, especially in cold weather. Give the warriors one small success to boast about, and they would very likely decide they had done enough and go quietly back to Ohio.

With the friendliest air he could assume, Boone told Blackfish he would himself go with him and persuade the young men to surrender. Blackfish must guarantee that they should not be tortured or forced to run the gauntlet. The latter ceremony was usually inevitable whenever a new captive was brought into a village.

Boone further explained that it was too cold to move the women and children now; but in the spring it would be easy enough to take them to Detroit. Blackfish agreed, but added that if Boone failed to persuade his salt-makers to surrender, his own life might be the penalty.

Next morning the war party set off. By noon they were within two hundred yards of the salt-makers and had entirely surrounded them without being discovered. Boone was then sent down a hill toward them through the snow, under surveillance of warriors following a little way behind him but near enough to shoot in case of treachery.

The spring had been flooded with fresh water for some days and the salt-makers, unable to work, were resting quietly in camp. Boone's absence occasioned no uneasiness. Scouts or hunters were likely to stay in the forest for days at a time and the other two scouts were also still out. Seeing men approaching through the woods, the salt-makers looked up from their blankets, supposing it was the relief coming in from Boonesborough. Then, seeing Indians, they leaped for their rifles.

"Don't fire!" yelled Boone. "If you do, all will be massacred."

Hurriedly he explained: "You are surrounded with Indians and I have agreed with these Indians that you are to be used well and you are to be prisoners of war and will be give up to the British officers at Detroit where you will be treated well." A militia lieutenant had been left in command. Under his orders, the salt-makers formed a circle and stacked arms. A larger circle of warriors then emerged from the woods on all sides, surrounded them, and ordered them to sit down. Including Boone himself, the haul of prisoners was either twenty-seven or twenty-eight, two salt-packers and two scouts being absent.

The Indians now held council to determine whether they should kill their prisoners in spite of promises. There was no possible excuse for such treachery; but it was exactly what the American soldiers had done to Cornstalk, and the war party had come out to avenge his murder. They proposed to spare no one but Boone. He would be useful at Boonesborough in the spring.

White, red, and black sat down together in the council. For two full hours the solemn debate proceeded, as warrior after warrior rose and spoke, for mercy or for death. The negro Pompey, sitting by Boone, translated for him, but in so low a voice that the other prisoners could not hear. With no knowledge of Shawnee, none of them had the least idea that their lives depended on the outcome of the ceremonious Indian council. The white agents whom the British had sent along sat silent through it all, but Daniel Boone was permitted to make the closing speech. Sixty-six years later, one of the salt-makers repeated what he remembered. It was not a speech likely to be forgotten:

"Brothers!" said Boone, as Pompey turned his words, sentence by sentence, into Shawnee. "What I have promised you, I can much better fulfill in the Spring than now; then the weather will be warm, and the women and children can travel from Boonesboro to the Indian towns, and all live with you as one people. You have got all the young men; to kill them, as has been suggested, would displease the Great Spirit, and you could not then expect future success in hunting nor war; and if you spare them they will make you fine warriors, and excellent hunters to kill game for your squaws and children. These young men have done you no harm; they were engaged in a peaceful occupation, and unresistingly surrendered upon my assurance that such a step was the only safe one; I consented to their capitulation on the express condition that they should be made prisoners of war and treated well; spare them, and the Great Spirit will smile upon you."

This was the first speech the startled prisoners had understood, and now for the first time they realized the peril they were in. The war club passed from hand to hand as the vote was taken, under the eyes of the captives. Fifty-nine warriors dashed it into the ground, as a vote for death; sixty-one let it pass as a token of mercy. There is a story that they let Boone vote. The group of reckless, brutal young braves who wanted blood had lost. Blackfish, who had allowed Pompey to translate for Boone, had won. The older chiefs seemed to approve.

All had turned out exactly as Daniel Boone had hoped. The Shawnees were entirely satisfied. Here was a big haul of prisoners and plenty of glory—plenty of profit, too. Prisoners were useful as slaves and could be sold to the British for cash. Why go on to Boonesborough through the snow and risk a hard fight for nothing, when they could now slip safely back to Ohio with prisoners, much glory, and no losses?

Boone is said to have pretended conversion to the British side. The pretense would have been credible enough, for even Simon Girty had served for a time with the Americans before joining the British, and Boone himself had been a Colonial officer under the British flag in 1774. He could point to the surrender of his men as proof of his conversion, and he painted an alarming picture of Boonesborough's strength. The fort was far too strong, he said, for any war party of this size to think of capturing. Why not let it alone for the time being, and return later with a larger band?

Blackfish was greatly impressed. When he actually did come back, six months later, he brought four or five hundred warriors.

In vain did their white comrades urge the Shawnees on to the attack, while Boone and the other prisoners listened in an agony of suspense. Charles Beaubien was disgusted with Boone's success. He doubted that the garrison of Boonesborough was any stronger than his own band. With Boone's large party absent, he argued, it was probably weaker. Capture would be easy.

Beaubien was entirely correct. But "the Savages could not be prevailed on to attempt the Fort, which by means of their prisoners might have been easily done with success," as the British lieutenant-governor at Detroit, Henry Hamilton, later complained. He did not know that it was Boone who had thwarted his whole enterprise.

Boone had, in fact, played his part altogether too well. He convinced the Indians and thereby saved the settlement. Blackfish probably expected that with his prisoner's intervention he could eventually take the town without even fighting for it. But what deceived Boone's enemies also deceived some of his friends. There was no chance for Boone to take his own men into his confidence. They had no knowledge of his plans. And his devious play-acting roused suspicions of his loyalty.

Once the retreat with the prisoners had been decided on, it was promptly carried out. Three hundred bushels of salt were thrown away. Then the war party filed off to the north through the white and silent winter woods, with their prisoners under close and careful guard.

Having been accepted as a friend, Boone was eager to keep up the pose. He joked and made friends with the warriors, and there may have been some surly and suspicious glances from the other whites at a leader who had first made them surrender to the redskins and now seemed to be on the best of terms with his savage captors.

Since there had been no fighting, there were no wounded. Since the prisoners were all seasoned woodsmen, there were no weaklings or laggards. There was, therefore, none of the usual dreadful tomahawking and scalping of prisoners who were unable to keep up with the rest of the party. Once they had agreed not to kill their prisoners, the Indians kept their bargain and, according to their lights, treated them well. When, in the division of the burdens, a warrior tried to make Daniel Boone carry a heavy brass kettle, he refused. When the brave insisted, Boone knocked him and the kettle down together, and was immediately protected by Blackfish.

They had barely reached camp that night, however, when Boone noticed warriors clearing a path in the snow. He inquired of Pompey what it was for. As he had suspected, the Indians were getting ready for the gauntlet. Boone went straight to Blackfish with a protest and a reminder of his promise, only to be met with:

"Oh, Captain Boone, this is not intended for your men but for you."

Blackfish was right. In his eagerness to protect his companions, Daniel Boone had quite forgotten to stipulate that he, too, should be exempted from the gauntlet, something every new captive normally must go through, even when the tribe intended to spare his life. Blackfish was offering his prisoner the honor of running the gauntlet among warriors only. Most captives were dragged to the villages and compelled to sing at the tops of their voices as they approached. Thus warned, the entire population—squaws, children, old men, and any warriors who happened to have stayed behind—seized clubs, sticks, stones, hatchets, deer's antlers, or anything else that seemed likely to hurt the prisoner, and raced out to help belabor him.

It was, as a brave once explained, "a sort of how do do." It was also a useful way of sorting out the stronger and braver captives from the weaker and more timid. The weak would not survive, and a timid man who hesitated stood a good chance of being beaten to death; but a bold man who dashed fearlessly through his tormentors was reasonably sure to escape with minor injuries. Practical purposes aside, the Indians found the gauntlet vastly diverting. It was their idea of innocent merriment.

Boone surprised the warriors by zigzagging from side to side, escaping the worst of the ordeal. When one man stepped squarely into the path, hoping to get in a good blow, Boone butted him in the chest with his head, knocking the eager redskin sprawling amid shouts of Shawnee laughter. Once the gauntlet was over, the band crowded around to offer congratulations on his courage, and Boone remained a prime favorite.

ROBERT SOUTHEY

An important and influential literary figure in his time (1774–1843), Robert Southey, who was England's Poet Laureate for thirty years, is little read today, outside academic circles. His poetry has had little appeal for our own period, and he is now best known, perhaps, for his *Life of Nelson,* published in 1813. I have reprinted here his account of the battle of Trafalgar—the culminating point of Nelson's life, and the occasion of his death. The story of Nelson's end has long been regarded as one of the prime instances of modern chivalric behavior. It has never been better told than in Southey's pages.

Lord Nelson at Trafalgar

THE station which Nelson had chosen was some fifty or sixty miles to the west of Cádiz, near Cape St. Mary. At this distance he hoped to decoy the enemy out, while he guarded against the danger of being caught with a westerly wind near Cádiz, and driven within the Straits. The blockade of the port was rigorously enforced, in hopes that the combined fleets might be forced to sea by want. The Danish vessels therefore, which were carrying provisions from the French ports in the bay, under the name of Danish property, to all the little ports from Aymonte to Algeciras, from whence they were conveyed in coasting boats to Cádiz, were seized. Without this proper exertion of power the blockade would have been rendered nugatory by the advantage thus taken of the neutral flag. The supplies from France were thus effectually cut off. There was now every indication that the enemy would speedily venture out; officers and men were in the highest spirits at the prospect of giving them a decisive blow—such, indeed, as would put an end to all further contests upon the seas.

On the 9th [October, 1805] Nelson sent Collingwood what he called in his diary the "Nelson touch." "I send you," said he, "my plan of attack, as far as a man dare venture to guess at the very uncertain position the enemy may be found in; but it is to place you perfectly at ease respecting my intentions, and to give full scope to your judgment for carrying them into effect. We can, my dear Coll, have no little jealousies. We have only one great object in view, that of annihilating our enemies, and getting a glorious peace for our country. No man has more confidence in another than I have in you, and no man will render your services more justice than your very old friend, Nelson and Bronte."

The order of sailing was to be the order of battle—the fleet in two lines, with an advanced squadron of eight of the fastest sailing two-deckers. The second in command, having the entire direction of his line, was to break through the enemy, about the twelfth ship from their rear; he would lead through the centre, and the advanced squadron was to cut off three or four ahead of the centre. This plan was to be adapted to the strength of the enemy, so that they should always be one-fourth superior to those whom they cut off. Nelson said that "his admirals and captains, knowing his precise object to be that of a close and decisive action, would supply any deficiency of signals and act accordingly. In case signals cannot be seen or clearly understood, no captain can do wrong if he places his ship alongside that of an enemy."

About half-past nine in the morning of the 19th the *Mars,* being the nearest to the fleet of the ships which formed the line of communication with the frigates inshore, repeated the signal that the enemy were coming out of port. The wind was at this time very light, with partial breezes, mostly from the S. S. W. Nelson ordered the signal to be made for a chase in the south-east quarter. About two the repeating ships announced that the enemy were at sea. All night the British fleet continued under all sail, steering to the south-east. At daybreak they were in the entrance of the Straits, but the enemy were not in sight. About seven, one of the frigates made signal that the enemy was bearing north. Upon this the *Victory* hove to, and shortly afterwards Nelson made sail again to the northward. In the afternoon the wind blew fresh from the south-west, and the English began to fear that the foe might be forced to return to port.

A little before sunset, however, Blackwood, in the *Euryalus,* telegraphed that they appeared determined to go to the westward. "And that," said the Admiral in his diary, "they shall not do, if it is in the power of Nelson and Bronte to prevent them." Nelson had signified to Blackwood that he depended upon him to keep sight of the enemy. They were observed so well that all their motions were made known to him, and as they wore twice, he inferred that they were aiming to keep the port of Cádiz open, and would retreat there as soon as they saw the British fleet; for this reason he was very careful not to approach near enough to be seen by them during the night. At daybreak the combined fleets were distinctly seen from the *Victory's* deck, formed in a close line of battle ahead, on the starboard tack, about twelve miles to leeward, and standing to the south. Our fleet consisted of twenty-seven sail of the line and four frigates; theirs of thirty-three and seven large frigates. Their superiority was greater in size and weight of metal than in numbers. They had four thousand troops on board, and the best riflemen that could be procured, many of them Tyrolese, were dispersed through the ships.

Soon after daylight Nelson came upon deck. The 21st of October was a festival in his family, because on that day his uncle, Captain Suckling, in the *Dreadnought,* with two other line-of-battle ships, had beaten off a French squadron of four sail of the line and three frigates. Nelson, with that sort of superstition from which few persons are entirely exempt, had more than once expressed his persuasion that this was to be the day of his battle also, and he was well pleased at seeing his prediction about to be verified. The wind was now from the west— light breezes, with a long heavy swell. Signal was made to bear down upon the enemy in two lines, and the fleet set all sail. Collingwood, in the *Royal Sovereign,* led the lee line of thirteen ships; the *Victory* led the weather line of fourteen. Having seen that all was as it should be, Nelson retired to his cabin, and wrote the following prayer—

"May the great God whom I worship, grant to my country, and for the benefit of Europe in general, a great and glorious victory, and may no misconduct in any one tarnish it, and may humanity after victory be the predominant feature in the British fleet! For myself individually, I commit my life to Him that made me, and may His blessing alight on my endeavours for serving my country faithfully! To Him I resign myself, and the just cause which is entrusted to me to defend. Amen, Amen, Amen."

Blackwood went on board the *Victory* about six. He found him in good spirits, but very calm; not in that exhilaration which he felt upon entering into battle at Aboukir and Copenhagen; he knew that his own life would be particularly aimed at, and seems to have looked for death with almost as sure an expectation as for victory. His whole attention was fixed upon the enemy. They tacked to the northward, and formed their line on the larboard tack; thus bringing the shoals of Trafalgar and St. Pedro under the lee of the British, and keeping the port of Cádiz open for themselves. This was judiciously done; and Nelson, aware of all the advantages which he gave them, made signal to prepare to anchor.

Villeneuve was a skilful seaman, worthy of serving a better master and a better cause. His plan of defence was as well conceived and as original as the plan of attack. He formed the fleet in a double line, every alternate ship being about a cable's length to windward of her second ahead and astern. Nelson, certain of a triumphant issue to the day, asked Blackwood what he should consider as a victory. That officer answered that, considering the handsome way in which battle was offered by the enemy, their apparent determination for a fair trial of strength, and the situation of the land, he thought it would be a glorious result if fourteen were captured. He replied: "I shall not be satisfied with less than twenty." Soon afterwards he asked him if he did not think there was a signal wanting. Captain Blackwood made answer that he thought the whole fleet seemed very clearly to understand what they were about. These words were scarcely spoken before that signal was made which will be remembered as long as the language or even the memory of England shall endure—"ENGLAND EXPECTS EVERY MAN WILL DO HIS DUTY!" It was received throughout the fleet with a shout of answering acclamation, made sublime by the spirit which it breathed and the feeling which it expressed. "Now," said Lord Nelson, "I can do no more. We must trust to the great disposer of all events and the justice of our cause. I thank God for this great opportunity of doing my duty."

He wore that day, as usual, his admiral's frock-coat, bearing on the left breast four stars of the different orders with which he was invested. Ornaments which rendered him so conspicuous a mark for the enemy were beheld with ominous apprehension by his officers. It was known that there were riflemen on board the French ships, and it could not be doubted but that his life would be particularly aimed at. They communicated their fears to each other, and the surgeon, Mr. Beatty, spoke to the chaplain, Dr. Scott, and to Mr. Scott, the public secretary, desiring that some person would entreat him to change his dress or cover the stars; but they knew that such a request would highly displease him. "In honour I gained them," he had said when such a thing had been hinted to him formerly, "and in honour I will die with them." Mr. Beatty, however, would not have been deterred by any fear of exciting his displeasure from speaking to him himself upon a subject in which the weal of England, as well as the life of Nelson, was concerned; but he was ordered from the deck before he could find an opportunity. This was a point upon which Nelson's officers knew that it was hopeless to remonstrate or reason with him; but both Blackwood and his own captain, Hardy, represented to him how advantageous to the fleet it would be for him to keep out of action as long as possible, and he consented at last to let the *Leviathan* and the *Temeraire,* which were sailing abreast of the *Victory,* be ordered to pass ahead.

Yet even here the last infirmity of this noble mind was indulged, for these ships could not pass ahead if the *Victory* continued to carry all her sail; and so far was Nelson from shortening sail, that it was evident he took pleasure in pressing on, and rendering it impossible for them to obey his own orders. A long swell was setting into the Bay of Cádiz. Our ships, crowding all sail, moved majestically before it, with light winds from the south-west. The sun shone on the sails of the enemy, but their well-formed line, with their numerous three-deckers, made an appearance which any other assailants would have thought formidable, but the British sailors only admired the beauty and the splendour of the spectacle, and in full confidence of winning what they saw, remarked to each other what a fine sight yonder ships would make at Spithead!

The French admiral, from the *Bucentaure,* beheld the new manner in which his enemy was advancing—Nelson and Collingwood, each leading his line; and pointing them out to his officers, he is said to have exclaimed that such conduct could not fail to be successful. Yet Villeneuve had made his own dispositions with the utmost skill, and the fleets under his command waited for the attack with perfect coolness. Ten minutes before twelve they opened their fire. Eight or nine of the ships immediately ahead of the *Victory,* and across her bows, fired single guns at her to ascertain whether she was yet within their range. As soon as Nelson perceived that their shot passed over him, he desired Blackwood and Captain Prowse, of the *Sirius,* to repair to their respective frigates, and on their way to tell all the captains of the line-of-battle ships that he depended on their exertions, and that, if by the prescribed mode of attack they found it impracticable to get into action immediately, they might adopt whatever they thought best, provided it led them quickly and closely alongside an enemy. As they were standing on the poop, Blackwood took him by the hand, saying he hoped soon to return and find him in possession of twenty prizes. He replied, "God bless you, Blackwood; I shall never see you again."

Nelson's column was steered about two points more to the north than Collingwood's, in order to cut off the enemy's escape into Cádiz. The lee line, therefore, was first engaged. "See," cried Nelson, pointing to the *Royal Sovereign,* as she steered right for the centre of the enemy's line, cut through it astern of the *Santa Anna,* three-decker, and engaged her at the muzzle of her guns on the starboard side; "see how that noble fellow Collingwood carries his ship into action!" Collingwood, delighted at being first in the heat of the fire, and knowing the feelings of his commander and old friend, turned to his captain and exclaimed: "Rotherham, what would Nelson give to be here!" Both these brave officers, perhaps, at this moment thought of Nelson with gratitude for a circumstance which had occurred on the preceding day. Admiral

Collingwood, with some of the captains, having gone on board the *Victory* to receive instructions, Nelson inquired of him where his captain was, and was told in reply that they were not upon good terms with each other. "Terms!" said Nelson; "good terms with each other!" Immediately he sent a boat for Captain Rotherham, led him, so soon as he arrived, to Collingwood, and saying, "Look, yonder are the enemy!" bade them shake hands like Englishmen.

The enemy continued to fire a gun at a time at the *Victory* till they saw that a shot had passed through her main-topgallant sail; then they opened their broadsides, aiming chiefly at her rigging, in the hope of disabling her before she could close with them. Nelson as usual had hoisted several flags, lest one should be shot away. The enemy showed no colours till late in the action, when they began to feel the necessity of having them to strike. For this reason the *Santissima Trinidad,* Nelson's old acquaintance, as he used to call her, was distinguishable only by her four decks, and to the bow of this opponent he ordered the *Victory* to be steered. Meantime an incessant raking fire was kept up upon the *Victory*. The Admiral's secretary was one of the first who fell; he was killed by a cannon shot while conversing with Hardy. Captain Adair, of the marines, with the help of a sailor, endeavoured to remove the body from Nelson's sight, who had a great regard for Mr. Scott, but he anxiously asked, "Is that poor Scott that's gone?" and being informed that it was indeed so, exclaimed, "Poor fellow!"

Presently a double-headed shot struck a party of marines who were drawn up on the poop, and killed eight of them, upon which Nelson immediately desired Captain Adair to disperse his men round the ship, that they might not suffer so much from being together. A few minutes afterwards a shot struck the fore-brace bits on the quarter-deck, and passed between Nelson and Hardy, a splinter from the bit tearing off Hardy's buckle and bruising his foot. Both stopped, and looked anxiously at each other: each supposed the other to be wounded. Nelson then smiled, and said: "This is too warm work, Hardy, to last long."

The *Victory* had not yet returned a single gun; fifty of her men had by this time been killed or wounded, and her maintopmast, with all her studding sails and their booms, shot away. Nelson declared that in all his battles he had seen nothing which surpassed the cool courage of his crew on this occasion. At four minutes after twelve she opened her fire from both sides of her deck. It was not possible to break the enemy's lines without running on board one of their ships; Hardy informed him of this, and asked him which he would prefer. Nelson replied: "Take your choice, Hardy; it does not signify much." The master was ordered to put the helm to port, and the *Victory* ran on board the *Redoubtable* just as her tiller-ropes were shot away. The

French ship received her with a broadside, then instantly let down her lower-deck ports for fear of being boarded through them, and never afterwards fired a great gun during the action. Her tops, like those of all the enemy's ships, were filled with riflemen. Nelson never placed musketry in his tops; he had a strong dislike to the practice, not merely because it endangers setting fire to the sails, but also because it is a murderous sort of warfare, by which individuals may suffer and a commander now and then be picked off, but which never can decide the fate of a general engagement.

Captain Harvey, in the *Temeraire,* fell on board the *Redoubtable* on the side; another enemy was in like manner on board the *Temeraire;* so that these four ships formed as compact a tier as if they had been moored together, their heads all lying the same way. The lieutenants of the *Victory* seeing this, depressed their guns of the middle and lower decks, and fired with a diminished charge, lest the shot should pass through and injure the *Temeraire;* and because there was danger that the *Redoubtable* might take fire from the lower deck guns, the muzzles of which touched her side when they were run out, the fireman of each gun stood ready with a bucket of water, which, as soon as the gun was discharged, he dashed into the hole made by the shot. An incessant fire was kept up from the *Victory* from both sides, her larboard guns playing upon the *Bucentaure* and the huge *Santissima Trinidad.*

It had been part of Nelson's prayer that the British fleet should be distinguished by humanity in the victory he expected. Setting an example himself, he twice gave orders to cease firing upon the *Redoubtable,* supposing that she had struck, because her great guns were silent; for, as she carried no flag, there was no means of instantly ascertaining the fact. From this ship, which he had thus twice spared, he received his death. A ball fired from her mizzen-top, which in the then situation of the two vessels was not more than fifteen yards from that part of the deck where he was standing, struck the epaulette on his left shoulder, about a quarter after one, just in the heat of action. He fell upon his face, on the spot which was covered with his poor secretary's blood. Hardy, who was a few steps from him, turning round, saw three men raising him up. "They have done for me at last, Hardy!" said he. "I hope not!" cried Hardy. "Yes," he replied, "my backbone is shot through!"

Yet even now, not for a moment losing his presence of mind, he observed as they were carrying him down the ladder, that the tiller-ropes, which had been shot away, were not yet replaced, and ordered that new ones should be rove immediately. Then, that he might not be seen by the crew, he took out his handkerchief and covered his face and his stars. Had he but concealed these badges of honour from the enemy, England perhaps would not have cause to receive with sorrow the news of the battle of Trafalgar. The cockpit was crowded with wounded and dying men, over whose bodies he was with some difficulty conveyed, and laid upon a pallet in the midshipmen's berth. It was soon perceived, upon examination, that the wound was mortal. This, however, was concealed from all except Captain Hardy, the chaplain, and the medical attendants. He himself being certain, from the sensation in his back and the gush of blood he felt momently within his breast, that no human care could avail him, insisted that the surgeon should leave him, and attend to those to whom he might be useful, "for," said he, "you can do nothing for me."

All that could be done was to fan him with paper, and frequently give him lemonade to alleviate his intense thirst. He was in great pain, and expressed much anxiety for the event of the action, which now began to declare itself. As often as a ship struck, the crew of the *Victory* hurrahed, and at every hurrah a visible expression of joy gleamed in the eyes and marked the countenance of the dying hero. But he became impatient to see Captain Hardy, and as that officer, though often sent for, could not leave the deck, Nelson feared that some fatal cause prevented him, and repeatedly cried, "Will no one bring Hardy to me? He must be killed! He is surely dead!"

An hour and ten minutes elapsed from the time when Nelson received his wound before Hardy could come to him. They shook hands in silence; Hardy in vain struggling to express the feelings of that most painful and sublimest moment. "Well, Hardy," said Nelson, "how goes the day with us?"—"Very well," replied Hardy; "ten ships have struck, but five in the van have tacked, and show an intention to bear down upon the *Victory*. I have called two or three of our fresh ships round, and have no doubt of giving them a drubbing."—"I hope," said Nelson, "none of our ships have struck." Hardy answered, "There was no fear of that." Then, and not till then, Nelson spoke of himself. "I am a dead man, Hardy," said he; "I am going fast; it will be all over with me soon. Come nearer to me." Hardy observed that he hoped Mr. Beatty could yet hold out some prospect of life. "Oh no!" he replied, "it is impossible; my back is shot through. Beatty will tell you so." Captain Hardy then once more shook hands with him, and with a heart almost bursting hastened upon deck.

By this time, all feeling below the breast was gone; and Nelson, having made the surgeon ascertain this, said to him: "You know I am gone. I know it. I feel something rising in my breast"—putting his hand on his left side—"which tells me so." And upon Beatty's inquiring whether his pain was very great, he replied, "So great that he wished he was dead." "Yet," said he in a lower voice, "one would like to live a little longer too!" Captain Hardy, some fifty minutes after he had left the cockpit, returned, and again taking the hand of his dying friend and commander, congratulated him on having gained a complete victory. How many of the enemy were taken he did not know, as it was impossible to perceive them distinctly; but fourteen or fifteen at least. "That's well!" cried Nelson; "but I bargained for twenty." And then in a stronger voice he said, "Anchor, Hardy, anchor." Hardy upon this hinted that Admiral Collingwood would take upon himself the direction of affairs. "Not while I live, Hardy," said the dying Nelson, ineffectually endeavouring to raise himself from the bed; "Do you anchor."

His previous order for preparing to anchor had shown how clearly he foresaw the necessity of this. Presently calling Hardy back, he said to him in a low voice: "Don't throw me overboard"; and he desired that he might be buried by his parents, unless it should please the king to order otherwise. Then turning to Hardy: "Kiss me, Hardy," said he. Hardy knelt down and kissed his cheek, and Nelson said: "Now I am satisfied. Thank God, I have done my duty!" Hardy stood over him in silence for a moment or two, then knelt again and kissed his forehead. "Who is that?" said Nelson; and being informed, he replied: "God bless you, Hardy." And Hardy then left him for ever.

Nelson now desired to be turned upon his right side, and said: "I wish I had not left the deck, for I shall soon be gone." Death was indeed rapidly approaching. He said to the chaplain: "Doctor, I have *not* been a *great* sinner." His articulation now became difficult, but he was distinctly heard to say: "Thank God, I have done my duty!" These words he repeatedly pronounced. And they were the last words that he uttered. He expired at thirty minutes after four, three hours and a a quarter after he had received his wound!

GEORGE WASHINGTON

It has never been customary, and we are unlikely ever, to regard George Washington (1732–1799) as a writing man. His has been pictured, time and again, as a one-track mind, not matching in brilliance the courage and integrity of his character. Hamilton has been credited with the wording of his Farewell Address, and the journal he kept at Mount Vernon, for anyone not interested in agricultural matters, is dull reading. My own conviction for a long time has been that Washington was a more interesting man, apart from his achievements as soldier and builder of the young republic, than his biographers, including even the late Douglas Freeman, have been able to make him appear. The statue dominates the legend, and sometimes, at least, has come perilously close to being transformed into a stuffed shirt. He was neither, but a full-blooded, often violent man, and capable, as Owen Wister pointed out in his *Seven Ages of Washington* (a more warmly human portrait than anyone else's), of rolling on the ground with laughter. But he was also intensely ambitious, with a sharp eye cocked on the main chance—and by that I do not mean to call him an opportunist, for his integrity was iron-clad, and his courage of the four-o'clock-in-the-morning variety.

I am reprinting here some pages from the journal he kept on his first important mission, when he went out to woo the Indians and circumvent the French. There are only eight copies of the original printing extant; it has now been made available to the general reader in an edition published by the Kingsport Press, of Kingsport, Tennessee.

That journal is a revealing document. In it we can sense the craving for advancement, and through its somewhat pedestrian understatements we are made aware of the intrepidity and fortitude of which Washington was so highly capable. It was this journal which first made his name known to the English, and marked him as a man to be watched.

Trial by Wilderness

GEORGE WASHINGTON was twenty-one years of age when on a crisp October day in 1753 he reached Williamsburg, capital of the colony of Virginia. A shy and solemn young man who rode a horse with natural grace, he jogged along Duke of Gloucester Street unmindful of the ducks and geese, the pigs and dogs scattering around him in shrill complaint. To the quiet, youthful squire of Mount Vernon, Williamsburg's taverns and shops, its dusty streets and sprawling Market Square seemed alive with people. Wealthy planters who came to drink and gamble and dance, sea captains and merchants with commercial business to transact, an occasional frontiersman leaning on his long rifle and gazing with bold, curious eyes at members of the House of Burgesses in powdered wigs, satin coats and ruffled shirts were all drawn to Williamsburg during those "Publick Times" when the courts and legislature convened. Colorful and exciting the old capital appeared that autumn day in 1753; yet the perceptive ear caught the note of anxiety in some voices, the knowing eye discerned the lines of tautness in some faces. Washington, young and anxious to make a name for himself as a military man, had come to Williamsburg seeking an audience with Governor Dinwiddie because he understood the risks of the impending crisis. A war could result. Not in decades had the colony faced a time when cool heads were more needed—and straight talk bolstered by the resolution to defend every inch of soil belonging to Virginia.

Even though the boundaries of the colony, as set by the Charter of 1609, had been reduced by grants to Maryland, the Carolinas and Pennsylvania, in 1753 Virginia remained a vast empire stretching into the mists of an unexplored wilderness. Today what is the western part of Pennsylvania and the states of West Virginia, Kentucky, Ohio, Indiana, Illinois, Michigan and Wisconsin then was included in the domain claimed by the government in Williamsburg. The French contended otherwise. It was no surprise, the French argued, that the British wanted everything—this was an old British habit. But, asked the French, had not Robert Cavelier, Sieur de la Salle, following Marquette and Joliet, descended the Mississippi River to its mouth in 1682? And the French, answering their own question by deed, began stringing trading posts and forts along the Ohio River. Occasionally an English frontiersman found himself dispossessed from a wilderness home, or his scalp lifted by a savage whose belly had been warmed by French brandy, or carried away to Canada for interrogation about British strength and plans—the rules were catch-as-catch-can in wilderness diplomacy. After all, the heartland of a continent was at stake. So big an end justified such small means.

The British bulldog, transported to America, lost neither its growl nor tenacity. For all the Governor's good humor, his benevolent manner, the gentleness in his blue-gray eyes, Dinwiddie could be square-jawed, stubborn, perhaps even hot-tempered. He intended to give the French fair warning—they must cease encroaching upon British land along the Ohio or they would be thrown out—and if the emissary who carried this message also judged the military strength of the French settlements, selected promising sites for forts and evaluated the allegiance of Indian tribes in the territory, so much the better. Dinwiddie was no fool; the expedition posed obstacles no one could foresee. How far the party must travel before reaching the French commandant was a guess where a thousand miles could be as accurate as five hundred. Only one fact could be stated with certainty—the whole way over strange mountains, through silent forests and across turbulent streams would embrace a country of wild Indians, bears and rattlesnakes. The time of year likewise worked against the expedition. November would bring bleak skies, rain, swollen rivers, cold days and raw nights. December would bring snow and ice, frozen roads that could become impassable, dangerous shortages of drinking water. Obviously, to lead such an expedition a man must possess courage and stamina, tact and intelligence, devotion to King and country. But Dinwiddie believed that Virginia claimed such a leader, even if Washington scarcely had come of age.

So the young man on horseback, scattering the ducks and geese along Duke of Gloucester Street, was called for the first time as the man for a crisis. Gossip—always a lively art in Colonial America—found him a new and fascinating subject. Those who knew his background and brief career described him accurately as a sober young fellow who had made the most of long odds. As for his family, he need apologize to no one. The Washingtons, originally from Northhamptonshire, had settled in America in 1657 when John Washington bought land in Westmoreland County, Virginia. His son, Lawrence, had sired Augustine who in turn had sired young George (the date of his birth, now that Britain had adopted the Gregorian calendar, was February 22, 1732, although the date at the time was February eleventh). Augustine's family—a Virginian's interest in such subjects even then seemed inexhaustible—consisted of three sons and a daughter by his first wife and four sons and two daughters by Mary Ball, his second wife. George was the first child of the second marriage.

The Washingtons moved shortly after George's birth to Ferry Farm on the Rappahannock, across from the village of Fredericksburg, and here happy boyhood years were spent. Young George came to know the old river the way a boy does pulling an oar against its tides, sailing its windy bends, swimming and fishing its deep pools. He came to know the surrounding green hills as a lad does riding a horse well and searching, gun in hand, for fox and wolf tracks, the heavy print of a bear, a glimpse of fleeing deer. His schooling was crude and sparse, really no more than a knowledge of simple arithmetic, a personal idea of how English words are spelled, an ability to read aloud with many stumbling hems and ahs, a smattering acquaintance with farming methods. Visitors today to the Library of Congress may see the "Rules of Civility" that in 1747 young George wrote down as he taught himself social manners.

This little copybook, homemade by George Washington in his fifteenth year, foreshadows much of the character, the temperament and personality of the future Father of the Country. "Play not the Peacock, looking everywhere about you, to See if you be well Deck't, if your Shoes fit well if your Stockings Sit neatly, and Cloths handsomely," wrote the boy who in later years would be equally at ease with ragged soldier and polished diplomat. "Gaze not on the marks or blemishes of Others and ask not how they came," repeated the boy who in a few years would contract smallpox and carry its scars on his face through the remainder of life. "Be not Curious to Know the Affairs of Others neither approach those that Speak in Private," the boy admonished himself, certainly sound advice for a gentleman, a statesman-to-be. "Labour to keep alive in your Breast that Little Spark of Celestial fire Called Conscience," the boy learned, and men grew to trust him implicitly.

Augustine Washington died when George was eleven, but the lad remained at Ferry Farm the next few years before Lawrence, his half brother and favorite, asked him to come live at Mount Vernon. In the rich, fertile tidewater country of the Potomac known as the Northern Neck, a dominant personality was gruff, irascible, unsociable Lord Fairfax, cousin of Colonel William Fairfax who was Lawrence's father-in-law. Neighbors often grumbled that a porcupine offered better companionship than this scowling, tart-tongued old nobleman, yet Lord Fairfax was drawn to George, liking his strength and vigor, his ease in handling horses, his skill on a fox hunt, his quiet shyness, his innate politeness. Soon George was working as a surveyor for Lord Fairfax, earning good wages and following the nobleman's advice in investing his money in property.

At the age of eighteen, as Lord Fairfax's friend and protégé, solemn-faced George had gained an inner contentment. He was a landowner. As a surveyor he had crossed the Blue Ridge Mountains and knew how frontiersmen were clearing the wilderness and cutting a path to future empire. He had talked with Indians, attended their conferences, won their confidence.

Yet grim experiences were ahead. Lawrence, a man of delicate constitution, hoped that his failing health might mend in the milder climate of the West Indies, and the one trip that George would make from the soil of his homeland came in the autumn of 1751 when he accompanied his half brother on a journey to Barbados. Here George suffered his attack of smallpox; but for Lawrence the adventure was more disheartening. He was no better in health in the West Indies than at Mount Vernon; alone, George returned to Virginia. Lawrence's death was only a few months away, and by his will when his widow remarried George became the owner of Mount Vernon.

In the management of this fine estate on the Potomac, Washington began to show his maturing judgment, his ability to get along with people, his competence for assuming community responsibility. Appointed a major in the Virginia militia, his administrative talent was at once obvious. For another reason, Dinwiddie thought of Mount Vernon and Washington as the tension along the Ohio mounted. The Governor was a member of the Ohio Company that Lawrence Washington once had headed, and what the trouble with the French was costing this company in the loss of men and valuable furs was as painful a subject at Mount Vernon as in Williamsburg. There was no need for Dinwiddie to state the case obliquely to George. The French were pinching pride, patriotism and pocketbook.

Washington had no wish to loiter, once his mind was set to a task. The letter Governor Dinwiddie handed him said, "The Lands upon the River Ohio in the Western Parts of the Colony of Virginia are so notoriously known to be the Property of the Crown of Great Britain, that is a Matter of equal Concern and Surprize to me to hear that a Body of French Forces are erecting Fortresses and Making Settlements upon that River within his Majesty's Dominions." That was fine, by Washington's standards—direct, unequivocal, its double-edged meaning clear. The planters, the merchants and ship captains, the Burgesses in powdered wigs could spend the remaining daylight over their ale and buttered rum in Raleigh Tavern; Washington had work to do, and with Governor Dinwiddie's letter in his saddlebag he left that same day for Fredericksburg.

To lead the party into the wilderness, the Governor selected hard-bitten Christopher Gist, an Indian trader with the Ohio Company who deserved his fame among early American frontiersmen. Gist was one

of the first to penetrate those canebrakes now called Kentucky; a restless fellow, who might feel hemmed-in if he saw his own shadow too
often, he was the kind of woodsman who one night chased a bear from
under a ledge so that he might have that sequestered spot for his own
sleeping quarters. Later he fought with Braddock, and five years after
this mission under Washington died of smallpox. A grandson, B.
Gratz Brown, became the vice-presidential candidate of the Democratic
Party in 1872.

Early in the journey Gist's own journal revealed the cut of the man
in its entry for November fifteenth: "We set out, and at night encamped at George's Creek, about eight miles, where a messenger came
with letters from my son, who was just returned from his people at the
Cherokees, and lay sick at the mouth of the Conegocheague. But as I
found myself entered again on public business, and Major Washington
and all the company unwilling I should return I wrote and sent
medicines to my son, and so continued my journey. . . ." Like Washington, Gist placed duty first, and one hopes that the medicines reached
his ailing son in time to be of help. Washington's reluctance to turn
back is understandable, for snow had begun to fall and three days later
Gist's journal would describe it as "ancle deep."

EARL SCHENCK MIERS

December, 1753

(4TH) This is an old Indian Town [Venango], situated at the Mouth
of French Creek on Ohio; and lies near N. about 60 Miles from the
Loggs-Town, but more than 70 the way we were obliged to go.

We found the French Colours hoisted at a House from which they
had driven Mr. John Frazier, an English Subject. I immediately
repaired to it, to know where the Commander resided. There were
three Officers, one of whom Capt. Joncaire, informed me, that he had
the command of the Ohio; But that there was a General Officer at the
near Fort, where he advised me to apply for an Answer. He invited
us to sup with them; and treated us with the greatest Complaisance.
The Wine, as they dosed themselves pretty plentifully with it, soon
banished the Restraint which at first appeared in their Conversation;
and gave a license to the Tongues to reveal their Sentiments more
freely. They told me, That it was their absolute Design to take Possession of the Ohio, and by G—— they would do it; For that altho'
they were sensible the English could raise two Men for their one; yet
they knew their Motions were too slow and dilatory to prevent any
Undertaking of theirs. They pretend to have an undoubted Right to
the River, from a Discovery made by one La Salle 60 Years ago; and
the Rise of this Expedition is, to prevent our settling on the River or

Waters of it, as they had heard of some Families moving-out in Order thereto. From the best Intelligence I could get, there have been 1500 Men on their Side of Ontario Lake: But upon the Death of the General all were recalled to about 6 or 700, who were left to garrison four Forts, 150 or thereabouts in each. The first of them is on French-Creek near a small Lake, about 60 Miles from Venango, near N.N.W. the next lies on Lake Erie, where the greater Part of their Stores are kept, about 15 Miles from the other. From this it is 120 Miles to the carrying Place at the Fall of Lake Erie [Niagara Falls] where there is a small Fort [Fort Niagara]; which they lodge their Goods at, in bringing them from Montreal, the Place whence all their Stores come from. The next Fort lies about 20 Miles from this, on Ontario Lake [Fort Toronto]. Between this Fort and Montreal there are three others, the first [Fort Frontenac] of which is near opposite to the English Fort Oswego. From the Fort on Lake Erie to Montreal is about 600 Miles, which they say requires no more, of good Weather, than four Weeks Voyage, if they go in Barks or Large Vessels, so that they may cross the Lake: But if they come in Canoes it will require 5 or 6 Weeks, for they are obliged to keep under the Shore.

5TH. Rain'd excessively all Day, which prevented our Travelling. Capt. Joncaire sent for the Half-King,[1] as he had but just heard that he came with me: He affected to be much concerned that I did not make free to bring them [the Indians] in before. I excused it in the best Manner I was capable, and told him, I did not think their company agreeable, as I had heard him say a good deal in Dispraise of Indians in general. But another Motive prevented me from bringing them into his Company: I knew he was Interpreter, and a Person of great, great Influence among the Indians, and had lately used all possible Means to draw them over to their Interest; therefore I was desirous of giving no Opportunity that could be avoided.

When they came in, there was great Pleasure expressed at seeing them. He wondered how they could be so near without coming to visit him; made several trifling Presents; and applied Liquor so fast, that they were soon rendered incapable of the Business they came about, notwithstanding the Caution which was given.

6TH. The Half-King came to my Tent, quite sober, and insisted very much that I should stay and hear what he had to say to the French. I fain would have prevented him speaking any Thing till he came to the

---

[1] Half-King's real name was Tanacharisson; although a Seneca chief, he owed an allegiance to the Six Nations, and so became known as Half-King.

Commandant, but could not prevail. He told me that at this Place a Council Fire was kindled, where all their Business with these People was to be transacted; and that the Management of the Indian affairs was left solely to Monsieur Joncaire. As I was desirous of knowing the Issue of this, I agreed to stay; But sent our Horses a little way up French Creek to raft over and encamp; which I knew would make it near Night.

About 10 o'Clock they met in Council. The King spoke much the same as he had before done to the General; and offered the French Speech-Belt which had before been demanded, with the Marks of four Towns on it, which Monsieur Joncaire refused to receive; but desired him to carry it to the Fort to the Commander.

14TH. As the Snow increased very fast, and our Horses daily became weaker, I sent them off unloaded; under the Care of Barnaby Currin, and two others, to make all convenient Dispatch to Venango, and there await our Arrival, if there was a prospect of the Rivers freezing: If not, then to continue down to Shanapin's Town, at the Forks of the Ohio, and there to wait till we came to cross the Aliganey; intending myself to go down by Water, as I had the Offer of a Canoe or two.

15TH. The Commandant ordered a plentiful Store of Liquor, Provision, &c., to be put on Board our Canoe; and appeared to be extremely complaisant, though he was exerting every Artifice which he could invent to set our own Indians at Variance with us, to prevent their going 'till after our Departure. Presents, Rewards, and every Thing which could be suggested by him or his Officers.—I can't say that ever in my Life I suffered so much Anxiety as I did in this Affair: I saw that every Stratagem which the most fruitful Brain could invent, was practised, to win the Half-King to their Interest; and that leaving him here was giving them the Opportunity they aimed at.—I went to the Half-King and press'd him in the strongest Terms to go: He told me the Commandant would not discharge him 'till the Morning. I then went to the Commandant and desired him to do their Business; and complain'd of ill Treatment: For keeping them, as they were Part of my Company, was detaining me. This he promised not to do, but to forward my Journey as much as he could. He protested he did not keep them, but was ignorant of the Cause of their Stay; though I soon found it out:—He had promised them a present of Guns, &c, if they would wait 'till the morning.

As I was very much press'd by the Indians, to wait this Day for them, I consented, on a Promise, That nothing should hinder them in the Morning.

16TH. The French were not slack in their inventions to keep the Indians this Day also: But as they were obligated, according to Promise, to give the Present, they then endeavored to try the Power of Liquor; which I doubt not would have prevailed at any other Time than this; But I urged and insisted with the King so closely upon his Word, that he refrained, and set off with us as he had engaged.

We had a tedious and very fatiguing Passage down the Creek. Several Times we were like to have been staved against Rocks; and many Times were obliged all Hands to get out and remain in the Water Half an Hour or more, getting over the Shoals. At one Place the Ice had lodged and made it impassable by Water; therefore we were obliged to carry our Canoe across a Neck of Land, a quarter of a Mile over. We did not reach Venango, till the 22d, where we met with our Horses.

This Creek is extremely crooked, I dare say the Distance between the Fort and Venango can't be less than 130 Miles, to follow the Meanders.

23D. When I got Things ready to set-off, I sent for the Half-King, to know whether he intended to go with us or by Water. He told me that White-Thunder had hurt himself much, and was sick and unable to walk; therefore he was obliged to carry him down in a Canoe. As I found he intended to stay here a Day or two, and knew that Monsieur Joncaire would employ every Scheme to set him against the English as he had before done; I told him I hoped he would guard against his Flattery, and let no fine Speeches influence him in their Favour. He desired I might not be concerned, for he knew the French too well, for anything to engage him in their Behalf; and that though he could not go down with us, he yet would endeavour to meet us at the Forks with Joseph Campbell, to deliver a Speech for me to carry to his Honour the Governor. He told me he would order the young Hunter to attend us, and get Provision, &c. if wanted.

Our Horses were now so weak and feeble, and the Baggage so heavy (as we were obliged to provide all the Necessaries which the Journey would require) that we doubted much their performing it; therefore myself and others (except the Drivers, who were obliged to ride) gave up our Horses for Packs, to assist along with the Baggage. I put myself in an Indian walking Dress, and continued with them three Days, till I found there was no Probability of their getting home in any reasonable Time. The Horses grew less able to travel every Day; the Cold increased very fast; and the Roads were becoming much worse by a deep Snow, continually freezing: Therefore as I was uneasy to get back, to make Report of my Proceedings to his Honour, the Governor,

I determined to prosecute my Journey the nearest Way through the Woods, on Foot.

Accordingly I left Mr. Vanbraam in Charge of our Baggage: with Money and Directions to Provide Necessaries from Place to Place for themselves and Horses, and to make the most convenient Dispatch in Travelling.

I took my necessary Papers; pulled off my Cloaths; and tied myself up in a Match Coat. Then with Gun in Hand and Pack at my Back, in which were my Papers and Provisions, I set-out with Mr. Gist, fitted in the same Manner, on Wednesday the 26th.

The Day following, just after we had passed a Place called the Murdering-[Murthering] Town (where we intended to quit the Path, and steer across the Country for Shannapins Town) we fell in with a Party of French Indians, who had lain in Wait for us. One of them fired at Mr. Gist or me, not 15 steps off, but fortunately missed. We took this fellow into Custody, and kept him till about 9 o'clock at Night; Then let him go, and walked all the remaining Part of the Night without making any Stop; that we might get the start, so far, as to be out of the Reach of their Pursuit the next Day, since we were well assured they would follow our Tract as soon as it was light. The next Day we continued travelling till quite dark, and got to the River [Allegheny] about two Miles above Shannapins. We expected to have found the River frozen, but it was not, only about 50 Yards from each Shore; The Ice I suppose had broken up above, for it was driving in vast Quantities.

There was no way for getting over but on a Raft; Which we set about with but one poor Hatchet, and finished just after Sun-setting. This was a whole Day's Work. Then set off; But before we were Half Way over, we were jammed in the Ice, in such a Manner that we expected every Moment our Raft to sink, and ourselves to perish. I put-out my setting Pole to try to stop the Raft, that the Ice might pass by; when the Rapidity of the Stream threw it with so much Violence against the Pole, that it jerked me out into ten Feet Water: but I fortunately saved myself by catching hold of one of the Raft Logs. Notwithstanding all our efforts we could not get the Raft to either Shore; but were obliged, as we were near an Island to quit our Raft and make to it.

The Cold was so extremely severe, that Mr. Gist had all his Fingers, and some of his Toes frozen; but the water was shut up so hard, that we found no Difficulty in getting-off the Island, on the Ice, in the Morning, and went to Mr. Frazier's. We met here about 20 Warriors who were going to the Southward to War, but coming to a Place upon the Head of the great Kunnaway [Kanawha], where they found seven

People killed and scalped (all but one Woman with very light Hair) they turned about and ran back for fear the Inhabitants should rise and take them as the Authors of the Murder. They report that the Bodies were lying about the House, and some of them much torn and eaten by Hogs. By the Mark which were left, they say they were French Indians of the Ottaway Nation, &c., who did it.

As we intended to take Horses here, and it required some Time to find them, I went-up about three Miles to the Mouth of Yaughyaughane to visit Queen Aliquippa, who had expressed great Concern that we passed her in going to the Fort. I made her a Present of a Matchcoat and a Bottle of Rum; which latter was thought much the best Present of the Two.

January, 1754

TUESDAY the 1st Day of January, we left Mr. Frazier's House, and arrived at Mr. Gist's at Monongahela the 2d, where I bought a Horse, Saddle, etc: the 6th we met 17 Horses loaded with Materials and Stores, for a Fort at the Forks of Ohio, and the Day after some Families going out to settle: This Day we arrived at Wills Creek, after as fatiguing a Journey as it is possible to conceive, rendered so by excessive bad Weather. From the first Day of December to the 15th, there was but one Day on which it did not rain or snow incessantly: and throughout the whole Journey we met with nothing but one continued Series of cold wet Weather, which occasioned very uncomfortable Lodgings: especially after we had quitted our Tent, which was some Screen from the Inclemency of it.

On the 11th I got to Belvoir: where I stopped one Day to take necessary Rest; and then set out and arrived in Williamsburg the 16th; when I waited upon his Honour the Governor with the Letter I had brought from the French Commandant; and to give an Account of the Success of my Proceedings. This I beg leave to do by offering the foregoing Narrative as it contains the most remarkable Occurrences which happened in my Journey.

I hope what has been said will be sufficient to make your Honour satisfied with my Conduct; for that was my Aim in undertaking the Journey, and chief Study throughout the Prosecution of it.

The long and bloody French and Indian War followed. Washington's habit of finishing whatever he started continued even after Braddock's costly defeat at Fort Duquesne. Sent out to survey the ground where Braddock had fared so disastrously, Washington stood among the ruins of Fort Duquesne and planted there, with pride and defiance, the British flag.

The rough-hewn quality of this narrative of Washington's mission to the Ohio country makes it a true product of the American frontier. The will to survive required dealing bluntly and unemotionally with reality. What Governor Dinwiddie and the Council needed were the facts of the case. Washington stated them brusquely, as his own nature and the spirit of the crisis demanded.

But even so, a great deal of Washington the man emerged. Here was the Washington of twenty-one taking a raft across the ice-packed Allegheny as on a Christmas night some years hence an older Washington would pay a surprise visit on the Hessians across the ice-packed Delaware at Trenton. Here was the Washington of twenty-one showing his future dimensions of leadership as he judged the strength of a French fort down to the last canoe blocked-out and waiting to be finished when spring came, or as he took the measure of Half-King and Joncaire and St. Pierre, or as he taught Christopher Gist how frozen mountain trails should be crossed in the dead of winter. Here at twenty-one was the hero of whom Lord Byron would one day sing:

> *The Cincinnatus of the West,*
> *Whom envy dared not hate,*
> Bequeathed the name of Washington
> *To make man blush there was but one!*

EARL SCHENCK MIERS

WALTER HAVIGHURST

One of our best regionalists, a novelist, biographer, and historian of the Middle West, Walter Havighurst was born in Appleton, on the Fox River, in Wisconsin, in 1901. Like an increasing number of our serious writers, he is a college teacher and is at present a member of the Department of English at Miami University, one of Ohio's many long-established centers of learning.

His first novel, *Pier 17,* was based on his memories of a Pacific coast water-front strike. It attracted the attention of the late Constance Lindsay Skinner, who asked him to write the volume on the Upper Mississippi in the Rivers of America series—one of the best books in the series. He has also written about the early trade routes on the Great Lakes. For the purposes of this anthology I have selected that portion of his biography of George Rogers Clark which tells the story of that frontier commander's memorable march on the British fortress of Vincennes. The audacity and fortitude with which that expedition was conceived and carried out make it the most famous of Rogers' many exploits. His conquest of the old Northwest was of great importance in securing the complete success of the War for Independence.

The March on Vincennes:
George Rogers Clark

IN THE desolate Illinois winter Kaskaskia huddled on its gray river-bank under a cold gray sky. Behind the little farmhouses cornstalks rattled in the wind; the pastures were gray, the orchards bare and rocking. As Clark stared from the blockhouse, a thin curtain of snow blurred the eastern plain. Weeks had passed, with no word from the spies he had sent across the prairie. He paced the puncheon floor and stood again at the porthole, as though his narrowed eyes could see across 200 bleak and frozen miles to the banks of the Wabash. But he could not see. He could only wait and wonder—about the fate of Captain Helm and his small garrison, about the loyalty of the French citizens of Vincennes, about the strength of the British in the fort and the Indians camped on the commons. In those gray days Kaskaskia was besieged by winter and by worry. Was Hamiliton even now marching across the desolate land?

A commander cannot wait for a blow to fall; he must make ready to parry or absorb it. So Clark set out over the iron roads to Cahokia: he could not protect that defenseless town, but he could instruct the French habitants about their conduct under siege or capture. His party moved briskly, mounted on shaggy ponies and bouncing in two-wheeled carts. But they never reached Cahokia.

Twelve miles the hoofbeats drummed on the Old Fort Chartres Road, between tattered cornfields and wheat stubble powdered with snow, and in the chilling dusk they reached the village of Prairie du Rocher. In that quiet place, in the empty winter season, the arrival of visitors was an event. After a smoking supper Clark's party was entertained at a ball. The fiddler twanged his strings and feet tapped briskly on the timbered floor. A cold wind moaned outside the windows, but firelight leapt in the chimney and a bowl of spiced cider steamed on the hearth. Clark danced a quadrille and talked with the French farmers around the smoking punch bowl. For a little while even a commander could forget the siege of winter and the weight of war.

At midnight the fiddle strings were lilting and French voices raised the refrain of a *voyageurs'* song, rhythmic as the dip of canoe paddles in swift water:

> *Lon, lon, laridon daine!*
> *Lon, lon, laridon dai!*

Now there was hot buttered rum and crisp-crusted French bread with mellow cheese. Suddenly the door burst open. A bitter wind swept the room and a mist of snow, fine and sharp like sand, stung the faces of the dancers.

Into the hall came a man gray with cold and grim with his message. He went straight to Clark in the ruddy light of the hearth fire. At that moment the fiddler's strings went silent and all the voices were still. Then came the stunning message—Governor Hamilton, the "Hair-buyer General," was within three miles of Kaskaskia, leading 800 troops and Indians against the fort. Kaskaskia must even now be in his possession.

The hall filled with murmur, with confusion, with alarm, and then, suddenly, it was strained with silence. Every eye was on the commander, where the firelight washed his rugged features and gleamed like copper in his hair. In that stillness the wind moaned overhead and the windows rattled.

Clark turned to his officers. "Saddle the horses. We must gain the fort before they gather their attack."

The voices murmured again, anxious now, begging the commander not to ride into the arms of the enemy. Already the town must be in British hands. They urged him to fly to the Mississippi, to cross the river to safety on the Spanish side, to take refuge in the friendly town of St. Louis. Clark shook his head. In war a commander sought not to save his life but to risk it when that was necessary. He must not turn his back on the enemy but go to meet them. Now he called to the fiddler, "Strike up the music!" and to the company he said, "On with the dance. The horses are not yet ready."

At that display of spirit the young Frenchmen were fired with boldness. They ran out to get their own ponies, to ride with the Americans in the face of an overwhelming enemy. While the fiddler played, Clark wrote a hurried message to Major Bowman at Cahokia. Soon an officer reported the horses ready. With a last word to the villagers Clark led his men outside.

In the cold wind under a starless sky that file of horsemen pounded over the frozen road toward Kaskaskia. Each man had a blanket rolled behind his saddle. Clark had instructed them in a border stratagem: if they found the fort under attack, they would wrap themselves in blankets and mingle with the enemy. At the gate of the fort they would give the recognition signal and immediately join in its defense.

For two hours they raced through darkness with a thin snow blowing, and as he neared Kaskaskia, Clark listened for the din of battle. There was only the uneasy wind and the creak of saddle leather—no crash and bang of gunfire, no piercing war whoops, no flickering torches or fiery arrows in the sky. They reined their horses and jogged into the quiet street, with the houses sleeping and the fort hunched darkly on the hill. With a creak of timber the gate swung open; all was in order there. From the blockhouse Clark peered over the vague dark prairie. Perhaps the attack was delayed in this bad weather; perhaps the British general was waiting for daylight. Perhaps he was giving the Americans time to withdraw, so that he could march unresisted into an empty fort. In that case Clark would disappoint him.

Before daybreak he sent men with smoking torches to burn the houses nearest to the fort; he would leave no cover for the enemy's attack. Soon a fierce light washed the faces of the defenders, standing at their cannon, crouching at loopholes with rifles ready. Outside the stockade frantic citizens milled in the snowy street. When Clark threatened to burn all houses containing stores of food that the enemy might seize, French householders streamed into the fort with boxes, baskets, barrels. Quickly the fort was provisioned, and with their stores inside, the citizens grew anxious to defend it. From the portholes they watched gray day break on the snowy prairie.

With full daylight the thin snow stopped, the wind died down. It was good weather for an attacking army, but no army came. Instead, from the other direction, over the Old Fort Chartres Road from Cahokia, galloped a file of men under Major Bowman. They brought cheering news. The approaching British force had not been Hamilton's great army; it was but a scouting party of forty men, sent out to raid Kaskaskia and to capture Colonel Clark. That band had lost the way and given up the mission. At this moment they were hurrying back toward Vincennes.

After that fearful and defiant night Kaskaskia waited tensely for a new attack. Clark's scouts rode off toward Vincennes, but they did not return. Apparently they were captured, and Clark was left to worry and wonder about the enemy's movements. At last, on a cold day in late January, 1779, a single horseman rode in from the frozen prairie. So came to Kaskaskia a Spanish merchant, Colonel Francis Vigo, who traded in all the Illinois towns and across the river at St. Louis. He rode straight to the fort, and a sentry led him into the commander's office.

A slight, shrewd, swarthy man with black eyes in a deeply wrinkled face, he stood before the young red-haired commander. Francis Vigo was a native of Sardinia in the blue Mediterranean; he had come to New Orleans as a young soldier in the Spanish army. Later he had located in St. Louis as a fur trader, traveling to and from the prairie posts. He was liked by the Indians and respected by the French; he made a fortune. A shrewd and knowing trader, he was also a man of wholehearted warmth and generosity.

Now he gave Clark fresh news from Vincennes: General Hamilton was there, making himself comfortable during the harsh season, with a large quantity of arms and ammunition, a warehouse full of supplies, and a force of British regulars, French volunteers, and tribal warriors. Some of the Indians he had sent to raid Kentucky, some of the regulars he had ordered back to Detroit. But his entire army of 700 men would reassemble in the spring to march against the Americans. Meanwhile his men were repairing the fort, patrolling the town, scouting the approaches—though they had no fear of attack from Clark's outnumbered men.

At this report Clark paced the room with long, devouring strides. When he turned to the wrinkled Spaniard, his blue eyes were smoldering. Did Vigo judge that an attack would take Hamilton by surprise?

Attack? Did Colonel Clark mean an American attack? In this season? The prairies were desolate, the bottom lands were flooded. Vincennes was a stronghold surrounded with a moat of ice and water. How would Clark get his army there?

The commander had his answer ready. They would march, wade, swim.

The merchant's face grew more wrinkled than ever. An American attack. The weak surprising the strong. . . . Then his shrewd black eyes began to burn. He understood the strategy of trade—catch the other off his guard, take him by surprise. In the fateful contest of war the same strategy might win.

Now the little merchant, still huddled in his great coat, was nodding his head. If the Americans could get there undiscovered, at a time when the British would least expect attack, they might capture Vincennes and make prisoners of their enemies. Yes—if they could attack without warning, if they could take them by surprise. . . .

Alone again, Clark peered out at the winter prairie. He stood quiet at the porthole, but his thoughts were seething. This was the kind of situation that fired his mind and roused his will. A weak force and a strong enemy. An unlikely time, a bold attack, a strategy of secrecy and daring. But his own troops were depleted by illness and desertion; he had hardly one full company. He turned to a big map on the wall and studied the Wabash Valley with Fort Vincennes marked out in bold black ink. His big fists clenched. At this moment he would have bound himself to seven years' imprisonment or slavery to have 500 troops for a fortnight's service. But he had barely 150 men. He might go to Kentucky to raise more volunteers; there was no time for that. He might send to Fort Pitt; that would take longer still. There was just one course—to attack the enemy without hesitation or delay, to do by daring what he could not do by reason. He would be defeated if he waited in Kaskaskia for Hamilton's campaign. He could be no more than defeated at Vincennes. And if he won. . . . if he won. . . . If he won. . . .

As he considered it, the very audacity of his purpose gave him confidence. He thought now, step by step: *The season being so formidable* —slush ice drifting in the rivers, the prairie sodden with melting snow, the swamps swollen to miles of sullen water, the bottoms drowned in a numbing waist-deep flood. It was a favorable season for a forced march into enemy country; the very madness of it made it favorable. *No enemy would suppose*—it was out of all order and logic, it was beyond all reason that a weak force would cross a flooded country in a bleak season to attack a stronghold. *An enemy off their guard*—in this desolation they would not even send out spies, and their scouting parties would huddle over the fire in some half-faced camp, not thinking it worth while to watch for an invasion. *A desperate situation needs a desperate resolution*—there was no alternative. The more he thought of it the more inevitable his plan became.

That night he called his captains and told them. They were silent, doubtful, fearful. He talked a little more, acknowledging the hardships and dangers of the march. But the season being so hostile, no enemy would suppose that an attack could come over an impassable country. An enemy off guard is an enemy half beaten; surprise is stronger than an arsenal. Slowly the doubting captains began to speak. "Yes, we took Kaskaskia by surprise." . . . "Yes, the time is favorable." . . . "Yes, we can capture the 'Hair-buyer'!"

Boldness is a strong contagion. Now all Kaskaskia came to life with courage and resolve. French volunteers offered to join the desperate march. Citizens brought provisions, blankets, boots, caps, mufflers, mittens. Clark would need stores of ammunition for his attack and a cannon to breach the heavy walls of the fort. With funds borrowed from Merchant Vigo, he bought a Mississippi flatboat, mounted six small cannon on the deck, and loaded the cabin with supplies. This was the *Willing*, the first gunboat on the western rivers. Aboard it marched Captain John Rogers, Clark's cousin, and forty men, mostly from Cahokia. On the gray fourth day of February, shortly after noon, they pushed into the current of the swollen Kaskaskia River. They would go down the Mississippi, up the Ohio, up the Wabash. Below Vincennes they would hide in the river thickets, waiting the arrival of Clark's regiment across the prairies.

While the *Willing* disappeared around a bend of the river, Clark sat in his office writing a message to Governor Patrick Henry: *". . . I know the case is desperate; but Sir, we must either quit the country or attack. . . . Great things have been effected by a few men well conducted. Perhaps we may be fortunate."*

It was a hazardous, perilous plan, against enormous odds. That night George Rogers Clark sat late beside the fire. *Perhaps we may be fortunate. . . .*

On the fifth day of February, 1779, while drums rolled in the fort yard, the citizens of Kaskaskia lined the street below. In the stockade Father Gibault raised his hand; the drums ceased and the priest said a simple, heartfelt blessing. As the drums rolled again, Clark's regiment filed out the fort gate in a thin cold rain. It was midafternoon; all morning the captains had been busy, inspecting the men's clothing, ammunition, and provisions, tallying the pack ponies and their loads of tents, baggage, and supplies. Now in mingled French and English the townsfolk cried out their last farewells.

The men marched steadily, followed by the plodding pack train. Soon they were on the empty prairie. Behind them, in the cold seep of the rain, lay the huddled houses of Kaskaskia; behind was Merchant Vigo who had counted out money for the campaign, the old men who had given rifle balls and powder, the women who had stitched twenty flags for their soldiers to raise from the roofs and bastions of Vincennes. Behind was the warmth of familiar hearth fires; ahead lay 200 miles of soaking prairie and drowned bottom land, and at the end a superior enemy waited in a massive fort. Hour after hour they tramped on. Some remembered what was behind them, some thought of what was ahead. Some, perhaps, just marched. Long-striding Virginians and Kentuckians in deerskin jackets, dark-eyed French-Americans in match coats and mackinaws, they marched together in the rain. In all they were 130 men.

Six miles out on the prairie the winter dusk came down. They made their camp on desolate ground; they ate a cold supper washed down with smoking tea. They huddled over reluctant fires, trying to dry their boots and mackinaws. They rolled in their blankets and slept on sodden earth; before daylight they were on their way again. Hour after hour they slogged through mud and mire under a sky the color of wet ashes. A file of stubborn, plodding men, they made twenty-seven miles before they pitched their square camp in the winter dusk, baggage in the middle, sentries posted all around. The third day brought great flat plains of standing water, and the rain kept falling. With a kind of incredulity the men remembered when sunlight washed a green and fragrant prairie; now they gave up thought of warmth and dryness. They splashed on toward a watery horizon.

But the commander kept their spirits burning. Each day he sent out mounted hunters at the sign of game. They came back with quarters of venison and buffalo, and at the end of the day's march one of the four companies gave a feast. They ate like a war party on a triumphant raid. Tearing juicy flesh from bones, grinning with greasy, bearded faces, gulping down their burning whisky ration, they feasted together. Clark passed from one supper fire to another, a hulking, mud-smeared man with a gruff humor, sampling the joints of smoking meat and nodding approval of the cooking. He was a commander with a kind of triumph in him, not seeming to think of the hardships, the hazards, the desperate test ahead. So, feasting and laughing, singing rowdy songs and whooping like savages, the men forgot the misery of the march. The hot food roused their blood, and the whooping raised their courage. They were young men, in a wild new country, on a mission of daring.

During the day's march Clark often gave his horse to the hunters and fell in with the men. Sometimes he swung along in silence, his big feet sloshing up and down. But he was mysteriously aware of the army's spirit. He knew when the men were grim with weariness and when their thoughts went ahead with uncertainty and fear. At those times his ragged voice lifted a song or raised a war whoop, and gradually the other voices took it up until the whole wretched regiment sang and shouted under the desolate sky. At weary stretches of mud he set out on a lumbering run, challenging them all to a footrace. At the edge of swollen creeks he held his rifle high and lunged into the water with a savage war cry. So he kept them going; they took fire, like wet faggots, from his own nerve and will. They finished the day's march and devoured their food like a gaunt wolf pack in the firelight. They held numb and swollen hands to the blaze; the leather steamed and stiffened on their feet. They slept in sodden blankets and they did not complain.

On February 13, a week away from Kaskaskia, they reached the Little Wabash. That small river was now a vast flood, five miles across, with the drowned bottoms of the Embarrass River and the swollen Wabash beyond. They were sixty-three forbidding miles from Vincennes. From that camp Clark stared at the gray water, knee-deep, waist-deep, sometimes shoulder-deep. Now a third of his men were shaking with chills and fever. It was five miles to the hills on the opposite shore, and over all that plain of water the cold rain kept falling. Clark ordered his strongest men to take axes, to fell poplar logs, to hollow out canoes. In the first crude craft he sent a party ahead to build a landing platform on the distant shore. Into other canoes they loaded their sick and their baggage. Then they were ready to march.

Clark took the lead, plunging into waist-deep water, lifting his long rifle overhead. The men splashed after him. In that numbing water he kept their courage alive. Time after time he promised land ahead; when the water rose about his waist, he broke into the strains of "A Soldier's Life" or "Billy of the Wild Woods" or "A Man Who Wouldn't Hoe Corn." At last they reached the wooded shore. They landed their baggage and helped their sick ashore. Provisions were short, but Clark was more concerned with secrecy than hunger. He ordered short rations and no firing of guns.

They made a cheerful camp, laughing over their nightmare march, repeating a dozen times how in deep water the drummer boy had crawled onto his drum and floated on it like a raft. Strengthened by hardship, made bold by difficulty, they thought nothing could stop them. Now they spoke of the formidable Wabash as a creek; they would find a way to cross it. And when they reached Vincennes—— Before the fires died down, there was talk of marching on Detroit.

That night, lying sleepless in a wet blanket, Clark had his own grim realization. They were now in the enemy's country, a flooded valley behind them, their horses abandoned, with no possibility of retreat. He wondered about the Wabash: could the *Willing* ascend a flooded river in time to keep their rendezvous below Vincennes?

Next day they marched through endless swamps and creek bottoms. Hour after hour they stumbled through freezing mud and splashed through ice-skimmed water. It was long after dark before they stumbled on dry ground and made their desolate camp. The day that followed, and the day that followed that, were the same. At night they gnawed a handful of parched corn and slept with exhaustion.

On the evening of February 17 they reached the Embarrass River at a point nine miles from Vincennes. Those nine miles were a vast drowned bottom, broken by islanded hills and ridges. Gaunt with fatigue and hunger they marched along the Embarrass to its juncture with the Wabash. They marched grimly. Clark and his captains shouted, but the men slogged on in silence. Mud, mud, mud, mud . . . water, water, water, water . . . cold, cold, cold, cold . . . war, war, war, war. . . . In a weary, aching trance they kept moving, one foot lifting, then another, one stride more.

So they reached the Wabash. Now Vincennes was upstream, still nine miles away, across the swollen channel and the drowned bottom lands. They had no rations left—not even a rind of bacon or a handful of corn. Here they were to meet the *Willing;* but the flooded Wabash lay empty between the wooded hills.

"Camp Hunger" the men called it. Clark promptly had a pair of axmen hollowing out a log, and in that canoe he sent a party downstream to find the *Willing.* The rest waited, remembering the bushels of corn and the stacks of dried buffalo meat they had loaded on the gunboat. They watched in silence while the canoe came back, and the gaunt faces of the paddlers told the news before they voiced it. The *Willing* had not arrived. (The gunboat had been delayed by floodwater and was now at the mouth of the Wabash, 100 miles away.)

It was a hungry night. In the cold gray daybreak they heard a boom of cannon—the morning gun from the frowning fort at Vincennes. At that moment General Hamilton was sitting down to a hot and hearty breakfast, but Clark gave his men no time to think of food. He kept them chopping trees and lacing logs together with fox vines from the branches; on those makeshift rafts he sent men toward Vincennes to steal boats. They poled the rafts away, and too soon they returned. A mile away they had found a camp of Indians around four large camp-fires; they dared not go farther for fear of being discovered. Again Clark sent men down river, to look for the *Willing*. He paced the muddy shore while his gaunt troops chewed the bark of slippery elm to quiet their stomach pains. They had not tasted food for two days.

Weak as they were, Clark kept his axmen hollowing canoes. All morning their blades hacked and thudded on wet poplar logs. At noon the river sentries brought in a captured boat, and five astonished Frenchmen were led to the commander. They answered Clark's questions readily, declaring that no one in Vincennes suspected the presence of American troops in the Wabash country. That evening a hunter came in with fresh-killed venison. One deer for 130 men—it made their hunger violent.

Next morning in the leaden dawn they ferried the Wabash, and still they were cut off from the town by miles of flooded lowland. With a muttered "March!" Clark plunged into knee-deep water. The men waded after him. All day the gray rain fell, all day they floundered on, pushing their canoes through drowned timber and across desolate bays of flood. The five Frenchmen from Vincennes were amazed at this march; they had told Clark it was impossible to reach Vincennes without a fleet of boats. When Clark asked the location of the nearest dry land, they described a sugar camp, a grove of maple trees on a rounded hill. A canoe went ahead through submerged thickets, but it could not find a passage. Then Clark went forward, wading into the deepening stream. It was cold as ice.

Waist-deep in sullen water, he turned to his men. They watched him in silence, eyes fearful and beaten, faces gaunt and hollow. Some were shaking with chills, some were dazed with fever; in all of them hunger was gnawing like an animal. Suddenly Clark raised his powder horn. He poured a pinch of precious gunpowder into his wet hand and smeared the black mixture on his face. His voice went up in a frenzied, yowling war whoop; in it sounded hunger, grimness, desperation, but it ended in a fierce defiance. He turned then and lunged into the stream. For a moment the men stared blankly, eyes dead as cinders in their famished faces. Then one man blacked his own cheeks and plunged in. Another followed, and another; the gaunt regiment was moving. Ahead of them Clark lifted his rifle. His ragged voice began a song, and behind him, in a thin and growing chorus, the men joined in. They were a wretched, starving, and exhausted army—singing.

At last they felt firm ground beneath their feet. They followed it through a chaos of brush and bending willow branches. It led to a half acre of mounded land, covered with bare maple trees. They made their camp in the sugar grove. It was a cold night but they slept like dead.

In the morning the Frenchmen from Vincennes pointed to the broad Horseshoe Plain—not a plain now but a gray sea covering a great sickle bend of the Wabash. The sky had cleared in the night and a yellow sun rose over the floodlands. Clark stood among his silent men. This was the final march, he told them. In two hours they would see the roofs of Vincennes. There could be no weakness now.

He stationed Major Bowman in the rear with orders to shoot any man who faltered or turned back. Then he led the way. Out in the desolate Horseshoe Plain there were no half-drowned bushes to grasp at, no trees to cling to. Clark ordered canoes to carry the weakest men, to land them on the far shore, and to return for others. The rest struggled on, arms around each other's shoulders, floundering toward the land. There was no singing now. Even the commander kept silent, but he kept advancing. When at last they reached a brushy ridge, they would have sunk down, numb and exhausted, but Clark kept them on their feet. They chopped branches and started fires. The strong men dragged the weak around and around the burning embers until their clothing had dried and the blood was brisk in their veins.

When a sentry reported a craft on the water, Clark sent a party after it. They captured a large canoe paddled by Indian women; in it were buffalo meat, corn, tallow, and a nest of blackened kettles. Hungry eyes glittered while the kettles warmed on the fire. Broth was fed to the weak and fevered men; all of them had a ration of corn. It was not a feast, but it was a taste of food; it quickened sluggish blood and put strength into exhausted muscles. With new spirit they pushed on.

In canoes and afoot they crossed another mile of floodland and came to the brushy knob of Warrior's Island, with sunlight slanting through its winter trees. From there Clark gazed across two miles of flat and open country to Post Vincennes—the houses scattered along the river, the timbered church and the long stockade of the fort with its five frowning blockhouses catching the rays of the sinking sun. Around him stood his men, staring at the goal of their impossible march.

BURTON HARRIS

A native son of Wyoming, Burton Harris is a businessman with a consuming interest in western history. He is a Dartmouth graduate, and after a brief fling at the oil business in Texas, spent seven years in Brazil, occupied with banking. At present he makes his home in the New York area.

His life of John Colter (1775–1813), one of the most interesting figures to emerge from the Lewis and Clark expedition, was the second book to tell the story of Colter's life. There is an earlier biography by Stallo Vinton. Colter, though much less known than Bridger or Fremont, both of whom he preceded, was one of the great pathfinders of the Rocky Mountain West. Born in Virginia, he enlisted in the Lewis and Clark expedition in 1803; three years later, on the return trip, he was granted a discharge, and joined a party of trappers. In 1807, on his way to St. Louis, he was engaged to guide Manuel Lisa's expedition to the mouth of the Big Horn. Lisa sent him on a mission to the Crow Indians, and although not much is known about his exact route, he is generally credited with having crossed both the Wind Rivers and the Tetons on foot, and is thought to be the first white man ever to see the country now included in Yellowstone Park.

The pages I have taken from the Harris biography describe his capture by a party of 800 Blackfeet, his escape, and his remarkable journey back to Lisa's fort on the Big Horn. Actually the account is from Thomas James's *Three Years Among the Indians,* one of Mr. Harris's sources.

John Colter Escapes from the Indians

H E [Colter] had gone with a companion named Potts to the Jefferson river, which is the most western of the three Forks, and runs near the base of the mountains. They were both proceeding up the river in search of beaver, each in his own canoe, when a war party of about eight hundred Black-Feet Indians suddenly appeared on the east bank of the river. The Chiefs ordered them to come ashore, and apprehending robbery only, and knowing the utter hopelessness of flight, and having dropped his traps over the side of the canoe from the Indians, into the water, which was here quite shallow, he hastened to obey their mandate. On reaching the shore, he was seized, disarmed and stripped entirely naked. Potts was still in his canoe in the middle of the stream, where he remained stationary, watching the result. Colter requested him to come ashore, which he refused to do, saying he might as well lose his life at once, as be stripped and robbed in the manner Colter had been. An Indian immediately fired and shot him about the hip; he dropped down in the canoe, but instantly rose with his rifle in his hands. 'Are you hurt?' said Colter. 'Yes, said he, too much hurt to escape; if you can get away do so. I will kill at least one of them.' He leveled his rifle and shot an Indian dead. In an instant, at least a hundred bullets pierced his body and as many savages rushed into the stream and pulled the canoe, containing his riddled corpse, ashore. They dragged the body up onto the bank, and with their hatchets and knives cut and hacked it all to pieces, and limb from limb. The entrails, heart, lungs &c., they threw into Colter's face. The relations of the killed Indian were furious with rage and struggled, with tomahawk in hand, to reach Colter, while others held them back. He was every moment expecting the death blow or the fatal shot that should lay him beside his companion. A council was hastily held over him and his fate quickly determined upon. He expected to die by tomahawk, slow, lingering and horrible. But they had magnanimously determined to give him a chance, though a slight one, for his life. After the council, a Chief pointed to the prairie and motioned him away with his hand, saying in the Crow language, 'go—go away.' He supposed they intended to shoot him as soon as he was out of the crowd and presented a fair mark to their guns. He started in a walk, and an old Indian with impatient signs and exclamations, told him to go faster, and as he still kept a walk, the same Indian manifested his wishes by still more violent gestures and adjurations. When he had gone a distance of eighty or a hundred yards from the army of his enemies, he saw the younger Indians throwing off their blankets, leggings, and other incumbrances, as if for a race. Now he knew their object. He was to run a race, of which the prize was to be his own life and scalp. Off he started with the speed of the wind. The war-whoop and yell immediately arose behind him; and looking back, he saw a large company of young warriors, with spears, in rapid pursuit. He ran with all his strength that nature, excited to the utmost, could give; fear and hope lent a supernatural vigor to his limbs and the rapidity of his flight astonished himself. The Madison Fork lay directly before him, five miles from his starting place. He had run half the distance when his strength began to fail and the blood to gush from his nostrils. At every leap the red stream spurted before him, and his limbs were growing rapidly weaker and weaker. He stopped and looked back; he had far outstripped all his pursuers and could get off if strength would only hold out. One solitary Indian, far ahead of the others, was rapidly approaching, with a spear in his right hand, and a blanket streaming behind from his left hand and shoulder. Despairing of escape, Colter awaited his pursuer and called to him in the Crow language, to save his life. The savage did not seem to hear him, but letting go his blanket, and seizing his spear with both hands, he rushed at Colter, naked and defenceless as he stood before him and made a desperate lunge to transfix him. Colter seized the spear, near the head, with his right hand, and exerting his whole strength, aided by the weight of the falling Indian, who had lost his balance in the fury of the onset, he broke off the iron head or blade which remained in his hand, while the savage fell to the ground and lay prostrate and disarmed before him. Now was his turn to beg for his life, which he did in the Crow language, and held up his hands imploringly, but Colter was not in a mood to remember the golden rule, and pinned his adversary through the body to the earth by one stab with the spear head. He quickly drew the weapon from the body of the now dying Indian and seizing his blanket as lawful spoil, he again set out with renewed strength, feeling, he said to me, as if he had not run a mile. A shout and yell arose from the pursuing army in his rear as from a legion of devils, and he saw the prairie behind him covered with Indians in full and rapid chase. Before him, if anywhere, was life and safety; behind him certain death; and running as never man before sped the foot, except, perhaps, at the Olympic Games, he reached his goal, the Madison River and the end of his five mile heat. Dashing through the willows on the bank he plunged into the stream and saw close beside him a beaver house, standing like a coal-pile about ten feet above the surface of the water, which was here of about the same depth. This presented to him a refuge from his ferocious enemies of which he immediately availed himself. Diving under the water he arose into the beaver house, where he found a dry and comfortable resting place on the upper floor or story of this singular structure. The Indians soon came up, and in their search for him they stood upon the roof of his house of refuge, which he expected every moment to hear them breaking open. He also feared that they would set it on fire. After a diligent search on that side of the river, they crossed over, and in about two hours returned again to his temporary habitation in which he was enjoying bodily rest, though with much anxious foreboding. The beaver houses are divided into two stories and will generally accommodate several men in a dry and comfortable lodging. In this asylum Colter kept fast till night. The cries of his terrible enemies had gradually died away, and all was still around him, when he ventured out of his hiding place, by the same opening under the water by which he entered and which admits the beavers to their building. He swam the river and hastened towards the mountain gap or ravine, about thirty miles above on the river, through which our company passed in the snow with so much difficulty. Fearing that the Indians might have guarded this pass, which was the only outlet from the valley, and to avoid the danger of a surprise, Colter ascended the almost perpendicular mountain before him, the tops and sides of which a great way down were covered with perpetual snow. He clambered up this fearful ascent about four miles below the gap, holding on by the rocks, shrubs and branches of trees, and by morning had reached the top. He lay there concealed all that day, and at night proceeded on in the descent of the mountain, which he accomplished by dawn. He now hastened on in the open plain towards Manuel's Fort on the Big Horn, about three hundred miles ahead in the northeast. He travelled day and night, stopping only for necessary repose, and eating roots and the bark of trees, for eleven days. He reached the Fort, nearly exhausted by hunger, fatigue and excitement. His only clothing was the Indian's blanket, whom he had killed in the race, and his only weapon, the same Indian's spear which he brought to the Fort as a trophy. His beard was long, his face and whole body were thin and emaciated by hunger, and his limbs and feet swollen and sore. The company at the Fort did not recognize him in this dismal plight until he made himself known. Colter now with me passed over the scene of his capture and wonderful escape, and described his emotions during the whole adventure with great minuteness. Not the least of his exploits was the scaling of the mountain, which seemed to me impassable even by the mountain goat. As I looked at its ragged and perpendicular sides I wondered how he ever reached the top—a feat probably never performed before by mortal man. The whole affair is a fine example of the quick and ready thoughtfulness and presence of mind in a desperate situation, and the power of endurance, which characterise the western pioneer."

Everyone who has experienced the chilling drop in temperature in the Rocky Mountain region that coincides with the setting of the sun, particularly during the fall months, will have realized the importance of the Indian blanket Colter acquired during his flight. That covering would have shielded him from the numbing exposure of the early morning as he made his way in the darkness along the protective sides of the hills. However, he was too large a man to have squeezed into a normal-sized beaver lodge, and this feature may have been added by James for effect.

The exhausted man who finally arrived at Manuel's Fort was not long in recovering his strength. The tremendous endurance that carried Colter through such an ordeal undoubtedly assisted his recovery. Shortly afterward he proved conclusively that his courage was a worthy companion to his stamina.

WALLACE STEGNER

Wallace Stegner, born at Lake Mills, Iowa, in 1909, is professor of English and director of the Creative Writing Center at Stanford University. He is best known to the reading public as a novelist, and his most popular work was *The Big Rock Candy Mountain,* the story of the struggles of a western family during the first half of the present century. Three years ago he published a life of Major John Wesley Powell, one of the titans of western history, under the title, *Beyond the Hundredth Meridian.* The book deals comprehensively and vividly with one of the more neglected chapters of the westward movement and with the sadly neglected figure of Major Powell, who, in Mr. Stegner's hands, is given his full stature as one of the most arresting personalities in our conquest of the continent.

The pages I have chosen for inclusion here are the most stirring in this excellent biography. They tell, in magnificent detail, the story of the hazardous descent of the Colorado River, and the terrifying passage made by Powell and his companions through the menacing gorges and rapids of the Grand Canyon. Of all the tales of fresh-water adventuring, this one, I believe, ranks supreme. The successful completion of Powell's expedition took just about everything that dauntless men can give.

The Descent of the Colorado: Major Powell

THERE IS a rough physical law to the effect that the carrying power of water increases as the sixth power of its velocity, which is to say that a stream moving two miles an hour will carry particles sixty-four times as large as the same stream moving one mile an hour, and that one moving ten miles an hour will carry particles a million times as great. A stream that in low water will deposit even its fine silt and sand, in high water will roll enormous boulders along its bed, and sometimes one can stand near the bank and see a rock that looks as big as a small house yield and sway with the force of the current.

Where the Colorado River entered the granite a few miles below the Little Colorado the channel was narrow, the river engorged, very deep, and very swift. It took hold of a boat irresistibly: the characteristic reaction of our diarists was awe. More times than once Bradley was led to report rapids as the worst of the trip so far, and all of them felt the gloom of that black inner gorge and the poverty of the narrow sky. To add to undernourishment and exhaustion and strain they had nights of rain that caught them miserable and unprotected on bouldery shores, days of alternating sun and rain that first drenched them and then boiled them in temperatures of 115°. Rarely was there a decent camping place; they stopped where daylight or endurance ran out on them. With very little shore, the river did not even provide adequate firewood. Curling up on the edges of cliffs, among boulders, on wet spits of sand, they made out as they could. And along with their discomforts there was an increasing but unspoken fear.

Partly the lack of shores did it, the way the river sometimes took up all the space and left them no place for lining, no trail for a portage. Rapids that they feared to run they ran because they could do nothing else, and as they came plunging through the waves, tossed from one side to the other by the cushion of the water piling against great rocks, they often had no chance to inspect the river ahead, to search out channels, to guard against falls. They went with the recklessness of Sam Adams, not for lack of better sense but in sheer helplessness.

The pretense that it was a scientific expedition had worn thin. Every barometer they had was out of commission, so that they had lost track of their altitude and had no way of telling how much fall there was before the Virgin. Even an accurate view of where they had been was denied them, after Howland lost in a swamping his map of the river from the Little Colorado down, and all his notes with it. Anxiety closed around them like the dark rock, and looking up lateral gorges to the outer walls so high and far above, to the buttes and towers and enormous pediments and alcoves of the cliff-edged plateaus that now rose above them more than a vertical mile, they could add claustrophobia to their burdens, and the haunting speculation of what it would mean if they had to try to climb out.

Unrelieved labor, incessant strain and anxiety, continuing rain, a river that seemed every day to grow worse, and for food the same moldy bread, spoiled bacon, stewed apples, and for commander a man who they felt would risk all their lives for an extra hour of geologizing, an extra night of squinting at a star.

When they ran into the granite on the second day below the Little

Colorado—one of the days that Bradley recorded as the wildest thus far—the *Emma Dean* was smashed under by a wave and ran swamped for half a mile before its crew got it into an eddy. Bradley and Walter Powell brought their boat through with the loss of an oar, the third escaped with a shaking up and a ducking. That night as they slept among boulders and on ledges so narrow that only Sumner and Major Powell found space wide enough to make a double bed, Bradley huddled off by himself and wrote up his secret diary in the rain. They had better lie quiet, he said, or one of them would be in the river before morning.

Some of them were in the river every day now. Hawkins capsized and lost his oars the next morning, and after only two and a half days in the Grand Canyon their supplies were again wet and spoiling. At the mouth of a beautiful clear creek coming in from the north they camped to saw out more oars and dry the food. That was Silver Creek, which Powell later, on a lecture tour, rechristened Bright Angel Creek to make a singularly happy contrast with the Dirty Devil above. The cutwater of the *Emma Dean* was broken and all of them were exhausted. Even Bradley was willing to lay over a day for a rest. Immediately Powell, seizing the opportunity, took off up the canyon to geologize.

As if to emphasize the need for haste, the Bright Angel layover was hard on the rations. There they finally threw away what remained of the bacon, so many times spoiled and dried and boiled and redried that they gagged at it. And Billy Hawkins, making biscuits on a rock, had the misfortune to let the saleratus get sawed off into the river by the line of one of the boats. From that time on they ate unleavened bread.

Below Bright Angel they got through one laborious day without accident. On the afternoon of the next a furious thunder shower drove them to what shelter they could find among the rocks, where they sat dripping and heard the thunder bounce from cliff to cliff and saw hundreds of flash-flood rivulets burst over the walls above them. The more their need for haste, the less haste they seemed able to make. "Hard work and little distance seems to be the characteristic of this canyon," Bradley wrote. Then on the 19th the *Emma Dean* swamped again, and Bradley's boat, sweeping to the rescue, struck on her cutwater with a jolt that started her nails. Two more oars went in that rapid, and all the boats now were so battered that they had to be calked every day. For the sixth day out of the last seven they lay down in soaking blankets. But that night when it cleared off, a great drying fire restored them. So bedraggled were they that they did not start until noon the next day. They were all looking ahead, watching for that break in the walls that might be the Grand Wash Cliffs.

It seemed as if they might have reached it, or neared it, for the walls did fall back a little and the rapids were further apart. In a half day's run, including a portage and two linings, they ran ten miles. The next day was again for Bradley "first for dashing wildness of any day we have seen or *will* see." Swept broadside down upon a rapid, Powell's boat rebounded from the cliff and was carried into a narrow slot with no shores to land on. Ahead a bend cut off the view. From around it came the "mad roar" that had taught them caution many times already. Here they could not be cautious if they would. Powell stood up, hanging to a strap that ran from gunwale to gunwale, trying to spot a channel through the long, winding chute of white water. Their luck held. All they got out of that one was a tremendously exhilarating ride for ten precious miles before the roar of another heavy fall below made them pull ashore to reconnoiter. By the time they had portaged that, they were out of the granite.

Their cheers had in them something of the hysteria of strain, and they did not stay cheerful long. Barely had they adjusted themselves to milder water when the river turned sharply from its north-by-west course and bored back almost straight east into the granite again. Overhead the clouds gathered blackly, and it rained.

Their hypnotized spirits now rose and fell with the river, and changed with its course. When, away back at the Little Colorado, they had discovered their latitude to be as low as that of Callville, they had been cheered, but the river taught them to wait and see, for it persisted in running back toward the north with them. Now it rubbed in the lesson of skepticism by taking them back into the hard rock they feared. "If it keeps on this way," Bradley wrote, "we shall be back where we started from, which would make us feel very much as I imagine the old hog felt when he moved the hollow log so that both ends came on the outside of the fence."

Still, there was nothing they could do except to keep rooting at the log. They fought their way down to spend another night on the rocks, with a bad rapid facing them as soon as they should wake up, and its roar an uneasy sound in their dreams. But next day the unpredictable river switched again. After two hard miles the hated granite sank under toward its home at the earth's core. The rapids, though tremendous, seemed by Grand Canyon standards lighter. On the afternoon when they ran out of the granite they made ten miles.

The following day they made twenty-two with great cheerfulness, and their cheer was doubled by the great marble cave in which the Major chose to camp—dry and spacious and out of the interminable rain. Around their fire they sat speculating on how far Grand Wash might be, for the Mormons whose notes on the river from Grand

Wash to Callville were in the Major's pocket put the Wash no more than seventy or eighty miles below the mouth of the Little Colorado. On the dogleg river they had already gone more than one hundred twenty. They must be very close, perhaps within a day's running. Ahead, they convinced themselves, the river seemed to widen and the current to slack off. They examined their flour—one sack plus enough for a meal or two—and gauged the skimpy supply against the possible miles ahead. They were half naked, bearded, skinny, and their dreams were haunted by visions of gargantuan meals, but they knew they would make it now.

The river relented. On August 25 they made thirty-five marvelous miles, in spite of a hard portage around what they called Lava Falls, where a basalt flow had first dammed the canyon and then been cut clean through, and in spite of a near accident when the iron strap in the bow of one boat pulled loose and almost let the boat get away in a rapid. All the boats, clearly, were about as used up as the men. They drove themselves.

The opening of their last sack of flour was a solemn moment, and a warning. Down a violent stretch of river where lava made continuous but not major rapids they ran the battered boats recklessly, lining only once in thirty-five miles when they landed on the wrong side of a rapid and couldn't get across to run it safely. Another good omen: the dry abandoned dwellings and granaries of ancient Indians that they had been seeing among the cliffs ever since Glen Canyon gave way to signs of life. In an Indian garden they found squash big enough to eat, and stole a dozen to make green squash sauce, their first fresh vegetable food since the disastrous potato-top greens in Uinta Valley fifty days before. Though the nearly vertical walls of the inner gorge grew higher and higher, their two-day run of seventy miles put them close to two hundred miles below the Little Colorado. "A few days like this," Powell said, "and we are out of prison."

It was a prison even to him now, not a happy hunting ground of science. And the river knew better than they did. On the morning of August 27 it swung south, and since the dip of the beds was to the north, they rapidly ran into lower and lower formations. If it kept up this way they would be back in the granite. By nine o'clock they saw the dreaded rock, brown here instead of black, but unmistakable, rising up from the shoreline. They had to portage at the very entrance to the granite gorge. By eleven they came to a place that forced them ashore with sinking hearts.

Later river runners, with some justification, have disputed Powell's description of that rapid, both as to its violence and to its shape. There can be no doubting the fact that it looked to them, in their demoralized

and discouraged state, like the worst thing on the river. Sumner's
journal calls it "a hell of foam"; Powell and Bradley agree in calling it
the worst they had met. "The billows are huge," said Bradley, "and I
fear our boats could not ride them if we could keep them off the rocks.
The spectacle is appalling to us."

It should have been. They had five days' rations remaining. Above
the narrow inner gorge the outer walls stepped back in lofty and perhaps unclimbable cliffs. The nearest Mormon settlement was miles
away to the north across unknown plateaus and deserts. To run the
rapid was, as far as Powell could see, pure self-destruction. Above the
pounding water rose abrupt granite cliffs. Trying the right bank, they
could find no way either to portage or to line. Crossing over above the
rapid, they tried the left, working along the craggy granite to try to
get a view of the river below the first fall. The cliff shut off the water.

Telling about that day in his published *Report,* Powell records an
adventure that neither his own daily notes nor the journals of Bradley
and Sumner mention. He says that, intent upon seeing and appraising
the rapid, he worked out upon the pinnacles and crags of the cliff and
once more, as in Desolation Canyon, got himself "rimmed." He was
four hundred feet above the boulder-strewn water, clinging to the
rock with his one hand, when he called for help. He says that the men
climbed close above him and dropped him a rope, but that he dared
not let go to grab for it. Hanging grimly, unable even to advise them
because he could not see his own position, he clung while two men
hurried down the cliff and came back with a pair of the largest oars.
Themselves working on a perilous edge, they reached out an oar and
finally jammed it in a crevice beyond Powell so that they could pinch
him in against the cliff and hold him there. Then they jammed the
second oar below him, and carefully he turned himself until he could
step on this oar and inch back to safety.

How they may have looked at one another, whether or not they may
have cursed him to themselves for being maimed and a burden, how
fully they may have laid their situation at his door, no one will ever
know. Since the journals do not mention the episode at all, it may not
even be true. It may be a piece of fiction suggested by his previous
rimming and inserted into the narrative as peculiarly effective here.
Perhaps it is part of that impulse to self-dramatization that had led
Powell to make speeches on top of Long's Peak, and sit on a spectacular
crag above Flaming Gorge producing rhetoric for the Chicago *Tribune.*
But even if the story is not true, it ought to be. There could have been
no more striking symbolic summary of the fix the whole expedition
was in than the spectacle of the maimed leader hanging perilously be-

tween advance and retreat, unable to move either way, on a crag of the hated granite.

Without getting a really good view, they spent another hour trying to see from the left-hand cliff and in the afternoon crossed again to try the right, but without success.

After almost a full day of studying the situation, Powell could see no way except to let down over the first fall, run the rapid to the head of the second, and then pull like fury to the left to avoid a great rock against which the river poured a curving, boiling wall of water. It was not a plan that appealed to him; it appealed even less to some of the men. Bradley, who had reported rebelliousness before, reported it again: "There is discontent in camp tonight and I fear some of the party will take to the mountains but hope not."

Crossing the river again and camping in the mouth of a lateral gorge, they had both certainties and uncertainties to contemplate as they chewed on their leathery unleavened bread. There were the alternative uncertainties of a fearful nest of rapids with an unknown river below, and a perhaps equally dangerous climb out some side gorge onto the plateau and across it to the Mormon settlements northward. And there were the desperate certainties of failing supplies, failing boats, failing strength, failing nerve. Sitting apart from the others and writing up his notes, Bradley called it "decidedly the darkest day of the trip."

Of all the men who had accompanied Major Powell through a summer of natural history in the Colorado parks, a winter of studying Indians and topography from the base camp on White River, and more than three tense months in the Canyons, O. G. Howland was best fitted by education and interests to be a companion for the commander. He was the oldest in the party, though at thirty-six, less than a year older than Powell, he was hardly decrepit to match his beard. Like Sumner, Hawkins, and his brother Seneca, he was technically entered on the expedition's roll as a hunter, but he was no buckskin savage. Since arriving in Denver in 1860 on the tide of the Colorado gold rush he had been a printer and editor of Byer's *Rocky Mountain News,* business agent for a Methodist Episcopal magazine known as the *Sunday School Casket,* member and later vice-president of the Denver Typographical Union Local No. 49, and secretary and member of the board of the Nonpareil Prospecting and Mining Company. Judged by his letters to the *News,* he was the most literate and articulate of the group. By Powell's own testimony, he was of a "faithful, genial nature." When Powell took a companion with him on his exploratory climbs around the canyon rims and up side gulches he almost always took his brother, Bradley, or the elder Howland. Bradley was the only member of the party over thirty, outside of Howland and

Powell, and he had been an army non-com long enough to learn discipline.

But the same qualities that made Howland a companion and friend for Powell half unfitted him for the grueling adventure of the river. He had a certain scientific and literary curiosity, and part of his job was to map the river and make notes as they went, but his appetite for knowledge was nothing like Powell's omnivorous passion, and though he was an outdoor man and a sportsman he had not quite the hardihood or the youth of the hunters and Andy Hall. Also, he had been the unlucky one. His momentary error of sight or judgment had led to the wreck of the *No-Name,* the loss of a third of their provisions, and their present starving and desperate condition. The comparative meagerness of their scientific results could be traced to his misfortune in twice losing his maps and notes in swampings. Possibly the sense of personal failure troubled him. Just possibly Powell or his brother, under the increasing strain, may in some moment of irritation have thrown it up to him. Conceivably too, as Sumner and Hawkins many years after the fact asserted, the Major and Bill Dunn may have rubbed each other the wrong way, or trouble may have brewed between the moody Walter Powell and Dunn. Bradley's journal mentions no such cause of discontent, however, and he was not one to spare the Major when he thought Powell needed criticism. Sumner's journal is equally bare.

Put it down to strain, to the steady corrosion of strength and nerve. Lay it to the dark oppressive granite, to the repeated hope that they had run out of it for good and the each-time-greater anger and disappointment when the river switched them back into it. Put it down to the rapid they now faced without a clear chance to run, line, or portage. Put it down to a growing lack of confidence in Powell's judgment or the reliability of his scientific observations, to the gnawing need for a square meal or to the arrival at an ultimate ceiling of endurance. Whatever it is put down to, it was clear to Powell on the night of August 27 that the whole expedition was close to where he himself had been that afternoon on the cliff, unable to go forward or back.

That was even clearer when Howland came to him after supper and asked him to walk up the side canyon for a little talk. Howland had been talking things over with his brother and Bill Dunn. It was madness and suicide to try to go on. He proposed that the whole expedition abandon the river and make its way out to the Mormon settlements on the Virgin. If Powell would not take the whole party out, the Howlands and Dunn would go by themselves. They had had enough.

Powell had strong arguments. He knew that they could not be more than a few days' run from Grand Wash, he knew that the river had

been falling so fast that it could not possibly have much further to fall
to the level of Callville. But Howland had a stronger one. He had only
to point to the furious string of rapids that blocked their way down-
river. Even if past them there were calm water all the rest of the way
to the Virgin, those were enough.

In the end they agreed not to say anything to the other men until
Powell had had time to plot their position by dead reckoning to find
out exactly where they were. It was a clear night; he got a meridian
observation with the sextant and found that it agreed pretty closely
with the plot. By airline, they could not be more than forty-five miles
from the mouth of the Virgin, twenty miles from which there were
Mormon towns. Moreover, for a good many miles above the Virgin
the Mormon party under Jacob Hamblin had found low walls and no
bad rapids on the Colorado. The eighty or ninety meandering miles of
river still ahead might contain no more than a day or two of bad water.

He was several hours establishing to his own satisfaction that there
was no possibility of serious error in his calculations. Then he woke
Howland and spread the plot on the sand and showed him. This is
how he told it later:

We have another short talk about the morrow, and he lies down
again; but for me there is no sleep. All night long, I pace up and
down a little path, on a few yards of sand beach, along by the river,
Is it wise to go on? I go to the boats again, to look at our rations.
I feel satisfied that we can get over the danger immediately before
us; what there may be below I know not. From our outlook
yesterday, on the cliffs, the cañon seemed to make another great
bend to the south, and this, from our experience heretofore, means
more and higher granite walls. I am not sure that we can climb out
of the cañon here, and, when at the top of the wall, I know
enough of the country to be certain that it is a desert of rock and
sand, between this and the nearest Mormon town, which, on the
most direct line, must be seventy-five miles away. True, the late
rains have been favorable to us, should we go out, for the proba-
bilities are that we shall find water still standing in holes, and, at
one time, I almost conclude to leave the river. But for years I have
been contemplating this trip. To leave the exploration unfinished,
to say that there is a part of the cañon which I cannot explore,
having already almost accomplished it, is more than I am willing
to acknowledge, and I determine to go on.

He woke Walter Powell and told him of the decision that must be
made. Walter promised to stay with him. He woke Billy Hawkins, the

irrepressible, and Andy Hall, the lighthearted, and Sumner, the hardy, and Bradley, the saturnine, and they promised the same. Though reduced, it would still be an expedition.

Breakfast on August 28 was "solemn as a funeral." In silence except for the pounding roar of the rapid, deep in the gloomy rock where the early sun could not reach, they ate Hawkins' flat biscuits and drank their coffee and avoided each others' eyes. They had finished eating when Powell asked his question. With five men behind him he could ask it bluntly. Did the three want to come along, or climb out?

Seneca Howland, left to himself, would have stuck, but neither he nor the other six could persuade his brother and Bill Dunn. They had all climbed enough on the walls to know the possibility of unbroken, unscalable cliffs stretching for miles. But they thought they could make their way out one of the side canyons, and they were sure they could kill game on the plateau. They were mountain men, the wilderness was their natural home. Listening to the arguments of the others, they shook their heads; in the end Seneca Howland decided to stay with his brother.

They were given two rifles and a shotgun and invited to take their share of the miserable rations. It was to their credit, and evidence of friendliness between the two groups, that they refused. The three crossed the river with the others, helped them unload the leaky *Emma Dean,* which was to be abandoned, and assisted in portaging the two large boats over a thirty-foot rock and lining them down the first fall. Hawkins left a pan of biscuits on the rock for them. Sumner gave Howland his watch to deliver to his sister, Mrs. William Byers, in Denver. Powell wrote a letter to his wife. The records of the expedition were, as Powell thought, divided, each party taking one complete copy. At the head of a two hundred yard rapid between the two falls each entreated the other to change its mind. They shook hands; there were tears. "They left us with good feelings," Bradley wrote, "though we deeply regret their loss for they are as fine fellows as I ever had the good fortune to meet." Bradley was a grumbler, but he rose nobly to occasions.

So the parting at Separation Rapid was not quite Sam Adams' experience of collecting a purse and sending someone home as a "common nuisance," nor was it marked by the quarreling and accusation and blame that attended the breakup of Adams' volunteers. Neither was it what some unaccountably virulent enemies of Powell asserted later: a harsh discharge of three men at a place and in circumstances that might mean their death. Neither was it what some of Powell's defenders have tried to make it, a craven desertion by three cowards.

It was a sad parting at the brink of two dangers, by men who respected one another.[1]

The original ten were now six, the four boats two. What had been rations for ten months was now rations for five days. What had been thrilling was grim. From up on the cliff the Howlands and Dunn watched as Powell stepped into the *Maid of the Canyon* and the men shoved off into the waves along the right-hand wall. The river seized them. They shot down a hollow, up a wave, past a rock half buried in the foaming water. The oarsmen pulled madly at the clumsy oars— a job of enormous difficulty in a boat leaping through waves at a speed of twenty miles an hour, tossed now up, now down, the water falling away suddenly so that the oarblade bites air, then surging up to bury the oar to the handle. To hit a hidden rock with an oar was to risk shattering it or having it driven into the oarsman's body; to catch a crab was to lose all chance of control. They rowed as the river had taught them to row, pulling hard for the tongue of the second fall. There the boat was all but snatched from under them. They shot down the fall and burst into the great back-cresting waves at its foot. Instantly they were full of water, but half swamped they still rowed like madmen, pulling across the current. The wild pile-up of water against the right-hand rock caught them only partially. They raced up the sloping wall of water, fell away to the left, down into a hole, and were through into the diminishing tailwaves. The whole rapid had taken perhaps a minute. While they pulled for shore to bail out, the *Kitty Clyde's Sister* plunged through the tailwaves and was with them, safe. Powell afterward thought the rapid, in spite of its fearful look, no worse than others they had run. Bradley continued to think it the worst to date, until they met another one that afternoon.

Below the rapid, according to Powell's *Report,* they landed and fired off their guns in the hope that the three hunters would climb down and rejoin them. But they did not come, and the boats went on. They had dangers enough of their own to occupy them. Powell's journal entry for the day of parting is indication of how even so serious an event had to take its place in the day's routine. His journal reads simply, "Boys left us. Ran rapid. Bradley boat. Make camp on left bank. Camp 44."

In that one brief entry are contained not merely the schism that all but destroyed the expedition, but the incident that of all their summer's adventures was perhaps most hair-raising. "Bradley boat," the Major says. What he thus reminded himself of was a climactic little

[1] The Howlands and Dunn successfully made the climb out of the mile-deep canyon but, on their way to the nearest Mormon settlement, were murdered by Indians as a result of a misunderstanding as to their identity.

episode. As the wreck of the *No-Name* in Lodore initiated them to disaster and taught them caution, so Bradley's adventure below Separation Rapid ended their river dangers in desperation and cool skill. They had come a long way from the initial amateurishness and inattention to Bradley's complete adequacy to his job, from Powell's first caution to his final recklessness.

Like many another rapid, the big one (Lava Cliff) six and a half miles below Separation struck Bradley as the worst they had met on the river. The stage of water has such an unpredictable, even unbelievable effect upon specific rapids that there would be little chance of checking his judgment, even if that rapid were not now silted up at the head of Lake Mead. But it was bad enough. Sumner referred to it as "another hell." Powell landed to look it over, and found that along one side a line could be taken up on the basalt cliff and the boats lined from above. But when he arrived back on the riverbank he found that the men had already started one boat, Bradley's, down toward the head of the fall. She was in fast water, too much in the sweep of the current for them to pull her back, and their line was not long enough to be taken up over the cliff. They took a bight around a rock and hung on while one went for more rope.

Meantime Bradley, in the very sag of the fall, found himself swinging at the end of a mighty pendulum. The current set in close and fierce against the basalt wall, and suspended as he was from above, he yawed in a wide arc out into the rapids and then was slammed back in against the cliff. Standing in the boat, he fended himself off with an oar, but the moment he stopped the inward swing the waves snatched him outward again. Powell saw him take quick looks down river, saw him look at the straining, worn line, saw him reach in his pocket for his knife.

Before he could cut the line the whole sternpost was jerked out of the boat, rope and cutwater flew thirty feet into the air, and the *Sister* was off like a horse from the starting line. Bradley dropped his knife and leaped to the steering oar, fighting to get her bow pointed downstream, for to go over broadside-on would be certain wreck. One stroke, two, three, and just as he hit the fall he turned her. She went clear under in a welter of white, came up on a huge crest, went down again and out of sight beyond some rocks. In half a breath she shot into the open, Bradley still standing, and swung into an eddy. Bradley waved his hat in triumph, but from where Powell stood it was impossible to see how badly the boat was damaged, and he feared both it and Bradley might go down into the whirlpool.

Powell shouted at his brother and Sumner to run along the cliff to help below. Then with Hawkins and Hall he leaped into the second boat, pushed off, and went over the falls any way the water took them, endways and sideways, blind with water, beaten almost out of the boat by waves. It was an act totally uncharacteristic, reckless beyond anything he had permitted himself or his men all the way down the river. It is as good documentation as any for the desperation of their case.

Bradley had to rescue them, capsized and strangling, and help them pull their boat to safety against the cliff. There was handshaking around to match that when the Howlands and Goodman were rescued from their island at Disaster Falls. Powell said nothing ever thrilled him so much as to see Bradley swing his hat from the spinning boat after running her through. It is clear from his various accounts of the trip that Bradley, more than any other member of the party, had his complete respect as a man of skill and courage. As for Bradley, his diary was getting used to superlatives. This ride, he said, "stands A No. 1 of the trip."

That was the last big roar from the river dragon. Two or three miles below that great rapid the river swung northwest. By nightfall they were out of the granite. By noon of the next day, after a swift uneventful run, they passed through the sudden portal in the Grand Wash Cliffs and saw rolling country, low walls, distant mountains.

Where they camped that night is not certain. To be appropriate, it should have been in the little loop that now, as part of Lake Mead, on the Nevada-Arizona boundary, is known as God's Pocket. They were in God's pocket sure enough. Their joy, Powell says, was almost ecstasy, though even in that relaxed and triumphant camp, in the clear night, with an unreal wide sky over them, they speculated a long time on how the Howlands and Dunn were faring, how they had managed on the cliffs, whether they might now be in the high plateau forest filling themselves with venison or wild mutton or whether they might be stuck in some gulch groping for a way up and out. They could say I-told-you-so; they could also, more generously, hope the others' luck had been equal to their own.

For there was no doubt that they were now "out of prison." On August 30 they scared away one band of naked Paiutes and talked to another family that Powell coaxed near by speaking Ute to them. From the Indians, however, they learned little and got no food, and so they pushed on. Just after the noon stop they saw four men pulling a seine in the river. They were a Mormon named Asa and his two sons and an Indian, and they were there on instructions from Church headquarters in Salt Lake City to watch the river for wreckage or bodies from the Powell Expedition, reported lost weeks ago in the depths of the Colorado canyons.

That was the first official notice Brigham Young ever paid to Major Powell. He would pay him more later; the two would become something like friends, and Brigham would draw on Powell for scientific information useful to his empire. His interest now was something more than mortuary, something more than merely humanitarian. For Powell's river party was in a way doing Brigham's business for him, exploring the heart of the country on whose fringes Brigham's colonists had scratched out precarious toeholds of settlement. If Asa and his sons and their Indian companion waiting in the glare of the red mudflats at the mouth of the Virgin saw no bodies floating by, they might at least intercept something else—records or wreckage—from which to piece together information about the canyons. They intercepted more than they expected, and yet their humanitarian and mortuary gesture was not to be entirely wasted either.

Nine men had plunged into the unknown from the last outpost of civilization in the Uinta Valley on the sixth of July, 1869. On August 30 six came out.

ROBERT FALCON SCOTT

No name in the annals of exploration commands deeper respect than that of Robert Falcon Scott (1868–1912). Generous in spirit, indomitable in courage, thinking always last of himself, a born leader of men, this British naval officer who led on foot the Antarctic expedition which arrived at the South Pole on January 18, 1912, only to learn that the Norwegian explorer Amundsen had got there just one month before him, left behind him in the icy wastes where he and his companions starved and froze to death one of the imperishable records of man's fortitude and frequent greatness of spirit. Scott's Journal of his last expedition will be read and remembered as long as men take pride in the summits of human unselfishness and heroic achievement.

Like a surprising number of British men of action (one thinks immediately of Sir Philip Sidney, Henry Fielding, Sir Richard Burton, Lawrence of Arabia, and Sir Winston Churchill, to name only a few), Robert Scott was an impressively articulate man, the master of a forthright and vigorous prose. To be sure his Journal derives much of its impact from the extraordinary circumstances of which it tells, but it could not have been written by a Colonel Blimp. The sections I have selected are from the latter part of the Journal, and describe the desperate march back from the Pole, its unflinching facing up to hardship great as men have ever endured, and the inspiring manner of these Englishmen's deaths. No one, I think, can read the pages that follow without a renewed and quickened sense of mankind at its best.

The interspersed commentary is from the notes by Leonard Huxley.

Death in the Antarctic

SUNDAY, February 11.—R. 25. Lunch Temp. +6:5°; Supper +3:5°. The worst day we have had during the trip and greatly owing to our own fault. We started on a wretched surface with light S.W. wind, sail set, and pulling on ski—horrible light, which made everything look fantastic. As we went on light got worse, and suddenly we found ourselves in pressure. Then came the fatal decision to steer east. We went on for 6 hours, hoping to do a good distance, which in fact I suppose we did, but for the last hour or two we pressed on into a regular trap. Getting on to a good surface we did not reduce our lunch meal, and thought all going well, but half an hour after lunch we got into the worst ice mess I have ever been in. For three hours we plunged on on ski, first thinking we were too much to the right, then too much to the left; meanwhile the disturbance got worse and my spirits received a very rude shock. There were times when it seemed almost impossible to find a way out of the awful turmoil in which we found ourselves. At length, arguing that there must be a way on our left, we plunged in that direction. It got worse, harder, more icy and crevassed. We could not manage our ski and pulled on foot, falling into crevasses every minute—most luckily no bad accident. At length we saw a smoother slope towards the land, pushed for it, but knew it was a woefully long way from us. The turmoil changed in character, irregular crevassed surface giving way to huge chasms, closely packed and most difficult to cross. It was very heavy work, but we had grown desperate. We won through at 10 P.M. and I write after 12 hours on the march. I *think* we are on or about the right track now, but we are still a good number of miles from the depôt, so we reduced rations to-night. We had three pemmican meals left and decided to make them into four. To-morrow's lunch must serve for two if we do not make big progress. It was a test of our endurance on the march and our fitness with small supper. We have come through well. A good wind has come down the glacier which is clearing the sky and surface. Pray God the wind holds to-morrow. Short sleep to-night and off first thing, I hope.

Monday, February 12.—R.26. In a very critical situation. All went well in the forenoon, and we did a good long march over a fair surface. Two hours before lunch we were cheered by the sight of our night camp of the 18th December, the day after we made our depôt—this showed we were on the right track. In the afternoon, refreshed by tea, we went forward, confident of covering the remaining distance, but by a fatal chance we kept too far to the left, and then we struck uphill and, tired and despondent, arrived in a horrid maze of crevasses and fissures. Divided councils caused our course to be erratic after this, and finally, at 9 P.M. we landed in the worst place of all. After discussion we decided to camp, and here we are, after a very short supper and one meal only remaining in the food bag; the depôt doubtful in locality. We *must* get there to-morrow. Meanwhile we are cheerful with an effort. It's a tight place, but luckily we've been well fed up to the present. Pray God we have fine weather to-morrow.

[At this point the bearings of the mid-glacier depôt are given, but need not be quoted.]

Tuesday, February 13.—Camp R.27, beside Cloudmaker. Temp. +10°. Last night we all slept well in spite of our grave anxieties. For my part these were increased by my visits outside the tent, when I saw the sky gradually closing over and snow beginning to fall. By our ordinary time for getting up it was dense all around us. We could see nothing, and we could only remain in our sleeping bags. At 8.30 I dimly made out the land of the Cloudmaker. At 9 we got up, deciding to have tea, and with one biscuit, no pemmican, so as to leave our scanty remaining meal for eventualities. We started marching, and at first had to wind our way through an awful turmoil of broken ice, but in about an hour we hit an old moraine track, brown with dirt. Here the surface was much smoother and improved rapidly. The fog still hung over all and we went on for an hour, checking our bearings. Then the whole plain got smoother and we turned outward a little. Evans raised our hopes with a shout of depôt ahead, but it proved to be a shadow on the ice. Then suddenly Wilson saw the actual depôt flag. It was an immense relief, and we were soon in possession of our 3½ days' food. The relief to all is inexpressible; needless to say, we camped and had a meal.

Marching in the afternoon, I kept more to the left, and closed the mountain till we fell on the stone moraines. Here Wilson detached himself and made a collection, whilst we pulled the sledge on. We camped late, abreast the lower end of the mountain, and had nearly our usual satisfying supper. Yesterday was the worst experience of the trip and gave a horrid feeling of insecurity. Now we are right, but we must march. In future food must be worked so that we do not run so short if the weather fails us. We mustn't get into a hole like this again. Greatly relieved to find that both the other parties got through safely. Evans seems to have got mixed up with pressures like ourselves. It promises to be a very fine day to-morrow. The valley is gradually clearing. Bowers has had a very bad attack of snow blindness, and Wilson another almost as bad. Evans has no power to assist with camping work.

Wednesday, February 14.—Lunch Temp. 0°; Supper Temp. +1°. A fine day with wind on and off down the glacier, and we have done a fairly good march. We started a little late and pulled on down the moraine. At first I thought of going right, but soon, luckily, changed my mind and decided to follow the curving lines of the moraines. This course has brought us well out on the glacier. Started on crampons; one hour after, hoisted sail; the combined efforts produced only slow speed, partly due to the sandy snowdrifts similar to those on summit, partly to our torn sledge runners. At lunch these were scraped and sandpapered. After lunch we got on snow, with ice only occasionally showing through. A poor start, but the gradient and wind improving, we did 6½ miles before night camp.

There is no getting away from the fact that we are not pulling strong. Probably none of us: Wilson's leg still troubles him and he doesn't like to trust himself on ski; but the worst case is Evans, who is giving us serious anxiety. This morning he suddenly disclosed a huge blister on his foot. It delayed us on the march, when he had to have his crampon readjusted. Sometimes I fear he is going from bad to worse, but I trust he will pick up again when we come to steady work on ski like this afternoon. He is hungry and so is Wilson. We can't risk opening out our food again, and as cook at present I am serving something under full allowance. We are inclined to get slack and slow with our camping arrangements, and small delays increase. I have talked of the matter to-night and hope for improvement. We cannot do distance without the hours. The next depôt[1] some 30 miles away and nearly 3 days' food in hand.

Thursday, February 15.—R.29. Lunch Temp. $+10°$; Supper Temp. $+4°$. 13.5 miles. Again we are running short of provision. We don't know our distance from the depôt, but imagine about 20 miles. Heavy march—did 13¾ (geo.). We are pulling for food and not very strong evidently. In the afternoon it was overcast; land blotted out for a considerable interval. We have reduced food, also sleep; feeling rather done. Trust 1½ days or 2 at most will see us at depôt.

Friday, February 16.—12.5 m. Lunch Temp. $+6.1°$; Supper Temp. $+7°$. A rather trying position. Evans has nearly broken down in brain, we think. He is absolutely changed from his normal self-reliant self. This morning and this afternoon he stopped the march on some trivial excuse. We are on short rations but not very short, food spins out till to-morrow night. We cannot be more than 10 or 12 miles from the depôt, but the weather is all against us. After lunch we were enveloped in a snow sheet, land just looming. Memory should hold the events of a very troublesome march with more troubles ahead. Perhaps all will be well if we can get to our depôt to-morrow fairly early, but it is anxious work with the sick man. But it's no use meeting troubles half way, and our sleep is all too short to write more.

Saturday, February 17.—A very terrible day. Evans looked a little better after a good sleep, and declared, as he always did, that he was quite well. He started in his place on the traces, but half an hour later worked his ski shoes adrift, and had to leave the sledge. The surface

---

[1] The Lower Glacier Depôt.

was awful, the soft recently fallen snow clogging the ski and runners at every step, the sledge groaning, the sky overcast, and the land hazy. We stopped after about one hour, and Evans came up again, but very slowly. Half an hour later he dropped out again on the same plea. He asked Bowers to lend him a piece of string. I cautioned him to come on as quickly as he could, and he answered cheerfully as I thought. We had to push on, and the remainder of us were forced to pull very hard sweating heavily. Abreast the Monument Rock we stopped, and seeing Evans a long way astern, I camped for lunch. There was no alarm at first, and we prepared tea and our own meal, consuming the latter. After lunch, and Evans still not appearing, we looked out, to see him still afar off. By this time we were alarmed, and all four started back on ski. I was first to reach the poor man and shocked at his appearance; he was on his knees with clothing disarranged, hands uncovered and frostbitten, and a wild look in his eyes. Asked what was the matter, he replied with a slow speech that he didn't know, but thought he must have fainted. We got him on his feet, but after two or three steps he sank down again. He showed every sign of complete collapse. Wilson, Bowers, and I went back for the sledge, whilst Oates remained with him. When we returned he was practically unconscious, and when we got him into the tent quite comatose. He died quietly at 12.30 A.M. On discussing the symptoms we think he began to get weaker just before we reached the Pole, and that his downward path was accelerated first by the shock of his frostbitten fingers, and later by falls during rough travelling on the glacier, further by his loss of all confidence in himself. Wilson thinks it certain he must have injured his brain by a fall. It is a terrible thing to lose a companion in this way, but calm reflection shows that there could not have been a better ending to the terrible anxieties of the past week. Discussion of the situation at lunch yesterday shows us what a desperate pass we were in with a sick man on our hands at such a distance from home.

At 1 A.M. we packed up and came down over the pressure ridges, finding our depôt easily.

Friday, March 2.—Lunch. Misfortunes rarely come singly. We marched to the [Middle Barrier] depôt fairly easily yesterday afternoon, and since that have suffered three distinct blows which have placed us in a bad position. First we found a shortage of oil; with most rigid economy it can scarce carry us to the next depôt on this surface [71 miles away]. Second, Titus Oates disclosed his feet, the toes showing very bad indeed, evidently bitten by the late temperatures. The third blow came in the night, when the wind, which we had hailed with some joy, brought dark overcast weather. It fell below — 40° in the night, and this morning it took 1½ hours to get our foot gear on, but we got away before eight. We lost cairn and tracks together and made as steady as we could N. by W., but have seen nothing. Worse was to come—the surface is simply awful. In spite of strong wind and full sail we have only done 5½ miles. We are in a *very* queer street since there is no doubt we cannot do the extra marches and feel the cold horribly.

Saturday, March 3.—Lunch. We picked up the track again yesterday, finding ourselves to the eastward. Did close on 10 miles and things looked a trifle better; but this morning the outlook is blacker than ever. Started well and with good breeze; for an hour made good headway; then the surface grew awful beyond words. The wind drew forward; every circumstance was against us. After 4¼ hours things so bad that we camped, having covered 4½ miles. [R.46.] One cannot consider this a fault of our own—certainly we were pulling hard this morning—it was more than three parts surface which held us back— the wind at strongest, powerless to move the sledge. When the light is good it is easy to see the reason. The surface, lately a very good hard one, is coated with a thin layer of woolly crystals, formed by radiation no doubt. These are too firmly fixed to be removed by the wind and cause impossible friction on the runners. God help us, we can't keep up this pulling, that is certain. Amongst ourselves we are unendingly cheerful, but what each man feels in his heart I can only guess. Putting on foot gear in the morning is getter slower and slower, therefore every day more dangerous.

Sunday, March 4.—Lunch. Things looking *very* black indeed. As usual we forgot our trouble last night, got into our bags, slept splendidly on good hoosh, woke and had another, and started marching. Sun shining brightly, tracks clear, but surface covered with sandy frostrime. All the morning we had to pull with all our strength, and in 4½ hours we covered 3½ miles. Last night it was overcast and thick, surface bad; this morning sun shining and surface as bad as ever. One has little to hope for except perhaps strong dry wind—an unlikely contingency at this time of year. Under the immediate surface crystals is a hard sustrugi surface, which must have been excellent for pulling a week or two ago. We are about 42 miles from the next depôt and have a week's food, but only about 3 to 4 days' fuel—we are as economical of the latter as one can possibly be, and we cannot afford to save food and pull as we are pulling. We are in a very tight place indeed, but none of us despondent *yet,* or at least we preserve every semblance of good cheer, but one's heart sinks as the sledge stops dead at some sastrugi behind which the surface sand lies thickly heaped. For the moment the temperature is in the —20°—an improvement which makes us much more comfortable, but a colder snap is bound to come again soon. I fear that Oates at least will weather such an event very poorly. Providence to our aid! We can expect little from man now except the possibility of extra food at the next depôt. It will be real bad if we get there and find the same shortage of oil. Shall we get there? Such a short distance it would have appeared to us on the summit! I don't know what I should do if Wilson and Bowers weren't so determinedly cheerful over things.

Monday, March 5.—Lunch. Regret to say going from bad to worse. We got a slant of wind yesterday afternoon, and going on 5 hours we converted our wretched morning run of 3½ miles into something over 9. We went to bed on a cup of cocoa and pemmican solid with the chill off. (R.47.) The result is telling on all, but mainly on Oates, whose feet are in a wretched condition. One swelled up tremendously last night and he is very lame this morning. We started march on tea and pemmican as last night—we pretend to prefer the pemmican this way. Marched for 5 hours this morning over a slightly better surface covered with high moundy sastrugi. Sledge capsized twice; we pulled on foot, covering about 5½ miles. We are two pony marches and 4 miles about from our depôt. Our fuel dreadfully low and the poor Soldier nearly done. It is pathetic enough because we can do nothing for him; more hot food might do a little, but only a little, I fear. We none of us expected these terribly low temperatures, and of the rest of us Wilson is feeling them most; mainly, I fear, from his self-sacrificing devotion in doctoring Oates' feet. We cannot help each other, each has enough to do to take care of himself. We get cold on the march when the trudging is heavy, and the wind pierces our worn garments. The others, all of them, are unendingly cheerful when in the tent. We mean to see the game through with a proper spirit, but it's tough work to be pulling harder than we ever pulled in our lives for long hours, and to feel that the progress is so slow. One can only say "God help us!" and plod on our weary way, cold and very miserable, though outwardly cheerful. We talk of all sorts of subjects in the tent, not much of food now, since we decided to take the risk of running a full ration. We simply couldn't go hungry at this time.

Tuesday, March 6.—Lunch. We did a little better with help of wind yesterday afternoon, finishing 9½ miles for the day, and 27 miles from depôt. [R.48.] But this morning things have been awful. It was warm in the night and for the first time during the journey I overslept myself by more than an hour; then we were slow with foot gear; then, pulling with all our might (for our lives) we could scarcely advance at rate of a mile an hour; then it grew thick and three times we had to get out of harness to search for tracks. The result is something less than 3½ miles for the forenoon. The sun is shining now and the wind gone. Poor Oates is unable to pull, sits on the sledge when we are track-searching—he is wonderfully plucky, as his feet must be giving him great pain. He makes no complaint, but his spirits only come up in spurts now, and he grows more silent in the tent. We are making a spirit lamp to try and replace the primus when our oil is exhausted. It will be a very poor substitute and we've not got much spirit. If we could have kept up our 9-mile days we might have got within reasonable distance of the depôt before running out, but nothing but a strong wind and good surface can help us now, and though we had quite a good breeze this morning, the sledge came as heavy as lead. If we were all fit I should have hopes of getting through, but the poor Soldier has become a terrible hindrance, though he does his utmost and suffers much I fear.

Wednesday, March 7.—A little worse I fear. One of Oates' feet *very* bad this morning; he is wonderfully brave. We still talk of what we will do together at home.

We only made 6½ miles yesterday. [R.49.] This morning in 4½ hours we did just over 4 miles. We are 16 from our depôt. If we only find the correct proportion of food there and this surface continues, we may get to the next depôt [Mt. Hooper, 72 miles farther] but not to One Ton Camp. We hope against hope that the dogs have been to Mt. Hooper; then we might pull through. If there is a shortage of oil again we can have little hope. One feels that for poor Oates the crisis is near, but none of us are improving, though we are wonderfully fit considering the really excessive work we are doing. We are only kept going by good food. No wind this morning till a chill northerly air came ahead. Sun bright and cairns showing up well. I should like to keep the track to the end.

Thursday, March 8.—Lunch. Worse and worse in morning; poor Oates' left foot can never last out, and time over foot gear something awful. Have to wait in night foot gear for nearly an hour before I start changing, and then am generally first to be ready. Wilson's feet giving trouble now, but this mainly because he gives so much help to others. We did 4½ miles this morning and are now 8½ miles from the depôt —a ridiculously small distance to feel in difficulties, yet on this surface we know we cannot equal half our old marches, and that for that effort we expend nearly double the energy. The great question is, What shall we find at the depôt? If the dogs have visited it we may get along a good distance, but if there is another short allowance of fuel, God help us indeed. We are in a very bad way, I fear, in any case.

Saturday, March 10.—Things steadily downhill. Oates' foot worse. He has rare pluck and must know that he can never get through. He asked Wilson if he had a chance this morning, and of course Bill had to say he didn't know. In point of fact he has none. Apart from him, if he went under now, I doubt whether we could get through. With great care we might have a dog's chance, but no more. The weather conditions are awful, and our gear gets steadily more-icy and difficult to manage. At the same time of course poor Titus is the greatest handicap. He keeps us waiting in the morning until we have partly lost the warming effect of our good breakfast, when the only wise policy is to be up and away at once; again at lunch. Poor chap! it is too pathetic to watch him; one cannot but try to cheer him up.

Yesterday we marched up the depôt, Mt. Hooper. Cold comfort. Shortage on our allowance all round. I don't know that anyone is to blame. The dogs which would have been our salvation have evidently failed.[2] Meares had a bad trip home I suppose.

This morning it was calm when we breakfasted, but the wind came from W.N.W. as we broke camp. It rapidly grew in strength. After travelling for half an hour I saw that none of us could go on facing such conditions. We were forced to camp and are spending the rest of the day in a comfortless blizzard camp, wind quite foul. [R.52.]

Sunday, March 11.—Titus Oates is very near the end, one feels. What we or he will do, God only knows. We discussed the matter after breakfast; he is a brave fine fellow and understands the situation, but he practically asked for advice. Nothing could be said but to urge him to march as long as he could. One satisfactory result to the discussion; I practically ordered Wilson to hand over the means of ending our troubles to us, so that anyone of us may know how to do so. Wilson had no choice between doing so and our ransacking the medicine case. We have 30 opium tabloids apiece and he is left with a tube of morphine. So far the tragical side of our story. [R.53.]

The sky completely overcast when we started this morning. We could see nothing, lost the tracks, and doubtless have been swaying a good deal since—3.1 miles for the forenoon—terribly heavy dragging—expected it. Know that 6 miles is about the limit of our endurance now, if we get no help from wind or surfaces. We have 7 days' food

---

[2] For the last six days the dogs had been waiting at One Ton Camp under Cherry-Garrard and Demetri. The supporting party had come out as arranged on the chance of hurrying the Pole travellers back over the last stages of their journey in time to catch the ship. Scott had dated his probable return to Hut Point anywhere between mid-March and early April. Calculating from the speed of the other return parties, Dr. Atkinson looked for him to reach One Ton Camp between March 3 and 10. Here Cherry-Garrard met four days of blizzard; then there remained little more than enough dog food to bring the teams home. He could either push south one more march and back, at imminent risk of missing Scott on the way, or stay two days at the Camp where Scott was bound to come, if he came at all. His wise decision, his hardships and endurance are recounted by Dr. Atkinson in Vol. II, *The Last Year at Cape Evans.*

and should be about 55 miles from One Ton Camp to-night, 6 × 7 = 42, leaving us 13 miles short of our distance, even if things get no worse. Meanwhile the season rapidly advances.

Monday, March 12.—We did 6.9 miles yesterday, under our necessary average. Things are left much the same, Oates not pulling much, and now with hands as well as feet pretty well useless. We did 4 miles this morning in 4 hours 20 min.—we may hope for 3 this afternoon, 7 × 6 =42. We shall be 47 miles from the depôt. I doubt if we can possibly do it. The surface remains awful, the cold intense, and our physical condition running down. God help us! Not a breath of favourable wind for more than a week, and apparently liable to head winds at any moment.

Wednesday, March 14.—No doubt about the going downhill, but everything going wrong for us. Yesterday we woke to a strong northerly wind with temp. — 37°. Couldn't face it, so remained in camp [R.54.] till 2, then did 5¼ miles. Wanted to march later, but party feeling the cold badly as the breeze (N.) never took off entirely, and as the sun sank the temp. fell. Long time getting supper in dark. [R.55.]

This morning started with southerly breeze, set sail and passed another cairn at good speed; half-way, however, the wind shifted to W. by S. or W.S.W., blew through our wind clothes and into our mits. Poor Wilson horribly cold, could [not] get off ski for some time. Bowers and I practically made camp, and when we got into the tent at last we were all deadly cold. Then temp. now midday down — 43° and the wind strong. We *must* go on, but now the making of every camp must be more difficult and dangerous. It must be near the end, but a pretty merciful end. Poor Oates got it again in the foot. I shudder to think what it will be like to-morrow. It is only with greatest pains rest of us keep off frostbites. No idea there could be temperatures like this at this time of year with such winds. Truly awful outside the tent. Must fight it out to the last biscuit, but can't reduce rations.

Friday, March 16 *or Saturday* 17.—Lost track of dates, but think the last correct. Tragedy all along the line. At lunch, the day before yesterday, poor Titus Oates said he couldn't go on; he proposed we should leave him in his sleeping-bag. That we could not do, and we induced him to come on, on the afternoon march. In spite of its awful nature for him he struggled on and we made a few miles. At night he was worse and we knew the end had come.

Should this be found I want these facts recorded. Oates' last thoughts were of his Mother, but immediately before he took pride in thinking that his regiment would be pleased with the bold way in which he met his death. We can testify to his bravery. He has borne intense suffering for weeks without complaint, and to the very last was able and willing to discuss outside subjects. He did not—would not—give up hope till the very end. He was a brave soul. This was the end. He slept through the night before last, hoping not to wake; but he woke in the morning —yesterday. It was blowing a blizzard. He said, "I am just going outside and may be some time." He went out into the blizzard and we have not seen him since.

I take this opportunity of saying that we have stuck to our sick companions to the last. In case of Edgar Evans, when absolutely out of food and he lay insensible, the safety of the remainder seemed to demand his abandonment, but Providence mercifully removed him at this critical moment. He died a natural death, and we did not leave him till two hours after his death. We knew that poor Oates was walking to his death, but though we tried to dissuade him, we knew it was the act of a brave man and an English gentleman. We all hope to meet the end with a similar spirit, and assuredly the end is not far.

I can only write at lunch and then only occasionally. The cold is intense, — 40° at midday. My companions are unendingly cheerful, but we are all on the verge of serious frostbites, and though we constantly talk of fetching through I don't think anyone of us believes it in his heart.

We are cold on the march now, and at all times except meals. Yesterday we had to lay up for a blizzard and to-day we move dreadfully slowly. We are at No. 14 pony camp, only two pony marches from One Ton Depôt. We leave here our theodolite, a camera, and Oates' sleeping-bags. Diaries, &c., and geological specimens carried at Wilson's special request, will be found with us or on our sledge.

Sunday, March 18.—To-day, lunch, we are 21 miles from the depôt. Ill fortune presses, but better may come. We have had more wind and drift from ahead yesterday; had to stop marching; wind N.W., force 4, temp. — 35°. No human being could face it, and we are worn out *nearly*.

My right foot has gone, nearly all the toes—two days ago I was proud possessor of best feet. These are the steps of my downfall. Like an ass I mixed a small spoonful of curry powder with my melted pemmican—it gave me violent indigestion. I lay awake and in pain all night; woke and felt done on the march; foot went and I didn't know it. A very small measure of neglect and have a foot which is not pleasant to contemplate. Bowers takes first place in condition, but there is not much to choose after all. The others are still confident of getting through—or pretend to be—I don't know! We have the last *half* fill of oil in our primus and a very small quantity of spirit—this alone between us and thirst. The wind is fair for the moment, and that is perhaps a fact to help. The mileage would have seemed ridiculously small on our outward journey.

Monday, March 19.—Lunch. We camped with difficulty last night, and were dreadfully cold till after our supper of cold pemmican and biscuit and a half a pannikin of cocoa cooked over the spirit. Then, contrary to expectation, we got warm and all slept well. To-day we started in the usual dragging manner. Sledge dreadfully heavy. We are 15½ miles from the depôt and ought to get there in three days. What progress! We have two days' food but barely a day's fuel. All our feet are getting bad—Wilson's best, my right foot worst, left all right. There is no chance to nurse one's feet till we can get hot food into us. Amputation is the least I can hope for now, but will the trouble spread? That is the serious question. The weather doesn't give us a chance—the wind from N. to N.W. and — 40° temp. to-day.

Wednesday, March 21.—Got within 11 miles of depôt Monday night; [3] had to lay up all yesterday in severe blizzard. To-day forlorn hope, Wilson and Bowers going to depôt for fuel.

Thursday, March 22 *and* 23.—Blizzard bad as ever—Wilson and Bowers unable to start—to-morrow last chance—no fuel and only one or two of food left—must be near the end. Have decided it shall be natural—we shall march for the depôt with or without our effects and die in our tracks.

[*Thursday*], *March* 29.—Since the 21st we have had a continuous gale from W.S.W. and S.W. We had fuel to make two cups of tea apiece and bare food for two days on the 20th. Every day we have been ready to start for our depôt 11 *miles* away, but outside the door of the door of the tent it remains a scene of whirling drift. I do not think we can hope for any better things now. We shall stick it out to the end, but we are getting weaker, of course, and the end cannot be far.

It seems a pity, but I do not think I can write more.

R. SCOTT.

For God's sake look after our people.

Wilson and Bowers were found in the attitude of sleep, their sleeping-bags closed over their heads as they would naturally close them.

Scott died later. He had thrown back the flaps of his sleeping-bag and opened his coat. The little wallet containing the three notebooks was under his shoulders and his arm flung across Wilson. So they were found eight months later.

[3] The 60th camp from the Pole.

With the diaries in the tent were found the following letters:

To Mrs. E. A. Wilson

MY DEAR MRS. WILSON,

If this letter reaches you Bill and I will have gone out together. We are very near it now and I should like you to know how splendid he was at the end—everlastingly cheerful and ready to sacrifice himself for others, never a word of blame to me for leading him into this mess. He is not suffering, luckily, at least only minor discomforts.

His eyes have a comfortable blue look of hope and his mind is peaceful with the satisfaction of his faith in regarding himself as part of the great scheme of the Almighty. I can do no more to comfort you than to tell you that he died as he lived, a brave, true man—the best of comrades and staunchest of friends.

My whole heart goes out to you in pity.

Yours,
R. Scott

To Mrs. Bowers

MY DEAR MRS. BOWERS,

I am afraid this will reach you after one of the heaviest blows of your life.

I write when we are very near the end of our journey, and I am finishing it in company with two gallant, noble gentlemen. One of these is your son. He had come to be one of my closest and soundest friends, and I appreciate his wonderful upright nature, his ability and energy. As the troubles have thickened his dauntless spirit ever shone brighter and he has remained cheerful, hopeful, and indomitable to the end.

The ways of Providence are inscrutable, but there must be some reason why such a young, vigorous and promising life is taken.

My whole heart goes out in pity for you.

Yours,
R. Scott.

To the end he has talked of you and his sisters. One sees what a happy home he must have had and perhaps it is well to look back on nothing but happiness.

He remains unselfish, self-reliant and splendidly hopeful to the end, believing in God's mercy to you.

To Sir J. M. Barrie

My dear Barrie,

We are pegging out in a very comfortable spot. Hoping this letter may be found and sent to you, I write a word of farewell. . . . More practically I want you to help my widow and my boy—your godson. We are showing that Englishmen can still die with a bold spirit, fighting it out to the end. It will be known that we have accomplished our object in reaching the Pole, and that we have done everything possible, even to sacrificing ourselves in order to save sick companions. I think this makes an example for Englishmen of the future, and that the country ought to help those who are left behind to mourn us. I leave my poor girl and your godson, Wilson leaves a widow, and Edgar Evans also a widow in humble circumstances. Do what you can to get their claims recognised. Goodbye. I am not at all afraid of the end, but sad to miss many a humble pleasure which I had planned for the future on our long marches. I may not have proved a great explorer, but we have done the greatest march ever made and come very near to great success. Goodbye, my dear friend,

Yours ever,

R. Scott.

We are in a desperate state, feet frozen, &c. No fuel and a long way from food, but would do your heart good to be in our tent, to hear our songs and the cheery conversation as to what we will do when we get to Hut Point.

Later.—We are very near the end, but have not and will not lose our good cheer. We have four days of storm in our tent and nowhere's food or fuel. We did intend to finish ourselves when things proved like this, but we have decided to die naturally in the track.

As a dying man, my dear friend, be good to my wife and child. Give the boy a chance in life if the State won't do it. He ought to have good stuff in him. . . . I never met a man in my life whom I admired and loved more than you, but I never could show you how much your friendship meant to me, for you had much to give and I nothing.

Message to the Public

The causes of the disaster are not due to faulty organisation, but to misfortune in all risks which had to be undertaken.

1. The loss of pony transport in March 1911 obliged me to start later than I had intended, and obliged the limits of stuff transported to be narrowed.

2. The weather throughout the outward journey, and especially the long gale in 83° S., stopped us.

3. The soft snow in lower reaches of glacier again reduced pace.

We fought these untoward events with a will and conquered, but it cut into our provision reserve.

Every detail of our food supplies, clothing and depôts made on the interior ice-sheet and over that long stretch of 700 miles to the Pole and back, worked out to perfection. The advance party would have returned to the glacier in fine form and with surplus of food, but for the astonishing failure of the man whom we had least expected to fail. Edgar Evans was thought the strongest man of the party.

The Beardmore Glacier is not difficult in fine weather, but on our return we did not get a single completely fine day; this with a sick companion enormously increased our anxieties.

As I have said elsewhere we got into frightfully rough ice and Edgar Evans received a concussion of the brain—he died a natural death, but left us a shaken party with the season unduly advanced.

But all the facts above enumerated were as nothing to the surprise which awaited us on the Barrier. I maintain that our arrangements for returning were quite adequate, and that no one in the world would have expected the temperatures and surfaces which we encountered at this time of the year. On the summit in lat. 85° 86° we had − 20°, − 30°. On the Barrier in lat. 82°, 10,000 feet lower, we had − 30° in the day, − 47° at night pretty regularly, with continuous head wind during our day marches. It is clear that these circumstances come on very suddenly, and our wreck is certainly due to this sudden advent of severe weather, which does not seem to have any satisfactory cause. I do not think human beings ever came through such a month as we have come through, and we should have got through in spite of the weather but for the sickening of a second companion, Captain Oates, and a shortage of fuel in our depôts for which I cannot account, and finally, but for the storm which has fallen on us within 11 miles of the depôt at which we hoped to secure our final supplies. Surely misfortune could scarcely have exceeded this last blow. We arrived within 11 miles of our old One Ton Camp with fuel for one last meal and food for two days. For four days we have been unable to leave the tent—the gale howling about us. We are weak, writing is difficult, but for my own sake I do not regret this journey, which has shown that Englishmen can endure hardships, help one another, and meet death with as great a fortitude as ever in the past. We took risks, we knew we took them; things have come out against us, and therefore we have no cause for complaint, but bow to the will of Providence, determined still to do our best to the last. But if we have been willing to give our lives to this enterprise, which is for the honour of our country, I appeal to our countrymen to see that those who depend on us are properly cared for.

Had we lived, I should have had a tale to tell of the hardihood, endurance, and courage of my companions which would have stirred the heart of every Englishman. These rough notes and our dead bodies must tell the tale, but surely, surely, a great rich country like ours will see that those who are dependent on us are properly provided for.

JOSHUA SLOCUM

The stories of man's struggle against the sea are endless in number. They were among the first of the battles he fought against his environment, and they will be, no doubt, among the last. Of them all, none, perhaps, has a stronger claim upon the imagination than the story of Captain Slocum, who, single-handed, sailed round the world in a sloop. He started on his memorable voyage in 1895, when he was fifty-one years old. As a feat of daring, carried out with superb skill, it has seldom been matched.

Slocum was born in Nova Scotia in 1844. He made his first ocean voyage at the age of sixteen. When he was twenty-five he headed an Alaskan expedition. Some years before his lone voyage round the globe he sailed 6,000 miles across the Pacific, accompanied only by his wife, and some years after it he put out from Bristol, Rhode Island, again alone, bound for the Orinoco in South America. This voyage, like the great one, was made in the *Spray*. He never returned.

The story of his round-the-world voyage was told by him in *Sailing Alone Around the World*. From that book I have chosen the pages which tell of his battle with storm off Cape Horn.

Storm off Cape Horn

IT was the 3rd of March when the *Spray* sailed from Fort Tamar direct for Cape Pillar, with the wind from the northeast, which I fervently hoped might hold till she cleared the land; but there was no such good luck in store. It soon began to rain and thicken in the northwest, boding no good. The *Spray* neared Cape Pillar rapidly, and, nothing loath, plunged into the Pacific Ocean at once, taking her first bath of it in the gathering storm. There was no turning back even had I wished to do so, for the land was now shut out by the darkness of night. The wind freshened, and I took in a third reef. The sea was confused and treacherous. In such a time as this the old fisherman prayed. "Remember, Lord, my ship is so small and thy sea is so wide!" I saw now only the gleaming crests of waves. They showed white teeth while the sloop balanced over them. "Everything for an offing," I cried, and to this end I carried on all the sail she would bear. She ran all night with a free sheet, but on the morning of March 4 the wind shifted to southwest, then back suddenly to northwest, and blew with terrific force. The *Spray,* stripped of her sails, then bore off under bare poles. No ship in the world could have stood up against so violent a gale. Knowing that this storm might continue for many days, and that it would be impossible to work back to the westward along the coast outside of Tierra del Fuego, there seemed nothing to do but to keep on and go east about, after all. Anyhow, for my present safety the only course lay in keeping her before the wind. And so she drove southeast, as though about to round the Horn, while the waves rose and fell and bellowed their never-ending story of the sea; but the Hand that held these held also the *Spray.* She was running now with a reefed forestaysail, the sheets flat amidship. I payed out two long ropes to steady her course and to break combing seas astern, and I lashed the helm amidship. In this trim she ran before it, shipping never a sea. Even while the storm raged at its worst, my ship was wholesome and noble. My mind as to her seaworthiness was put to ease for aye.

When all had been done that I could do for the safety of the vessel, I got to the fore-scuttle, between seas, and prepared a pot of coffee over a wood fire, and made a good Irish stew. Then, as before and afterward on the *Spray,* I insisted on warm meals. In the tide-race off Cape Pillar, however, where the sea was marvellously high, uneven, and crooked, my appetite was slim, and for a time I postponed cooking. (Confidentially, I was seasick!)

The first day of the storm gave the *Spray* her actual test in the worst sea that Cape Horn or its wild regions could afford, and in no part of the world could a rougher sea be found than at this particular point, namely, off Cape Pillar, the grim sentinel of the Horn.

Farther offshore, while the sea was majestic, there was less apprehension of danger. There the *Spray* rode, now like a bird on the crest of a wave, and now like a waif deep down in the hollow between seas; and so she drove on. Whole days passed, counted as other days, but with always a thrill—yes, of delight.

On the fourth day of the gale, rapidly nearing the pitch of Cape Horn, I inspected my chart and pricked off the course and distance to Port Stanley, in the Falkland Islands, where I might find my way and refit, when I saw through a rift in the clouds a high mountain, about seven leagues away on the port beam. The fierce edge of the gale by this time had blown off, and I had already bent a square-sail on the boom in place of the mainsail, which was torn to rags. I hauled in the trailing ropes, hoisted this awkward sail reefed, the forestaysail being already set, and under this sail brought her at once on the wind heading for the land, which appeared as an island in the sea. So it turned out to be, though not the one I had supposed.

I was exultant over the prospect of once more entering the Strait of Magellan and beating through again into the Pacific, for it was more than rough on the outside coast of Tierra del Fuego. It was indeed a mountainous sea. When the sloop was in the fiercest squalls, with only the reefed forestaysail set, even that small sail shook her from keelson to truck when it shivered by the leech. Had I harboured the shadow of a doubt for her safety, it would have been that she might spring a leak in the garboard at the heel of the mast; but she never called me once to the pump. Under pressure of the smallest sail I could set she made for the land like a race-horse, and steering her over the crests of the waves so that she might not trip was nice work. I stood at the helm now and made the most of it.

Night closed in before the sloop reached the land, leaving her feeling the way in pitchy darkness. I saw breakers ahead before long. At this I wore ship and stood offshore, but was immediately startled by the tremendous roaring of breakers again ahead and on the lee bow. This puzzled me, for there should have been no broken water where I supposed myself to be. I kept off a good bit, then wore round, but finding broken water also there, threw her head again offshore. In this way, among dangers, I spent the rest of the night. Hail and sleet in the fierce squalls cut my flesh till the blood trickled over my face; but what of that? It was daylight, and the sloop was in the midst of the Milky Way of the sea, which is northwest of Cape Horn, and it was the white breakers of a huge sea over sunken rocks which had threatened to engulf her through the night. It was Fury Island I had sighted and steered for, and what a panorama was before me now and all around! It was not the time to complain of a broken skin. What could I do but fill away among the breakers and find a channel between them, now that it was day? Since she had escaped the rocks through the night, surely she would find her way by daylight. This was the greatest sea adventure of my life. God knows how my vessel escaped.

The sloop at last reached inside of small islands that sheltered her in smooth water. Then I climbed the mast to survey the wild scene astern. The great naturalist Darwin looked over this seascape from the deck of the *Beagle,* and wrote in his journal, "Any landsman seeing the Milky Way would have nightmare for a week." He might have added "or seaman" as well.

The *Spray's* good luck followed fast. I discovered, as she sailed along through a labyrinth of islands, that she was in the Cockburn Channel, which leads into the Strait of Magellan at a point opposite Cape Froward, and that she was already passing Thieves' Bay, suggestively named. And at night, March 8, behold, she was at anchor in a snug cove at the Turn! Every heartbeat on the *Spray* now counted thanks.

Here I pondered on the events of the last few days, and, strangely enough, instead of feeling rested from sitting or lying down, I now began to feel jaded and worn; but a hot meal of venison stew soon put me right, so that I could sleep. As drowsiness came on I sprinkled the deck with tacks, and then I turned in, bearing in mind the advice of my old friend Samblich that I was not to step on them myself. I saw to it that not a few of them stood "business end" up; for when the *Spray* passed Thieves' Bay two canoes had put out and followed in her wake, and there was no disguising the fact any longer that I was alone.

Now, it is well known that one cannot step on a tack without saying something about it. A pretty good Christian will whistle when he steps on the "commercial end" of a carpet-tack; a savage will howl and claw the air, and that was just what happened that night about twelve o'clock, while I was asleep in the cabin, where the savages thought they "had me," sloop and all, but changed their minds when they stepped on deck, for then they thought that I or somebody else had them. I had no need of a dog; they howled like a pack of hounds. I had hardly use for a gun. They jumped pell-mell, some into their canoes and some into the sea, to cool off, I suppose, and there was a deal of free language over it as they went. I fired several guns when I came on deck, to let the rascals know that I was home, and then I turned in again, feeling sure I should not be disturbed any more by people who left in so great a hurry.

The Fuegians, being cruel, are naturally cowards; they regard a rifle with superstitious fear. The only real danger one could see that might come from their quarter would be from allowing them to surround one within bowshot, or to anchor within range where they might lie in ambush. As for their coming on deck at night, even had I not put the tacks about, I could have cleared them off by shots from the cabin and hold. I always kept a quantity of ammunition within reach in the hold and in the cabin and in the forepeak, so that retreating to any of these places I could "hold the fort" simply by shooting up through the deck.

Perhaps the greatest danger to be apprehended was from the use of fire. Every canoe carries fire; nothing is thought of that, for it is their custom to communicate by smoke-signals. The harmless brand that lies smouldering in the bottom of one of their canoes might be ablaze in one's cabin if he were not on the alert. The port captain of Sandy Point warned me particularly of this danger. Only a short time before they had fired a Chilean gunboat by throwing brands in through the stern windows of the cabin. The *Spray* had no openings in the cabin or deck, except two scuttles, and these were guarded by fastenings which could not be undone without waking me if I were asleep.

On the morning of the 9th, after a refreshing rest and a warm breakfast, and after I had swept the deck of tacks, I got out what spare canvas there was on board, and began to sew the pieces together in the shape of a peak for my square-mainsail, the tarpaulin. The day to all appearances promised fine weather and light winds, but appearances in Tierra del Fuego do not always count. While I was wondering why no trees grew on the slope abreast of the anchorage, half minded to lay by the sail-making and land with my gun for some game and to inspect a white boulder on the beach, near the brook, a williwaw came down with such terrific force as to carry the *Spray,* with two anchors down, like a feather out of the cove and away into deep water. No wonder trees did not grow on the side of that hill! Great Boreas! a tree would need to be all roots to hold on against such a furious wind.

From the cove to the nearest land to leeward was a long drift, however, and I had ample time to weigh both anchors before the sloop came near any danger, and so no harm came of it. I saw no more savages that day or the next; they probably had some sign by which they knew of the coming williwaws; at least, they were wise in not being afloat even on the second day, for I had no sooner gotten to work at sail-making again, after the anchor was down, than the wind, as on the day before, picked the sloop up and flung her seaward with a vengeance, anchor and all, as before. This fierce wind, usual to the Magellan country, continued on through the day, and swept the sloop by several miles of steep bluffs and precipices overhanging a bold shore of wild and uninviting appearance. I was not sorry to get away from it, though in doing so it was no Elysian shore to which I shaped my course. I kept on sailing in hope, since I had no choice but to go on, heading across for St. Nicholas Bay, where I had cast anchor February 19. It was now the 10th of March! Upon reaching the bay the second time I had circumnavigated the wildest part of desolate Tierra del Fuego. But the *Spray* had not yet arrived at St. Nicholas, and by the merest accident her bones were saved from resting there when she did arrive. The parting of a staysailsheet in a williwaw, when the sea was turbulent and she was plunging into the storm, brought me forward to see instantly a dark cliff ahead and breakers so close under the bows that I felt surely lost, and in my thoughts cried, "Is the hand of fate against me, after all, leading me in the end to this dark spot?" I sprang aft again, unheeding the flapping sail, and threw the wheel over, expecting, as the sloop came down into the hollow of a wave, to feel her timbers smash under me on the rocks. But at the touch of her helm she swung clear of the danger, and in the next moment she was in the lee of the land.

It was the small island in the middle of the bay for which the sloop had been steering, and which she made with such unerring aim as nearly to run it down. Farther along in the bay was the anchorage, which I managed to reach, but before I could get the anchor down another squall caught the sloop and whirled her round like a top and carried her away, altogether to leeward of the bay. Still farther to leeward was a great headland, and I bore off for that. This was retracing my course toward Sandy Point, for the gale was from the southwest.

I had the sloop soon under good control, however, and in a short time rounded to under the lee of a mountain, where the sea was as smooth as a mill-pond, and the sails flapped and hung limp while she carried her way close in. Here I thought I would anchor and rest till morning, the depth being eight fathoms very close to the shore. But it was interesting to see, as I let go the anchor, that it did not reach the bottom before another williwaw struck down from this mountain and carried the sloop off faster than I could pay out cable. Therefore, instead of resting, I had to "man the windlass" and heave up the anchor with fifty fathoms of cable hanging up and down in deep water. This was in that part of the strait called Famine Reach. Dismal Famine Reach! On the sloop's crab-windlass I worked the rest of the night, thinking how much easier it was for me when I could say, "Do that thing or the other," than now doing all myself. But I hove away and sang the old chants that I sang when I was a sailor. Within the last few days I had passed through much and was now thankful that my state was no worse.

It was daybreak when the anchor was at the hawse. By this time the wind had gone down, and cat's-paws took the place of williwaws, while the sloop drifted slowly toward Sandy Point. She came within sight of ships at anchor in the roads, and I was more than half minded to put in for new sails, but the wind coming out from the northeast, which was fair for the other direction, I turned the prow of the *Spray* westward once more for the Pacific, to traverse a second time the second half of my first course through the strait.

CHARLES AUGUSTUS
LINDBERGH

There is little need for me to epitomize here the story of one of the
most famous men of our time. At the age of twenty-five he electrified
the world by his lone flight across the Atlantic, that unforgettable
May day of 1927. He served with distinction in World War II, and by
his repeated missions in the Pacific theater of that war, won back the
esteem of a people, many of whom had unjustly judged him during
the days preceding our entrance into the conflict.

The rather inarticulate boy who had won the world's affection and
admiration has in the intervening years developed into a thoughtful
and eloquent writer, with a keen awareness of man's spiritual needs
in the midst of his technological triumphs. The man who did so much
to advance the cause of aviation has come to the point where he can
even question the desirability of man's increasing conquest of the air,
unless his moral strength and wisdom can match his technical
achievement.

I have taken something from each of his two more recent books—
very different works from the *We* he does not acknowledge in his
Who's Who biography. I have chosen a section from *Of Flight and
Life,* and others from *The Spirit of St. Louis*—passages which tell
the story of his desperate efforts to keep awake and to function long
enough to insure his landing, if not in Paris, then at least somewhere
on the shores of Ireland or of Europe. Few ventures of man alone,
fighting against odds, make a more heroic tale than this.

Back from the Border of Death

FORTY thousand feet and still climbing. I am running an ignition
breakdown test on the engine of a Thunderbolt fighter. Research
in the higher air is a relief from my wartime routine of conferences,
production lines, and bomber shakedown flights.

Under one wing, an off-shaded patch on the great quilt of earth, is the city of Detroit. Under the other, slightly hazed by smoke, lies Toledo. The thumb of Michigan presses flat against the gray waters of Lake Huron. To the eastward, Canada and Lake Erie merge into fog; while a dim band on the western horizon marks Wisconsin's shore. Almost lost in the expanse of land and water, requiring a careful search of the eyes to locate them, fine parallel and intersecting lines on a postage-stamp-size field are actually the mile-long runways of Willow Run. Eight thousand feet closer to earth, edging a thin veil of cirrus cloud, an angular vapor trail shows where my ascending fighter has pierced the crystalline sky. The temperature gage registers 55 degrees below zero outside my cockpit.

At 41,000 feet, I level off, set the trim tabs, and adjust the turbo. I must hold five minutes of level flight while plane and engine settle down to normal readings. The oil temperature's at the peg again— oil's probably foaming out of the vent. Well, can't do anything about that up here. I'll let it foam as long as the pressure holds. But it'll mean another cleaning job for the ground crew. There just isn't enough air above 40,000 feet to keep an R–2800 engine cool.

Shall I try radio contact with the Tower? Not much use at this altitude—reception's bad and, with the thinness of atmosphere, the best you can do is a word to a breath. Still, they'd probably like to hear from me. I must try to get each word's last syllable formed before my lungs run out of air. I press the "mike" button:

"WILLOW . . . . . RUN . . . . . TOWER . . . . . FROM . . . . . ARMY . . . . . SIX . . . . . ZERO . . . . . THREE . . . . . EIGHT . . . . . OVER."

(You don't speak, you pant out words, at high altitude.) I turn up the volume control to maximum. A voice replies in my earphones, but the words don't come through:

"#**¢MY-*@ZERO#;&EIGHT-*(*¢@-*%OWRUNO
#-*¢":/*#*#."

That's for me, all right. Maybe *they* can hear better:

"TOWER . . . . . FROM . . . . . ZERO . . . . . THREE . . . . . EIGHT . . . . . POSITION . . . . . TWENTY . . . . . MILES . . . . . SOUTH . . . . . WILLOW . . . . . RUN . . . . . ALTITUDE . . . . . FORTY . . . . . ONE . . . . . THOUSAND . . . . . OUT."

There are more jumbled noises in my earphones. I don't know how much of the message they received, but I'm not going to send it again. My head's already swimming slightly from the effort, and it's time to take instrument readings.

Air speed, manifold pressure, engine r.p.m. (Careful; one's mind doesn't work as clearly at altitude, and each figure's got to go in the right box on the log sheet.) Oil pressure, fuel pressure . . . There goes the rate-of-climb needle!—left rudder; level up wing and nose; watch the turbo speed—these fighters balance on a pinpoint at high altitude. Cylinder head temperatures, base temperatures, carburetor air. The engine's a little rough on the left magneto, ambient; smooth on each mag, pressurized. Pretty good results for the new distributor heads—I might make 43,000 feet today.

All goes well until, tests run and readings logged, I start to descend. Then, at 36,000 feet: something happens to clarity of air, to pulse of life, perception of eye. I grow aware of that vagueness of mind and emptiness of breath which warn a pilot of serious lack of oxygen. I force myself to alertness—I must think or die! The idea lashes brain and body like the bow of a whip. Mask leaking? I shove it up with my left hand—no, tight against my face. Out of oxygen? No. (A glance at the gage shows 50 pounds.) Then something must be wrong with the oxygen system. I know from altitude-chamber experience [1] that I have about 15 seconds of consciousness left at this altitude—neither time nor clearness of mind to check hoses and connections. Life demands oxygen and the only sure supply lies 4 miles beneath me.

I shove the stick forward. The earth slants upward and the dive begins . . . 35,000 feet . . . 34,000 . . . my cockpit roars through the air . . . the earth fades out . . . the instrument dials darken . . . breath's thin; lungs, empty—I'm blacking out—losing sight . . . I push the nose down farther . . . faster . . . 33,000 . . . 30,000 . . . the dials become meaningless . . . down . . . down . . . I am dimly aware of a great shriek, as though a steam whistle were blowing near my ears . . . Compressibility dive? . . . I'm not thinking about compressibility . . . it's oxygen I need . . . I'm blind . . . I can't see the needles . . . there are no more seconds left—it's a razor edge—a race between decreasing consciousness and increasing density of air. . . .

17,000 . . . 16,000 . . . 15,000 . . . a white needle moves over white figures . . . it's the altimeter—I can see—I'm reading its dial again—I'm aware of the cockpit, the plane, the earth and sky—I've already begun to pull out of the dive—the stick is free; the nose, rising; the seat pressing against me.

The air in my lungs has substance. Perception floods through nerve and tissue. How clear the sky is above me, how wonderful the earth

[1] Experiments carried out September-October, 1942, at the Aero Medical Unit, Mayo Clinic, Rochester, Minn., Dr. Walter M. Boothby, Chairman.

below, its villages and farms, its forests, lakes and fields! They seem a part of me, not distant as before. I'm no longer confined to my cockpit, no longer imprisoned by plane or body. I become a part of all things, feeling them, being them, as well as seeing them through my eyes. What more could be desired than the pure joy of existence, the beauty of planet, sun, and space? How could I have been so blinded by instrument dials and figures? How false material values are; how trivial, human problems. Simply to appreciate is more important than any material accomplishment of man.

Returning from the border of death always makes one more aware of life. Relationships take on a higher value and the senses penetrate to new depths with new perspective. I brought life rather than an airplane back to ground. My fighter was only a method of carrying it. The rows of camouflaged bombers and the line of huge brick hangars I taxied past seemed unimportant. The flight report was a ruled sheet of paper to be filled in quickly. The mechanic who told me that my pressure gage read 50 pounds too high carried dull news. Then the oxygen tank had simply run empty at 36,000 feet. That had caused all my trouble—a quarter-inch error of a needle. I felt a sudden revulsion for such details, an impatience with needles, instruments, and readings. What fools men were to impress their minds, enslave their bodies, with figures and machines when life lay everywhere around them, free for the taking, unperceived.

My office was at the opposite end of the factory from the airfield. As I drove back, the great door of an assembly line opened and a four-engined bomber rolled out onto the concrete apron. Behind it, stretching as far as the eye could see, were dozens of uncompleted bombers. A few hours before, I would have viewed this production line as a marvelous feat of engineering. I would have felt proud of even the small part I had taken in bringing it into being. Now, it seemed a terrible giant's womb, growling, clanging, giving birth to robots which were killing people by the thousands each day as they destroyed the culture of Europe. Inside, crawling over jigs and wings like ants, were thousands of men and women, sacrificing sunlit hours, home and family, shop and farm, to serve this hellish monster.

This was a temple of the god of science at which we moderns worshiped. Here was the power, the efficiency, the superhuman magic of which we had dreamed. Only two years before on this same spot, I would have been surrounded by hickories, maples, and oaks. Scientific man could now touch a forest in Michigan with his wand, and by so doing wipe out European cities.

In "temples" such as this, the western world was prostrating itself in peace and war. For what? For material possessions, for speed, for power. Somehow man must be made to see that science was hypnotizing him with its machines, dulling his senses with its knowledge, destroying his culture with its bombs. How blind we were—how time and space misled our eyes! Here I watched a steel door lift and an airplane roll outside; while, in reality, the walls of a cathedral fell and children died.

Why squander life slaving in factories, gathering technical data, building planes to fly faster and higher? Why risk death for a thousand feet of height or ten extra miles an hour? How could we further human progress by striving for such scientific goals when the very concentration on them blinded us to higher values, mocked the brotherhood of man, shielded us from God?

This altitude flight at Willow Run taught me that in worshiping science man gains power but loses the quality of life.

The Enemy Sleep

On a long flight, after periods of crisis and many hours of fatigue, mind and body may become disunited until at times they seem completely different elements, as though the body were only a home with which the mind has been associated but by no means bound. Consciousness grows independent of the ordinary senses. You see without assistance from the eyes, over distances beyond the visual horizon. There are moments when existence appears independent even of the mind. The importance of physical desire and immediate surroundings is submerged in the apprehension of universal values.

For unmeasurable periods, I seem divorced from my body, as though I were an awareness spreading out through space, over the earth and into the heavens, unhampered by time or substance, free from the gravitation that binds men to heavy human problems of the world. My body requires no attention. It's not hungry. It's neither warm nor cold. It's resigned to being left undisturbed. Why have I troubled to bring it here? I might better have left it back at Long Island or St. Louis, while this weightless element that has lived within it flashes through the skies and views the planet. This essential consciousness needs no body for its travels. It needs no plane, no engine, no instruments, only the release from flesh which the circumstances I've gone through make possible.

Then what am I—the body substance which I can see with my eyes and feel with my hands? Or am I this realization, this greater understanding which dwells within it, yet expands through the universe outside; a part of all existence, powerless but without need for power; immersed in solitude, yet in contact with all creation? There are moments when the two appear inseparable, and others when they could be cut apart by the merest flash of light.

While my hand is on the stick, my feet on the rudder, and my eyes on the compass, this consciousness, like a winged messenger, goes out to visit the waves below, testing the warmth of water, the speed of wind, the thickness of intervening clouds. It goes north to the glacial coasts of Greenland, over the horizon to the edge of dawn, ahead to Ireland, England, and the continent of Europe, away through space to the moon and stars, always returning, unwillingly, to the mortal duty of seeing that the limbs and muscles have attended their routine while it was gone.

In a period of physical awakeness between these long excursions, I find the clouds around me covered with a whiter light. In the area of sky where my plane is flying, night is giving way to day. The night—so long—so short—is ending. This is the dawn of Europe, of Paris, of Le Bourget. But how dull appreciation is! Dawn—it's tremendously important. I've waited for it the whole night through. But my senses perceive it only vaguely, separately, indifferently, like pain through too weak an anaesthetic. It is intellectual knowledge, while my normal thoughts and actions are mechanical. In flesh, I'm like an automaton geared to a previously set routine.

The minute hand has just passed 1:00 a.m. It's dawn, one hour after midnight. But it's one hour after midnight only on the clock, and back at the longitude of New York where I set it before take-off in the morning—yesterday morning, it is, now. The clock simply shows the number of hours I've been in the air. It relates only to my cockpit and my plane, not to time outside. It no longer marks the vital incidents of day—dawn, and noon, and sunset. My flight is disconnected from all worldly measures. It passes through different frames of time and space.

With this faint trace of day, the uncontrollable desire to sleep falls over me in quilted layers. I've been staving it off with difficulty during the hours of moonlight. Now it looms all but insurmountable. This is the hour I've been dreading; the hour against which I've tried to steel myself. I know it's the beginning of my greatest test. This will be the worst time of all, this early hour of the second morning—the third morning, it is, since I've slept.

I've lost command of my eyelids. When they start to close, I can't restrain them. They shut, and I shake myself, and lift them with my fingers. I stare at the instruments, wrinkle forehead muscles tense.

Lids close again regardless, stick tight as though with glue. My body has revolted from the rule of its mind. Like salt in wounds, the light of day brings back my pains. Every cell of my being is on strike, sulking in protest, claiming that nothing, nothing in the world, could be worth such effort; that man's tissue was never made for such abuse. My back is stiff; my shoulders ache; my face burns; my eyes smart. It seems impossible to go on longer. All I want in life is to throw myself down flat, stretch out—and sleep.

I've struggled with the dawn often enough before, but never with such a background of fatigue. I've got to muster all my reserves, all the tricks I've learned, all remaining strength of mind, for the conflict. If I can hold in air and close to course for one more hour, the sun will be over the horizon and the battle won. Each ray of light is an ally. With each moment after sunrise, vitality will increase.

Something's wrong on the instrument board—the compass needle —it's strayed ten degrees off course while I was making resolutions to hold it on its mark. I tense my muscles, shake my body, bounce up and down in the cockpit, bring the nose back onto its heading. I can't afford to waste time and fuel like this. Why spend weeks studying navigation and laying out charts precisely, if I'm going to let my plane swing ten degrees off course? I simply *must* keep that compass needle in the center—good God, it's off again. This is like a feverish dream.

I've *got* to find some way to keep alert. There's no alternative but death and failure. *No alternative but death and failure,* I keep repeating, using the thought as a whip on my lagging mind; trying to make my senses realize the importance of what I'm saying. I kick rudder over sharply, skid back into position. But there's no use taking it out on the plane; that's unfair; it's not the plane's fault; it's mine. I try running fast on the floorboards with my feet for as many seconds as the *Spirit of St. Louis* will hold to course. Then, I clamp the stick between my knees while I simulate running with my hands. I push first one wing low and then the other, to blow fresh air through the cockpit and change pressures on my body. I shake my head until it hurts; rub the muscles of my face to regain feeling. I pull the cotton from my ears, fluff it out, and wad it in again. I must keep glancing at the turn-indicator, hold the needle in center with my feet.

I'll set my mind on the sunrise—think about that—watch the clouds brighten—the hands of the clock—count the minutes till it comes. It will be better when the full light of day has broken. It's always better after the sun comes up. As that dazzling ball of fire climbs into the sky, night's unpaid claims will pass. The desire for sleep will give way to waking habits of the day---That's always happened before---

And yet, I'm not sure---It's never been like this before---I never wanted so badly---to sleep---

I'm leaning against my father's side. I hear the clump of horses' hoofs, smell their sweat-damped bodies. Wheels crunch through sand. It's still a long way to our farm. My mother pulls me over, rolls me up in the driving robe, lays me in a hammock formed by the folded carriage hood behind her. Half-turned in the seat, she sings softly:
"A Span-ish cav-a-lier stood in his re-treat,---"
The evening is black; the stars, bright; the carriage rocks on its springs---
"Say, dar-ling, say, when I'm far away,---"
Ah, if I could only sleep like that tonight; if I could only land on one of these clouds, even for a moment, and let its feathery billows cover me up. If I could give way to sleep for five minutes while the plane flew itself! What wouldn't I give for five minutes of sleep? Anything ---except life---

Right rudder—twelve degrees!

My leg is cramped from holding the Ford's clutch in low. Wheels bump, spin, and stop. Water is steaming from the radiator. We step out into the mud—my father, his two friends, and I. Our car is mired to its hubcaps. All evening we've been grinding over wet, rough, and deeply rutted Minnesota roads. In this tamarack swamp the corduroy logs have rotted out.

I climb back into the driver's seat and push down on the clutch pedal, while the three men put shoulders to the car. We gain six inches, no more. We wade into the swamp to gather sticks and brush. One of the men gets a long pole to pry the wheels up while the rest of us fill the ruts beneath them. Twenty feet ahead is more solid ground.

We make it this time. The men scrape their feet on the running boards and climb in, splattered and muddy. We grind through another quarter mile, and get caught in another mire.

About midnight, we reach a crossroad with a house and country store. We've pushed, strained, and lifted until it's painful to move at all. And the nearest town is more than ten miles away, over the same kind of roads. I drive onto a higher bit of ground and switch off the engine. There's dead silence except for swamp cheepers. Our feet are wet, and it's much too cold to sleep in the car. My father makes his way to the dimly outlined porch. No light shows inside the house. My father's knocks are loud and clear. Minutes pass. There are flickers on glass. The door scrapes open. A lantern and legs appear.

It's a small house with only one bed for the storekeeper and his wife.

But we're welcome to sleep on the parlor chairs. Or maybe we'd prefer sleeping in the store. There's plenty of room on the floor there, and we can have two new horse blankets for bedding. We choose the store.

It's hard, the rough plank floor, with only one blanket under us. Sleep is fitful. My father's friends are large men. One kicks, and the other snores. The top blanket, too small to cover four of us, moves constantly back and forth. I'm in between, and warm enough; but my clothes are sticky damp. I doze, and turn, and wake as heavy shoulders crowd against me and press my bones onto the floor - - -

It had seemed a hardship then, when I was thirteen years of age; but what luxury a bed like that would be in this mid-Atlantic dawn! I'd never feel the hardness of the boards, hear a sound, or notice movement, if I could only sleep - - -

Six degrees right rudder!

Girls' voices shrill out through open windows. Wheels splash in water. Our river boat throbs with its engine's beat. I wake, sway forward, lean back against the wall, and doze and wake again. I'm in a group of Field Artillery cadets off on a week-end leave, in the summer of '21. We move slowly up the Ohio. It's still more than an hour to our landing and a bed. If I didn't carry the dignity of a soldier's uniform, I'd lie down on deck and sleep soundly till we get there. All day long, before this excursion started, I was loading our Battery's guns on the range at Camp Knox, hooking up caissons, riding my wheel horse. Now, if I could even sit down, I'd close my eyes and sleep. But every bench is full. So I wake and doze and wake again, propped up against this wall.

I'd thought that was the ultimate in tiredness, to doze standing up against a wall. But how I'd welcome a wall tonight to sleep against! I hadn't appreciated the relaxation one can have, leaning against a wall, the freedom of mind, the security of body. One doesn't need comfort to sleep. Cushions and beds are unimportant. All one needs is the knowledge that one can - - - sleep - - - and - - - live - - -

* * * * *

Strength - - - It's not strength I need tonight in the *Spirit of St. Louis* - - - it's sleep - - - sleep - - - I take off my helmet - - - rub my head - - - pull the helmet on again - - - I drink some water from the canteen - - - that helps. Possibly if I eat a sandwich - - - the grease-spotted bag lies unopened at my side. I've had nothing since breakfast yesterday; but my mouth wants no food, and eating might make me sleepier. Should I have taken along a thermos of coffee? Would that keep me awake? No, I don't want coffee either. It wouldn't do any good. It wouldn't have any effect when I'm feeling like this. Coffee may be all right for school pre-examination nights; but it would be worse than useless here.

If I could get down through the clouds and fly close to the waves, maybe that would help me stay awake. It did yesterday. But there isn't light enough yet. To glide down into those clouds would be like going back into night. Even if there's a ceiling underneath, it would be too dark to fly close to the water --- I'll have to wait another hour at least --- unless the clouds break up --- The crevasses are still black and bottomless ---

There's a great, steep hollow in the mist --- No, not mist --- rock --- hard, reddish yellow walls --- broken, crumbling slopes, cupping a mile-wide crater. See the deep, blue sky above, through which a meteor once hurtled to make this giant pockmark on the earth. My mother, my uncle Charles, and I stand on the blasted rim, near Winslow, Arizona. A hot wind blows dust against our eyes, and whistles through stone crevices. Almost a thousand feet below us lies the brush-spotted desert floor, a group of abandoned mine buildings in its center. Far in the distance, a puff of dust marks another car's struggle with the sands. Beyond that, there's not a sign of life for as far as we can see.

It's late summer of 1916. I'm driving our Saxon car from Little Falls to California. We've been over thirty days on the road, and we've been pushing fairly hard. Weather and mechanical troubles have held us up —a worn-out timer-trigger in Iowa, mud in Missouri (oh, those dismal hotel rooms, where we waited for the roads to dry!), a broken spring-bolt in Kansas, a wheel shimmy that started on the Raton Pass. The list is long; we add new items almost every day, and we still have half a thousand miles to go. My uncle picks up a chunk of brownish rock. I wish we could find a fragment of the meteor --- No, it's not rock --- It's mist --- soft, gray walls --- billowing --- sloping ---

Shaking my body and stamping my feet no longer has effect. It's more fatiguing than arousing. I'll have to try something else. I push the stick forward and dive down into a high ridge of cloud, pulling up sharply after I clip through its summit. That wakes me a little, but tricks don't help for long. They're only tiring. It's better to sit still and conserve strength.

My mind strays from the cockpit and returns. My eyes close, and open, and close again. But I'm beginning to understand vaguely a new factor which has come to my assistance. It seems I'm made up of three personalities, three elements, each partly dependent and partly independent of the others. There's my body, which knows definitely that what it wants most in the world is sleep. There's my mind, constantly making decisions that my body refuses to comply with, but which itself is weakening in resolution. And there's something else, which seems to become stronger instead of weaker with fatigue, an element of spirit, a directive force that has stepped out from the background and taken control over both mind and body. It seems to guard them as a wise father guards his children; letting them venture to the point of danger, then calling them back, guiding with a firm but tolerant hand.

When my body cries out that it *must* sleep, this third element replies that it may get what rest it can from relaxation, but that sleep is not to be had. When my mind demands that my body stay alert and awake, it is informed that alertness is too much to expect under these circumstances. And when it argues excitedly that to sleep would be to fail, and crash, and drown in the ocean, it is calmly reassured, and told it's right, but that while it must not expect alertness on the body's part, it can be confident there'll be no sleep.

My eyes, under their weighted lids, seem completely disconnected from my body, to have within themselves no substance, to be conscious rather than to see. They became a part of this third element, this separate mind which is mine and yet is not, this mind both far away in eternity and within the confines of my skull, within the cockpit and outside of it at the same moment, connected to me and yet unlimited to any finite space.

During long ages between dawn and sunrise, I'm thankful we didn't make the *Spirit of St. Louis* a stable plane. The very instability which makes it difficult to fly blind or hold an accurate course at night now guards me against excessive errors. It's again a case of the plane and me compensating for each other. When I was fresh and it was overloaded, my quickness of reaction held its nose from veering off. Now that I'm dreaming and ridden by sleep, its veering prods my lagging senses. The slightest relaxation of pressure on either stick or rudder starts a climbing or a diving turn, hauling me back from the borderland of sleep. Then, I fix my eyes on the compass and determine again to hold it where it belongs.

There's no use; within a few minutes the needle swings over to one side. No mental determination within my control has more than fleeting value. That third quality has taken over. It knows and holds a limit I can't consciously define, letting my mind and body stay relaxed as long as the *Spirit of St. Louis* flies reasonably straight and level, giving the alarm to both when needles move too fast or far. So far, no farther, the nose can veer off course; so far, no farther, the plane can dive or climb. Then I react from my stupor, level out, kick the rudder back onto the compass heading, shake myself to half awakeness---

and let the needle creep again. I'm asleep and awake at the same moment, living through a reality that is a dream.

The clock's minute hand shows quarter of two. It's almost time for my hourly routine of log and tanks and heading. Previously, I've looked forward to this as welcome diversion, as something to sharpen my senses, to force mental concentration, to bring movement to muscles cramped from the fixed position of long, straightforward flight. Now, the effort seems too much to bear. It's all I can do to rouse my senses sufficiently to pull out the pencil and lay the log sheet on my chart.

THE NINETEENTH HOUR
Over the Atlantic
TIME — 1:52 A.M.

WIND VELOCITY	*Unknown*	VISIBILITY	*Unlimited*
WIND DIRECTION	*Unknown*		*outside of*
TRUE COURSE			*clouds*
VARIATION		ALTITUDE	9000 *feet*
MAGNETIC COURSE		AIR SPEED	87 *m.p.h.*
DEVIATION		TACHOMETER	1625 *r.p.m.*
COMPASS COURSE		OIL TEMPERATURE	35° C.
DRIFT ANGLE		OIL PRESSURE	59 *lbs.*
COMPASS HEADING	96°	FUEL PRESSURE	3 *lbs.*
CEILING	*Unlimited*	MIXTURE	4
	above clouds	FUEL TANK	*Nose*

Eighteen hundred miles behind. Eighteen hundred miles to go. Halfway to Paris. This is a point I planned on celebrating out here over the ocean as one might celebrate a birthday anniversary as a child. I've been looking forward to it for hours. It would be a time to eat a sandwich and take an extra swallow of water from the canteen. But now all this seems unimportant. Food, I definitely don't want. And water—I'm no longer thirsty; why trouble to take another drink? I have as far to go as I've come. I must fly for eighteen endless hours more, and still hold a reserve for weather. Time enough for food and water after the sun rises and I wake; time enough after the torture of dawn is past.

Shall I shift fuel tanks again? I've been running a long time on the fuselage tank. I put another pencil mark on the instrument board to register the eighteenth hour of fuel consumed. That wasn't so difficult; it didn't require any thought—just a straight line, a quarter inch long, one more in those groups of fives. But shall I shift tanks? Let's see;

how did I plan to keep the balance? Oh, yes; it's best not to let the center of gravity move too far forward, so the plane won't dive under the surface in case of a forced landing. I turn on the nose tank, and shut off the flow from the fuselage tank, instinctively.

There's one more thing—the change of course—each hour it has to be done. But what difference do two or three degrees make when I'm letting the nose swing several times that much to one side or the other of my heading? And there are all the unknown errors of the night. Sometime I'll have to figure them out—make an estimate of my position. I should have done it before; I should do it now; but it's beyond my ability and resolution. Let the compass heading go for another hour. I can work it all out then. Let the sunrise come first; with it, new life will spring. My greatest goal now is to stay alive and pointed eastward until I reach the sunrise.

LAURENS VAN DER POST

Now one of the best-known writers about Africa, Laurens van der
Post was born there in 1907 of Dutch parentage. His first language
was Afrikaans, and he knew no English until he was ten. He grew up
on what might be called the South African frontier, where his family
had been pioneers for generations. His adult life had been divided between Africa and England. He was a Commando in World War II,
and altogether spent ten years as a soldier. Since 1949 he has carried
out a number of special missions for the British government, most of
them in exploration of little-known parts of Africa.

The selection from his work that follows is drawn from the book
which made him famous—*Journey to the Interior*. In these opening
pages he tells the story of his remarkable mother, who was the kind
of woman bred on frontiers the world over. She had the courage, as
you will see, to stand alone.

Woman Alone

AFRICA is my mother's country. I do not know exactly how long
my mother's family has lived in Africa; but I do know that Africa
was about and within her from the beginning, as it was for me. Her
mother, my grandmother, was cradled, if not actually born, in an ox-
wagon driving in the thirties of the last century steadfastly deeper into
the unknown interior of Southern Africa. The ox-wagon was part of
the small and ill-fated Liebenberg Trek. My mother's grandfather was
its leader. This little caravan consisting of no more than seven or eight
wagons, this small group of people numbering no more than forty or
fifty souls, had moved in the far forefront of a vast exodus. They
formed part of the great trek of Dutch farmers from British rule at
the Cape.

They had crossed the Karroo safely; hauled their wagons laboriously
through the boulder-strewn drifts of the Orange River; crossed the

wide, melancholy plains of the Free State and forded the deep, yellow Vaal River. They had gone safely across the high veld of the Transvaal, which was plundered bare and still smoked after the raids of Zulu and Matabele, and were moving into the Bushveld, somewhere near where the town of Louis Trichardt stands to-day, when they in their turn were attacked. We shall never know precisely what happened.

My grandmother was little more than a baby; she could just run about and speak. All that is known about the attack is what was gathered afterwards from the incoherent account in broken Afrikaans given by the half-caste maid, who looked after my grandmother and her baby sister.

According to the maid, the wagons, after a long and exhausting trek, had come to rest the night before on the banks of a fairly big stream. During the night the two little children were very restless and had kept their parents awake with their crying. As a result, the maid was ordered just before dawn to dress the children and take them out of earshot of the wagons. One gets a clear impression from this order of how little the sleeping lager suspected what fate had in store for it. The maid had collected the children and had taken them down to the stream, as she had some washing to do.

She had not been there many minutes when the quiet—that lovely, musical, rhythmical quiet of the Bushveld at dawn—was broken with the war-cries and yells of the attacking Kaffirs. She must have walked through a gap in the encircling *impi*[1] just before it drew its horns tight around the sleeping wagons. She snatched the two little girls and, with one under each arm, ran ducking along the side of the stream until she came to a wide, shallow waterfall. The stream fell, as I myself have so often seen them do in Africa, over a wide, overhanging ledge of stone. Behind the water there was a dry hollow, and shelter. The nurse dodged in behind this curtain of water and sat there fearfully all day with her terrified, uncomprehending charges. Late that night she crept out. She found the wagons burnt out and the battered, disfigured bodies of all who had been in them strewn far around.

Somehow, sheltering behind the waterfall by day and going out to forage when it became dark, she kept herself and the children alive. Nearly a week later they were picked up by a party of horsemen, who were wisely patrolling the disturbed country ahead of a much bigger trek following in the Liebenberg tracks.

I have no intention of writing a family history, but this much ap-

[1] "Impi" is the Zulu or Sindabile for an army or regiment. This force usually attacked in a formation shaped like a crescent moon: thin and light at the tips of the horns; deep and solid in the centre. The task of the horns was to spread out and surround the enemy; that of the centre constantly to reinforce its extreme flanks.

peared necessary because it shows, as nothing else can show, how much Africa is my mother's country. Her mother told her the story repeatedly from as early as she could remember; I heard it similarly from her. I heard it over and over again from my aunts, each telling it with their own slight, colourful variations; but, alas, I never heard it from my grandmother, because she died before I was born. I heard it, however, from my grandfather who lived to be nearly a hundred.

And he, too, whatever his ancestral origin, was essentially a part of that same Africa. He also, as a young boy, was involved in the great trek to the north; at the age of fourteen and a half he was carrying a man's rifle on his shoulder and was captured by the redoubtable Sir Harry Smith at the battle of Boomplaas in 1848. He fought in the Kaffir and Basuto wars and helped to clear the Free State hills of their last marauding bushmen.

His own farm was called Boesmans Fontein, the fountain of Bushman. And what a farm it was! I remember, as a child, sitting with him on a hill one Sunday morning, and his pointing out to me how his land stretched as far as we could see in every direction. He had twelve miles of river running through it; a river with a name that suggests an individual and special history of its own: the Knapsack River. His land had long ranges of hills down the centre of it; wide, flower-covered vleis; plains thick with sheep, wild horses, cattle and flickering springbuck.

We were told with an air of implied, delightful and flattering secrecy by my mother that he had bought it all from the Griquas for a couple of barrels of Cape Brandy—red lavender the Griquas called it—and two dozen frock coats and top hats.

My grandfather's house was filled with the strangest, most colourful collection of warm-hearted human relics and harmless scoundrels from Free State's great and vanishing past. When they became too much for his generous but circumspect spirit, they fled to my mother, whom they had known ever since she was born. In defiance of the cold convention already being thrust on the country by self-conscious patriots from the Cape, who had never risked life and limb in war or trek, they never used the formal "mistress" or even the slightly warmer "Nonna" of the Cape Malayas, but insisted on calling her, as her family always did, "The Little Lamb."

There were two little Bushmen, for instance, whom my grandfather had brought back with him from the Commando which went to clean up the bands of Jacob Jaer and Pieter Windvoel, the last of the Bushmen marauders in the Free State. They were tiny little men, extremely highly strung and at the age of sixty still unashamedly terrified of the dark. But they had a fascinating fund of stories that were religion to them, about animals, insects and worms, about spiders, praying mantises and the moon.

There were also the last lingering strains of the Hottentots, with skins like newly strung telephone wires and haunted Nylotic faces. They too told us endless stories about animals, about wolves, jackals, hares and tortoises, about elephants, birds and baboons, but also about beings half-animal, half-human, and stories of witchcraft and magic under the moon.

Again there were serious, rather businesslike Basutos who, under my grandfather's firm hand, carried the real responsibility of working his vast lands. And there were disreputable old Griquas, who knew intuitively that no matter how drunk they became or how often they were jailed for petty theft, they were certain of forgiveness and a sure sustenance, because of my grandfather's conscience. And they knew that they were loved by my mother and her entire family.

There was in particular one old Griqua, Jan Kok, too old for either virtue or sin. He was so old that his age was popularly estimated at anything between one hundred and one hundred twenty years. But no one, least of all he himself, knew for sure. He was a nephew of Adam Kok, the greatest of the Griqua kings, who had in his day concluded treaties with the British Government. He would sit all day long sunning himself in the kitchen courtyard and often he would tell me, in a blurred voice, the strangest things about Africa. He told me, for instance, that one part of the Griqua people—the other part, of course, was European—had come from the far northern interior of Africa, from the other side of mountains which shook and rumbled, sending fire and smoke into the sky.

When his dim old eyes were troubled, he would frequently sing to himself a hymn learnt nearly a hundred years before from the great missionary Dr. Philip, who is hated by so many of my countrymen to this day as though he were still alive. It began: "Lord, how does thy light fall towards the sea," and as he sang I used to think, "Poor old Jan, he has never seen the sea and never will."

After supper in the evenings, all that was human in and about my grandfather's home gathered in the dining-room to listen to him reading from THE BOOK. At those moments there could be seen by the lamplight, lifted attentively to catch some terrible words from the Old Testament, a wrinkled old face of almost every race and colour that had contributed to the history of the country. I have never forgotten the eyes of those Bushmen and Hottentots, on those evenings forty years ago. Those dark eyes that were solemn and glowing with the first light of the world's history; warm and content with the secret of man's earliest days. Some of those races have since vanished for good, and those places that once knew them so well are now only occupied, as though by ghosts, by people of our own colour. And so I could continue for a long time, but these fragments must suffice to suggest how it was at the beginning.

One final word about my mother. At the age of seventy she suddenly distressed her children, grandchildren and her vast circle of friends and acquaintances by refusing, in the most resolute and absolute fashion, to live peacefully, quietly and comfortably in civilized surroundings. Instead, she installed herself, with a European maid, on one of her largest farms which had deteriorated under hired management. It proved too lonely and rough a life for the maid, who soon left. My mother, however, continued for some years alone with her Basuto servants, until the property was completely rehabilitated and once more pleasing to her fastidious eye. Her children then hoped that she would have had enough, and tried to persuade her to come and live in comfort, where they could see and visit her regularly. But she refused, for she had only ended the first stage of another life.

She moved on to an even more remote and backward farm. In due course that too was restored to the semblance of a well-cared-for establishment, and my mother promptly gave it to a son who had just come back from the war in Italy. Then, before the old argument could again be raised by her children, she went even further away.

Many years ago my father had bought a vast tract of land on the edge of the Kalahari Desert. For fifty years no one had made any effort to develop it, and those broad acres were left there, lying parched and unwanted in the desert sun. There my mother went at the age of eighty. The only people who seemed willing to accompany her were displaced persons; there was a German geologist who had been interned during the war; a delicate Bavarian missionary, whom she made her secretary; and an Italian carpenter and mason, and ex-prisoner of war, who became her foreman.

A hundred miles from the nearest village, they pitched their tents and started looking for water, without which no permanent settlement was possible. At first they hired from private contractors the machines to drill for the water. The German geologist's knowledge of his science and my mother's intuitive assessment between them determined where the drilling should take place. The first contractor drilled down to 150 feet, struck iron stone—or so he said—and refused to continue.

There was a terrible scene out there in the desert between the determined old lady who refused to change the site of the contractor's task, for she was convinced that water was there, and the cynical technician whose profits, if any, decreased the deeper he drilled. In the end the contractor departed.

A second contractor, drilling a few feet away from the first hole, after going down 147 feet, lost all his tackle in the shaft and moved away in dusgust. A third contractor, drilling still in the same narrow area, found after 153 feet that he had sunk his shaft at an angle, and could not continue. He too went, bitter and deeply out-of-pocket. By this time no new contractor could be tempted to try his fortune at this notorious site. There was nothing for it but for my mother to buy her own drilling machine. The aged geologist was apprenticed for some months to one of the few remaining unestranged drilling contractors in the area, in order to acquire this new craft; then drilling was resumed in earnest.

Nearly three years had gone by out there in the Kalahari Desert, with the burning suns of its summer, and the searing, cold winds of its winter. One of the worst droughts in memory, bringing great storms of dust and sand, broke over them. But the party continued confidently.

Every morning at six my mother rang a hand-bell and handed her employees steaming bowls of coffee that she had made herself. "Men are like that," she says, "they are like children who will get out of bed for food if for nothing else."

Having thus enticed them out of bed, she set them drilling. At 157 feet, only four feet deeper than the deepest shaft sunk by a contractor, they struck water.

"It was most dramatic," my mother said. "I was watching the machine at that moment quite by chance"—of course, her eyes never left it—"when suddenly I saw it lurch slightly. All the slack in the rope of the drill disappeared. The bore was through the stone and in a deep vein of water. It came gushing up the shaft."

So sure had she been all along that water would be found that the pumps were there waiting; they had been waiting for three years ready to go up the moment that water was found.

There my mother is to this day, a slim, lovely, upright, gracious old lady, whose skin looks as if it has never known anything but a European sun. She is still active, vigorous, young in spirit and convinced that she will live to be a hundred and twenty. She builds, plants trees and orchards, and grows corn in a desert where neither corn nor grass grew before.

We, her children, have all been bitterly reproached by close friends and well-meaning relations for letting her live in this way. Frankly I have not even the excuse that the others have, for they have done their best to dissuade her, whereas I have actively and whole-heartedly encouraged her. She seems to me happier now than she has ever been, in spite of the difficulties, anxieties and extreme discomforts of this new way of life.

It has often occurred to me that the heavy burden of bearing and rearing children—and my mother reared thirteen—has, in a sense, been irrelevant to the deepest and most vital purpose of her life. I have never been able to believe that a woman's task in life is limited to her children. I can quite well conceive that in my mother, as with more and more women of our own day, there is an urge to creativeness which lies underneath and deeper, above and beyond the begetting of children. These women have a contract with life itself, which is not discharged by the mere procreation of their species. Men recognize and try to honour this contract in themselves as a matter of course. Their contribution to life vibrates with their passionate rebellion against the narrowly conceived idea that would restrict their role to that of protectors and feeders of women and children. They do not acknowledge and respect the same thing so readily in women. Perhaps until they do the world will not see the full creative relationship that life intends there should be between men and women.

As far as my mother is concerned, I was moved and reassured by this development so late in her life. For me her story is a source of unfailing confidence in the future. After many years in which the need to create must have been consciously forgotten, overlaid by a thousand anxieties of birth and death, war and peace, when it should, by all the dictates of reason, have vanished for good, then suddenly as an old lady my mother was able to turn round and find the same urge close beside her, throwing, in the gathering darkness round her feet, the clear, familiar light she had known as a child. For this it is that Mother has done and I would like it to be told as a memorial of her. After sixty uninterrupted years as a wife and a mother she turned confidently to the authentic and original vision of her life, and was at once enabled to pursue the dream of her African girlhood.

ANTOINE DE SAINT-EXUPÉRY

On July 21, 1944, Antoine de Saint-Exupéry (1900–1944), distinguished
flier and philosophic spokesman for Western Europe, was reported
missing in action. He had by that time, and for several years past, been
well known as a writer in the United States. He was a yea-sayer, unlike some of his countrymen who have followed him (I refer to Sartre
& Co.), and a passionate believer in the dignity of man. Though he
published no poetry, his prose writing sometimes rose to poetic heights.
Action and meditation were fused in him; both were essential to his
vision of what life should be.

His contribution to this book is taken from *Wind, Sand and Stars,*
the first volume in a kind of trilogy now published as *Airman's Odyssey,* of which the second part and third parts are *Night Flight* and
Flight to Arras. The passage I have chosen does not describe an experience of his own; it is the story of a comrade in arms, the pilot
Guillaumet, and was written in homage to him. It concerns Guillaumet's flight over the Andes, and what happened to him when he
crashed. It is a story to take heart from.

Crash Over the Andes

IT WAS winter and you had been gone a week over the Andes. I
had come up from farthest Patagonia to join Deley at Mendoza.
For five days the two of us, each in his plane, had ransacked the
mountains unavailingly. Two ships! It seemed to us that a hundred
squadrons navigating for a hundred years would not have been enough
to explore the endless, cloud-piercing range. We had lost all hope. The
very smugglers themselves, bandits who would commit a crime for a
five-peso note, refused to form a rescue party out of fear of those
counterforts. "We should surely die," they said; "the Andes never give
up a man in winter."

And when Deley and I landed at Santiago, the Chilean officers also advised us to give you up. "It is midwinter," they said; "even if your comrade survived the landing, he cannot have survived the night. Night in those passes changes a man into ice."

And when, a second time, I slipped between the towering walls and giant pillars of the Andes, it seemed to me I was no longer seeking, but was now sitting up with, your body in the silence of a cathedral of snow.

You had been gone a week, I say, and I was lunching between flights in a restaurant in Mendoza when a man stuck his head in the door and called out:

"They've found Guillaumet!"

All the strangers in the restaurant embraced.

Ten minutes later I was off the ground, carrying two mechanics, Lefebvre and Abri. Forty minutes later I had landed alongside a road, having recognized from the air, I know not by what sign, the car in which you were being brought down from San Rafael. I remember that we cried like fools; we put our arms about a living Guillaumet, resuscitated, the author of his own miracle. And it was at that moment that you pronounced your first intelligible sentence, a speech admirable in its human pride:

"I swear that what I went through, no animal would have gone through."

Later, you told us the story. A storm that brought fifteen feet of snow in forty-eight hours down on the Chilean slope had bottled up all space and sent every other mail pilot back to his starting point. You, however, had taken off in the hope of finding a rift in the sky. You found this rift, this trap, a little to the south, and now, at twenty thousand feet, the ceiling of clouds being a couple of thousand feet below you and pierced by only the highest peaks, you set your course for Argentina.

Down currents sometimes fill pilots with a strange uneasiness. The engines run on, but the ship seems to be sinking. You jockey to hold your altitude: the ship loses speed and goes mushy. And still you sink. So you give it up, afraid that you may have jockeyed too much; and you let yourself drift to right or left, striving to put at your back a favorable peak, that is, a peak off which the winds rebound as off a springboard.

And yet you go on sinking. The whole sky seems to be coming down on you. You begin to feel like the victim of some cosmic accident. You cannot land anywhere, and you try in vain to turn round and fly back into those zones where the air, as dense and solid as a pillar, had held you up. That pillar has melted away. Everything here is rotten and you slither about in a sort of universal decomposition while the cloud-bank rises apathetically, reaches your level, and swallows you up.

"It almost had me in a corner once," you explained, "but I still wasn't sure I was caught. When you get up above the clouds you run into those down currents that seem to be perfectly stationary for the simple reason that in that very high altitude they never stop flowing. Everything is queer in the upper range."

And what clouds!

"As soon as I felt I was caught I dropped the controls and grabbed my seat for fear of being flung out of the ship. The jolts were so terrible that my leather harness cut my shoulders and was ready to snap. And what with the frosting on the panes, my artificial horizon was invisible and the wind rolled me over and over like a hat in a road from eighteen thousand feet down to ten.

"At ten thousand I caught a glimpse of a dark horizontal blot that helped me right the ship. It was a lake, and I recognized it as what they call Laguna Diamante. I remembered that it lay at the bottom of a funnel, and that one flank of the funnel, a volcano called Maipu, ran up to about twenty thousand feet.

"There I was, safe out of the clouds; but I was still blinded by the thick whirling snow and I had to hang on to my lake if I wasn't to crash into one of the sides of the funnel. So down I went, and I flew round and round the lake, about a hundred and fifty feet above it, until I ran out of fuel. After two hours of this, I set the ship down on the snow—and over on her nose she went.

"When I dragged myself clear of her I stood up. The wind knocked me down. I stood up again. Over I went a second time. So I crawled under the cockpit and dug me out a shelter in the snow. I pulled a lot of mail sacks round me, and there I lay for two days and two nights. Then the storm blew over and I started to walk my way out. I walked for five days and four nights."

But what was there left of you, Guillaumet? We had found you again, true; but burnt to a crisp, but shriveled, but shrunken into an old woman. That same afternoon I flew you back to Mendoza, and there the cool white sheets flowed like a balm down the length of your body.

They were not enough, though. Your own foundered body was an encumbrance: you turned and twisted in your sleep, unable to find lodgment for it. I stared at your face: it was splotched and swollen, like an overripe fruit that has been repeatedly dropped on the ground.

You were dreadful to see, and you were in misery, for you had lost the beautiful tools of your works: your hands were numb and useless, and when you sat up on the edge of your bed to draw a free breath, your frozen feet hung down like two dead weights. You had not even finished your long walk back, you were still panting; and when you turned and stirred on the pillow in search of peace, a procession of images that you could not escape, a procession waiting impatiently in the wings, moved instantly into action under your skull. Across the stage of your skull it moved, and for the twentieth time you fought once more the battle against these enemies that rose up out of their ashes.

I filled you with herb-teas.

"Drink, old fellow."

"You know ... what amazed me ..."

Boxer victorious, but punch-drunk and scarred with blows, you were re-living your strange adventure. You could divest yourself of it only in scraps. And as you told your dark tale, I could see you trudging without ice-axe, without ropes, without provisions, scaling cols fifteen thousand feet in the air, crawling on the faces of vertical walls, your hands and feet and knees bleeding in a temperature twenty degrees below zero.

Voided bit by bit of your blood, your strength, your reason, you went forward with the obstinacy of an ant, retracing your steps to go round an obstacle, picking yourself up after each fall to earth, climbing slopes that led to abysses, ceaselessly in motion and never asleep, for had you slept, from that bed of snow you would never have risen. When your foot slipped and you went down, you were up again in an instant, else had you been turned into stone. The cold was petrifying you by the minute, and the price you paid for taking a moment too much of rest, when you fell, was the agony of revivifying dead muscles in your struggle to rise to your feet.

You resisted temptation. "Amid snow," you told me, "a man loses his instinct of self-preservation. After two or three or four days of tramping, all you think about is sleep. I would long for it; but then I would say to myself, 'If my wife still believes I am alive, she must believe that I am on my feet. The boys all think I am on my feet. They have faith in me. And I am a skunk if I don't go on.'"

So you tramped on; and each day you cut out a bit more of the opening of your shoes so that your swelling and freezing feet might have room in them.

You confided to me this strange thing:

"As early as the second day, you know, the hardest job I had was to force myself not to think. The pain was too much, and I was really up against it too hard. I had to forget that, or I shouldn't have had the heart to go on walking. But I didn't seem able to control my mind. It kept working like a turbine. Still, I could more or less choose what

I was to think about. I tried to stick to some film I'd seen, or book I'd read. But the film and the book would go through my mind like lightning, and I'd be back where I was, in the snow. It never failed. So I would think about other things...."

There was one time, however, when, having slipped, and finding yourself stretched flat on your face in the snow, you threw in your hand. You were like a boxer emptied of all passion by a single blow, lying and listening to the second drop one by one into a distant universe, until the tenth second fell and there was no appeal.

"I've done my best and I can't make it. Why go on?" All that you had to do in the world to find peace was to shut your eyes. So little was needed to blot out that world of crags and ice and snow. Let drop those miraculous eyelids and there was an end of blows, of stumbling falls, of torn muscles and burning ice, of that burden of life you were dragging along like a worn-out ox, a weight heavier than any wain or cart.

Already you were beginning to taste the relief of this snow that had now become an insidious poison, this morphia that was filling you with beatitude. Life crept out of your extremities and fled to collect round your heart while something gentle and precious snuggled in close at the centre of your being. Little by little your consciousness deserted the distant regions of your body, and your body, the beast now gorged with suffering, lay ready to participate in the indifference of marble.

Your very scruples subsided. Our cries ceased to reach you, or, more accurately, changed for you into dream-cries. You were happy now, able to respond by long confident dream-strides that carried you effortlessly towards the enchantment of the plains below. How smoothly you glided into this suddenly merciful world! Guillaumet, you miser! You had made up your mind to deny us your return, to take your pleasures selfishly without us among your white angels in the snows. And then remorse floated up from the depth of your consciousness. The dream was spoilt by the irruption of bothersome details. "I thought of my wife. She would be penniless if she couldn't collect the insurance. Yes, but the company..."

When a man vanishes, his legal death is postponed for four years. This awful detail was enough to blot out the other visions. You were lying face downward on a bed of snow that covered a steep mountain slope. With the coming of summer your body would be washed with this slush down into one of the thousand crevasses of the Andes. You knew that. But you also knew that some fifty yards away a rock was jutting up out of the snow. "I thought, if I get up I may be able to reach it. And if I can prop myself up against the rock, they'll find me there next summer."

Once you were on your feet again, you tramped two nights and three days. But you did not then imagine that you would go on much longer:

"I could tell by different signs that the end was coming. For instance, I had to stop every two or three hours to cut my shoes open a bit more and massage my swollen feet. Or maybe my heart would be going too fast. But I was beginning to lose my memory. I had been going on a long time when suddenly I realized that every time I stopped I forgot something. The first time it was a glove. And it was cold! I had put it down in front of me and had forgotten to pick it up. The next time it was my watch. Then my knife. Then my compass. Each time I stopped I stripped myself of something vitally important. I was becoming my own enemy! And I can't tell you how it hurt me when I found that out.

"What saves a man is to take a step. Then another step. It is always the same step, but you have to take it."

"I swear that what I went through, no animal would have gone through." This sentence, the noblest ever spoken, this sentence that defines man's place in the universe, that honors him, that re-establishes the true hierarchy, floated back into my thoughts. Finally you fell asleep. Your consciousness was abolished; but forth from this dismantled, burnt, and shattered body it was to be born again like a flower put forth gradually by the species which itself is born of the luminous pulp of the stars. The body, we may say, then, is but an honest tool, the body is but a servant. And it was in these words, Guillaumet, that you expressed your pride in the honest tool:

"With nothing to eat, after three days on my feet...well...my heart wasn't going any too well. I was crawling along the side of a sheer wall, hanging over space, digging and kicking out pockets in the ice so that I could hold on, when all of a sudden my heart conked. It hesitated. Started up again. Beat crazily. I said to myself, 'If it hesitates a moment too long, I drop.' I stayed still and listened to myself. Never, never in my life have I listened as carefully to a motor as I listened to my heart, me hanging there. I said to it: 'Come on, old boy. Go to work. Try beating a little.' That's good stuff my heart is made of. It hesitated, but it went on. You don't know how proud I was of that heart."

As I said, in that room in Mendoza where I sat with you, you fell finally into an exhausted sleep. And I thought: If we were to talk to him about his courage, Guillaumet would shrug his shoulders. But it

would be just as false to extol his modesty. His place is far beyond
that mediocre virtue.

If he shrugs his shoulders, it is because he is no fool. He knows that
once men are caught up in an event they cease to be afraid. Only the
unknown frightens men. But once a man has faced the unknown, that
terror becomes the known.

Especially if it is scrutinized with Guillaumet's lucid gravity. Guillaumet's courage is in the main the product of his honesty. But even
this is not his fundamental quality. His moral greatness consists in his
sense of responsibility. He knew that he was responsible for himself,
for the mails, for the fulfilment of the hopes of his comrades. He was
holding in his hands their sorrow and their joy. He was responsible
for that new element which the living were constructing and in which
he was a participant. Responsible, in as much as his work contributed
to it, for the fate of those men.

Guillaumet was one among those bold and generous men who had
taken upon themselves the task of spreading their foliage over bold
and generous horizons. To be a man is, precisely, to be responsible. It
is to feel shame at the sight of what seems to be unmerited misery. It is
to take pride in a victory won by one's comrades. It is to feel, when
setting one's stone, that one is contributing to the building of the
world.

There is a tendency to class such men with toreadors and gamblers.
People extol their contempt for death. But I would not give a fig for
anybody's contempt for death. If its roots are not sunk deep in an acceptance of responsibility, this contempt for death is the sign either of
an impoverished soul or of youthful extravagance.

I once knew a young suicide. I cannot remember what disappointment in love it was which induced him to send a bullet carefully into
his heart. I have no notion what literary temptation he had succumbed
to when he drew on a pair of white gloves before the shot. But I remember having felt, on learning of this sorry show, an impression not
of nobility but of lack of dignity. So! Behind that attractive face,
beneath that skull which should have been a treasure chest, there had
been nothing, nothing at all. Unless it was the vision of some silly little
girl indistinguishable from the rest.

And when I heard of this meagre destiny, I remembered the death
of a man. He was a gardener, and he was speaking on his deathbed:
"You know, I used to sweat sometimes when I was digging. My
rheumatism would pull at my leg, and I would damn myself for a
slave. And now, do you know, I'd like to spade and spade. It's beautiful
work. A man is free when he is using a spade. And besides, who is
going to prune my trees when I am gone?"

That man was leaving behind him a fallow field, a fallow planet. He was bound by ties of love to all cultivable land and to all the trees of the earth. There was a generous man, a prodigal man, a nobleman! There was a man who, battling against death in the name of his Creation, could like Guillaumet be called a man of courage!

ARTHUR D. DIVINE

Arthur Divine might be called a British-American. Born in Capetown in 1904, he traveled widely after World War I, settled down in England, and got into World War II as one of the volunteer yachtsmen who took their small boats over to Dunkirk for the evacuation, in the course of which he was seriously wounded. Barred from the armed services because of his wounds, he became a war correspondent, landed with our First Division in North Africa, stayed ashore and joined up with an American tank-destroyer battalion which was our first unit to make contact with the Germans, went back to sea after Tunis, went ashore again during the preliminary bombardment on D-Day, then served at sea with American destroyers in the Cherbourg action. After that he shifted to the Pacific theater, joined the U.S.S. *Lexington* at Ulithi, was at Iwo Jima with the U.S.S. *Tennessee,* and landed in Tokyo Bay with the United States Marines.

He now lives in England, but is tempted to take up residence in the United States. What follows is his eyewitness account of the Dunkirk miracle, for his part in which he received the British Distinguished Service Medal. It is a piece of first-rate reporting and vividly records one of the most heroic episodes in military history. Under the pseudonym of David Rame, he has written thrillers and books for boys, and has published one serious novel, *Wine of Good Hope.*

Dunkirk

I AM STILL amazed about the whole Dunkirk affair. There was from first to last a queer, medieval sense of miracle about it. You remember the old quotation about the miracle that crushed the Spanish Armada, "God sent a wind." This time "God withheld the wind." Had we had one onshore breeze of any strength at all, in the first days, we would have lost a hundred thousand men.

The pier at Dunkirk was the unceasing target of bombs and shellfire throughout, yet it never was hit. Two hundred and fifty thousand men embarked from that pier. Had it been blasted ...

The whole thing from first to last was covered with that same strange feeling of something supernatural. We muddled, we quarreled, everybody swore and was bad-tempered and made the wildest accusations of inefficiency and worse in high places. Boats were badly handled and broke down, arrangements went wrong.

And yet out of all that mess we beat the experts, we defied the law and the prophets, and where the Government and the Board of Admiralty had hoped to bring away 30,000 men, we brought away 335,000. If that was not a miracle, there are no miracles left.

When I heard that small boats of all sorts were to be used at Dunkirk, I volunteered at once, having no vast opinion of the navy as small-boat handlers. I had been playing with the navy off and on since the beginning of the year, mine sweeping and submarine hunting, convoying, and so on. So friends of mine at the Admiralty passed me through without formalities, and within two hours of my first telephone call I was on my way to Sheerness. From Sheerness I acted as navigator for a party of small boats round to Ramsgate, and at Ramsgate we started work. The evacuation went on for something over a week, but to me the most exciting time was the night before the last.

I was given a motorboat about as long as my drawing room at home, 30 feet. She had one cabin forward and the rest was open, but she had twin engines and was fairly fast. For crew we had one sub-lieutenant, one stoker and one gunner. For armament we had two Bren guns— one my own particular pet which I had stolen—and rifles. In command of our boat we had a real live Admiral—Taylor, Admiral in charge of small boats.

We first went out to French fishing boats gathered off Ramsgate, boats from Caen and Le Havre, bright little vessels with lovely names —*Ciel de France, Ave Maria, Gratia Plena, Jeanne Antoine.* They had helped at Calais and Boulogne and in the preceding days at Dunkirk, and the men were very tired, but when we passed them new orders they set out again for Dunkirk.

They went as the leaders of the procession, for they were slow. With them went a handful of Dutch *schouts,* stumpy little coasting vessels commandeered at the collapse of Holland, each flying the white ensign of the Royal Navy, sparkling new, and each fitted out with a Lewis gun. Next went coasters, colliers, paddle steamers that in time of peace had taken trippers around the harbor for a shilling, tugs towing mud scows with brave names like *Galleon's Reach* and *Queen's Channel.*

There was a car ferry, surely on its first trip in the open sea. There were yachts; one the *Skylark*—what a name for such a mission! There were dockyard tugs, towing barges. There were sloops, mine sweepers, trawlers, destroyers. There were Thames fire floats, Belgian drifters, lifeboats from all around the coast, lifeboats from sunken ships. I saw the boats of the old *Dunbar Castle,* sunk eight months before. Rolling and pitching in a cloud of spray were open speedboats, wholly unsuited for the Channel chop.

There was the old *Brighton Belle* that carried holiday crowds in the days before the Boer War. She swept mines in the Great War, and she swept mines in this war through all the fury of last winter. I know; I sailed with her then. Coming back from her second trip to Dunkirk, she struck the wreck of a ship sunk by a magnetic mine and slowly sank. Her captain, a Conservative party agent in civil life, got 400 men safely off and at the last even saved his dog.

There was never such a fleet went to war before, I think. As I went round the western arm of the harbor near sunset, passing out orders, it brought my heart into my throat to watch them leave. They were so small! Little boats like those you see in the bight of Sandy Hook fishing on a fine afternoon. Some were frowsy, with old motorcar tires for fenders, and some of them were bright with paint and chromium— little white boats that were soon lost to view across the ruffled water. And as they went there came round from the foreland a line of fishing boats—shrimp catchers and what not, from the east coast—to join the parade.

When this armada of oddments was under way, we followed with the faster boats—Royal Air Force rescue launches, picket boats and the like—and with us went an X-lighter, a flatboat, kerosene-powered built for landing troops at Gallipoli and a veteran of *that* evacuation more than 20 years ago.

It was the queerest, most nondescript flotilla that ever was, and it was manned by every kind of Englishman, never more than two men, often only one, to each small boat. There were bankers and dentists, taxi drivers and yachtsmen, longshoremen, boys, engineers, fishermen and civil servants. There were bright-faced Sea Scouts and old men whose skin looked fiery red against their white hair. Many were poor; they had no coats, but made out with old jerseys and sweaters. They wore cracked rubber boots. They were wet, chilled to the bone, hungry; they were unarmed and unprotected, and they sailed toward the pillars of smoke and fire and the thunder of the guns, into waters already slick with the oil of sunken boats, knowing perfectly well the special kind of hell ahead. Still, they went, plugging gamely along.

I had a feeling, then and after, that this was something bigger than organization, something bigger than the mere requisitioning of boats.

In a sense it was the naval spirit that has always been the foundation of England's greatness, flowering again and flowering superbly. I believe 887 was the official figure for the total of boats that took part over the ten days of the evacuation. But I think there were more than a thousand craft in all. I myself know of fishermen who never registered, waited for no orders, but, all unofficial, went and brought back soldiers. Quietly, like that.

It was dark before we were well clear of the English coast. It wasn't rough, but there was a little chop, sufficient to make it very wet, and we soaked the Admiral to the skin. Soon, in the dark, the big boats began to overtake us. We were in a sort of dark traffic lane, full of strange ghosts and weird, unaccountable waves from the wash of the larger vessels. When destroyers went by, full tilt, the wash was a serious matter to us little fellows. We could only spin the wheel to try to head into the waves, hang on, and hope for the best.

Mere navigation was dangerous in the dark. Clouds hung low and blotted out the stars. We carried no lights, we had no signals, no means of recognition of friend or foe. Before we were halfway across we began to meet the first of the returning stream. We dodged white, glimmering bow waves of vessels that had passed astern, only to fall into the way of half-seen shapes ahead. There were shouts in the darkness, but only occasionally the indignant stutter of a horn. We went "by guess and by God."

From the halfway mark, too, there were destroyers on patrol crossing our line of passage, weaving a fantastic warp of foam through the web of our progress. There were collisions, of course. Dover for days was full of destroyers with bows stove in, coasting vessels with great gashes amidships, ships battered, scraped and scarred. The miracle is that there were not ten for every one that happened.

Even before it was fully dark we had picked up the glow of the Dunkirk flames, and now as we drew nearer the sailing got better, for we could steer by them and see silhouetted the shapes of other ships, of boats coming home already loaded, and of low dark shadows that might be the enemy motor torpedo boats.

Then aircraft started dropping parachute flares. We saw them hanging all about us in the night, like young moons. The sound of the firing and the bombing was with us always, growing steadily louder as we got nearer and nearer. The flames grew, too. From a glow they rose up to enormous plumes of fire that roared high into the everlasting pall of smoke. As we approached Dunkirk there was an air attack on the destroyers and for a little the night was brilliant with bursting bombs and the fountain sprays of tracer bullets.

The beach, black with men, illumined by the fires, seemed a perfect target, but no doubt the thick clouds of smoke were a useful screen.

When we got to the neighborhood of the mole there was a lull. The aircraft had dispersed and apparently had done no damage, for there was nothing sinking. They had been there before, however, and the place was a shambles of old wrecks, British and French, and all kinds of odds and ends. The breakwaters and lighthouse were magnificently silhouetted against the flames of burning oil tanks—enormous flames that licked high above the town. Further inshore and to the east of the docks the town itself was burning furiously, but down near the beach where we were going there was no fire and we could see rows of houses standing silent and apparently empty.

We had just got to the eastward of the pier when shelling started up. There was one battery of 5.9's down between La Panne and Nieuport that our people simply could not find and its shooting was uncannily accurate. Our place was in the corner of the beach at the mole and as they were shelling the mole, the firing was right over our heads. Nothing, however, came near us in the first spell.

The picture will always remain sharp-etched in my memory—the lines of men wearily and sleepily staggering across the beach from the dunes to the shallows, falling into little boats, great columns of men thrust out into the water among bomb and shell splashes. The foremost ranks were shoulder deep, moving forward under the command of young subalterns, themselves with their heads just above the little waves that rode in to the sand. As the front ranks were dragged aboard the boats, the rear ranks moved up, from ankle deep to knee deep, from knee deep to waist deep, until they, too, came to shoulder depth and their turn.

Some of the big boats pushed in until they were almost aground, taking appalling risks with the falling tide. The men scrambled up the sides on rope nets, or climbed hundreds of ladders, made God knows where out of new, raw wood and hurried aboard the ships in England.

The little boats that ferried from the beach to the big ships in deep water listed drunkenly with the weight of men. The big ships slowly took on lists of their own with the enormous numbers crowded aboard. And always down the dunes and across the beach came new hordes of men, new columns, new lines.

On the beach was a destroyer, bombed and burned. At the water's edge were ambulances, abandoned when their last load had been discharged.

There was always the red background, the red of Dunkirk burning. There was no water to check the fires and there were no men to be spared to fight them. Red, too, were the shell bursts, the flash of guns, the fountains of tracer bullets.

The din was infernal. The 5.9 batteries shelled ceaselessly and brilliantly. To the whistle of shells overhead was added the scream of falling bombs. Even the sky was full of noise—anti-aircraft shells, machine-gun fire, the snarl of falling planes, the angry hornet noise of dive bombers. One could not speak normally at any time against the roar of it and the noise of our own engines. We all developed "Dunkirk throat," a sore hoarseness that was the hallmark of those who had been there.

Yet through all the noise I will always remember the voices of the young subalterns as they sent their men aboard, and I will remember, too, the astonishing discipline of the men. They had fought through three weeks of retreat, always falling back, often without orders, often without support. Transports had failed. They had gone sleepless. They had been without food and water. Yet they kept ranks as they came down the beaches, and they obeyed commands.

Veterans of Gallipoli and of Mons agreed this was the hottest spot they had ever been in, yet morale held. I was told stories of French troops that rushed the boats at first so that stern measures had to be taken, but I saw nothing like that. The Frenchmen I brought off were of the rear guard, fine soldiers, still fighting fit.

Having the Admiral on board, we were not actually working the beaches but were in control of operations. We moved about as necessary, and after we had spent some time putting small boats in touch with their towing boats, the 5.9 battery off Nieuport way began to drop shells on us. It seemed pure spite. The nearest salvo was about 20 yards astern, which was close enough.

We stayed there until everybody else had been sent back, and then went pottering about looking for stragglers. While we were doing that, a salvo of shells got one of our troopships alongside the mole. She was hit clean in the boilers and exploded in one terrific crash. There were then, I suppose, about 1,000 Frenchmen on the mole. We had seen them crowding along its narrow crest, outlined against the flames. They had gone out under shellfire to board the boat, and now they had to go back again, still being shelled. It was quite the most tragic thing I ever have seen in my life. We could do nothing with our little park dinghy.

While they were still filing back to the beach and the dawn was breaking with uncomfortable brilliance, we found one of our stragglers —a navy whaler. We told her people to come aboard, but they said that there was a motorboat aground and they would have to fetch off her crew. They went in, and we waited. It was my longest wait, ever. For various reasons they were terribly slow. When they found the captain of the motorboat, they stood and argued with him and he wouldn't come off anyway. Damned plucky chap. He and his men lay quiet until the tide floated them later in the day. Then they made a dash for it, and got away.

We waited for them until the sun was up before we got clear of the mole. By then, the fighting was heavy inshore, on the outskirts of the town, and actually in some of the streets.

Going home, the Jerry dive bombers came over us five times, but somehow left us alone though three times they took up an attacking position. A little down the coast, towards Gravelines, we picked up a boatload of Frenchmen rowing off. We took them aboard. They were very much bothered as to where our "ship" was, said quite flatly that it was impossible to go to England in a thing like ours. Too, too horribly dangerous!

One of the rare touches of comedy at Dunkirk was the fear of the sea among French poilus from inland towns. They were desperately afraid to forfeit solid land for the unknown perils of a little boat. When, on the last nights of the evacuation, the little boats got to the mole many refused to jump in, despite the hell of shells and bombs behind them. I saw young sublieutants grab poilus by the collar and the seat of the pants and rush them overside into waiting launches.

There was comedy of a sort, too, in the misadventures of the boats. The yachting season hadn't begun and most of the pleasure boats had been at their winter moorings when the call came; their engines had not been serviced and they broke down in the awkwardest places. The water supply at Dunkirk had been bombed out of use in the first days, and the navy ferried water across to keep the troops alive. Some of the water went in proper water cans, but most of it was put into two-gallon gasoline tins. *Of course* some of these tins got into the gasoline dumps, with lamentable results. I ran out of gasoline myself in the angle between Dunkirk mole and the beach, with heavy shelling going on and an Admiral on board. He never even said "damn." But we were lucky. A *schout* with spare fuel was lying a mile or so from the beach, near a buoy. I got to her with my last drop of reserve.

Then, for grim humor, there is the tale of the young sublieutenant, no more than a boy, whom I saw from time to time on one side of the Channel or the other. He was sent in the early days of the show to the beach east of Gravelines, where he was told there was a pocket of English troops cut off. He landed at the beach with only a revolver and walked off into the sand dunes to hunt for them. In the darkness he suddenly saw two faint shapes moving, and called out, "Here we are, boys, come to take you off."

There was silence, and then a guttural, *"Lieber Gott!"*

"So," the boy told me, "I shot them and came away."

He had walked right into the German army.

One of the greatest surprises of the whole operation was the failure of the German E-boats—motor torpedo boats. We crossed by a path that was well lit by light buoys, spread clean across from Goodwins to Dunkirk Roads. Well-handled E-boats could have got among us in the dark and played havoc—either in the Channel or in Dunkirk Roads.

I had stopped once off one of the light buoys when a division of destroyers passed me. They could see me only as a small dark shape on the water, if at all, and had I had torpedoes I could have picked off the leaders. I might have been a German motorboat, and if the German navy had any real fighting spirit I ought to have been a German motorboat. They did send a few boats in, and I believe they claimed one of our destroyers somewhere off La Panne, but they never pressed the attack home, never came in force against our motley armada off the beaches. The German navy lost a great chance.

Germany, in fact, failed in three ways at Dunkirk. Against a routed army she failed on land to drive home her advantage, though she had strategic and numerical superiority. She failed in the air, though with half a million men narrowed into one small semi-circle, she should have been able—if air power ever could be decisive—to secure decisive victory. And at sea, her motorboats were so lamentably handled that we almost disregarded them. For long hours on end we were sheep for the slaughtering, but we got back to Ramsgate safely each time. There we watched the debarkations, two and three hundred men from each of the larger boats marching in an endless brown stream down the narrow curve of the east harbor wall. Among each load would be five or six wounded. The hospital ships went in to Dover; at Ramsgate we saw mainly the pitiful survivors of ships bombed on the way over —men with their skin flayed by oil burns, torn by bomb splinters, or wounded by machine-gun fire from the air. Most of them were un-bandaged and almost untended. They were put ashore just as they were pulled from the water, the most pitiful wrecks of men. Yet they were surprisingly few.

Well, that's the story of Dunkirk, as I saw the show.

SIDNEY STEWART

An Oklahoman, Sidney Stewart was born in 1919. While in medical school, he was drafted into the army, and soon after training was sent to the Philippines, arriving in Manila six weeks before Pearl Harbor. He was one of those who endured the Bataan march, and was a prisoner of the Japanese for more than three years. In his first book, *Give Us This Day,* published in 1957, he has told, in vivid prose, the story of that harrowing experience. The quiet bravery that shines through this record will be long remembered and cherished by all Americans. Mr. Stewart began by hating his captors; he ended his ordeal by realizing that they were simply a different breed of men. The pages I have chosen describe the march itself.

Bataan

WE REACHED the road and the Japanese motioned haughtily for us to stand in the depressions along the sides of the old coral highway. Holding their rifles flat and ready, they moved among us slowly, coolly suspicious, their eyes glaring.

With the gasping breath of relief the word was passed along, "They're going to make us prisoners." Suddenly the deafening roar of the explosions stopped. All firing ceased.

The quick silence was an odd sound to our ears, so used to the war. An occasional rifle shot cracked in the distance, ringing with a hollow echo over the jungle. When I looked at the dust-covered faces of our captors, I felt the cold hatred in their eyes, and wondered how we would be treated. We laid our stuff out on the ground in front of us and unrolled our packs. Most of us had very little, as a soldier throws everything away but the very essential.

The Japanese officers walked back and forth in the road, their samurai swords clacking against their black boots. By contrast the Jap enlisted men were dressed in patched and ragged uniforms and wrapped to the knees in puttees like those the American soldiers had worn in the First World War. An order was screamed in Japanese. I don't know why we all looked at John, expecting him to translate for us. But of course he couldn't. The Japs began knocking our helmets off with the tips of their bayonets. They fell to the ground with the clamour of tin wash pans.

"You don't have any Japanese souvenirs, do you?" John asked me out of the corner of his mouth.

"No, I got rid of everything," I whispered.

The Jap guards began to feel us over, searching us. I had a little medical kit strapped to my belt. A Japanese soldier, half grinning, ripped it from my belt and emptied it upon the ground. Grunting, he stooped forward and picked up a bottle of Sodium Amytal, a potent sleeping medicine. Each green tablet contained three grains. He looked into my face with contempt and hatred in his eyes, questioning me. Then he uncorked the bottle and poured the tablets out into his hand.

"*Yoroshi?* Are they good?" He asked in Japanese. I looked at him, sensing his feeling of superiority and hating him for it.

"*Tien yoroshi,*" I said, remembering the words I had learned from a prisoner we had taken. He poured a few more into his hand. "Yes," I repeated. "They are very good."

Lifting his hand to his mouth, he gulped them down and walked to the next man and began searching him. I felt a small triumph. I knew he would live only a few minutes. He would not vomit because they would act as a sedative. Slowly he would fall asleep and die. I felt glad of it as I looked at the glaring mahogany faces of our captors. They didn't know it yet, but I had notched one more to our score, right under their noses.

"Just look at these poor guys," Rass whispered. I looked around at the Filipinos and the Americans lined up in the road. Their faces were half-starved and dirty from the swirling chalky dust of the coral road glaring in the sun. Their clothes were in rags and there was fear and hatred in their tired red eyes. They were expecting something very bad and now it was coming.

Suddenly the Japanese soldiers began to lose restraint. They jerked off watches and fountain pens. Then they lost their tempers, slugging and beating the men up and down the line. A boy who stood near me cried out with pain as one of the Jap guards smashed a fist into his face. The guard laughed, then raised the butt of his rifle, crashing it down over the boy's head. Groaning, the kid sagged to his knees. With all his strength the guard swung the butt again and the boy's head made a dull, splattering sound as it split open before our eyes.

The body convulsed, shuddering, and the fingers grabbed the ground.

Then it lay still. One of the Jap soldiers laughed and kicked the dead American with the toe of his shoe. Suddenly I hated them with a violent hatred.

Never had I wanted to kill for the sheer pleasure of killing before. But now, good God, how I wanted to tear them limb from limb. I despised myself for the times when I had felt sorry for them.

"The dirty bastards!" Weldon was rasping through set teeth.

"Shut up!" John's whisper was firm. "This is no time to lose your head. Hold your temper and take it easy. You don't want to end up like that guy!" The black hatred still boiled in my brain, but gradually I got control of myself.

"*Yahura!*" the guards began to yell. "Start moving!"

We started out on the road, leaving our little handful of possessions behind us. Every few yards more Japanese materialized from the bushes around us. We were covered by the white dust stirred up by the horse-drawn artillery and the trucks. Jap soldiers, as they filed along, would jerk an American out of line and beat him, then shove him back into the line. There was no reason in the performance. They did it purely for entertainment.

Before we had gone two miles our shirts were stripped from our bodies. The sun reached straight above us, beating down on our bare heads. My head began to ache in the blistering heat. My eyes seemed to bulge from my head. I wanted water more than anything. We kept walking and the heat seemed to search out all the strength in me.

"Oh, God, where are we going? Where are we going?" Hughes whimpered. John gave him a savage "Sshh!"

The afternoon wore on and the Japanese soldiers lining the road became more ferocious. The sun beat on my head and it ached almost to splitting with the heat of it. My skin felt pierced by a million needles of fire. I passed a man lying in the road with his head smashed in, and then another, writhing in misery, clutching his belly in bloody hands. A bayonet had been driven through his intestines. Soon it became commonplace and I saw scores and finally hundreds like them. I began to think only of lifting my feet one at a time and putting them down.

"Keep up, Sid," Weldon said grimly. "Keep up, don't be falling back. I hear they're going to let us rest up ahead."

"They'll have trucks up there to move us out," someone passed the word. Just the thought refreshed me. They were going to put us on trucks, surely, and we would have water.

Slowly the darkness fell. The coolness of night descended. I watched men fall to the ground. The Japanese rushed in among us, kicking them with their heavy boots and jabbing them with their bayonets. If the men could not rise they were beaten to death. My hatred gave me strength. Then I remembered the Jap who had taken the Sodium Amytal from my medical kit. I began to laugh hysterically.

Rass reached over and shook me. "What's wrong, fella? Hold on. What's wrong?"

"I got one of the bastards, Rass. I got one of the bastards."

"Get hold of yourself, Sid." John gripped my shoulder.

"I got one of the bastards, the dirty bastards." I laughed hysterically. In a whisper I told them how the Jap had swallowed twenty of the Sodium Amytal tablets.

"Won't he vomit them up?" Hughes asked.

"No, he won't." Rass shook his head. "He'd just fall over and sleep and pretty soon he'd be dead. Oh, God, if we only could give it to them all!"

We laughed at that and it helped.

We walked all night and when the dawn came it brought the sun again. The temperature rose slowly as the sun climbed in the sky. The noon hour came and the midday heat was blistering, searing our skins. But we straggled on, afraid to fall by the side. The heat and the choking dust filled our noses, tearing at our raw throats.

Hughes kept stumbling and whimpering. He walked bent almost in half and the white coral dust covering his hair gave him the appearance of a very old man. John, who never complained, began a rasping cough and his dirt mask was criss-crossed with lines of running sweat.

During the afternoon we came to a cool mountain stream and the Japanese yelled for us to stop. We stood there, knowing we were to get water. The dampness of the ground smelled mossy and wonderful. Looking down at the cool stream bubbling and gurgling over the rocks, I licked my cracked and gritty lips. It looked so clear, so cool, so delicious. If only I could throw myself down into the water and lie there feeling it rush over my body.

We waited and waited, but still they did not allow us to drink. Suddenly one of the men could bear it no longer. He rushed forward, fell on his hands and knees, threw his face into the water. A Japanese noncom ran up, unsheathing his sword and swinging it high.

I heard a quick, ugly swish. Before I could realize what had happened, I saw the head roll away in the stream. The blood and water mingled together, a violent red. The body was stationary for a moment and suddenly the blood gushed out of the gaping hole at the neck like a waterfall. The body lunged forward in the stream bed, the hands opening and closing. Feeling sick, I thought, "It is like a chicken with its neck wrung." I hated myself for the thought. I closed my eyes and gritted my teeth.

The guards yelled for us to go on. They were not going to let us have water. Without stopping or turning we headed up the dusty road glaring in the tropical sun.

"I don't think I can make it much farther," I heard Hughes whisper. "I don't feel like I can make it another block."

"I don't think I can either," Rass gasped. But then a mile passed.

"Just keep thinking that you're gonna get water up ahead," Weldon begged, the strength almost gone from his deep voice.

I began to fasten my mind on the thought of water, how good it would taste. My mouth was terribly dry and my tongue felt rough and swollen in my mouth. The dust tasted gritty on my cracked lips. I licked my tongue across them, thinking of water and its taste. Somehow the night passed and the morning sun came again. I remembered passing through Orion and then Pilar.

The sun beat down on my throbbing head. I thought only of bringing my feet up, putting them down, bringing them up. Along the road the jungle was a misty green haze, swimming before my sweat-filled eyes.

The hours dragged by, and a great many of the prisoners reached the end of their endurance. The drop-outs became more numerous. They fell by the hundreds in the road. Some made an effort to rise. Groaning and weeping, they tried to get to their feet. Some succeeded, others fell back helplessly. I wondered that the Jap guards paid no attention. Why? Why did they leave them, when they had killed them before?

Suddenly I knew. There was the crack of a pistol and the shot rang out across the jungle. There was another shot, and more shots, and I knew that, straggling along behind us, was a clean-up squad of Japanese, killing their helpless victims on the white dusty road. The shots rang out through the night, making orange flashes in the darkness. I wondered how soon our bodies would be with the rest. The shots continued, goading us on. I gritted my teeth. "Oh, God, I've got to keep going. I can't stop. I can't die like that."

When morning came, John said, "I can't make it this day. I cannot make it."

"I can't either, John."

But we kept on and the sun climbed slowly higher and higher. We passed thousands of American and Filipino bodies bloating and rotting in the sun.

At noon they stopped us. There was a flurry of activity up ahead. There were carabao holes beside the road, like pig wallows, with greenish water and slimy scum covering the top. Small gnats and flies buzzed around them. Even so, it was water.

We looked, asking the question with our eyes of our Jap guards. Surprisingly, they nodded, and we ran for it. Falling on our knees, we pushed the scum back from the top of the water with our hands. The stenching liquid was water. When we started down the road again, somehow I felt better.

The murders went on. Death was always at our heels. We struggled to keep going. Weldon pushed Hughes with his shoulder, trying to keep him from falling. Rass half-carried John at times. Then he would shift him to me. We would change positions and I would walk in front with John's hands on my shoulders, holding him up.

On the fifth day we arrived at Orani. They herded us on to the cement patio of an old Spanish church. They motioned for us to sit down, but we were so crowded that we had to sit with our knees hunched up in front of us. After a little while huge caldrons of steaming rice were brought forward and a small handful was ladled out to each one of us. We ate ravenously. But no sooner had we finished eating than the guards ran in among us, screaming, kicking us with their boots, making us get to our feet.

The rest had cramped my muscles and my legs jerked with the effort as we started up the road. Gradually I began to lose consciousness. I was surrounded by a scorching, thirsty haze. My eyes grew dim and I thought only of keeping my feet moving. I had to keep going. Walking, Walking. I no longer noticed when the men in my Company fell out. No longer counted the bodies in the road.

Sometime late in the night we started through the outskirts of the Filipino city of Lubao. It may have been a day later, for Weldon told me we had been walking for eight days. In Lubao the Filipinos stood at the open windows of their homes and threw food to us. A scramble started among the prisoners. I watched them through a haze, wondering how they had the strength to fight. The guards screamed in frenzy, stamping and grinding the food under their feet, and beating a man if he picked up a piece of it.

We were herded on through the streets of the city, much like the other cities, with bamboo homes set on stilts. At the end of one street there was an ancient Alamo-style church. My eyes burned with the sun and sweat and dust, but when I looked at the compassion and pity on the faces of the Filipinos I became more determined. I will go on, I thought. I'll live to see these bastards die.

Somehow we reached the other side of the city. They marched us into an open field. An interpreter screamed that we were not to sit down. The nerves in my legs began an uncontrollable jerking and I wondered what we were waiting for. Weldon stood as though propped up by some unseen force, his eyes staring without focus. Hughes leaned against him with his knees sagging. His once-blond hair was muddy with sweat and dust, and his face was drawn and cadaverous. John swayed drunkenly, his hand gripping Rass' shoulder. Rass' bloodshot eyes grew suddenly alive. I followed the look in them.

A guard walked by with an American head stuck on the end of his bayonet. My stomach turned over at the sight. Blood was running from the neck and from the open lips. The teeth were clenched in a ghastly smile and the eyes protruded. I turned my eyes away, but I saw three other Japs, each of them with an American head on a bayonet. They walked in among us and we fell silent, watching them with black, deadly hatred.

Night came at last, yet we continued to stand there. If a man slumped to his knees the guards rushed in, jabbing him with their bayonets or kicking him until he either stood or fell groaning to the ground.

When morning came we started again. The day was like the rest, horribly hot and thirsty. But we walked and the day passed and the night passed.

"We're on the outskirts of San Fernando," Rass said. His voice sounded like an echo in a cave. "They'll give us food here. They're going to put us on a train."

I shook my head. I could not trust myself to speak. I did not believe it. The only thing that gave me hope was the fact that they didn't kill us. They must have some reason for marching us, goading us, beating us on like this. Surely somewhere was the end of this trail of blood and death.

"We've been walking nine days now," John said. The words rasped from his parched throat.

We went on through the streets of San Fernando. My head was bursting under the constant glare of the sun, and I lost consciousness. When my head cleared again I was on a boxcar.

"I don't know what happened to you. I dragged you that last two miles," Rass said quietly. "You kept falling. You were kicked and beaten but you always managed to get back on your feet."

I looked around. John and Weldon and Hughes were still there. They sat holding their heads in their hands. The jolting and jarring of the boxcar racked every muscle in my body. I looked down. My feet were wet with blood.

On April 21st, twelve days after our surrender, we reached Camp O'Donnell. It was said that more than fourteen thousand men died on the march. The living also were dying men at the end, haunted by fear, eaten by pain and fever.

Sometimes I think we all died on the march. Sometimes I feel sure that all the things that came later were just a fevered dream, and that somewhere back on those blood-soaked miles there is another body....

MAURICE HERZOG

The conqueror of Annapurna was born in 1919 in Lyons, France, of a mountain-climbing family. Both his father and his seven brothers and sisters are all devotees of the sport. He holds bachelor degrees in science and in law, and also was graduated from the French equivalent of the Harvard Business School. He fought for four years in World War II, commanding at its end a company of Alpine troops. He now makes his home in Paris.

Herzog began to write in 1951, while in the American Hospital at Neuilly, where he was recovering from the severe injuries he had received on his descent from Annapurna, at that time the highest mountain yet climbed by man. Lucien Devies, president of the Fédération Française de la Montagne, said of him in the preface to *Annapurna:* "The other members of the party have been the first to confirm the wisdom of our choice of a leader by the affection and even reverence in which they hold him. But it was not the Himalaya which revealed Maurice Herzog to us, for his past record had convinced us that we had entrusted the Expedition to the most valiant of them all.... What a range of gifts he has shown! His intelligence and character opened many fields of activity to him. His grasp of the practical side of life debarred him neither from the poetry of Mallarmé nor from the Pensées of Pascal. He was as much at home in a city office as on one of the great Italian ridges of Mont Blanc. His great goodness of heart, which won him so many friends, did not prevent him from taking firm decisions when necessary, or forming a clear-sighted judgment of people. A level head controlled the natural exuberance of abounding vitality."

In the selections from *Annapurna* made for this book I have spared you the agonies endured by Herzog while the Expedition's surgeon tried to save his fingers and toes. I have chosen instead Herzog's account of the final assault on the summit, and then, skipping the terrible night spent in the crevasse, the chapter telling of escape from the avalanche and the safe arrival at Camp II, where medical aid was waiting for Herzog and his exhausted companions.

As Justice Douglas has observed of this book, to read it is to have been the companion of greatness.

The Ascent of Annapurna

O N THE third of June, 1950, the first light of dawn found us still clinging to the tent poles at Camp V, at 24,600 feet. Gradually the wind abated and, with daylight, died away altogether. I made desperate attempts to push back the soft, icy stuff which stifled me, but every movement became an act of heroism. My mental powers were numbed: thinking was an effort, and we did not exchange a single word.

What a repellent place it was! To everyone who reached it, Camp V became one of the worst memories of their lives. We had only one thought—to get away. We should have waited for the first rays of the sun, but at half-past five we felt we couldn't stick it any longer.

"Let's go, Biscante," I muttered. "Can't stay here a minute longer."

"Yes, let's go," repeated Lachenal.

Which of us would have the energy to make tea? Although our minds worked slowly we were quite able to envisage all the movements that would be necessary—and neither of us could face up to it. It couldn't be helped—we would just have to go without. It was quite hard enough work to get ourselves and our boots out of our sleeping bags—and the boots were frozen stiff so that we got them on only with the greatest difficulty. Every movement made us terribly breathless. We felt as if we were being stifled. Our gaiters were stiff as a board, and I succeeded in lacing mine up; Lachenal couldn't manage his.

"No need for the rope, eh, Biscante?"

"No need," replied Lachenal laconically.

That was two pounds saved. I pushed a tube of condensed milk, some nougat, and a pair of socks into my sack; one never knew, the socks might come in useful—they might even do as Balaclavas. For the time being I stuffed them with first-aid equipment. The camera was loaded with a black and white film; I had a color film in reserve. I pulled the movie camera out from the bottom of my sleeping bag, wound it up, and tried letting it run without film. There was a little click, then it stopped and jammed.

"Bad luck after bringing it so far," said Lachenal.

In spite of our photographer, Ichac's, precautions taken to lubricate it with special grease, the intense cold, even inside the sleeping bag, had frozen it. I left it at the camp rather sadly: I had looked forward to taking it to the top. I had used it up to 24,600 feet.

We went outside and put on our crampons, which we kept on all day. We wore as many clothes as possible; our sacks were very light. At six o'clock we started off. It was brilliantly fine, but also very cold. Our super-lightweight crampons bit deep into the steep slopes of ice and hard snow up which lay the first stage of our climb.

Later the slope became slightly less steep and more uniform. Sometimes the hard crust bore our weight, but at others we broke through and sank into soft powder snow which made progress exhausting. We took turns in making the track and often stopped without any word having passed between us. Each of us lived in a closed and private world of his own. I was suspicious of my mental processes; my mind was working very slowly and I was perfectly aware of the low state of my intelligence. It was easiest just to stick to one thought at a time— safest, too. The cold was penetrating; for all our special eiderdown clothing we felt as if we'd nothing on. Whenever we halted, we stamped our feet hard. Lachenal went as far as to take off one boot which was a bit tight; he was in terror of frostbite.

"I don't want to be like Lambert," he said. Raymond Lambert, a Geneva guide, had to have all his toes amputated after an eventful climb during which he got his feet frostbitten. While Lachenal rubbed himself hard, I looked at the summits all around us; already we overtopped them all except the distant Dhaulagiri. The complicated structure of these mountains, with which our many laborious explorations had made us familiar, was now spread out plainly at our feet.

The going was incredibly exhausting, and every step was a struggle of mind over matter. We came out into the sunlight, and by way of marking the occasion made yet another halt. Lachenal continued to complain of his feet. "I can't feel anything. I think I'm beginning to get frostbite." And once again he undid his boot.

I began to be seriously worried. I realized very well the risk we were running; I knew from experience how insidiously and quickly frostbite can set in if one is not extremely careful. Nor was Lachenal under any illusions. "We're in danger of having frozen feet. Do you think it's worth it?"

This was most disturbing. It was my responsibility as leader to think of the others. There was no doubt about frostbite being a very real danger. Did Annapurna justify such risks? That was the question I asked myself; it continued to worry me.

Lachenal had laced his boots up again, and once more we continued to force our way through the exhausting snow. The whole of the Sickle glacier was now in view, bathed in light. We still had a long way to go to cross it, and then there was that rock band—would we find a gap in it?

My feet, like Lachenal's, were very cold and I continued to wriggle my toes, even when we were moving. I could not feel them, but that was nothing new in the mountains, and if I kept on moving them it would keep the circulation going.

Lachenal appeared to me as a sort of specter—he was alone in his world, I in mine. But—and this was odd enough—any effort was slightly *less* exhausting than lower down. Perhaps it was hope lending us wings. Even through dark glasses the snow was blinding—the sun beating straight down on the ice. We looked down upon precipitous ridges which dropped away into space, and upon tiny glaciers far, far below. Familiar peaks soared arrowlike into the sky. Suddenly Lachenal grabbed me:

"If I go back, what will you do?"

A whole sequence of pictures flashed through my head: the days of marching in sweltering heat, the hard pitches we had overcome, the tremendous efforts we had all made to lay siege to the mountain, the daily heroism of all my friends in establishing the camps. Now we were nearing our goal. In an hour or two, perhaps, victory would be ours. Must we give up? Impossible! My whole being revolted against the idea. I had made up my mind, irrevocably. Today we were consecrating an ideal, and no sacrifice was too great. I heard my voice clearly:

"I should go on by myself."

I would go alone. If he wished to go down it was not for me to stop him. He must make his own choice freely.

"Then I'll follow you."

The die was cast. I was no longer anxious. Nothing could stop us now from getting to the top. The psychological atmosphere changed with these few words, and we went forward now as brothers.

I felt as though I were plunging into something new and quite abnormal. I had the strangest and most vivid impressions, such as I had never before known in the mountains. There was something unnatural in the way I saw Lachenal and everything around us. I smiled to myself at the paltriness of our efforts, for I could stand apart and watch myself making these efforts. But all sense of exertion was gone, as though there were no longer any gravity. This diaphanous landscape, this quintessence of purity—these were not the mountains I knew: they were the mountains of my dreams.

The snow, sprinkled over every rock and gleaming in the sun, was of a radiant beauty that touched me to the heart. I had never seen such complete transparency, and I was living in a world of crystal. Sounds were indistinct, the atmosphere like cotton wool.

An astonishing happiness welled up in me, but I could not define it. Everything was so new, so utterly unprecedented. It was not in the least like anything I had known in the Alps, where one feels buoyed up by the presence of others—by people of whom one is vaguely aware, or even by the dwellings one can see in the far distance.

This was quite different. An enormous gulf was between me and the world. This was a different universe—withered, desert, lifeless; a fantastic universe where the presence of man was not foreseen, perhaps not desired. We were braving an interdict, overstepping a boundary, and yet we had no fear as we continued upward. I thought of the famous ladder of St. Theresa of Avila. Something clutched at my heart.

Did Lachenal share these feelings? The summit ridge drew nearer, and we reached the foot of the ultimate rock band. The slope was very steep and the snow interspersed with rocks.

"Couloir!"

A finger pointed. The whispered word from one to another indicated the key to the rocks—the last line of defense.

"What luck!"

The couloir up the rocks though steep was feasible.

The sky was a deep sapphire blue. With a great effort we edged over to the right, avoiding the rocks; we preferred to keep to the snow on account of our crampons and it was not long before we set foot in the couloir. It was fairly steep, and we had a minute's hesitation. Should we have enough strength left to overcome this final obstacle?

Fortunately the snow was hard, and by kicking steps we were able to manage, thanks to our crampons. A false move would have been fatal. There was no need to make handholds—our axes, driven in as far as possible, served us for an anchor.

Lachenal went splendidly. What a wonderful contrast to the early days! It was a hard struggle here, but he kept going. Lifting our eyes occasionally from the slope, we saw the couloir opening out on to ... well, we didn't quite know, probably a ridge. But where was the top —left or right? Stopping at every step, leaning on our axes, we tried to recover our breath and to calm down our racing hearts, which were thumping as though they would burst. We knew we were there now —that nothing could stop us. No need to exchange looks—each of us would have read the same determination in the other's eyes. A slight detour to the left, a few more steps—the summit ridge came gradually nearer—a few rocks to avoid. We dragged ourselves up. Could we possibly be there?

Yes!

A fierce and savage wind tore at us.

We were on top of Annapurna! 8,075 meters, 26,493 feet.

Our hearts overflowed with an unspeakable happiness.

"If only the others could know ..."

If only everyone could know!

The summit was a corniced crest of ice, and the precipices on the far side which plunged vertically down beneath us, were terrifying, unfathomable. There could be few other mountains in the world like this. Clouds floated halfway down, concealing the gentle, fertile valley of Pokhara, 23,000 feet below. Above us there was nothing!

Our mission was accomplished. But at the same time we had accomplished something infinitely greater. How wonderful life would now become! What an inconceivable experience it is to attain one's ideal and, at the very same moment, to fulfill oneself. I was stirred to the depths of my being. Never had I felt happiness like this—so intense and yet so pure. That brown rock, the highest of them all, that ridge of ice—were these the goals of a lifetime? Or were they, rather, the limits of man's pride?

"Well, what about going down?"

Lachenal shook me. What were his own feelings? Did he simply think he had finished another climb, as in the Alps? Did he think one could just go down again like that, with nothing more to it?

"One minute, I must take some photographs."

"Hurry up!"

I fumbled feverishly in my sack, pulled out the camera, took out the little French flag which was right at the bottom, and the pennants. Useless gestures, no doubt, but something more than symbols—eloquent tokens of affection and goodwill. I tied the strips of material—stained by sweat and by the food in the sacks—to the shaft of my ice ax, the only flagstaff at hand. Then I focused my camera on Lachenal.

"Now, will you take me?"

"Hand it over—hurry up!" said Lachenal.

He took several pictures and then handed me back the camera. I loaded a color film and we repeated the process to be certain of bringing back records to be cherished in the future.

"Are you mad?" asked Lachenal. "We haven't a minute to lose: we must go down at once."

And in fact a glance round showed me that the weather was no longer gloriously fine as it had been in the morning. Lachenal was becoming impatient.

"We must go down!"

He was right. His was the reaction of the mountaineer who knows his own domain. But I just could not accustom myself to the idea that we had won our victory. It seemed inconceivable that we should have trodden those summit snows.

It was impossible to build a cairn; there were no stones; everything was frozen. Lachenal stamped his feet; he felt them freezing. I felt

mine freezing too, but paid little attention. The highest mountain to
be climbed by man lay under our feet! The names of our predecessors
on these heights raced through my mind: Mummery, Mallory and
Irvine, Bauer, Welzenbach, Tilman, Shipton. How many of them
were dead—how many had found on these mountains what, to them,
was the finest end of all?

My joy was touched with humility. It was not just one party that had
climbed Annapurna today, but a whole expedition. I thought of all
the others in the camps perched on the slopes at our feet, and I knew
it was because of their efforts and their sacrifices that we had succeeded.
There are times when the most complicated actions are suddenly
summed up, distilled, and strike you with illuminating clarity: so it
was with this irresistible upward surge which had landed us two here.

Pictures passed through my mind—the Chamonix valley, where I
had spent the most marvelous moments of my childhood; Mont Blanc,
which so tremendously impressed me! I was a child when I first saw
"the Mont Blanc people" coming home, and to me there was a queer
look about them; a strange light shone in their eyes.

"Come on, straight down," called Lachenal.

He had already done up his sack and started going down. I took
out my pocket aneroid: 8,500 meters. I smiled. I swallowed a little
condensed milk and left the tube behind—the only trace of our passage. I did up my sack, put on my gloves and my glasses, seized my
ice ax; one look around and I, too, hurried down the slope. Before
disappearing into the couloir I gave one last look at the summit which
would henceforth be all our joy and all our consolation.

Lachenal was already far below; he had reached the foot of the
couloir. I hurried down in his tracks. I went as fast as I could, but it
was dangerous going. At every step one had to take care that the snow
did not break away beneath one's weight. Lachenal, going faster than
I thought he was capable of, was now on the long traverse. It was my
turn to cross the area of mixed rock and snow. At last I reached the
foot of the rock band. I had hurried and I was out of breath. I undid
my sack. What had I been going to do? I couldn't say.

"My gloves!"

Before I had time to bend over, I saw them slide and roll. They
went further and further straight down the slope. I remained where
I was, quite stunned. I watched them rolling down slowly, with no
appearance of stopping. The movement of those gloves was engraved
in my sight as something irredeemable, against which I was powerless.
The consequences might be most serious. What was I to do?

"Quickly, down to Camp V."

Rébuffat and Terray would be there. My concern dissolved like magic. I now had a fixed objective again: to reach the camp. Never for a minute did it occur to me to use as gloves the socks which I always carry in reserve for just such a mishap as this.

On I went, trying to catch up with Lachenal. It had been two o'clock when we reached the summit; we had started out at six in the morning, but I had to admit that I had lost all sense of time. I felt as if I were running, whereas in actual fact I was walking normally, perhaps rather slowly, and I had to keep stopping to get my breath. The sky was now covered with clouds, everything had become gray and dirty-looking. An icy wind sprang up, boding no good. We must push on! But where was Lachenal? I spotted him a couple of hundred yards away, looking as if he was never going to stop. And I had thought he was in indifferent form!

The clouds grew thicker and came right down over us; the wind blew stronger, but I did not suffer from the cold. Perhaps the descent had restored my circulation. Should I be able to find the tents in the mist? I watched the rib ending in the beaklike point which overlooked the camp. It was gradually swallowed up by the clouds, but I was able to make out the spearhead rib lower down. If the mist should thicken I would make straight for that rib and follow it down, and in this way I should be bound to come upon the tent.

Lachenal disappeared from time to time, and then the mist was so thick that I lost sight of him altogether. I kept going at the same speed, as fast as my breathing would allow.

The slope was now steeper; a few patches of bare ice followed the smooth stretches of snow. A good sign—I was nearing the camp. How difficult to find one's way in thick mist! I kept the course which I had set by the steepest angle of the slope. The ground was broken; with my crampons I went straight down walls of bare ice. There were some patches ahead—a few more steps. It was the camp all right, but there were *two tents!*

So Rébuffat and Terray had come up. What a mercy! I should be able to tell them that we had been successful, that we were returning from the top. How thrilled they would be!

I got there, dropping down from above. The platform had been extended, and the two tents were facing each other. I tripped over one of the guy-ropes of the first tent; there was movement inside, they had heard me. Rébuffat and Terray put their heads out.

"We've made it. We're back from Annapurna!"

The Descent Begins

Rébuffat and Terray received the news with great excitement.

"But what about Biscante?" asked Terray anxiously.

"He won't be long. He was just in front of me! What a day—started out at six this morning—didn't stop ... got up at last."

Words failed me. I had so much to say. The sight of familiar faces dispelled the strange feeling that I had experienced since morning, and I became, once more, just a mountaineer.

Terray, who was speechless with delight, wrung my hands. Then the smile vanished from his face: "Maurice—your hands!" There was an uneasy silence. I had forgotten that I had lost my gloves: my fingers were violet and white and hard as wood. The other two stared at them in dismay—they realized the full seriousness of the injury. But, still blissfully floating on a sea of joy remote from reality, I leaned over toward Terray and said confidentially, "You're in such splendid form, and you've done so marvelously, it's absolutely tragic you didn't come up there with us!"

"What I did was for the expedition, my dear Maurice, and anyway you've got up, and that's a victory for the whole lot of us."

I nearly burst with happiness. How could I tell him all that his answer meant to me? The rapture I had felt on the summit, which might have seemed a purely personal, egotistical emotion, had been transformed by his words into a complete and perfect joy with no shadow upon it. His answer proved that this victory was not just one man's achievement, a matter for personal pride; no—and Terray was the first to understand this—it was a victory for us all, a victory for mankind itself.

"Hi! Help! Help!"

"Biscante!" exclaimed the others.

Still half-intoxicated and remote from reality I had heard nothing. Terray felt a chill at his heart, and his thoughts flew to his partner on so many unforgettable climbs; together they had so often skirted death, and won so many splendid victories. Putting his head out, and seeing Lachenal clinging to the slope a hundred yards lower down, he dressed in frantic haste.

Out he went. But the slope was bare now; Lachenal had disappeared. Terray was horribly frightened, and he could only utter unintelligible cries. It was a ghastly moment for him. A violent wind sent the mist tearing by. Under the stress of emotion Terray had not realized how it falsified distances. "Biscante! Biscante!"

He had spotted him, through a rift in the mist, lying on the slope much lower down than he had thought. Terray set his teeth and glissaded down like a madman. How would he be able to brake without crampons, on the wind-hardened snow? But Terray was a first-class skier, and with a jump turn he stopped beside Lachenal, who was suffering from concussion after his tremendous fall. In a state of collapse, with no ice ax, Balaclava, or gloves, and only one crampon, he gazed vacantly around him.

"My feet are frostbitten. Take me down . . . take me down, so that Oudot can see to me."

"It can't be done," said Terray sorrowfully. "Can't you see we're in the middle of a storm . . . It'll be dark soon."

But Lachenal was obsessed by the fear of amputation. With a gesture of despair he tore the ax out of Terray's hands and tried to force his way down; but soon saw the futility of his action and resolved to climb up to the camp. While Terray cut steps without stopping, Lachenal, ravaged and exhausted as he was, dragged himself along on all fours.

Meanwhile I had gone into Rébuffat's tent. He was appalled at the sight of my hands and, as rather incoherently I told him what we had done, he took a piece of rope and began flicking my fingers. Then he took off my boots with great difficulty for my feet were swollen, and beat my feet and rubbed me. We soon heard Terray giving Lachenal the same treatment in the other tent.

For our comrades it was a tragic moment: Annapurna was conquered, and the first eight-thousander had been climbed. Every one of us had been ready to sacrifice everything for this. Yet, as they looked at our feet and hands, what can Terray and Rébuffat have felt?

Outside the storm howled and the snow was still falling. The mist grew thick and darkness came. As on the previous night we had to cling to the poles to prevent the tents being carried away by the wind. The only two air-mattresses were given to Lachenal and myself while Terray and Rébuffat both sat on ropes, rucksacks, and provisions to keep themselves off the snow. They rubbed, slapped, and beat us with a rope. Sometimes the blows fell on the living flesh, and howls arose from both tents. Rébuffat persevered; it was essential to continue, painful as it was. Gradually life returned to my feet as well as to my hands, and circulation started again. Lachenal, too, found that feeling was returning.

Now Terray summoned up the energy to prepare some hot drinks. He called to Rébuffat that he would pass him a mug, so two hands stretched out toward each other between the two tents and were instantly covered with snow. The liquid was boiling though scarcely more than 60 degrees Centigrade (140 degrees Fahrenheit). I swallowed it greedily and felt infinitely better.

The night was absolute hell. Frightful onslaughts of wind battered us incessantly, while the never-ceasing snow piled up on the tents.

Now and again I heard voices from next door—it was Terray massaging Lachenal with admirable perseverance, only stopping to ply him with hot drinks. In our tent Rébuffat was quite worn out, but satisfied that warmth was returning to my limbs.

Lying half-unconscious I was scarcely aware of the passage of time. There were moments when I was able to see our situation in its true dramatic light, but the rest of the time I was plunged in an inexplicable stupor with no thought for the consequences of our victory.

As the night wore on the snow lay heavier on the tent, and once again I had the frightful feeling of being slowly and silently asphyxiated. I tried, with all the strength of which I was capable, to push off with both forearms the mass that was crushing me. These fearful exertions left me gasping for breath and I fell back into the same exhausted state. It was much worse than the previous night.

"Rébuffat! Gaston! Gaston!"

I recognized Terray's voice.

"Time to be off!"

I heard the sounds without grasping their meaning. Was it light already? I was not in the least surprised that the other two had given up all thought of going to the top, and I did not at all grasp the measure of their sacrifice.

Outside the storm redoubled in violence. The tent shook and the fabric flapped alarmingly. It had usually been fine in the mornings: did this mean the monsoon was upon us? We knew it was not far off—could this be its first onslaught?

"Gaston! Are you ready?" Terray called again.

"One minute," answered Rébuffat. He did not have an easy job: he had to put my boots on and do everything to get me ready. I let myself be handled like a baby. In the other tent Terray finished dressing Lachenal whose feet were still swollen and would not fit into his boots. So Terray gave him his own, which were bigger. To get Lachenal's on to his own feet he had to make slits in them. As a precaution he put a sleeping bag and some food into his sack and shouted to us to do the same. Were his words lost in the storm? Or were we too intent on leaving this hellish place to listen to his instructions?

Lachenal and Terray were already outside.

"We're going down!" they shouted.

Then Rébuffat tied me on the rope and we went out. There were only two ice axes for the four of us, so Rébuffat and Terray took them as a matter of course. For a moment as we left the two tents of Camp V, I felt childishly ashamed at leaving all this good equipment behind.

Already the first rope seemed a long way down below us. We were blinded by the squalls of snow and we could not hear each other a yard away. We had both put on our *cagoules,* for it was very cold. The snow was apt to slide and the rope often came in useful.

Ahead of us the other two were losing time. Lachenal went first and, safeguarded by Terray, he forced the pace in his anxiety to get down. There were no tracks to show us the way, but it was engraved on all our minds—straight down the slope for four hundred yards then traverse to the left for one hundred fifty to two hundred yards to get to Camp IV. The snow was thinning and the wind less violent. Was it going to clear? We hardly dared to hope so. A wall of seracs brought us up short.

"It's to the left," I said, "I remember perfectly."

Somebody else thought it was to the right. We started going down again. The wind had dropped completely, but the snow fell in big flakes. The mist was thick, and, not to lose each other, we walked in line: I was third and I could barely see Lachenal, who was first. It was impossible to recognize any of the pitches. We were all experienced enough mountaineers to know that even on familiar ground it is easy to make mistakes in such weather. Distances are deceptive, one cannot tell whether one is going up or down. We kept colliding with hummocks which we had taken for hollows. The mist, the falling snowflakes, the carpet of snow, all merged into the same whitish tone and confused our vision. The towering outlines of the seracs took on fantastic shapes and seemed to move slowly around us.

Our situation was not desperate, we were certainly not lost. We would have to go lower down; the traverse must begin further on—I remembered the serac which served as a milestone. The snow stuck to our *cagoules* and turned us into white phantoms noiselessly flitting against a background equally white. We began to sink in dreadfully, and there is nothing worse for bodies already on the edge of exhaustion.

Were we too high or too low? No one could tell. Perhaps we had better try slanting over to the left! The snow was in a dangerous condition, but we did not seem to realize it. We were forced to admit that we were not on the right route, so we retraced our steps and climbed up above the serac which overhung us. No doubt, we decided, we should be on the right level now. With Rébuffat leading, we went back over the way which had cost us such an effort. I followed him jerkily, saying nothing, and determined to go on to the end. If Rébuffat had fallen I could never have held him.

We went doggedly on from one serac to another. Each time we thought we had recognized the right route, and each time there was a fresh disappointment. If only the mist would lift, if only the snow would stop for a second! On the slope it seemed to be growing deeper every minute. Only Terray and Rébuffat were capable of breaking the trail and they relieved each other at regular intervals, without a word and without a second's hesitation.

I admired this determination of Rébuffat's for which he is so justly famed. He did not intend to die! With the strength of desperation and at the price of superhuman effort he forged ahead. The slowness of his progress would have dismayed even the most obstinate climber, but he would not give up, and in the end the mountain yielded in face of his perseverance.

Terray, when his turn came, charged madly ahead. He was like a force of nature: at all costs he would break down these prison walls that penned us in. His physical strength was exceptional, his will power no less remarkable. Lachenal gave him considerable trouble. Perhaps he was not quite in his right mind. He said it was no use going on; we must dig a hole in the snow and wait for fine weather. He swore at Terray and called him a madman. Nobody but Terray would have been capable of dealing with him—he just tugged sharply on the rope and Lachenal was forced to follow.

We were well and truly lost.

The weather did not seem likely to improve. A minute before we had still had ideas about which way to go—now we had none. This way or that ... we went on at random to allow for the chance of a miracle which appeared increasingly unlikely. The instinct of self-preservation in the two fit members of the party alternated with a hopelessness which made them completely irresponsible. Each in turn did the maddest things: Terray traversed the steep and avalanchy slopes with one crampon badly adjusted. He and Rébuffat performed incredible feats of balance without the least slip.

Camp IV was certainly on the left, on the edge of the Sickle. On that point we were all agreed. But it was very hard to find. The wall of ice that gave it such magnificent protection was now ironical, for it hid the tents from us. In mist like this we should have to be right on top of them before we spotted them.

Perhaps if we called, someone would hear us? Lachenal gave the signal, but snow absorbs sound and his shout seemed to carry only a few yards. All four of us called out together: "One ... two ... three ... HELP!"

We got the impression that our united shout carried a long way, so we began again: "One ... two ... three ... HELP!" Not a sound in reply!

Now and again Terray took off his boots and rubbed his feet; the sight of our frostbitten limbs had made him aware of the danger and he had the strength of mind to do something about it. Like Lachenal, he was haunted by the idea of amputation. For me, it was too late: my feet and hands, already affected from yesterday, were beginning to freeze up again.

We had eaten nothing since the day before, and we had been on the go the whole time, but men's resources of energy in the face of death are inexhaustible. When the end seems imminent, there still remain reserves, though it needs tremendous will power to call them up.

Time passed, but we had no idea how long. Night was approaching, and we were terrified, though none of us made any complaint. Rébuffat and I found a way that we thought we remembered, but were brought to a halt by the extreme steepness of the slope—the mist turned it into a vertical wall. We were to find next day that at that moment we had been only thirty yards from the camp, and that the wall was the very one that sheltered the tent which would have been our salvation.

"We must find a crevasse."

"We can't stay here all night!"

"A hole—it's the only thing."

"We'll all die in it."

Night had suddenly fallen and it was essential to come to a decision without wasting another minute; if we remained on the slope, we should be dead before morning. We would have to bivouac. What the conditions would be like, we could guess, for we all knew what it meant to bivouac above 23,000 feet.

With his ax Terray began to dig a hole. Lachenal went over to a snow-filled crevasse a few yards further on, then suddenly let out a yell and disappeared before our eyes. We stood helpless: should we, or rather would Terray and Rébuffat, have enough strength for all the maneuvers with the rope that would be needed to get him out? The crevasse was completely blocked up save for the one little hole which Lachenal had fallen through.

"Lachenal!" called Terray.

A voice, muffled by many thicknesses of ice and snow, came up to us. It was impossible to make out what it was saying.

"Lachenal!"

Terray jerked the rope violently; this time we could hear.

"I'm here!"

"Anything broken?"

"No! It'll do for the night! Come along."

This shelter was heaven-sent. None of us would have had the strength to dig a hole big enough to protect the lot of us from the wind. Without hesitation Terray let himself drop into the crevasse, and a loud "Come on!" told us he had arrived safely. In my turn I let myself go: it was a regular toboggan slide. I shot down a sort of twisting tunnel, very steep, and about thirty feet long. I came out at great speed into the opening beyond and was literally hurled to the bottom of the crevasse. We let Rébuffat know he could come by giving a tug on the rope.

The intense cold of this minute grotto shriveled us up, the enclosing walls of ice were damp and the floor a carpet of fresh snow; by huddling together there was just room for the four of us. Icicles hung from the ceiling and we broke some of them off to make more head room and kept little bits to suck—it was a long time since we had anything to drink.

That was our shelter for the night. At least we should be protected from the wind, and the temperature would remain fairly even, though the damp was extremely unpleasant. We settled ourselves in the dark as best we could. As always in a bivouac we took off our boots; without this precaution the constriction would cause immediate frostbite. Terray unrolled the sleeping-bag which he had had the foresight to bring, and settled himself in relative comfort. We put on everything warm that we had, and to avoid contact with the snow I sat on the movie camera. We huddled close up to each other, in our search for a hypothetical position in which the warmth of our bodies could be combined without loss, but we couldn't keep still for a second.

We did not open our mouths—signs were less of an effort than words. Every man withdrew into himself and took refuge in his own inner world. Terray massaged Lachenal's feet; Rébuffat felt his feet freezing too, but he had sufficient strength to rub them himself. I remained motionless, unseeing. My feet and hands went on freezing, but what could be done? I attempted to forget suffering by withdrawing into myself, trying to forget the passing of time, trying not to feel the devouring and numbing cold which insidiously gained upon us.

Terray shared his sleeping-bag with Lachenal, putting his feet and hands inside the precious eiderdown. At the same time he went on rubbing.

Anyhow the frostbite won't spread further, he was thinking.

None of us could make any movement without upsetting the others, and the positions we had taken up with such care were continually being altered so that we had to start all over again. This kept us busy. Rébuffat persevered with his rubbing and complained of his feet; like Terray he was thinking: We mustn't look beyond tomorrow—afterward we'll see. But he was not blind to the fact that "afterward" was one big question mark.

Terray generously tried to give me part of his sleeping-bag. He had understood the seriousness of my condition, and knew why it was that

I said nothing and remained quite passive; he realized that I had abandoned all hope for myself. He massaged me for nearly two hours; his feet, too, might have frozen, but he didn't appear to give the matter a thought. I found new courage simply in contemplating his unselfishness; he was doing so much to help me that it would have been ungrateful of me not to go on struggling to live. Though my heart was like a lump of ice itself, I was astonished to feel no pain. Everything material about me seemed to have dropped away. I seemed to be quite clear in my thoughts and yet I floated in a kind of peaceful happiness. There was still a breath of life in me, but it dwindled steadily as the hours went by. Terray's massage no longer had any effect upon me. All was over, I thought. Wasn't this cavern the most beautiful grave I could hope for? Death caused me no grief, no regret—I smiled at the thought.

After hours of torpor a voice mumbled "Daylight!"

This made some impression on the others. I only felt surprised—I had not thought that daylight would penetrate so far down.

"Too early to start," said Rébuffat.

A ghastly light spread through our grotto and we could just vaguely make out the shapes of each other's heads. A queer noise from a long way off came down to us—a sort of prolonged hiss. The noise increased. Suddenly I was buried, blinded, smothered beneath an avalanche of new snow. The icy snow spread over the cavern, finding its way through every gap in our clothing. I ducked my head between my knees and covered myself with both arms. The snow flowed on and on. There was a terrible silence. We were not completely buried, but there was snow everywhere. We got up, taking care not to bang our heads against the ceiling of ice, and tried to shake ourselves. We were all in our stockinged feet in the snow. The first thing to do was to find our boots.

Rébuffat and Terray began to search and realized at once that they were blind. Yesterday they had taken off their glasses to lead us down and now they were paying for it. Lachenal was the first to lay hands upon a pair of boots. He tried to put them on, but they were Rébuffat's. Rébuffat attempted to climb up the chute down which we had come yesterday, and which the avalanche had followed in its turn.

"Hi, Gaston! What's the weather like?" called up Terray.

"Can't see a thing. It's blowing hard."

We were still groping for our things. Terray found his boots and put them on awkwardly, unable to see what he was doing. Lachenal helped him, but he was all on edge and fearfully impatient, in striking contrast to my immobility. Terray then went up the icy channel, puffing and blowing, and at last reached the outer world. He was met by terrible gusts of wind that cut right through him and lashed his face.

Bad weather, he said to himself, this time it's the end. We're lost ... we'll never come through.

At the bottom of the crevasse there were still two of us looking for our boots. Lachenal poked fiercely with an ice ax. I was calmer and tried to proceed more rationally. We extracted crampons and an ax in turn from the snow, but still no boots.

Well—so this cavern was to be our last resting place! There was very little room—we were bent double and got in each other's way. Lachenal decided to go out without his boots. He called frantically, hauled himself up on the rope, trying to get a hold or to wiggle his way up, digging his toes into the snow walls. Terray from outside pulled as hard as he could. I watched him go; he gathered speed and disappeared.

When he emerged from the opening he saw the sky was clear and blue, and he began to run like a madman, shrieking, "It's fine, it's fine!"

I set to work again to search the cave. The boots *had* to be found, or Lachenal and I were done for. On all fours, with nothing on my hands or feet I raked the snow, stirring it around this way and that, hoping every second to come upon something hard. I was no longer capable of thinking—I reacted like an animal fighting for its life.

I found one boot! The other was tied to it—a pair! Having ransacked the whole cave I at last found the other pair. But in spite of all my efforts I could not find the movie camera, and gave up in despair. There was no question of putting my boots on—my hands were like lumps of wood and I could hold nothing in my fingers; my feet were very swollen—I should never be able to get boots on them. I twisted the rope around the boots as well as I could and called up the chute:

"Lionel ... Boots!"

There was no answer, but he must have heard for with a jerk the precious boots shot up. Soon after the rope came down again. My turn. I wound the rope around me. I could not pull it tight so I made a whole series of little knots. Their combined strength, I hoped, would be enough to hold me. I had no strength to shout again; I gave a great tug on the rope, and Terray understood.

At the first step I had to kick a notch in the hard snow for my toes. Further on I expected to be able to get up more easily by wedging myself across the runnel. I wriggled up a few yards like this and then I tried to dig my hands and my feet into the wall. My hands were stiff and hard right up to the wrists and my feet had no feeling up to the ankles, the joints were inflexible and this hampered me greatly.

Somehow or other I succeeded in working my way up, while Terray pulled so hard he nearly choked me. I began to see more distinctly and so knew that I must be nearing the opening. Often I fell back, but I clung on and wedged myself in again as best I could. My heart was bursting and I was forced to rest. A fresh wave of energy enabled me to crawl to the top. I pulled myself out by clutching Terray's legs; he was just about all in and I was in the last stages of exhaustion. Terray was close to me and I whispered:

"Lionel ... I'm dying!"

He supported me and helped me away from the crevasse. Lachenal and Rébuffat were sitting in the snow a few yards away. The instant Lionel let go of me I sank down and dragged myself along on all fours.

The weather was perfect. Quantities of snow had fallen the day before and the mountains were resplendent. Never had I seen them look so beautiful—our last day would be magnificent.

Rébuffat and Terray were completely blind; as he came along with me Terray knocked into things and I had to direct him. Rébuffat, too, could not move a step without guidance. It was terrifying to be blind when there was danger all around. Lachenal's frozen feet affected his nervous system. His behavior was disquieting—he was possessed by the most fantastic ideas:

"I tell you we must go down ... down there ..."

"You've nothing on your feet!"

"Don't worry about that."

"You're off your head. The way's not there ... it's to the left!"

He was already standing up; he wanted to go straight down to the bottom of the glacier. Terray held him back, made him sit down, and, though he couldn't see, helped Lachenal put his boots on.

Behind them I was living in my own private dream. I knew the end was near, but it was the end that all mountaineers wish for—an end in keeping with their ruling passion. I was consciously grateful to the mountains for being so beautiful for me that day, and as awed by their silence as if I had been in church. I was in no pain and had no worry. My utter calmness was alarming. Terray came staggering toward me, and I told him: "It's all over for me. Go on ... you have a chance ... you must take it ... over to the left ... that's the way."

I felt better after telling him that. But Terray would have none of it: "We'll help you. If we get away, so will you."

At this moment Lachenal shouted: "Help! Help!"

Obviously he didn't know what he was doing ... Or did he? He was the only one of the four of us who could see Camp II down below. Perhaps his calls would be heard. They were shrieks of despair, reminding me tragically of some climbers lost in the Mont Blanc massif whom

I had endeavored to save. Now it was our turn. The impression was vivid: we were lost.

I joined in with the others: "One ... two ... three ... HELP! One ... two ... three ... HELP!" We tried to shout together, but without much success; our voices could not have carried more than ten feet. The noise I made was more of a whisper than a shout. Terray insisted that I should put my boots on, but my hands were dead. Neither Rébuffat nor Terray, who were unable to see, could help much, so I said to Lachenal: "Come and help me to put my boots on."

"Don't be silly, we must go down!"

And off he went once again in the wrong direction, straight down. I was not in the least angry with him; he had been sorely tried by the altitude and by everything he had gone through.

Terray resolutely got out his knife, and with fumbling hands slit the uppers of my boots back and front. Split in two like this I could get them on, but it was not easy and I had to make several attempts. Soon I lost heart—what was the use of it all anyway since I was going to stay where I was? But Terray pulled violently and finally he succeeded. He laced up my now-gigantic boots, missing half the hooks. I was ready now. But how was I going to walk with my stiff joints?

"To the left, Lionel!"

"You're crazy, Maurice," said Lachenal, "it's to the right, straight down."

Terray did not know what to think of these conflicting views. He had not given up like me, he was going to fight; but what, at the moment, could he do? The three of them discussed which way to go.

I remained sitting in the snow. Gradually my mind lost grip—why should I struggle? I would just let myself drift. I saw pictures of shady slopes, peaceful paths, there was a scent of resin. It was pleasant—I was going to die in my own mountains. My body had no feeling—everything was frozen.

"Aah ... aah!"

Was it a groan or a call? I gathered my strength for one cry: "They're coming!" The others heard me and shouted for joy. What a miraculous apparition! "Schatz ... it's Schatz!"

Barely two hundred yards away Marcel Schatz, waist-deep in snow, was coming slowly toward us like a boat on the surface of the slope. I found this vision of a strong and invincible deliverer inexpressibly moving. I expected everything of him. The shock was violent, and quite shattered me. Death clutched at me and I gave myself up.

When I came to again the wish to live returned and I experienced a violent revulsion of feeling. All was not lost! As Schatz came nearer my eyes never left him for a second—twenty yards—ten yards—he came straight toward me. Why? Without a word he leaned over me, held me close, hugged me, and his warm breath revived me.

I could not make the slightest movement—I was like marble. My heart was overwhelmed by such tremendous feelings and yet my eyes remained dry.

"It is wonderful—what you have done!"

ELLIOTT ARNOLD

Elliott Arnold, born in New York City in 1912, is a former newspaper-man of long and varied experience who has written fiction, biography, and war history. During World War II he served in the North African, Italian, and South Pacific theaters. As an Air Force officer, he collaborated on two books dealing with air warfare: *Mediterranean Sweep* and *Big Distance,* which, as its title suggests, had its setting in the Pacific Theater. His other books include *Finlandia: The Story of Sibelius, The Commandos,* and several novels. He has also written a number of books for children. He is represented here by a selection from his most recent book. *Rescue!,* a stirring account of the worldwide work of the Air Rescue Service of the United States Air Force—one field of its activities about which too little has been written.

For the purpose of this book I have chosen a most unusual story. It is Arnold's account of the miracles performed—and I use that word with due deliberation—by the Air Force crew that came to the rescue of hundreds of people who had been trapped in one of the great avalanches which are one of the hazards of life in the Walser Valley of western Austria. The experiences here recounted are so alien to our own experience that most readers will, I am sure, be as spellbound as I was myself by this extraordinary story.

Death by Avalanche

FOR almost three hundred years the people of the Walser Valley in western Austria have remembered the Great Avalanche of 1670. There have been wars, and dynasties have changed and the world has moved from one century to another, but nothing that happened anywhere was so important in the Grosses Walsertal as that time when the snow slid down the mountains. That was theirs alone, the personal catastrophe of the dwellers in the valley, and in the winters, when the new snow fell, they held close to their fires and repeated the stories they had heard from their fathers. And each detail remained sharp and clear as though it had happened not almost three centuries ago but the year before or the year before that. It was even easy to remember exact names—in this remote valley near the borders of Liechtenstein and Switzerland family names have not changed in 300 years.

The Grosses Walsertal, in Vorarlberg Province, is called a valley but it is more of a giant gorge, a great cleft, a narrow-angled V without even a flat floor, the sharp, steep sides meeting at a trickling stream. There are little villages along the hillsides where men have to lean almost sideways to keep erect—Blons is closest to the mouth, Sonntag, Fontanello, Buchboden, others—and so precipitous are the slopes that even in midsummer one side of the valley is in twilight from early afternoon on.

There have been other avalanches, many of them, some great and some small, but none could measure up to the Great Avalanche. The danger was always there in the winter when the snow gathered on the roofs of the hills and men always asked themselves why they lived there under the hanging blanket of death, but there was no answer. None was needed. It was their home. Even though there were those who said it should not be called Walser Valley but Death Valley.

On the afternoon of Thursday, January 7, 1954, snow began to fall upon Grosses Walsertal. The men and women noted that it was the dreaded *Staublawinen*—the dry snow. There are two kinds of avalanches, the wet and the dry. In the wet avalanche the snow packs as it falls and it destroys by brute force, by weight and impact. It is bad but it is a physical thing that can be seen and understood and perhaps with luck even be avoided.

The dry avalanche is different. The snow remains a powder, a fine dust almost. It builds up a solid wall of *air pressure* in front of it, invisible and deadly, and it destroys houses it never touches directly, and it strangles people standing in the open air. Because people smother and homes crumble from something that is unseen and many yards from them the people look upon the *Staublawinen* as something supernatural, something strange and mystic that belongs to the powers of darkness.

The dry snow continued to fall through the night and through that Friday and Saturday. On Sunday morning it was still falling. And on that day Maria Tuertscher, a husky, unmarried woman of thirty-two who worked with her father on his farm, dressed in her warmest clothes and left her home in Blons to go to church. It was a time to pray to Saint Nikolaus.

"Two of my sisters and my cousin went with me," Fräulein Tuertscher told me many months later when I visited her in Blons. "The
church was a mile from our house and the snow was very high but
we were able to go there and return. On the way back I saw several
smaller snowfalls started from their deep pathway above. We spent all
Sunday and all that night in our house and on Monday morning my
sister, Adelheid, looked out through the window and saw that a thick
blanket of snow was blown along the house and at the same moment
we heard a loud crack and the house moved."

There was sudden darkness, as though night had sprung upon them,
and then the house wrenched itself from its foundations and toppled
over on its side, the way a tree might fall. Then there was a great
smashing sound, and heavy timbers broke through and the air filled
with dust and snow and the people inside began to choke. Then there
was a deep silence. After a little while the people called out to each
other.

"We were all laid out, more or less covered by wooden beams from
the barn that had been driven into the house. The ceiling and the floor
of the room were almost vertical. My sisters and my cousin could get
out by themselves but they had to carry me out because I had a terrible
pain in my neck.

"When we were all outside, we saw that the whole house had moved
down about a hundred yards and that the barn with the hay was on
top of the building where we had been. The roof of the barn and the
cattle in it were all thrown over the roof of the house and were wiped
down to the river.

"They carried me, and then we noticed that the house of another
sister of mine, a sister with ten children, which had been about a hundred yards from our house, was now about ten yards away. In that
ruined house we heard voices calling: 'Mamma! Mamma!' They put
me down for a minute and went over there and they found my sister
lying upside down, all broken from falling beams, and five of her
children. They could not find the others. Then men came down and
they took us all into the village."

For a little while it seemed as though the village itself might escape
the full force of the *Staublawinen,* Frau Maria Schiebel, wife of Rudolf
Schiebel, an engineer in Blons, told me. "The electric lights went out
on Sunday," she said. "The telephone connection with the main valley
was interrupted by avalanches. On Monday morning our house was
snowed in almost completely. They tried to dig a pathway up to the
church but they could not do it until the afternoon. It was not until
that afternoon that the avalanche alarm was given.

"The first big avalanche had come down already at Esch, a mile farther up the valley. Ten houses were hit and wiped away there completely. There were deaths in every family living there and all those who were not killed were injured. Some of them managed to escape. All who could move came to Blons and gathered in a house near the dairy which was believed to be safe. The injured people who could be rescued from nearby were also brought out to that place and to the Inn Kroner close to the church of Blons.

"At seven o'clock on Monday the whole hillside of Blons moved down in a huge avalanche and also the people who were thought to be safe in the house near the dairy were wiped away with the house and most of them were killed. It was still snowing heavily through the night and nobody could leave the few houses and spots that were a little safe on the edges of the gorges. On Tuesday morning two men went out to Thüringen to give the word on what had happened."

By then twenty of the twenty-three buildings in Blons were swept away by the powder snow. Debris was scattered 1,000 feet down the mountainside. Standing were only the old church with its image of Saint Nikolaus, the inn, and one dwelling. It was, as Dr. Bruno Haid said, "as though the hand of God—or the Devil—had swept down across the mountain and the valley."

The snow fell almost everywhere across Austria, on Bludenz, just outside the Grosses Walsertal, down the long Klostertal, on Arlberg and St. Christoph's Pass, on St. Anton and Landeck, on all the valleys and mountains and villages that look like pictures in a storybook or settings on a stage, on Innsbruck, the lovely city on the river Inn. Innsbruck is a popular skiing center. The snow that fell upon it was dry snow, too, which was excellent for the runs. Those who had come to holiday were joyful.

From his office window in the University Hospital in Innsbruck— a hospital that treats many skiers when they break an arm or a leg— Dr. Haid stared at the falling snow. Dr. Haid is a skier himself—he has won many prizes in championship competitions—but on that morning he was not thinking of the ecstasy of skimming swiftly down a slope. The reports from Grosses Walsertal had just come in.

Bruno Haid is a young, tall, blue-eyed, flaxen-haired man of great charm, a doctor and surgeon, and more recently a specialist in anesthesiology. He is regarded as one of the finest anesthesiologists in Austria, perhaps in all Europe. He was born in Oetz, a little village in a valley near Innsbruck, where his father runs a resort hotel, the Drei Mohren— Three Moors. A skillful mountain climber, hunter, fisherman, Haid served as a lieutenant physician in the Austrian Army, first in Russia and then in the Rhineland and Holland....

When the full extent of the disaster that had befallen the Walser Valley became known in Innsbruck on that January morning, Dr. Haid consulted immediately with his chief, Professor Burghard Breitner, director of the Department of Surgery at University Hospital and head of the Austrian Red Cross. "Professor Breitner instantly started to investigate the possibility of getting a helicopter into Blons," Dr. Haid told me. "There was no possibility of an airplane in the situation. He telephoned the United States Army Headquarters at Salzburg and asked for help." The appeal went direct to the Air Rescue group in Sembach, Germany, the commanding officer of which was Bob Rizon.

To the north the falling snow was swept by high winds as a Rescue pilot, Captain Bill K. Sayers, carefully flew a new-model helicopter he was ferrying from England toward his base at Fürstenfeldbruck, near Munich. The helicopter was a model "B" of the H-19 and there were several important modifications in it with which Bill was not yet too familiar. He felt a great sense of relief when he brought the chopper down on a snowbank at Fursty.

The base was closed down because of the blizzard. Nothing was moving. The helicopter was hauled off into a hangar and mechanics got to work on checking it out, a three-day process required for all newly arrived helicopters during which everything on it is tested and inspected. Bill, a sturdy young veteran of the Korean war, now half-dead with weariness, wondered how he was going to get home—snow had closed the road between the base and his quarters. Somebody found a weasel and Bill climbed in. A path was broken to his house. Bill took a hot bath and fell into bed. That was the night of Monday the eleventh.

The next day word about Blons came down from Bob Rizon to the Rescue squadron at Fursty. "The helicopter was still in inspection," Sayers said. "But the man in charge of maintenance, Master Sergeant Bill Tostanoski, and the aircraft inspector, Master Sergeant George Arndt, went to work fast. They headed up a crew of fifteen mechanics and inspectors who worked without rest, all that day and night and part of the next day. I got out on Wednesday, in the first helicopter, the one I had brought from England."

Bill was off the ground at 1100. With him was his copilot Lieutenant Harold Cooley, and two crew members, Staff Sergeant John Harwood, a mechanic, and Staff Sergeant John Lowe, a medical technician. "They told us to fly to Innsbruck and pick up some doctors and then fly them to Bludenz," Sayers said. "At that time I didn't think I was going to participate in Rescue work—I thought we were just flying the doctors in. The weather was horrible all the way. We were down in the deep valleys of the Alps. I flew down to Rosenheim and up the valley to Innsbruck. It was snowing terrifically, with a low ceiling. The visibility was about half a mile.

"We had to fly right on the treetops. There were lots of high telephone wires across the valleys. We had to duck under them or over them. The whole thing was nip and tuck. When you're cruising along you can't see but just a few hundred yards and you are going sixty or seventy knots. If something should happen up ahead you're in real trouble. When we got to Innsbruck they had to stamp the snow out—a square about ten or twelve feet—so we could land."

Dr. Haid spent that morning with his colleague, Dr. Wolfgang Baumgartner, and with Professor Breitner, discussing every possible way to help the people in the Grosses Walsertal and assembling what they would need. "I remember thinking at the time how they use sticks to look for people under the snow," Haid said. "They poke them down wherever the snow is deep. I had an idea of linking together hollow tubes to shoot oxygen under the snow to trapped people. We tried to think of all kinds of things.

"Then we heard the helicopter was on its way. We went out to the airfield in an ambulance with equipment for surgery and resuscitation. We also took two dog leaders and two avalanche dogs. These dogs are trained by special men to find human beings under the snow. They train them in the early wintertime up at the mountain huts. They bury somebody under the snow and let the dog find the person. They then pet the dog and feed him.

"One of the dogs was a *Riesenschnauzer,* a giant schnauzer. The other was a *Schaeferhund,* a shepherd dog. We were all waiting when the helicopter came in about one-thirty. I think it was the first time I ever saw this kind of helicopter. It looked to me like a giant bumblebee. Then Captain Sayers and Lieutenant Cooley climbed down from the cockpit."

Professor Breitner, a tall, white-haired man with a very distinguished appearance, listened with sparkling eyes as Dr. Haid was speaking to me. Now he interrupted, pounding his fist excitedly on his desk. "I have only one impression. They came here not to ask questions, not to speak, but to *do!* The only thing they asked was: 'Who is coming with us?' Not 'Can we get there?' but 'Who is coming with us?'

"And when we told them two doctors and two dogs and two trainers they said: 'It can be done.' And they started to throw out all their luggage. They were in such a hurry! Not 'Where can we store this?' but 'Out it comes!' And then they said they would have to leave their two enlisted men here because of the weight crossing the pass. And off they went! What an impression—work! work! And for our poorest people. Not for a rich and famous person, but for our poorest, poorest people."

Sergeant Lowe, a Negro raised in the British West Indies, briefed Dr. Haid on how to use the intercommunication system in the helicopter so that Haid, riding in the cabin, could speak to Sayers while in flight. "After we took off we kept the cabin door open and I navigated," Haid said. "Although I know the area very well I noticed it was not so easy to say at any place exactly where you were. We saw where we had been but not where we were going. At one place we had to turn around because we went up a wrong valley."

The two dogs became restive in the small cabin and the trainers had difficulty controlling them.

Sayers: "We had to cross this 6,000-foot St. Christoph's Pass. When we got up there the valley got so narrow that we couldn't have turned around in case we couldn't get over the pass. We didn't know whether we could make it or not. It was snowing all the time and there was a strong wind.

"We finally got over the top. When we hit the top we hit an extreme amount of turbulence. We thought we lost control completely for a while. On the way down from the top of the pass we saw a snow slide where it took out a railroad station and a train and everything and killed six people. Later on we went in there and helped evacuate."

Haid: "We arrived at Bludenz where we were supposed to land. There were about 200 people at the railroad station there, pointing toward Ludesch, which was closer to Blons."

Sayers: "When we got to Ludesch, about four o'clock in the afternoon, they marked a place for us to land. And we set down."

The equipment for surgery and resuscitation was taken out at Ludesch, loaded in a small truck, and rushed off to Bludenz with Dr. Baumgartner, who set up shop in the small hospital there. A couple of Austrian rescue experts climbed into the cabin of the helicopter and Sayers took off again for Blons.

Sayers: "We flew up the valley with the help of an Austrian map that cost twenty cents and showed the mountains. It was far better for our purpose than our own flight map. We got about a mile and a half in the mouth of the Walsertal. There was a kind of three-cornered place there. Blons sets in a corner. We had to approach it from one side, against the wind."

Haid: "On the way up we saw on top of the hills where the snow broke away deep, deep crevasses. People were digging everywhere. There were ruins of houses—just parts of them above the snow. It was a complete scene of desolation and catastrophe. When they saw the helicopter coming they waved and directed us toward Blons. And when we first saw Blons it looked like the hand of God—or the Devil —had swept down across the mountain and the valley."

Sayers: "When we went in the whole town had been wiped out. The only possible place to land was where there had been a building and part of the floor was still there. But I couldn't really land there—I couldn't get on the platform because the hill rose too steeply in front of it and my rotors would have hit the ground in front."

And so Bill Sayers, at the controls of a helicopter that was still largely unfamiliar to him, set down on the edge of the floor of the ruined house with his two *front* wheels and the two rear wheels *off the ground,* and he held the helicopter in a hover in that position against a maddening wind that smote the aircraft as though in anger at its defying the destruction of the elements.

"I had the feeling," said Dr. Haid, "as if a swallow had set down at its nest. The rotors were two feet from the hillside." The dogs and their trainers and the Austrian rescue experts and the remaining equipment were off-loaded and then the first patient was taken aboard. She was Maria Tuertscher.

Haid: "She had a displacement of the seventh vertebra at the neck. We had to move her very carefully so she would not get paralyzed and be unable to breathe. We put others in the helicopter, a girl who was frozen up to her waist, she was black all the way to her waist, and there was another woman. And all the time we all kept watching the mountainside and we wondered whether the sound vibrations from the helicopter would start a new avalanche."

While they loaded on the patients Bill Sayers watched the hover and Cooley, who, as it happened, was fresh out of helicopter school and on his first mission, watched the instruments. And when there were as many persons aboard as the helicopter could carry Bill made his take off—by just falling off the side of the hill and then backing away.

Sayers brought his patients to Ludesch where they were moved on to Bludenz and put under the care of Dr. Baumgartner. Sayers got some more gasoline from a representative of the Swiss Red Cross, loaded his helicopter with more rescue experts, and returned to Blons. In all, that first night, during constant snowfall, he made three round trips, bringing in volunteers and carrying out patients, four or five each time. The last trip was made in almost total darkness. Each time he set down in Blons on just two front wheels.

Sayers: "We have a landing light that shines on a fixed spot and we have a searchlight that you can swing in a 360-degree arc. You can go into a place at maybe ten or fifteen miles an hour and check for wires and posts and trees. We tried usually to cruise between twenty-five and thirty knots, but it varied. If I got into a tight spot I would slow down. Dr. Haid flew with me and he loaded and unloaded patients and then between trips, whenever he got free time, he would run up to the hospital in Bludenz and treat people. After the last trip we couldn't make it any more that night. They gave us a hot dinner—wiener schnitzel, I think—and they gave us a place to sleep. They were extremely nice. They wouldn't let us pay for anything, room or food."

But Bill wouldn't permit himself the luxury of sleep, not just yet, although he had flown that day from Fürstenfeldbruck to Innsbruck to Ludesch and then three times back and forth in the snow-swept Walsertal. He drove over to the hospital in Bludenz and asked Dr. Baumgartner what additional medical supplies he needed and then he telephoned his commanding officer, Major Edward J. Ontko, up at Fursty, and he told him how bad it was and what Haid and Baumgartner had to have.

At Fürstenfeldbruck maintenance men were working tirelessly getting other newly arrived helicopters in commission. Ontko went out to the hangars and urged them to work even harder, and then he called Bob Rizon at Sembach. He related the facts that Sayers had given him and Rizon, a full colonel now, immediately turned over almost the entire facilities of his group to the suffering people in the Grosses Walsertal. The group surgeon, Major Rufus Hessberg, took off from Sembach the next morning and went to Fürstenfeldbruck to together the supplies Sayers had pleaded for.

A word about Doc Hessberg. He is a deceptive-looking little man. He is quiet, small, hardly ever speaks above a whisper. As I mentioned earlier in this book he is a jumper and has helped develop many new types of chutes now in use, always trying them out himself first. In the 1949 blizzard in the United States he flew day and night in temperatures reaching twenty-six below zero in the memorable Operation Snowbound, bringing medicines and food to people isolated in the Midwest. In February 1953 he worked indefatigably with Bob Rizon in flood-ravaged Holland. Later in the year 1954 he jumped into the mountains of Italy when a C-47 crashed there, killing twenty-one Air Force boys.

As soon as he landed at Fürstenfeldbruck he set to work with pararescue personnel and the base hospital commander collecting the medi-

cal equipment and supplies—plasma, bandages, antibiotics. By four
o'clock the next morning he had everything loaded on a plane and
a couple of hours later he took off for Austria.

He arrived at Ludesch about the same time Bob Rizon pulled in
from Sembach. There was time for only the briefest greetings between
Dr. Haid and Rizon, and then Haid filled in Hessberg on the medical
situation and Bill Sayers gave Rizon the Rescue picture. And then the
four of them piled into Sayers' chopper and went up to Blons. When
Rizon saw how dangerous was the flight into "Death Valley" he issued
an order: no helicopter pilot was to make the trip up the Walsertal
without going first with a pilot who had already been there.

Sayers and Cooley split up and checked out two pilots who came
down later that day, and when the new arrivals had their initiation
they in turn checked out others. And then Rizon set up a shuttling
system with his fleet of helicopters, taking in Red Cross workers,
Austrian rescue experts, and food, bringing out the sick, frozen, and
maimed.

During the day Haid and Hessberg flew with the choppers, gave
first aid on the spot in the valley, loaded the seriously injured and frostbitten aboard the aircraft and delivered them to Baumgartner. At night,
when the flights had to stop, Haid and Hessberg went to the hospital
and worked there until the small hours of the morning—the former
Austrian Army doctor and the American Air Force doctor laboring
side by side to make whole the broken and gangrenous bodies of the
people from the Walsertal Valley. For a four-day period neither Haid
nor Hessberg nor Baumgartner got more than three hours' sleep a
night. And the avalanche was not the only emergency.

Hessberg: "In the midst of all this we got an SOS call for a *maternity*
case up another valley. The local doctor who called Bruno said it was
a matter of life and death. One of the chopper pilots resting between
trips to the Walsertal offered to take Bruno up to this other valley. The
doctor who had called in was not at the place where he was supposed
to meet Bruno. Night was falling and the helicopter had to return.

"Bruno remained up the valley. When the chopper returned for him
the next day he had not one but *two* women—both pregnant with
complications. They were brought to the hospital and on top of everything else Dr. Haid delivered the two babies."

Now that the other helicopters were making the round trip to Blons,
Sayers and Cooley began to probe deeper into the Walsertal, to the
remote villages, Sonntag, Buchboden, Fontanello, seeking out people
who needed help. They were almost booby-trapped.

Sayers: "The valley itself is extremely narrow, much narrower than the section below Blons. They have cables strung across it where they go up and cut hay and let it slide across the cables.

"I was driving through there the first time and it was snowing and visibility was very poor and I came to one of these cables. It was about a thousand feet above the bottom of the valley. I threw the plane into a quick stop and started falling straight down on autorotation. I thought I would go under it. I thought there was just one strand. But there was another cable about a hundred feet under the first one and a third just under that and a fourth under that. Just like a wall. I got down to the bottom one and still had to go down.

"I was about thirty or forty feet off the ground. I did not have much room from there. If I had hit one of those cables I wouldn't be here. The top one that I saw was almost in the clouds and I didn't know if there was any above that. I managed to slip under the bottom one and I had to be pretty careful going up the rest of the valley. They had cables strung across everywhere at all different altitudes and you'd never see them until you were right on them and then you'd never know whether to try to go over them or under them. We were lucky."

And they saw how the hand that either God's or the Devil's had smitten the entire length of the Grosses Walsertal. It was a white hell. Houses uprooted and tumbled over on their sides, some of them a mile or more from their foundations. The stream that coursed along the valley bed choked with bodies of human beings and animals. Solitary dark figures of men and women and dogs burrowing in the snow like moles seeking out those who had been engulfed and buried. And the sudden cessation of digging and the raising of heads and hands beseechingly as the helicopter passed slowly with its shadow dark on the sparkling snow, and then the hysterical rush when the aircraft came down.

Sayers: "People fought to get on the helicopter, and we were loaded up so much we were in danger in getting off the snow. People would just have to be pushed off."

For three days Sayers and Cooley flew up and down the length of the Walsertal, dodging cables in the continuing snow.

Sayers: "I guess we flew about forty or fifty round trips. All the villages were wiped out to a great extent. The people would stamp out in the snow what they needed and we would put it down and then bring them what they asked for. Some of them needed bread and they would stamp out 'brot.' Others wanted potatoes and others wanted meat. So many people wanted onions. They would ask specifically for onions. We would drop fifty-pound sacks out. I will never forget one place where we couldn't land and people had 'brot' stamped out and

I picked up a big sack of bread and kicked it out the side. It fell right in the middle of the 'o' of the word 'brot.' And on each trip we would land somewhere and bring out the injured.

"One thing they kept talking about was the 'white death.' It is a complete lack of oxygen from these avalanches. It must be a vacuum because there is a white mist and they cannot breathe. Lots of people smothered without being under the snow. People kept muttering about it all the time.

"I didn't have any trouble with the helicopter until the second day and then it scared me half to death because I was on my way up the valley at a pretty low altitude and I was losing my fuel and oil pressure. I thought I was going to drop into that valley. There was no place to land and there was just this stream at the bottom.

"I just made it to the mouth of the valley when my fuel and oil pressure hit zero. But it turned out there was no trouble at all. It was just that my instrument had gone out but I didn't know it at the time. Remember, I was brand new to that airplane. I was just new to the airplane and I didn't know what was wrong.

"We got out at a place one day and walked into the church and they had all the people laid out there. All the dead. I think there were thirty dead adults and fifteen children. They had all the children on the pulpit. It was terrible.

"Another time we took one fellow out who had been pinned on top of a stove by the snowslide. The whole front of him was burned. The back of him was frozen. Burned on one side, frozen on the other! Dr. Haid told me how another fellow was buried while he was milking a cow. The avalanche came and hit him and he was buried under the snow in the hay with the cow for three days. He was real snug and warm and both of them were pulled out all right.

"I caught a terrific cold from tramping around in that snow. I had boots on but they got wet and never did get dry. Once in a while I got a stiff shot of cognac from Dr. Haid. I was as nervous as a cat. Toward the end of the day I would get tense and short-tempered. I would yell on the radio. It was a terrific strain.

"Then next to the last day they got in some more helicopters and Colonel Rizon told me to take a rest. He said I looked like I needed one. I remember it was raining then. I went over to the helicopter and climbed into it. It was leaking. I wrapped up in some blankets. One of the boys brought along a bottle of scotch. He said: 'You're not going to fly any more, take a drink.' "

Bill had himself a stiff shot and was just starting to warm up a little when Rizon came over and told him a new pilot had just arrived and had to be taken up the valley for his first trip. Bill said nothing about the drink. He threw off his blankets and told the newcomer to hop in, and he flew him to Blons.

Bill Sayers from Lubbock, Texas, told me of these things on a sunny afternoon in Sembach. He did not speak of the impact the Rescue operation had upon the people of Grosses Walsertal because Bill's mind doesn't work that way. He did tell me the impact it had upon him. "You realize how completely cut off they were, these people. There was no way they could get in or out. I can't imagine what would have happened to them if we did not have helicopters. They were just about frozen to death and you could not get to them from the ground.

"This was my first major mission for Air Rescue. To me, it sold me on Air Rescue. I kept thinking that a few years ago these people would have blown me out of the sky and now we were saving their lives. It gives you a very funny feeling when you are risking your own life and the lives of your crew." Bill paused. His forehead wrinkled. "I would do it again."

During the entire operation there was only one serious helicopter accident. It was the time when Major Ontko was flying Doc Hessberg into Blons to pick up some more survivors. Hessberg: "We came in once and because of a tricky wind we had to go around again in emergency flight. In the second approach for a landing we sheared off the tail rudder shaft."

The tail rudder shaft is what operates the rotor on the rear of the helicopter and that rotor is what keeps the chopper from spinning in circles. With it out of commission Ontko struggled with his controls and kept the aircraft aloft although it turned around and around, faster and faster. He dropped it as gently as he could, revolving like a whirling dervish, in deep snow on a steep incline. The men inside sat there for a little while waiting to see whether the chopper was going to slide down, then they cautiously crept out.

Hessberg: "We were not sick from the spinning. We were more scared. But we almost did get sick when we got out. Just about fifty feet from where we had set down there was a sheer drop of about fifteen hundred feet—straight down."

Major Ontko's comment later was this: "We set a lot of records on this mission and we almost set another. If we'd hit about twenty yards farther down we'd have become the biggest snowball ever seen in Austria."

By Saturday, the sixteenth of January, Austrian ground rescue workers broke a trail through to Blons and some two thousand ski-borne volunteers poured into the valley and shuttling by air no longer was necessary. Bob Rizon's gang were able to leave for their bases in Germany, leaving behind them as a memento a helicopter crashed into the side of a hill. They also left behind a memory.

The number of men and women and children close to death who were brought out of the Grosses Walsertal by helicopter ran well into the hundreds—Bill Sayers alone brought out between seventy and eighty persons. Rescue workers with equipment and dogs were brought into the valley by the same helicopters—which also hauled in almost four tons of food, giving life to people, many of whom quite possibly would have starved to death before succor could reach them on the ground.

A year and a half later, on a beautiful Saturday in June, Bill Sayers and I flew down from Sembach to Innsbruck. We were met at the airport by Dr. Haid. We visited for a little while with Professor Breitner at the University Hospital and they told me many of the things you have just read. And then Bill and I got into Dr. Haid's little car and we drove almost a hundred miles, over St. Christoph's Pass, to the village of Blons. It was the first time since the avalanche that Bill Sayers had gone back to the people who exist, in a certain degree, due to him.

Word had gone ahead that the American helicopter pilot was coming to visit them and when we arrived in Blons the people of the community and of other communities up the valley were gathered in front of the church. They were scrubbed clean and they wore their best clothes and as Dr. Haid stopped the car and Bill got out they walked slowly toward him, their faces radiant. Bill began to look uncomfortable.

They stopped a few feet from him and just looked at him, and then a plump woman rushed up to him, paused, and reached out and touched him slowly on the face. "Do you remember me?" she asked. "I am Frau Schiebel." Her eyes filled with tears. She smoothed her green dress. "That morning, do you not remember?"

Maria Tuertscher stepped forward. "I was the one with the neck injury."

Another woman, in her early thirties, her blond hair braided elaborately over her ears, cried out: "I am Annamarie Metzler. Do you not remember me?" At Frau Metzler's side was her husband, Hermann, a soldier in the German Army during the war. He shifted self-consciously and then he straightened and raised his hand in salute to Captain Sayers. Frau Metzler seized Bill's hand and pressed it to her bosom and began to talk rapidly. Dr. Haid translated her words.

"How I remember! I was five months with child at the time. I was working so hard those days and nights and I didn't get anything to eat

and I could not stand any more to see all the people getting hurt
around me and some of them dying in front of me. I broke down, and
I had the feeling it was the end of my life and I lay there for days
almost out of my mind. Then they told me that an American helicopter
is coming to fly me away. I was never in a helicopter before.

"I remember how they put me in Captain Sayers' helicopter and I
was crying for my children and how Captain Sayers would not leave
until they found the children and put them in the cabin with me. And
then Captain Sayers took us out—to think he did it, without knowing
any of us, or the danger of the area! How dangerous it was for him!

"I know he rescued me risking his own life. I thank my life and good
health only to him. A rescue group in an air force is almost a holy
thing. It was only through their help so many people were saved."

Now all the people pressed closer to Bill Sayers, all talking at once,
Dr. Haid trying to translate what everybody was saying as they re-
minded Bill of the things he had done for them. The burgomaster of
Blons, Herr Josef Bischof, spoke a few words in the name of his people,
and Bill got redder and redder, and he ran his fingers around his collar.
When Herr Bischof was finished Bill said to Dr. Haid: "Tell them
I'd like to see how they are rebuilding their village."

When Dr. Haid translated this the people swept Bill away, struggling
to get close to him, to be nearest to him, to touch some part of his
clothing, and they led him around Blons and showed him the new
homes and barns that had been built and were being built.

Bruno Haid bit his lip and lowered his eyes. Herr Bischof shook his
head slowly. "They will never forget him. This was our greatest avalanche since the one of 1670. They will not talk of that one any more
but of the one of 1954. We have never been able to find out how many
lives were lost. In Blons alone it was well over a hundred—dead and
missing. We still find bodies. But we do not think of the dead, only of
those who were given back to us by men like Captain Sayers and the
others who came after him."

Late that night we drove back through the mountains to the little
town of Oetz where Bruno Haid was born. Although it was well after
three o'clock in the morning Dr. Haid's father was waiting for us in
the Drei Mohren and he led us to the dining room. A table was laden
with a cold buffet and bottles of rare Austrian wine from Herr Haid's
private stock. We lingered over the wine until after dawn that Sunday
morning. The Oetz church bell began to toll slowly.

Bruno Haid stared at his glass. "You saw them in Blons, the way
they feel, even now, after all this time. But you should have seen them

then. I had the opportunity to listen closely to them and I saw how much they appreciated this help and how grateful they were.

"I saw people crying in gratitude and happiness when your people brought in injured relatives whom they thought were dead. And they knew this was not for money or for reward, even not for the expectation of gratitude."

Dr. Haid looked up. His fine features seemed to take on an illumination. "Today you have seen for yourself. I do not have anything to add, except that on that day when your people left, I wept when I said farewell to Colonel Rizon and Dr. Hessberg and Captain Sayers. I never experienced such generosity as this was."

JOHN STEWART COLLIS

An Irish-born writer living now in England, John Stewart Collis has had two books published in the United States. The first, *The Triumph of the Tree,* is a remarkable evocation of the part trees have played in the history of man: in his physical development, his mythologies, and in his so-called "conquest of nature." I regard it as one of the most fascinating and original books published during recent years. It has been followed by *The Moving Waters,* which is an equally imaginative, yet scientifically soundly based book dealing with what may be roundly described as the role of water in the economy of nature.

For the purpose of this book I have selected a passage describing one of the more recent frontiers in man's exploration of the world about him. Not as much has yet been written about it as we have had concerning the sea around us, the skies above us, or the land under our feet. This new frontier is that of the underground world—the world of the speleologists—the men who venture into the bowels of the earth, who follow subterranean watercourses to their unpredictable source. The hazards which they accept are breath-taking. Mr. Collis tells you what they are like, and what the world is like that these daring men have penetrated. It is unlike any other that we know.

In the Bowels of the Earth: The Speleologists

IN THE nineteenth century various mountain caves were known, in Austria, in Australia, in France, in England, and in America, where the seventy-mile accumulation of avenues which compose the Kentucky Mammoth Cave is still considered, according to Martel, to be "one of the most impressive phenomena to be seen on this planet of ours." But it is only recently that men began to realize that here was a new world to be conquered. It had seemed that the earth now offered nothing further to explorers; that the virgin forest, the untrodden desert, the mapless mountain, the unjourneyed sea were all things of the past and that there were no realms remaining which were completely undiscovered. We were tempted to say, "It is finished: there is nothing left now for the iron-souled adventurers, the active visionaries, who in all ages have sought to penetrate into uncharted places, and with nothing more than an intuition to go by, and with the possibility of irretrievable calamity facing them at every step, have yet endured all things, overcome all things, and discovered new realms. Now there is only the moon left." Yet we need not say this. There is spelaeology. We can still go where others have not dared to tread or have not found the way. We can enter regions still waiting to be explored by brave men. We can open gates hitherto closed and pass into territories of inconceivable beauty and alarm. We can find chambers once known before the dawn of history by cave men, and then penetrate beyond into places which have never previously echoed to the trampling of any feet. This is the country of the spelaeologists, this their playground; here lies all their ambition, their desperate endeavour. They are not as other men: unexampled fortitude, steel-like patience, sublime audacity, the nerves of acrobats and the blood of fishes, belong to the adventurers whose way of life is cast in those lonely lands.

The French spelaeologists have been the most articulate, and it is to them that we chiefly owe our knowledge, and through them we may experience marvellous and terrifying adventures by proxy. The honoured pioneer is Edouard Martel, who led the way at the close of the last century and the beginning of this one. "Here was a man," says Norbert Casteret, his generous-minded follower, "who descended to terrifying depths to look at underground France, and who discovered the Palace of the Thousand and One Nights for the greater glory of science. He thought nothing of risking his life daily by having himself let down on a rope tied to the middle of a stick; he rode his broomstick clad in a bowler hat and a sack coat like a Jules Verne scientist. Martel was 'the man of the chasms.'...He explored hundreds in many countries." Now the number of spelaeologists increases yearly and tales come in not only from France but from Italy, Switzerland, Austria, Algeria, Yugoslavia, Montenegro, and the United States. Pierre Chevalier, who has spent 960 hours underground and gone on fifty-nine out of the sixty-five of the expeditions carried out by the Speleo-Alpine Club between 1935 and 1947, lists forty cave systems having a total drop of over eight hundred feet—though some go down more than twice that depth. And these underground systems, as I have mentioned, are but few in comparison with those yet to be discovered, and are nothing in numbers when we think of the systems which offer no means of approach.

What are the means of approach? Roughly two: either you see a stream disappearing into a cavity in the mountain, or merely a hole—perhaps not very obvious save to the trained person who is looking for it. They may be too small to offer any entrance to a man, or just large enough, or extremely large at the outset. This is where the underground mountaineer starts his adventure.

Often he starts alone. Later on, if he has found something interesting opening up, he will seek company; later still a team may prove necessary. I am thinking especially of Norbert Casteret. He was born with a genius for spelaeology. Caves called to him at the age of five. From then onwards they reigned supreme in the empire of his thoughts. He opens one of his books with the words: "I know and love caverns, abysses, and subterranean rivers. Studying and exploring them has been my passion for years. Where can one find such excitement, see such strange sights, enjoy such intellectual satisfactions as in exploration below ground?" In recounting his search for the true source of the Garonne (an important geographical and political point) he drops the remark: "For three years I had not passed a day without asking myself, 'Where does that stream go?'" That is typical of the truly dedicated man—the counterpart of which question could easily be quoted from the utterances of all such men in many different fields, especially in science and art.

Casteret loved exploring alone. In fact, in the course of his cave career he made the most dramatic solo adventure in the annals of spelaeology. He came to a crack in a mountain at Montespan in the Pyrenees, from which a stream was running out. He undressed, squeezed through the hole and found himself in a corridor about 12 feet wide and 8 feet high. Wading in the water, he progressed about 60 yards when the ceiling began to dip, the water to deepen, after which presently the roof and water joined. Thus he was stopped.

Explore farther? When men, as opposed to fishes, come upon the roof of a cave dipping down into the water, they can go no farther. Yes, but your passionate spelaeologist is not as other men are. Why not dive into this depth and this darkness, Casteret asked himself, and see if it is an underwater tunnel through which one could swim and perhaps come up again into the air at the other end? True, the risk was appalling to contemplate: the tunnel might go on indefinitely, he might go over a high waterfall, he might run into a cul-de-sac, and if tempted too far might fail to get back before his lungs burst. Almost up to his neck now in water, with one hand clutching a candle, Casteret stood there in the awful loneliness and silence weighing his chances. Then sticking his candle on to a ledge, with a mixture of confident intuition and sublime audacity he dived into the unknown, using his finger-tips for eyes—*and came up the other side.*

He had forced what they call a siphon, a tunnel with a submerged ceiling. Then with a good sense only equalled by his courage he immediately turned about and dived back again—for to lose sense of direction in that total darkness would be as easy as it would be fatal. So back he went to his candle shining on the black water.

Next day he returned with more equipment, consisting of a rubber bathing-cap full of matches and extra candles. Once more, clothed only with these things, he entered the freezing water in the dark, cold underworld, and again successfully swam through the siphon. His candle now showed him a roof parallel to the water with a thin airspace between. After a hundred yards he came to a clay bank at the entrance to a chamber rising to a height of forty feet and decorated with stalagmite cascades. Accustomed as he was to caverns, he confesses that he had never known such a feeling of "isolation, oppression, and terror"—for these men do not possess less sensitivity than others, only more courage. He found himself now faced with another siphon. He dived again. It was longer than the first, but he again got through. Now he was locked below by a double barrier, and in the untellable solitude and black silence he "struggled against an uneasiness slowly turning to anguish." Shaking with cold, numbed by the glacial water, he yet pursued his way, and crawling on for some distance, he reached a larger hall than the last. He continued his exploration for five hours through further chambers and corridors and galleries with ever more perspectives opening up and leading him on whenever he thought he had come to some impassable bottle-neck. At last he went back, nearly losing his way when confronted with forks he had not noticed on his way in, and failing to get through the worst siphon at the first attempt.

A year later he returned to the attack, this time accompanied by a friend. Having once more passed the second siphon, Casteret began to probe in a nook with an excavating tool he had brought with him on this occasion, and came upon a primitive flint which had obviously been used. No sooner had he discovered this than he came upon a clay statue of a bear which he had not noticed in the feeble candlelight.

He had stumbled upon a piece of sculpture that was soon to be acknowledged by scientists from many countries as the oldest statue in the world.

Then for an hour discovery followed discovery—horses in relief, clay lions, engravings, designs, mysterious symbols. All the important large animals of the Magdalenian period were engraved on the walls and rocks. Many of them showed mutilations—as if javelins had been hurled at them. Sometimes they found claw-marks beside human footprints in the clay, and sometimes both were mixed together where there had been a struggle for possession of the cave. A footprint in a lonely place is always a pathetic and a tragic sight. Here were footprints, forlorn and fearful, that had remained in solitude for two hundred centuries of speechless night.

Thus was the courage of Casteret rewarded. He had plunged into the unknown—and had come up into the Past to roam in ages before the dawn of history.

It is no doubt a commonplace of archaeological adventure to come upon cave drawings—though never less than thrilling—and to contemplate the combination of art and magic. We started in caves, and at the death of civilization the other day, when the three necessities of man became food, clothing, and shelters, we returned to them—and may yet be compelled to do so on a much larger scale. In between these extremes caves have provided habitation for hermits and other lovers of solitude throughout the ages, for many saints in many countries, for professional wise men, for beggars, and for those of whom it was written that they "went about in sheepskins, in goatskins: being destitute, afflicted, evil entreated (of whom the world was not worthy), wandering in deserts and mountains and caves and the holes of the earth." There is nothing exceptional in discovering the relics of habitation in caves, but it must be conceded to Casteret that the way to his discovery no less than what he found provides the most dramatic instance in the history of such enterprise. It is with some amusement that one learns how, when the distinguished scientists arrived to check his claims, they were baulked by the siphons, and the water had to be considerably drained and diverted before they could attend at the primitive exhibition.

That adventure and triumph of Casteret's is moving and thrilling, but perhaps one is even more moved when the explorer pursues his way and comes, after frightful hardship and danger, into regions which hitherto no man had ever penetrated since the foundation of the world—that surely is the ultimate of exploration. To emerge from a cat-hole into the soundless blackness of eternal night, to stand alone in the unspeakable isolation of a sepulchral hall—imagine the anguish and the ecstasy!

A cat-hole is horrifying to contemplate. It is a hole which the explorer thinks he may possibly be able to squeeze his way through if he lies on his stomach and worms his way along. He cannot tell what length the hole is, or whether he may fail to get through, and perhaps stick. It has happened more than once that a spelaeologist, on his own, miles from all human succour, has got stuck, neither able to advance nor retreat, and there has perished. Yet nothing seems to daunt these

men, and they have frequently unlocked their door by climbing
through the keyhole. Also, entrance to this underworld often must be
effected by descending grim perpendicular holes for about 800 feet.
These pot-holes are nearly as frightening as the cat-holes. One of the
bravest of these adventurers, after gazing down into his first pit,
declared afterwards (though too modestly) : "I realized with shame and
despair that I was no explorer. I would never dare attempt such a
chasm—the very sight of it scared me to death." Worse in a way are
the journeys down the waterfalls. After descending a pot-hole of 500 to
800 feet, perhaps, and finding a landing-place at last, he may thence
make his way through a hall or a corridor—the possibilities are many.
He may be compelled to wade through a lake and along a river which
suddenly falls over into another shaft. Is this the end of his journey?
By no means. If he has enough rope with him he will tie it to a rock
and go down with the waterfall. If the rope is not long enough and he
fails to reach the bottom, though already soaking and frozen, he will be
obliged to climb up again against the cruel buffeting of the torrent.

Worse possibly is their special method of being hanged. When a
party of spelaeologists are tackling some formidable cave they sometimes place a windlass at the top of one of those terrible holes which
confront them as they proceed. By this means a man can be lowered
by cable down into the darkness. The cable is ⅕ inch thick. Its composition is such that it is very strong, but its thinness strikes terror into
the toughest of these men, and they always feel that they are literally
hanging by a thread. The man is lowered, sometimes hundreds of
feet, until some landing-place is established where he can be joined
by a comrade, and together they will continue their journey into the
bowels of the mountains. But in due course it is necessary to get back
and be hauled up. On these occasions the windlass does not always
work. It frequently breaks down, gets stuck, advances upwards in
jerks, or suddenly lets the man down a few feet while he hangs there
in agony of expectation. Casteret gives an account of how his companion, Vander Elst, thus ascended from a pit in the Basque country.
It was a question of stoppage after stoppage, a succession of jerks,
prolonged halts—repeated for nearly an hour as he hung there. Casteret speaks of his anxiety for his friend as he watched from below,
seeing him swing slowly higher, when the breaking of the cable would
be fatal, and how if the winding apparatus broke down definitely he
would be suspended there indefinitely without any possibility of rescue;
and he adds these words (without emphasis) : "Not for one moment
did he show the slightest sign of being worried, *nor did he address a
single question to the men above,* who must have been having an

awful time with the winding, coupled with the dread of not being able to get us up."

They are rewarded for these labours. The raindrop has seen to that. The landscape which it has opened up for travellers in this far country exceeds their expectations and justifies their toil. They are amazed at the revelations resulting from the hydrogeological ablutions carried out through centuries of dawnless dark in the depths of the earth. The explorer never knows where his steps will take him, what he may encounter next. At the other end of this siphon or that cat-hole, at the bottom of this shaft, what will declare itself? Will it lead him to a narrow corridor or a cathedral nave, to a river or a waterfall, to a lovely sea-green lake or another yawning pit?

A huge vault may open before him, a chamber so vast that, like the giant cave near Trieste, the massive St. Peter's in Rome could be put inside it, or like the Cavern of Cagire, into which a football field would fit, together with the Cathedral of Notre Dame with its thirty-seven chapels; or the chamber itself may be like a cathedral, and it was right for Casteret and his companions to celebrate Mass in the Grotto of Esparros with its Gothic nave, its pillars of stalagmite, its altar, shrine, and font.

He may discover at the bottom of a chasm a grim chaos of boulders and all about him the results of explosive pressure and primitive savagery of convulsion; and yet just beyond this he is likely to come to a miniature grotto bearing witness to the delicate, graceful work of water falling drop by drop to create slender, translucent stalactites, filigrees of gypsum, and embossed draperies upon the many-coloured walls; and roaming farther he may find himself gazing across at a dream country with stalagmitic mosques, minarets, and towers on a rounded white and yellow hill, belonging to the *Arabian Nights* realm of the mind; while at his feet is a limpid lakelet with water so clear and quiet that he can see the bottom as sharply as through glass, a submarine landscape starred with crystalline fronds like a coral carpet —perhaps the source from which Alph the sacred river ran.

He may pass into a void, or what seems to him a void, and wrestle with impenetrable nothingness, his candle revealing only a hall of empty darkness. Alone he has entered into a loneliness unmeasured; a solitary in a solitude like no solitude upon the earth, he is suspended in centuries of accumulated silence, broken only by the steady fall of a single waterdrop like the ticking of the clock of eternity. He may stumble on into a deafening region of roaring rivers and sounding cataracts; and then come to another place where the waters have been stopped and stilled: the waterfall frozen into silence and chiselled into peace; an ice curtain hanging free; the lake a mirror of glass; the river like a glacier; and huge towers rising in the abyss like icy arms up-raised to stay the further steps of human feet.

He may come to a spot where he hears and is sure that he hears voices, where no voices are; where he is positive that a conversation is going on, for he can all but catch the words, though there is no one to converse; where sighs and wailings come to him from places where there is no one to lament. If he reaches a cavern above which a gleam of light shows that there is a hole leading to the surface, he may stumble upon a charnel-house of decaying corpses of animals that have fallen down. Sometimes mouldy wood is also found in such a spot, and the astonished spelaeologist may encounter phosphorescent mush-rooms gleaming in the darkness like glow-worms, such as were seen in a pot-hole in the Basque country—a vegetation as extraordinary as that nightmare meadow of thick white grass that graced the bottom of a chasm, three hundred and twenty-six feet down in the Moroccan Atlas.

He will not often see such monstrous shapes of tragic growth in sunless soil; his gaze will be turned far more often to the true plants that furnish these regions with appointments more resplendent than in the palaces of kings. The stalagmites rising from the ground, the stalactites hanging from the roof, are the most enthralling of all the marvels of water-work. They grow at the rate of about an inch in 1,000 years, or perhaps the thickness of a sixpence in the compass of a man's lifetime. Often they meet; but not in the middle, not halfway, for it is obvious (or so it seems to me) that the stalagmites build up a good deal faster than the stalactites build down. When they meet they look like pillars supporting their temple. A small *forest* of them, numbering 400, from 60 to 100 feet high, were found in the Chasm of Armand in Lozère. Gazing upon them, the stupefied explorers felt that all their toils and dangers were as little against the reward of such a revelation of Nature's engineering: first the raising of vapour by vir-tue of the sun, and its housing in the lofts of the sky; thence its descent upon the mountain and into the rocks, followed by the excavation of the chasm; and, finally, the tribute of the pale deposit which through further centuries had built up these silver trunks of stone.

We generally think of stalactites as daggers and spears and Damoc-lean swords, but they assume all sorts of shapes and all sorts of colours, sometimes looking exactly like bunches of carrots (pink and yellow), or so like curtains that you feel you could easily take them down and fold them over your arm. We need not go far to see these things, but we must go a long way, we must climb up to an opening in a cliff, and then crawl through a cat-hole, to see what shows itself in the deep-

est abyss in France, the Cirque de Lez. The first man who got through
the cat-hole shouted frantically back to his comrades, *"The white sea!"*
Scrambling through after him, they beheld a brilliantly white surface
spread under their feet, terminated by high white cliffs—none of it
made of water or ice, but of stalagmite. The white expanse narrowed
and became like a fjord between those Dover cliffs, until it ended at
the foot of a petrified waterfall. They continued their journey, encountering fresh marvels which their most experienced leader was
quite unprepared for. Advancing through chambers and vestibules
now, unable to avoid trampling on flowers, crushing masses of crystal
with their hobnailed boots, breaking glass rods and swords and coral-
bushes, they stepped into a fairy palace. "Stalactites and crystals sparkled
everywhere; their profusion, their whiteness, their shapes were fantastic beyond belief. We were inside a precious stone; it was a palace
of crystal." As they walked on they brushed against strange cobwebs
that broke at a breath, and against "silver strings with the brilliance of
silk yarn," dangling from roof and walls, which could be tied in knots
and wound into balls. These mineral cords and cobwebs were a form
of gypsum, which provides the most varied floral display in this kingdom, in crosier and plume and cluster and gem. Was this the thread of
which Blake spoke, which if you held on to would lead you in at
Heaven's gate?

We must now leave these scenes. It has been encouraging to meet
these men. As we go from their presence many images come before the
mind. We think of them passing from the sight of peaceful forests,
down the pitiless shaft into a world totally and endlessly dark, to wage
their battle and match their skill against indefinite difficulties and
obstacles, pushing their way ever farther into the heart of a mountain.
We think of their special and dreadful hazards: getting lost in a
labyrinth, or stuck in a cat-hole, or drowned by a sudden inundation,
or injured by falling stones, or nearly frozen to death in drenching
clothes. We think of the patience of men who can perch on ledges or
narrow balconies 400 feet down a chasm overhanging pitch-black space
for fifteen to twenty hours while their comrades in front carry on the
exploration, hearing nothing save the shrill little cries of bats, sad
children of eternal night. We think of the perseverance that drove
them to return again and again to the attack of some desperate, ever-
opening cave such as the Henne-Morte (after the dead woman whose
winding-sheet was snow and her tomb a mountain), which was attacked eleven times during ten years before yielding to conquest.

It was during this saga of assault that two men were terribly injured
in the depths, one by slipping, the other by a stone falling on him, and
had to be got back to the surface—a terrible and wonderful story. When

thinking of those two men, whose one desire as they lay in agony was to be able to climb and search again, my mind turned to another scene: I thought of Philip Wills's glider-flight over the Italian mountains and of his dying comrade who had met with disaster, declaring that he would yet live to fly again. I thought of the two lots of men: the glider pilots who, mounting through the shafts and potholes in the air, hold acquaintance with the clouds, and stride the blast, and range the kingdoms of the sky: and these their fellows who leave the light of heaven for the darkness of the pit to search the secrets of the caves, and stand beside the Styx in the empty hall of Hades.

PART II

Man Against the Inner World

JOB

Few would question that the lamentations of Job make one of the greatest books of the Old Testament. I do not pretend to know the Bible as well as I am sure my five Scottish great-grandparents did, but out of what they would consider my skimpy knowledge I should vote for Job, Ecclesiastes, Ruth, and the Psalms. Job should really be printed in full, but available space forbade. I trust my butchery will not enrage the readers of this book, for Job is all magnificent stuff, or, as Somerset Maugham would say (in preference to "majestic"), majestical. I cannot forbear remarking that it gives us one of the comparatively few happy endings among the great Bible stories.

The Trials of Job

IS THERE not an appointed time to man upon earth?
Are not his days also like the days of an hireling?
As a servant earnestly desireth the shadow,
And as an hireling looketh for the reward of his work:
So am I made to possess months of vanity,
And wearisome nights are appointed to me.
When I lie down, I say,
When shall I arise, and the night be gone?
And I am full of tossings to and fro unto the dawning of the day.
My flesh is clothed with worms and clods of dust;
My skin is broken, and become loathsome.
My days are swifter than a weaver's shuttle,
And are spent without hope.
O remember that my life is wind:
Mine eye shall no more see good.
The eye of him that hath seen me shall see me no more:
Thine eyes are upon me, and I am not.
As the cloud is consumed and vanisheth away:

So he that goeth down to the grave shall come up no more.
He shall return no more to his house,
Neither shall his place know him any more.
Therefore I will not refrain my mouth;
I will speak in the anguish of my spirit;
I will complain in the bitterness of my soul.
Am I a sea, or a whale,
That thou settest a watch over me?
When I say, My bed shall comfort me,
My couch shall ease my complaint;
Then thou scarest me with dreams,
And terrifiest me through visions:
So that my soul chooseth strangling,
And death rather than my life.
I loathe it; I would not live alway:
Let me alone; for my days are vanity.
What is man, that thou shouldest magnify him?
And that thou shouldest set thine heart upon him?
And that thou shouldest visit him every morning,
And try him every moment?
How long wilt thou not depart from me,
Nor let me alone till I swallow down my spittle?
I have sinned; what shall I do unto thee,
O thou preserver of men?
Why hast thou set me as a mark against thee,
So that I am a burden to myself?
And why dost thou not pardon my transgression,
And take away mine iniquity?
For now shall I sleep in the dust;
And thou shalt seek me in the morning, but I shall not be."

"My soul is weary of my life;
I will leave my complaint upon myself;
I will speak in the bitterness of my soul.
I will say unto God, Do not condemn me;
Shew me wherefore thou contendest with me.
Is it good unto thee that thou shouldest oppress,
That thou shouldest despise the work of thine hands,
And shine upon the counsel of the wicked?
Hast thou eyes of flesh?
Or seest thou as man seeth?
Are thy days as the days of man?
Are thy years as man's days,

That thou enquirest after mine iniquity,
And searchest after my sin?
Thou knowest that I am not wicked;
And there is none that can deliver out of thine hand.
Thine hands have made me and fashioned me
Together round about; yet thou dost destroy me.
Remember, I beseech thee, that thou hast made me as the clay;
And wilt thou bring me into dust again?
Hast thou not poured me out as milk,
And curdled me like cheese?
Thou hast clothed me with skin and flesh,
And hast fenced me with bones and sinews.
Thou hast granted me life and favour,
And thy visitation hath preserved my spirit.
And these things hast thou hid in thine heart:
I know that this is with thee.
If I sin, then thou markest me,
And thou wilt not acquit me from mine iniquity.
If I be wicked, woe unto me;
And if I be righteous, yet will I not lift up my head.
I am full of confusion; therefore see thou mine affliction;
For it increaseth. Thou huntest me as a fierce lion:
And again thou shewest thyself marvellous upon me.
Thou renewest thy witnesses against me,
And increasest thine indignation upon me;
Changes and war are against me.
Wherefore then hast thou brought me forth out of the womb?
Oh that I had given up the ghost, and no eye had seen me!
I should have been as though I had not been;
I should have been carried from the womb to the grave.
Are not my days few? cease then,
And let me alone, that I may take comfort a little,
Before I go whence I shall not return,
Even to the land of darkness and the shadow of death;
A land of darkness, as darkness itself;
And of the shadow of death, without any order,
And where the light is as darkness."

"Man that is born of a woman
Is of a few days, and full of trouble.
He cometh forth like a flower, and is cut down:
He fleeth also as a shadow, and continueth not.
And dost thou open thine eyes upon such an one,

And bringest me into judgement with thee?
Who can bring a clean thing out of an unclean?
Not one.
Seeing his days are determined,
The number of his months are with thee,
Thou hast appointed his bounds that he cannot pass;
Turn from him, that he may rest,
Till he shall accomplish, as an hireling, his day.
For there is hope of a tree,
If it be cut down, that it will sprout again,
And that the tender branch thereof will not cease.
Though the root thereof wax old in the earth,
And the stock thereof die in the ground;
Yet through the scent of water it will bud,
And bring forth boughs like a plant.
But man dieth, and wasteth away:
Yea, man giveth up the ghost, and where is he?
As the waters fail from the sea,
And the flood decayeth and drieth up:
So man lieth down, and riseth not:
Till the heavens be no more, they shall not awake,
Nor be raised out of their sleep.
O that thou wouldest hide me in the grave,
That thou wouldest keep me secret, until thy wrath be past,
That thou wouldest appoint me a set time, and remember me!
If a man die, shall he live again?
All the days of my appointed time will I wait,
Till my change come.
Thou shalt call, and I will answer thee:
Thou wilt have a desire to the work of thine hands.
For now thou numberest my steps:
Dost thou not watch over my sin?
My transgression is sealed up in a bag,
And thou sewest up mine iniquity.
And surely the mountain falling cometh to nought,
And the rock is removed out of his place.
The waters wear the stones:
Thou washest away the things which grow out of the dust of the earth;
And thou destroyest the hope of man.
Thou prevailest for ever against him, and he passeth:
Thou changest his countenance, and sendest him away.
His sons come to honour, and he knoweth it not;

And they are brought low, but he perceiveth it not of them.
But his flesh upon him shall have pain,
And his soul within him shall mourn."

"Surely there is a vein for the silver,
And a place for gold where they fine it.
Iron is taken out of the earth,
And brass is molten out of the stone.
He setteth an end to darkness,
And searcheth out all perfection:
The stones of darkness, and the shadow of death.
The flood breaketh out from the inhabitant;
Even the waters forgotten of the foot:
They are dried up, they are gone away from men.
As for the earth, out of it cometh bread:
And under it is turned up as it were fire.
The stones of it are the place of sapphires:
And it hath dust of gold.
There is a path which no fowl knoweth,
And which the vulture's eye hath not seen:
The lion's whelps have not trodden it,
Nor the fierce lion passed by it.
He putteth forth his hand upon the rock;
He overturneth the mountains by the roots.
He cutteth out rivers among the rocks;
And his eye seeth every precious thing.
He bindeth the floods from overflowing;
And the thing that is hid bringeth he forth to light.
But where shall wisdom be found?
And where is the place of understanding?
Man knoweth not the price thereof;
Neither is it found in the land of the living.
The depth saith, "It is not in me":
And the sea saith, "It is not with me."
It cannot be gotten for gold,
Neither shall silver be weighed for the price thereof.
It cannot be valued with the gold of Ophir,
With the precious onyx, or the sapphire.
The gold and the crystal cannot equal it:
And the exchange of it shall not be for jewels of fine gold.
No mention shall be made of coral, or of pearls:
For the price of wisdom is above rubies.

The topaz of Ethiopia shall not equal it,
Neither shall it be valued with pure gold.
Whence then cometh wisdom?
And where is the place of understanding?
Seeing it is hid from the eyes of all living,
And kept close from the fowls of the air.
Destruction and death say,
'We have heard the fame thereof with our ears.'
God understandeth the way thereof,
And he knoweth the place thereof.
For he looketh to the ends of the earth,
And seeth under the whole heaven;
To make the weight for the winds;
And he weigheth the waters by measure.
When he made a decree for the rain,
And a way for the lightning of the thunder:
Then did he see it, and declare it;
He prepared it, yea, and searched it out.
And unto man he said, 'Behold, the fear of the Lord, that is wisdom;
And to depart from evil is understanding.' "

Then the Lord answered Job out of the whirlwind, and said,
"Who is this that darkeneth counsel
By words without knowledge?
Gird up now thy loins like a man;
For I will demand of thee, and answer thou me.
Where wast thou when I laid the foundations of the earth?
Declare, if thou hast understanding.
Who hath laid the measures thereof, if thou knowest?
Or who hath stretched the line upon it?
Whereupon are the foundations thereof fastened?
Or who laid the corner stone thereof;
When the morning stars sang together,
And all the sons of God shouted for joy?
Or who shut up the sea with doors,
When it brake forth, as if it had issued out of the womb?
When I made the cloud the garment thereof,
And thick darkness a swaddlingband for it,
And brake up for it my decreed place,
And set bars and doors,
And said, Hitherto shalt thou come, but no further:
And here shall thy proud waves be stayed?
Hast thou commanded the morning since thy days;

And caused the dayspring to know his place;
That it might take hold of the ends of the earth,
That the wicked might be shaken out of it?
It is turned as clay to the seal;
And they stand as a garment.
And from the wicked their light is withholden,
And the high arm shall be broken.
Hast thou entered into the springs of the sea?
Or hast thou walked in the search of the depth?
Have the gates of death been opened unto thee?
Or hast thou seen the doors of the shadow of death?
Hast thou perceived the breadth of the earth?
Declare if thou knowest it all.
Where is the way where light dwelleth?
And as for darkness, where is the place thereof,
That thou shouldest take it to the bound thereof,
And that thou shouldest know the paths to the house thereof?
Knowest thou it, because thou wast then born?
Or because the number of thy days is great?
Hast thou entered into the treasures of the snow?
Or hast thou seen the treasures of the hail,
Which I have reserved against the time of trouble,
Against the day of battle and war?
By what way is the light parted,
Which scattereth the east wind upon the earth?
Who hath divided a watercourse for the overflowing of waters,
Or a way for the lightning of thunder;
To cause it to rain on the earth, where no man is;
On the wilderness, wherein there is no man;
To satisfy the desolate and waste ground;
And to cause the bud of the tender herb to spring forth?
Hath the rain a father?
Or who hath begotten the drops of dew?
Out of whose womb came the ice?
And to hoary frost of heaven, who hath gendered it?
The waters are hid as with a stone,
And the face of the deep is frozen.
Canst thou bind the sweet influences of Pleiades,
Or loose the bands of Orion?
Canst thou bring forth Mazzaroth in his season?
Or canst thou guide Arcturus with his sons?
Knowest thou the ordinances of heaven?

Canst thou set the dominion thereof in the earth?
Canst thou lift up thy voice to the clouds,
That abundance of waters may cover thee?
Canst thou send lightnings, that they may go,
And say unto thee, 'Here we are'?
Who hath put wisdom in the inward parts?
Or who hath given understanding to the heart?
Who can number the clouds in wisdom?
Or who can stay the bottles of heaven,
When the dust groweth into hardness,
And the clods cleave fast together?

"Wilt thou hunt the prey for the lion?
Or fill the appetite of the young lions,
When they couch in their dens,
And abide in the covert to lie in wait?

"Who provideth for the raven his food?
When his young ones cry unto God,
They wander for lack of meat."

"Knowest thou the time when the wild goats of the rock bring forth?
Or canst thou mark when the hinds do calve?
Canst thou number the months that they fulfil?
Or knowest thou the time when they bring forth?
They bow themselves, they bring forth their young ones,
They cast out their sorrows.
Their young ones are in good liking, they grow up with corn;
They go forth, and return not unto them.

"Who hath sent out the wild ass free?
Or who hath loosed the bands of the wild ass?
Whose house I have made the wilderness,
And the barren land his dwellings.
He scorneth the multitude of the city,
Neither regardeth he the crying of the driver.
The range of the mountains is his pasture,
And he searcheth after every green thing.

"Will the unicorn be willing to serve thee,
Or abide by thy crib?
Canst thou bind the unicorn with his band in the furrow?

Or will he harrow the valleys after thee?
Wilt thou trust him, because his strength is great?
Or wilt thou leave thy labour to him?
Wilt thou believe him, that he will bring home thy seed,
And gather it into thy barn?

"Gavest thou the goodly wings unto the peacocks?
Or wings and feathers unto the ostrich?
Which leaveth her eggs in the earth,
And warmeth them in dust,
And forgetteth that the foot may crush them,
Or that the wild beast may break them.
She is hardened against her young ones, as though they were not hers:
Her labour is in vain without fear;
Because God hath deprived her of wisdom,
Neither hath he imparted to her understanding.
What time she lifteth up herself on high,
She scorneth the horse and his rider.

"Hast thou given the horse strength?
Hast thou clothed his neck with thunder?
Canst thou make him afraid as a grasshopper?
The glory of his nostrils is terrible.
He paweth in the valley, and rejoiceth in his strength:
He goeth on to meet the armed men.
He mocketh at fear, and is not affrighted;
Neither turneth he back from the sword.
The quiver rattleth against him,
The glittering spear and the shield.
He swalloweth the ground with fierceness and rage:
Neither believeth he that it is the sound of the trumpet.
He saith among the trumpets, 'Ha, ha';
And he smelleth the battle afar off,
The thunder of the captains, and the shouting.

"Doth the hawk fly by thy wisdom,
And stretch her wings toward the south?
Doth the eagle mount up at thy command,
And make her nest on high?
She dwelleth and abideth on the rock,
Upon the crag of the rock, and the strong place.
From whence she seeketh the prey,
And her eyes behold afar off.

Her young ones also suck up blood:
And where the slain are, there is she."

Moreover the Lord answered Job, and said,
"Shall he that contendeth with the Almighty instruct him?
He that reproveth God, let him answer it."

  Then Job answered the Lord, and said,
"Behold, I am vile; what shall I answer thee?
I will lay mine hand upon my mouth.
Once have I spoken; but I will not answer:
Yea, twice; but I will proceed no further."

  Then answered the Lord unto Job out of the whirlwind, and said,
"Gird up thy loins now like a man:
I will demand of thee, and declare thou unto me.
Wilt thou also disannul my judgment?
Wilt thou condemn me, that thou mayest be righteous?
Hast thou an arm like God?
Or canst thou thunder with a voice like him?
Deck thyself now with majesty and excellency;
And array thyself with glory and beauty.
Cast abroad the rage of thy wrath:
And behold every one that is proud, and abase him.
Look on every one that is proud, and bring him low;
And tread down the wicked in their place.
Hide them in the dust together;
And bind their faces in secret.
Then will I also confess unto thee
That thine own right hand can save thee.

"Behold now behemoth,
Which I made with thee;
He eateth grass as an ox.
Lo now, his strength is in his loins,
And his force is in the navel of his belly.
He moveth his tail like a cedar:
The sinews of his stones are wrapped together.
His bones are as strong pieces of brass;
His bones are like bars of iron.
He is the chief of the ways of God:
He that made him can make his sword to approach unto him.
Surely the mountains bring him forth food,

Where all the beasts of the field play.
He lieth under the shady trees,
In the covert of the reed, and fens.
The shady trees cover him with their shadow;
The willows of the brook compass him about.
Behold, he drinketh up a river, and hasteth not:
He trusteth that he can draw up Jordan into his mouth.
He taketh it with his eyes:
His nose pierceth through snares."

"Canst thou draw out leviathan with an hook?
Or his tongue with a cord which thou lettest down?
Canst thou put an hook into his nose?
Or bore his jaw through with a thorn?
Will he make many supplications unto thee?
Will he speak soft words unto thee?
Will he make a covenant with thee?
Wilt thou take him for a servant for ever?
Wilt thou play with him as with a bird?
Or wilt thou bind him for thy maidens?
Shall the companions make a banquet of him?
Shall they part him among the merchants?
Canst thou fill his skin with barbed irons?
Or his head with fish spears?
Lay thine hand upon him,
Remember the battle, do no more.
Behold, the hope of him is in vain:
Shall not one be cast down even at the sight of him?
None is so fierce that dare stir him up:
Who then is able to stand before me?
Who hath prevented me, that I should repay him?
Whatsoever is under the whole heaven is mine.
I will not conceal his parts,
Nor his power, nor his comely proportion.
Who can discover the face of his garment?
Or who can come to him with his double bridle?
Who can open the doors of his face?
His teeth are terrible round about.
His scales are his pride,
Shut up together as with a close seal.
One is so near to another,
That no air can come between them.
They are joined one to another,

They stick together, that they cannot be sundered.
By his neesings a light doth shine,
And his eyes are like the eyelids of the morning.
Out of his mouth go burning lamps,
And sparks of fire leap out.
Out of his nostrils goeth smoke,
As out of a seething pot or caldron.
His breath kindleth coals,
And a flame goeth out of his mouth.
In his neck remaineth strength,
And sorrow is turned into joy before him.
The flakes of his flesh are joined together:
They are firm in themselves; they cannot be moved.
His heart is as firm as a stone;
Yea, as hard as a piece of the nether millstone.
When he raiseth up himself, the mighty are afraid:
By reason of breakings they purify themselves.
The sword of him that layeth at him cannot hold:
The spear, the dart, nor the habergeon.
He esteemeth iron as straw,
And brass as rotten wood.
The arrow cannot make him flee:
Slingstones are turned with him into stubble.
Darts are counted as stubble:
He laugheth at the shaking of a spear.
Sharp stones are under him:
He spreadeth sharp pointed things upon the mire.
He maketh the deep to boil like a pot:
He maketh the sea like a pot of ointment.
Me maketh a path to shine after him;
One would think the deep to be hoary.
Upon earth there is not his like,
Who is made without fear.
He beholdeth all high things:
He is a king over all the children of pride."

Then Job answered the Lord, and said,
"I know that thou canst do every thing,
And that no thought can be withholden from thee.
Who is he that hideth counsel
Without knowledge?
Therefore have I uttered that I understood not;
Things too wonderful for me, which I knew not.

Hear, I beseech thee, and I will speak:
I will demand of thee, and declare thou unto me.
I have heard of thee by the hearing of the ear:
But now mine eye seeth thee.
Wherefore I abhor myself, and repent
In dust and ashes."

And it was so, that after the Lord had spoken these words unto Job, the Lord said to Eliphaz the Temanite, "My wrath is kindled against thee, and against thy two friends: for ye have not spoken of me the thing that is right, as my servant Job hath. Therefore take unto you now seven bullocks and seven rams, and go to my servant Job, and offer up for yourselves a burnt offering; and my servant Job shall pray for you: for him will I accept: lest I deal with you after your folly, in that ye have not spoken of me the thing which is right, like my servant Job." So Eliphaz the Temanite and Bildad the Shuhite and Zophar the Naamathite went, and did according as the Lord commanded them: the Lord also accepted Job. And the Lord turned the captivity of Job, when he prayed for his friends: also the Lord gave Job twice as much as he had before. Then came there unto him all his brethren, and all his sisters, and all they that had been of his acquaintance before, and did eat bread with him in his house: and they bemoaned him, and comforted him over all the evil that the Lord had brought upon him: every man also gave him a piece of money, and every one an earring of gold. So the Lord blessed the latter end of Job more than his beginning: for he had fourteen thousand sheep, and six thousand camels, and a thousand yoke of oxen, and a thousand she asses. He had also seven sons and three daughters. And he called the name of the first Jemima; and the name of the second, Kezia; and the name of the third, Kerenhappuch. And in all the land were no women found so fair as the daughters of Job: and their father gave them inheritance among their brethren. After this lived Job an hundred and forty years, and saw his sons, and his sons' sons, even four generations. So Job died, being old and full of days.

PLATO

Plato, who played Boswell to Socrates, and, like his Scottish descendant, was a creative spirit in his own right, was born about 427 B.C. He was twenty when he came under the influence of the older man whose great part in the intellectual life of ancient Greece he was to immortalize. He founded a school in the grove of Academus—the Academy—where he taught mathematics and philosophy until his death in about 347 B.C.

The accounts we have from him of the trial and death of Socrates, who was charged with corrupting the youth of Athens, are among the most moving and noble documents in the intellectual and spiritual history of man. I have reprinted Socrates' own defense, his speech after the sentence of death was pronounced, and the wonderfully vivid record of the manner of his dying.

The Trial and Death of Socrates

SOME ONE will say: And are you not ashamed, Socrates, of a course of life which is likely to bring you to an untimely end? To him I may fairly answer: There you are mistaken: a man who is good for anything ought not to calculate the chance of living or dying; he ought only to consider whether in doing anything he is doing right or wrong—acting the part of a good man or of a bad.

Fear of death is indeed the pretence of wisdom, and not real wisdom, being the appearance of knowing the unknown; since no one knows whether death, which they in their fear apprehend to be the greatest evil, may not be the greatest good. Is there not here conceit of knowledge, which is a disgraceful sort of ignorance? And this is the point in which, as I think, I am superior to men in general, and in which I might perhaps fancy myself wiser than other men,—that whereas I know but little of the world below, I do not suppose that I know: but I do know that injustice and disobedience to a better, whether God or man, is evil and dishonorable, and I will never fear or avoid a possible good rather than a certain evil. And therefore if you let me go now—if you say to me, Socrates, this time we will let you off, but upon one condition, that you are not to inquire and speculate in this way any more, and that if you are caught doing this again you shall die;—if this was the condition on which you let me go, I should reply: Men of Athens, I honor and love you; but I shall obey God rather than you, and while I have life and strength I shall never cease from the practice and teaching of philosophy, exhorting any one whom I meet after my manner, and convincing him, saying: My friend, why do you, who are a citizen of the great and mighty and wise city of Athens, care so much about laying up the greatest amount of money and honor and reputation, and so little about wisdom and truth and the greatest improvement of the soul, which you never regard or heed at all? Are you not ashamed of this? And if the person with whom I am arguing, says: Yes, but I do care; I do not depart or let him go at once; I interrogate and examine and cross-examine him, and if I think that he has no virtue, but only says that he has, I reproach him with undervaluing the greater, and overvaluing the less. And this I should say to everyone whom I meet, young and old, citizen and alien, but especially to the citizens, inasmuch as they are my brethren. For this is the command to God, as I would have you know; and I believe that to this day no greater good has ever happened in the state than my service to the God. For I do nothing but go about persuading you all, old and young alike, not to take thought for your persons or your properties, but first and chiefly to care about the greatest improvement of the soul. I tell you that virtue is not given by money, but that from virtue come money and every other good of man, public as well as private. This is my teaching, and if this is the doctrine which corrupts the youth, my influence is ruinous indeed. But if any one says that this is not my teaching, he is speaking an untruth. Wherefore, men of Athens, I say to you, either acquit me or not; but whatever you do, know that I shall never alter my ways, not even if I have to die many times.

Meletus and Anytus will not injure me: they can not; for it is not in the nature of things that a bad man should injure a better than himself. I do not deny that he may, perhaps, kill him, or drive him into exile, or deprive him of civil rights; and he may imagine, and others may imagine, that he is doing him a great injury: but in that I do not agree with him; for the evil doing as Anytus is doing—of unjustly taking away another man's life—is greater far. And now, Athenians, I am not going to argue for my own sake, as you may think, but for yours, that you may not sin against the God, or lightly reject his boon by condemning me. For if you kill me you will not easily find another like me, who, if I may use such a ludicrous figure of speech, am a sort of gadfly, given to the state by the God; and the state is like a great and noble steed who is tardy in his motions owing to his very size, and requires to be stirred into life. I am that gadfly which God has given the state, and all day long and in all places am always fastening upon you, arousing and persuading and reproaching you. And as you will not easily find another like me, I would advise you to spare me. I dare say that you may feel irritated at being suddenly awakened when you are caught napping; and you may think that if you were to strike me dead as Anytus advises, which you easily might, then you would sleep on for the remainder of your lives, unless God in his care of you gives you another gadfly. And that I am given to you by God is proved by this:—that if I had been like other men, I should not have neglected all my own concerns or patiently seen the neglect of them during all these years, and have been doing yours, coming to you individually like a father or elder brother, exhorting you to regard virtue; this, I say, would not be like human nature. And had I gained anything, or if my exhortations had been paid, there would have been some sense in that; but now, as you will perceive, not even the impudence of my accusers dares to say that I have ever exacted or sought pay of any one; they have no witness of that. And I have a witness of the truth of what I say; my poverty is a sufficient witness.

There is great reason to hope that death is a good, in one of two ways:—either death is a state of nothingness and utter unconsciousness, or, as men say, there is a change and migration of the soul from this world to another. Now if you suppose that there is no consciousness, but a sleep like the sleep of him who is undisturbed even by the sight of dreams, death will be an unspeakable gain. Eternity is then only a single night. But if death is the journey to another place, and there, as men say, all the dead are, what good can be greater than this? If indeed when the pilgrim arrives in the world below, he is delivered from the professors of justice in this world, and find the true judges who are said to give judgment there, Minos and Rhadamanthus and Aeacus and Triptolemus, and other sons of God who were righteous in their own life, that pilgrimage will be worth making. What would not a man give if he might converse with Orpheus and Musaeus and Hesiod and Homer? Nay, if this be true, let me die again and again. I, too, shall have a wonderful interest in a place where I can converse with Palamedes, and Ajax the son of Telamon, and other heroes of old, who have suffered death through an unjust judgment; and there will be no small pleasure, as I think, in comparing my own sufferings with theirs. Above all, I shall be able to continue my search into true and false knowledge; as in this world, so also in that; I shall find out who is wise, and who pretends to be wise, and is not. What would not a man give to be able to examine the leader of the great Trojan expedition; or Odysseus or Sisyphus, or numberless others, men and women too! What infinite delight would there be in conversing with them and asking them questions! For in that world they do not put a man to death for this; certainly not. For besides being happier in that world than in this, they will be immortal, if what is said is true.

Wherefore, my judges, be of good cheer about death, and know this of a truth—that no evil can happen to a good man, either in life or after death. He and his are not neglected by the gods; nor has my own approaching end happened by mere chance. But I see clearly that to die and be released was better for me; and therefore the oracle gave no sign. For which reason, also, I am not angry with my accusers or my condemners; they have done me no harm, although neither of them meant to do me any good; and for this I may gently blame them.

Still I have a favor to ask of them. When my sons are grown up, I would ask you, my friends, to punish them; and I would have you trouble them, as I have troubled you, if they seem to care about riches, or anything, more than about virtue; or if they pretend to be something when they are really nothing—then reprove them, as I have reproved you, for not caring about that for which they ought to care, and thinking that they are something when they are really nothing. And if you do this, I and my sons will have received justice at your hands.

The hour of departure has arrived, and we go our ways—I to die, and you to live. Which is better God only knows.

Adorned in her own proper jewels, which are temperance, and justice, and courage, and nobility, and truth—in these arrayed a man's soul is ready to go on her journey to the world below, when her time comes. You, Simmias and Cebes, and all other men, will depart at some time or other. Me already, as the tragic poet would say, the voice of fate calls. Soon I must drink the poison; and I think that I had better repair to the bath first, in order that the women may not have the trouble of washing my body after I am dead.

When he had done speaking, Crito said: And have you any commands for us, Socrates—anything to say about your children, or any other matter in which we can serve you?

Nothing particular, he said: only, as I have always told you, I would have you look to yourselves; that is a service which you may always be doing to me and mine as well as to yourselves. And you need not make professions; for if you take no thought for yourselves, and walk not according to the precepts which I have given you, not now for the first time, the warmth of your professions will be of no avail.

We will do our best, said Crito. But in what way would you have us bury you?

In any way that you like; only you must get hold of me, and take care that I do not walk away from you. Then he turned to us, and added with a smile:—I can not make Crito believe that I am the same Socrates who has been talking and conducting the argument; he fancies that I am the other Socrates whom he will soon see, a dead body—and he asks, How shall he bury me? And though I have spoken many words in the endeavor to show that when I have drunk the poison I shall leave you and go to the joys of the blessed,—these words of mine, with which I comforted you and myself, have had, as I perceive, no effect upon Crito. And therefore I want you to be surety for me now, as he was surety for me at the trial: but let the promise be of another sort; for he was my surety to the judges that I would remain, but you must be my surety to him that I shall not remain, but go away and depart; and then he will suffer less at my death, and not be grieved when he sees my body being burned or buried. I would not have him sorrow at my hard lot, or say at the burial, Thus we lay out Socrates, or, Thus we follow him to the grave or bury him; for false words are not only evil in themselves, but they infect the soul with evil. Be of good cheer, then, my dear Crito, and say that you are burying my body only, and do with that as is usual, and as you think best.

When he had spoken these words, he arose and went into the bath-chamber with Crito, who bid us wait; and we waited, talking and thinking of the subject of discourse, and also of the greatness of our sorrow; he was like a father of whom we were being bereaved, and we were about to pass the rest of our lives as orphans. When he had taken the bath his children were brought to him—(he had two young sons and an elder one); and the women of his family also came, and he talked to them and gave them a few directions in the presence of Crito; and he then dismissed them and returned to us.

Now the hour of sunset was near, for a good deal of time had passed while he was within. When he came out, he sat down with us again after his bath, but not much was said. Soon the jailer, who was the servant of the eleven, entered and stood by him, saying:—To you, Socrates, whom I know to be the noblest and gentlest and best of all who ever came to this place, I will not impute the angry feelings of other men, who rage and swear at me, when, in obedience to the authorities, I bid them drink the poison—indeed, I am sure that you will not be angry with me; for others, as you are aware, and not I, are the guilty cause. And so fare you well, and try to bear lightly what must needs be; you know my errand. Then bursting into tears he turned away and went out.

Socrates looked at him and said: I return your good wishes, and will do as you bid. Then turning to us, he said, How charming the man is: since I have been in prison he has always been coming to see me, and at times he would talk to me, and was as good as could be to me, and now see how generously he sorrows for me. But we must do as he says, Crito; let the cup be brought, if the poison is prepared: if not, let the attendant prepare some.

Yet, said Crito, the sun is still upon the hill-tops, and many a one has taken the draught late, and after the announcement has been made to him, he has eaten and drunk, and indulged in sensual delights; do not hasten then, there is still time.

Socrates said: Yes, Crito, and they of whom you speak are right in doing thus, for they think that they will gain by the delay; but I am right in not doing thus, for I do not think that I should gain anything by drinking the poison a little later; I should be sparing and saving a life which is already gone; I could only laugh at myself for this. Please then to do as I say, and not to refuse me.

Crito, when he heard this, made a sign to the servant; and the servant went in, and remained for some time, and then returned with the jailer carrying the cup of poison. Socrates said: You, my good friend, who are experienced in these matters, shall give me directions how I am to proceed. The man answered: You have only to walk about until your legs are heavy, and then to lie down, and the poison will act. At the same time he handed the cup to Socrates, who in the easiest and gentlest manner, without the least fear or change of color or feature, looking at the man with all his eyes, Echecrates, as his manner was, took the cup and said: What do you say about making a libation out of this cup to any god? May I, or not? The man answered: We only prepare, Socrates, just so much as we deem enough. I understand, he said: yet I may and must pray to the gods to prosper my journey from this to that other world—may this then, which is my prayer, be granted to me. Then holding the cup to his lips, quite readily and cheerfully he drank off the poison. And hitherto most of us had been able to control our sorrow; but now when we saw him drinking, and saw too that he had finished the draught, we could no longer forbear, and in spite of myself my own tears were flowing fast; so that I covered my face and wept over myself, for certainly I was not weeping over him, but at the thought of my own calamity in having lost such a companion. Nor was I the first, for Crito, when he found himself unable to restrain his tears, had got up and moved away, and I followed; and at that moment, Apollodorus, who had been weeping all the time, broke out into a loud cry which made cowards of us all. Socrates alone retained his calmness: What is this strange outcry? he said. I sent away the women mainly in order that they might not offend in this way, for I have heard that a man should die in peace. Be quiet then, and have patience. When we heard that, we were ashamed, and refrained our tears; and he walked about until, as he said, his legs began to fail, and then he lay on his back, according to the directions, and the man who gave him the poison now and then looked at his feet and legs; and after a while he pressed his foot hard, and asked him if he could feel; and he said No; and then his leg, and so upwards and upwards, and showed us that he was cold and stiff. And he felt then himself and said: When the poison reaches the heart, that will be the end. He was beginning to grow cold about the groin, when he uncovered his face, for he had covered himself up, and said (they were his last words)—he said: Crito, I owe a cock to Asclepius; will you remember to pay the debt? The debt shall be paid, said Crito; is there anything else? There was no answer to this question; but in a minute or two a movement was heard, and the attendants uncovered him; his eyes were set, and Crito closed his eyes and mouth.

Such was the end, Echecrates, of our friend, whom I may truly call the wisest, and justest, and best of all men whom I have ever known.

ST. MATTHEW

The Gospel according to St. Matthew is generally regarded as on the whole the most satisfying of the New Testament accounts of the life, death, and resurrection of Jesus Christ. For this telling of the world's greatest story I have used the King James Version, as printed in *The Reader's Bible,* published by the Oxford University Press.

Among all the other things which it is, and which have made it the precious possession of twenty centuries, the gospel story sets before us the greatest trial scene in history. There are two others which approach it in grandeur—one which preceded it in time and one which came after—the trials of Socrates and of Joan of Arc, both of which appear in this anthology. If I may presume to draw a parallel between them all, it is this: All three of the accused made no effort to buy acquittal by argument. Socrates told his judges that if they were to say to him, we will let you off, on condition that "you are not to inquire and speculate in this manner any more...if this was the condition on which you let me go, I should reply: Men of Athens, I honor and love you; but I shall obey God rather than you." The Maid, time after time, when she could have saved herself, said to the inquisitors, "Pass on," even as Jesus, facing Pontius Pilate, replied merely, when Pilate asked, "Art Thou the King of the Jews?" "Thou sayest." He did not say, as He might have, "I make no such claim." And again, to continue the parallel, in all three trials the accusers are now the condemned.

The Trial and Crucifixion of Jesus

THEN cometh Jesus with them unto a place called Gethsemane, and saith unto the disciples, "Sit ye here, while I go and pray yonder." And he took with him Peter and the two sons of Zebedee, and began to be sorrowful and very heavy. Then saith he until them, "My soul is exceeding sorrowful, even unto death: tarry ye here, and watch with me." And he went a little further, and fell on his face, and prayed, saying, "O my Father, if it be possible, let this cup pass from me: nevertheless not as I will, but as thou wilt." And he cometh unto the disciples, and findeth them asleep, and saith unto Peter, "What, could ye not watch with me one hour? Watch and pray, that ye enter not into temptation: the spirit indeed is willing, but the flesh is weak." He went away again the second time, and prayed, saying, "O my Father, if this cup may not pass away from me, except I drink it thy will be done." And he came and found them asleep again: for their eyes were heavy. And he left them, and went away again, and prayed the third time, saying the same words. Then cometh he to his disciples, and saith unto them, "Sleep on now, and take your rest: behold, the hour is at hand, and the Son of man is betrayed into the hands of sinners. Rise, let us be going: behold, he is at hand that doth betray me."

And while he yet spake, lo, Judas, one of the twelve, came, and with him a great multitude with swords and staves, from the chief priests and elders of the people. Now he that betrayed him gave them a sign, saying, "Whomsoever I shall kiss, that same is he: hold him fast." And forthwith he came to Jesus, and said, "Hail, Master"; and kissed him. And Jesus said unto him, "Friend, wherefore art thou come?" Then came they, and laid hands on Jesus, and took him. And, behold, one of them which were with Jesus stretched out his hand, and drew his sword, and struck a servant of the high priest's, and smote off his ear. Then said Jesus unto him, "Put up again thy sword into his place: for all they that take the sword shall perish with the sword. Thinkest thou that I cannot now pray to my Father, and he shall presently give me more than twelve legions of angels? But how then shall the scriptures be fulfilled, that thus it must be?" In that same hour said Jesus to the multitudes, "Are ye come out as against a thief with swords and staves for to take me? I sat daily with you teaching in the temple, and ye laid no hold on me. But all this was done, that the scriptures of the prophets might be fulfilled." Then all the disciples forsook him, and fled.

And they that had laid hold on Jesus led him away to Caiaphas the high priest, where the scribes and the elders were assembled. But Peter followed him afar off unto the high priest's palace, and went in, and sat with the servants, to see the end. Now the chief priests, and elders, and all the council, sought false witness against Jesus, to put him to death; but found none: yea, though many false witnesses came, yet found they none. At the last came two false witnesses, and said, "This fellow said, 'I am able to destroy the temple of God, and to build it in three days.'" And the high priest arose, and said unto him, "Answerest thou nothing? what is it which these witness against thee?" But Jesus held his peace. And the high priest answered and said unto him, "I adjure thee by the living God, that thou tell us whether thou be the Christ, the Son of God." Jesus said unto him, "Thou hast said: nevertheless I say unto you, Hereafter shall ye see the Son of man sitting on the right hand of power, and coming in the clouds of heaven." Then the high priest rent his clothes, saying, "He hath spoke blasphemy; what further need have we of witnesses? behold, now ye have heard his blasphemy. What think ye?" They answered and said, "He is guilty of death." Then did they spit in his face, and buffeted him; and others smote him with the palms of their hands, saying, "Prophesy unto us, thou Christ, Who is he that smote thee?"

Now Peter sat without in the palace: and a damsel came unto him, saying, "Thou also wast with Jesus of Galilee." But he denied before them all, saying, "I know not what thou sayest." And when he was gone out into the porch, another maid saw him, and said unto them that were there, "This fellow was also with Jesus of Nazareth." And again he denied with an oath, "I do not know the man." And after a while came unto him they that stood by, and said to Peter, "Surely thou also art one of them; for thy speech betrayeth thee." Then began he to curse and to swear, saying, "I know not the man." And immediately the cock crew. And Peter remembered the word of Jesus, which said unto him, "Before the cock crow, thou shalt deny me thrice." And he went out, and wept bitterly.

When the morning was come, all the chief priests and elders of the people took counsel against Jesus to put him to death: and when they had bound him, they led him away, and delivered him to Pontius Pilate the governor.

Then Judas, which had betrayed him, when he saw that he was condemned, repented himself, and brought again the thirty pieces of silver to the chief priests and elders, saying, "I have sinned in that I have betrayed the innocent blood." And they said, "What is that to us? see thou to that." And he cast down the pieces of silver in the temple, and departed, and went and hanged himself. And the chief priests took the silver pieces, and said, "It is not lawful for to put them into the treasury, because it is the price of blood." And they took counsel, and bought with them the potter's field, to bury strangers in. Wherefore that field was called, The field of blood, unto this day. Then was fulfilled that which was spoken by Jeremy the prophet, saying, "And they took the thirty pieces of silver, the price of him that was valued, whom they of the children of Israel did value; and gave them for the potter's field, as the Lord appointed me."

And Jesus stood before the governor: and the governor asked him, saying, "Art thou the King of the Jews?" And Jesus said unto him, "Thou sayest." And when he was accused of the chief priests and elders, he answered nothing. Then said Pilate unto him, "Hearest thou not how many things they witness against thee?" And he answered him to never a word; insomuch that the governor marvelled greatly. Now at that feast the governor was wont to release unto the people a prisoner, whom they would. And they had then a notable prisoner, called Barabbas. Therefore when they were gathered together, Pilate said unto them, "Whom will ye that I release unto you? Barabbas, or Jesus which is called Christ?" For he knew that for envy they had delivered him. When he was set down on the judgment seat, his wife sent unto him, saying, "Have thou nothing to do with that just man: for I have suffered many things this day in a dream because of him." But the chief priests and elders persuaded the multitude that they should ask Barabbas, and destroy Jesus. The governor answered and said unto them, "Whether of the twain will ye that I release unto you?" They said, "Barabbas." Pilate saith unto them, "What shall I do then with Jesus which is called Christ?" They all say unto him, "Let him be crucified." And the governor said, "Why, what evil hath he done?" But they cried out the more, saying, "Let him be crucified." When Pilate saw that he could prevail nothing, but that rather a tumult was made, he took water, and washed his hands before the multitude, saying, "I am innocent of the blood of this just person: see ye to it." Then answered all the people, and said, "His blood be on us, and on our children." Then released he Barabbas unto them: and when he had scourged Jesus, he delivered him to be crucified.

Then the soldiers of the governor took Jesus into the common hall, and gathered unto him the whole band of soldiers. And they stripped him, and put on him a scarlet robe. And when they had platted a crown of thorns, they put it upon his head, and a reed in his right hand: and they bowed the knee before him, and mocked him, saying, "Hail, King of the Jews!" And they spit upon him, and took the reed, and smote him on the head. And after that they had mocked him, they took the robe off from him, and put his own raiment on him, and led him away to crucify him.

And as they came out, they found a man of Cyrene, Simon by name: him they compelled to bear his cross. And when they were come unto a place called Golgotha, that is to say, a place of a skull, they gave him vinegar to drink mingled with gall: and when he had tasted thereof, he would not drink. And they crucified him, and parted his garments, casting lots: that it might be fulfilled which was spoken by the prophet, "They parted my garments among them, and upon my vesture did they cast lots." And sitting down they watched him there;

and set up over his head his accusation written, THIS IS JESUS THE KING OF THE JEWS. Then were there two thieves crucified with him, one on the right hand, and another on the left. And they that passed by reviled him, wagging their heads, and saying, "Thou that destroyest the temple, and buildest it in three days, save thyself. If thou be the Son of God, come down from the cross." Likewise also the chief priests mocking him, with the scribes and elders, said, "He saved others; himself he cannot save. If he be the King of Israel, let him now come down from the cross, and we will believe him. He trusted in God; let him deliver him now, if he will have him: for he said, 'I am the Son of God.'" The thieves also, which were crucified with him, cast the same in his teeth.

Now from the sixth hour there was darkness over all the land unto the ninth hour. And about the ninth hour Jesus cried with a loud voice, saying, "ELI, ELI, LAMA SABACHTHANI?" that is to say, "My God, my God, why hast thou forsaken me?" Some of them that stood there, when they heard that, said, "This man calleth for Elias." And straightway one of them ran, and took a spunge, and filled it with vinegar, and put it on a reed, and gave him to drink. The rest said, "Let be, let us see whether Elias will come to save him." Jesus, when he had cried again with a loud voice, yielded up the ghost. And, behold, the veil of the temple was rent in twain from the top to the bottom; and the earth did quake, and the rocks rent; and the graves were opened; and many bodies of the saints which slept arose, and came out of the graves after his resurrection, and went into the holy city, and appeared unto many. Now when the centurion, and they that were with him, watching Jesus, saw the earthquake, and those things that were done, they feared greatly, saying, "Truly this was the Son of God." And many women were there beholding afar off, which followed Jesus from Galilee, ministering unto him: among which was Mary Magdalene, and Mary the mother of James and Joses, and the mother of Zebedee's children.

When the even was come, there came a rich man of Arimathaea, named Joseph, who also himself was Jesus' disciple: he went to Pilate, and begged the body of Jesus. Then Pilate commanded the body to be delivered. And when Joseph had taken the body, he wrapped it in a clean linen cloth, and laid it in his own new tomb, which he had hewn out in the rock: and he rolled a great stone to the door of the sepulchre, and departed. And there was Mary Magdalene, and the other Mary, sitting over against the sepulchre.

Now the next day, that followed the day of the preparation, the chief priests and Pharisees came together unto Pilate, saying, "Sir, we remember that that deceiver said, while he was yet alive, 'After three

days I will rise again.' Command therefore that the sepulchre be made
sure until the third day, lest his disciples come by night, and steal him
away, and say unto the people, 'He is risen from the dead': so the last
error shall be worse than the first." Pilate said unto them, "Ye have a
watch: go your way, make it as sure as ye can." So they went, and
made the sepulchre sure, sealing the stone, and setting a watch.

In the end of the sabbath, as it began to dawn toward the first day
of the week, came Mary Magdalene and the other Mary to see the
sepulchre. And, behold, there was a great earthquake: for the angel
of the Lord descended from heaven, and came and rolled back the
stone from the door, and sat upon it. His countenance was like lightning, and his raiment white as snow: and for fear of him the keepers
did shake, and became as dead men. And the angel answered and said
unto the women, "Fear not ye: for I know that ye seek Jesus, which
was crucified. He is not here: for he is risen, as he said. Come, see
the place where the Lord lay. And go quickly, and tell his disciples
that he is risen from the dead; and, behold, he goeth before you into
Galilee; there shall ye see him: lo, I have told you." And they departed
quickly from the sepulchre with fear and great joy; and did run to
bring his disciples word. And as they went to tell his disciples, behold,
Jesus met them, saying, "All hail." And they came and held him by
the feet, and worshipped him. Then said Jesus unto them, "Be not
afraid: go tell my brethren that they go into Galilee, and there shall
they see me."

Now when they were going, behold, some of the watch came into
the city, and shewed unto the chief priests all the things that were
done. And when they were assembled with the elders, and had taken
counsel, they gave large money unto the soldiers, saying, "Say ye, 'His
disciples came by night, and stole him away while he slept.' And if
this come to the governor's ears, we will persuade him, and secure
you." So they took the money, and did as they were taught: and this
saying is commonly reported among the Jews until this day.

Then the eleven disciples went away into Galilee, into a mountain
where Jesus had appointed them. And when they saw him, they worshipped him: but some doubted. And Jesus came and spake unto
them, saying, "All power is given unto me in heaven and in earth.
Go ye therefore, and teach all nations, baptizing them in the name of
the Father, and of the Son, and of the Holy Ghost: teaching them to
observe all things whatsoever I have commanded you: and, lo, I am
with you alway, even unto the end of the world." Amen.

ST. AUGUSTINE

Aurelius Augustinus, to give him his Latin name, was born near the Mediterranean port of Hippo, in what is now Algeria, in 354. His mother, St. Monica, brought him up as a Christian, but when he went to study in Carthage, where he concentrated on rhetoric, he abandoned his religion and embarked on a dissolute life. At one time in his youth he embraced Manichaeanism, and it was not until 387, when he was thirty-three, that he returned to Christianity. Four years later he became a priest, ending his days as Bishop of Hippo. He died in 430.

Among St. Augustine's works, in addition to the famous *Confessions,* are his *City of God,* in which he discussed the impact of Christianity upon society, his *On the Trinity,* and *On the Work of Monks.* The *Confessions,* generally regarded as a classic of Christian mysticism, is notable also as the fullest source of information about his life, and is one of the outstanding records of Christian conversion. I have reprinted here a portion of Book Three, in which he looks back on what he had come to regard as his misspent youth, and in which, addressing himself directly to God, he expresses his repentance. The translation is that of Dr. E. B. Pusey.

The Youth of St. Augustine

[I.] 1. To Carthage I came, where there sang all around me in my ears a cauldron of unholy loves. I loved not yet, yet I loved to love, and out of a deep-seated want, I hated myself for wanting not. I sought what I might love, in love with loving, and safety I hated, and a way without snares. For within me was a famine of that inward food, Thyself, my God; yet, through that famine I was not hungered; but was without all longing for incorruptible sustenance, not because filled therewith, but the more empty, the more I loathed it. For this cause my soul was sickly and full of sores, it miserably cast itself forth, desiring to be scraped by the touch of objects of sense. Yet if these had not a soul, they would not be objects of love. To love then, and to be beloved, was sweet to me; but more, when I obtained to enjoy the person I loved. I defiled, therefore, the spring of friendship with the filth of concupiscence, and I beclouded its brightness with the hell of lustfulness; and thus foul and unseemly, I would fain, through exceeding vanity, be fine and courtly. I fell headlong then into the love, wherein I longed to be ensnared. My God, my Mercy, with how much gall didst thou out of thy great goodness besprinkle for me that sweetness? For I was both beloved, and secretly arrived at the bond of enjoying; and was with joy fettered with sorrow-bringing bonds, that I might be scourged with the iron burning rods of jealousy, and suspicions, and fears, and angers, and quarrels.

[II.] 2. Stage-plays also carried me away, full of images of my miseries, and of fuel to my fire. Why is it, that man desires to be made sad, beholding doleful and tragical things, which yet himself would by no means suffer? yet he desires as a spectator to feel sorrow at them, and this very sorrow is his pleasure. What is this but a miserable madness? for a man is the more affected with these actions, the less free he is from such affections. Howsoever, when he suffers in his own person, it used to be styled misery: when he compassionates others, then it is mercy. But what sort of compassion is this for feigned and scenical passions? For the auditor is not called on to relieve, but only to grieve: and he applauds the actor of these fictions the more, the more he grieves. And if the calamities of those persons (whether of old times, or mere fiction) be so acted, that the spectator is not moved to tears, he goes away disgusted and criticising; but if he be moved to passion, he stays intent, and weeps for joy.

3. Are griefs then too loved? Verily all desire joy. Or whereas no man likes to be miserable, is he yet pleased to be merciful? which because it cannot be without passion, for this reason alone are passions loved? This also springs from that vein of friendship. But whither goes that vein? whither flows it? wherefore runs it into that torrent of pitch bubbling forth those monstrous tides of foul lustfulness, into which it is wilfully changed and transformed, being of its own will precipitated and corrupted from its heavenly clearness? Shall compassion then be put away? by no means. Be griefs then sometimes loved. But beware of uncleanness, O my soul, under the guardianship of my God, the *God of our fathers, who is to be praised and exalted above all for ever,* beware of uncleanness. For I have not now ceased to pity; but then in the theatres I rejoiced with lovers, when they wickedly enjoyed one another, although this was imaginary only in the play. And when they lost one another, as if very compassionate, I sorrowed with them, yet had my delight in both. But now I much

more pity him that rejoiceth in his wickedness, than him who is thought to suffer hardship, by missing some pernicious pleasure, and the loss of some miserable felicity. This certainly is the truer mercy, but in it, grief delights not. For though he that grieves for the miserable, he commended for his office of charity; yet had he, who is genuinely compassionate, rather there were nothing for him to grieve for. For if good will be ill willed, (which can never be,) then may he, who truly and sincerely commiserates, wish there might be some miserable, that he might commiserate. Some sorrow may then be allowed, none loved. For thus dost Thou, O Lord God, who lovest souls far more purely than we, and has more incorruptibly pity on them, yet are wounded with no sorrowfulness. *And who is sufficient for these things?*

4. But I, miserable, then loved to grieve, and sought out what to grieve at, when in another's and that feigned and personated misery, that acting best pleased me, and attracted me the most vehemently, which drew tears from me. What marvel that an unhappy sheep, straying from Thy flock, and impatient of Thy keeping, I became infected with a foul disease? And hence the love of griefs; not such as should sink deep into me; for I loved not to suffer, what I loved to look on; but such as upon hearing their fictions should lightly scratch the surface; upon which as on envenomed nails, followed inflamed swelling, impostumes, and a putrified sore. My life being such, was it life, O my God?

[III.] 5. And Thy faithful mercy hovered over me afar. Upon how grievous iniquities consumed I myself, pursuing a sacrilegious curiosity, that having forsaken Thee, it might bring me to the treacherous abyss, and the beguiling service of devils, to whom I sacrificed my evil actions, and in all these things thou didst scourge me! I dared even, while Thy solemnities were celebrated within the walls of Thy Church, to desire, and to compass a business, deserving death for its fruits, for which Thou scourgedst me with grievous punishments, though nothing to my fault, O Thou my exceeding mercy, my God, my refuge from those terrible destroyers, among whom I wandered with a stiff neck, withdrawing further from Thee, loving mine own ways, and not Thine; loving a vagrant liberty.

6. Those studies also, which were accounted commendable, had a view to excelling in the courts of litigation; the more bepraised, the craftier. Such is men's blindness, glorying even in their blindness. And now I was chief in the rhetoric school, whereat I joyed proudly, and I swelled with arrogancy, though (Lord, Thou knowest) far quieter and altogether removed from the subvertings of those "Subverters" (for this ill-omened and devilish name, was the very badge of gal-

lantry) among whom I lived, with a shameless shame that I was not even as they. With them I lived, and was sometimes delighted with their friendship, whose doings I ever did abhor, i.e. their "subvertings," wherewith they wantonly persecuted the modesty of strangers, which they disturbed by a gratuitous jeering, feeding thereon their malicious mirth. Nothing can be liker the very actions of devils than these. What then could they be more truly called than "subverters"? themselves subverted and altogether perverted first, the deceiving spirits secretly deriding and seducing them, wherein themselves delight to jeer at, and deceive others.

[IV.] 7. Among such as these, in that unsettled age of mine, learned I books of eloquence, wherein I desired to be eminent, out of a damnable and vain glorious end, a joy in human vanity. In the ordinary course of study, I fell upon a certain book of Cicero, whose speech almost all admire, not so his heart. This book of his contains an exhortation to philosophy, and is called *"Hortensius."* But this book altered my affections, and turned my prayers to Thyself, O Lord; and made me have other purposes and desires. Every vain hope at once became worthless to me; and I longed with an incredibly burning desire for an immortality of wisdom, and began now to arise, that I might return to Thee. For not to sharpen my tongue, (which thing I seemed to be purchasing with my mother's allowances, in that my nineteenth year, my father being dead two years before,) not to sharpen my tongue did I employ that book; nor did it infuse into me its style, but its matter.

8. How did I burn then, my God, how did I burn to re-mount from earthly things to Thee, nor knew I what Thou wouldest do with me? For with Thee is wisdom. But the love of wisdom is in Greek called "philosophy," with which that book inflamed me. Some there be that seduce through philosophy, under a great, and smooth, and honourable name colouring and disguising their own errors: and almost all who in that and former ages were such, are in that book censured and set forth: there also is made plain that wholesome advice of Thy Spirit, by Thy good and devout servant; *Beware lest any man spoil you through philosophy and vain deceit, after the tradition of men, after the rudiments of the world, and not after Christ. For in Him dwelleth all the fulness of the Godhead bodily.* And since at that time (Thou, O light of my heart, knowest) Apostolic Scripture was not known to me, I was delighted with that exhortation, so far only, that I was thereby strongly roused, and kindled, and inflamed to love, and seek, and obtain, and hold, and embrace not this or that sect, but wisdom itself whatever it were; and this alone checked me thus enkindled, that the name of Christ was not in it. For this name, accord-

ing to Thy mercy, O Lord, this name of my Saviour Thy Son, had my tender heart, even with my mother's milk, devoutly drunk in, and deeply treasured; and whatsoever was without that name, though never so learned, polished, or true, took not entire hold of me.

[V.] 9. I resolved then to bend my mind to the holy Scriptures, that I might see what they were. But behold, I see a thing not understood by the proud, nor laid open to children, lowly in access, in its recesses lofty, and veiled with mysteries; and I was not such as could enter into it, or stoop my neck to follow its steps. For not as I now speak, did I feel when I turned to those Scriptures; but they seemed to me unworthy to be compared to the stateliness of Tully: for my swelling pride shrunk from their lowliness, nor could my sharp wit pierce the interior thereof. Yet were they such as would grow up in a little one. But I disdained to be a little one; and, swoln with pride, took myself to be a great one.

[VI.] 10. Therefore I fell among men proudly doting, exceeding carnal and prating, in whose mouths were the snares of the Devil, lined with the mixture of the syllables of Thy name, and of our Lord Jesus Christ, and of the Holy Ghost, the Paraclete, our Comforter. These names departed not out of their mouth, but so far forth, as the sound only and the noise of the tongue, for the heart was void of truth. Yet they cried out "Truth, Truth," and spake much thereof to me, yet *it was not in them:* but they spake falsehood, not of Thee only, (who truly art Truth,) but even of those elements of this world, Thy creatures. And I indeed ought to have passed by even philosophers who spake truth concerning them, for love of Thee, my Father, supremely good, Beauty of all things beautiful. O Truth, Truth, how inwardly did even then the marrow of my soul pant after Thee, when they often and diversely, and in many and huge books, echoed of Thee to me, though it was but an echo? And these were the dishes wherein to me, hungering after Thee, they, instead of Thee, served up the Sun and Moon, beautiful works of Thine, but yet Thy works, not Thyself, no nor Thy first works. For Thy spiritual works are before these corporeal works, celestial though they be, and shining. But I hungered and thirsted not even after those first works of Thine, but after Thee Thyself, the Truth, *in whom is no variableness, neither shadow of turning:* yet they still set before me in those dishes, glittering fantasies, than which better were it to love this very sun, (which is real to our sight at least), than those fantasies which by our eyes deceive our mind. Yet because I thought them to be Thee, I fed thereon; not eagerly, for Thou didst not in them taste to me as Thou art; for Thou wast not these emptinesses, nor was I nourished by them, but exhausted rather. Food in sleep shews very like our food awake;

yet are not those asleep nourished by it, for they are asleep. But those
were not even any way like to Thee, as Thou hast now spoken to me;
for those were corporeal fantasies, false bodies, than which these true
bodies, celestial or terrestrial, which with our fleshly sight we behold,
as far more certain: these things the beasts and birds discern as well
as we, and they are more certain than when we fancy them. And again,
we do with more certainty fancy them, than by them conjecture other
vaster and infinite bodies which have no being. Such empty husks
was I then fed on; and was not fed. But Thou, my soul's Love, *in
looking for whom I fail,* that I may become strong, art neither those
bodies which we see, though in heaven; nor those which we see not
there; for Thou hast created them, nor dost Thou account them
among the chiefest of Thy works. How far then art Thou from those
fantasies of mine, fantasies of bodies which altogether are not, than
which the images of those bodies, which are, are far more certain, and
more certain still the bodies themselves, which yet Thou art not; no
nor yet the soul, which is the life of the bodies. So then, better and
more certain is the life of the bodies, than the bodies. But Thou art
the life of souls, the life of lives, having life in Thyself; and changest
not, life of my soul.

11. Where then wert Thou then to me, and how far from me? Far
verily was I straying from Thee, barred from the very husks of the
swine, whom with husks I fed. For how much better are the fables
of poets and grammarians, than these snares? For verses, and poems,
and "Medea flying," are more profitable truly, than these men's five
elements, variously disguised, answering to five dens of darkness,
which have no being, yet slay the believer. For verses and poems I
can turn to true food, and "Medea flying," though I did sing, I maintained not; though I heard it sung, I believed not: but those things I
did believe. Woe, woe, by what steps was I brought down to *the
depths of hell!* toiling and turmoiling through want of Truth, since
I sought after Thee, my God, (to Thee I confess it, who hadst mercy
on me, not as yet confessing,) not according to the understanding of
the mind, wherein Thou willedst that I should excel the beasts, but
according to the sense of the flesh. But Thou were more inward to me,
than my most inward part; and higher than my highest. I lighted
upon that bold woman, *simple and knoweth nothing,* shadowed out
in Solomon, *sitting at the door, and saying, Eat ye bread of secrecies
willingly, and drink ye stolen waters which are sweet:* she seduced
me, because she found my soul dwelling abroad in the eye of my
flesh, and ruminating on such food, as through it I had devoured.

[VII.] 12. For other than this, that which really is I knew not;
and was, as it were through sharpness of wit, persuaded to assent to

foolish deceivers, when they asked me, "whence is evil?" "is God bounded by a bodily shape, and has hairs and nails?" "are they to be esteemed righteous, who had many wives at once, and did kill men, and sacrificed living creatures?" At which I, in my ignorance, was much troubled, and departing from the truth, seemed to myself to be making towards it; because as yet I knew not that evil was nothing but a privation of good, until at last a thing ceases altogether to be; which how should I see, the sight of whose eyes reached only to bodies, and of my mind to a phantasm? And I knew not *God to be a Spirit,* not One who hath parts extended in length and breadth, or whose being was bulk; for every bulk is less in a part, than in the whole: and if it be infinite, it must be less in such part as is defined by a certain space, than in its infinitude; and so is not wholly every where, as Spirit, as God. And what that should be in us, by which we were like to God, and might in Scripture be rightly said to be *after the Image of God,* I was altogether ignorant.

13. Nor knew I that true inward righteousness, which judgeth not according to custom, but out of the most rightful law of God Almighty, whereby the ways of places and times were disposed, according to those times and places; itself meantime being the same always and every where, not one thing in one place, and another in another; according to which Abraham, and Isaac, and Jacob, and Moses, and David, were righteous, and all these commended by the mouth of God; but were judged unrighteous by silly men, *judging out of man's judgment,* and measuring by their own petty habits, the moral habits of the whole human race. As if in an armory, one ignorant what were adapted to each part, should cover his head with greaves, or seek to be shod with a helmet, and complain that they fitted not: or as if on a day, when business is publicly stopped in the afternoon, one were angered at not being allowed to keep open shop, because he had been in the forenoon; or when in one house he observeth some servant take a thing in his hand, which the butler is not suffered to meddle with; or something permitted out of doors, which is forbidden in the dining-room; and should be angry, that in one house, and one family, the same thing is not allotted every where, and to all. Even such are they, who are fretted to hear something to have been lawful for righteous men formerly, which now is not; or that God, for certain temporal respects, commanded them one thing, and these another, obeying both the same righteousness: whereas they see, in one man, and one day, and one house, different things to be fit for different members, and a thing formerly lawful, after a certain time not so; in one corner permitted or commanded, but in another rightly forbidden and punished. Is justice therefore various or mutable? No, but the times,

over which it presides, flow not evenly, because they are times. But men, whose *days are few upon the earth,* for that by their senses, they cannot harmonize the causes of things in former ages and other nations, which they had no experience of, with these which they have experience of, whereas in one and the same body, day, or family, they easily see what is fitting for each member, and season, part, and person; to the one they take exceptions, to the other they submit.

14. These things I then knew not, nor observed; they struck my sight on all sides, and I saw them not. I indited verses, in which I might not place every foot every where, but differently in different metres; nor even in any one metre the self-same foot in all places. Yet the art itself, by which I indited, had not different principles for these different cases, but comprised all in one. Still I saw not how that righteousness, which good and holy men obeyed, did far more excellently and sublimely contain in one all those things which God commanded, and in no part varied; although in varying times it prescribed not every thing at once, but apportioned and enjoined what was fit for each. And I, in my blindness, censured the holy Fathers, not only wherein they made use of things present as God commanded and inspired them, but also wherein they were foretelling things to come, as God was revealing in them.

[VIII.] 15. Can it at any time or place be unjust *to love God with all his heart, with all his soul, and with all his mind; and his neighbour as himself?* Therefore are those foul offences which be against nature, to be every where and at all times detested and punished; such as were those of the men of Sodom: which should all nations commit, they should all stand guilty of the same crime, by the law of God, which hath not so made men, that they should so abuse one another. For even that intercourse which should be between God and us is violated, when that same nature, of which He is Author, is polluted by the perversity of lust. But those actions which are offences against the customs of men, are to be avoided according to the customs severally prevailing; so that a thing agreed upon, and confirmed, by custom or law of any city or nation, may not be violated at the lawless pleasure of any, whether native or foreigner. For any part, which harmonizeth not with its whole, is offensive. But when God commands a thing to be done, against the customs or compact of any people, though it were never by them done heretofore, it is to be done; and if intermitted, it is to be restored; and if never ordained, is now to be ordained. For lawful if it be for a king, in the state which he reigns over, to command that, which no one before him, nor he himself heretofore, had commanded, and to obey him cannot be against the common weal of the state; (nay, it were against it if he were not obeyed, for to obey princes is a general compact of human society;) how much more unhesitatingly ought we to obey God, in all which He commands, the Ruler of all His creatures! For as among the powers in man's society, the greater authority is obeyed in preference to the lesser, so must God above all.

16. So in acts of violence, where there is a wish to hurt, whether by reproach or injury; and these either for revenge, as one enemy against another; or for some profit belonging to another, as the robber to the traveller; or to avoid some evil, as towards one who is feared; or through envy, as one less fortunate to one more so, or one well thriven in any thing, to him whose being on a par with himself he fears, or grieves at, or for the mere pleasure at another's pain, as spectators of gladiators, or deriders and mockers of others. These be the heads of iniquity, which spring from the lust of the flesh, of the eye, or of rule, either singly, or two combined, or all together; and so do men live ill against the three, and seven, that psaltery of *ten strings,* Thy Ten Commandments, O God, most high, and most sweet. But what foul offenses can there be against Thee, who canst not be defiled? or what acts of violence against Thee, who canst not be harmed? But Thou avengest what men commit against themselves, seeing also when they sin against Thee, they do wickedly against their own souls, and *iniquity gives itself the lie,* by corrupting and perverting their nature, which Thou hast created and ordained, or by an immoderate use of things allowed, or in *burning* in things unallowed, *to that use which is against nature;* or are found guilty, raging with heart and tongue against Thee, *kicking against the pricks;* or when, bursting the pale of human society, they boldly joy in self-willed combinations or divisions, according as they have any object to gain or subject of offence. And these things are done when Thou art forsaken, O Fountain of Life, who art the only and true Creator and Governor of the Universe, and by a self-willed pride, any one false thing is selected therefrom and loved. So then by a humble devoutness we return to Thee; and Thou cleansest us from our evil habits, and art merciful to their sins who confess, and *hearest the groaning of the prisoner,* and loosest us from the chains which we made for ourselves, if we lift not up against Thee the horns of an unreal liberty, suffering the loss of all, through covetousness of more, by loving more our own private good, than Thee, the Good of all.

JOAN OF ARC

What can one say of Joan of Arc that has not been said before? Hers is one of the world's greatest stories—the greatest, perhaps, aside from that of the Man of Galilee. It has fascinated the best minds of every age since her own, and no doubt will continue to do so as long as men have the capacity to think, to doubt, and to believe. It has engaged the creative efforts of some of the greatest workers in the arts, beginning with Shakespeare himself, whose dismissal of her as a female mounte-bank (natural, perhaps, in a patriotic Englishman not far in time from the events in which she played so dramatic a part) makes one of the few debit marks against his all-embracing genius. In our own era she has held enthralled such diverse minds and powers as those of Mark Twain and Bernard Shaw. In the words that Tennyson applied to Maud, "there is none like her, none."

Certainly none of the men or women who figure in the pages of this book has higher claim to representation. For the revelation of the spirit in which she faced calumny and death I have gone to the words of the Maid herself. The pages that follow are taken from the Orleans Manuscript, the verbatim, day-to-day report of St. Joan's trial and execution. This document was only recently discovered; it gives for the first time a complete and exact transcription of her testimony, together with the questions of her inquisitors. It reveals not only the extraordinary agility, clarity, and strength of her mind, but the full measure, as well, of the agony of spirit endured by this peasant girl, who emerged from her ordeal as one of the greatest champions of spiritual liberty the world has ever known. The passages chosen are from the final days of what might be called the most dramatic trial in history, save one.

The Trial of Joan of Arc

The Public Admonition

THE same day [1] Jeanne was brought before the judges in this trial. The bishop, in their presence, admonished her that she should follow the advice and admonitions which had been given to her by

[1] In fact a fortnight later, 2 May.

Maître Jean de Châtillon, doctor in theology, for the salvation both of her soul and her body, and if she were unwilling so to do, she would fall into grave danger both of body and soul.

And then the judges begged de Châtillon to proceed charitably to the said admonitions.

To which de Châtillon answered that he would gladly do so.

Firstly, he pointed out to her that all loyal Christians are obliged to believe and hold the articles of the Faith.

And he showed her the form and manner thereof, as she had previously been shown.

He then asked her whether she was willing to correct herself and amend her faults in accordance with the deliberation.

To which she answered: Read your book,

That is to say, the schedule which the bishop [2] was holding.

And then I will answer you. I wait upon God my Creator in all. I love Him with all my heart.

Questioned as to whether she desires to answer to this general admonition,

She answered: I trust in my judge, that is the King of Heaven and earth.

She was then told: Formerly you said that your deeds were seen and cross-examined, as is contained in the schedule.

She answered that she gives the same answer now.

When it was explained to her what the Church Militant meant, and [she was] admonished to believe and hold the article *Unam Sanctam Ecclesiam,* etc., and to submit to the Church Militant,

She answered: I believe in the Church on earth; but for my deeds and words, as I have previously said, I refer the whole matter to God, Who caused me to do what I have done.

She said also that she submits to God her Creator, Who caused her to do what she did; and refers it to Him in His own Person.

Asked if she means that she has no judge on earth, and our Holy Father the Pope is not her judge,

She replied: I will tell you nothing else. I have a good Master, Our Lord, in Whom I trust for everything, and not in any other.

She was told that if she did not wish to believe in the Church and in the article *Ecclesiam Sanctam Catholicam,* she would be a heretic to uphold [her views], and that she would be punished by other judges who would sentence her to be burned.

She answered: I will tell you nothing else. And [even] if I saw the fire, I should tell you what I have told you, and nothing else.

[2] This should read: Archdeacon.

Questioned as to whether, if the General Council, that is to say our Holy Father, the Cardinals [and the rest] were here, she would be willing to submit,

She answered: You will drag nothing else from me.

Asked if she is willing to submit to our Holy Father the Pope,

She said: Bring me to him, and I shall answer him.

She was unwilling to answer further,

Concerning her dress, etc.

She answered that in the matter of her clothing, she was most willing to wear a long dress and a woman's hood in which to go to church and receive her Saviour, as she has previously said; provided that immediately afterwards she may take it off and put on again that which she is wearing.

It was also explained to her that in the matter of her taking man's dress, there was now no necessity [for her to continue to do so], and especially since she was in prison,

She answered: When I shall have done that for which I have been sent by God, I shall take a woman's dress.

Asked if she believes she does well to wear male dress,

She answered: I trust in Our Lord.

Questioned on the explanation that she was given, that is on her saying that she did well and did not sin in wearing the said dress, together with the circumstances touching the fact of taking and wearing this dress, and in saying that God and the saints made her do so, she was guilty of blasphemy, and, as is more fully contained in the schedule, she erred and did evil,

She answered that she blasphemed neither God nor His saints.

Being admonished to leave off wearing this dress, and to cease believing that she did well to wear it; and being ordered to take a woman's dress,

She answered that she would not do otherwise.

Asked whether, every time that Saint Catherine and Saint Margaret come, she signs herself,

She answered that sometimes she makes the sign of the Cross, and other times she does not.

Concerning the revelations,

She answered that in this matter she refers to her judge, that is to say, God. And she says that her revelations come from God, without any intermediary.

Asked whether, concerning the sign given to her king, she would refer to the Archbishop of Rheims, the elder de Boussac, and to the knights de Bourbon, de la Trémoïlle and la Hire, to whom or to one of whom she said she had formerly shown this crown, they being present when the angel brought the crown and gave it to the archbishop, or if she would refer to others of her party, who would write under their seals of what they know,

She said: Send a messenger, and I will write to them all about this trial.

And otherwise she would neither believe nor refer to them.

As to her rash faith [in prophesying future events],

She answered: I refer to my judge, that is, God; and to what I have previously said, which is in the book.

Asked, if they gave her two, three or four knights [3] of her party, who would come under a safe conduct, whether she would be willing to refer herself to them concerning her apparitions and the matters contained in this trial,

She said, let them come, and then she would answer. Otherwise she was not willing to refer herself or submit herself in this trial.

Asked whether in the church of Poitiers, where she was examined, she was willing to refer and submit herself,

She answered: Do you think you can catch me that way, and draw me to you?

In conclusion, she was abundantly and newly admonished to submit to the Church, under pain of being abandoned by the Church. And if the Church abandoned her, she would be in great danger both of body and soul; her soul in peril of everlasting fire, and her body in danger of the flames of this world, by the sentence of other judges,

To which she answered: You will not do as you say against me without suffering evil, both of body and soul.

Asked to give one reason why she will not submit to the Church,

She will give no other answer.

And afterwards, a number of doctors of different sciences and faculties admonished and charitably exhorted her to submit to the Universal Church Militant and to the General Council; explaining to her the peril and danger to which she exposed herself as much in body as in soul, if she does not submit to the Church Militant.

To which she answered as before.

Finally the bishop told her that she should think well and advisedly over these monitions, and that she should change her mind.

To which Jeanne answered: How long do you give me to think it over?

The bishop told her that she must do so immediately, and that she should answer as she wished.

And at that time nothing further was done.

---

[3] D'Urfé also gives *chevaliers*, but in Courcelles the word used is *clericorum*.

The Threat of Torture

On the Wednesday, IXth of May, in the great dungeon of the castle of Rouen,

Jeanne was led into the presence of her judges, who were accompanied by Maîtres Jean de Châtillon, Guillaume Erard, the Abbot of Saint Cornille, Guillaume Eston, André Marguerie, Nicolas de Venderès, Aubert Morel, Nicolas Loiseleur and Messire Jean Massieu, Dean of the Christendom of Rouen.

The monitions and exhortations being done,[4]

Jeanne replied to the judges and assessors: Truly, if you were to tear me limb from limb and make my soul leave my body, I would not say to you anything else. [And if you force me to do so], then afterwards I shall say that you made me say so by force.

She said also that on Holy Cross Day [5] she received comfort from Saint Gabriel. And that her voices had told her that it was Saint Gabriel.

She said further that she had asked them whether she ought to submit to the Church, since the churchmen were pressing her strongly to do so, and they told her that if she wished Our Lord to help her, she should wait on Our Lord for all her deeds.

She said that she well knew that Our Lord was always master of her deeds; and that the Enemy never had power over them.

Furthermore she said that she had asked Saint Michael and her other voices if she would be burned; and that the voices had told her that she must wait on Our Lord and He would help her.

Concerning the sign of the crown which she said had been given to the Archbishop of Rheims, being asked whether she wished him to be consulted about it,

She answered: Have him come here, that I may hear him speak; then I shall answer you. He would not dare to tell you the contrary of what I have said to you.

Deliberation as to Torture

The XIIth day of May, in the house of my lord the Bishop of Beauvais, at the hour of Vespers,

---

[4] Jeanne was shown the instruments of torture and was told that if she did not answer truthfully she would be put to the torture, in order to procure the salvation of her soul. Many years afterwards, the Master Executioner said: "On this occasion she answered with such prudence that all present marvelled. I retired without doing anything."

[5] The Feast of the Invention of the Cross is May 3. In 1431 it fell on a Thursday, the day after the Public Admonition was made to Jeanne.

The judges being assembled in the presence of the Vice-Inquisitor of the Faith: Maître Raoul Roussel, Treasurer of the [Cathedral] Church of Rouen, Nicolas de Venderès, archdeacon, André Marguerie, Guillaume Erard, doctors in theology, Robert Barbery, Denis Gastinel, Aubert Morel, Thomas de Courcelles, Nicolas Couppequesne, Jean le Doulx, Ysambard de la Pierre, and Nicolas Loiseleur, jurists.

After they had been told what had been done the previous Wednesday, they were asked what still remained to be done; and whether it were expedient to put Jeanne to the torture.

They answered as follows:

Firstly, Maître Raoul Roussel said no; in order that the trial which had been held could not be calumniated.

Maître Nicolas de Venderès said that it was not expedient to put her to the torture as yet.

Maître André Marguerie said that it was not expedient at the moment.

Maître Guillaume Erard, in no circumstances should she be put to the torture; that the matter was clear enough without torture.

Maître Robert Barbery said as the afore-mentioned. But that she should again be admonished, once for all; and then, if she was unwilling to submit to the Church, one should proceed otherwise.

Maître Denis Gastinel said that it was not expedient to put her to the torture in order to know the truth of her falsehoods.

Maître Thomas de Courcelles said that it seemed to him she ought to be put to the torture; [6] and that she should be questioned as to whether she would submit to the judgment of the Church.

Maître Nicolas Couppequesne said it is not expedient that she should be put to the torture; and that she should be admonished time and again to submit to the Church's judgment.

Maître Jean le Doulx said the same as Couppequesne.

Brother Ysambard de la Pierre, as the above; but that she should still be admonished to submit herself to the Church Militant.

Maître Nicolas Loiseleur said that it seemed to him that, for her [soul's] health, she should be put to the torment; but that nevertheless he would stand by the opinion of those who had previously [given their views].

Maître Guillaume Haiton, who arrived later, was of the opinion that she ought not to be put to the torture.

Maître Jean Le Maître, Vice-Inquisitor, was of the opinion that she should be questioned frequently, to know if she would be willing to submit to the Church Militant.

[6] In his deposition at the Trial of Rehabilitation Courcelles said: "I never gave an opinion as to her being put to the torture."

The Consideration of the Opinion of the University of Paris

In the year one thousand four hundred XXXI, on Saturday, the XIXth day of May,

The judges assembled in the chapel of the archiepiscopal manor of Rouen, before the Bishop of Beauvais and the Vice-Inquisitor of the Faith: Maîtres Raoul Roussel, Nicolas de Venderès, the Abbot of Fécamp, André Marguerie, Jean Pichon, Jean de Châtillon, Evrard Emengard, Guillaume Le Boucher, the Prior of Longueville, Jean Beaupère, Nicolas Midi, Maurice du Chêne, Pierre de Hodeng, Jean Lefèvre, the Abbot of Mortemer, the Prior of Saint Lô, Pierre Maurice, Jacques Quesdon, Jean Foucher, the Abbot of Cormeilles, Jean Foucher, Thomas de Courcelles, Nicolas de Couppequesne, Raoul Silvestre, Jean Pigache, Richard Gruchel, Nicolas Loiseleur, Pasquier de Vaux, Denis Gastinel, Jean Mauger, Jean Secart, Jean Adensem, Geoffroi du Crotoy, Guillaume de la Chambre, Jean du Quemyn, Martin Ladvenu, Ysambard de la Pierre, Guillaume de Lyvet, Jean Le Doulx, Jean Colombel, Richard Dessaul, Laurens du Bosc, Pierre le Mynier, Pierre Carré and Raoul Auguy.

In the presence of all of these, the Bishop of Beauvais read at length the report of the trial of Jeanne.

This done, on the advice of all the judges it was ordered that the Articles that had been sent to the University of Paris should be read in their presence.

[After the Opinion of the University had been considered by the doctors and masters assembled at Rouen, these latter agreed with it, and advised that it should be read to Jeanne, and that she should be charitably admonished and warned before a final Sentence was pronounced.]

The Reading of the Censures of the University

Read and pronounced by Maître Pierre Maurice, doctor in theology, together with the University's deliberations upon each of the Articles. Firstly, he addressed himself to Jeanne, saying to her:

[I]

You, Jeanne, have said that from the age of thirteen you have had revelations and apparitions of angels, of Saint Catherine and of Saint Margaret, and that you have frequently seen them with your bodily eyes; and that they have spoken to you.

On this first point the clerks of the University of Paris have considered the form of the said revelations and apparitions and the purpose and matter of the things revealed, and the condition of the person. Taking all these things into consideration, they have said and declared that all the afore-mentioned things are lies, untrue, pernicious and evil; and that all such revelations are superstitious, and proceed from evil and devilish spirits.

II

You have said that your king had a sign whereby he knew that you were sent from God; for Saint Michael, accompanied by several angels, some having wings, and others crowns, and with them Saint Catherine and Saint Margaret, came to you in the castle of Chinon, and climbed the steps of the castle as far as the hall of your king, before whom the angel who carried a crown, bowed. On one occasion you said that when your king received this sign, he was alone; on another occasion you said that this crown, which you call "a sign," was given to the Archbishop of Rheims, who handed it to your king in the presence of several princes and lords whom you named.

As for this Article, the clerks say that it is not true; but is a presumptuous lie, seductive and pernicious, and a pretence that is derogatory of both ecclesiastical and angelic dignity.

III

You have said that you recognized the angels and the saints by the good advice, and the comfort and teaching that they gave you. And you also believe that it was Saint Michael who appeared to you; and you declare that their deeds and words are good; and that you believe this as firmly as you believe the Faith of Jesus Christ.

As for this Article, the clerks say that such things are not sufficient to [enable you to] recognize these angels and saints; that you believed too lightly and affirmed your belief too rashly; and that inasmuch as you make a comparison saying you believe these things as firmly as you believe in the Faith of Jesus Christ, you err in the faith.

IV

You have said that you are aware of certain things to come, and that you have known hidden secrets; and that you have recognized people whom you had never seen before; and that you have done so by means of the voices of Saint Catherine and Saint Margaret.

As for this Article, they say that in this matter there are both superstition and divination, presumptuous assertion, and vain boasting.

V

You have said that, by God's command, you have continually worn man's dress, wearing the short robe, doublet, and hose attached by points; that you have also worn your hair short, cut *en rond* above your ears, with nothing left that could show you to be a woman; and that on many occasions you received the Body of our Lord dressed in this fashion, although you have been frequently admonished to leave it off, which you have refused to do, saying that you would rather die than leave it off, save by God's command. And you said further that if you were still so dressed and with the king and those of his party, it would be one of the greatest blessings for the kingdom of France; and you have said that not for anything would you take an oath not to wear this dress or carry arms; and concerning all these matters you have said that you did well, and obediently to God's command.

As for these points, the clerks say that you blaspheme God in His sacraments; that you transgress divine law, the Holy Scriptures and the canon law; you hold the Faith doubtfully and wrongly; you boast vainly; you are suspect of idolatry; and you condemn yourself in being unwilling to wear the customary clothing of your sex, and following the custom of the Gentiles and the heathen.

VI

You have said that often in your letters you have put the two names Jesus Maria and the sign of the Cross, in token that those to whom you have written should not do that which is contained in your letters; and in others of your letters you have boasted that you would see by the result who had the best right; and on many occasions you said that you had done nothing save by revelation and by God's command.

As for this Article, the clerks say that you are cruel and a murderess, desirous of the shedding of human blood, seditious, provoking to tyranny, and blaspheming God and His commandments and revelations.

VII

You have said that, following the revelations you had had, at the age of seventeen you left your father and mother against their will, causing them such anxiety that they went almost our of their minds. And you went to Robert de Baudricourt, who, at your request, gave you a man's garments and a sword, and also men to lead you to your king, to whom you said that you had come to drive out his enemies; and you promised him that you would install him in his kingdom;

and that he would have victory over all his enemies; and that God had sent you to do so. And you said that you had done all these things in obedience to God's revelation.

As for this Article, the clerks say that you have acted wrongly and impetuously towards your father and mother, therein transgressing the commandment of God to honour thy father and thy mother; that you have behaved scandalously, blaspheming God and erring in the Faith. And the promise that you made to your king was presumptuous and rash.

VIII

You have said that of your own will you leaped from the tower of Beaurevoir into the moat, preferring to die rather than to be put in the hands of the English and to live on after the destruction of Compiègne; and that Saint Catherine and Saint Margaret forbade you to leap, but you could not refrain from doing so, although you sinned greatly in leaping contrary to their orders; but you have since learned from your voices that God had forgiven the sin, after you had confessed it.

As for this Article, the clerks say that in this was cowardice tending to despair and to suicide; and that you have made a rash and presumptuous assertion in saying that God had forgiven the sin; showing that you wrongly understand [the doctrine of] free-will and man's right to choose.

IX

You have said that Saint Catherine and Saint Margaret promised to bring you to heaven, provided you kept your virginity which you vowed and promised them. And of this you are as certain as if you were already in the glory of Paradise; and you do not believe that you have committed mortal sin; for if you were in mortal sin, Saint Catherine and Saint Margaret would not come to you as they do.

As for this Article, the clerks say that herein you are guilty of a rash and presumptuous assertion and of pernicious lies; that you contradict what you previously said, and that you incorrectly understand the Christian Faith.

X

You have said that you are well assured that God loves certain others living more than yourself, and that you know this by revelation from these saints, who speak in the French language; and not in English, because they are not of their party. And that, ever since you learned that the voices were on your king's side, you have not loved the Burgundians.

As for this Article, the clerks say that this is a rash presumption and assertion, blasphemy against the saints, and transgression of God's commandment to love one's neighbour.

XI

You have said that to those whom you call Saint Michael, Saint Catherine and Saint Margaret you made several reverences, kneeling and kissing the ground they walked on, and vowing your virginity to them; and even that you have kissed and embraced them, and from the beginning [believed] that they came from God, without asking advice from your curé or from any churchman; but that none the less you believe that this voice has come from God, as firmly as you believe in the Christian Faith and that Jesus Christ suffered His death and passion; and that if any evil spirits were to appear in the form and feature of Saint Michael, you would know it. You have also said that not for anyone in the world would you tell the sign given to your king, save by God's command.

To which the clerks say that, supposing you have had the revelations and apparitions of which you boast, in the way that you say, you are an idolater, and invoker of demons, a wanderer from the Faith, and have rashly taken an unlawful oath.

XII

You have said that if the Church desired you to do the opposite of the commandment which you say you have received from God, you would not do so for anything in the world. And you know for certain that what is contained in your trial came by God's command; and that it would be impossible for you to do the contrary. And that, concerning all the afore-mentioned matters, you are not willing to refer them to the judgment of the Church on earth, nor of any man alive, but only to God alone. And you say further that you do not give your answers of your own intelligence, but by command of God, regardless of the fact that the article of the Faith which says that everyone must believe in the Catholic Church has been several times explained to you; and that every good Catholic Christian must submit all his deeds to the Church, and especially facts concerning revelations and such-like.

As for this Article, the clerks say that you are schismatic, having no comprehension of the truth and authority of the Church; and that up to the present you have perniciously erred in the faith of God.

The Charitable Admonition

After the Articles had been read to Jeanne, together with the Opinion of the University of Paris, she was admonished by the said doctor that she should carefully consider her words and deeds, especially with reference to the final Article; speaking to her as follows:

Jeanne, my very dear friend, it is now time, at the end of your trial, to think carefully of what you have said and done.

For since both by the Bishop of Beauvais, the Vice-Inquisitor, and other doctors sent to you to admonish you, both in public and in secret, for the honour of the Faith and law of Jesus Christ, for the peace of Christian people, and on account of the scandal which it causes, as well as for the salvation of your soul and of your body, you have been very carefully warned; you have also been told of the punishments which may be inflicted upon you, both in soul and body, if you do not correct and amend your words and deeds, and submit to the judgment of the Church.

Up to the present you have been unwilling to heed these warnings. And although in your own deeds and words there has been matter enough to find you guilty, yet the judges, desiring your salvation both of body and soul, sent to the University of Paris, the light of all knowledge and the extirpation of all error, in order that your words and deeds at your trial might be thoroughly examined.

In accordance with the opinion of the University, the judges ordered that you should be over and over again charitably admonished, warning you of the errors, scandals and other sins you have committed, and begging and praying for the love of Our Lord Jesus Christ, Who suffered so cruel a death to redeem mankind, that you should correct your words and deeds, and submit to the judgment of the Church, as every loyal Christian is obliged to do; and not allow yourself to be separated from Our Lord Jesus Christ, that you may be a partaker of His glory; nor choose the way of eternal damnation with the enemies of God, who are always endeavouring to molest and disturb men, sometimes counterfeiting the likeness of angels or saints, and pretending to be such, as appears in the lives of the Fathers. Therefore if such apparitions appear to you, do not believe them, but reject and cast out such follies and imaginations, in agreement with the statements and opinions of the University of Paris and the other doctors, who are conversant with and understand God's law and the Holy Scriptures; to whom it seems that one should give no credence to such apparitions and other novelties, unless they are justified in Holy Scripture or by some other sign as being miraculous. In these you have believed most lightly, without having recourse to God in devout prayer, in order that you might be made certain in the matter; nor have you had recourse to any prelate or other wise and learned churchman, who would have been able to inform you of the truth; which, considering your condition and the simplicity of your knowledge, you ought to have done.

Take for example: if your king in the exercise of his power had given you charge of a certain place, forbidding you to let anyone enter; and [some-one came], saying he came by the king's authority, you would not allow him to enter unless he brought you letters or some other certain sign that he came with the king's authority; likewise Our Lord Jesus Christ, when He ascended into heaven, leaving the government of the Church to Saint Peter and his successors, forbade them to receive any coming in His Name, if they were not sufficiently assured, other than by their own words, that they came from God.

Thus we should not have faith in your words, since God has forbidden it.

Wherefore, Jeanne, you must understand that, if in your king's realms, when you were there, a knight or some other subject had arisen and said, I will not obey the king, nor will I submit to any of his officers, would you not have said that he should be condemned? What would you say therefore of yourself, brought up in the Faith of Jesus Christ by the sacrament of baptism, and made the spouse of Jesus Christ, if you do not obey His officers, the prelates of the Church? What judgment would you pass upon yourself? Cast off, I beg you, these opinions, if you love God your Spouse and your Salvation, and be obedient to the Church and submit yourself to its judgment. And be well assured that if you do not do so, but persevere in your errors, your soul will be condemned to eternal torment in hell; and as for your body, I do not doubt that it will come to perdition.

I beg you not to allow yourself to be held back by human shame and useless fear, by which perchance you are detained, that you may lose the great honours in which you formerly lived. Put first God's honour and the salvation of your body and your soul, and remember that if you do not do what I say, but continue in your errors, you will separate yourself from the Church and the Faith which you promised [to hold] in the holy sacrament of baptism, and will despise the authority of God and the Church, which is led and governed by Our Lord; for He has said to its prelates, He that heareth you heareth Me; and he that despiseth you despiseth Me. Therefore if you will not submit to the Church, you are unwilling to submit yourself to God, and you err in this article of faith: We believe in the Catholic Church, whose authority has been sufficiently explained to you in the preceding Articles and admonitions.

Therefore, in view of these matters, on behalf of my lord the bishop, here present, and of my lord the Inquisitor of the Faith, your judges, I do admonish, beg and exhort you, by the pity that you feel for the Passion of Our Saviour your Creator, and the desire you must have for the salvation of your soul and body, to correct and amend your faults and return into the way of truth, obeying and submitting yourself to the judgment and decision of the Church. And in so doing you will save your soul, and deliver, as I hope, your body from death. But if you do contrary, and persist [in your evil courses], be assured that your soul will be damned, and I fear also the destruction of your body. From which may God preserve you. Amen.

After Jeanne had been thus admonished, and had heard all the exhortations, she answered in the manner following:

As for my words and deeds, I refer to what I said at my trial, and I will maintain them.

Questioned by the said Maître Pierre [Maurice] if she believes that she is not bound to submit her words and deeds to the Church Militant or to any other than God,

She answered: I will maintain what I have always said at my trial.

And if I were to be condemned and saw the fire lit and the wood prepared and the executioner who was to burn me ready to cast me into the fire, still in the fire would I not say anything other than I have said. And I will maintain what I have said until death.

After this, the judges asked the promoter of the trial and Jeanne herself if either of them wished to say anything further, to which they both answered no.

Then the bishop proceeded to the conclusion of the trial, according to a schedule which he held in his hands, of which the tenor follows.

We, the judges competent in this trial, declare and have declared Ourselves so to be, as much as is required, and declare this trial ended. And We do assign to-morrow to hear Our verdict in this matter, and to proceed further in accordance with law and equity.

In the presence of Brother Ysambard de la Pierre and Messire Matthew le Basteur,[7] priests; and Louis Coursel, clerk; of the dioceses of Rouen, London and Noyon; witnesses.

[Here in the Orleans manuscript is a statement that the writer intends to include the opinion of Jean Gerson, who believed Jeanne innocent of all the charges. For some reason unknown to us, this opinion was never included in the manuscript.]

[7] Presumably Mathew Shepherd, an English priest.

The Abjuration

[At a solemn assembly publicly held in the cemetery of Saint Ouen at Rouen, before the lord Bishop of Beauvais and the Vice-Inquisitor, in the presence of the most reverend father in Christ Henry, Cardinal of England, the reverend fathers in Christ the lord Bishops of Thérouanne, Noyon and Norwich, together with the lords and masters, Jean Beaupère, Nicolas Midi, Nicolas de Venderès, André Marguerie, Denis Gastinel, Jean de Châtillon, the lord abbots of Saint Ouen, Fécamp and Saint Michel-au-péril-de-la-mer, Maurice du Chêne, Jean Pinchon and Jean Alespée ... after the sermon (from the fifteenth chapter of Saint John, 'A branch cannot bear fruit of itself except it abide in the vine')[8] the preacher said to Jeanne: "Here are my lords the judges, who have time and again summoned and required you to submit your words and deeds to our Mother Holy Church, inasmuch as it seems to the learned clerks that there are many things contained in these words and deeds which it is not good either to say or to uphold."

To which Jeanne replied: "I will answer you." As to submission to the Church she said, "I have already told you that concerning all that I have done I appeal, after God, to our Holy Father the Pope. Everything that I have done, I have done at God's command." ... And she was told that this did not suffice, for it was not possible to send to the Holy Father, being so far away, and that the Ordinaries were each one judge in his own diocese, and that therefore she must submit to our Mother Holy Church. She was thus admonished three times.

And when the Sentence was partly read, she said that she was willing to hold all that the judges and the Church desired, and to be obedient to them.[9]

Then, in the presence of the afore-named persons and a great multitude of people, she recanted and made her abjuration in the manner following.]

HERE FOLLOWS THE ABJURATION OF JEANNE THE PUCELLE, MADE THE XXIIIith OF MAY, IN THE YEAR MIIIIXXXI

[8] In his sermon the preacher Erard grossly insulted the king, at which she could not keep silence, but called out "Speak of me, not of the king." Pointing at her, he repeated "Your king, since he listened to you, is heretic and schismatic." Despite the imminent danger in which she stood Jeanne could not refrain from answering, saying, "I dare swear that my king is the most noble Christian of all Christians!" Marvellous fidelity to a worthless sovereign, who had left her succourless to die!

[9] While the sentence was being read, Loiseleur, one of the assessors, and Massieu the usher, together with Erard, began to urge Jeanne to submit rather than be burnt. Jeanne, worn out with the long strain, and but half understanding what was being said, conscious only of the imminence of the fire, at last gave in.

All those who have erred and been at fault in the Christian Faith, and have since by God's grace returned into the light of truth, and into the unity of our Mother Holy Church, must take extreme care that the enemy of hell does not cause them to relapse into error and damnation.

Here follows the tenor of the schedule which the Bishop of Beauvais and the other judges said was made by the said Jeanne and signed by her hand,

The which I do not believe,

And it is not believable that she intended that which is here shown.[10]

I JEANNE, CALLED THE PUCELLE, A MISERABLE SINNER, AFTER I RECOGNIZED THE SNARE OF ERROR IN WHICH I WAS HELD; AND NOW THAT I HAVE, BY GOD'S GRACE, RETURNED TO OUR MOTHER HOLY CHURCH; IN ORDER THAT IT MAY BE APPARENT THAT NOT FEIGNEDLY BUT WITH GOOD HEART AND WILL I HAVE RETURNED TO HER; I DO CONFESS THAT I HAVE GRIEVOUSLY SINNED, IN FALSELY PRETENDING THAT I HAVE HAD REVELATIONS FROM GOD AND HIS ANGELS, SAINT CATHERINE AND SAINT MARGARET, ETC.

AND ALL MY WORDS AND DEEDS WHICH ARE CONTRARY TO THE CHURCH, I DO REVOKE; AND I DESIRE TO LIVE IN UNITY WITH THE CHURCH, NEVERMORE DEPARTING THEREFROM.

IN WITNESS WHEREOF MY SIGN MANUAL,

signed JHENNE +

The Reading of the Sentence

Here follows the Definitive Sentence, pronounced by the Bishop of Beauvais, after the abjuration and the [signing of the] schedule, beginning:

IN THE NAME OF THE LORD, AMEN

All pastors of the Church who would faithfully lead God's people, must carefully and diligently watch lest the devil, through his subtle arts, seduces and deceives the flock of Jesus Christ, to do which he labours ceaselessly. Wherefore there is need of great diligence to resist his false and sinful wiles.

Since you, Jeanne, commonly called the Pucelle, have been found guilty of many errors in the Faith of Jesus Christ, for which you have been called to judgment, and concerning which you have been heard; and since all the points and articles of your trial, your confessions,

10 An allusion to Jeanne's later retraction.

answers and assertions have been examined by Us, and the whole trial has been seen and deliberated upon by the masters and doctors of the Faculty of Theology in Paris, as well as by a number of prelates and doctors in law, both canon and civil, who are in this town of Rouen, by whom you have been charitably admonished with long appeals for your change of heart.

Notwithstanding these warnings and remonstrances, and after the abjuration made to you, you have rashly and wantonly fallen into sin.

Wherefore, that you may make salutary penance, We have condemned you, and do now condemn you by this Definitive Sentence to perpetual imprisonment,[11] with the bread of sorrow and the water of affliction, that you may weep for your sins, and nevermore commit them. Saving Our grace and moderation, if hereafter you shall deserve them.

[Here, and out of chronological order, Orleans inserts an incorrect version of the scene at St. Ouen. This I have replaced above by the correct version taken from d'Urfé.]

Visit of the Inquisitor to the Prison

After the Sentence was pronounced, as has been said, the Vice-Inquisitor and several others who had been present at the Sentence, went to see Jeanne after dinner in the prison in which she was kept. They remonstrated with her, pointing out that the Church had dealt kindly with her, and that she should accept the Sentence with humility and be obedient to the Church; that she should leave her revelations and other stupidities; warning her that if she should again fall into such sins, the Church would not take her back; and begging her to leave off man's clothes and wear a woman's dress.

To this Jeanne replied that she would willingly wear woman's dress and be obedient to the Church.

And immediately she put on a woman's dress, and allowed her hair, which had been cut *en rond,* to be cut off.[12]

---

[11] There is a doubt as to the especial meaning attached to the word *carcer perpetuas.* The Rev. Father Thurston, S.J., in *Studies* for September 1924, writes: " 'Lifelong prison' . . . is, undoubtedly, the natural and obvious translation; but the phrase, I submit, is shown by sundry Inquisition records to mean simply a permanent prison as opposed to the makeshift buildings which were casually employed for the purpose." I think, however, that the usual meaning of *perpetuas,* perpetual or lifelong, is more likely to be correct.

[12] Jeanne's hair had grown during her imprisonment. After the Abjuration, it was shaved off completely.

Visit of the Judges to the Prison

The following Monday, the twenty-eighth day of May, the judges went to the prison, and found [Jeanne] dressed in man's clothing, that is, a robe, hood, and the other garments normally worn by men, which garments she had left off by order of the Church.

Asked for what reason she had again taken man's dress,

She answered that she had done so just now.

Asked why, and who had induced her to do so,

She said, of her own will. And that nobody had forced her to do so. And that she preferred man's dress to woman's.

Wherefore she was reminded that she had sworn and promised never again to wear male clothing,

To which she replied that she had never intended to take an oath not to take man's dress again.

Being asked several times why she had taken it again,

She said that she had done so because it seemed to her more suitable and convenient to wear man's dress being with men, than to wear a woman's dress.

She said further that she had again taken it because they had not kept their promise that she should hear Mass; that she should receive the Body of the Lord; and that she should be relieved of her fetters.

And that she would rather die than be kept in irons. But if they promised that she should go to Mass and have her fetters removed, she would do everything the Church ordered and required.

Questioned whether since last Thursday she had heard the voices of Saint Catherine and Saint Margaret,

She answered yes.

And that they told her that God had sent her word by them that she had put herself in great danger of perdition in that she had consented to make the abjuration and renunciation in order to save her life; and that she was damned for doing so.

And she said that, before Thursday, her voices had told her what she ought to do, and that she had done it.

She said also that her voices had told her that, when she was on the platform, she should answer the preacher boldly. And she said that the preacher was a false preacher, for he said that she had done many things which she had never done.

She said further that in saying that God had not sent her she had damned herself, for truly God had sent her. And since Thursday her voices had told her that she had done great wrong to God in confessing that what she had done was not well done.

She said also that everything she had said and revoked, she had done only through fear of the fire.

Asked if she believes that the voices are those of Saint Catherine and Saint Margaret,

She answered yes; and that they come from God.

Asked to tell the truth about the afore-mentioned crown,

She answered that she had told the truth in everything, as best she could.

It was then said to her that when she was on the platform before the judges and the people, when she made her abjuration, she had been adjured to tell the truth. And you admitted [they said], that you had boasted falsely that the voices you said you heard were those of Saint Catherine and Saint Margaret.

To which she answered that she never intended to have denied her apparitions, that is, that they were Saint Catherine and Saint Margaret. And what she said, she said for fear of the fire. And if she recanted, it was untrue.

She also said that she would rather do penance by dying, than bear any longer the agony of imprisonment.

And she said that never had she done anything contrary to God and the Faith, anything that they had made her revoke; and as for what was contained in the schedule of abjuration, she never intended it.

And she never intended to revoke anything, unless it was pleasing to God that she should do so.

She said further, if the judges desire it, she will wear a woman's dress again. For the rest, she knows no more.

Decision of the Judges to Hand Over Jeanne to the Secular Arm

On Tuesday the twenty-ninth day of May, We, the Bishop of Beauvais, called together the doctors and other ecclesiastics in great number in the chapel of the Archiepiscopal Manor, and explained to them that Jeanne had been again and again admonished to return into the way of truth. And how, after being so admonished before the people, she had sworn that never would she relapse, and had signed a schedule with her own hand; and on Thursday after dinner, being the day of her Sentence, she had been charitably admonished by the Vice-Inquisitor and others that she should continue in her good intentions and take great care she did not relapse.

But, being persuaded by the devil, she had declared time and again, in the presence of several persons, that her voices, who had been accustomed to appear to her, had come again; and she had taken off her woman's dress and again taken man's clothing.

And after this, before all the clerks who were present in the chapel, the confessions and assertions which she had made the day before were read; after which, their opinions were asked as to what should be done, and they were all of the opinion and stated that she ought to be considered a heretic, and should be left to secular justice, with a request that they should treat her more kindly than she had deserved.

[*At seven the next morning Jeanne was visited in her cell by the two Dominicans, Ladvenu and Toutmouillé, who came to prepare her for death. The former heard her in confession, and (most inconsistently in the case of a judgment for relapse) Cauchon permitted her to receive Holy Communion.*

It is impossible to understand what Cauchon meant when he gave this permission; the reception of the Sacrament by a relapsed person, necessarily unabsolved, is not consonant with the fact that communion demands the prerequisite of absolution. If she were absolved, she could no longer be in lapse.

The Host was brought to her cell, as Massieu said, "irreverently, without stole and lights, at which Brother Martin, who had confessed her, was ill-content, and so a stole and lights were sent for, and thus Brother Martin administered It to her." It is on record that Jeanne said to her confessor, "Where shall I be to-night?" to which he replied, "Have you no faith in Our Lord?" "Yes, God helping me, to-day I shall be with Him in Paradise."]

The Definitive Sentence

And on Wednesday the penultimate day of May, being the last day of the trial,

By Us the said Jeanne was cited to hear the law and to appear in person before Us in the Old Market of the town of Rouen at eight o'clock in the morning, to see herself declared relapsed into her errors, heretic and excommunicate; together with the intimations customary to be made in such a case.

Later on the same day, at about nine o'clock in the morning, We the bishop and judges being in the Old Market of Rouen, near to the church of Saint Sauveur, in the presence of the Bishops of Thérouanne and Noyon, and several other doctors, clerks and masters, after the sermon had been preached, We admonished Jeanne, for the salvation of her soul, that she should repent her evil deeds and show true contrition, by means of counsel from two Friar Preachers, who were near her in order that they might continually advise her, whom for this purpose, We had appointed.

All these matters referred to being done, We, the aforesaid bishop and Vice-Inquisitor, having regard to the afore-mentioned matters wherein it appeared that Jeanne remained obstinate in her errors, and through malice and devilish obstinacy had falsely shown signs of contrition and penitence; and that she had blasphemed the holy and divine Name of God; and showing herself an incorrigible heretic had relapsed into heresy and error, and was unworthy and incapable of any pity,

We proceeded to the Definitive Sentence in the manner following:

IN THE NAME OF THE LORD, AMEN

We Pierre, by Divine pity, humble Bishop of Beauvais, and We, Brother Jean le Maître, deputy of the Inquisitor of the Faith, judges competent in this matter,

Since you, Jeanne, called the Pucelle, have been found by Us relapsed into divers errors and crimes of schism, idolatry, invocation of devils, and various other wickednesses.

And since for these reasons by just judgment We have found you so to be,

Nevertheless, since the Church never closes her arms to those who would return to her, We did believe that, with full understanding and unfeigned faith, you had left all the errors which you had renounced, vowing, swearing and publicly promising that never again would you fall into such errors, nor into any other heresies, but would live in Catholic unity and communion with our Church and our Holy Father the Pope, as is stated in a schedule signed by your own hand.

None the less time and again you have relapsed, as a dog that returns to its vomit, as We do state with great sorrow.

Wherefore We declare that you have again incurred the Sentence of excommunication which you formerly incurred, and are again fallen into your previous errors, for which reasons We now declare you to be a heretic.

And by this Sentence, seated upon Our tribunal of justice, as it is herein written, We do cast you forth and reject you from the communion of the Church as an infected limb, and hand you over to secular justice, praying the same to treat you with kindness and humanity in respect of your life and of your limbs.[13]

---

[13] This was a sheer formality, and never meant to be acted upon.

The Execution

After the Sentence was read, the bishop, the Inquisitor, and many of the judges went away, leaving Jeanne upon the scaffold.

Then the Bailli of Rouen, an Englishman, who was there, without any legal formality and without reading any Sentence against her, ordered that she should be taken to the place where she was to be burned.

When Jeanne heard this order given, she began to weep and lament in such a way that all the people present were themselves moved to tears.

The said Bailli immediately ordered that the fire should be lighted, which was done.

And she was there burned and martyred tragically, an act of unparalleled cruelty.

And many, both noble and peasant, murmured greatly against the English.

J. W. N. SULLIVAN

John William Nazin Sullivan, English by birth, was born in 1886 and died in 1937. A graduate of University College in London, he had a passionate dual interest in science and in music. He wrote voluminously on scientific subjects, both for British periodicals and in a long list of books. He also wrote a novel or two, but is best known to American readers for his lives of Galileo and Beethoven.

I have selected for this book several pages from his life of the great composer: that section of it which describes Beethoven's struggle with his deafness, an affliction which obviously cut more deeply in his case than in that of the average person. He first became aware of that handicap when he was twenty-eight years old, and about three years later he made his first written reference to it; he wrote to Amanda, "Your Beethoven is most unhappy, and at strife with nature and Creator ... Only think that my noblest faculty, my hearing, has greatly deteriorated." And to his doctor friend, Wegeler, a week or two later, he wrote: "I am living a wretched life; for two years I have avoided almost all social gatherings because it is impossible for me to say to people: 'I am deaf.'"

As Sullivan makes clear in the passages from his biography which are reprinted here, Beethoven's battle with himself in facing up to this blow of fate was to have profound effect upon his spiritual health, and is reflected in the power and grandeur of the music he wrote after he had met and conquered the enemy he had so greatly feared.

Beethoven in Deafness

ONE OF THE most significant facts, for the understanding of Beethoven, is that his work shows an organic development up till the very end. The longer Beethoven lived, the more and more profound was what he had to say. The greatest music Beethoven ever wrote is to be found in the last string quartets, and the music of every decade before the final period has greater music than its predecessor. Such sustained development, in the case of an artist who reaches years of maturity, is a rare and important phenomenon. Bach, for instance, who may be likened to Beethoven for the seriousness and maturity of his mind, lost himself at the end in the arid labyrinths of pure technique. Wagner, as the fever in his blood grew less, had nothing to express at the end but exhaustion and ineffectual longing. Beethoven's music continually developed because it was the expression of an attitude toward life that had within it the possibility of indefinite growth.

Some attitudes toward life are not susceptible of development. They may achieve greater richness and subtlety, but they are incapable of organic growth. The cynic, for example, may become more bitter and penetrating, but unless he suffers a catastrophic change he remains at the same distance from reality. The man who has sincerely accepted a religious scheme in which all the major problems of life are provided with solutions is likely to go through life without ever experiencing the direct impact of those problems. That is, in fact, the weakness of Bach as compared with Beethoven. Wagner, the great apostle of the pride of life, finds, as the bright world slips past him, that he is left alone with his yearning and his pain. The attitude of both Bach and Wagner toward life was not sufficient to support all their length of days. Beethoven on his deathbed could say, *Plaudite, amici, comoedia finita est.* But the "comedy" had been in play up to the last moment.

The chief characteristic of the fully mature Beethoven's attitude toward life is to be found in his realization of suffering and in his realization of the heroism of achievement. The character of life as suffering is an aspect that our modern civilization, mercifully for the great majority of people, does a great deal to obscure. Few men have the capacity fully to realize suffering as one of the great structural lines of human life. Bach, as we have said, escaped the problem with his religious scheme. Wagner, on the basis of a sentimental philosophy, finds the reason and anodyne of suffering in the pity it awakens. Mozart, with his truer instinct, is bewildered. The G minor quintet is the most poignant expression of his angelic anguish at his late discovery of this earth's pain. To Beethoven the character of life as suffering became a fundamental part of his outlook. The deep sincerity and naïveté of his nature, combined with the circumstances of his life, made this knowledge inevitable. The quality of this realization has nothing in common with the pessimism of such a man as Schopenhauer. It is the direct, simple, and final acceptance of an obvious fact. This attitude of mind is perhaps rarer today than at any previous period of history. To the modern mind suffering is essentially remediable. Suffering is primarily due to physical and moral maladjustment, and with the spread of science and correct social theories we shall be able to abolish it. For an increasing number of people suffering is already practically abolished. They may go through life without meeting one problem they cannot evade until they reach their deathbed, while they find the sufferings of others easier to endure through their conviction that they are the temporary consequences of the imperfect state of society. But to the vast majority of people suffering is still one of the fundamental characteristics of life, and it is their realization that an experience of suffering, pure and profound, enters as an integral part into Beethoven's greatest work, that helps to give that work its unique place in the minds and hearts of men.

Beethoven's capacity for a deep and passionate realization of suffering necessitated, if he were not to be reduced to impotence, a corresponding capacity for endurance and an enormous power of self-assertion. No artist ever lived whose work gives a greater impression of indomitable strength than we find in some of Beethoven's most characteristic movements. The force that triumphs through the scherzo of the Ninth symphony, for example, is indeed indestructible, while the fugue of the Hammerclavier sonata is an almost insensate outburst of unconquerable self-assertion. As he grew older his force increased. "I will take Fate by the throat," he said as a young man, à propos of his increasing deafness, and there is plenty of the "will to victory" in the Fifth symphony he proceeded to write. But a stronger, although a more subtle pulse, is to be found in some of the last string quartets. In his last years he had more to carry and he carried it more lightly.

The "personality" of such a man as Beethoven is a slowly developed synthetic whole. It is formed by the gradual combination of its constituent elements into an organic unity. For the development of a personality a rich and profound inner life is necessary, and for that reason it is usually only great artists and religious leaders who impress us as being complete persons. Among the elements constitutive of Beethoven's personality we must include his lack of malleability. This quality made him almost immune from purely external influences. Thus he was impervious to criticism; his manners were atrocious; he ignored conventions; he was permanently subject to no social passions, not even sexual love. The low standard of education he achieved seemed to have been as much due to his lack of plasticity as to his lack of opportunities. He was not an educable man. He accepted none of the schemes of thought or conduct current in his time; it is doubtful whether he was even fully aware of their existence. He remained utterly faithful to his own experience. It is for this reason that his affirmative utterances, as in the Credo of the Mass in D, have such unexampled weight. Such utterances spring solely from his own personal and tested experience.

Beethoven's capacity for realizing the fundamental character of life in its two aspects of suffering and achievement, combined with his lack of flexibility, was the necessary condition for the development of his attitude toward life. That development takes the form of a synthesis. The Beethoven of the C minor symphony finds the meaning of life in achievement in spite of suffering. Fate is an enemy to be defied. The Beethoven of the last quartets finds that the highest achievement is reached through suffering. Suffering is accepted as a necessary condition of life, as an illuminating power. That the reconciliation he thus effected was genuine and complete is made evident by the music, for none of Beethoven's music is more obviously the expression of an authentic experience. The quality of this experience has led many writers to call this music "mystical" or "metaphysical." But whatever meanings these terms may be intended to convey, the music in question is really Beethoven's expression of the final synthesis he achieved between the primary elements of his experience. He did not turn away from life toward some mystical Nirvana. He forgot none of the joy, the effort, or the pain. He abandoned nothing. What he achieved is something much more wonderful than an old man's serenity. The life in the last string quartets is as full, varied, and intense as anywhere in Beethoven's music. But those aspects of life that Beethoven formerly presented as contrasted he now presents as harmoniously flowering from a single stem. Life's experiences are still presented with all their diversity, but no longer as conflicting.

Within the iron framework of Beethoven's permanent attitude toward life flourished a highly sensitive and passionate emotional nature. Although his vision had the stern strength of the Puritan outlook it had none of its bleakness. He was fully alive to the countless lovely and tender things in life. No one's reaction to simple pastoral scenes, for example, was ever more intense and innocent than Beethoven's. He had none of the doubts that troubled the Victorian romantics after their acquaintance with the doctrine of the "struggle for existence," neither had he any of the eighteenth-century cultured affectation of a "love for nature." His reaction was spontaneous, direct, and unsophisticated. Only a man pure in heart could have written the Pastoral symphony. The same quality is shown in what may be called his love music. The Opus 78 sonata expresses that exquisite, shy, and yet joyful tenderness that only the truly chaste have ever achieved. In this it is typical. In spite of music's unexampled power of expressing eroticism, most powerfully exemplified by Wagner's work, there is no trace of this quality in Beethoven. He knows nothing, even in his most abandoned moods (as in the finale of the Seventh symphony), of the ecstasy of sexual delirium. We know from Beethoven's own words that he was what is called a "moralist" in sexual matters, but we know from his music that this was owing to no asceticism, to no principles, but to the presence of very strong feelings which could allow nothing inferior in that kind to coexist with them. To the man of the world Beethoven's love for music may be that of a romantic; to the youth who is just awakening to the awe and rapture of this great experience Beethoven is one of the very few true poets of the heart. Beethoven's attitude toward sexual love never became sophisticated. This very intense and rich emotional nature was, in truth, very simple and very pure. There were no feigned or borrowed emotions, and nerve storms never took the place of feelings. He had no need to complicate his joy with bitterness or to distort his rapture with cynicism. These are the devices of a man who wishes to come to terms with his suffering without facing it in all its darkness. But Beethoven had the innocence of his courage.

We have, then, in the person of Beethoven a musical genius with all the conditions for writing great music. He has a realization of the ultimate character of life, he has a force adequate to any trial, however arduous, his growth will be free from the distorting effects of mere convention, and his response is pure and sincere to a wide range of experience. No other musician who ever lived has united so many advantages.

It would appear that Beethoven first noticed symptoms of his deafness in 1798. His first reference to it, however, occurs in a letter to Amenda, dated June 1, 1801. The letter is most interesting as showing us Beethoven's attitude, at this time, toward the impending calamity. His first reaction, as we should expect, is rage at the *senselessness* of the hideous affliction. That he, of all men, should lose this particular sense must, indeed, have seemed the most abominable of ironies.

"Your Beethoven is most unhappy," he writes, "and at strife with nature and Creator. I have often cursed the latter for exposing his creatures to the merest accident, so that often the most beautiful buds are broken or destroyed thereby. Only think that my noblest faculty, my hearing, has greatly deteriorated."

But still he has hopes, although he fears the worst, and his self-confidence remains indomitable.

"It is said to be due to my bowels, and so far as they are concerned, I am nearly restored to health. . . . I hope, indeed, that my hearing will also improve, but I am dubious, because such diseases are the most incurable. How sad is my lot! I must avoid all things that are dear to me. . . . Oh, how happy could I be if my hearing were completely restored; then would I hurry to you, but as it is I must refrain from everything and the most beautiful years of my life must pass without accomplishing the promise of my talent and powers. A sad resignation to which I must resort, although, indeed, I am resolved to rise superior to every obstacle. But how will that be possible? ..."

In a letter to his doctor friend Wegeler, written at the end of the same month, he goes more into detail.

"I am living a wretched life; for two years I have avoided almost all social gatherings because it is impossible for me to say to people: 'I am deaf.' If I belonged to any other profession it would be easier, but in my profession it is an awful state, the more since my enemies, who are not few, what would they say? In order to give you an idea of this singular deafness of mine I must tell you that in the theatre I must get very close to the orchestra in order to understand the actor. If I am a little distant I do not hear the high tones of the instruments, singers, and if I be put a little farther away I do not hear at all. Frequently I can hear the tones of a low conversation, but not the words, and as soon as anybody shouts it is intolerable. It seems singular that in conversation there are people who do not notice my condition at all, attributing it to my absent-mindedness. Heaven knows what will happen to me. *Vering says that there will be an improvement if no complete cure.* I have often—cursed my existence. *Plutarch* taught me resignation. If possible I will bid defiance to my fate, although there will be moments in my life when I shall be the unhappiest of God's creatures.... Resignation! What a wretched refuge—and yet the only one open to me."

In November he again writes to Wegeler. His hearing has become no better, but rather worse. The slight hope of improvement that he had seems to have abandoned him, so that now he clutches eagerly at any chance. He thinks of changing his physician, accusing Vering of negligence....

"Oh, if I were rid of this affliction I could embrace the world! I feel that my youth is just beginning and have I not always been ill? My physical strength has for a short time past been steadily growing more than ever and also my mental powers. Day by day I am approaching the goal which I apprehend but cannot describe. It is only in this that your Beethoven can live. Tell me nothing of rest. I know of none but sleep, and woe is me that I must give up more time to it than usual. Grant me but half freedom from my affliction and then—as a complete, ripe man I shall return to you and renew the old feelings of friendship. You must see me as happy as it is possible to be here below—not unhappy. No! I cannot endure it. I will take Fate by the throat; it shall not wholly overcome me. Oh, it is so beautiful to live—to live a thousand times! I feel that I am not made for a quiet life."

During the winter of 1801–2 Beethoven did change his physician, the new one being Dr. Schmidt, and on his advice spent the summer of 1802 at the near but quiet and secluded village of Heiligenstadt. Schmidt seems to have given Beethoven hopes that the quiet, by lessening the demands on his hearing, would effect an improvement. Up till now, as we see quite clearly from the letters, Beethoven's reaction to the impending calamity was defiance. He felt that he must assert his will in order not to be overcome. He would summon up all his strength in order to go on living and working in spite of his fate. "I will take Fate by the throat." He was, as it were, *defending* his creative power. But by the end of this summer he found that his genius, that he had felt called upon to cherish and protect, was really a mighty force using him as a channel or servant. It is probable that every genius of the first order becomes aware of this curious relation towards his own genius. Even the most fully conscious type of genius, the scientific genius, as Clerk Maxwell and Einstein, reveals this feeling of being *possessed*. A power seizes them of which they are not normally aware except by obscure premonitions. With Beethoven, so extraordinarily creative, a state of more or less unconscious tumult must have been constant. But only when the consciously defiant Beethoven had succumbed, only when his pride and strength had been so reduced that he was willing, even eager, to die and abandon the struggle, did he find that his creative power was indeed indestructible and that it was its deathless energy that made it impossible for him to die. This new and profound realization of his nature is the most significant thing in the famous Heiligenstadt Testament, written in the autumn of this year, but not discovered till after his death. It marks the complete collapse of the old morality of power, and shows the experiences that made possible the erection of a new morality of power on the ruins of the old. The document must be quoted in full.

"For my brothers Carl and — Beethoven

"O ye men who think or say that I am malevolent, stubborn or misanthropic, how greatly do ye wrong me, you do not know the secret causes of my seeming so, from childhood my heart and mind were disposed to the gentle feelings of good will, I was even ever eager to accomplish great deeds, but reflect now that for 6 years I have been in a hopeless case, aggravated by senseless physicians, cheated year after year in the hope of improvement, finally compelled to face the prospect of a *lasting malady* (whose cure will take years or, perhaps, be impossible), born with an ardent and lively temperament, even susceptible to the diversions of society, I was compelled early to isolate myself, to live in loneliness, when I at times tried to forget all this, O how harshly was I repulsed by the doubly sad experience of my bad hearing, and yet it was impossible for me to say to men speak louder, shout, for I am deaf. Ah how could I possibly admit an infirmity in the one sense which should have been more perfect in me than in others, a sense which I once possessed in highest perfection, a perfection such as few surely in my profession enjoy or ever have enjoyed—O I cannot do it, therefore forgive me when you see me draw back when I would gladly mingle with you, my misfortune is doubly painful because it must lead to my being misunderstood, for me there can be no recreation in society of my fellows, refined intercourse, mutual exchange of thought, only just as little as the greatest needs command may I mix with society. I must live like an exile, if I approach near to people a hot terror seizes upon me, a fear that I may be subjected to the danger of letting my condition be observed—thus it has been during the last year which I spent in the country, commanded by my intelligent physician to spare my hearing as much as possible, in this almost meeting my present natural disposition, although I sometimes ran counter to it yielding to my inclination for society, but what a humiliation when one stood beside me and heard a flute in the distance and *I heard nothing,* or someone heard *the shepherd singing* and again I heard nothing, such incidents brought me to the verge of despair, but little more and I would have put an end to my life—only art it was that withheld me, ah it seemed impossible to leave the world until I had produced all that I felt called upon to produce, and so I endured this wretched existence—truly wretched, an excitable body which a sudden change can throw from the best into the worst state. *Patience* it is said I must now choose for my guide, I have done so, I hope my determination will remain firm to endure until it pleases the inexorable parcae to break the thread, perhaps I shall get better, perhaps not, I am prepared. Forced already in my 28th year to become a philosopher, O it is not easy, less easy for the artist than for anyone else—Divine One thou lookest into my inmost soul, thou knowest it, thou knowest that love of man and desire to do good live therein. O men, when some day you read these words, reflect that ye did me wrong, and let the unfortunate one comfort himself if he can find one of his own kind who despite all the obstacles of nature yet did all that was in his power to be accepted among worthy artists and men. You my brothers Carl and — as soon as I am dead if Dr. Schmidt is still alive ask him in my name to describe my malady and attach this document to the history of my illness so that so far as possible at least the world may become reconciled with me after my death. At the same time I declare you two to be the heirs to my small fortune (if so it can be called), divide it fairly, bear with and help each other, what injury you have done me you know was long ago forgiven. To you brother Carl I give special thanks for the attachment you have displayed towards me of late. It is my wish that your lives may be better and freer from care than I have had, recommend virtue to your children, it alone can give happiness, not money, I speak from experience, it was virtue that upheld me in misery, to it next to my art I owe the fact that I did not end my life by suicide. —Farewell and love each other—I thank all my friends, particularly *Prince Lichnowsky* and *Professor Schmidt*—I desire that the instruments from Prince L. be preserved by one of you but let no quarrel result from this, so soon as they can serve you a better purpose sell them, how glad will I be if I can still be helpful to you in my grave— with joy I hasten towards death—if it comes before I shall have had an opportunity to show all my artistic capacities it will still come too early for me despite my hard fate and I shall probably wish that it had come later—but even then I am satisfied, will it not free me from a state of endless suffering? Come when thou will I shall meet thee bravely. —Farewell and do not wholly forget me when I am dead, I deserve this of you in having often in life thought of you and how to make you happy; be so.

"Ludwig Van Beethoven

Heiglnstadt, *October 6th, 1802.*

"For my brothers Carl and — to be read and executed after my death.

"Heiglnstadt, October 10th, 1802, thus do I take my farewell of thee —and indeed sadly—yes that beloved hope—which I brought with me when I came here to be cured at least in a degree—I must wholly abandon, as the leaves of autumn fall and are withered so hope has been blighted, almost as I came—I go away—even the high courage— which often inspired me in the beautiful days of summer—has disappeared—O Providence—grant me at last but one day of pure joy— it is so long since real joy echoed in my heart—O when—O when, O Divine One—shall I find it again in the temple of nature and of men— Never? no—O that would be too hard."

This document marks a crisis in Beethoven's life. Never again was his attitude towards life one of defiance, where the defiance was an expression of what is called his "strength of character." He had no such need of defiance, for he no longer had any fear. He had become aware within himself of an indomitable creative energy that nothing could destroy.

It is this realization, become exultant, that makes him break off, in sketching the theme of the great C major fugue of the third Rasoumowsky quartet, to write in the margin that nothing can now hinder his composing. "In the same way that you are now able to throw yourself into the whirlpool of society, so you are able to write your works in spite of all social hindrances. Let your deafness be no longer a secret—even for art." He is no longer afraid for his art.

The first piece of music he composed that has a really profound and important spiritual content is the Eroica symphony. Indeed, the difference from the earlier music is so startling that it points to an almost catastrophic change, or extremely rapid acceleration, in his spiritual development. We have found that such a change is witnessed to by the Heiligenstadt Testament, and we shall see that the Eroica symphony is an amazingly realized and co-ordinated expression of the spiritual experiences that underlay that document. The ostensible occasion of the symphony appears to have been the career of Napoleon Bonaparte, but no amount of brooding over Napoleon's career could have given Beethoven his realization of what we may call the life-history of heroic achievement as exemplified in the Eroica. This is obviously a transcription of personal experience. He may have thought Napoleon a hero, but his conception of the heroic he had earned for himself. It has been objected to the symphony that the funeral march is in the wrong place and that it should follow the scherzo. But this objection entirely misses the organic connection of the whole work. The most profound experience that Beethoven had yet passed through was when his courage and defiance of his fate had been followed by despair. He was expressing what he knew when he made the courage and heroism of the first movement succeeded by the black night of the second. And he was again speaking of what he knew when he made this to be succeeded by the indomitable uprising of creative energy in the scherzo. Beethoven was here speaking of what was perhaps the cardinal experience of his life, that when, with all his strength and courage, he had been reduced to despair, that when the conscious strong man had tasted very death, there came this turbulent, irrepressible, deathless creative energy surging up from depths he had not suspected. The whole work is a miraculously realized expression of a supremely important experience, and is justly regarded as a turning-point in Beethoven's music. The last movement is based on what we know to have been Beethoven's "Prometheus" theme. Having survived death and despair the artist turns to creation. By adopting the variation form Beethoven has been able to indicate the variety of achievement that is now open to his "Promethean" energy. The whole work is a most close-knit psychological unity. Never before in music has so important, manifold, and completely coherent an experience been communicated.

At the time that he wrote the Hammerclavier sonata, finished in 1818, Beethoven's realization of his essential loneliness was terrible and complete. But we may suppose that even then he was becoming aware that his separation from the world was the entry into a different and more exalted region. But the Hammerclavier sonata is the expression of a man of infinite suffering, of infinite courage and will, but without God and without hope. At the time that he depicted this experience it is possible that Beethoven had already passed beyond it. The sonata is the complete expression of an important stage in Beethoven's spiritual development, but it was only after passing through this stage that the wonderful new world lay open before him, and that all his greatest work was achieved. From the Hammerclavier sonata itself nothing more could come. Its spiritual content is at the end of a process, an end that contains within itself no new beginning. The completely naked Beethoven, relying upon nothing whatever but his inner resources, has said his last word in the Hammerclavier sonata. Unless some new life is added to him, without some new organization of his experience, the undying energy of the Hammerclavier fugue can be used only to say over again what it has already said. The Hammerclavier sonata does not, in its spiritual content, belong to what is called Beethoven's third period. Neither does it belong to his second. It stands alone, a great and grim memorial to the long and painful journey between the two worlds.

The courage and resolution we find in the first movement is curiously austere. The old experience is once again to be lived through, but the spirit in which it is approached is very different. Those cold harmonies, so characteristic of Beethoven's later work, no longer convey the warm human confidence of a man who knows that victory lies at the end. There is expressed a stark, bare resolution, courageous enough, but uncoloured by any joy in conflict. And the other elements that go to make up the wealth of a Beethoven first movement have all become colder. The man who wrote this music is already a great solitary. He has abated nothing of his courage, but it has become more grim. Suffering, it would appear, has hardened him; never again, one would think, can this man melt. And there is no good humour in the scherzo. A curiously laconic savagery, with hints of the formidable passion that is expressing itself so abruptly, entirely separates this movement from the frank energy of the earlier scherzos. The slow movement is the deliberate expression, by a man who knows no reserves, of the cold and immeasurable woe in whose depths, it would seem, nothing that we could call life could endure. It seems as inimical to human existence as the icy heart of some remote mountain lake. Whether it be faithfulness to psychological experience, or whether it be the instinct of an unmatched artist, the largo that follows the slow movement is a miracle of art. To end with the slow movement would be unendurable, and any sudden shattering of the hypnotic state it produces would be equally unendurable. The gradual awakening effected by the largo from our state of dumb suspension fulfils a craving of the spirit that surely only this one artist could ever have formulated. And we awake to what? To the blind and desperate energy left in this man when there was no longer any reason to live. We are presented here with a will to live which is inexpressibly furious and inexpressibly bare. It is the expression of the final refusal of annihilation, even if no hope and no object be left in life. This sheer blind energy, this insistence on mere existence, does not contain within itself dramatic contrasts. To be expressed at all it must be expressed in a form within which its swift-ness and violence can rage unchecked. No form permits so unidirec-tional and unhampered a flow as the fugue, and Beethoven chose the fugue. And having chosen it, he exhausts its resources to keep his mass moving with the requisite momentum. At one point the mass rises to a climax and there is an interruption. We are given a glimpse, a few bars, dolce and cantabile, of that serene, inhuman eternity that sur-rounds this blind, furious striving. But it is only a glimpse, a meaning-less stare, and we are once more involved in this headlong rush, this most primitive, fundamental, and unconquerable of the impulses that manifest themselves in creatures that have life.

Of the three great last quartets, the one in C sharp minor is the most unearthly and serene. The first of them, in A minor, is the least mystical and the one most full of human pain. It is, as a matter of historical fact, connected with a serious illness of Beethoven's and he himself wrote over the slow movement "Heiliger Dankgesang an die Gottheit eines Genesenen, in der lydischen Tonart." ... The whole quartet may be taken as illustrating the normal aspect that life presented to the late Beethoven. Witness after witness testifies to the expression of pro-found sorrow that was habitual with him in the last years of his life, so that in mere contemplation of that dumb countenance the more emotional of them felt moved to tears. As we have said, we believe that in his most profound moments of insight and abstraction Beetho-ven was granted the solace of a more complete understanding. But such moments must have been comparatively rare, and could have occurred only in the midst of the artist's most profound isolation. We can well believe that no man ever saw the face of the transfigured Beethoven. We believe that this man had suffered so greatly that the Beethoven men saw was the normal Beethoven of those days, poor, ill, stone-deaf, wretchedly housed, utterly alone, betrayed and abandoned by the one human being whose love he so desperately and pitifully craved. And from the depths of this man rose that solemn, pure and profound song of thanksgiving to the Godhead. The yearning and the pain of the first movement (which ends, as only Beethoven would end, with what

sounds like a startling and celestial trumpet call) is but little lightened
in the second movement where there reigns a spiritual weariness which
is quite unmistakable. But again there comes that intimation of something celestial in an *alternativo* (that some writers find "curious" and
others "humorous"!) where the first violin soars high over a pedal,
and then comes the first moment of joy, real joy without any *arrière-
pensée,* in the whole quartet. The first part is then repeated; the dominant mood is re-established. From this matrix rises the slow movement,
the most heartfelt prayer from the most manly soul that has expressed
itself in music. From this pure and sincere communion with his God
there comes a quickened life, a rush of celestial joy, in the passage
marked "Neue Kraft fühlend." The psychological resemblance between
this transition and that in the second movement is obvious. Relief from
pain, in this most pessimistic of Beethoven's quartets, comes only from
above. Two main experiences form the texture of this quartet, exhaustion and defeat, and the new life bestowed as an act of grace from on
high. With this "new strength" the next movement steps forth, but
there is a wistfulness in its bravery. This is one of those movements,
that occur only in the late Beethoven, where the very quality of the
heroism reveals the heartache it is intended to conceal. This forlorn
and lonely little march is marching to no victory. It is a gesture, brave
but pathetic. With the *Più allegro* section our forebodings are realized.
Here is a shudder of realization, a resigned and hopeless cry, and we
are again in the darkness of the struggle. Great waves of anguish seem
to sweep over the struggling soul and at moments it seems that no
resolution and faith can prevail against them. But a permanent strength,
we may suppose, has come from those earlier celestial visions, from that
pure and profound prayer, and the theme which before seemed to
strive with difficulty against despair accelerates, until, in the final presto,
it rings out victoriously, but victor in a victory so hard-won that we are
left with none of that feeling of exultant triumph with which we have
watched so many of Beethoven's victories, but rather with a feeling of
slightly incredulous relief, of thankfulness still tinged with doubt....

It so happens that Beethoven's last complete work, the quartet in
F major, op. 135, makes a fitting end to his great series of explorations.
It is the work of a man who is fundamentally at peace. It is the peace
of a man who has known conflict, but whose conflicts are now remi-
niscent. This quality is most apparent in the last movement, with its
motto "Muss es sein? Es muss sein!" According to Schindler this motto
had its origin in a joke, but, as used here, it is a summary of the great
Beethovenian problem of destiny and submission. But Beethoven had
found his solution of that problem, and he treats the old question here
with the lightness, even the humour, of one to whom the issue is

settled and familiar. There is no real conflict depicted in this last movement; the portentous question meets with a jovial, almost exultant answer, and the ending is one of perfect confidence. The question raised here is, indeed, seen in the light of the profound peace which dominates the slow movement of this quartet. If we may judge from this quartet and also from Beethoven's actual last composition, the present finale of the B flat quartet, it would appear that at the end of his life the inner Beethoven, the Beethoven who expressed himself in music, was content.

JOHN MASON BROWN

Wit, critic, and essayist, John Mason Brown, who has probably delighted more lecture audiences than any other living American, was born in Kentucky in 1900. One of this country's best-known writers on the theater, he is the author of numerous books, the latest of which, an appraisal of some of our leading contemporary political figures, found him reaching out for new domains in which to shine.

As editor of the Viking *Portable Charles Lamb,* he contributed an introduction which tells in human terms the moving story of Lamb's unselfish devotion to his periodically demented sister. It is that portion of his biographical and critical sketch which I have included here. There are certain instances of this type of devotion that are open to the suspicion of being a kind of self-sought martyrdom. We are all familiar with them, but Lamb's solicitous and tender care of Mary, undertaken at such cost to himself that it unquestionably hastened the death of a man who was capable of the greatest delight in life, is not one of them. The story of it is a record of true spiritual bravery.

The Sacrifice of Charles Lamb

AMONG the tantalizing "ifs" of literature is what Charles Lamb might have been like as man and writer if, in a fit of madness, his sister Mary had not slain their mother when he was only twenty-one. The "gentle Elia" the world loves was the product of ungentle and terrible events. He was the stepchild of a calamity as bloody as any to be found in the most bloodstained Elizabethan dramas of which Lamb was later to become a champion. To a tragic extent Lamb's life, hence Elia's character, was carved out for him by the case knife which poor deluded Mary drove straight and deep into their mother's heart.

Surely never in the strange annals of authorship has the world gained so much in pleasure or an innocent man lost more in freedom than in the instance of the catastrophe which resulted in Lamb's becoming the most beloved bachelor of letters literature has produced.

When he quit his desk at the East India House on the afternoon of September 22, 1796, and started to walk home through the London he loved, Lamb was not without his worries. His sister Mary, ten years his senior, had already shown symptoms of insanity. Not for the first time, either. As a person who had himself been confined the previous year for six weeks in a madhouse at Hoxton, these symptoms may have had a special meaning for him. In any case, Mary's condition was sufficiently disturbing to have sent Lamb, on his way to work that very morning, in search of a doctor who was not to be found. Aware though he was of the gathering clouds, Lamb could not have been prepared for the violence of the storm which had broken out in the house where he lived with his old father, his invalid mother, his sister, and his Aunt Hetty.

The sight he beheld when he opened the door was of tabloid gruesomeness. Above the bustle of Little Queen Street, he may have heard the cries of his father and the shrieks of Mary and her apprentice as he approached his home. If he had not, the landlord's presence was in itself a warning. Certainly his eyes must have disbelieved the nightmare of reality which confronted them. The room, in which the table was laid for dinner, was in a turmoil. Charles' aged aunt was unconscious on the floor, "to all appearance like one dying." His senile father was bleeding from a wound in his forehead. His mother was dead in a chair, stabbed to the heart by Mary, who was standing over her with the case knife still in her hand. Lamb arrived only in time to snatch the knife from her grasp.

What had provoked this scene no one knows. Perhaps, as a professional seamstress, Mary had been overworking, and the stress of a dependent household had become too great for her. Perhaps the final straw had been the additional cares which had come her way because of the leg injury recently suffered by her brother John, her elder by a year and a half. Perhaps, as moderns have hinted, an ugly, long-suppressed animosity between her and her mother had at last erupted. In any event, Mary had had an altercation with the young woman who, in her mantua-making, was her helper. Mary had reached for the knives and forks on the table, throwing them at this frightened girl in the hope of driving her from the house. It was one of the forks thus thrown which had struck her father. Her mother might have been spared had she not attempted to intercede in the apprentice's behalf.

"I date from the day of horrors," wrote Lamb to Coleridge soon after the disaster. Although by this he meant merely to place in time events described in his letter, he unwittingly summarized the rest of his adult life. To these sensational occurrences which cost him dearly, we owe, in part at least, the writer we cherish as one of the least sensational of authors. For the next thirty-eight years Lamb lived a gallant and, on the whole, a cheerful prisoner to the happenings of that fatal afternoon. In no sense of the word a tragic hero, he emerged as the hero of a tragedy. We pity him the more because he was without self-pity.

There are people, luckless mortals, who by the injustices of circumstance or because of a certain granite in their character are doomed to be caryatids for the suffering of others. Charles Lamb was one of these. He could have fallen back on the law and allowed his sister to be committed to a public insane asylum. He could have walked out on Mary. In other words, he could have done what his older brother John did and wanted him to do.

Yet even when John washed his hands of the whole problem, Lamb was able to rise, "not without tenderness," to his brother's defense. He knew John to be "little disposed ... at any time to take care of old age and infirmities." Charles went so far as to persuade himself that John, "with his bad leg, had an exemption from such duties." He was well aware that John would make speeches about the money needed to maintain Mary in a private institution. But Charles and John, though brothers, were made of very different stuff. Young and poor as he was, Charles faced without complaining the fact that "the whole weight of the family" had been thrown upon him. From the outset he was determined, regardless of the sacrifices, that Mary should not go into a public asylum.

Nor did she. Instead, he assumed full responsibility for her. More than that, he devoted his life to her. Because of this utter devotion his own life was altered inescapably. Had it not been for Mary, age would not have fallen so suddenly and engulfingly upon him. Without her, we might be able to imagine Lamb as a young man rather than always picturing him as a smoky and eccentric oldish fellow, settled in both his habits and his singleness, whose youth had come to an abrupt end with his childhood. Without Mary, Charles' dream-children might have been real. The "fair Alice W——n," she of the light yellow hair and the pale blue eyes for whom he claimed to have pined away seven of his "goldenest years," might have been the "passionate ... love-adventure" he once described her as being instead of a reference, true or fanciful, which biographers have been unable to track down. He might not have waited so many years to propose to Fanny Kelly, the actress with the "divine plain face," and Fanny might even have accepted him.

Without his "poor dear dearest" Mary, Charles might have continued longer to try his hand at poetry and not so soon, as he put it (with wonderful inaccuracy, in his case), have "dwindled into prose and criticism." His spirit would have been gayer; his laughs less like sighs. He might not have been so "shy of novelties, new books, new faces, new years." The present, not the past, might have been his delight. He would not have been driven, as driven he was by the events of that appalling afternoon, to find happiness by thinking back to happier days. Retrospection would not have become his refuge. The "boy-man" that he felt himself to be would not have clung with such tenacious affection to his own boyhood. The texture, the range, the very tone and temper of his work would have been different.

From the moment of his mother's murder and the time that he stepped forward to become Mary's legal guardian Lamb knew that he and Mary were "in a manner *marked*." This was bound to be a portion of their fate. There was no hushing their story. It not only pursued them; it ran ahead of them. Sometimes it even forced them to change their lodgings. No shelter could be found from the nudgings, the whisperings, the stares, and the embarrassments it provoked. Charles' determination to care for Mary involved more than living with her. It also meant his living with the knowledge that everyone around them knew her case and their history. If this increased his shyness, it also brought Mary and him closer together. It was only one more of the many bonds, tender and tragic, which united them.

Fortunately, theirs was a relationship based upon more than the perilous stuffs of gratitude or an embittering sense of obligation. Positive as each of them was as a personality, they were united not only by misfortune but by shared tastes and minds which, in spite of dissimilarities, were complementary. When dedicating a volume of his verse, Charles called Mary his best friend. From the dedication of his life she knew she had no better friend than he. Their devotion to each other was genuine and abiding. It shines through their letters. It is unmistakable in every reference to Mary as Bridget in Charles' essays. They were collaborators in life no less than in literature. No brother and sister in history are more inseparably linked. To Lamb their life as old bachelor and maid was "a sort of double singleness."

The glimpses we have of them together are at once heartwarming and heartbreaking. "You would like to see us," wrote Mary to Sarah Stoddart, "as we often sit, writing on one table (but not on one cushion sitting), like Hermia and Helena in the *Midsummer's Night's Dream;* or, rather, like an old literary Darby and Joan: I taking snuff, and he groaning all the while and saying he can make nothing of it, which he always says till he has finished, and then he finds out he has made something of it."

That is a picture of them at their happiest. It belongs with those
other pictures we conjure when we imagine them together: playing
cards; seeing a play; going to exhibitions; reading books, she doting
on narratives—any narratives; he delighting in the reflective passages
of the older authors. Visiting friends. Enjoying the adventure of one
of their short summer journeys. Presiding over one of their delectable
"evenings" at home (held first on Wednesdays, later on Thursdays),
which Hazlitt immortalized with his "How often did we cut into the
haunch of letters, while we discussed the haunch of mutton on the
table!" Or discussing, in the financial comfort of their later years, the
greater pleasures they had known when, in their youth, they had been
forced to skimp, save, and plan in order to make a purchase or crowd
their way into the pit.

Against these brighter moments must be set the darker ones. These
are black indeed. By common agreement Mary, in her right mind, was
one of the most amiable and admirable of women. But Mary was not
always in her right mind. She was "perpetually on the brink of madness." If this was Mary's tragedy, it was also Lamb's. Their sunniest
days together were never cloudless. The threat under which they lived
was fearful and incessant. At all times the Furies stalked them. Small
wonder this brother and this sister have been likened to a cockney
Orestes and Electra.

Mary's was a recurrent illness. There was no telling when it would
return. There was only the certainty that return it would, with ever-
increasing frequency, with ever-mounting seriousness. Some hints, such
as a sudden moroseness or irritability on Mary's part, preceded its
coming. For these dreaded signs Charles watched anxiously. Apparently Mary did, too.

"You would laugh, or you would cry, perhaps both," Mary wrote
in another letter to Miss Stoddart, "to see us sit together, looking at
each other with long and rueful faces, and saying, 'How do you do?'
and 'How do *you* do?' and then we fall a-crying and say we will be
better on the morrow. Charles says we are like tooth-ache and his
friend gum-boil, which though a kind of ease is an uneasy kind of ease."

Their ease at its best was the epitome of uneasiness. Surely few scenes
could be more touching than the one several of their friends had witnessed. It was the common sequel to each reappearance of Mary's
symptoms. When these had shown themselves, Charles would get ready
to take her to the private asylum at Hoxton. She would gather together
a few clothes, replace with a bonnet the mobcap she wore indoors, and
prepare for the street. He would lead her, unresisting, to the door. Then
they would start out hand-in-hand, two figures as somberly dressed as

Quakers, walking the whole way, weeping as they walked, and carrying Mary's straitjacket with them.

Even so, Mary, between interruptions, brought Charles a happiness almost as complete as was the unhappiness her madness had brought upon them both. The debt we owe her is at once incalculable and unpayable. If, as readers, we delight in Lamb as he is, we do so because his writing is the product of his life as it was. He never objected to his lot. He faced it squarely, gaily, without whining, and with inexhaustible courage.

The world that knows him as the "gentle Elia" does Lamb an injustice. Gentle he always was with Mary and in most of his writings. It was, however, his strength which enabled him to be gentle and not any softness which forced him into being so. He hated the phrase "gentle-hearted" when applied to him as much as Sir James Barrie abhorred the word "whimsical." "For God's sake (I never was more serious)," wrote Charles to Coleridge, "don't make me ridiculous any more by terming me gentle-hearted in print, or do it in better verse. ... The meaning of gentle is equivocal at best, and almost always means poor-spirited."

Certainly Lamb was anything but poor-spirited. He had a resilience unknown to noisier men and a toughness unsuspected by those who have read him sparingly, and then only in his fanciful or sentimental moods. Did he look like a clerk? He did not act like one. He was no timid soul. He was fiercely independent. His father may have been a servant, but in a snobbish age Lamb was subservient to no one. He was at all times ready to stammer out his opinions without fear. Everyone who described him noted the sadness of his brown eyes, the thoughtfulness of his expansive brow, the sweetness of his expression, and the smallness of his body. Lamb knew that physically he was "less than the least of the Apostles." A friend thought he looked so fragile that "a breath would overthrow him." But there was iron in his "immaterial legs." His slight body contradicted the largeness of his spirit.

EDGAR JOHNSON

Edgar Johnson, who has written what seems likely to stand as the modern counterpart to John Forster's life of Dickens, is a professor of English who was born in New York City in 1901. His biography of the novelist, besides being documented with the greatest care, is excellent as narrative, perceptive as literary criticism, and probingly sympathetic in its reading of Dickens' complex character.

For inclusion here I have chosen two sections from the second volume, in which Mr. Johnson, with a wealth of illuminating detail, tells the story of Dickens' self-punishing and almost hysterical spending of his energies during his later years on the reading platform. As almost everyone knows, Dickens delighted in theatricals, amateur and otherwise. He was at heart as much an actor as he was a novelist. He poured all his immense vitality into the public readings from his works, which represented, in the period covered by the passages that follow, a compulsion by which he was truly obsessed. He did not merely read from his books; he acted, with enormous gusto, the part provided by each of his characters. As Mr. Johnson suggests, there is ground for belief, because the long-endured frustration of his marriage contributed so much to his deep unhappiness, that this prodigal expenditure of energy, leaving him completely exhausted time after time, was perhaps unconsciously suicidal. There is no doubt that it materially hastened his death, but nothing and nobody could dissuade him from his course.

It is difficult for us now to realize the overwhelming emotional impact which Dickens' readings had upon his audiences both at home and in the United States. They were literally transported; by turns amused, saddened, and terrified to the point of hysteria, while the man who had played upon their emotions as a virtuoso plays upon an instrument, would make his exit and collapse.

Actually, then, it may be argued that this ordeal which Dickens endured was self-imposed, and consequently not authentically a trial of the spirit. Yet Dickens carried himself through it with such amazing fortitude, and sometimes with such generous thought for others, that his story would seem to warrant inclusion.

The Last Years of Charles Dickens

BEFORE heading south for Philadelphia, Baltimore, and Washington, Dickens had another week of readings in New York. This time he also read in Brooklyn, where the only available place turned out to be the Plymouth Church, of which the pastor was Harriet Beecher Stowe's brother, the Reverend Henry Ward Beecher. The usual riotous scenes attended the sale of tickets, with "the noble army of speculators" building bonfires and fighting in the streets and greeting Dolby with roars of "Hallo! Dolby! So Charley has let you have the carriage, has he, Dolby? How is he, Dolby? Don't drop the tickets, Dolby! Look alive, Dolby!" The receipts were so enormous that the manager was "always going about with an immense bundle that looks like a sofa-cushion, but is in reality paper-money, and it had risen to the proportions of a sofa on the morning he left for Philadelphia."

Dickens's cold, however, still would not "stir an inch. It distresses me greatly at times, though it is always good enough to leave me for the needful two hours. I have tried allopathy, homeopathy, cold things, warm things, sweet things, bitter things, stimulants, narcotics, all with the same result. Nothing will touch it." He was hardly able to eat. "I rarely take any breakfast but an egg and a cup of tea, not even toast or bread-and-butter. My dinner at three, and a little quail or some such light thing when I come home at night, is my daily fare. At the Hall I have established the custom of taking an egg beaten up in sherry before going in, and another between the parts. I think that pulls me up; at all events, I have since had no return of faintness."

He had determined by now that he would confine the readings to the East, in spite of anguished outcries from St. Louis, Cincinnati, and Chicago. "Good heavens, sir!" exclaimed George W. Childs, the publisher of the Philadelphia *Public Ledger*, "if you don't read in Chicago the people will go into fits!" "Well," Dickens replied, "I would rather they went into fits than I did." Chicago in fact led a violent assault upon Dickens, with bitter imputations against his reasons for avoiding that city. His brother Augustus, who had deserted his wife in 1858, had died there in 1866, leaving a "widow" and three children. Dickens refused to explain that he had long supported the only legitimate Mrs. Augustus Dickens or that since his brother's death he had been sending £50 a year to Chicago. The newspapers painted lugubrious pictures of his "brother's wife and her helpless children." "Of course my lips are sealed. Osgood and Dolby have

really been lashed into madness, and but for my strict charge would
have blown the whole thing to pieces regardless of every other consideration. I have imposed silence on them, and they really writhe
under it." ...

Baltimore, Dickens felt, was haunted by "the ghost of slavery" and
still wore "a look of sullen remembrance." It was here that "the ladies
used to spit when they passed a Northern soldier.... The ladies are
remarkably handsome, with an Eastern look upon them, dress with
a strong sense of colour, and made a brilliant audience." For the first
reading in Washington, President Andrew Johnson, the chief members
of the Cabinet, the Supreme Court, ambassadors, naval and military
officers in full uniform, leading government officials and political
figures came almost in a body. The President had a whole row for
every reading of the week. During one of the *Carol* evenings there was
a dog who kept turning up in different parts of the house looking at
Dickens intently. "He was a very comic dog, and it was well for me
that I was reading a very comic part of the book. But when he bounced
out in the center aisle again ... and tried the effect of a bark ... I was
seized with such a paroxysm of laughter, that it communicated itself
to the audience, and we roared at one another loud and long."

On February 5th the President invited Dickens to call at the White
House. He found the Executive quiet and composed in spite of the
political storms that were gathering about him (he was impeached
on February 24th). "A man not to be turned or trifled with," Dickens
thought. "A man ... who must be killed to be got out of the way."
Dickens also dined with his old friend Charles Sumner, and met Secretary of War Stanton, whose dismissal by the President was to set the
nation on fire.

Stanton told him a strange anecdote about Abraham Lincoln. Attending a Cabinet meeting one day, Stanton found the President sitting with grave dignity instead of "lolling about" in "ungainly attitudes" and telling "questionable stories," as he usually did. He had
had, Lincoln told them, a dream. "And I have now had the same
dream three times. Once, on the night preceding the Battle of Bull
Run. Once, on the night preceding" another battle unfavorable to the
North. His chin sank upon his breast. "Might one ask the nature of
this dream, sir?" said the Attorney-General. "Well, I am on a great
broad rolling river—and I am in a boat—and I drift—and I drift!—but
this is not business—" he suddenly raised his head and looked around
the table, "—let us proceed to business, gentlemen." That night he
was shot.

On Dickens's birthday in Washington flowers from countless people
came pouring into his room in garlands, bouquets, and green baskets,

together with other gifts and "letters radiant with good wishes." But his cold was so bad that when Sumner came in at five and found him voiceless and covered with mustard poultice, he said, "Surely, Mr. Dolby, it is impossible that he can read tonight." "Sir, I have told the dear Chief so four times today, and I have been very anxious." But by some mysterious act of will Dickens always managed to overcome his affliction so that "after five minutes of the little table" he was not even hoarse. "The frequent experience of this return of force when it is wanted saves me a vast amount of anxiety," he wrote; "but I am not at times without the nervous dread that I may some day sink altogether."

Immediately after his birthday, Dickens turned north again on the second half of his tour. He gave farewell readings in Baltimore and Philadelphia, and then made a week's swing through the New England towns of New Haven, Hartford, Worcester, and Providence. Going on ahead, Dolby discovered that his own advance ticket-agent, a man named Kelly, was responsible for a good deal of the dissatisfaction about sales. Kelly had been speculating in tickets and taking bribes from speculators. In New Haven there was an indignation meeting presided over by the Mayor. Dolby brought consternation to the meeting by promptly canceling the reading and refunding the price of the tickets; but after a scene in which, as Dickens said, he and the Mayor alternately embraced and exchanged mortal defiances, agreed that he would try to work in another evening there later.

Kelly was peremptorily dismissed, and was about to be sent back to England. After a few days, however, Dickens relented and allowed him to remain, although in disgrace and "within very reduced limits." Employees about Steinway Hall swore to give him a beating when he returned to New York. "It is curious," Dickens wrote, "that I conceived a great dislike towards this man, aboard the *Cuba* coming out. He was ill all the voyage, and I only saw him two or three times, staggering about the lower deck; but I underwent a change of feeling towards him, as if I had taken it in at the pores of the skin."

On February 24th Dickens was back in Boston for another fortnight's reading there. The impeachment of the President, however, cut so drastically the audiences for all entertainments that for the first time there were empty seats. Dickens decided to cancel the second week, which had not yet been announced, and see if his cold would yield to rest. Dolby and Osgood, who were always doing ridiculous things to keep Dickens in spirits, had decided at the beginning of the month to hold a walking match on the 29th. "Beginning this design in joke, they have become tremendously in earnest, and Dolby has

actually sent home (much to his opponent's terror) for a pair of seam-
less socks to walk in."

In Baltimore, Dickens had given them "a breather" of five miles in
the snow, half the distance uphill, at a pace of four and a half miles
an hour, from which the two returned "smoking like factories." In
Washington, coming back from some farewell calls and seeing Dickens
looking out of the window, they "put on a tremendous spurt," as if
they had been training, and, "rushing up the staircase, and bursting
into the sitting-room,...sat on the floor, gasping for breath." "They
have the absurdest ideas," Dickens wrote, "of what are tests of walking
power, and continually get up in the maddest manner and see *how high
they can kick* the wall!... To see them doing this—Dolby, a big man,
and Osgood, a very little one, is ridiculous beyond description."

Dickens drew up burlesque articles of agreement for this "Great
International Walking Match," in which Dolby was given the sport-
ing nickname of the "Man of Ross" and Osgood was the "Boston
Bantam." The umpires were Fields, "Massachusetts Jemmy," and
Dickens, "whose surprising performances (without the least variation)
on that truly national instrument, the American catarrh, have won
for him the well-merited title of the Gad's Hill Gasper." Going at a
tremendous pace, Dickens and Fields laid out the course: six and a half
miles along the Mill Dam Road to Newton Centre and then back. It
was covered with snow and sheets and blocks of ice.

Despite his cold, Dickens turned up for the race. There was a biting
wind and furious snow. "It was so cold, too, that our hair, beards, eyelashes, eyebrows, were frozen hard, and hung with icicles." Just
before the turning point Dickens put on a great spurt to establish
himself there ahead of the contestants. "He afterwards declared that
he received a mental knock-downer...to find bright Chanticleer
close in upon him, and Rossius steaming up like a locomotive." After
the turning the Bantam forged ahead and "pegged away with his little
drum-sticks as if he saw his wives and a peck of barley waiting for him
at the family perch." "We are not quite decided whether Mrs. Fields
did not desert our colours, by coming on the ground in a carriage,
and having *bread soaked in brandy* put into the winning man's mouth
as he steamed along. She pleaded that she would have done as much
for Dolby, if *he* had been ahead, so we are inclined to forgive her."

Afterward, in honor of the contestants, Dickens gave an elaborate
dinner for eighteen in the Crystal Room at the Parker House. Among
the guests were Fields, James Russell Lowell, Holmes, Charles Eliot
Norton, Ticknor, Aldrich, and their wives, "and an obscure poet named
Longfellow (if discoverable), and Miss Longfellow." Around ten
o'clock, when the other guests had gone, Dickens went upstairs to his

room with Dolby and Osgood, in joking high spirits. Water had been drawn for his bath and he entertained his companions by giving an imitation of Grimaldi on the rolling edge of the tub. In the midst of the complicated feat, he lost his balance and, with a tidal wave of a splash, fell in, evening dress, boutonnière, gold chains, brilliantined earlocks, and all.

At a bachelor dinner a few nights later Dickens was in his wildest form. John Bigelow, the ex-Minister Plenipotentiary to France, was one of the guests, and they enacted a burlesque of an English election scene, with Bigelow as Fields's candidate and Dolby as Dickens's. Dickens made a campaign speech pretending that Dolby's superiority to his rival lay in his lack of hair. "We roared and writhed," said Fields, "in agonies of laughter, and the candidates themselves were literally choking and crying..." When Fields tried to speak for his man, Dickens interrupted all his attempts to be heard "with imitative jeers of a boisterous election mob," in a variety of voices, including "a pretended husky old man bawling out at intervals, 'Three cheers for the bald 'un!' 'Down with the hairy aristocracy!' 'Up with the little shiny chap on top!'"

With the exposure and exertion of the walking match, the true American had taken "a fresh start, as if it were quite a novelty," and was "on the whole rather worse than ever." Dickens terrified Dolby "out of his wits, by setting in for a paroxysm of sneezing." Under these circumstances, Dickens began a ten days' circuit of one-night stands in western and upstate New York, Syracuse, Rochester, Buffalo, ending with two nights in Albany. At Syracuse he began to have trouble walking, although this time it was something that he called an eruption on his right leg. The hotel there fascinated him with a printed menu which listed "chicken de pullet," "Turpin Soup," "Rolard mutton," and "Paettie de Shay." The last of these, the Irish waiter said with a broad grin, was "the Frinch name the steward giv' to oyster pattie." "You wash down these choice dishes with copious draughts of 'Mooseux,' 'Abasinth,' 'Curraco,' 'Maraschine,' 'Annise,' 'Margeaux'... We had an old Buffalo for supper, and an old Pig for breakfast, and we are going to have I don't know what for dinner at 6."

In spite of these jokes, Dickens was constantly tired and depressed and homesick. He was saddened to hear of the death of his old friend Chauncey Townshend. Between Rochester and Albany floods stranded them overnight at Utica after their train had crept on for miles and miles through water. Next day they continued slowly through "drowned farms, barns adrift like Noah's arks, deserted villages," with a hundred booted men pushing blocks of ice out of the way with long poles. On the way they released "a great train of cattle and sheep that had been in the water I don't know how long, and that had begun in their imprisonment to eat each other. I never could have realized the strong and dismal expressions of which the faces of sheep are capable, had I not seen the haggard countenances of this unfortunate flock ..." Dickens arrived at his hotel in Albany "pretty well knocked up" at half-past ten that night.

On March 20th he entered the last stage of his journeyings. There were still to be ten days of moving through Springfield, Worcester, New Haven, Hartford, and New Bedford, up to Portland, Maine. Then there would remain only the farewell series of readings in Boston and New York. But he reached Portland sick and exhausted. "With the return of snow, nine days ago, the 'true American' (which had lulled) came back as bad as ever. I have coughed from two or three in the morning until five or six, and have been absolutely sleepless. I have had no appetite besides, and no taste. Last night I took some laudanum, and it is the only thing that has done me good." To Forster he admitted, "I am nearly used up. Climate, distance, catarrh, travelling, and hard work have begun (I may say so, now they are nearly over) to tell heavily upon me." If he had engaged to go on into May, he thought he must have broken down.

But the killing odyssey was nearly over. On the train back to Boston, Dickens felt more cheerful and talked briskly with Osgood. From the rear of the car, near the water cooler and the trainboy with his popcorn balls and molasses candy, he was watched by an adoring little girl later known as Kate Douglas Wiggin. When Osgood got up to go to the smoking car, she speeded up the aisle and planted herself timorously "in the seat of honor."

"God bless my soul," Dickens exclaimed, "where did you come from?" "I came from Hollis, Maine," she stammered, "and I'm going to Charlestown to visit my uncle. My mother and her cousin went to your reading last night, but, of course, three couldn't go from the same family, so I stayed at home.... There was a lady there who had never heard of Betsey Trotwood, and had only read two of your books." "Well, upon my word! you do not mean to say that *you* have read them!" "Of course I have," she replied; "every one of them but the two that we are going to buy in Boston, and some of them six times."

Under pressing she admitted that she skipped "some of the very dull parts once in a while," and Dickens laughed heartily. Taking out a notebook and pencil, he examined her elaborately on the books in which the dull parts predominated. "He chuckled so constantly during this operation that I could hardly help believing myself extraordinarily agreeable, so I continued dealing these infant blows, under the delusion that I was flinging him bouquets. It was not long before one of my hands was in his, and his arm around my waist..."

"Did you want to go to my reading very much?" asked Dickens. This was a question that stirred the depths of her disappointment and sorrow. Her lips trembled as she faltered, *"Yes; more than tongue can tell."* Only when she was sure the tears in her eyes were not going to fall did she look up, and then she saw that there were tears in his eyes too. "Do you cry when you read out loud?" she asked. "We all do in our family. And we never read about Tiny Tim, or about Steerforth when his body is washed up on the beach, on Saturday nights, or our eyes are too swollen to go to Sunday School." "Yes, I cry when I read about Steerforth," Dickens answered quietly.

They were now fast approaching Boston, and passengers were collecting their wraps and bundles. Several times Osgood had come back, but had been waved away by Dickens. "You are not travelling alone?" he now asked. "Oh, no, I had a mother, but I forgot all about her." "You are a passed-mistress of the art of flattery!" Dickens said.

The return was not too soon. Dickens was not sure his lungs had not been done a lasting injury. On Forster's birthday—and his own marriage day—he coughed constantly and was sunk in gloom. He petulantly refused to see two of Osgood's friends from New Bedford: "No, I'll be damned if I will!" "I think, too," adds Mrs. Fields, "only $1,300 in the house was bad for his spirits!" But although Longfellow and all his Cambridge friends urged him to give in, he astonished them and even himself by his rendering of the last Boston readings.

He could hardly eat now, and had established a fixed system: "At seven in the morning, in bed, a tumbler of cream and two table-spoonsful of rum. At twelve, a sherry cobbler and a biscuit. At three (dinner time), a pint of champagne. At five minutes to eight, an egg beaten up with a glass of sherry. Between the parts, the strongest beef tea that can be made, drunk hot. At a quarter past ten, soup, and anything to drink that I can fancy. I don't eat more than a half a pound of solid food in the whole twenty-four hours, if so much."

The final New York readings were all that remained. Only the daily attention of Dr. Fordyce Barker and the devoted care of Dolby brought Dickens through the ordeal. "Dolby is as tender as a woman," he wrote, "and as watchful as a doctor. He never leaves me during the readings now, but sits at the side of the platform and keeps his eye upon me all the time." But Dickens's condition was frightful. In the excitement and exertion of the readings, the blood rushed into his hands until they became almost black, and his face turned red and white and red again without his knowing it. After one of the last three, Mrs.

Fields, who had come on to New York with her husband to be with their friend to the end, found him prostrated, "his head thrown back without support on the couch, the blood suffusing his throat and temples again where he had been very white a few minutes before."

There was still a great press banquet at Delmonico's on April 18th which Dickens had promised to attend. Two hundred and four tickets were sold at fifteen dollars a plate. The eight large tables were a mass of confections and flowers. But at five o'clock Dickens felt so unwell that it was not certain he would leave the Westminster Hotel. Messengers ran back and forth between there and Delmonico's with inquiries and bulletins about his condition. Dickens was determined to make the effort, and by the application of lotions and a careful bandaging of his foot and leg Dr. Barker enabled him to get out. He was an hour late when he limped into the restaurant leaning heavily on the arm of Horace Greeley.

The staggering affair progressed through course after course in which the diners had choices of at least three dozen elaborate dishes, including such items as "Crème d'asperges à la Dumas," "Timbales à la Dickens," "Filets de boeuf à la Lucullus," "Coutelettes à la Fenimore Cooper," "aspic de foie gras historiés," and "Soupirs à la Mantalini." The confectionery triumphs of the pastry cooks included a "temple de la Littérature; trophées à l'auteur; Stars and Stripes; pavilion internationale; armes Britanniques; la loi du Destin; monument de Washington; and colonne triomphale." "Sairey Gamp and Betsy Prig, and Poor Joe and Captain Cuttle blossomed out of charlotte russe, and Tiny Tim was discovered in pâté de foie gras."

Unaware of how severe was the pain from which Dickens was suffering, Greeley was "One vast, substantial smile." In response to his welcoming speech, with its concluding health, Dickens rose. He was henceforth charged with a duty, he said, "on every suitable occasion ...to express my high and grateful sense of my second reception in America, and to bear my honest testimony to the national generosity and magnanimity. Also, to declare how astounded I have been by the amazing changes I have seen around me on every side—changes moral, changes physical, changes in the amount of land subdued and peopled, changes in the rise of vast new cities, changes in the growth of older cities almost out of recognition, changes in the graces and amenities of life, changes in the press, without whose advancement no advancement can be made anywhere. Nor am I, believe me, so arrogant as to suppose that in twenty-five years there have been no changes in me, and that I had nothing to learn and no extreme impressions to correct when I was here first."

Though he had no intention of writing any other book on America, he wished "to record that wherever I have been, in the smallest places equally with the largest, I have been received with unsurpassable politeness, delicacy, sweet temper, hospitality, consideration, and with unsurpassable respect for the privacy daily enforced upon me by the nature of my advocation here, and the state of my health. This testimony, so long as I live, and so long as my descendants have any legal right in my books, I shall cause to be republished as an appendix to those two books of mine in which I have referred to America. And this I will do and cause to be done, not in mere love and thankfulness, but because I regard it as an act of plain justice and honour."

His feelings he believed representative of those of the majority of the English people. Essentially the two peoples were one, with a common heritage of great achievement. "And if I know anything of my countrymen... the English heart is stirred by the fluttering of those Stars and Stripes, as it is stirred by no other flag that flies except its own." In conclusion, "I do believe that from the great majority of honest minds on both sides, there cannot be absent the conviction that it would be better for this globe to be riven by an earthquake, fired by a comet, overrun by an iceberg, and abandoned to the Arctic fox and bear, than that it should present the spectacle of these two great nations, each of which has, in its own way and hour, striven so hard and so successfully for freedom, ever again being arrayed the one against the other."

So severe was Dickens's agony by the end of this speech that he was forced to beg to be excused. Hobbling painfully on Greeley's arm, he could not conceal his sufferings. The mechanism of the body, indeed, was disastrously weakened, but the steel-coiled will that dominated it would not surrender. Two nights later, on April 20th, he forced himself to the final reading and bade his American listeners farewell forever. "My future life lies over the sea." But though in some miraculous way the vessel had not been dashed to pieces against the Loadstone Rock and sunk, all its fabric was twisted and broken with the dreadful strain. Could it attempt another such voyage and not go down? Yet it was precisely such a course that Dickens even now was charting.

The summer and mild autumn days following Dickens's breakdown passed swiftly and quietly. It was the Indian summer of his life. During the mornings he worked in the chalet on the book his hand would leave unfinished. In the sunny afternoons he strolled among the trees and rhododendrons of Cobham Park, or ruminated in straw hat and velvet jacket along Rochester High Street, through the old gatehouse into the green Cathedral close, and thence past the quaint old houses of Minor Canon Row.

His health was still uncertain, but he was in cheerful spirits. Teas-
ing his friend Fields's mania for antiques, he pretended to have found
for him a decrepit chair without a bottom, "very ugly and wormy," of
which it was claimed that "on one occasion Washington declined to
sit down in it." He had made further improvements at Gad's Hill,
each one "positively the last," and now watched with pleasure the
growth of his limes and chestnuts. Indoors, there was a new staircase
with a parquet floor on the first landing. October saw the beginning
of a conservatory, "glass and iron," opening from both the drawing
room and the dining room, "brilliant but expensive, with foundations as
of an ancient Roman work of horrible solidity." "You are not expected
to admire," he wrote Macready, "but there *is* a conservatory building
at this moment—be still my soul!" . . .

Christmas Dickens spent at Gad's Hill. His left foot was again
painful, and he sat in the library all day having it poulticed; at dinner
it rested bandaged on a chair. But he was feeling pleased: [his son]
Harry had done so well at Cambridge that the family confidently expected him to win a fellowship. Shortly after the new year, Dickens
entered him at the Temple, where he was to take the first steps toward
the successful career he later pursued at the bar. Dickens was also looking forward excitedly to the last twelve readings, which would, in some
degree at least, make up for the twenty-six canceled by his breakdown
the previous spring. Partly to cut out the railway traveling he would
otherwise have to do between Gad's Hill and London, and partly for
[his daughter] Mary's sake, he rented the Milner Gibson house at 5
Hyde Park Place, just opposite the Marble Arch, from January to the
1st of June. New Year's Eve he spent at Forster's, where his old friend,
none too well himself, was troubled by observing that Dickens's left foot
and left hand both gave him pain. Dickens, however, made light of his
uncertainties of touch and tread, and read the second installment of
Edwin Drood with such overflowing humor that Forster forgot his
worry in enjoyment and enthusiastically pronounced the number "a
clincher."

On January 6th, as President of the Birmingham and Midland
Institute, Dickens awarded the prizes and certificates won by its most
successful students. He seized the occasion to reaffirm his declaration
of the preceding fall that he had "very little faith in the people who
govern us," but that he had "great confidence in the People whom
they govern." Severely shaken by the railway journey and the fatigue
of these ceremonies, he returned to London for his last appearances as
a reader.

He began at St. James's Hall on the evening of January 11th.
Throughout most of the remainder of that month he was to read twice

a week, on Tuesdays and Fridays, and thereafter once a week until March 15th. Two of his performances were scheduled for afternoons, and there was a morning one given at the request of actors and actresses, who could not come later in the day. Dickens's family and friends feared he might break down again under the strain, but in the face of his determination they could do nothing except see that instant help was available in case of need. Dr. Frank Beard came to every reading, and he privately bespoke Charley's attendance as well. "I have had some steps put up at the side of the platform," he told him. "You must be there every night, and if you see your father falter in the least, you must run and catch him and bring him off to me, or, by Heaven, he'll die before them all."

David Copperfield and the "Trial," on the opening night went "with the greatest brilliancy." But afterward Beard found that Dickens's pulse had gone from its normal 72 to 95. From that night on, it rose ominously. Even before the first "Murder" reading, on the morning of the 21st, his fermenting anticipation raised it to 90; at the end it was 112, and even fifteen minutes later had descended only to 100. Dickens was so prostrated that he could not get back his breath for some time and was meanwhile, as he said himself, the "express image" of a man who had lost a fight. But the pretty actresses in his audience delighted him with their rapture; he was thrilled that even those professional observers who were bent on watching how he achieved his effects were carried out of themselves. Two days later, when he saw Carlyle for the last time, his arm was once more in a sling.

Nevertheless, he went on, his pulse rising to 114—to 118—to 124. During intermissions he had to be helped into his retiring room and laid on a sofa; fully ten minutes would pass before he could speak a rational or consecutive sentence. Then he would swallow a wineglassful of weak brandy and water and rush back on the platform. Throughout February his hand never ceased to be swollen and painful. As he wiped the readings out one by one his feverish excitement and bodily pain grew ever greater.

His audiences, however, were almost hysterical with enthusiasm. A boy whose father was a friend of Dickens brought him to one of the *Pickwick* readings, where they sat in the front row, and the youngster laughed, roared, wept, and howled; "I must have been a terrible nuisance to Dickens," he said in later years, "for I was at his feet, and at least twice I remember very distinctly he looked at me, I am sure with the idea of having me removed." On their left, however, they were wedged in by a fat man who roared even louder, and he *couldn't* be removed. At the end, stepping down to speak to the father, Dickens looked quizzically at the boy, "but he gave me a friendly tap or pat of forgiveness on the head."

As the suicidal ordeals drew to their close, Dickens's energies were visibly exhausted. During one of the last three readings Charley noticed that he was unable to articulate "Pickwick" correctly, "calling it 'Pickswick,' 'Picnic,' 'Peckwicks,' " and "all sorts of names except the right one, with a comical glance of surprise" at friends in the front row. On the last evening of all he read the *Christmas Carol* and the "Trial." An audience of over two thousand, cramming the hall to capacity, gave him a tumultuous ovation that made the glittering chandeliers vibrate. Dickens's granddaughter, little Mekitty, had been brought for the first time that night to hear him read, and she was frightened by the apparition of her "Wenerables" as a terrible and unfamiliar figure a long way off "speaking in unknown voices." And, worst of all, came "the dreadful moment when he *cried*."

He had been called back to the platform at the end by thunders of applause, and looked tremulously at his audience, striving to speak, while tears rolled down his cheeks. It was the end. These clamors that had meant so much to him were sounding in his ears for the last time; this ferment of excitement which for twelve years had filled so much of his life, which had often been almost all his life, would soon be irrevocably over. With effort he restrained himself sufficiently to say the words of appreciation and love on which he had determined. His voice was controlled, but weighted with emotion. "From these garish lights," he concluded, "I now vanish forevermore, with a heartfelt, grateful, respectful, affectionate farewell." Mournfully he limped from the stage, only to be recalled again by repeated demonstrations. His cheeks still wet, he kissed his hand, and then walked off for the last time.

All told, the paid readings had numbered 423, including 111 given under the management of Arthur Smith, 70 under Thomas Headland, and 242 under Dolby. Dickens had no exact record of his net profits under Smith and Headland, but he always estimated them at about £12,000. Under Dolby he cleared nearly £33,000. The impressive total of £45,000 represented an average of more than £100 a reading and amounted to almost half of the £93,000 that proved to be the value of his estate when he died.

But the great sum was bought at more than a dear sacrifice of health; it was at the cost of life itself. In melancholy inversion of one of those legendary bards at whose singing palaces and towers rose in the enchanted air, Dickens's voice had been sinking his grave. His reckless and burning energy hardly more than veils a weariness almost indistinguishable from that which Macaulay expressed in his journal shortly before he died: "A month more of such days as I have been passing of late would make me impatient to get to my narrow little crib, like a weary factory child." Despite the sparkling face Dickens still turned on the world, the warehouse child that time had so transformed was hastening to his rest.

Though the readings were over, his impetuosity continued, working, walking, hurrying excitedly. There were invitations to dinners, invitations to speak at public functions, an invitation to Buckingham Palace from the Queen. Not long since, Dickens had chanced to show some American Civil War photographs to Arthur Helps, the Clerk of the Privy Council, and Helps in turn had mentioned them to the Queen. At her request, Dickens had sent them for her to look at, and presently Helps brought a message that the Queen would like to thank him in person. Formally responding that he would be "proud and happy to wait upon Her Majesty," Dickens also sent Helps a facetious little note pretending to believe that he was about to be made a baronet. "We will have 'Of Gad's Hill Place' attached to the title of the Baronetcy, please—on account of the divine William and Falstaff," he wrote jestingly. "With this stipulation, my blessing and forgiveness are enclosed."

The meeting took place shortly after the middle of March. Court etiquette did not allow Dickens to sit down, but Victoria herself remained standing throughout the entire hour and a half of their interview, leaning over the back of a sofa. Gracious though the gesture was, she could do so with less strain than if she had been an ailing man with a swollen foot. Under like circumstances the preceding year, Carlyle had bluntly announced that he was a feeble old man and helped himself to a chair. But except in private surroundings Dickens's pride would have driven him to collapse before he would have yielded to an infirmity....

Little more than a week later Dickens was bidden to Her Majesty's next levee, which he attended, making merry with Dolby beforehand over his court dress and joking about whether he should wear his cocked hat "fore and aft" or "th'wart ships." Dickens sent the Queen the first number of *Edwin Drood,* which was to be published on March 31st, and offered, if she "should ever be sufficiently interested in the tale to desire to know a little more of it in advance of her subjects," to send advance copies of its further installments. Soon after, Mary was presented to the Queen. Later still, in May, Dickens was invited to dinner at Lord Houghton's to meet the Prince of Wales and the King of the Belgians. He was by this time so lame again that he could not ascend the staircase to meet the company, and had to be helped immediately into the dining room. All these events, and possibly a circulation of his little joke about a baronetcy, gave rise to rumors that he was to be made a member of the Privy Council, even offered a peerage. "You will probably have read before now," he wrote a correspondent, "that I am going to be everything the Queen can make me. If my authority be worth anything believe on it that I am going to be nothing but what I am, and that includes my being as long as I live,—Your faithful and heartily obliged, Charles Dickens." He had already won for himself, in fact, every significant distinction he could possibly possess.

His bodily health continued to give reason for alarm. Less than a week after the last reading, he confessed to Forster that once more, walking along Oxford Street, he had found himself unable to read more than the right-hand halves of the names over the shops. Other grave symptoms presented themselves, although as usual he tried to make light of them. "My uneasiness and hemorrhage, after having quite left me, as I supposed, has come back with an aggravated irritability that it has not yet displayed. You have no idea what a state I am in today from a violent rush of it; and yet it has not the slightest effect on my general health that I know of." ...

His foot was by now a source of distress that would "yield to nothing but days of fomentation and horizontal rest." "Last night," he wrote Georgina on May 11th, "I got a good night's rest under the influence of Laudanum but it hangs about me very heavily today. I have had the poultices constantly changed, hot and hot, day and night..." On the 16th the foot was "a mere bag of pain." The following evening, despite having "viciously bubbled and blistered it in all directions," he was unable to go with Mary to the Queen's Ball, to which they had both been invited.

Deep within his consciousness he must have known that the end was near. Receiving a young girl with literary aspirations whom Lord Lytton had sent to him, he spoke of his habits of publication while his work was still in progress. "But suppose," she said diffidently, "suppose you died before all the book was written?" "Ah-h!" he said, and paused. "That has occurred to me at times." His long, future-piercing gaze seemed to her to be penetrating golden veils. Then, looking at her kindly, he said cheerfully, "One can only work on, you know—work while it is day."

Forster saw him for the last time on May 22nd. Not long before, an admirer had written Dickens from Liverpool, describing himself as a self-raised man, attributing his prosperous career to what he had learned of kindness and sympathy from Dickens's writings, and asking in gratitude that Dickens accept an enclosed check for £500. Dickens refused the gift, but replied that he would be glad to accept any small memorial in some other form. Presently there arrived a silver basket, and a silver centerpiece designed to portray Spring, Summer, and Autumn. The giver explained that he desired to connect Dickens "with none save the brighter and milder days." "I never look at it," Dickens told Forster, "that I don't think most of the Winter." The gift, Forster mournfully observed, foreshadowed that season which Dickens was never again to see.

Throughout all the month of May the pace of his engagements had never slackened. Gladstone, the Prime Minister, invited him to breakfast; he dined with John Lothrop Motley and Disraeli at Lord Stanhope's. He met Arthur Stanley, the Dean of Westminster, at Frederick Locker-Lampson's, and a little later dined at Stanley's with the Russells, the Clarendons, and Connop Thirlwall, the Bishop of St. David's, who had been, with Mill and Macaulay, among the three child-prodigies of the age. He attended the theater with Lady Molesworth and Lord Redesdale, and was so full of droll thoughts tumbling out one after another that he kept himself and his companions "laughing at the majesty of his own absurdities"; his talk, Lord Redesdale said, "had all the sparkle of champagne."

It was almost the last flare of that delight in the theater that had burned brightly throughout Dickens's entire life. Walking with a friend only a short time before, Dickens had paused in the shadow of Westminster Abbey and asked, "What do you think would be the realization of one of my most cherished day-dreams?" Without waiting for a reply, he instantly continued that it would be to "hold supreme authority" in the direction of a great theater, with "a skilled and noble company." "The pieces acted should be dealt with according to my pleasure, and touched up here and there in obedience to my own judgment; the players as well as the plays being absolutely under my command. That," he ended, laughing and glowing at the fancy, *"that's* my day-dream!"

Toward the end of May he took charge of some private theatricals being given by his London neighbors, Mr. and Mrs. Freake, at Cromwell House. Mary and Katey were among the actors and Millais painted the scenery. Dickens rehearsed the company daily, brilliantly showing them how to do all the parts, from the "old man" to the "young lover." He had meant to take a role himself but was prevented by his lameness. Though June 2nd, the night of the production, was a stifling one, he acted as stage manager, ringing all the bells, working all the lights, and between these activities sitting in the prompter's corner.

Dolby had been with him at the office that very afternoon. Rising to leave, and extending his hand across the table at which they had been sitting, Dolby was shocked by the pain mirrored in his Chief's face, and noticed that his eyes were suffused with tears. Throwing off his emotions, Dickens also rose. Grasping Dolby's hand, and looking him full in the face, instead of using the words "Good day" or "Good night," as he usually did, Dickens earnestly said, "Goodbye, Dolby, old man."

On June 3rd he was back at Gad's Hill. The country was delicious with the foliage and flowers of early summer. Dickens rejoiced in his escape from London and "the preposterous endeavour to dine at preposterous hours and preposterous places." On the suggestion of an actress friend, he had sent off for a "Voltaic Band" which he hoped might give some relief to his foot. He was looking forward to uninterrupted morning hours among the leaves and mirrors and fresh scents of the chalet. But coming down on Saturday to spend the week-end, Katey was heavy-hearted to see him looking so worn. Dickens, however, was talkative and cheerful. The new conservatory had been completed while he was in London, and he delighted in its perfumed brightness of massed blossoms. "Well, Katey," he exclaimed gaily, "you now see POSITIVELY the last improvement of Gad's Hill"; and they all laughed at the joke against himself.

On Sunday Dickens seemed refreshed on returning from a quiet afternoon walk. When dinner was over, he and Katey remained sitting in the dining room to be near the flowers in the conservatory, while they listened to Mary singing in the drawing room. At eleven o'clock Mary and Georgina retired, but Dickens and Katey sat on, with the lamps turned low, enjoying the warm, sweet-scented summer air coming in through the open windows. He and his daughter talked long and affectionately. He wished, Dickens told her, that he had been "a better father, and a better man." Later he spoke of his hopes that he might make a success of *Edwin Drood,* "if, please God, I live to finish it." Katey looked startled: "I say *if,*" Dickens told her, "because you know, my dear child, I have not been strong lately." It was three o'clock, and the summer dawn was creeping into the conservatory before they went upstairs and parted at his chamber door.

It was long before Katey slept. When she arose late in the morning, he had already gone to the chalet. She had to go up to London that morning and would be unable to return to Gad's Hill until the following Saturday. But she felt uneasy about her father. Confiding in Mary and her aunt, she drew a promise from Georgina to write the next day with news of how he was. Knowing his dislike of partings, she was going only to leave her dear love for him without any farewell. As she waited on the porch for the carriage, however, she felt an uncontrollable impulse, and went down the tunnel, through the Shrubbery to the chalet, and climbed the stairs to the upper room.

"His head was bent low down over his work, and he turned an eager and rather flushed face towards me as I entered." Usually, Dickens merely raised his cheek for a kiss, "saying a few words, perhaps, in 'the little language'" he had used when his daughters were children, "but on this morning, when he saw me," Katey remembered, "he pushed his chair back from the writing table, opened his arms, and took me into them." She hurried back to the house, saying to herself, without knowing why, "I am so glad I went—I am so glad."

In the afternoon Dickens walked with the dogs to mail some letters in Rochester. Tuesday morning, Mary left for a visit to Katey in London. Dickens felt tired, and only drove in the carriage to Cobham Wood with Georgina, where he strolled about under the trees of the park. That evening he strung some Chinese lanterns in the conservatory, and sat long with Georgina enjoying their shimmering illumination on the flowers. He was glad, he told her, at having finally abandoned London for Gad's Hill. Only a few days before, he had said that he wished his name to be more and more associated with this place while he lived, and repeated a hope he had often expressed before, that he might lie in the little Cathedral graveyard at the foot of the Castle wall when he died.

On the 8th of June, in violation of his usual habits, he worked all day, returning to the house only for lunch, and then going directly back to the chalet to write again. The last page that he wrote there, among the dappled sunshine and shadow of the leaves, has a picture of a brillant morning in Rochester: "Changes of glorious light from moving boughs, songs of birds, scents from gardens, woods, and fields —or, rather, from the one great garden of the whole cultivated island in its yielding time—penetrated the Cathedral, subdue its earthy odour, and preach of the Resurrection and the Life. The cold stone tombs of centuries ago grow warm; and flecks of brightness dart into the sternest marble corners of the building, fluttering there like wings." The words, so serene and still elegiac, are a fitting valedictory to the exalted, laughing, despairing, tormented, and triumphant career.

He was late leaving the chalet, but in the study before dinner he wrote a few letters. In one of them he quoted Friar Laurence's warning to Romeo: "These violent delights have violent ends." It was true. Looking at him across the table, Georgina was alarmed by the expression of pain on his face. "For an hour," he told her, "he had been very ill." Nevertheless he desired dinner to go on. He made a few other random and disconnected remarks. Suddenly he said he had to go to London at once. Pushing back the crimson-damasked chair in which he had been sitting, he rose, but would have fallen where he stood if Georgina had not hurried around the table to support him. She tried to help him to a sofa. His body was too heavy for her strength, however, and after a slight struggle she was obliged to lower him to the floor, where he sank heavily on his left side. "On the ground," he murmured faintly.

With the aid of the servants Georgina placed him on the sofa. She at once summoned a local surgeon, and dispatched telegrams to Mary and Katey and Dr. Beard. Charley also received a telegram instructing him to bring a London physician for consultation. Mary and Katey arrived late that night with Frank Beard. It was judged safer not to move him, and all night he remained unconscious on the dining-room sofa. Early next morning Charley brought the London doctor. But nothing could be done. It was a paralytic stroke; an effusion of blood on the brain left no gleam of hope. Katey was sent back to London to break the news to her mother, and returned that afternoon, when Ellen Ternan also came. All day Dickens's body lay, breathing heavily, in the bright dining room opening on the scarlet geraniums, musk, and blue lobelias in the conservatory. The day was mild and the windows were wide. Katey and Charley sat outside on the steps, where the scent of syringa was heavy in the air. Afterward, Charley could never bear that flower near him.

Just before six o'clock Dickens's breathing grew fainter. At ten minutes past that hour, he gave a deep sigh. His eyes were closed, but a tear welled from under his right eye and trickled down his cheek. Then he was gone. "Like a weary factory child," he had sunk to his narrow bed. It was just four months and two days past his fifty-eighth birthday.

VAN WYCK BROOKS

Van Wyck Brooks is, I should say, our foremost living American man of letters. I use that term in its general sense, as of a writer whose working life has been dedicated to the interests of literature. He has written neither novels nor poetry—or if he has, they have been carefully kept secret from the reading public. But he has been our foremost literary liaison officer between American books and American life. He has not been the creator of a system of aesthetic theory, unless his insistence upon the relationship I have just referred to may be so regarded. He has been our most interesting and suggestive literary historian, and his major work, a series of books known as *Makers and Finders; A History of the Writer in America,* should prove to be a lasting record of the literary life in this country.

Of Francis Parkman, the story of whose career he told in *New England: Indian Summer,* I have already spoken. His pages on Parkman are here reprinted in full. I shall mention here also, rather than by way of preface to his own story of ordeal, his most recent book, an autobiographical account of the Twenties in literary America. Its concluding chapter, "A Season in Hell," is an absorbing account of the three-year nervous breakdown which Brooks suffered toward the end of that decade. He emerged from it a stronger and more confident man. His account will mean most to those who have made a similar journey to hell and returned, but I do not think it can fail to hold and impress any sensitive and intelligent reader.

Ordeals of Francis Parkman

DURING these years, Francis Parkman was at work in his Boston study. He was a lonely man, detached from his time and place and their interests and causes. A classmate of Hunt, with whom he had travelled in Italy, he was also an old friend of Norton, who had helped him with the proofs of *The Oregon Trail.* He was indifferent to painting and sculpture, however, and European opinion meant nothing to him. He was still more remote from everything Higginson represented, or all but his admiration for Epictetus and his love of out-door life. Parkman detested reformers, though he also detested the worship of money. He despised the "morality of commerce," and he made common cause with Godkin in his efforts to save the republic. He had no use for "flintlock business men." He was a soldier in all his instincts, although fate had made him something else, a writer, and one of the greatest of his age and country. The state of his health had prevented him from taking part in the Civil War, and for him the post-war years were so ignoble that he wished for no part or lot in their concerns. He was only at home in his own mind, where he lived with explorers, borderers, adventurers and woodsmen.

Some years before the war, Parkman had published a novel bearing the name of the hero, *Vassall Morton*. This Morton was a rich young man with a preference for young ladies who were wild and lawless. He did not admire the tamer virtues that prevailed in his little Boston world. He refused any fixed and stated calling. Ardent and energetic, a lover of hardship, with a mind formed for action, he planned to devote his life to the study of primitive races, resolving to gain his ends at any cost. In this he succeeded, the reader was led to suppose, but only after encountering incredible odds and disasters. He spent four years in an Austrian dungeon, and he was condemned to die and imprisoned again, a "death in life," a "slow-consuming horror." But he hardened his heart, in this inferno, against himself and his own troubles; and, when he escaped at last and returned to Boston, he felt he was proof against all further woes. With a mind that had ripened in solitude and suffering, he was ready to face the future with golden hopes.

The novel was one of those still-born books that no one reads but the friends of the author. When the author is a man of genius who has put his worst foot forward, these books are always interesting, however; and Parkman's friends saw at once that he had pictured himself in Morton.[1] This impetuous young man, who had learned to be patient, —strenuous, eager, proud, confident, manly,—was certainly the son of Dr. Parkman, the minister, the friend of Dr. Channing, who had lived in a spacious old house in Bowdoin Square. It was Dr. Parkman's brother, the physician, who had been murdered by Professor Webster in the laboratory of the Harvard Medical School. In college, Francis Parkman, the grandson of a rich old merchant, had constantly read

---

[1] It may be noted that Morton is also the name of the hero of Motley's first novel. Perhaps in both cases this name was suggested by that of the rebel of "Merry Mount," who disliked the ways of the Puritans as much as Parkman and Motley. These two Mortons were totally different, but both were rough self-portraits of men who found their vocation in historical writing.

Cooper, Scott and Byron. He had "Injuns on the brain," his friends remembered, and he had crossed the plains, on the Oregon Trail, when it was as dangerous to do so as ever it was for Columbus to cross the Atlantic. The book he had written about his adventures was boyishly vigorous, fresh and frank, and he wrote as if he rather wished his pen had been a sword. One saw in Morton all these traits of Parkman, with his ethnological interests and his plans for historical writing. Parkman had published *The Conspiracy of Pontiac* five years before he wrote the novel. But even his friends might have been puzzled by some of the scenes in *Vassall Morton*. If the picture of the Tyrolese woods and mountains was highly circumstantial, they were aware that Parkman knew the Alps. He had visited the wilder Alpine regions, which recalled to him at once the American woods. No forester knew these woods better than Parkman. But what about Morton's anguish in the Austrian dungeon? What gave these prison-scenes their unmistakable air of reality? Had the writer of this novel been in prison? Or was the dungeon a symbol of something else? One could only say, though one said it with conviction, "Eccovi, this child has been in hell."

It was true. Parkman had lived in hell, and his life, at best, remained a purgatory. As a delicate, sensitive boy, with a passion for adventure, he had lived in a state of constant tension. Fascinated by Cooper's heroes and Byron's wanderers and outlaws, he was bent on surpassing the Indians in strength and endurance. He had spent all his summers in the woods, with his rifle, "Satan," riding the wildest horses without saddle or stirrups. He had tried to crush, in the Indian fashion, every personal weakness; and, while his will and energy were super-normal, his constitution could not bear the strain. He had broken down at one point,—overtaxed his heart,—then at another and another. His eyes had given way from excessive reading. To rest his eyes, while studying Indian life, he had undertaken the Oregon journey. This had destroyed his digestion and given him chronic insomnia. Arthritis attacked his knee and left him crippled, and, finally, a nervous disorder engulfed his mind. At any attempt to think or write, he felt an iron band about his head that seemed to contract with force. He could not enlist in the Civil War, the bitterest disappointment of his life, and the doctor he consulted in Paris threatened him with insanity if he ever tried to use his brain again. He was reduced to the kind of inaction that men of his type can least endure; for, while he exulted in danger and almost exulted in suffering, he could not bear stagnation and confinement. For two long periods, one lasting four years, he could not use his mind for any purpose; and at best he was able to work two hours a day. Two or three hours, of the twenty-four, was the most he ever slept. He could not read continuously for more than five minutes, and he usually read a minute at a time. "Prescott could see a little," he wrote in one of his early letters; "confound him, he could even look over his proofs, but I am no better off than an owl in the twilight." He had composed his first books, *The Oregon Trail* and *Pontiac,* pacing back and forth in the garret of the old colonial house in Bowdoin Square. Sometimes he sat in the dark, with bandaged eyes and drawn curtains, memorizing his work, chapter by chapter, dictating or using his writing-machine; for he had what he called a "gridiron," like Prescott's noctograph, a wooden frame with horizontal wires, with which he could write in pencil,— at an average of six lines a day,—when he could not even see to write his name. Then, for fourteen years, he published nothing, or nothing but the novel, *Vassall Morton,* which showed, at least, his gift for story-telling. His mind ran riot in the darkness.

Not until 1865, when Parkman was forty-two, was he able to resume his historical writing. Then appeared *The Pioneers of France in the New World,* the first, or the first but one, of his great series. He had published *Pontiac,* the last of the series,—in chronological order,—as if he feared he could never round out the subject; and he had been preparing ever since, when he was able to work, for the other volumes. He collected his books and documents and had them read aloud to him. He jotted down his notes, which were later deciphered and read to him again till he knew them by heart. It was wonderful to follow his dictation, to watch the scenes unfold and the persons come to life out of the crabbed notes that he held in his hand. Although he could scarcely see these notes, he had lived them, in a sense, from his earliest boyhood; and he had formed a plan for his life during his student-years at Harvard. This plan was to write what he called the "history of the American forest"—the history of the "old French war,"—the contest of the Indians, the French and the English for the control of the continent. He had met with little encouragement. No one seemed to care about this old French war, a dim and squalid struggle, as people supposed it, between savages and bushrangers, with nothing but a wilderness as the stake; and even *The Conspiracy of Pontiac* had aroused little interest in it.[2] But this war had decided the fate of the continent, and

[2] In spite of the success of Bancroft's American history, the reading public long remained indifferent to the subject of it. John Fiske referred to an incident, in this connection, that occurred about 1875: "A gentleman in a small New England town was asked if some lectures of mine on 'America's Place in History' would be likely to find a good audience there. He reflected a moment, then shook his head gravely. 'The subject,' he said, 'is one which would interest very few people.' In the state of mind thus indicated there is something so bewildering that I believe I have not yet recovered from it."— John Fiske, *Essays Historical and Literary,* II, 126.

"The preferences of sentient creatures are what *create* the importance of topics."— William James.

Parkman knew how important it was. Moreover, he knew that he had a chance, the last and only chance, to picture, in the Indians, who were disappearing,—at least, in their primitive form,—authentic American men of the Stone Age, the forbears of civilization. No one could have been better prepared to carry out this project, nor was any project ever achieved with a more tenacious will.

From his earliest childhood, Parkman's tastes and interests had converged to form this will. For, while he was a man of the world, he was a woodsman born. As a little boy, he had caught horned pouts in the Frog Pond,—a stone's-throw from Prescott's later dwelling,— and broiled them over a fire in his father's garden. At eight, he was taken to live on his grandfather's farm at Medford, in the woods of the Middlesex Fells, with their cliffs, ravines, marshes, streams and lakes, a patch of primitive wilderness that still remained within eight miles of Boston. He had four years of freedom in the fields and forests, riding, shooting, trapping, fishing, camping. He carried snakes in his pockets, he botanized; he even raised silkworms for a while. He knew all the animals and imitated their calls. In Boston, he was observed, on a Sunday morning, following his father and mother on their way to church, carrying by the tail a rat which he meant to take home and stuff. Then one day Cooper's novels came alive in Boston: a party of Sacs and Foxes, in deerskins and feathers, performed a war-dance on the Common. His college rooms at Harvard were the rooms of a sportsman. He spent all his summer vacations tramping through New England, western Massachusetts, New Hampshire and Maine, crossing the Canadian border, following the Indian trails, tracing the routes of the French and the *coureurs de bois*. He kept careful diaries on all these journeys.

He was highly systematic, though not by nature. With his temperamental zest for adventure, he found research repulsive.[3] He despised "emasculate" scholarship all his days. But he forced his tastes to gain his ends. He was ferociously accurate and savagely thorough. No one was ever more reckless, as *The Oregon Trail* showed, and no one was more methodical in pursuing an object. He directed his travels and reading like a Jesuit novice. He divided his time in college between rhetoric, history and gymnastics; and when he was sent abroad, at nineteen, to spend some months in Italy, for the sake of his health, he stayed for several weeks at a convent of the Passionists, near the Coliseum in Rome. The monks did their best to convert him, but Parkman was intractable. Neither then nor later was his positive mind open to

[3] In this he resembled Prescott and Motley. The tension created by this repulsion is characteristic of first-rate minds. No good writer has ever liked drudgery, nor has any good writer ever permitted anyone else to do his drudgery for him.

religious exaltations. He had an extreme distaste for the clergy at home, in spite of his excellent father. He had fallen away from the faith of Channing, although he was drawn to Theodore Parker, with whom he climbed Vesuvius and talked in Rome. Parker was a muscular man, who preached a robust religion, while Channing had always been Parkman's special aversion,—because he was frail and small and his habits too sedentary and he preached the superiority of mind over muscle. Parkman thought the clergy as a class were soft, gushing, vague and spoiled by women. He liked to describe them as "vermin"; and, having small use for the Puritans, he had still less for the Catholics. He was an agnostic, somewhat harsh in temper. Then why did he visit these amiable monks and get himself presented to the Pope? Because he wished to carry out his plan. He haunted the churches and monasteries, in Italy and Sicily, because to write his history, as he knew, he had to understand the Church, the methods of the missionaries, the ecclesiastical system, from top to bottom. He wished to live in a monastery and see it from the inside, as later he wished to live in an Indian lodge.

In the same systematic way, he studied human nature, to learn what he called the springs of emotion and action. His journal bristled with accurate sketches of soldiers, sailors, farmers, priests and scholars. He went through the Law School, not for the sake of the law, but to study history and statesmanship and, still more, human character; and in Boston, after his breakdown, when he could not sleep, he rose and prowled all night in the open, watching the tramps on the Common. Just so, he had watched the reformers in the days of the "Newness." The Chardon Street Chapel, the haunt of the "Friends of Reform," had once been the Parkmans' family stable, and Dr. Parkman, who disliked reformers quite as much as his son, always spoke of the chapel as "my mother's barn." Parkman abhorred these eccentric people,—he called the Brook Farmers the "she-philosophers,"—but he went to their meetings just the same. He had no shred of sympathy with their causes, but they were types to examine. Visionaries, idealists, fanatics,—they were all one to Parkman,—had played a part in Canadian history, and he took pains to observe them. He had a contempt for physical weakness that grew with his own infirmities and suggested the "hard-boiled" mind of a later epoch. "How I hate 'em!" he would say, referring to men who were frail or sickly; but he noted their manners and motives, and their conversation, and set them all down among the rest. What he really hated was the weakness in himself, in this resembling all the "hard-boiled" writers. Of Thoreau, in later years, he spoke with respect, for Thoreau had known the Indians as he knew the woods; but he was too self-conscious and introspective to please this Boston Spartan.

Wordsworth he could not abide. Everything that savoured of speculation, the dreamy, the sentimental, the philanthropic,—philosophy, metaphysics, the inward eye,—was antipathetic to Parkman. He disliked the words "culture" and "refinement" because they suggested the artificial. What he called the "improved savage" was Parkman's favourite type, delicate in his feelings and decent in behaviour and also virile, natural, resourceful and strong.

Such was this lover of action, this literary soldier who was to picture himself in describing his heroes, Frontenac, La Salle, Lord Howe and Wolfe. His element was the Border, and the life of the Border, where the primitive and the civilized were in conflict, where civilization prevailed, but only by means of the primitive virtues, and human nature appeared in its utmost starkness. In Italy, on Lake Como, he had written, "Give me Lake George, and the smell of the pine and fir!" He had preferred Vesuvius to all the ruined temples; and in England, with its smooth green hills and hedges, he had longed for the shaggy mountains, the cedars and the scrub-oak, the "fiery glare of the sun . . . its wild and ruddy light." In Scotland and Switzerland alone, among the crags and cataracts, he had felt at home. No one knew better than he the depths of the forests, dim and silent as a cavern, the cedar-bordered streams of the northern lakes, with their water-girdled rocks and verdurous islets, where the muskrats swam and plunged, the rock-maples rearing their shadowy masses, the sombre balsam-firs, the coves where the wild ducks dived beneath the alders, and the moose, neck-deep in water to escape the flies, vanished among the trees with clumsy trot. Many a time, on Lake Champlain, as the sun set behind the western mountains, piled in mist along the sky, he had watched some dead pine stretching its arms athwart the burning heaven, with a crow perched on its top like an image carved in jet. He had observed the night-hawk, circling in its flight, pitching through the air, on whirling wing, for the unseen prey that flew beneath it. To the farthest outposts of Canada, to the Rocky Mountains, Parkman knew the wilderness, the savage forests and the open woodlands, the mighty rivers and the lakes and prairies; and he knew the inhabitants of all these regions, the Indians, the half-breeds and the traders, the settlers, soldiers, trappers and pioneers. Before he was twenty-three, he had seen most of the Indian tribes from Maine to Colorado and Nevada and had visited many of the spots he described in his books. He had explored the sites of the Indian towns and villages, measured the ruined forts and talked with the oldest settlers. He had gathered from survivors of the tribes the legends of the Ojibways and the Mohawks, the Iroquois, the Foxes and the Hurons. An ancient brave at Old Town, Maine, patching his canoe, had described the attacks of the Mohawks, as the tribe recalled them: they had roasted the children on forked sticks like apples. He had heard fireside tales and wild recitals of necromancy and witchcraft, tales of the magic drums of the conjurors, of grisly weendigoes and bloodless geebi, of evil manitoes in the dens of the woods and malignant sorcerers dwelling on lonely islands, in lakes they had bound with spells. He had heard of pygmy champions, mighty in soul, who had subdued the monsters of the wilds, and heroes who had achieved marvellous triumphs over the brute force of their assailants. He knew the secret places of the woods where the Indians had held their councils; and he read the signs of the forest himself, the whistle of a bird that stood for danger, the rustle of a leaf that stood for death. In the perilous depths of the mountains, he had lodged with lonely trappers, in time-worn buckskins, gripping their rifles in sinewy hands, sleeping on the rough earth, with dried meat and water for their food and drink. The wild, hard life of these pioneers had for him a resistless charm. He had even found *coureurs de bois,* still dwelling beyond the solitudes of the northern lakes, unchanged in life and character since the far-off days when the Sun-king claimed this cheerless empire.

By the time he was able to write again, Parkman was almost ready to carry out his whole ambitious plan,—for all his historical writings, taken together, were to form a single work in eleven volumes. Now and then he went abroad, to extend his investigations, for his studies were based on original manuscript sources. He made four visits to Paris. He had to take a secretary into the libraries with him and listen while the documents were read aloud; and all the income from his books scarcely paid for the copyists who collected manuscripts for him in Paris and London. But most of his notes were assembled in 1865, and he was already prepared for his double task: to picture the forest and its history and drama and to "realize a certain ideal of manhood,— a little mediaeval," as he called it. He had been all the better fitted to live the story that he wrote because, like La Salle, he was a "man of thought, trained amid arts and letters." [4] Meanwhile, unable to use his eyes, and threatened with insanity, he turned aside for a while into horticulture. He took refuge in his garden at Jamaica Plain; and there, confined to his wheel-chair, he rapidly moved about, sowing seeds,

---

[4] "The pioneer of western pioneers was no rude son of toil, but a man of thought, trained amid arts and letters."—*La Salle and the Discovery of the Great West.*

Parkman observed in a note appended to this: "A Rocky Mountain trapper, being complimented on the hardihood of himself and his companions, once said to the writer, 'That's so; but a gentleman of the right sort will stand hardship better than anybody else.' The history of Arctic and African travel, and the military records of all time, are a standing evidence that a trained and developed mind is not the enemy, but the active and powerful ally, of constitutional hardihood. The culture that enervates instead of strengthening is always a false or partial one."

raking and weeding, planting and cutting his borders and splitting wood. Active and methodical, as elsewhere, he studied the art of gardening. He even served for a year as professor of horticulture at the Bussey Institute. He developed the "Parkman lily" and brought out new varieties of larkspur, phlox and poppy. He was a famous grower of roses, like Bancroft and Prescott before him, and like John Fiske and Henry Adams and Henry Cabot Lodge. He had a thousand varieties of roses. He even wrote a handbook on this flower of historians, describing its groups and families, its cultivation and propagation. Parkman was severe with roses as with men, an aristocrat in horticulture, an aristocrat in human culture. He would have liked to subject his race to the methods that governed the growing of flowers. If it was good for roses, why not for men? He expressed his social faith in *The Book of Roses*.[5]

Thenceforward, at 50 Chestnut Street, where he always spent his winters, one might have seen Parkman forever at work in the shadow of his third-floor study. Two of the walls were covered with books; the others were hung with portrait-engravings. The light from the north windows was subdued. A few Indian relics stood on the mantel, with statuettes of animals by Barye, whom Hunt, his friend, had more or less discovered. One saw two or three photographs of the statue of Colleoni, which he kept for the sake of the subject, not for the sculpture. Colleoni was never out of his eye or mind. Solitary and silent mostly, usually sleepless, often in pain, stoical as an Indian struck by an arrow, he could be amusing with his daughters,—his wife and son were dead, —who knew he had a capital sense of humour. He appeared on the streets, at a rapid gait, a tall, slender figure in a long grey coat, with the fur cap that rose in winter over the prow-like chin. But he was obliged to restrain his passion for action, and he who could so ill endure confinement, and who studied as it were against the grain, could not relax indeed but had to sit. Or, rather, he rode his chair as if it were a saddle. He had to sublimate his love of danger, he had to repress his energy to save his nerves. His mind was like a bow, too tightly strung; and this tension appeared in his work, in its frequent speed and picturesqueness. One felt the virile force of the writer, his pleasure in the savage and the vast, while his eagerness, transformed into patience,

---

[5] "The art of horticulture is no leveller. Its triumphs are achieved by rigid systems of selection and rejection, founded always on the broad basis of intrinsic worth. The good cultivator propagates no plants but the best. He carefully chooses those marked out by conspicuous merit; protects them from the pollen of inferior sorts, intermarries them, perhaps, with other varieties of equal vigour and beauty; saves the seed and raises from it another generation. . . . Thus the rose and other plants are brought slowly to their perfect development. . . . We cultivate the parent, and look for our reward in the offspring."—*The Book of Roses*, 95–98.

made him thorough and accurate.[6] One felt his impetuosity in the drive of his writing. With his cordial dislike of Puritanism, which he thought narrow and bookish, he retained its passionate fervour and its rigorous tenseness. No doubt, the isolation and strain of his life intensified his natural harshness. He loved hard truth, and he neither gave nor expected praise or pity; but this, with his positive mind, his New England practicality and like for the useful, limited his sympathies and imagination. Of all the figures in his books, the one he most resembled was La Salle, the stern and self-reliant Roman Frenchman, masterful, martial, serious, austere and shy. For all his distaste for priests, he admired the courage and heroism of the Jesuit martyrs, and he followed the priestly model in his own career. The heir of a long line of divines, like many of the New England writers of the previous age, he shared their sacerdotal temper and all their pride of learning and pride of power. Parkman was a Brahmin of the Brahmins.

This mediæval strain of the priest and soldier, marked in Parkman's nature, fitted him for the theme that filled his life. He had something in common with all the types, English, French and Indian, that appeared in the drama, and the drama itself was mediæval, or, rather, it covered the whole age, from Champlain to Montcalm and Wolfe, during which the mediæval became the modern. It was a conflict, as Parkman revealed it, between the past and the future, the old and the new, between feudalism and monarchism, an autocratic Church and State, and the democratic freedom that replaced them. That all the fervour of the Middle Ages revived in the enterprise of Montreal, with the spirit of Godfrey de Bouillon, that the settlement was another crusade,—a moment of faith that became a political movement, as the economic motive grew in power,—Parkman was the first to show, in any conclusive fashion, while he showed the meaning of the old French war as a cause of the American Revolution. He understood the protagonists, French and English, who had shared his romantic feeling and his feeling for action, and his imagination failed him only with the Indians, whose virtues, for the rest, he admired and knew. His Indians were visibly real. They were not operatic, like Prescott's, or the noble savages of Cooper. Parkman had lived with them, and his Indian scenes and portraits were drawn from life. But he had preconceived ideas about them, and he took no pains to keep up with later investigations and observations. Ethnology scarcely existed at the time when he began to write, and the Indians he had known best were the Sioux,

---

[6] See, however, the strictures of Charles Francis Adams the second on Parkman's account of the capture of Quebec, a matter in which, according to Adams, no one could have been right who had not actually taken part in military operations.—C. F. Adams, *Lee at Appomattox and Other Papers*, 347–354.

at the very worst period to judge them. He had approached them, moreover, as a young New England man whose mind was filled with legends of Haverhill and Deerfield. He saw them as Miles Standish might have seen them, with his inelastic nature, from the outside only. His ungenerous treatment of Pontiac was a case in point. He had made up his mind in regard to racial and moral questions and he never expanded or changed it. He had no feeling whatever for evolution. But as, volume by volume, his work advanced till the series came to an end in the early nineties, everyone became aware that he was a great historian, the greatest perhaps who had ever appeared in the country. While *The Conquest of Mexico* was finer than any of Parkman's books, as a masterpiece of historical story-telling, he was more original than Prescott or Motley, for he had established the taste by which he was read. He had made Champlain and La Salle historic figures like Charlemagne, Peter the Great and Robert Bruce. Until he wrote, students who thought the Tudors all-important saw nothing in the conflict in the forest that had made the American nation what it was; and Parkman, who had discovered his theme, or first perceived its real significance, created a form that matched his theme in grandeur.

J. VAN GOGH-BONGER

Everyone who has seen the excellent motion picture, *Lust for Life,* that was made from Irving Stone's biographical novel about Vincent Van Gogh, will remember the affection with which that deeply troubled man was received by the young wife of his beloved brother Theo. It is she who contributes the warmly sympathetic memoir of her brother-in-law, part of which I have used here to describe Van Gogh's desperate struggle with himself and the demons by which he was possessed.

She has told in her preface to Vincent's letters to his brother how when she came as a bride to the Paris flat in which Theo was living she found in the bottom of a small desk a drawer full of letters from Vincent, and how "week after week I saw the soon familiar yellow envelopes with the characteristic handwriting increase in number." After Vincent's death she and Theo discussed the possibility of their publication, but he, too, soon died, and it was not until twenty-four years later, in 1914, that the letters were published. She observes in her preface that they would have appeared earlier had she not chosen to wait until the work to which Vincent had given his life "was recognized and appreciated as it deserved."

To have given the picture of Vincent Van Gogh's heart-rending struggle to achieve the mastery which was to be his would have been an almost impossible task if I had included here only such excerpts from his correspondence as space afforded. It seemed much preferable to give the story, or part of it, as it is told in the Memoir his sister-in-law wrote as introduction to the letters themselves. No man so tortured could have wished for a more understanding portrayal than the one which emerges from her pages.

Ordeals of Vincent Van Gogh

IN OCTOBER Theo, who has got a permanent position at Goupil's in Paris, comes to visit him [Vincent] on his journey thither and tries in vain to bring him to some fixed plan for the future; he is not yet ripe to take any resolution; before he becomes conscious of his real power he has still to struggle through the awful winter of 1879–'80, that saddest, most hopeless time of his never very fortunate life. In these days he undertakes, with ten francs in his pocket, the hopeless expedition to Courrières, the dwelling place of Jules Breton, whose pictures and poems he so much admires, and with whom he secretly hopes to come in contact in some way or other. But the only thing that becomes visible to him is the inhospitable exterior of Breton's newly built studio and he lacks the courage to introduce himself. Disappointed in his hope, he has to undertake the long journey home; his money is all spent, generally he sleeps in the open air or in a hay loft. Sometimes he exchanges a drawing for a piece of bread, and he undergoes so much fatigue and want that his health always suffered from the consequences. In spring he comes once more to the vicarage of Etten and speaks again about going to London. "If he really wants it, I shall enable him to go," writes his father, but finally he returns again to the Borinage and lives that summer of 1880 at the house of the miner, Charles Decrucq at Cuesmes. There he writes in July the wonderfully touching letter (133) that tells of what is going on in his innermost self —"My only anxiety is what can I do ... could I not be of use, and good for something?" It is the old wish, the old longing to serve and comfort humanity, which made him write afterwards, when he had found his calling, "And in a picture I wish to say something that would console as music does." Now in the days of deepest discouragement and darkness at last the light begins to dawn. Not in books shall he find satisfaction, not in literature find his work, as his letters sometimes suggested, he turns back to his old love, "I said to myself, I'll take up my pencil again, I will take up drawing, and from that moment everything has changed for me." It sounds like a cry of deliverance, and once more, "do not fear for me, if I can continue my work I will succeed." At last he has found his work and herewith the mental equilibrium is restored; he no longer doubts of himself and however difficult or heavy his life may become, the inward serenity, the conviction of his own calling never more deserts him.

The little room in the house of the miner Decrucq, which he has to share with the children, is his first studio. There he begins his painter's career with the first original drawing of miners who go to work in the early morning. There he copies with restless activity the large drawings after Millet, and when the room is getting too narrow for him, he takes his work out into the garden.

When the cold autumn weather prevents his doing this, and as his surroundings at Cuesmes are getting too narrow for him, he moves in October to Brussels where he settles in a small hotel on the Bd. du Midi

72. He is longing to see pictures again, but above all he hopes to become acquainted with other artists. Deep in his heart there was such a great longing for sympathy, for kindness and friendship, and though his difficult character generally prevented him from finding this and left him isolated in life, yet he always kept on longing for somebody with whom he could live and work.

Theo, who meanwhile had acquired a good position in Paris, could now assist him in word and deed. He brought Vincent into relation with the young Dutch painter van Rappard, who had worked some time in Paris and now studied at the academy at Brussels. At first the acquaintance did not progress, for the outward difference between the rich young nobleman and the neglected wanderer from the Borinage was too great to ripen the acquaintance at once into friendship; yet the artistic taste and opinions of both were too similar for them not to find each other; a friendship arose—perhaps the only one that Vincent ever had in Holland—it lasted for five years and then was broken through a misunderstanding, which van Rappard always regretted, though he acknowledged that intercourse with Vincent was very difficult.

"I remember as if it happened yesterday the moment of our first meeting at Brussels when he came into my room at nine o'clock in the morning, how at first we did not get on very well together, but so much the better after we had worked together a few times," writes van Rappard to Vincent's mother after the latter's death. And again, "whoever has witnessed this wrestling, struggling and sorrowful existence could not but feel sympathy for the man who demanded so much of himself, that it ruined body and mind. He belonged to the race that produces the great artists.

"Though Vincent and I had been separated the last years by a misunderstanding which I have often regretted—I have never ceased to remember him and the time we spent together with great sympathy.

"Whenever in the future I shall remember that time, and it is always a delight for me to recall the past, the characteristic figure of Vincent will appear to me in such a melancholy but clear light, the struggling and wrestling, fanatic, gloomy Vincent, who used to flare up so often and was so irritable, but who still deserved friendship and admiration for his noble mind and highly artistic qualities."

Vincent's own opinion of van Rappard is clearly shown in his letters. A second acquaintance that Vincent made through Theo, with the painter Roelofs, was of less-during importance. Roelof's advice to enter the Academy was not followed by Vincent, perhaps they did not admit him because he was not far enough advanced, but probably he had more than enough of academical institutions and theories, and in painting as well as in theology he preferred to go his own way; that is the reason he did not come into contact with other Dutch painters who were at that same time at the Academy at Brussels, for instance, Haverman.

He studied anatomy by himself, drew diligently from the living model, and from a letter to his father it seems that he took lessons in perspective from a poor painter at 1.50 fr. a lesson of two hours: it has not been possible to fix the name of the painter, it may have been Madiol.

At the end of the winter when van Rappard goes away, in whose studio he has often worked because his own little bedroom was too small, he longs for other surroundings, especially for the country; the expenses in Brussels are also somewhat heavy, and he thinks it will be cheapest to go to his parents at Etten where he has board and lodging free and can use all the money he receives for his work.

He stays there for eight months, and this summer of 1881 is again a happy time for him. First, van Rappard comes to stay with and he too always remembers with pleasure his stay at the vicarage, "And my visit at Etten! I see you still sitting at the window when I came in," he writes to Vincent's mother in the letter quoted above, "I still enjoy that beautiful walk we all took together that first evening, through the fields and along the small path! And our excursions to Seppen, Passievaart, Liesbosch, I often look through my sketch books for them."

In the beginning of August Theo comes over from Paris; shortly after Vincent makes an excursion to the Hague to consult about his work with Mauve, who firmly encourages him, so that he continues with great animation, and finally in those days he meets for the second time a woman who has great influence on his life. Among the guests who spent that summer at the vicarage at Etten was a cousin from Amsterdam—a young widow with her little four-year-old son. Quite absorbed in her grief over the loss of her husband, whom she had loved so tenderly, she was unconscious of the impression which her beauty and touching sorrow made on the cousin, who was a few years her junior. "He was so kind to my little boy," she said when she afterwards remembered that time. Vincent, who had great love for children, tried to win the heart of the mother by great devotion to the child. They walked and talked much together, and he has also drawn a portrait of her (which seems to have been lost), but the thought of a more intimate relation did not occur to her, and when Vincent spoke to her at last about his love, a very decided *no* was the immediate reply. She went back to Amsterdam and never saw him again. But Vincent could not abide by her decision, and with his innate tenacity he keeps on persevering and hoping for a change in her feelings for him; when his letters are not answered, he accuses both his and her parents of opposing the match, and only a visit to Amsterdam, where she refuses to see him, convinces him of the utter hopelessness of his love.

"He fancied that he loved me," she said afterwards, but for him it was sad earnest, and her refusal becomes a turning point in his life. If she had returned his love it would perhaps have been a spur to him to acquire a social position, he would have had to provide for her and her child; as it is he loses all worldly ambition and in the future lives only for his work, without taking one step to make himself independent. He cannot bear to stay in Etten any longer, he has become irritable and nervous, his relations to his parents become strained, and after a violent altercation with his father, in December he leaves suddenly for the Hague.

The two years he spends there are, for his work, a very important period of which his letters give a perfect description. His low spirits rise at first, by the change of surroundings and the intercourse with Mauve, but the feeling of having been slighted and wronged does not leave him and he feels himself utterly abandoned. When he meets in January a poor neglected woman approaching her confinement, he takes her under his protection, partly from pity but also to fill the great void in his life. "I hope there is no harm in his so-called model. Bad connections often arise from a feeling of loneliness, of dissatisfaction," writes his father to Theo, who is always the confidant of both parties and has to listen to all the complaints and worries; father is not far wrong. Vincent could not be alone, he wanted to live for somebody, he wanted a wife and children, and as the woman he loved had rejected him, he took the first unhappy woman who crossed his path, with children that were not his own. At first he feigns to be happy and tries to convince Theo in every letter how wisely and well he has acted, and the touching care and tenderness with which he surrounds the woman when she leaves the hospital after her confinement, strike us painfully when we think on whom that treasure of love was lavished. He prides himself now on having a family of his own, but when their living together has become a fact and he is continually associated with a coarse, uneducated woman, marked by smallpox, who speaks with a low accent and has a spiteful character, who is addicted to liquor and smokes cigars, whose past life has not been irreproachable, and who draws him into all kinds of intrigues with her family, he soon writes no more about his home life; even the posing, by which she won him (she sat for the beautiful drawing, "Sorrow"), and of which he had expected so much, soon ceases altogether. This unfortunate adventure deprives him of the sympathy of all in the Hague who took an interest in him. Neither Mauve nor Tersteeg could approve of his taking upon himself the cares of a family, and such a family! while he was financially dependent on his younger brother. Acquaintances and relatives are shocked to see him walk about with such a slovenly woman; nobody cares to associate with him any longer and his home life is such that nobody comes to visit him. The solitude around him becomes greater and greater and as usual it is only Theo who understands and continues to help him.

When the latter comes to visit Vincent for the second time in the Hague, in the summer of 1883, and witnesses the situation—finds the household neglected, everything in bad condition and Vincent deeply in debt—he too advises to let the woman go her own way as she is not fit for a regulated life. She herself had already felt that things could not continue like that, because Vincent wants too much money for his painting to leave enough for the support of her and the children, and she was already planning with her mother to earn money in another way. Vincent himself feels that Theo is right, and in his heart he longs for a change of surroundings, and liberty to go where his work calls him, but it costs him a bitter struggle to give up what he had taken upon himself, and to leave the poor woman to her fate. Till the last he defends her, and excuses her for her faults with the sublime words, "she has never seen what is good, so how can she be good?"

In those days of inward strife he allows Theo to read deeper than ever into his heart. These last letters from the Hague (letters 313 to 322) give the key to many things that were incomprehensible until now. For the first time he speaks openly about what has happened at the time of his dismissal from Goupil, for the first time he explains his strange indifference to show his own work or to try to make it productive, when he writes, "it is so painful for me to speak to people. I am not afraid to do so, but I know I make a disagreeable impression; I am so much afraid that my efforts to introduce myself will do me more harm than good," and how naïvely he adds, "human brains cannot bear everything as is shown by van Rappard, who had brain fever and now has gone to Germany to recover." As if he wanted to say: "do not let me make efforts to know strange people, as the same thing might happen to me." Once more he touches the old love story of Etten, "a single word made me feel that nothing is changed in me about it, that it is and remains a wound, which I carry with me, but it lies deep and will never heal, it will remain in after years just what it was the first day." And he expresses openly how different his life would have been without this disappointment in his love.

When at last he starts alone in September for Drenthe, he has made all possible provisions for the woman and the children, and there is a sorrowful parting, especially from the little boy to whom he had become attached as if it were his own child.

The trip to Drenthe proves a failure instead of doing him good. But some of his most beautiful letters date from those days. The season was too far advanced, the country too inhospitable, and what Vincent so ardently desired—to come into contact with some artists, for instance, Lieberman—was not realized.

Bitter loneliness and want of money put a too heavy strain on his nerves. He is afraid of falling ill, and in December 1883 hastens back to the parental vicarage, the only place where he can find a safe shelter.

His father had meanwhile left Etten and been nominated to Nuenen, a village in the neighbourhood of Eindhoven, and the new place and surroundings pleased Vincent so well that instead of paying a short visit, as first was his intention, he stays there for two years.

To paint the Brabant landscape and the Brabant types is now his aim, and to accomplish that aim he overlooks all other difficulties.

To live together with his parents was for him as well as for them a very difficult thing. In a small village vicarage, where nothing can happen without the whole village knowing it, a painter is obviously an anomaly; how much more a painter like Vincent, who had so completely broken with all formalities, conventionalities and with all religion, and who was the last person in the world to conform himself to other people. On both sides there must have been great love and great patience to put up with it so long. When his letters from Drenthe to his parents became more and more melancholy, his father anxiously had written to Theo, "it seems to me that Vincent is again in a wrong mood. He seems to be in a melancholy state of mind; but how can it be otherwise? Whenever he looks back into the past and recalls to his memory how he has broken with all former relations, it must be very painful to him. If he had only the courage to think of the possibility that the cause of much which has resulted from his eccentricity lies in himself. I don't think he ever feels any self-reproach, only soreness against others, especially against the gentlemen at the Hague. We must be very careful with him for he seems to be in a fit of contrariness."

And they *are* so careful. When he comes back to them of his own will, they receive him with so much love and try all in their power to make him comfortable; they are proud too of the progress in his work, of which it must be said they had no great expectations at first. "Do you not like the pen drawings of the tower that Vincent sent you? It seems to come to him so easily," writes his father in the first days of December to Theo, and then on the twentieth of December, "You will be longing to know how things are getting on with Vincent. At first it seemed hopeless, but by and by things have arranged themselves, especially since we approved of his staying here for some time to make studies. He wanted the inner room fitted up for him; we did not think it a very fit abode for him, but we had a nice stove put there; as the room had a stone floor we had it covered with boards, and made it as comfortable as possible: we put a bed in it on a wooden stand, that it might not be too damp. Now we will make the room nicely warm and dry, so that it may turn out better than we expected. I proposed to have a large window made in it but he did not want that. In short, with real courage we undertake this new experiment and we intend to leave him perfectly free in his peculiarities of dress, etc. The people here have seen him anyhow, and though it is a pity he is so reserved in manner, we cannot change the fact of his being eccentric...." "He seems to occupy himself a great deal with your plans for the future, but you will be wise enough not to let yourself be influenced to do things that are not practical, for alas that certainly is his foible. One thing is certain, he works hard and finds here lots of subjects, he has made already several drawings, which we like very much." Such is the feeling from their side; but Vincent is not satisfied with all that kindness and wants a deeper understanding of his innermost self than his parents can give, however much they try. When about the middle of January '84 his mother meets with an accident and is brought home from Helmond with a broken leg, the relations become less strained. Vincent, who has become an expert nurse in the Borinage, helps to nurse his mother with the greatest devotion, and in every letter of that time they praise him for his faithful help. "Vincent is untiring, and the rest of his time he devotes to his painting and drawing with the greatest zeal." "The doctor praised Vincent for his ability and care." "Vincent proves an ideal nurse and at the same time he works with the greatest ambition." "I fervently hope that his work may find success for it is edifying to see how much he works," is told in the letters of February.

Vincent's own letters at that time are gloomy and full of complaints and unjust reproaches to Theo that he never sells anything for him and does not even try to, ending at last with the bitter cry: "A wife you cannot give me, a child you cannot give me, work you cannot give me —money yes, but what is the use of it when I must miss all the rest!" And Theo, who always understands him, never gives a sharp or angry answer to those reproaches: a light sarcasm is the only reply he sometimes gives to such outbursts. In May Vincent's spirits rise somewhat on his moving into a new, larger studio, two rooms in the house of the sexton of the Catholic church. Shortly after, van Rappard comes to spend some time with him again, and besides, Vincent had during his mother's illness come more in contact with neighbours and friends in the village, who daily came to visit the patient, so that he writes in those days, "I have had a much pleasanter time with the people here than at first, which is worth a great deal to me, for one must have some distraction now and then, and when one feels too lonely the work suffers from it." But with a prophetic glance he continues, "One must keep in mind however that these things do not always last." Indeed, difficult times were approaching for him again. With one of his mother's visitors, the youngest of three sisters who lived next door to the vicarage, he had soon got into a more intimate relation; she was much older than he and neither beautiful nor gifted, but she had an active mind and a kind heart. She often visited the poor with Vincent; they walked much together, and on her part at least the friendship soon changed into love. As to Vincent, though his letters do not give the impression of any passionate feeling for her (the fact is he writes very little about it), yet he seems to have been inclined to marry her, but the family vehemently protested against the plan, and violent scenes took place between the sisters, which were not conducive to keep Vincent in a pleasant mood.

"Vincent works hard but he is not very sociable," writes his mother in July, and it will get worse still, for the young woman, violently excited by the scenes with her sisters, tries to commit suicide, which fails, but shocks her health so much that she had to be nursed at a doctor's in Utrecht. She quite recovered and after half a year she came back to Nuenen, but their relations were broken for ever and the whole affair left Vincent in a gloomy, bitter mood.

For his parents the consequences were also painful, because the neighbours avoided the vicarage from that time, not wishing to meet Vincent, "which is a great privation for me, but it is not your mother's way to complain," the latter writes in October of that year. It is in those days that van Rappard once more comes to stay with them. "He is not a talkative person, but a hard worker," writes mother, and van Rappard himself writes in 1890, in the letter to her, quoted above, "how often do I think of the studies of the weavers which he made in Nuenen, with what intensity of feeling did he depict their lives, what deep melancholy pervaded them, however clumsy the execution of his work may have been then. And what beautiful studies he made of the old church tower in the churchyard. I always remember a moonlight effect of it, which particularly struck me at that time. When I think of those studies in those two rooms near the church, it recalls to my mind so many memories, and reminds me of the whole surroundings, the cheerful hospitable vicarage with its beautiful garden, the family Begemann, our visits to the weavers and peasants, how I did enjoy it all."

After van Rappard's visit Vincent has no other distraction than a few acquaintances in Eindhoven, with whom he has come into contact through the house painter, who furnishes his colours. They are a former goldsmith, Hermans, a tanner, Kersemakers, and also a telegraphist whose name is not mentioned, all of whom Vincent initiates into the art of painting. Mr. Kersemakers has recorded his reminiscences of that time in the weekly "De Amsterdammer" of the 14th and 21st of April 1912, and gives among others the following description of Vincent's studio, which according to him looked quite "Bohemian."

"It was quite astonishing to see how crowded the place was with pictures, with drawings in water-colour and chalk; heads of men and women whose negro-like turned up noses, projecting jawbones and large ears were strongly accentuated, the fists callous and furrowed; weavers and weavers' looms, women driving the shuttle, peasants planting potatoes, women busy weaving, innumerable still-lives, at least ten studies in oil of the old church tower at Nuenen, of which he was so fond, and which he had painted in all seasons of the year and in all weathers (afterwards this old tower was demolished by the Nuenen Vandals, as he called them).

"Heaps of ashes around the stove, which never had seen brush or polish, a few frayed out rush-bottomed chairs, and a cupboard with at least thirty different birds' nests, all kinds of moss and plants brought from the heath, some stuffed birds, shuttles, spinning-wheel, bed-warmer, all sorts of farmers' tools, old caps and hats, dirty women's bonnets, wooden shoes, etc." He also tells about their trip to Amsterdam (in the autumn of 1885) to see the "Ryksmuseum," how Vincent in his rough ulster and his inseparable fur cap was calmly sitting painting a few small views of the town in the waiting room of the station; how they saw the Rembrandts in the museum, how Vincent could not tear himself away from the "Jewish Bride" and said at last, "Do you know that I would give ten years of my life if I could sit here before this picture a fortnight, with nothing but a crust of dry bread for food."

Dry bread was nothing unusual to him; according to Kersemakers, Vincent never ate it otherwise, in order not to indulge himself too much. His impression of Vincent's work is given as follows: "At my first visit in Nuenen I could not understand it at all, it was so totally different from what I expected, it was so strong, so coarse and unfinished that I could not possibly admire it or see anything in it.

"At my second visit the impression was already much better, though I thought in my ignorance that he could not draw, or totally neglected the drawing of the figures, and I took the liberty of telling him straight out. I did not make him angry, he only laughed and said: 'You will think differently about it later on.'"

Meanwhile the winter days passed on gloomily enough at the vicarage. "For Vincent I should wish that the winter were over, he cannot work out of doors and the long evenings are not profitable for his work. We often think that it would be better for him to be among people of his own profession, but we cannot dictate to him," writes his father in December, and mother complains, "how is it possible to behave so unkindly. If he has wishes for the future, let him exert himself, he is still young enough; it is almost impossible to bear it. I think he wants a change, perhaps he might find something that would give him inspiration, here it is always the same thing and he never speaks to anyone." But still she finds one luminous point to mention: "We saw that Vincent received a book from you, he seems to read it with much pleasure. I heard him say 'that is a fine book,' so you have given him great pleasure. I am glad that we regularly get books from the reading club; the illustrations in the magazines interest him most, and then there is the Nouvelle Revue, etc., every week something new is a great pleasure to him." Incessantly Vincent continues his work in the gloomy cottages of peasants and weavers. "I never began a year of a more gloomy aspect, in a more gloomy mood," he writes on New Year's Day '85. "He seems to become more and more estranged from us," complains his father, whose letters became more and more melancholy, as if he is not equal to the difficulties of living together with his gifted, unmanageable son, and feels himself helpless against his unbridled violence. "This morning I talked things over with Vincent; he was in a kind mood and said there was no particular reason for his being depressed," says the latter, "may he meet with success anyhow," are the last words he writes about Vincent in a letter of the 25th of March. Two days later, coming home from a long walk across the heath, he fell down on the threshold of his home and was carried lifeless into the house. Hard times followed in the vicarage; mother could remain there another year, but for Vincent it brought immediate changes. In consequence of several disagreeable discussions with the other members of the family, he resolved to live no longer at the vicarage, but took up his abode in the studio, where he stayed from May to November. Henceforth there is not a single thing to distract him from his aim—to paint the peasant life. He spends those months in the cottages of the weavers or with the peasants in the field. "It is a fine thing to be right in the snow in the winter, right in the yellow leaves in autumn, in summer right in the ripe corn, in spring right in the grass, always with the peasant girls and reapers, in summer under the open skies, in winter near the open fireplace, and to know that it has always been so and will always be" (letter 425). He is now in harmony with himself and his surroundings, and when he sends Theo his first great picture, "The Potato-Eaters," he can say in good reason that it is "from the heart of peasant life."

An uninterrupted series of studies follow each other; the cottages of the old peasants and their witch-like wives, the old church tower of the cemetery, the autumn landscapes and the birds' nests, a number of still-lives and the strong drawings of the Brabant peasants. In Nuenen he also writes the beautiful passages about colour, in reference to Delacroix's laws of colours. It seems strange to hear him, who was called afterwards one of the first Impressionists, even Neo-impressionists, declare, "there is a school I think of impressionists, but I do not know much about it" (letter 402), and in his usual spirit of contradiction he afterwards adds, "from what you have told me about impressionism I have learned that it is different from what I thought it was, but as to me I find Israëls for instance so enormous that I am little curious about or desirous of anything different or new. I think I shall change a great deal in touch and colour but I expect to become rather more dark than lighter." As soon as he came to France he thought differently of it.

During the last days of his stay in Nuenen difficulties arise between him and the Catholic priest, who has long since looked askance at the studio next to his church, and now forbids his parishioners to pose for Vincent. The latter was already thinking about a change. He gives notice of leaving his studio the first of May, but starts for Antwerp, towards the end of November, leaving all his Brabant work behind. When in May his mother also leaves Nuenen, everything belonging to Vincent is packed in cases, left in care of a carpenter in Breda and— forgotten! After several years the carpenter finally sold everything to a junk dealer.

What Theo's opinion about his brother was at that time is shown in the letter to his sister of the 13th of October '85, in which he writes: "Vincent is one of those who has gone through all the experiences of life and has retired from the world, now we must wait and see if he has genius. I think he has.... If he succeeds in his work he will be a great man. As to the worldly success, it will perhaps be with him as with Heyerdahl [1]: appreciated by some but not understood by the public at large. Those however who care whether there is really something in the artist, or if it is only outward shine, will respect him, and in my opinion that will be sufficient revenge for the animosity shown him by so many others."

In Antwerp Vincent rents for 25 fr. a month a little room over a small paint-dealer's shop in the "Rue des Images" 194. It is but a very small room but he makes it cosy with Japanese prints on the wall, and when he has rented a stove and a lamp, he feels himself safe and writes with profound satisfaction, "no fear of my being bored I can assure you." On the contrary he spends the three months of his stay in one feverish intoxication of work. The town life which he missed so long

---

[1] Norwegian painter, then in Paris.

fascinates him; he has not eyes enough to see, nor hands enough to paint: to make portraits of all the interesting types he meets is his delight, and in order to pay the models he sacrifices everything he has. As for food he does not bother. "If I receive money my first hunger is not for food, though I have fasted ever so long, but the desire for painting is ever so much stronger, and I start at once hunting for models till there is nothing left," he writes.

When he sees in January that he cannot go on like that, the expenses being too heavy, he becomes a pupil of the Academy, where the teaching is free and where he finds models every day. Hageman and de Baseleer were there among his fellow pupils and from Holland there was Briët. In the evening he worked again in the drawing class and after that, often till late at night, at a club where they also draw from life. His health cannot stand such a strain and in the beginning of February he writes that he is literally worn out and exhausted, according to the doctor it is complete prostration. He seems not to think about giving up his work, however, though he begins to make projects for a change, for the course at the Academy is almost finished and he has already had many disagreements with his teachers, for he is much too independent and self-willed to follow their guidance. Something must be done. Theo thinks it better for Vincent to go back to Brabant, but he himself wants to go to Paris. Then Theo proposes to wait at least till June, when he shall have rented a larger apartment, but with his usual impetuosity Vincent cannot wait so long, and one morning in the end of February, Theo receives in his office at the Boulevard a little note written in chalk, that Vincent had arrived and awaits him in the Salon Carré of the Louvre. Probably he left all his work in Antwerp, perhaps his landlord the paint-dealer kept it for the unpaid rent of the room. Certain it is that none of the studies about which he writes, the view of the Park, of the Cathedral, Het Steen, etc., ever has been found again.

The meeting in the Louvre took place, and since then Vincent lived with Theo in the latter's apartment in the Rue de Laval. As there was no room for a studio he worked during the first month at Cormon's studio, which did not satisfy him at all, but when they moved in June to the Rue Lepic 54, on Montmarte, he had there a studio of his own and never went back to Cormon.

At Arles, Vincent reaches the summit of his art. After the oppressiveness of Parisian life, he, with his innate love of nature, revives in sunny Provence. There follows a happy time of undisturbed and immense productivity. Without paying much attention to the town of Arles itself with its famous remains of Roman architecture, he paints the landscape, the glorious wealth of blossoms in Spring in a series of orchards in bloom, the cornfields under the burning sun at harvest time, the almost intoxicating richness of colours of the autumn, the glorious beauty of the gardens and parks, "The Poet's Garden," where he sees as in a vision the ghosts of Dante and Petrarcha roaming about. He paints "The Sower," "The Sunflowers," "The Starlit Night," the sea at St. Marie: his creative impulse and power are inexhaustible. "I have a terrible lucidity at moments, when nature is so glorious in those days I am hardly conscious of myself and the picture comes to me like in a dream," and rapturously he exclaims, "Life is after all enchanting."

His letters henceforth, written in French, give a complete image of what passes within him. Sometimes when he has written in the morning, he sits down again in the evening to tell his brother how splendid the day has been. "I never had such a chance, nature is extraordinarily beautiful here," and a day later, "I know that I wrote to you yesterday but the day has been again so glorious. My only regret is that you cannot see what I see here."

Completely absorbed in his work as he is, he does not feel the burden of the great loneliness that surrounds him in Arles, for except a short acquaintance with MacKnight, Bock and the Zouave lieutenant Milliet, he has no friends whatever. But when he has rented a little house of his own on the Place Lamartine, and arranges it after his own taste, decorates it with his pictures, makes it a "maison d'artiste," then he feels the old longing again, which he has already uttered at the beginning of his painting career in 1880, to associate himself with another artist, to live together and to work together. Just then he receives a letter from Paul Gauguin from Bretagne, who is in the greatest pecuniary embarrassment, and who tries in this roundabout way to ask Theo to try to sell some of his pictures for him: "I wanted to write to your brother but I am afraid to bother him, he being so busy from morning until night. The little I have sold is just enough to pay some urgent debts and in a month I shall have absolutely nothing left. Zero is a negative force...I do not want to importune your brother, but a little word from you on this head would set my mind at ease or at least help me to have patience. My God, how terrible are these money questions for an artist."

At once Vincent grasps at the idea of helping Gauguin. He must come to Arles and they will live and work together. Theo will pay the expenses and Gauguin will give him pictures in exchange. Again and again he insists on this plan with his innate perseverance and stubbornness, though Gauguin at first did not seem at all inclined to it. They had made each other's acquaintance in Paris, but it had been no more than a superficial acquaintance, and they were too different in talent and character ever to harmonize in the daily intercourse.

Gauguin, born in Paris in 1848, was the son of a Breton father, a journalist in Paris, and a Creole mother. His youth was full of adventures, he had gone to sea as cabin boy, and worked in a banker's office and had only painted in his leisure hours. Then after he had married and had a family, he devoted himself wholly to his art. His wife and children returned to her native city Copenhagen, as he was not able to provide for them, and he himself made a journey to Martinique where he painted, among others, his famous picture "The Negresses." He was now in Pont Aven in Brittany, without any source of income, so that the great need of money made him accept Vincent's proposition and come to Arles. The whole undertaking was a sad failure and had for Vincent a fatal end.

Notwithstanding the months of superhuman exertion which lay behind him, he strained every nerve in a last manifestation of power before the arrival of Gauguin. "I am conceited enough to want to make a certain impression on Gauguin by my painting. I have finished as far as possible the things I had undertaken, pushed by the great desire to show him something new, and not to undergo his influence before I have shown him indisputably my own originality," writes Vincent in letter 556. When we know that to this last work belongs one of Vincent's most famous pictures, "la chambre à coucher," and the series, "The Poet's Garden," it makes us feel rather sceptical about Gauguin's later assertion that before his arrival Vincent had only been bungling a little, and that he only made progress after Gauguin's lessons. We know then what to think of Gauguin's whole description of the episode at Arles, which is such a mixture of truth and fiction.[2]

The fact is that Vincent was completely exhausted and overstrained, and was no match for the iron Gauguin with his strong nerves and cool arguing. It became a silent struggle between them, and the endless discussions held while smoking in the little yellow house were not fit to calm Vincent. "Your brother is indeed a little agitated and I hope to calm him by and by," Gauguin writes to Theo, shortly after his arrival at Arles. And to Bernard he tells more intimately how little sympathy there really is between Vincent and himself. "Vincent and I generally agree very little especially about painting. He admires Daudet, Daubigny, Ziem, and the great Rousseau, all people whom I cannot bear. And on the contrary he detests Ingres, Raphaël, Degas, all people whom I admire. I answer, 'Brigadier, you are right,' in order to have peace. He loves my pictures very much, but when I make them

2 "Paul Gauguin," by Chas. Morice, Mercure de France, 1903.

he always finds I am wrong in this or that. He is romantic and I rather inclined to the primitive state." [3] And in later years when Gauguin again remembers this period he writes, "between two beings, he and I, he like a Vulcan, and I boiling too, a kind of struggle was preparing itself...." [4] The situation in consequence becomes more and more strained. In the latter half of December Theo receives from Gauguin the following letter: "Dear Mr. van Gogh,—I would be greatly obliged to you for sending me a part of the money for the pictures sold. After all I must go back to Paris, Vincent and I simply cannot live together in peace, in consequence of incompatibility of temper, and he as well as I, we need quiet for our work. He is a man of remarkable intelligence, whom I highly respect and leave with regret, but I repeat it is necessary. I appreciate all the delicacy in your conduct towards me, and I beg you to excuse my decision." Vincent also writes, in letter 565, that Gauguin seems to be tired of Arles, of the yellow house, and of himself. But the quarrel is made up, Gauguin asks Theo to consider his return to Paris as an imaginary thing, and the letter he had written him as a bad dream. But it is only the calm before the storm.

The day before Christmas,—Theo and I were just engaged to be married and intended to go together to Holland—(I was staying in Paris with my brother A. Bonger, the friend of Theo and Vincent)—a telegram arrived from Gauguin which called Theo to Arles. Vincent had on the evening of the 24th of December, in a state of violent excitement, "un accès de fièvre chaude," (an attack of high fever) cut off a piece of his ear and brought it as a gift to a woman in a brothel. A big tumult had been raised. Roulin the postman had seen Vincent home, the police had interfered, had found Vincent bleeding and unconscious in bed, and sent him to the hospital. Theo found him there in a severe crisis, and stayed with him during the Christmas days. The doctor considered his condition very serious. "There were moments while I was with him that he was well, but very soon after he fell back into his worries about philosophy and theology. It was painfully sad to witness, for at times all his suffering overwhelmed him and he tried to weep but he could not; poor fighter and poor, poor sufferer; for the moment nobody can do anything to relieve his sorrow and yet he feels deeply and strongly. If he might have found somebody to whom he could have disclosed his heart, it would perhaps never have gone thus far," Theo wrote to me after he had come back to Paris with Gauguin, and a day later, "there is little hope, but during his life he has done more than many others, and he has suffered and struggled more than

3 "Paul Gauguin," by Chas. Morice, *Mercure de France,* 1903.
4 Emile Bernard, Paris, 1901, "Letters of V. van Gogh."

most people could have done. If it must be that he dies, be it so, but my heart breaks when I think of it." The anxiety lasted a few more days. Dr. Rey, the house doctor of the hospital, to whose care Theo had entrusted him so urgently, kept him constantly informed. "I shall always be glad to send you tidings, for I too have a brother, I too have been separated from my family," he writes the 29th of December when the tidings are still very bad. The Protestant clergyman, the Rev. Salles, also visits Vincent and writes to Theo about his condition, and then there is last but not least the postman, Roulin, who is quite dismayed at the accident that befell his friend Vincent, with whom he spent so many pleasant hours at the "Café de la Gare" of Joseph Ginoux, and who has painted such beautiful portraits of him and his whole family! Every day he goes to the hospital for tidings and conveys them faithfully to Paris; as he is not a good penman, his two sons, Armand and Camille, serve him in turn as secretary. His wife too who posed for the "Berceuse" (Mme. Ginoux was the original of the "Arlésienne") visits her sick friend, and the first sign of recovery is when Vincent asks her about little Marcelle, the handsome baby he had painted such a short time ago. Then there comes a sudden change for the better in his condition. The Rev. Salles writes on the 31st of December, that he had found Vincent perfectly calm, and that he is longing to start work again. A day later, Vincent himself writes a short note in pencil to reassure Theo, and on the second of January there comes another note from him, to which Dr. Rey had added a word of reassurance. The 3rd of January an enthusiastic letter of Roulin's, "Vincent has quite recovered. He is better than before that unfortunate accident happened to him," and he, Roulin, will go to the doctor and tell him to allow Vincent to go back to his pictures. The following day they had been out and spent four hours together. "I am very sorry my first letters were so alarming and I beg your pardon; I am glad to say I have been mistaken in this case. He only regrets all the trouble he has given you, and he is sorry for the anxiety he has caused. You may be assured that I will do all I can to give him some distraction," writes Roulin.

On the 7th of January Vincent leaves the hospital, apparently entirely recovered, but, alas, at every great excitement or fatigue, the nervous attacks return ... they last long or shorter, but leave him also periods of almost perfect health, during which he goes back to his work with the old vigour. In February he is taken back to the hospital for a short time, but after his return to his little house, the neighbours have grown afraid of him and send a petition to the mayor, saying that it is dangerous to leave him at liberty, in consequence of which he is actually again sent to the hospital on the 27th of February—this time without any cause. Vincent himself for a whole month keeps the deepest silence about this unhappy affair, but the Rev. Salles sends Theo a faithful report. On the 2nd of March he writes, "The neighbours have raised a tumult out of nothing. The acts with which they have reproached your brother (even if they were exact), do not justify taxing a man with alienation or depriving him of his liberty. Unfortunately, the foolish act which necessitated his first removal to the hospital made people interpret in a quite unfavourable way every singular deed which the poor young man might perform; from anyone else it would remain unobserved, from him, everything takes at once a particular importance.... As I told you yesterday, at the hospital he has won everybody's favour and after all it is the doctor and not the chief of police who has to judge in these matters." The whole affair makes a deep impression on Vincent and again causes an attack from which he recovers with astonishing rapidity. It is again the Rev. Salles who tells Theo of Vincent's recovery. On the 18th of March he writes, "Your brother has spoken to me with perfect calmness and lucidity of mind about his condition and also about the petition signed by his neighbours. The petition grieves him very much. 'If the police,' he says, 'had protected my liberty by preventing the children and even the grown-ups from crowding around my house and climbing the windows as they have done, (as if I were a curious animal), I should have more easily retained my self-possession, at all events I have done no harm to anyone.' In short, I found your brother transformed, may God maintain this favourable change. His condition has something indescribable, and it is impossible to understand the sudden and complete changes which have taken place in him. It is evident that as long as he is in the condition in which I found him, there can be no question of interning him in an asylum; nobody, as far as I know, would have this sinister courage." A day after this interview with the Rev. Salles, Vincent himself for the first time writes again to Theo and justly complains that such repeated emotions might become the cause of a passing nervous attack changing to a chronic evil. And with quiet resignation, he adds, "to suffer without complaint is the only lesson we have to learn in this life."

He soon recovers his liberty but continues to live in the hospital for a short time, until the Rev. Salles shall have found him new lodgings in a different part of the town. His health is so good that the Rev. Salles writes on the 19th of April, "sometimes even no traces seem left of the disease which has affected him so vividly." But when he was going to arrange with the new landlord, he suddenly avowed to the Rev. Salles that he lacked the courage to start again a new studio, and that he himself thought it best to go to an asylum for a few months. "He is fully conscious of his condition, and speaks with me about his illness, which he fears will come back, with a touching openheartedness and simplicity," writes the Rev. Salles. "I am not fit," he told me the day before yesterday, "to govern myself and my affairs. I feel quite different than I was before." The Rev. Salles had then looked around and advised the asylum of St. Rémy, situated quite near Arles; he adds that the doctors at Arles approve of it, "given the state of isolation in which your brother would find himself upon leaving the hospital."

It was that which troubled Theo mostly. "Yes," he wrote to me, shortly before our marriage, in answer to my question if Vincent would not rather return to Paris, or spend some time with his mother and sisters in Holland, as he was so alone in Arles, "one of the greatest difficulties is, that whether in good or bad health his life is so barren of distraction. But if you knew him you would feel doubly how difficult is the solution of the question what must and can be done for him.

"As you know he has long since broken with what is called convention. His way of dressing and his manners show directly that he is an unusual personality and people who see him say, 'he is mad.' To me it does not matter, but for mother that is impossible. Then there is something in his way of speaking that makes people either like or dislike him strongly. He has always people around him, who sympathize with him, but also many enemies. It is impossible for him to associate with people in an indifferent way. It is either the one or the other, even to those who are his best friends it is difficult to remain on good terms with him, as he spares nobody's feelings. If I had time for it, I would go to him and, for instance, take a walking tour with him. That is the only thing, I imagine, that would do him good. If I can find somebody among the painters who would like to do it, I will send him. But those with whom he would like to go, are somewhat afraid of him, a circumstance which the visit of Gauguin did not change, on the contrary.

"Then there is another thing which makes me afraid to have him come here. In Paris he saw so many things which he liked to paint, but again and again it was made impossible for him to do so. Models would not pose for him, he was forbidden to paint on the street, and with his irascible temper this caused many unpleasant scenes, which excited him so much that he became unapproachable to everybody and at last he got a great dislike of Paris. If he himself had wanted to come back here, I would not hesitate for a moment...but again I think I can do no better than to let him follow his own wishes. A quiet life is impossible for him, except alone with nature or with very simple people like the Roulins, for wherever he passes he leaves the trace of his passing. Whatever he sees that is wrong he must criticize and that often occasions strife.

"I hope that he will find, some time, a wife who will love him so much that she will share his life but it will be difficult to find one who would be fit for that. Do you remember that girl in 'Terre Vierge' by Tourgenief, who is with the nihilists and brought the compromising papers across the frontiers? I imagine she should be like that, somebody who has gone through life's misery to the bottom. . . . It pains me not to be able to do something for him, but for uncommon people uncommon remedies are necessary and I hope these will be found where ordinary people would not look for them."

When Vincent himself now resolves to go to St. Rémy, Theo's first impression is that this may be a kind of self-sacrifice so as to be in nobody's way, and he writes to him once more asking with emphasis, whether he would not rather go to Pontaven or go to Paris.

But as Vincent sticks to his resolution Theo writes to him: "I do not consider your going to St. Rémy a retreat as you call it, but simply as a temporary rest cure which will make you come back with renewed strength. I for my part attribute your illness principally to the fact that your material existence has been too much neglected. In an establishment like that of St. Rémy there is a great regularity in the hours for meals, etc., and I think that regularity will do you no harm, on the contrary." When Theo has arranged everything with the director of the establishment, Dr. Peyron, a free room for Vincent and a room where he can paint, and as much liberty as possible to wander about as he likes, Vincent leaves for St. Rémy on the 8th of May accompanied by the Rev. Salles who writes to Theo the next day: "Our voyage to St. Rémy has been accomplished under the most excellent conditions; Monsieur Vincent was perfectly calm and himself has explained his case to the director as a man who is fully conscious of his condition. He remained with me till my departure and when I took leave of him he thanked me warmly and seemed somewhat moved, thinking of the new life he was going to lead in that house. Monsieur Peyron has assured me that he will show him all the kindness and consideration which his condition demands." How touching sounds that, "somewhat moved," at the departure of the faithful companion! His leave-taking broke the last tie that united Vincent with the outer world and he stayed behind in what was worse than the greatest loneliness, surrounded by neurotics and lunatics, with nobody to whom he could talk, nobody who understood him. Dr. Peyron was kindly disposed, but he was a reserved silent character, and the monthly letters by which he keeps Theo informed of the situation are not full of the warm sympathy which the doctors in the hospital at Arles showed him.

A full year Vincent spent amid these cheerless surroundings, struggling with unbroken energy against the ever returning attacks of his illness, but continued his work with the old restless zeal, which alone can keep him living now that everything else has failed him. He paints the desolate landscape which he sees from his window at sunrise and sunset, he undertakes long wanderings to paint the wide fields, bordered by the range of hills of the Alps, he paints the olive orchards with their dismally twisted branches, the gloomy cypresses, the sombre garden of the asylum, and he painted also the "Reaper," "that image of death as the great book of Nature represents it to us."

It is no longer the buoyant, sunny, triumphant work from Arles; there sounds a deeper sadder tone than the piercing clarion sound of his symphonies in yellow of the last year: his palette has become more sober, the harmonies of his pictures have passed into a minor key.

"To suffer without complaint," well had he learned that lesson; and when in August the treacherous evil attacks him again, just when he had hoped to be cured for good, he only utters a desponding sigh, "I can see no possibility of again having hope or courage."

Having painfully struggled through the winter, in which however he paints some of his most beautiful works, the "Piéta" after Delacroix, the "Resurrection of Lazarus," and the "Good Samaritan" after Rembrandt, the "Quatre heures du jour" after Millet; a few months follow during which he is not able to work, but now he feels that he would lose his energy for ever if he stayed longer in those fatal surroundings, he must get away from St. Rémy. For sometime Theo had been looking around for a fit opportunity—near Paris and yet in the country—where Vincent could live under the care of a physician, who would at the same time be a friend to him, and when he had found this at last, by the recommendation of Pissarro at Auvers sur Oise, an hour by train from Paris, where lived Dr. Gachet who had been in his youth a friend of Cézanne, Pissarro and the other Impressionists, then Vincent returns from the south on the 17th of May 1890. First he was going to spend a few days with us in Paris; a telegram from Tarascon informed us that he was going to travel that night and would arrive at ten in the morning. Theo could not sleep that night for anxiety—if anything happened to Vincent on the way, he had but scarcely recovered from a long and serious attack and had refused to be accompanied by anyone. How thankful we were when it was at last time for Theo to go to the station!

From the Cité Pigalle to the Gare de Lyon is a long distance, it seemed an endless time before they came back and I began to be anxious that something had happened, when I saw at last an open fiacre enter the Cité, two merry faces nodded to me, two hands waved—a moment later Vincent stood before me.

I had expected to see a patient and there stood before me a strong, broad-shouldered man, with a healthy colour, a smile on his face and an expression of great resoluteness in his whole appearance; from all the self-portraits the one before the easel is most like him at that period. Apparently there had again come such a sudden puzzling change in his state as the Rev. Salles had already observed to his great surprise at Arles.

"He seems perfectly well, he looks much stronger than Theo," was my first thought.

Then Theo drew him to the room where was the cradle of our little boy, that had been named after Vincent; silently the two brothers looked at the quietly sleeping baby—both had tears in their eyes. Then Vincent turned smilingly to me and said, pointing to the simple crocheted cover on the cradle: "Do not cover him too much with lace, little sister."

He stayed with us three days and was all the time cheerful and lively. St. Rémy was not mentioned. He went out by himself to buy olives which he used to eat every day and which he insisted on our eating too; the first morning he was up very early and was standing in his shirt-sleeves looking at his pictures of which our apartment was full; the walls were covered with them—in the bedroom the "Blooming Orchards," in the dining-room over the mantelpiece the "Potato Eaters," in the sitting-room (salon was too solemn a name for the cosy little room) the great "Landscape from Arles," and the "Night View on the Rhône," besides to the great despair of our *femme de ménage,* there were under the bed, under the sofa, under the cupboards, in the little spare room, huge piles of unframed canvases, that were now spread out on the ground and studied with great attention.

We had also many visitors, but Vincent soon perceived that the bustle of Paris did him no good and he was longing to set to work again. So he started the 21st of May for Auvers, with an introduction to Dr. Gachet, whose faithful friendship was to become his greatest support during the short time he was to spend at Auvers. We promised to come and see him soon, and he also wanted to come back to us in a few weeks to paint our portraits. In Auvers he took up his lodgings at an inn and immediately set to work.

The hilly landscape with the sloping fields and thatched roofs of the village pleased him, but what he enjoyed most was to have models again, and again to paint figures. One of the first portraits he painted was that of Dr. Gachet, who immediately felt great sympathy for Vincent, so that they spent most of their time together and became great friends—a friendship not ended by death, for Dr. Gachet and his children continued to honour Vincent's memory with rare piety, that became a form of worship, touching in its simplicity and sincerity. "The more I think of it the more I think Vincent was a giant. Not a day passes that I do not look at his pictures, I always find there a new idea, something different each day.... I think again of the painter and I find him a colossus. Besides he was a philosopher...."

So Gachet wrote to Theo shortly after Vincent's death and speaking of the latter's love for art he says: "The word love of art is not exact, one must call it *faith,* a faith to which Vincent fell a martyr!" None of his contemporaries had understood him better.

It was curious to note that Dr. Gachet himself somewhat resembled Vincent physically (he was much older) and his son Paul—then a boy of fifteen years—resembled Theo a little.

Their house, built on a hill, was full of pictures and antiques, which received but scanty daylight through the small windows; before the house there was a splendid terraced flower-garden, behind, a large yard where all kinds of ducks, hens, turkeys and peacocks walked about in the company of four or five cats; it was the home of an original, but an original of great taste.

The doctor no longer practised in Auvers, but had an office in Paris where he gave consultations a few days a week, the rest of the time he painted and etched in his room, that looked most like the workshop of an alchemist of the Middle Ages. Soon after, the 10th of June, we received an invitation from him to come with the baby and spend a whole day in Auvers. Vincent came to meet us at the train and he brought a bird's nest as a plaything for his little nephew and namesake. He insisted upon carrying the baby himself and had no rest until he had shown him all the animals in the yard, where a too-loudly crowing cock made the baby red in the face for fear and made him cry, whilst Vincent cried laughingly, "the cock crows cocorico," and was very proud that he had introduced his little namesake to the animal world. We lunched in the open air and after lunch took a long walk; the day was so peacefully quiet, so happy, that nobody would have suspected how tragically a few weeks later our happiness was to be destroyed for ever. In the first days of July, Vincent visited us once more in Paris; we were exhausted by a serious illness of the baby—Theo was again considering the old plan of leaving Goupil and setting up his own business, Vincent was not satisfied with the place where the pictures were kept, and our removal to a larger apartment was talked of; so those were days of much worry and anxiety. Many friends came to visit Vincent, among others, Aurier, who had written recently his famous article about Vincent,[5] and who now came again to look at the pictures

[5] "Les Isolés," *Mercure de France,* Janvier 1890.

with the painter himself, and Toulouse Lautrec who stayed for lunch with us and made many jokes with Vincent about an undertaker they had met on the stairs. Guillaumin was also expected to come, but it became too much for Vincent, so he did not wait for this visit but hurried back to Auvers—overtired and excited, as his last letters and pictures show, in which the threatening catastrophe seems approaching like the ominous black birds that dart through the storm over the cornfields.

"I hope he is not getting melancholy or that a new attack is threatening again, everything has gone so well lately," Theo wrote to me the 20th of July, after he had taken me with the baby to Holland and himself had returned to Paris for a short time, till he also should take his holidays. On the 25th he wrote to me, "there is a letter from Vincent which seems very incomprehensible; when will there come a happy time for him? He is so thoroughly good." That happy time was never to come for Vincent; fear of the again threatening attack or the attack itself, drove him to death.

On the evening of the 27th of July, he tried to kill himself with a revolver. Dr. Gachet wrote that same evening to Theo the following note, "With the greatest regret I must bring you bad tidings. Yet I think it my duty to write to you immediately. At nine o'clock in the evening of to-day, Sunday, I was sent for by your brother Vincent who wanted to see me at once. I went there and found him very ill. He has wounded himself . . . as I did not know your address and he refused to give it to me, this note will reach you through Goupil." The letter reached Theo in consequence only the next morning and he immediately started for Auvers. From there he wrote to me the same day, the 28th of July: "This morning a Dutch painter [6] who also lives in Auvers brought me a letter from Dr. Gachet that contained bad tidings about Vincent and asked me to come. Leaving everything I went and found him somewhat better than I expected. I will not write the particulars, they are too sad, but you must know, dearest, that his life may be in danger. . . .

"He was glad that I came and we are together all the time . . . poor fellow, very little happiness fell to his share and no illusions are left him. The burden grows too heavy for him, at times he feels so alone. He often asks for you and the baby, and said that you would not imagine there was so much sorrow in life. Oh! if we could give him some new courage to live. Don't make yourself too anxious, his condition has been so hopeless before, but his strong constitution deceived the doctors." That hope proved idle. Early in the morning of the 29th of July Vincent passed away.

[6] Hirschig.

Theo wrote to me, "one of his last words was: 'I wish I could die now,' and his wish was fulfilled. A few moments and all was over. He had found the rest he could not find on earth.... The next morning there came from Paris and elsewhere eight friends who decked the room where the coffin stood with his pictures, which came out wonderfully. There were many flowers and wreaths. Dr. Gachet was the first to bring a large bunch of sunflowers, because Vincent was so fond of them....

"He rests in a sunny spot amidst the cornfields...."

From a letter of Theo's to his mother: "One cannot write how grieved one is nor find any comfort. It is a grief that will last and which I certainly shall never forget as long as I live; the only thing one might say is, that he himself has the rest he was longing for ... life was such a burden to him; but now, as often happens, everybody is full of praise for his talents.... Oh! mother he was so my own, own brother."

Theo's frail health was broken. Six months later, on the 25th of January 1891, he had followed his brother.

They rest side by side in the little cemetery between the cornfields of Auvers.

T. E. LAWRENCE

A controversial and dramatic figure, Lawrence of Arabia (who, in his last years preferred to be known as Aircraftsman Shaw) became one of the most-publicized men of his period, and a legend in his own time (1888–1935). Thomas Edward Lawrence was born in Wales, was graduated from Oxford in 1911, served an apprenticeship in archaeological expeditionary research, entered the British Army in 1914, and rose to attract the world's attention by his exploits in winning over the Arab world to the Allied cause in World War I. After service as a member of the British delegation to the Peace Conference and as adviser to the Colonial Office on Arab affairs, he came to feel that his efforts had been wasted, and that the British Government had betrayed its Arab friends. Neurotic by nature, he retired from public affairs, and retreated within himself, enlisting as a private in the British Air Force. He was killed in a motorcycle accident in 1935.

Besides his *Seven Pillars of Wisdom* (an account of his campaigns in World War I), some pages of which are reprinted here, he wrote in *The Mint* the story of his service in the Air Force, and published a new translation of the *Odyssey*. Lawrence was an exceedingly complex and self-tortured character, with some of the qualities of greatness and genius. The passage I have chosen recounts his physical and moral humiliation while a prisoner of the Turks, and his battle with himself to overcome that humiliation.

Ordeal in Arabia

RAIN had set in steadily, and the country was sodden wet.... Azrak lay favourably for us, and the old fort would be convenient headquarters if we made it habitable, no matter how severe the winter.

So I established myself in its southern gate-tower, and set my six Haurani boys (for whom manual labour was not disgraceful) to cover with brushwood, palm-branches, and clay the ancient split stone rafters, which stood open to the sky. Ali took up his quarters in the southeast corner tower, and made that roof tight. The Indians weatherproofed their own northwest rooms. We arranged the stores on the ground floor of the western tower, by the little gate, for it was the soundest, driest place. The Biasha chose to live under me in the south gate. So we blocked that entry and made a hall of it. Then we opened a great arch from the court to the palm-garden, and made a ramp, that our camels might come inside each evening.

Hassan Shah we appointed Seneschal. As a good Moslem his first care was for the little mosque in the square. It had been half unroofed and the Arabs had penned sheep within the walls. He set his twenty men to dig out the filth, and wash the pavement clean. The mosque then became a most attractive house of prayer. What had been a place shut off, dedicated to God alone, Time had broken open to the Evanescent with its ministering winds and rain and sunlight; these entering into the worship taught worshippers how the two were one.

Our prudent Jemadar's next labour was to make positions for machine-guns in the upper towers, from whose tops the approaches lay at mercy. Then he placed a formal sentry (a portent and cause of wonder in Arabia) whose main duty was the shutting of the postern gate at sundown. The door was a poised slab of dressed basalt, a foot thick, turning on pivots of itself, socketed into threshold and lintel. It took a great effort to start swinging, and at the end went shut with a clang and crash which made tremble the west wall of the old castle. . . .

Then began our flood of visitors. All day and every day they came, now in the running column of shots, raucous shouting and rush of camel-feet which meant a Bedouin parade, it might be of Rualla, or Sherarat, or Serahin, Serdiyeh, or Beni Sakhr, chiefs of great name like ibn Zuhair, ibn Kaebir, Rafa el Khoreisha, or some little father of a family demonstrating his greedy goodwill before the fair eyes of Ali ibn el Hussein. Then it would be a wild gallop of horse: Druses, or the ruffling warlike peasants of the Arab plain. Sometimes it was a cautious, slow-led caravan of ridden camels, from which stiffly dismounted Syrian politicians or traders not accustomed to the road. One day arrived a hundred miserable Armenians, fleeing starvation and the suspended terror of the Turks. Again would come a spick and span group of mounted officers, Arab deserters from the Turkish armies, followed, often as not, by a compact company of Arab rank and file. Always they came, day after day, till the desert, which had been trackless when we came, was starred out with grey roads. . . .

In these slow nights we were secure against the world. For one thing, it was winter, and in the rain and the dark few men would venture either over the labyrinth of lava or through the marsh—the two approaches to our fortress; and, further, we had ghostly guardians. The first evening we were sitting with the Serahin, Hassan Shah had made the rounds, and the coffee was being pounded by the hearth, when there rose a strange, long wailing round the towers outside. Ibn Bani seized me by the arm and held to me, shuddering. I whispered to him, "What is it?" and he gasped that the dogs of the Beni Hillal, the mythical builders of the fort, quested the six towers each night for their dead masters.

We strained to listen. Through Ali's black basalt window-frame crept a rustling, which was the stirring of the night-wind in the withered palms, an intermittent rustling, like English rain on yet-crisp fallen leaves. Then the cries came again and again and again, rising slowly in power, till they sobbed round the walls in deep waves to die away choked and miserable. At such times our men pounded the coffee harder while the Arabs broke into sudden song to occupy their ears against the misfortune. No Bedouin would lie outside in wait for the mystery, and from our windows we saw nothing but the motes of water in the dank air which drove through the radiance of our firelight. So it remained a legend: but wolves or jackals, hyenas, or hunting dogs, their ghost-watch kept our ward more closely than arms could have done.

In the evening, when we had shut-to the gate, all guests would assemble, either in my room or in Ali's, and coffee and stories would go round until the last meal, and after it, till sleep came. On stormy nights we brought in brushwood and dung and lit a great fire in the middle of the floor. About it would be drawn the carpets and the saddle-sheepskins, and in its light we would tell over our own battles, or hear the visitors' traditions. The leaping flames chased our smoke-ruffled shadows strangely about the rough stone wall behind us, distorting them over the hollows and projections of its broken face. When these stories came to a period, our tight circle would shift over, uneasily, to the other knee, or elbow; while coffee-cups went clinking round, and a servant fanned the blue reed of the fire towards the loophole with his cloak, making the glowing ash swirl and sparkle with his draught. Till the voice of the story-teller took up again, we would hear the rain-spots hissing briefly as they dripped from the stone-beamed roof into the fire's heart.

At last the sky turned solidly to rain, and no man could approach us. In loneliness we learned the full disadvantages of imprisonment within such gloomy and ancient unmortared palaces. The rains guttered down within the walls' thickness and spouted into the rooms from their chinks. We set rafts of palm-branches to bear us clear of the streaming floor, covered them with felt mats, and huddled down on them under sheepskins, with another mat over us like a shield to throw off the water. It was icy cold, as we hid there, motionless, from the murky daylight until dark, our minds seeming suspended within these massive walls, through whose every shot-window the piercing mist streamed like a white pennant. Past and future flowed over us like an uneddying river. We dreamed ourselves into the spirit of the place; sieges and feasting, raids, murders, love-singing in the night....

As I was thinking how I would ride, there came to us, unheralded, one morning in the rain, Talal el Hareidhin, sheikh of Tafas. He was a famous outlaw with a price upon his head; but so great that he rode about as he pleased. In two wild years he had killed, according to report, some twenty-three of the Turks. His six followers were splendidly mounted, and himself the most dashing figure of a man in the height of Hauran fashion. His sheepskin coat was finest Angora covered in green broadcloth, with silk patches and designs in braid. His other clothes were silk; and his high boots, his silver saddle, his sword, dagger, and rifle matched his reputation.

He swaggered to our coffee-hearth, as a man sure of his welcome, greeting Ali boisterously (after our long sojourn with the tribes all peasants sounded boisterous), laughing broad-mouthed at the weather and our old fort and the enemy. He looked about thirty-five, was short and strong, with a full face, trimmed beard and long, pointed moustaches. His round eyes were made rounder, larger and darker by the antimony loaded on in villager style. He was ardently ours, and we rejoiced, since his name was one to conjure with in Hauran. When a day had made me sure of him, I took him secretly to the palm-garden, and told him my ambition to see his neighbourhood. The idea delighted him, and he companioned me for the march as thoroughly and cheerfully as only a Syrian on a good horse could. Halim and Faris, men specially engaged, rode with me as guards....

Properly to round off this spying of the hollow land of Hauran, it was necessary to visit Deraa, its chief town. Talal, however, could not venture in with me since he was too well known in the place. So we parted from him with many thanks on both sides, and rode southward along the line until near Deraa. There we dismounted. The boy, Halim, took the ponies, and set off for Nisib, south of Deraa. My plan was to walk round the railway station and town with Faris, and reach Nisib after sunset. Faris was my best companion for the trip, because he was an insignificant peasant, old enough to be my father, and respectable ...I was in Halim's wet things, with a torn Hurani jacket, and was yet limping from the broken foot acquired when we blew up Jemal's train. The slippery track made walking difficult, unless we spread out our toes widely and took hold of the ground with them: and doing this for mile after mile was exquisitely painful to me. Because pain hurt me so, I would not lay weight always on my pains in our revolt: yet hardly one day in Arabia passed without a physical ache to increase the corroding sense of my accessory deceitfulness towards the Arabs, and the legitimate fatigue of responsible command....

At the corner of the aerodrome by the south end of the station we struck over towards the town. There were old Albatros machines in the sheds, and men lounging about. One of these, a Syrian soldier, began to question us about our villages, and if there was much "government" where we lived. He was probably an intending deserter, fishing for a refuge. We shook him off at last and turned away. Someone called out in Turkish. We walked on deafly; but a sergeant came after, and took me roughly by the arm, saying "The Bey wants you." There were too many witnesses for fight or flight, so I went readily. He took no notice of Faris.

I was marched through the tall fence into a compound set about with many huts and a few buildings. We passed to a mud room, outside which was an earth platform, whereon sat a fleshy Turkish officer, one leg tucked under him. He hardly glanced at me when the sergeant brought me up and made a long report in Turkish. He asked my name: I told him Ahamed ibn Bagr, a Circassian from Juneitra. "A deserter?" "But we Circassians have no military service." He turned, stared at me, and said very slowly "You are a liar. Enrol him in your section, Hassan Chowish, and do what is necessary till the Bey sends for him."

They led me into a guard-room, mostly taken up by large wooden cribs, on which lay or sat a dozen men in untidy uniforms. They took away my belt, and my knife, made me wash myself carefully, and fed me. I passed the long day there. They would not let me go on any terms, but tried to reassure me. A soldier's life was not all bad. To-morrow, perhaps, leave would be permitted, if I fulfilled the Bey's pleasure this evening. The Bey seemed to be Nahi, the Governor. If he was angry, they said, I would be drafted for infantry training to the depot in Baalbek. I tried to look as though, to my mind, there was nothing worse in the world than that.

Soon after dark men came for me. It had seemed a chance to get away, but one held me all the time. I cursed my littleness. Our march crossed the railway, where were six tracks, besides the sidings of the engine-shop. We went through a side gate, down a street, past a square, to a detached, two-storied house. There was a sentry outside, and a glimpse of others lolling in the dark entry. They took me upstairs to the Bey's room; or to his bedroom, rather. He was another bulky man, a Circassian himself, perhaps, and sat on the bed in a nightgown, trembling and sweating as though with fever. When I was pushed in he kept his head down, and waved the guard out. In a breathless voice he told me to sit on the floor in front of him, and after that was dumb; while I gazed at the top of his great head, on which the bristling hair stood up, no longer than the dark stubble on his cheeks and chin. At last he looked me over, and told me to stand up: then to turn round. I obeyed; he flung himself back on the bed, and dragged me down with him in his arms. When I saw what he wanted I twisted round and up again, glad to find myself equal to him, at any rate in wrestling.

He began to fawn on me, saying how white and fresh I was, how fine my hands and feet, and how he would let me off drills and duties, make me his orderly, even pay me wages, if I would love him.

I was obdurate, so he changed his tone, and sharply ordered me to take off my drawers. When I hesitated, he snatched at me; and I pushed him back. He clapped his hands for the sentry, who hurried in and pinioned me. The Bey cursed me with horrible threats: and made the man holding me tear my clothes away, bit by bit. His eyes rounded at the half-healed places where the bullets had flicked through my skin a little while ago. Finally he lumbered to his feet, with a glitter in his look, and began to paw me over. I bore it for a little, till he got too beastly; and then jerked my knee into him.

He staggered to his bed, squeezing himself together and groaning with pain, while the soldier shouted for the corporal and the other three men to grip me hand and foot. As soon as I was helpless the Governor regained courage, and spat at me, swearing he would make me ask pardon. He took off his slipper, and hit me repeatedly with it in the face, while the corporal braced my head back by the hair to receive the blows. He leaned forward, fixed his teeth in my neck and bit till the blood came. Then he kissed me. Afterwards he drew one of the men's bayonets. I thought he was going to kill me, and was sorry: but he only pulled up a fold of the flesh over my ribs, worked the point through, after considerable trouble, and gave the blade a half-turn. This hurt, and I winced, while the blood wavered down my side and dripped to the front of my thigh. He looked pleased and dabbled it over my stomach with his finger-tips.

In my despair I spoke. His face changed and he stood still, then controlled his voice with an effort, to say significantly, "You must understand that I know: and it will be easier if you do as I wish." I was dumbfounded, and we stared silently at one another, while the men who felt an inner meaning beyond their experience, shifted uncomfortably. But it was evidently a chance shot, by which he himself did not, or would not, mean what I feared. I could not again trust my twitching mouth, which faltered always in emergencies, so at last threw up my chin, which was the sign for "No" in the East; then he sat down, and half-whispered to the corporal to take me out and teach me everything.

They kicked me to the head of the stairs, and stretched me over a guard-bench, pommelling me. Two knelt on my ankles, bearing down on the back of my knees, while two more twisted my wrists till they cracked, and then crushed them and my neck against the wood. The corporal had run downstairs; and now came back with a whip of the Circassian sort, a thong of supple black hide, rounded, and tapering from the thickness of a thumb at the grip (which was wrapped in silver) down to a hard point finer than a pencil.

He saw me shivering, partly I think, with cold, and made it whistle over my ear, taunting me that before his tenth cut I would howl for mercy, and at the twentieth beg for the caresses of the Bey; and then he began to lash me madly across and across with all his might, while I locked my teeth to endure this thing which lapped itself like flaming wire about my body.

To keep my mind in control I numbered the blows, but after twenty lost count, and could feel only the shapeless weight of pain, not tearing claws, for which I had prepared, but a gradual cracking apart of my whole being by some too-great force whose waves rolled up my spine till they were pent within my brain, to clash terribly together. Somewhere in the place a cheap clock ticked loudly, and it distressed me that their beating was not in its time. I writhed and twisted, but was held so tightly that my struggles were useless. After the corporal ceased, the men took up, very deliberately, giving me so many, and then an interval during which they would squabble for the next turn, ease themselves, and play unspeakably with me. This was repeated often, for what may have been no more than ten minutes. Always for the first of every new series, my head would be pulled round, to see how a hard white ridge, like a railway, darkening slowly into crimson, leaped over my skin at the instant of each stroke, with a bead of blood where two ridges crossed. As the punishment proceeded the whip fell more and more upon existing weals, biting blacker or more wet, till my flesh quivered with accumulated pain, and with terror of the next blow coming. They soon conquered my determination not to cry, but while my will ruled my lips I used only Arabic, and before the end a merciful sickness choked my utterance.

At last when I was completely broken they seemed satisfied. Somehow I found myself off the bench, lying on my back on the dirty floor, where I snuggled down, dazed panting for breath, but vaguely comfortable. I had strung myself to learn all pain until I died, and no longer

actor, but spectator, thought not to care how my body jerked and
squealed. Yet I knew or imagined what passed about me.

I remembered the corporal kicking with his nailed boot to get me
up; and this was true, for the next day my right side was dark and
lacerated, and a damaged rib made each breath stab me sharply. I remembered smiling idly at him, for a delicious warmth, probably
sexual, was swelling through me: and then he flung up his arm and
hacked with the full length of his whip into my groin. This doubled
me half-over, screaming, or, rather, trying impotently to scream, only
shuddering through my open mouth. One giggled with amusement.
A voice cried, "Shame, you've killed him." Another slash followed. A
roaring, and my eyes went black: while within me the core of life
seemed to heave slowly up through the rending nerves, expelled from
its body by this last indescribable pang.

By the bruises perhaps they beat me further; but I next knew that I
was being dragged about by two men, each disputing over a leg as
though to split me apart: while a third man rode me astride. It was
momently better than more flogging. Then Nahi called. They splashed
water in my face, wiped off some of the filth, and lifted me between
them retching and sobbing for mercy, to where he lay: but he now
rejected me in haste, as a thing too torn and bloody for his bed, blaming
their excess of zeal which had spoilt me: whereas no doubt they had
laid into me much as usual, and the fault rested mainly upon my
indoor skin, which gave way more than an Arab's.

So the crestfallen corporal, as the youngest and best-looking of the
guard, had to stay behind, while the others carried me down the narrow
stair into the street. The coolness of the night on my burning flesh,
and the unmoved shining of the stars after the horror of the past hour,
made me cry again. The soldiers, now free to speak, warned me that
men must suffer their officer's wishes or pay for it, as I had just done,
with greater suffering.

They took me over an open space, deserted and dark, and behind
the Government house to a lean-to wooden room, in which were many
dusty quilts. An Armenian dresser appeared, to wash and bandage me
in sleepy haste. Then all went away, the last soldier delaying by my
side a moment to whisper in his Druse accent that the door into the
next room was not locked.

I lay there in a sick stupor, with my head aching very much, and
growing slowly numb with cold, till the dawn light came shining
through the cracks of the shed, and a locomotive whistled in the
station. These and a draining thirst brought me to life, and I found
I was in no pain. Pain of the slightest had been my obsession and secret
terror, from a boy. Had I now been drugged with it, to bewilderment?

Yet the first movement was anguish: in which I struggled nakedly to my feet, and rocked moaning in wonder that it was not a dream, and myself back five years ago, a timid recruit at Khalfati, where something, less staining, of the sort had happened.

The next room was a dispensary. On its door hung a suit of shoddy clothes. I put them on slowly and unhandily, because of my swollen wrists: and from the drugs chose corrosive sublimate, as safeguard against recapture. The window looked on a long blank wall. Stiffly I climbed out, and went shaking down the road towards the village, past the few people already astir. They took no notice: indeed there was nothing peculiar in my dark broadcloth, red fez and slippers: but it was only by the full urge of my tongue silently to myself that I refrained from being foolish out of sheer fright. Deraa felt inhuman with vice and cruelty, and it shocked me like cold water when a soldier laughed behind me in the street.

By the bridge were the wells, with men and women about them. A side trough was free. From its end I scooped up a little water in my hands, and rubbed it over my face; then drank, which was precious to me; and afterwards wandered along the bottom of the valley, towards the south, unobtrusively retreating out of sight. This valley provided the hidden road by which our projected raid could attain Deraa town secretly, and surprise the Turks. So, in escaping I solved, too late, the problem which had brought me to Deraa.

Further on, a Serdi, on his camel, overtook me hobbling up the road towards Nisib. I explained that I had business there, and was already footsore. He had pity and mounted me behind him on his bony animal to which I clung the rest of the way, learning the feelings of my adopted name-saint on his gridiron. The tribe's tents were just in front of the village, where I found Faris and Halim anxious about me, and curious to learn how I had fared. Halim had been up to Deraa in the night, and knew by the lack of rumour that the truth had not been discovered. I told them a merry tale of bribery and trickery, which they promised to keep to themselves, laughing aloud at the simplicity of the Turks.

During the night I managed to see the great stone bridge by Nisib. Not that my maimed will now cared a hoot about the Arab Revolt (or about anything but mending itself); yet, since the war had been a hobby of mine, for custom's sake I would force myself to push it through. Afterwards we took horse, and rode gently and carefully towards Azrak, without incident, except that a raiding party of Wuld Ali let us and our horses go unplundered when they heard who we were. This was an unexpected generosity, the Wuld Ali being not yet of our fellowship. Their consideration (rendered at once, as if we had de-

served men's homage) momently stayed me to carry the burden, whose
certainty the passing days confirmed: how in Deraa that night the
citadel of my integrity had been irrevocably lost. . . .

I had never been a lofty person; on the contrary I had tried to be
accessible to everyone, even if it continually felt as though most of
them came and saw me every day. I had striven as eloquently as I
could by my own example to keep plain the standard of existence. I had
had no tents, no cooks, no body-servants: just my guards, who were
fighting men, not servile: and behold these Byzantine shopkeepers endeavouring to corrupt our simplicity! So I flung away from them in a
rage, determined to go south and see if anything active could be done,
in the cold weather, about the Dead Sea, which the enemy held as a
trench dividing us from Palestine.

My remaining money was handed over to Sherif Ali, for his maintenance till the spring; and the Indians were commended to his care.
Particularly we bought them fresh riding-camels, in case the need to
move came suddenly upon them in the winter; though the daily news
of a threat by the Turks against Azrak was scornfully discounted by
young Ali. He and I took affectionate leave of one another. Ali gave
me half his wardrobe: shirts, head-cloths, belts, tunics. I gave him an
equivalent half of mine, and we kissed like David and Jonathan, each
wearing the other's clothes. Afterwards, with Rahail only, on my two
best camels, I struck away southward.

We left Azrak one evening, riding into a glowing west, while over
our heads schools of cranes flew into the sunset like the out-drawn
barbs of arrows. It was toilsome from the start. Night was deep by
Wadi Butum, where the conditions became even worse. All the plain
was wet, and our poor camels slithered and fell time and again. We
fell as often as they did, but at least our part of sitting still, between
falls, was easier than their part of movement. By midnight we had
crossed the Ghadaf and the quag felt too awful for further progress.
Also the mishandling at Deraa had left me curiously faint; my muscles
seemed at once pappy and inflamed, and all effort frightened me in
anticipation. So we halted.

We slept where we were, in the mud; rose up plated with it at
dawn; and smiled crackily at one another. The wind blew, and the
ground began to dry. It was important, for I wanted to reach Akaba
before Wood's men had left it with the return caravan, and their eight
days' start called for speed. My body's reluctance to ride hard was
another (and perverse) reason for forcing the march. Until noon we
made poor travelling, for the camels still broke through the loose crust
of flints, and foundered in the red under-clay. After noon, on the

higher ground, we did better, and began rapidly to close the white sky-tents which were the Thlaithakhwat peaks.

Suddenly shots rang out at close range, and four mouthing men dashed down the slope towards us. I stopped my camel peaceably. Seeing this they jumped off, and ran to us brandishing their arms. They asked who I was: volunteering that they were Jazi Howeitat. This was an open lie, because their camel-brands were Faiz. They covered us with rifles at four yards, and told us to dismount. I laughed at them, which was good tactics with Bedouin at a crisis. They were puzzled. I asked the loudest if he knew his name. He stared at me, thinking I was mad. He came nearer, with his finger on the trigger, and I bent down to him and whispered that it must be *"Teras"* since no other tradesman could be so rude. As I spoke, I covered him with a pistol hidden under my cloak.

It was a shooting insult, but he was so astonished that anyone should provoke an armed man, as to give up for the moment his thought of murdering us. He took a step back, and looked around, fearful that there was a reserve somewhere, to give us confidence. At once I rode off slowly, with a creepy feeling in my back, calling Rahail to follow. They let him go too, unhurt. When we were a hundred yards away, they repented themselves, and began to shoot, but we dashed over the watershed into the next depression, and across it cantered more confidently into safe ground.

From the ridge at sunset we looked back for an instant upon the northern plain, as it sank away from us greyly, save that here and there glowed specks or great splashes of crimson fire, the reflection of the dying sun in shallow pools of rain-water on the flats. These eyes of a dripping bloody redness were so much more visible than the plain that they carried our sight miles into the haze, and seemed to hang detached in the distant sky, tilted up, like mirage.

We passed Bair long after dark, when only its latest tent-fires still shone. As we went we saw the stars mirrored in a valley bottom, and were able to water our breathless camels in a pool of yesterday's rain. After their drink, we eased them for half an hour. This night-journeying was hard on both men and animals. By day the camels saw the irregularities of their path, and undulated over them; and the rider could swing his body to miss the jerk of a long or short stride: but by night everything was blinded, and the march racked with shocks. I had a heavy bout of fever on me, which made me angry, so that I paid no attention to Rahail's appeals for rest. That young man had maddened all of us for months by his abundant vigour, and by laughing at our weaknesses; so this time I was determined to ride him out, showing no mercy. Before dawn he was blubbering with self-pity; but softly, lest I hear him.

Dawn in Jefer came imperceptibly through the mist like a ghost of sunlight, which left the earth untouched, and demonstrated itself as a glittering blink against the eyes alone. Things at their heads stood matt against the pearl-grey horizon, and at their feet melted softly into the ground. Our shadows had no edge: we doubted if that faint stain upon the soil below was cast by us or not. In the forenoon we reached Auda's camp; and stopped for a greeting, and a few Jauf dates. Auda could not provide us a relay of camels. We mounted again to get over the railway in the early night. Rahail was past protest now. He rode beside me white-faced, bleak and silent, wrought up only to outstay me, beginning to take a half pride in his pains.

Even had we started fair, he had the advantage anyhow over me in strength, and now I was nearly famished. Step by step I was yielding myself to a slow ache which conspired with my abating fever and the numb monotony of riding to close up the gate of my senses. I seemed at last approaching the insensibility which had always been beyond my reach: but a delectable land for one born so slug-tissued that nothing this side fainting would let his spirit free. Now I found myself dividing into parts. There was one which went on riding wisely, sparing or helping every pace of the wearied camel. Another hovering above and to the right bent down curiously, and asked what the flesh was doing. The flesh gave no answer, for, indeed, it was conscious only of a ruling impulse to keep on and on; but a third garrulous one talked and wondered, critical of the body's self-inflicted labour, and contemptuous of the reason for effort.

The night passed in these mutual conversations. My unseeing eyes saw the dawn-goal in front; the head of the pass, below which that other world of Rumm lay out like a sunlit map, and my parts debated that the struggle might be worthy, but the end foolishness and a rebirth of trouble. The spent body toiled on doggedly and took no heed, quite rightly, for the divided selves said nothing which I was not capable of thinking in cold blood; they were all my natives. Telesius, taught by some such experience, split up the soul. Had he gone on, to the furthest limit of exhaustion, he would have seen his conceived regiment of thoughts and acts and feelings ranked around him as separate creatures; eyeing, like vultures, the passing in their midst of the common thing which gave them life.

Rahail collected me out of my death-sleep by jerking my head-stall and striking me, while he shouted that we had lost our direction, and were wandering toward the Turkish lines at Aba el Lissan. He was right, and we had to make a long cut back to reach Batra safely. We walked down the steeper portions of the pass, and then stumbled along Wadi Hafira. In its midst a gallant little Howeiti, aged perhaps fourteen, darted out against us, finger on trigger, and told us to stand and explain; which we did, laughing. The lad blushed, and pleaded that his father's camels kept him always in the field so that he had not known us either by sight or by description. He begged that we would not do him shame by betraying his error. The incident broke the tension between Rahail and myself; and, chatting, we rode ou. upon the Gaa. There under the tamarisk we passed the middle hour of the day in sleep, since by our slowness in the march over Batra we had lost the possibility of reaching Akaba within the three days from Azrak. The breaking of our intention we took quietly. Rumm's glory would not let a man waste himself in feverish regrets.

We rode up its valley in the early afternoon; easier now and exchanging jests with one another, as the long winter evening crept down. When we got past the Khazail in the ascent we found the sun veiled behind level banks of low clouds in the west, and enjoyed a rich twilight of the English sort. In Itm the mist steamed up gently from the soil, and collected into wool-white masses in each hollow. We reached Akaba at midnight, and slept outside the camp till breakfast, when I called on Joyce, and found the caravan not yet ready to start: indeed Wood was only a few days returned.

Later came urgent orders for me to go up at once to Palestine by air. Croil flew me to Suez. Thence I went up to Allenby's headquarters beyond Gaza. He was so full of victories that my short statement that we had failed to carry a Yarmuk bridge was sufficient, and the miserable details of failure could remain concealed.

While I was still with him, word came from Chetwode that Jerusalem had fallen; and Allenby made ready to enter in the official manner which the catholic imagination of Mark Sykes had devised. He was good enough, although I had done nothing for the success, to let Clayton take me along as his staff officer for the day. The personal Staff tricked me out in their spare clothes till I looked like a major in the British Army. Dalmeny lent me red tabs, Evans his brass hat; so that I had the gauds of my appointment in the ceremony of the Jaffa gate, which for me was the supreme moment of the war....

On our return to Akaba domestic affairs engaged the remaining free days. My part mostly concerned the bodyguard which I formed for private protection, as rumour gradually magnified my importance. On our first going up country from Rabegh and Yenbo, the Turks had been curious: afterwards they were annoyed; to the point of ascribing to the English the direction and motive force of the Arab

Revolt, much as we used to flatter ourselves by attributing the Turkish efficiency to German influence.

However, the Turks said it often enough to make it an article of faith, and began to offer a reward of one hundred pounds for a British officer alive or dead. As time went on they not only increased the general figure, but made a special bid for me. After the capture of Akaba the price became respectable; while after we blew up Jemal Pasha they put Ali and me at the head of their list; worth twenty thousand pounds alive or ten thousand dead.

Of course, the offer was rhetorical; with no certainty whether in gold or paper, or that the money would be paid at all. Still, perhaps, it might justify some care. I began to increase my people to a troop, adding such lawless men as I found, fellows whose dash had got them into trouble elsewhere. I needed hard riders and hard livers; men proud of themselves, and without family. By good fortune three or four of this sort joined me at the first, setting a tone and standard....He examined the applicants for my service, and thanks to him and to the Zaagi, my other commander (a stiff man of normal officer cut), a wonderful gang of experts grew about me. The British at Akaba called them cut-throats; but they cut throats only to my order. Perhaps in others' eyes it was a fault that they would recognize no authority but mine. Yet when I was away they were kind to Major Marshall, and would hold him in incomprehensible talk about points of camels, their breeds and ailments, from dawn till night time. Marshall was very patient; and two or three of them would sit attentive by his bedside, from the first daylight, waiting to continue his education as soon as he became conscious.

A good half (nearly fifty of the ninety) were Ageyl, the nervous limber Nejdi villagers who made the colour and the parade in Feisal's army, and whose care for their riding camels was such a feature of their service. They would call them by name, from a hundred yards away, and leave them in charge of the kit when they dismounted. The Ageyl, being mercenaries, would not do well unless well paid, and for lack of that condition had fallen into disrepute: yet the bravest single effort of the Arab war belonged to that one of them who twice swam down the subterranean water-conduit into Medina, and returned with a full report of the invested town.

I paid my men six pounds a month, the standard army wage for a man and camel, but mounted them on my own animals, so that the money was clear income: this made the service enviable, and put the eager spirits of the camp at my disposal. For my time-table's sake, since I was more busy than most, my rides were long, hard and sudden. The ordinary Arab, whose camel represented half his wealth, could not afford to founder it by travelling my speed: also such riding was painful for the man.

Consequently, I had to have with me picked riders, on my own beasts. We bought at long prices the fastest and strongest camels to be obtained. We chose them for speed and power, no matter how hard and exhausting they might be under the saddle: indeed, often we chose the hard-paced as the more enduring. They were changed or rested in our own camel-hospital when they became thin; and their riders were treated likewise. The Zaagi held each man bodily responsible for his mount's condition, and for fitness of his saddlery.

Fellows were very proud of being in my bodyguard, which developed a professionalism almost flamboyant. They dressed like a bed of tulips, in every colour but white; for that was my constant wear, and they did not wish to seem to presume. In half an hour they would make ready for a ride of six weeks, that being the limit for which food could be carried at the saddle-bow. Baggage camels they shrank from as a disgrace. They would travel day and night at my whim, and made it a point of honour never to mention fatigue. If a new man grumbled the others would silence him, or change the current of his complaint, brutally.

They fought like devils, when I wanted, and sometimes when I did not, especially with Turks or with outsiders. For one guardsman to strike another was the last offence. They expected extravagant reward and extravagant punishment. They made boast throughout the army of their pains and gains. By this unreason in each degree they were kept apt for any effort, any risk.

Abdulla and the Zaagi ruled them, under my authority, with a savagery palliated only by the power of each man to quit the service if he wished. Yet we had but one resignation. The others, though adolescents full of carnal passion, tempted by this irregular life, well-fed, exercised, rich, seemed to sanctify their risk, to be fascinated by their suffering. Servitude, like other conduct, was profoundly modified to Eastern minds by their obsession with the antithesis between flesh and spirit. These lads took pleasure in subordination; in degrading the body: so as to throw into greater relief their freedom in equality of mind: almost they preferred servitude as richer in experience than authority, and less binding in daily care.

Consequently the relation of master and man in Arabia was at once more free and more subject than I had experienced elsewhere. Servants were afraid of the sword of justice and of the steward's whip, not because the one might put an arbitrary term to their existence, and the other print red rivers of pain about their sides, but because these were the symbols and the means to which their obedience was vowed. They had a gladness of abasement, a freedom of consent to yield to their master the last service and degree of their flesh and blood, because their spirits were equal with his and the contract voluntary. Such boundless engagement precluded humiliation, repining and regret.

In this pledging of their endurance, it disgraced men, if from weakness of nerve or insufficiency of courage, they fell short of the call. Pain was to them a solvent, a cathartic, almost a decoration, to be fairly worn while they survived it. Fear, the strongest motive in slothful man, broke down with us, since love for a cause—or for a person—was aroused. For such an object, penalties were discounted, and loyalty became open-eyed, not obedient. To it men dedicated their being, and in its possession they had no room for virtue or vice. Cheerfully they nourished it upon what they were; gave it their lives; and, greater than that, the lives of their fellowship: it being many times harder to offer than to endure sacrifice. . . .

However, for the time the Arabs were possessed, and cruelty of governance answered their need. Besides, they were blood enemies of thirty tribes, and only for my hand over them would have murdered in the ranks each day. Their feuds prevented them combining against me; while their unlikeness gave me sponsors and spies wherever I went or sent, between Akaba and Damascus, between Beersheba and Bagdad. In my service nearly sixty of them died.

With quaint justice, events forced me to live up to my bodyguard, to become as hard, as sudden, as heedless. The odds against me were heavy, and the climate cogged the die. In the short winter I outdid them, with my allies of the frost and snow: in the heat they outdid me. In endurance there was less disparity. For years before the war I had made myself trim by constant carelessness. I had learned to eat much one time: then to go two, three, or four days without food; and after to overeat. I made it a rule to avoid rules in food; and by a course of exceptions accustomed myself to no custom at all.

So, organically, I was efficient in the desert, felt neither hunger nor surfeit, and was not distracted by thought of food. On the march I could go dry between wells, and, like the Arabs, could drink greatly to-day for the thirst of yesterday and of to-morrow.

In the same way, though sleep remained for me the richest pleasure in the world, I supplied its place by the uneasy swaying in the saddle of a night-march, or failed of it for night after laborious night without undue fatigue. Such liberties came from years of control (contempt of use might well be the lesson of our manhood), and they fitted me peculiarly for our work: but, of course, in me they came half by training, half by trying, out of mixed choice and poverty, not effortlessly, as with the Arabs. Yet in compensation stood my energy of motive. Their less taut walls flagged before mine flagged, and by comparison made me seem tough and active.

Into the sources of my energy of will I dared not probe. The conception of antithetical mind and matter, which was basic in the Arab self-surrender, helped me not at all. I achieved surrender (so far as I did achieve it) by the very opposite road, through my notion that mental and physical were inseparably one: that our bodies, the universe, our thoughts and tactilities were conceived in and of the molecular sludge of matter, the universal element through which form drifted as clots and patterns of varying density. It seemed to me unthinkable that assemblages of atoms should cogitate except in atomic terms. My perverse sense of values constrained me to assume that abstract and concrete, as badges, did not denote oppositions more serious than Liberal and Conservative.

The practice of our revolt fortified the nihilist attitude in me. During it, we often saw men push themselves or be driven to a cruel extreme of endurance: yet never was there an intimation of physical break. Collapse rose always from a moral weakness eating into the body, which of itself, without traitors from within, had no power over the will. While we rode we were disbodied, unconscious of flesh or feeling: and when at an interval this excitement faded and we did see our bodies, it was with some hostility, with a contemptuous sense that they reached their highest purpose, not as vehicles of the spirit, but when, dissolved, their elements served to manure a field....

REAR-ADMIRAL
RICHARD E. BYRD

Richard Evelyn Bird (1888–1957), descendant of one of America's oldest and most distinguished families, was born in Virginia, and after a term at Virginia Military Institute went on to Annapolis, where he was graduated from the Naval Academy in 1912. The urge to travel to far places was one that woke in him early, and at the age of twelve he had an experience that falls to the lot of few boys—he traveled around the world alone. He had been one of those who aspired to make the New York-to-Paris flight in 1927, but when Charles Lindbergh stole the march on his competitors, Byrd turned to the Antarctic and became this country's most famous explorer in that field.

On his 1934 expedition he determined to spend the winter alone at the Bolling Advance Weather Base, which, in his own words, "was planted in the dark immensity of the Ross Ice Barrier, on a line between Little America and the South Pole. It was the first inland station ever occupied in the world's southernmost continent." It had originally been planned to man the base with several men; this proved impossible, and Byrd had to choose between giving up the base or staying there alone. He chose to man it by himself. He has written that apart from the objective of obtaining certain meteorological data he wanted to do this out of a strong desire "to know that kind of experience to the full.

"I wanted," he wrote, "something more than just privacy in the geographical sense. I wanted to seek roots into some replenishing philosophy.... Out there on the South Polar barrier, in cold and darkness as complete as that of the Pleistocene, I should have time to catch up, to study and think and listen to the phonograph; and, for maybe seven months, remote from all but the simplest distractions, I should be able to live exactly as I chose, obedient to no necessities but those imposed by wind and night and cold, and to no man's laws but my own.

"You might think that a man whose life carries him into remote places would have no special need for quietude. Whoever thinks that has little knowledge of expeditions. Most of the time they move in fearful congestion and uproar, and always under the lash of time. Nor will they ever be different, so long as explorers are not rich men and so long as exploration itself deals with uncertainties. No doubt the world thinks it is a fine thing to reach one pole, or both poles, for that matter. Thousands of men have devoted the best part of their lifetimes to reaching one pole or the other, and a good many have died on the way. But among the handful who have actually arrived at Latitude 90, whether north or south, I doubt that even one found the sight of the pole itself particularly inspiring. For there is little enough to see: at one end of the earth a mathematical spot in the center of a vast and empty ocean, and at the other end an equally imaginary spot in the midst of a vast and windy plateau. It's not getting to the pole that counts. It's what you learn of scientific value on the way. Plus the fact that you get there and back without being killed.

"Now, I had been to both poles. But for me there was little sense of true achievement. Rather, when I finished the stocktaking, I was conscious of a certain aimlessness. This feeling centered on small but increasingly lamentable omissions. For example, books. There was no end to the books I was forever promising myself to read; but, when it came to reading them, I seemed never to have the time or the patience. With music, too, it was the same way; the love for it—and I suppose the indefinable need—was also there, but not the will or opportunity to interrupt for it more than momentarily the routine which most of us come to cherish as existence.

"This was true of other matters: new ideas, new concepts, and new developments about which I knew little or nothing. It seemed a restricted way to live. One might ask: Why not try to bring these things into daily existence? Must you go off and bury yourself in the middle of polar cold and darkness just to be alone? After all, a stranger walking down Fifth Avenue can be just as lonely as a traveler wandering in the desert. All of which I grant, but with the contention that no man can hope to be completely free who lingers within reach of familiar habits and urgencies. Least of all a man in my position, who must go to the public for support and render a perpetual accounting of his stewardship. Now, it is undeniably true that our civilization has evolved a marvelous system for safeguarding individual privacy; but those of us who must live in the limelight are outside its protection."

His adventure brought him to despair, and close to death. In the pages that follow, from his book *Alone,* he tells how he saw it through.

Alone

ROLLING ADVANCE WEATHER BASE, which I manned alone during the Antarctic winter night of 1934, was planted in the dark immensity of the Ross Ice Barrier, on a line between Little America and the South Pole. It was the first inland station ever occupied in the world's southernmost continent. My decision to winter there was harder, perhaps, than even some of the men at Little America appreciated. For the original plan had been to staff the base with several men; but...this had proved impossible. In consequence, I had to choose whether to give up the base entirely—and the scientific mission with it—or to man it by myself. I could not bring myself to give it up.

This much should be understood from the beginning: that above everything else, and beyond the solid worth of weather and the auroral observations in the hitherto-unoccupied interior of Antarctica and my interest in these studies, I really wanted to go for the experience's sake. So the motive was in part personal. Aside from the meteorological and auroral work, I had no important purposes. There was nothing of that sort. Nothing whatever, except one man's desire to know that kind of experience to the full, to be by himself for a while and to taste peace and quiet and solitude long enough to find out how good they really are.

It was all that simple. And it is something, I believe, that people beset by the complexities of modern life will understand instinctively. We are caught up in the winds that blow every which way. And in the hullabaloo the thinking man is driven to ponder where he is being blown and to long desperately for some quiet place where he can reason undisturbed and take inventory.... For fourteen years or so, various expeditions, one succeeding the other, had occupied my time and thoughts, to the exclusion of nearly everything else. In 1919 it was the Navy's transatlantic flight; in 1925, Greenland; in 1926, the North Pole; in 1927, the Atlantic Ocean; 1928–30, the South Pole; and 1933–35, the Antarctic again. In between there was no rest. An expedition was hardly finished before I was engaged in putting a new one together; and meanwhile I was lecturing from one end of the country to the other in order to make a living and pay off the debts of the completed expedition, or else scurrying around to solicit money and supplies for a new one....

I wanted something more than just privacy in the geographical sense. I wanted to sink roots into some replenishing philosophy. And so it occurred to me, as the situation surrounding Advance Base evolved, that here was the opportunity. Out there on the South Polar barrier, in cold and darkness as complete as that of the Pleistocene, I should have time to catch up, to study and think and listen to the phonograph; and, for maybe seven months, remote from all but the simplest distractions, I should be able to live exactly as I chose, obedient to no necessities but those imposed by wind and night and cold, and to no man's laws but my own.

Snow was still falling on Thursday, the thirty-first of May. The morning was dreary and stagnant; the temperature about 5° above. The calendar warned: "Radio schedule." I went about the preparations methodically. Before me now are the messages which I dispatched to Little America that day. One was to Chief Pilot June and Navigator Rawson, reminding them to swing the planes for compass deviations. Another was to my wife [in Virginia], suggesting that she take up with my secretary, Miss McKercher, and my representatives in the United States ways and means of reducing the expedition's expenses.

Dyer took these messages down, then read them back. . . . We talked back and forth nearly an hour and a half. From my desk in the shack I could hear the engine in the tunnel; for some reason it started skipping. "Wait," I spelled out to Dyer.

Unhooking the lantern, I went into the tunnel. The air was thick with exhaust gases. Thinking the mixture was at fault, I bent over the carburetor and tinkered with the needle valve. This had little effect. I remember straightening up. And that was the last conscious act of mine that I do remember.

The next thing I recall, I was down on my hands and knees; and through the drowsiness, like an echo from far away, came an insistent notion that something terribly important ought to be done. What it was exactly my mind couldn't tell; and I felt helpless to do anything about it. I don't know how long I remained in that position. It may be that the cold aroused me. Anyhow, after a little while I crawled into the shack. The radio desk emerged from the blur, and then I remembered what I was supposed to do. I fumbled for the key and signed off, thinking how hard it was to spell out what I had to say. If any acknowledgment came, I did not hear it; for I couldn't get the earphones on.[1]

My actions thereafter are uncertain; I don't really know which were nightmare and which were fact. I remember lying on the bunk, fully dressed, and hearing, as if with surprise, the irregular beat of the

[1] The radio log at Little America shows that twenty minutes or so elapsed between the time I said, "Wait" and the time I signed off, saying, "See you Sunday." This fixes approximately the interval I was in the tunnel.

engine in the tunnel and realizing that I must shut it off to escape asphyxiation. I rolled off the bunk and staggered to the door. Dizziness seized me, and my heart turned fantastic somersaults; but, as from a great distance, I could see the gray fumes of the exhaust smoke curling under the top sill; and the upper half of the tunnel, when I entered, was so foggy that I could not see as far as the alcove where the engine lay.

Very probably I dropped to my hands and knees, as I must have appreciated the necessity for keeping my head under the fumes and in the uncontaminated air near the floor. Anyhow, I was on my knees when I reached into the recess and threw the ignition switch. When I turned around, the light was gone in the doorway; this was puzzling until I recalled that the only light in the shack was the electric bulb over the radio desk, which burned only while the engine supplied current. Luckily the lantern was still burning on a box, where I had set it down before adjusting the engine. Pushing the lantern ahead of me, I crawled back to the shack and to the bunk.

Whatever did, in fact, occur during the rest of this last day in May, this I do know: that much of it was probably fantasy—a slow and wearying fantasy. Perhaps I did in truth roll off the bunk and try to replace the sheets on the register drum; else how to account for the vague recollection of seeing the glass frame on the floor some time in the afternoon? But the rest of it—the skyrocketing pain in my fore-head and eyes, the nausea, the violent beating of my heart, the illusion of being a thin flame drawn between two voids—they could not have been real. Only the cold was real: the numbness in the hands and feet, creeping like a slow paralysis through my body. At least, I could cope with cold. I grasped for the throat of the sleeping bag and eased in.

Once the ticking of the clocks roused me out of the stupor. I have no sure memory of winding them; but, so strong was the compulsion of habit, I do remember thinking bitterly that they ought to be wound and that register and thermograph sheets ought to be changed. Evi-dently I performed these tasks; for the instruments were still going next day; and the records, now in the possession of the U. S. Weather Bureau, show that the sheets were shifted at 2:00 P.M., two hours late. My only distinct memory from that period was arousing and thinking that I was blind. My eyes were open, but I could see nothing. Then I realized that I must be facing the wall. The lantern was out (from lack of fuel, I learned presently), but a dim glow showed in the side of the stove.

There is nothing more panicky than the loss of sight. I shall never forget the agony in Floyd Bennett's voice when we pulled him, terribly smashed up, from the debris of our crash landing. "I'm done for," he whispered; "I can't see anything." His face was a smear of oil; when I wiped it away and he could see again, the expression that transfigured his face was beautiful.

It is painful for me to dwell on the details of my collapse, particularly as the affairs of Advance Base are now receding into the gentling haze of the past. The subject is one that does not easily bear discussion, if only because a man's hurt, like his love, is more seemly when concealed. From my youth I have believed that sickness was somehow humiliating, something to be kept hidden. But the consequences of this collapse were never to depart during the rest of my stay at Advance Base; and my struggle against the one universal certainty played too large a part in my experience there to be omitted from this account.

I have a pretty clear idea concerning much that happened, almost too clear, in fact. I shall not, however, depend upon memory alone. During the days that followed, I set forth in the diary—as far as I was able —what I knew and remembered. How natural is the instinct which drives a man alone to pencil and paper, as if his destiny required the right last word and period.

The afternoon ran out its time; though my eyes would not stop aching and the pain would not quit my temples, just lying in the sleeping bag quieted the hammering of my heart. Gradually my mind cleared, and I tried to reconstruct the events preceding the episode in the tunnel. The exhaust vent over the engine, I decided, must have filled with rime, causing the poisonous gases to back into the tunnel. I was pretty sure that it was carbon monoxide. The instantaneous way I was struck down, the absence of any consciousness of suffocation bespoke these things, plus the symptoms—the splitting headaches, the nausea, the stabbing pains in my body and eyes, the hot and cold rushes of dizziness. What had saved me in the tunnel was the fact of my being dropped as though poleaxed. Since monoxide rises, the air at the bottom of the tunnel must have been all right; and the oxygen entering my blood brought me around.

All this represented a mind groping for bearings. To know I had escaped disaster in one form was only a preliminary step in the process of preparing to avert it in another. The fact was manifest that I was helpless, at least for the time being. I barely had strength to light the candle standing on the tin ledge directly over my head. If so simple a movement could empty me of the little strength that had returned, what chance did I have of bringing in food and fuel from the tunnels, let alone attending to the instruments? I could live many days without food. I could suck snow to quench thirst. But, ill and weak as I was, I could not live long without heat; and the fuel tank had to be filled every three days. Pondering such difficult matters was too much for me; my mind went blank again. When I awakened and looked at my wrist watch, the time was seven o'clock. I wasn't quite so weak, and my body craved water.

So I drew the flashlight from the sleeping bag and propped it on the edge of the bunk in order to direct the beam toward the stove. With this to guide me, I slipped from the bunk, clinging to the side for support. Waves of dizziness swept from head to foot, but after a little while I was able to reach the chair and push it toward the stove. A little water remained in the bucket on the stove; I dipped it out with a can. The first few swallows my stomach threw up; nevertheless, I persevered until I had at least a cupful down. Wondering why my teeth chattered so, I put my hand against the stove. It was out—no longer than a few minutes, evidently, else the water would have frozen. *Thursday . . . Thursday . . . the day to fill the tank.* So the tank was dry, as was the lantern; and if I wanted to have light and warmth, both must be filled at once.

The notes which I jotted down a few days afterward insist this stranger reeling in the dark acted with the utmost deliberation. Perhaps so. Between the pain and the weakness it was hard for more than one thought to find a lodgment. I managed to pull on my parka and mittens. Then I lifted the empty tank from the stand. Holding it by the handle with one hand and the flashlight with the other, I started into the tunnel. The nearest fuel drum—by the grace of God equipped with a spigot—was only fourteen feet from the door; but to make the distance I had to stop and put around my neck the loop attached to the flashlight so as to free one hand with which to steady myself. I walked slowly and uncertainly; as, years ago, I had walked for the first time after being desperately ill of typhoid fever while on a midshipman cruise to England.

The funnel lay on top of a barrel. I fitted it into the tank; and, while the tank was filling, I rested on a box. But, though I had the strength to lift the tank (it weighed about twenty-one pounds filled to the brim), I could not carry it far. After a few steps my heart was pounding, and the dizziness returned. I let go and slumped on the tool box, near the head of the tunnel. For how long? I really don't know. Long enough, anyhow, to be shaken by the cold. If I couldn't carry the tank, perhaps I could pull it, which was what I did—a few feet at a time. At least I remember doing that.

Inside the shack, I poured half a gallon or so of the precious stuff into a pitcher; this would do for the lantern. A lot spilled on the floor. Presently I succeeded in lifting the tank itself to the stand behind the stove. With that a feeling of relief possessed me for a moment. I could

now hold off the cold for at least two days, and maybe three if I
economized. Nevertheless, I didn't attempt to light the stove, dreading
the effort and knowing that I ought to be in the bunk; but, craving
light after the long darkness, I did light the lantern. The light was so
cheery that I was encouraged to attempt an observation at 10:00 P.M.
(Actually 8:00 P.M. my old time; for, a day or two previously, I had
advanced my clock two hours, as an experiment in moonlight saving,
so to speak.)

That was a mistake. I was able to climb the ladder all right, resting
at every rung; I pushed the door back with my head, waited a moment, and then hobbled to the instrument shelter, feeling dizzy and
utterly forlorn. I guessed the wind's velocity as being seventeen miles
per hour (the register trace shows an actual wind speed of only seven
miles), and noted the absence of aurora. But I was unspeakably weak
and sick again when I reached the bottom of the ladder. I must sleep,
I must sleep, something was saying inside me. In the escape tunnel I
groped around until I found the box of Phenobarbital pills. With the
box in my hand I stumbled to the hut. I got my parka, pants, and
shoes off; but the shirt was beyond me. Using the chair as a step, I
hung the lantern from its peg above the bunk, then climbed in, weighed
down by a sense of complete futility.

The instant the candle died, the darkness dropped like a blow.
Sleep was the great hunger; but it would not come, so cruel was the
pain in my head and back and legs. As I lay there, the intimation came
that I would not recover. Carbon monoxide poisoning is an insidious
thing. Once the haemoglobin in the blood stream and the lungs is
broken down, it takes the liver and spleen a long time to restore the
oxygen-carrying material. Even with the best of hospital care this is a
matter of weeks and sometimes months. For me the worst of the cold
and the darkest part of the night were yet to come. The sun was nearly
three months away. I could not persuade myself that I had the strength
to meet it. To some men sickness brings a desire to be left alone;
animal-like, their one instinct is to crawl into a hole and lick the hurt.
It used to be so with me. But that night, as never before, I discovered
how alone I was; and the realization evoked an indescribable desire
to have about me those who knew me best. Remembering the meticulous preparations, the safeguards which I had thrown about myself,
my soul was bitter with reproaches. My fort had become an ambush.
Nothing within the power of the night or cold had made it so. My
stupidity was to blame, and this I should have feared before the others.

Even in my stupor I seem to have recognized that the gasoline engine was not solely responsible. The engine dealt the blow which
knocked me down, but long before then I had partially perceived a

developing weakness. I remembered the notches I had taken up in my belt; the headaches and hurt in my eyes earlier in the month. Maybe the frost in my lungs was at fault. Maybe something was organically wrong with me. But I doubted that these by themselves could have depleted me so much. What reason I could muster indicted the stinking stove as the principal villain. Monoxide poisoning is not necessarily an instantaneous matter. It may be a gradual and cumulative process, brought about by intermittent exposure to the chemistry of the fumes. And the more I thought about the leaky joints in the stove, the more I blamed it.

But all this was shadowy in my mind that last night in May. I wavered between self-recrimination and hopefulness, between pain and an emptiness devoid of feeling. I knew that I was in a frightful mess, one that would involve my family, the expedition, and God only knew whom else. But it was hard to see what could be done about that. I lighted the candle, intending to write certain messages; but no paper was within reach. After a little while I blew out the candle. In my hand was the box of sleeping pills. I was reluctant to take one, not from squeamishness but from the fear that the drug would weaken me further. So, telling myself I would wait until four o'clock before resorting to the sedative, I put the box down. Sometime after three o'clock I drifted off into a dream of horrors....

June 1 was a Friday. A black Friday for me. The nightmare left me, and about nine o'clock in the morning I awakened with a violent start, as if I had been thrown down a well in my sleep. I found myself staring wildly into the darkness of the shack, not knowing where I was. The weakness that filled my body when I turned in the sleeping bag and tried to throw the flashlight on my wrist watch was an eloquent reminder. I was Richard E. Byrd, United States Navy (Ret.), temporarily sojourning at Latitude 80° 08' south, and not worth a damn to myself or anybody else. My mouth was dry and tasted foul. God, I was thirsty. But I had hardly strength to move. I clung to the sleeping bag, which was the only source of comfort and warmth left to me, and mournfully debated the little that might be done.

Two facts stood clear. One was that my chances of recovering were slim. The other was that in my weakness I was incapable of taking care of myself. These were desperate conclusions, but my mood allowed no others. All that I could reasonably hope for was to prolong my existence for a few days by hoarding my remaining resources; by doing the necessary things *very slowly* and with *great deliberation*. So long as he did that and maintained the right frame of mind, even a very ill man should be able to last a time. So I reasoned, anyway.

There was no alternative. My hopes of survival had to be staked on the theory.

But you must have *faith*—you must have faith in the outcome, I whispered to myself. It is like a flight, a flight into another unknown. You start and you cannot turn back. You must go on and on and on, trusting your instruments, the course you have plotted on the charts, and the reasonableness of events. Whatever goes wrong will be mostly of your own making; if it is to be tragedy, then it will be the commonplace tragedy of human vulnerability.

My first need was warmth and food. The fire had been out about twelve hours; I had not eaten in nearly thirty-six. Toward providing those necessities I began to mobilize my slender resources. If there had been a movie camera to record my movements, the resulting picture could have been passed off as slow motion. Every act was performed with the utmost patience. I lifted the lantern—and waited. I edged out of the sleeping bag—and rested on the chair beside the stove. I pulled on my pants, hiking them up a little bit at a time. Then the shirt. Then the socks. And shoes. And finally the parka. All this took a long time. I was shaking so from the cold that, when my elbow struck the wall, the sound was like a peremptory knock at the door. Too miserable to stick it out, I retreated to the sleeping bag; half an hour later the chill in my body drove me into a fresh attempt to reach the stove.

Faintness seized me as I touched foot to the floor. I barely made the chair. There I sat for some minutes, not moving, just staring at the candle. Then I turned the valve, and with the stove lids off waited for the wick to become saturated with the cold, sluggish oil. Thirst continued to plague me. Several inches of ice were in the water bucket. I dropped it on the floor, bottom up. A sliver of ice fell out, which I sucked until my teeth rattled from the cold. A box of matches was on the table. I touched one to the burner. A red flame licked over the metal ring; it was a beautiful thing to see. I sat there ten or fifteen minutes at least, absorbing the column of warmth. The flame burned red and smoky, when it should have been blue and clear; and studying it, I knew that this was from faulty combustion and was one source of my misfortunes. This fire was my enemy, but I could not live without it.

Thus this never-ending day began. To describe it all would be tedious. Nothing really happened; and yet, no day in my life was more momentous. I lived a thousand years, and all of them were agonizing. I won a little and lost a lot. At the day's end—if it can be said to have had an end—all that I could say was that I was still alive. Granting the conditions, I had no right to expect more. Life seldom ends gracefully or sensibly. The protesting body succumbs like a sinking ship going down with the certificate of seaworthiness nailed fast to the wheelhouse bulkhead; but the mind, like the man on the bridge, realizes at last the weakness of the hull and ponders the irony. If the business drags out long enough, as mine did, the essence of things in time becomes pitifully clear; except that by then it is wadded into a tight little scrap ready to be thrown away, as the knowledge is of no earthly use.

My thirst was the tallest tree in a forest of pain. The escape tunnel was a hundred miles away, but I started out, carrying the bucket and lantern. Somewhere along the way I slipped and fell. I licked the snow until my tongue burned. The escape tunnel was too far. But in the food tunnel my boots had worn a rut eighteen inches wide and six inches deep, which was full of loose snow. The snow was dirty, but I scraped the bucket along until it was nearly full, then pulled it into the shack, a foot or so at a time.

Snow took a long time to melt in the bucket, and I could not wait. I poured a little into a pan and heated it with alcohol tablets. It was still a soggy mass of snow when I raised it to my lips. My hands were shaking, and the water spilled down the front of my parka; then I vomited, and all that I had drunk came up. In a little while I tried again, taking sips too small to be thrown up. Then I crawled on top of the sleeping bag, drawing a heavy blanket over my shoulders, hoping I should somehow regain strength.

Nevertheless, I was able to do a number of small things, in a series of stealthy, deliberate sorties from the bunk. I attended to the inside thermograph and register, changing the sheets, winding the clocks, and inking the pens. The outlet ventilator was two thirds filled with ice; I could just reach it from the bunk with a stick which had a big nail in the end. After every exertion I rested; the pain in my arms and back and head was almost crucifying. I filled a thermos jug with warm water, added powdered milk and sugar, and carried the jug into the sleeping bag. My stomach crawled with nauseous sensation; but, by taking a teaspoonful at a time, I finally managed to get a cupful down. After a while the weakness left me, and I felt strong enough to start for the instrument shelter. I reached the hatch and pushed it open, but could go no farther. The night was a gray fog, full of shadows, like my mood. In the shack I lost the milk I had drunk. On the verge of fainting, I made for the bunk.

I won't even attempt to recall all the melancholy thoughts that drifted through my mind that long afternoon. But I can say truthfully that at no time did I have any feeling of resignation. My whole being re-

belled against my low estate. As the afternoon wore on, I felt myself
sinking. Now I became alarmed. This was not the first time I had
ever faced death. It had confronted me many times in the air. But
then it had seemed altogether different. In flying things happen fast:
you make a decision; the verdict crowds you instantly; and, when the
invisible and neglected passenger comes lunging into the cockpit, he
is but one of countless distractions. But now death was a stranger sitting in a darkened room, secure in the knowledge that he would be
there when I was gone.

Great waves of fear, a fear I had never known before, swept through
me and settled deep within. But it wasn't the fear of suffering or even
of death itself. It was a terrible anxiety over the consequences of those
at home if I failed to return. I had done a damnable thing in going to
Advance Base, I told myself. Also, during those hours of bitterness, I
saw my whole life pass in review. I realized how wrong my sense of
values had been and how I had failed to see that the simple, homely,
unpretentious things of life are the most important.

Much as I should have liked to, I couldn't consider myself a martyr
to science; nor could I blame the circumstances that had prevented
staffing the base with three men, according to the original plan. I had
gone there looking for peace and enlightenment, thinking that they
might in some way enrich my life and make me a more useful man. I
had also gone armed with the justification of a scientific mission. Now
I saw both for what they really were: the first as a delusion, the second
as a dead-end street. My thoughts turned to gall and wormwood. I was
bitter toward the whole world except my family and friends. The
clocks ticked on in the gloom, and a subdued whir came from the
register at my feet. The confidence implicit in these unhurried sounds
emphasized my own debasement. What right had they to be confident
and unhurried? Without me they could not last a day.

The one aspiration I still had was to be vindicated by the tiny heap
of data collected on the shelf in the escape tunnel. But, even as I seized
upon this, I recognized its flimsiness; a romanticized rationalization,
as are most of the things which men are anxious to be judged by. We
men of action who serve science serve only a reflection in a mirror.
The tasks are difficult, the objectives remote; but scholars sitting in
bookish surroundings tell us where to go, what to look for, and even
what we are apt to find. Likewise, they pass dispassionate judgment on
whatever we bring back. We are nothing more than glamorous middle-
men between theory and fact, materialists jobbing in the substance of
universal truths.

Beyond the fact that I had suffered to secure them, what did I know
about the theoretical significance of the records in the escape tunnel, of

the implications which might differentiate them from a similar heap of records gathered at Keokuk? I really didn't know. I was a fool, lost on a fool's errand, and that was how I should be judged.

At the end only two things really matter to a man, regardless of who he is; and they are the affection and understanding of his family. Anything and everything else he creates are insubstantial; they are ships given over to the mercy of the winds and tides of prejudice. But the family is an everlasting anchorage, a quiet harbor where a man's ships can be left to swing to the moorings of pride and loyalty.

The chill went out of the shack; and the heat from the stove, accumulating in a layer under the ceiling, wrapped the bunk as in a blanket. A little after six o'clock, as nearly as I could remember afterward, I sipped the last of the milk in the thermos jug. My body needed stronger nourishment, but I possessed nothing like the strength to cook a meal. I nibbled an Eskimo biscuit and a piece of chocolate, but my stomach was turning somersaults. So I got up and refilled the thermos jug with hot water and powdered milk, a really desperate task, as I had to cling to the table to keep from falling. The next several hours are a blank. Later, when I was able to make notes of what had happened to me, I could not remember anything at all. Perhaps I slept. When I looked at my watch again the time was about nine thirty. I was dazed and exhausted. The idea came to me that I ought to put out the stove to give myself a needed rest from the fumes; besides, there was no telling when I should have strength to fill the tank again. As I twisted the valve, the room went black. The next thing I knew I was on the floor. I pulled myself up by the stove. It was still warm; so I could not have been out very long.

I dropped into the chair, convinced that the end was near. Up till now I had been sustained by a conviction that the only way I could nullify my mistake and make reparation to my family was by transcending myself and surviving. But I had lost. I flung my arms across the table, and put my head down, spilling a cup of water I had in my hand. My bitterness evaporated, and the only resentment I felt was concentrated on myself. I lay there a long time, sobbing, "What a pity, what an infinite pity!" So my pride was gone as well. A Virginian, I was brought up to believe that a gentleman never gives way to his feelings. I felt no shame then, although I do now. Fear was gone, also. When hope goes, uncertainty goes, too; and men don't fear certainties.

The only conscious resolve left was to write a message to my wife— a last groping touch of the hand. Beyond the very personal things, I wanted her to understand why I had not tried to inform Little America of my plight (forgetting that it needed no explanation) and my reasons for going to Advance Base. There had to be that. Pencil and paper were on a shelf nearby. When I went to reach out, my arm would not come free; my sleeve had frozen in the spilled water. I wrenched it loose. The frenzy to write supplied its own strength. After the first few paragraphs my mind calmed. But I was too weak to write sitting up. My head kept jerking forward; and, now that the fire was out, the shack was unbearably cold.

The bunk was a continent's breadth away, and I had to cross an interminable plateau to reach it. Safe at last in the sleeping bag, I lay still many minutes, shivering and gasping for breath. Then I finished the letter; and, as I did so, I thought of the last entry in Scott's diary: "For God's sake, look after our people." I had often pondered that simple phrase, but only intellectually. That night I understood what Scott meant. It seemed a pity that men must undergo a cataclysmic experience to perceive this simplest of truths.

The lantern flicked and grew dim. I managed to light two candles which stood on a ledge over the bunk. Just as the second one flamed, the lantern went out. Then, after a while, I wrote a letter to my mother, and another to my children, a few messages, very brief, of instruction to Dr. Poulter and Charlie Murphy concerning the welfare of the expedition, and a final letter to the men at Little America. On the shelf was the green metal box which held my personal papers. I have had it for years. In this I stowed the letters to my family. The ensuing periods are not very clear. I may have lapsed into a coma. A sensation of freezing came; my next recollection is of hoisting myself into a sitting position and composing a message to Murphy regarding the disposal of my papers. This, with the other messages, I secured with a string to the nail from which the lantern usually hung.

Something approaching gratitude flowed into me. Over my head the two candles still burned. Both were red. One stood in a cracked china holder. The other was planted in its own tallow. I looked up at them, thinking vaguely that, when they went out, I should never again see anything so friendly. After a little while I doused the wicks against the wall. Presently another reaction set in. My mind wandered off into a vision of the past, in which I seemed to be wrestling again for the welterweight championship of the naval academy. An agonizing pain was in my body; I had given up all hope of winning; there remained only an insane determination not to bring shame to my mother in the gallery. It was vivid, and the reason it was vivid was that I was again in almost the same situation, except that the stakes were infinitely greater and the chances of winning even less. Then the same determination that had kept me fighting on to the finish that day again came surging back. I saw that, although I seemed absolutely washed up, there was a chance I was mistaken. Anyway, I would have another try.

About three o'clock on the morning of June 2, I had another lucid phase. I tried without success to force my body into sleep. The sleeping pills were on the shelf. The flashlight fingered the bottle. I took it down and dumped the pellets into my cupped palm. There were more than two dozen, white and round; they bespoke a lovely promise. I reached for the bottle. But then I stopped. It was impossible to go on like this. I should become a madman, shrinking from every shadow and touch of pain. I found a match and lighted a candle. An unused sheet of paper lay on the bunk, on top of the diary. I wrote:

The universe is not dead. Therefore, there is an Intelligence there, and it is all pervading. At least one purpose, possibly the major purpose, of that Intelligence is the achievement of universal harmony.

Striving in the right direction for Peace (Harmony), therefore, as well as the achievement of it, is the result of accord with that Intelligence.

It is desirable to effect that accord.

The human race, then, is not alone in the universe. Though I am cut off from human beings, *I* am not alone.

For untold ages man has felt an awareness of that Intelligence. Belief in it is the one point where all religions agree. It has been called by many names. Many call it God.

This was the gist of the philosophy which had come to me out of April's hush. Dousing the candle, I slipped into the bag and repeated the sentiments over and over again. Sleep came after a while. It was intruded upon by another nightmare in which I seemed to be struggling desperately to awaken and take charge of my faculties. The struggle went on interminably in a half-lighted borderland divided by a great white wall. Several times I was nearly across the wall into a field flooded with a golden light, but each time I slipped back into a spinning darkness. Instinct plucked at my sleeve: You must wake up. You must wake up. I pinched the flesh over my ribs. I pulled my long hair. Then the tension eased; I fell across the wall; and, instead of warm sunlight, I found myself in darkness, shivering from cold and thirsting for water.

June 2 was a Saturday and a prolongation of the melancholy events of the day before. I was as weak as ever, and just as certain that I was at the end of my tether. The anemometer cups rattled most of the day; drift sifted down the ventilator in a fine haze, and dripped in hot, pinging pellets from the stovepipe to the deck. From the register I learned that the wind was in the northeast and blowing about twenty miles an hour. I prayed for it to stay in that quarter, since it would mean a continuation of the warm weather. Although the temperature did drop to — 19° in the evening, it was above zero part of the day. If the cold held off, I could do without the stove for long periods and give my system a chance to throw off the effects of the fumes. Altogether, I could not have been out of the bunk more than two or three hours during the day.

As before, I did what had to be done piecemeal, doling out my strength in miserly driblets, creeping rather than walking, and resting long intervals after each small effort. Toward the middle of the day I made several sorties into the tunnels, once after snow and three times after fuel. I relayed the fuel in a tin pitcher, which held about a gallon, since the stove tank was too heavy for me. Later, when the snow had melted, I mixed more milk in the thermos jug. My stomach would not hold anything more solid, although I did manage to down a cup of tea.

I have a vague memory of climbing the ladder to see what the day was like. This was the period of the moon; but, if it showed, I have no recollection of it; my mind remembered a depressing darkness and drift burning against the cheek. In the late afternoon, when the shack had warmed up, I shut down the stove. The thermograph trace shows a minimum temperature of — 22° for the day—a really moderate reading. But the water which I had spewed up was frozen on the floor; a film of ice was creeping up the shack walls; and the slop pail was a solid, messy chunk of ice.

That night, as well as I could estimate, I slept seven or eight hours. Sunday morning brought another anguished struggle to awaken. Sunday meant a radio schedule with Little America and a lie about my condition which every pain-ridden fiber entreated me not to make. God knows where the strength came from to slide the thirty-five-pound engine into the shack, get it up on the stove, and push it back into the tunnel again, a distance of some forty feet, all told. It was my good fortune to find the tank nearly half full of gasoline. The last thing I did was to pick the rime out of the surface ventilator pipe with a spiked stick. The pipe was almost solidly clogged. No wonder the tunnel had filled with fumes during the last schedule.

By the Little America radio log, I was about twenty minutes late reporting. Dyer's voice was saying, "KFZ calling KFY," in the same crisp, matter-of-fact way; but the sound was a surpassing miracle.

It took only the pressure of a finger to work the key; I knew that code would not betray me. Some days before, Charlie Murphy had asked me to give him certain weather information. The data had been lying on my desk for nearly a week. I sent that. Then some of the camp officers took up certain aspects of the proposed spring operations. I am not sure that I wholly understood everything that was said, for the sickness was coming on again. My answers were a simple yes or no or, "Will think over." Finally Dyer's stately, "Thank you, sir. We shall meet you again Thursday," came through the confusion. I shut off the engine, utterly spent.

I have often been asked why I did not tell Little America what had happened. My answer is that it was too dangerous for the men to come to me. This conviction was so strong that I took it for granted. But I was no automaton. When contact was made and Dyer remarked at the outset, as he always did, "We hope that everything is well with you," it was hard to say "OK." But it would have been harder to say anything else. The intervening darkness, the cold, the rolling vacancies of the Barrier, and the crevasses were all immutable facts. Advance Base was my responsibility. It was unthinkable that willing men at Little America should be made to suffer.

That afternoon I may have been close to going out of my mind; the strain of preparing for the schedule had raised Cain with me. I know that I was in torment, and the notion that I was dying would not leave me. Sometime during the evening I came out of the delirium, thirsty and hungry. Along with some milk, I managed to down half a dozen salt crackers, the first solid food since Thursday morning. That night I slept a little longer, though my slumber was lighted by unspeakable nightmares. Monday I scarcely left the sleeping bag. The rest did me good: as did, perhaps, my keeping the fire out most of the afternoon. At night I got up and supped on malted milk, salted crackers, almonds, and dried apples soaked in warm water. A queer mixture, which I myself cannot explain otherwise than by a dim notion that of all the edibles in the shack, these were the only ones that my stomach would tolerate.

I still had no endurance. The pain came and went in my eyes and head and back. And I was always cold.

That night, as before, I ranged the whole broad reaches of hell before finding sleep. Next morning I had much less difficulty waking up, which heartened me. Indeed, matters went somewhat easier. I even managed to empty the slop pail in the food tunnel. In the afternoon I had strength enough to crank the phonograph. The song "In the Gypsy's Life" from *Bohemian Girl* was on the disc. I played that, then the drinking song in *Heidelberg.* And "Adeste Fidelis." It was magnificent to hear the sound of many voices throbbing in every corner of the shack. *You are on the mend,* an inner voice said; *you really have a chance. One in a hundred, perhaps, but still a chance.*

HANS ZINSSER

Hans Zinsser (1878–1940), author of *Rats, Lice and History,* and of the autobiographical *As I Remember Him,* was a distinguished bacteriologist. The son of a chemist, he was educated at Columbia University, where his literary interests were kindled and fostered by George Edward Woodberry. His professional career carried him through World War I as a colonel in the medical corps and caused him to be chosen by the League of Nations in 1923 to go to Russia as Sanitary Commissioner on Cholera. His greatest contribution to bacteriology soon followed: his isolation of the germ of typhus.

I have always been fascinated by the blood alliance between physicians and biologists and creative writing. I shan't enlarge on that here; suffice it to say that besides publishing a volume of poetry (*Spring, Summer and Autumn*), Hans Zinsser, in *As I Remember Him,* wrote one of the most delightful autobiographies (told partly in the third person) of recent years. I reprint here the final chapter. When Dr. Zinsser wrote it, he had known for a year that he must soon die from an incurable disease of the blood.

Sentence of Death

R.S. returned from his last professional journey badly damaged. On the steamer he was humiliated by the fact that not only occasional youngsters but even a British general of approximately his own age could outlast him at deck tennis. Also the sun, instead of tinging his skin a healthy brown, turned him the lemon yellow of the sunburned anaemic. He made a tentative diagnosis of himself before arrival in port.

So when he got home, he went to see an old friend, a doctor, who had pulled him through a nasty infection a few years before. This friend to whom he had gone was one of those precious individuals whom nature had meant to be physicians. He was fond of R.S. and

showed it most helpfully by his affectionate abstinence from any expression of sympathy. And R.S. told me that, together, this good friend
and he stood for a long time at the office window, looking out at the
Charles River Basin. It was one of Lowell's June days, in the early
afternoon. Bright sunshine was reflected from the water and from
dozens of little white sails on the dinghies that were racing along
the Cambridge shore. The Esplanade was alive with contented men
and women, strolling and sitting on the benches; and the sounds of
playing children came up through the open window like the voices of
many birds. The world looked a bright and attractive place.

But in those few minutes, R.S. told me, something took place in his
mind that he regarded as a sort of compensatory adjustment to the
thought that he would soon be dead. In the prospect of death, life
seemed to be given new meaning and fresh poignancy. It seemed, he
said, from that moment, as though all that his heart felt and his senses
perceived were taking on a "deep autumnal tone" and an increased
vividness. From now on, instead of being saddened, he found—to his
own delighted astonishment—that his sensitiveness to the simplest experiences, even for things that in other years he might hardly have
noticed, was infinitely enhanced. When he awoke in the mornings, the
early sun striking across the bed, the light on the branches of the trees
outside his window, the noise of his sparrows, and all the sounds of the
awakening street aroused in him all kinds of gentle and pleasing
memories of days long past which had left their imprints—indelible but,
until now, not consciously realized—of contentment and happiness. It
was quite the opposite of the "woe of the remembering of happy times"
in Canto V of the *Inferno,* beginning: *"Nessun maggior dolore"* and so
on. R.S. felt a deeper tenderness for the people whom he loved, and a
warmer sympathy and understanding for many whose friendship he
had lost in one way or another. Each moment of the day, every prospect
on meadow or hill or sea, every change of light from dawn to dusk,
excited him emotionally with an unexpected clarity of perception and
a new suggestiveness of association. Thinking of the shortness of the
time still left, he reread—as though for a sort of P.P.C. conversation—
the books that had meant much to him at the various stages of his life,
and found them more moving, more deeply wise, or more hilariously
robust, according to their natures. Everything that went on about him
or within him struck upon his heart and mind with a new and powerful resonance. So, on the whole, he was far from either meriting or desiring sympathy. The only thing that depressed him at all in those days
was the thought of horses. He couldn't stand the sight of his saddles,
his bridles, and the various bits that hung about his bedroom—and
which he now packed out of sight in the cellar.

As his malady progressed, he had another variety of experience which, to some others more conditioned to religious belief than he was, might have signified an intimation of the separateness of body and soul.

He said to me: "Here I am, *me* as always. My mind more alive and vivid than ever before; my sensitiveness keener; my affections stronger. I seem for the first time to see the world in clear perspective; I love people more deeply and more comprehensively; I seem to be just beginning to learn my business and see my work in its proper relationship to science as a whole; I seem to myself to have entered into a period of stronger feelings and saner understanding. And yet here am I— essentially unchanged except for a sort of distillation into a more concentrated *me*—held in a damaged body which will extinguish me with it when it dies. If it were a horse I was riding that went lame or broke its neck, or a ship on which I was traveling that sprang a leak, I could transfer to another one and leave the old vehicle behind. As it is, my mind and my spirit, my thoughts and my love, all that I really am, are inseparably tied up with the failing capacities of these outworn organs.

"Yet," he continued, apostrophizing in a serio-comic mood, "poor viscera, I can hardly blame you! You have done your best, and have served me better than could be expected of organs so abused. When I think of the things that have flowed over and through you! Innumerable varieties of fermented hops and malt and of the grapes of all countries and climates: Vouvray, Anjou, Chablis, Haut Sauternes, Chambertain, Nuits-Saint-Georges, Riesling, Lachryma Christi, Johannisthaler, Berncastler, Saint-Julien, Clos de Mouche, Liebfrauenmilch; endless amounts of pinard and vin du pays; the sour wines of Alsace, of North Africa, and of the Pyrenees; the stronger ones of Spain— Oporto, Sherry, Madeira, Malaga; the Tokay of Hungary; sparkling vintages of Burgundy and of Champagne; Veuve Cliquot and her brothers Mumm and Pommery; and the California brews bought in demijohns; to say nothing of the distillates—flavored and unflavored; cognac, Three-Star Hennessy; whiskies—Scotch, Irish, Canadian, rye, bourbon, and the yellowish moonshine, colored with chicken droppings, from the Blue Hills; and gin—genuine and synthetic; Schlibovitz from the Balkans, Starka from Poland, and the vodka of the Steppes; crème de menthe and cacao, Marie Brizard Cointreau, and Calyados.

"No, no, my organs! I cannot feel that you have let me down. It is quite the other way round. Only now it seems so silly that you must take me with you when I am just beginning to get dry behind the ears."

Though he had these spells of half-humorous revolt against the idea that his personality and his increasing joy of living should be so helplessly at the mercy of his deteriorating body, he was still grateful that, in his case, it was this and not the mind that was going to pieces first.

He was not, at any time, tempted to seek strength in wishful surrender to a religious faith in which far greater men than he had taken refuge just before death. When this had, astonishingly, happened in the cases of several of his intimate friends, he regarded it as a capitulation of the mind to the fatigue of suffering. Indeed, he became more firm in his determination to see things out consistently along his own lines of resignation to agnostic uncertainty—as his father had done before him. Moving further away, therefore, from faith in any comprehensible conception of God, he yet grew closer in conviction of the wisdom and guiding integrity of the compassionate philosophy of Christ.

As his disease caught up with him, R.S. felt increasingly grateful for the fact that death was coming to him with due warning, and gradually. So many times in his active life he had been near sudden death by accident, violence, or acute disease; and always he had thought that rapid and unexpected extinction would be most merciful. But now he was thankful that he had time to compose his spirit, and to spend a last year in affectionate and actually merry association with those dear to him. He set down this feeling in his last sonnet:—

> Now is death merciful. He calls me hence
> Gently, with friendly soothing of my fears
> Of ugly age and feeble impotence
> And cruel disintegration of slow years.
> Nor does he leap upon me unaware
> Like some wild beast that hungers for its prey,
> But gives me kindly warning to prepare:
> Before I go, to kiss your tears away.
>
> How sweet the summer! And the autumn shone
> Late warmth within our hearts as in the sky,
> Ripening rich harvests that our love had sown.
> How good that 'ere the winter comes, I die!
> Then, ageless, in your heart I'll come to rest
> Serene and proud, as when you loved me best.

It is apparent, therefore, that in his last months R.S. achieved a certain degree of philosophical tranquillity and resignation. It would be a mistake, however, to suppose that, apart from his purely personal reactions to his own fate and his immediate environment, he was less confused at the time of his death than I have described him in my introductory chapter. When he gazed beyond the circle of his own work, his family and friends, into the rushing world about him, he was completely bewildered. He had a little the same resentful feeling that he remembered having when, as a boy, he had walked through Normandy and had to jump into the ditch to let one of the recently invented automobiles rattle by—knowing that its passengers would have dinner at the town where he expected to arrive two days later. It was all moving too fast for him. Indeed, he was not sure whether the world that was rushing by was going forward or backward. He wondered whether he had not, perhaps, been born a little too soon and remained unable to catch up with his time. The world to which he had been born had not alone speeded up with that acceleration of which Henry Adams complained, but it had actually seemed to change direction. Scientific progress had brought as much sorrow as happiness. With immensely enhanced powers of production, millions were out of work and starving. Ideas of democracy and individual freedom which he had accepted as the gradually evolved goals of centuries of struggle were not only being denied, but entire nations were frantically intent on destroying them. Great racial masses seemed willing to fight and perish, if necessary, for their own enslavement. New so-called "ideologies" were tearing up the foundations of all that men had thought firm and permanently established. Something had cracked in the old Western civilization, and its walls and lofty towers—cemented with the sweat and blood of their forefathers—were tumbling about men's ears. And the intellectual calamity seemed to be that no one could say whether the turmoil was the result of avoidable stupidity or of the operation of laws of economic and social evolution that were acting on mankind as other laws had acted on the dinosaur and the sabre-toothed tiger.

But in all these things he could never tell, before he died, whether the fault was in him or in the trends he disliked. He didn't admit this, of course, and remained, to the last, argumentatively arrogant. But I knew that at the time of his death he was as thoroughly bewildered as any thoughtful individual of our time is bound to be.

All of which goes to prove that, as I pointed out in the first chapter, R.S. was really a quite ordinary person about whom it was hardly worth while to write a book.

FRANCIS BEAUCHESNE
THORNTON

The story of the four chaplains—Fox the Vermont Methodist, Poling, another Protestant from upstate New York, Goode, a rabbi from Brooklyn, and Washington, a New Jersey Catholic priest—is one of the most moving episodes of World War II. The man who tells about it here, the Reverend Francis Thornton, is literary critic of *The Catholic Digest* and the author of two books of poetry. He was a chaplain in the war himself, and spent four years gathering his material for *Sea of Glory,* interviewing and writing to the families and friends of these men who went cheerfully to their deaths in the seas off Labrador. The *Dorchester,* on which they served, a little freighter pressed into service as a troopship, was under way to Greenland when she was torpedoed by a German submarine. The four chaplains went down with her, although three hundred or more men were rescued. The passages which follow form the Prologue and Epilogue to Father Thornton's book. I know of no more convincing record of the selflessness of which man, in his finest moments, is capable.

The Four Chaplains

THE freighter rose and fell sluggishly at her pier, her spring lines alternately slack and tight. In the darkness beneath the flooring, down at the waterline of the rusty ship, there was a slap of the waves—one of the loneliest sounds that can haunt man's ears.

Floodlamps turned the New England night into a garish noon, a noon full of shadows, and full of the sound of winches, of screeching cranes and booms and of the shuffling cadence of weary troops, keeping step out of habit rather than from conscious desire.

One of the shadows the lights didn't reach hung near the stern of the freighter, almost obliterating her name—the *Dorchester*—but neither the glare of the light nor the kindness of the shadows could hide the fact that the vessel was old, and small, and probably slow—or that she would undoubtedly pitch and roll even in good weather, and would yaw crazily in heavy seas.

Soldiers climbing the gangplank looked at the *Dorchester* as though they had been cheated in a poker game even before the cards were dealt. One whose humor had not been erased by hours of standing and marching spoke over his shoulder to another man behind him.

"She'd fit in a funnel of the *Queen Mary*. She's no bigger than a life-boat."

He was right. She was devoid of class. Whatever dignity she was to possess would have to go aboard her in the hearts and breasts of the soldiers using her as a ferry to the bloody fields of war. She had none of her own.

She was listed with Lloyds' at five thousand tons, and the symbols in the Register, when translated, meant that she was just another work-horse of the sea, intended to carry slow cargo in her holds. Only the exigencies of total war had forced her transformation into a troopship.

On this night in January, 1943, she was being loaded with troops at a Massachusetts port, her destination hidden in an envelope of secret orders, the seal of which would stay unbroken until she had lumbered into position in a convoy, hours out of sight of land.

Deckhands, fighting the winter cold in reefers close-collared against the wind, moved about her decks with the slow precision of veteran seamen. Lights atop the king posts and the bridge illuminated the open hatches through which was being lowered the gear and apparatus of war. The booms, swinging from ship to pier and back again, com-plained with the strident sound of steel rasping against steel.

The tide was running out and the freighter chafed at her moorings, moving in a short arc within the confines of her hawsers. The motion caused the gangplank to move back and forth too, the lower end, sup-ported by small wheels, rolling unevenly on the floorboards of the pier.

Each enlisted man, his duffel bag on his shoulder, had to break step as he reached the gangplank. Sometimes a foot would be poised for the first step and then the plank would pull away like a hoydenish thing. Again it would move drunkenly the other way, forcing the soldier to quickstep to protect himself.

Historians could speak of this contrivance in later years as a bridge to man's victory against the forces of totalitarian evil. It was a narrow, unstable link between the known and the unknown, between the safety of the shore and home and the awful dangers of the sea. Each man, tired and cold as he was that January night, must have thought about it as he plodded up the incline and stepped upon the steel plates of the freighter's deck.

There were humble GIs and equally humble officers who made the crossing from the pier to the *Dorchester*. A nameless fear quickened the pulse of every one of them, whether they spoke of it or not.

Among their number, carrying duffel bags like the rest, but without the reassuring strength that comes from rifle or sidearms, walked four chaplains. Their names—Fox, Goode, Poling, and Washington—told nothing.

On that night in January, 1943, destiny was curtained off completely. One by one, the army chaplains judged the eccentric behavior of the plank, adjusted their strides to match it, and stepped aboard the freighter, never dreaming the contraption was also a gangplank to everlasting glory.

Fox was a Methodist, called to duty from a snowbound parish in Vermont. Poling, another Protestant, had quit a comfortable existence in upstate New York. Goode, a Jewish rabbi born in Brooklyn, was fresh from a synagogue in rural Pennsylvania. Washington, the man with the odd name, was a Catholic priest born and bred in industrial New Jersey.

They shared a cabin on the *Dorchester*—a cabin in name only, not much different from the sleeping quarters of the enlisted men—dreary, airless, and heavy with the stench of fuel oil and bilge slop.

Fox was one up on his companions. He had gone overseas in the First World War—that time as a fighting man—and he knew the dirty business at its worst.

"I've been through this before," he said, stowing away his belongings to save space in the cramped room. "But with all these green kids and civilian workers it won't be any picnic. We'll make it all right, though."

Young Poling let the words hang suspended in the stuffy air, as they hung in each man's mind, while his stomach adjusted itself to the ship's motion.

"I'm a pretty good sailor," he said finally, "but when I crossed before I wasn't responsible for anyone but myself."

Soldiers tramped through the companionway outside, down into the bowels of the *Dorchester*. Naked light bulbs showed them their quarters—bunks hastily built into the holds, four tiers high, six niggardly feet of space per man—just enough room for a night's sleep, or for that last, long sleep from which there is no awakening.

The scrape of hobnails on steel decks, the creaking of the booms, and the whole mad cacophony of sound that grew out of the process of packing hundreds of men into narrow confines almost drowned out Father Washington's words.

"At least you've been to sea," he laughed. "I can't swim well enough to paddle across a duck pond. How about you, Alex?"

Rabbi Goode thrust his hands out. The other chaplains saw that his fingers were crossed and they guffawed.

"The way I see it," said Goode, "is this. We'll be so doggone busy with the men we won't have time to think of ourselves. Let's go topside for a minute. Maybe we aren't handsome, but if they catch us there smiling as they come aboard maybe it will kid them along a bit."

So they went up, making wrong turns in the narrow passageways as landlubbers always do, emerging on the starboard side aft when they had expected to come out forward on the port side. They laughed at their mistake and crossed to watch the dogfaces coming aboard like ants toiling to the top of their hill to disappear suddenly at the summit.

The men's faces were bleak, as only fighting men's faces can be, shoving off for overseas, or moving out on a patrol when the high brass, warm and safe at the rear, sends up orders to bring in prisoners for questioning or to apply more pressure in a diversion to protect the next division on one's flank.

It's the eyes that tell the story. The healthy glint that is any man's birthright grows lackluster on the eve of battle or danger. The sockets become a little deeper, stretching the skin into shadowed crow's-feet. So it was with these men coming aboard the *Dorchester*. They could only guess at the future.

The port of embarkation camp had been one vast rumor factory. They were going to Africa. They were going to Northern Ireland. They were part of a secret movement destined for a landing up some Norwegian fjord. There was a vital plant to be destroyed—something about heavy water—it didn't make any sense, but they were going to pull the Limey's chestnuts out of the fire again.

On board the *Dorchester* it was worse. Scuttlebutt passed from mouth to ear and on again with the speed of light. It was Africa. No, it wasn't. It was Greenland. The Nazis had executed their promised invasion of England and they'd all be thrown into the fighting somewhere in Cornwall the minute they hit land.

The sky pilots knew they were bound for Greenland...the godforsaken, ice-covered, glacier-tortured end of the world.

As preachers of the Word and as ministers to the sick of heart and body, the chaplains knew what life in a hurriedly thrown-together outpost on the Greenland coast could be. Worse than the front. There would be bitter cold, nights and days when the sun could be only a memory, far below the horizon, and there would be the monotony and the boredom and the bitterness and the grousing and the endlessness of time unsweetened by the music of a woman's voice.

Fox and Poling and Goode knew this better than the priest, since each had left a wife behind, but Father Washington understood well enough the heavy duty that lay on all four if they were to make life a little more bearable for the youngsters coming over the side, being herded by top kicks and ship's officers in the fetid compartments below....

At Point Option—the preselected rendezvous off the Massachusetts coast—the *Dorchester* found herself the seventh and last ship of a small convoy. If she had had two or three more knots in her she might have been the Lucky Seventh. As she didn't, she was placed smack in the middle of the convoy, much to the shame of her crew and the joy of the troops.

In January of 1943 the North Atlantic was perhaps the bitterest battleground of all the fronts. Allied shipping, under constant attack by wolf-packs of Nazi U-boats, was being sunk almost as fast as it could be built. Men-of-war and planes to combat the submarines were still in perilously short supply.

The newest destroyers went with the fleet to guard the carriers and battle-wagons pounding Japanese islands in the far Pacific. The bulk of those that were left stood guard with the fast convoys to the United Kingdom or formed the screens for baby aircraft carriers to constitute the killer groups that played such a large part in the ultimate defeat of the U-boats.

For such as the lumbering *Dorchester* and her sisters there were only a few Coast Guard cutters, refitted yachts, and other make-do craft.

The GIs, watching the *Dorchester* take station that first morning out, saw that three Coast Guard cutters were their only escort.... If they joked and kidded and laughed, maybe the steely fingers of fear would loosen a little about their hearts.

There was reason for the fear.

Word seeped down from the bridge and the radio shack that "Sparks," although never daring to send off a word, had heard many a dot-and-dash code message while listening to the endless chatter that even a war doesn't shut off.

There were lots of kraut subs around and they knew, it seemed, where the convoys were, and they must have been talking back and forth among themselves about a rendezvous at some not-too-distant "torpedo junction."...

Rolling and yawing, the *Dorchester* beat her slow way northeastward, unmindful of the comfort of her precious cargo. The cutters watched their brood with endless devotion and the ship's bells beat out their muffled count.

Somewhere up ahead, well north of the great circle route, in the impatient wilderness of the ocean, destiny was altering the *Dorchester's* course to a rendezvous with history.

From where the four chaplains stood at the lee rail there was nothing to be seen except the ships of the convoy and their escorts, heading into the wind but bucking a current that seemed to be sliding southward off the shelf of Labrador.

On their last visit to the chart room Captain Greenspun had shown them exactly where they were, making a little dot on the map with the help of dividers and parallel rules.

An inch or so away—on the chart—the coast of Greenland seemed to be extending her peninsulate fingers in greetings, urging the little convoy on to safe haven.

After that everyone felt better for a day or so. Then word was bruited about that both Captain Greenspun and Lieutenant Arpaia had a feeling they were being followed by enemy submarines. They couldn't explain it. It was just their psychological radar.

Lookouts were doubled, and the man in the crow's-nest was relieved every hour so that his eyes wouldn't be tired or his faculties dulled by the numbing cold. A rough assignment it was, lookout on the ship's main deck. High above the bridge and deck a little roost no cozier than a barrel was fastened to the mast and in it the lookout stood, straining his eyes for signs of a snorkel tube, a torpedo's wake, or any other hostile movement. The rim of the crow's-nest hit him at the armpits. His face was lashed by the wind and sleet and snow.

When the boat rolled, which was most of the time, the main mast swung back and forth like a great inverted pendulum, and the sailor in the crow's-nest felt like a pea in a bucket that some small boy was swinging around his head.

The chaplains could sense that the men were worried. They knew that every man aboard the *Dorchester* had a mysterious feeling that the ship was in critical danger.

The month of January was torn off the calendar in the main mess, and the act made the trip seem interminable. The men thought they had been at sea two months now and began to doubt whether the skipper and the navigator knew where they were. At night, when most of the lights had been extinguished, there was the sound of sobbing from some of the youngsters who had never been away from home before and who, overnight, were expected to be grown men. It was a funny thing that even the toughest of the old-timers never mentioned the nocturnal weeping. Even the four sky pilots had no cure for such heartache.

On the evening of the second day of the new month one of the three

Coast Guard cutters blinked a message across the water to the troop-ship.

We are being followed by a submarine.

Captain Greenspun alerted his officers. The PA system crackled with orders and the gun crews jumped to their guns. In the engine room, in response to the telegraph from the bridge, the *Dorchester's* machinery whined and labored, but the best it could do was to push the ungainly freighter along at ten knots.

Ten knots is incredibly slow. A man can run as fast for a short while. If you subtract the distance lost by constant zigzagging it is easy to see how helpless the *Dorchester* was, wallowing along in the winter seas.

The old man, pacing up and down the bridge, silent, troubled, deeply concerned for the safety of all the lives in his care, never seemed to rest. He had slept no more than three hours in midday since leaving port, and the quartermaster had to keep hot coffee going to the bridge in a steady stream to prevent the skipper from falling asleep.

Out of the overcast the next day came a slow, lumbering patrol plane bearing Canadian insignia on the undersides of her wings. She looked frail and antique, but nonetheless "Sparks" flashed her a message by blinker, giving the *Dorchester's* position and asking for assistance. Back came the stuttering light flashes:

Planes on duty elsewhere. Impossible to send any at this time.

That night the soldiers were sure that fate had kicked them squarely in the seat of the pants. They felt sorry for themselves and cursed the rust-bucket the government had given them for a transport. They wrote letters home in a blind rebellion against their miserable lot, against the bitter winds and the raw cold that made every minute on deck a trial. Many a letter was blurred by tears that wouldn't stay back.

Men ate in subdued anger and fear. They fell into the chow lines with their life jackets on, the strings securely fastened, and no one thought it strange or cowardly.

After the evening meal the tables were moved and the equipment cleared away, and the GIs had a party. Mess boys from Cuba and Puerto Rico brought out instruments. An old upright piano that had been lashed to a bulkhead was freed of its fetters, moved into the mess hall, secured again, and made to give forth music. There were hot rumbas and hotter jazz and, best of all, the old familiar, popular songs that any American kid over eight knows how to sing.

The four chaplains led the singing. When the lads were a little slow on suggesting the next tune, Fox or Goode or one of the others would slip in a request for a hymn. They seemed a little out of place sand-wiched in between "Mademoiselle from Armentières" and "Every-thing's up to Date in Kansas City," but the troops never let the chaplains down. They sang the hymns as lustily as they did the pop tunes. . . .

Although it seemed that every man could fairly taste submarines in the seething water behind them, the *Dorchester* plowed on that night of February 2 and the next day gained shelter behind the boom at St. John's, Newfoundland.

The sun came out and while the freighter was tied up to the pier, safe from all danger, the GIs shouted at the few girls who wandered down to the docks, sang happily, and acted as if they had won the war already.

The chaplains, with special passes, went ashore to mail the letters written by the troops too late to go off in the regular pouches. In the Bachelor Officers' Quarters they shot the breeze with American officers from the Argentia base, with Canadian pilots, and with the skippers of the little Canadian corvettes with which the Dominion was battling bravely against the hordes of undersea craft that Admiral Doenitz and Hitler thought could win the war by strangulation.

They'd have been better off—in a way—if they'd stayed on board the *Dorchester*.

The news was bad. At sea, with little to go on, the four chaplains had guessed how bad it was. On shore, where men were closer to day-to-day operations, the picture in all its somber colors unfolded—threatening, bleak, blood-curdling.

To the four chaplains the word was passed that sinkings were averaging as high as a hundred a month. The landings in North Africa, the top-priority convoys to Montgomery in Tripoli, the big U.K. runs from New York to Liverpool—all these were extending the Allied sea power too thin. Subs, fitted with their snorkel tubes, able to remain submerged with only a device the size of a mackerel above the surface, were raiding convoys and cutting out the prize targets like cowboys roping fat heifers from a moving herd.

"The Murmansk run is pure poison," the chaplains were told. "Almost no one comes back from that. It's a little better on the runs to England but those ships are faster. That rust-bucket of yours can't be any bargain. Must be mighty slow."

Slow? Lord in Heaven, that she was, and the sky pilots knew it and had to go on acting as if it were the *Queen Elizabeth* or the *Wakefield*. There was nothing for them to do but put on an act and try to kid the soldiers along, and whenever there was any spare time or when they were getting the little bit of horizontal drill they needed each night they could pray to God for a safe landing in Greenland.

There isn't much else to do with an elephantine five-thousand-ton freighter whose engines couldn't turn up another knot if they were fed aviation gas.

The respite in port was too short to do anyone much good.

A little after the church bells of St. John's had marked eight o'clock in the evening the *Dorchester* quit the pier and passed out to sea, through the submarine boom at the harbor mouth.

The convoy moved on northeastward, through the strange white darkness of an Arctic night. Each ship, it seemed to the men at the *Dorchester's* rail, stuck up like a clay target in a shooting gallery, inviting a torpedo from any sub that was within miles of the wallowing convoy.

On deck the crew made last-minute moves to secure odd gear and to lash the canvas covers on the hatches. In the brittle silence of the northern night each sound seemed maddeningly loud, each noise a gilt-edged invitation to a sub commander....

In the middle of the night some of the soldiers sleeping in the compartments farthest below decks heard the engine-room telegraph bells jingle, and after that the *Dorchester* moved through the water more slowly. Up on the bridge Captain Greenspun had ordered speed reduced because he was running into pan ice, and knew that at any minute an iceberg might loom ahead out of the harmless slush.

From here on into port in Greenland engines would run at half-speed, the propeller blades would turn even more slowly because of the new threat.

Strangely the slower speed brought a sense of relief, both on the bridge and among the men bunking in the holds. The old man, knowing that the knife-sharp edges of an iceberg could rip a U-boat as a can opener splits open a tin of sardines, figured no submarine would operate in such dangerous waters.

The chaplains congratulated each other. They knew about the ice and its double portent—of danger and of safety both—and they knew that probably by now the convoy had moved far enough to the north to come under the protecting umbrella of patrol planes flying off Greenland's runways.

The weather grew nastier with each passing hour. Long ground swells battered the stumbling *Dorchester,* and in between white-capped waves hammered malignantly against her bows and shook her to her keel plates....

The Arctic night was beautiful but it was deadly. Like a toy being dragged by a loitering child the *Dorchester* made her way through the early hours of the darkness—a darkness overcast with an eerie glimmering of whiteness. It zigged and zagged and it seemed to stumble from one crest to another, being punished by each in turn, yet staggering slowly on.

Below decks the passage of time was a slow gnawing at the mind, a dull sawing on the raw and open nerve ends of the soul.

There seemed to be an apprehensive silence that brooded over the ship. Men in their bunks sensed it, their eyes wide and their muscles tense. With the cutting of the speed the screws no longer threshed half the time out of water. The silence of the Arctic night muffled the clank of the engines.

The ship's bells struck twice. It was one o'clock in the morning. They never sounded again.

A minute or so later a torpedo smashed into the *Dorchester,* well below the waterline amidships.

The stricken ship staggered from the explosion. Men lying fully clothed in their bunks were tossed to the decks like walnuts from an upset basket. Others were catapulted against the bulkheads.

Blackout lights went out instantly, plunging the entire ship into darkness and leaving the men to grope in terror as they fought their way topside.

The German submarine skipper had caught the freighter fair on his periscope's crossed hairs. The torpedo, running swift and true, ripped open the tender skin of the ship and exploded in all its fury in the engine room.

Steam lines burst, letting their vapor escape to kill and scald and torture the engineers and oilers. Fuel tanks split open, spewing their oily contents over the scene of terror, making each ladder and catwalk a place of peril.

A wiper, checking the bearings in the shaft alley, heard the explosion, felt the ship tremble, and died in a sudden tidal wave of water and oil.

A junior engineer, standing at the side of a boiler, was flung against the water jacket unconscious, and awoke to die in a searing, blinding burst of steam.

In thirty seconds a hundred men were dead, scalded, mutilated, or drowned like rats in a trap.

Soldiers scrambled toward the companionways, already leaning crazily as the *Dorchester* listed to port, and fought their way, cursing and screaming, to the windy deck.

Abandon-ship drills, lectures on survival in torpedoings and the military discipline so newly acquired by civilians-suddenly-turned-soldiers went by the boards. In each man's mind was the single thought of how to save himself. The mores and the teachings of civilization were cast aside as a snake sheds its skin in the spring.

Then out of chaos came brief signs of order as men conquered the fear that had short-circuited their thinking. Doctors and medics snatched up their kits and headed below, bucking the tide of men seeking the open decks. If they sensed their own danger they brushed it aside and went on to rescue the injured. Their flashlights stabbed feebly at the blackness of the holds, already reeking with the choking fumes of ammonia.

Far below them in the engine room a boiler blew up, mangling bodies already mangled by the torpedo's warhead.

Up above things were no better. Even before the *Dorchester* had recovered from the first shock the skipper clawed for the siren lanyard to send off the six-blast signal agreed upon before the convoy quit home waters.

Three times the siren roared. The fourth blast died in the whistle's metal throat, a hollow, mocking cough.

Because of the freighter's list, lifeboats on the starboard side hung inboard, and men struggled to free them. Some were lowered, bumping crazily down the ship's sloping sides. Others broke away and fell free, hurtling down upon men who had jumped overboard in the first seconds of terror.

The wind meanwhile had chopped around to the northwest and some of the lifeboats, safely launched, were breached by heavy seas which filled them to the thwarts. Men on the troopship saw them disappear, spewing soldiers into the water. Everywhere there were the red lights of the life jackets, twinkling on the water like sparks of fire.

Life rafts went over the side as frantic men hacked at their lashings. Some bobbled away in the darkness before anyone could reach them. Others were so crowded with survivors that men died struggling to get a grip on their handlines.

Here and there about the deck battle lanterns flickered fitfully, doing little to pierce the blackness of the night.

Men shouted and men wept. Soldiers made their way out of the hold without their life jackets and went back to get them, dying in the smothering holds.

The devout cried to God for help, while others cursed His name. Kids who should have been in bed back home, resting for a day in the fields or at football practice, called for their mothers. Some just huddled at the rail, already awash, like frightened sheep.

Hysteria compelled weak men to jump into the Atlantic with mad words upon their lips, but the bitter cold of the ocean stilled their cries as if the words thickened in their throats.

Through this scene of terror moved a few strong men, purposeful, calm, and seemingly unafraid.

A soldier who couldn't have been out of his teens cut away a rope that had tangled in the block of a davit, setting a lifeboat, crowded with men, free upon the surface of the sea.

Captain Greenspun was everywhere, encouraging the soldiers, helping the crew to launch anything that would float, and issuing the few commands there were left to issue on a floundering, mortally wounded ship.

Army surgeons and medics behaved as though participating in a briefing session on how to care for the wounded at sea. Injured men were brought topside, bandaged, and helped into lifeboats when these were available. Men who might have died lived because of their ministration.

And everywhere about the ship, in the terror-ridden interior and on the crazily tilted deck, the four chaplains moved among the men with helpful words, giving some the strength to live and some the courage to die.

Knowing that the life expectancy of a man in such frigid waters was somewhere between 18 and 40 minutes, the three men with crosses on their collars and the one with the Tablets of the Law on his, urged the soldiers to stay aboard as long as possible after the smallboats had been cast off.

"Take it easy, soldier. It will be all right."

Strange how such simple, meaningless words could still panic in a man's heart. Stranger still how they could inject starch into a coward's spine.

The *Dorchester* by now had lost all way and was lying dead in the water. Fitful winds plucked spume from the wave crests and whipped it into the faces of the men on deck.

Suddenly the ship shivered and men everywhere cried out.

"She's going down. She's going down. We'll be sucked under."

Even the GIs who had never seen the ocean until they embarked on the *Dorchester* knew the added danger that accompanies a ship's last plunge.

Like old wives' tales feeding on themselves, lurid stories of the swirling, sucking vortex created when a vessel went down had gone the rounds among the men. What had made it worse was the knowledge that the evil couldn't be exaggerated.

Now, in the blackness of the night, the terror was multiplied a thousandfold.

The chaplains sensed the threat.

"Over the side, men, make it fast." The wind tore the words from their lips.

"Swim to the lifeboats," they cried. "Get away from the ship."

Men looked at the four chaplains with new wonder. They saw them move together as though that way they could be of greater help.

Soldiers lifted their eyes to them as if for a sign, some symbol to carry with them into the valley of death.

A man—more boy than man—made his way to the group at the rail.

"Padre, I've lost my life jacket. I can't swim. I'll..."

One of the chaplains tore off his own and put it about the boy's shoulders.

"Take this. I'm staying. I won't need it."

The soldier tied the jacket's strings, mounted the rail, and slipped into the sea, now almost level with the deck.

Of the three hundred or so men who survived not one can remember which chaplain it was who first voiced the decision to stay with the ship.

Was it Father Washington, who couldn't swim across a duck pond? Was it Fox, survivor of one war and victim of another? Poling, heir to a great name in preaching, or Goode, the rabbi from the Pennsylvania Dutch country?

What does it matter now? If the first had not spoken, another would. Catholic, Jew, and Protestant; each proved that night that courage knows no distinction of creed, bravery no division of caste.

Violent squalls confused the dying moments of the freighter. Flares on the bridge revealed the deck, now awash, at an ugly slant. Men fought for places on the last raft, and the losers cursed and wept.

The four chaplains stood with arms linked, each one without a life jacket. Somewhere off in the seething seas four other men were cheating death, supported by the chaplains' gifts.

Icy waters reached their knees as their lips moved in prayer.

"Our Father which art in Heaven, Hallowed be Thy name. Thy kingdom come, Thy will be done..."

The troopship labored to rise from a trough and staggered on. Water sluiced along the sloping deck.

"...ego te absolvo a peccatis tuis, in nomine Patris, et Filii, et Spiritus Sancti..."

A soldier, bleeding through his bandages, crawled to where the four were standing. His voice was barely audible.

"God bless you," he said, and crawled into the sea.

A wave breached clear across the tilted deck.

"Hear, O Israel, the Lord Our God, the Lord is one..."

For an instant the light of a flare cast an effulgence upon the four of them for all who were left aboard to see.

"...forgive us our trespasses, as we forgive those who trespass against us..."

Once more the ship labored to breast the next wave. There was a great noise of water and air churning in the darkness.

The *Dorchester* fought to right herself, failed, and plunged beneath the surface.

ANNE MORROW LINDBERGH

The wife of General Lindbergh, herself an accomplished flier who has accompanied her husband on some of his important flights, was born in 1906. The mother of five living children, she has made for herself a shining record as a writer. *North to the Orient,* her first book, published in 1935, and its successor, *Listen, the Wind,* established her as one of the best prose stylists of her period. *The Wave of the Future,* cause of a good deal of popular misunderstanding, for a time somewhat adversely affected her reputation. It was followed by *The Steep Ascent,* a brief piece of fiction which foreshadowed her deepening interest in the problems confronting women in the modern world. This interest was given fuller and subtler treatment in *Gift from the Sea,* published two years ago, which rapidly became one of the most widely read books of this century in the United States. Last year she published a collection of her verse, *The Unicorn and Other Poems.* The title poem and a few others have great delicacy and charm; it is, however, as a prose stylist that she shows the greater artistry.

I have reproduced here her introduction to the biography of Edward Sheldon by Eric Wollencott Barnes, *The Man Who Lived Twice.* To read her tribute to that remarkable man is to sense the heights to which human selflessness can reach.

The Man Who Lived Twice: Edward Sheldon

I REMEMBER lying in bed in the hospital, after the birth of a child, on an autumn morning crisp as an apple, rosy on one side, chilled on the other. The sun was pouring in my window and, outside, every yellow leaf, touched by frost the night before, stood still in the golden air. The nurse brought me a telegram from Edward Sheldon which read:

THIS IS A BEAUTIFUL MORNING. I AM SURE YOU AND YOUR DAUGHTER ARE HAPPY.

435

I felt full of joy at such a swift and magical sharing of my mood. Then suddenly I thought, shocked almost to tears, "But how does he know it is a beautiful morning? The man who sent that telegram is blind. He has not seen a tree for twenty years."

I remember very well the first time I met him. I felt rather shy as I rode up on the elevator to his penthouse and I wondered nervously whether I would say the right thing, how I should be able to talk to such a man. A nurse met me and ushered me into the long room with windows on two sides opening out onto the roof. On one side of the room, in front of the windows, there was an enormous table, piled high with books, stacks of them, seven or eight deep, current books which he was "reading." At the end of the room was a high bed, rather like a bier ("Like the last act of *Tristan*," someone once described it), with a thronelike canopy towering over it. The man lying in the shadow of this velvet canopy was covered with a Persian shawl, intricately patterned in soft reds and browns. Only his head and shoulders were visible. He was immaculately dressed as if he were lying down for a few minutes only. His eyes were bandaged. He greeted you with a rather breathless whisper.

I mention these details because the first time one entered the room they picked at one sharply and uncomfortably. After five minutes one never noticed them again. They were not even a barrier to be leapt across; they simply ceased to exist, so overshadowed were they by the personality of the man one went to see.

The nurse directed me to the comfortable chair and low table by the side of the bed where tea or lunch was always laid for his guests, even though he did not partake of it. But before I could sit down, Edward Sheldon had thrown a verbal life line to me, across that gulf of shyness that exists between two people meeting for the first time.

"Tell me, Mrs. Lindbergh," he said, referring to a line in a book of mine he had read, "did you ever get that crust of French bread and that piece of runny cheese you were thinking about over the Alps?"

I laughed; the life line fell neatly; the gulf had been bridged; we talked all afternoon.

As I have said, one went shyly the first time, on faith, perhaps because one had been asked to go, or even out of kindness. After that, one went for oneself, to fill a need. One talked to him as to an old friend, on all subjects; daily life, literature, politics or problems of morality—how to live the good life. On one occasion we had a long discussion, suggested by a quotation of Pascal's about men "of the middle." We were alike in our sympathy with the man in the middle, the moderate who will not be classified with this or that extreme group, who is never violent in his judgment or his praise, who has humility about his opinions, who sees the world and most of his fellow human beings as neither black nor white but gray. I ventured the opinion that, in one's critical judgment, the ideal attitude would be "black and white about oneself but gray about the rest of the world."

"Oh, no," Ned Sheldon corrected me quickly. "Oh, no, you must be gray about yourself, too; you must forgive yourself, too. That is the hardest thing of all."

He gave abundantly, advice, encouragement, stimulus, criticism. But he also allowed you to give to him (most subtle form of giving). He knew how to receive so graciously that the gift was enhanced by its reception. It was the rarest pleasure to bring things to him, books one had found, passages of poetry or philosophy, a seventeenth-century mystic or a modern poet, comments on life by a soldier one had met in a train, or by a child in a school bus. He took them all in eagerly. Warmed by his welcome, how beautiful became the things that one brought him. So often one has the opposite experience, gifts shrivel under the critical gaze of the recipient. One is like a child running in from the beach with a jewel found in the retreating rim of the tide, only to have it fade to an ordinary stone on the dry palm of another. With Edward Sheldon everything became more beautiful in the light of his appreciation. Seen through those translucent depths, sea shells became pearls; ordinary stones were jewels.

No, I should not have worried about having nothing to say to this man. One always talked too much and stayed too long. One went away refreshed and stimulated, with a hundred new paths shooting off in the mind, and the quiet certainty that there was infinite time in which to follow them. The world opened up from those four closed walls.

Why did one feel this way about him? How explain this extraordinary influence over other people? In what resided his power? The question is not answered by any listing of his qualities, saintlike though they were. Of course, all who knew him were fired by his sustained gallantry, were quickened by the unquenchable flame of his spirit, were overcome by his princely prodigality of heart. And you had only to walk into his room to be won by his chivalrous courtesy. Courtesy is generally considered a social value only, but in this case it passed the bounds of ordinary courtesy and took its place in the scale of moral values. It was, in fact, a combination of courage and extreme consideration.

He never mentioned his infirmities or referred to them in any way, even by implication or negatively. And he took the greatest pains to create and preserve in the minds of others the delicate illusion that he was just like everyone else. So perfect was the spell he cast over his bedroom that you ceased to think of him as an invalid. You had almost the impression, as a small boy once expressed it after a first visit, that he was "a prince under an enchantment." He spoke of "reading" books, "seeing" friends, and "meeting" people in a way that was physically impossible for him. But he spoke like this not out of any vanity, I am sure, but simply not to burden his friends with the constant awareness of his difficulties. Such an awareness might have stood between him and them, as a barrier—or a bridge. Either would have been distasteful to him. He would have abhorred the thought that people came to him *because* of his invalidism or even in *spite* of it. And they did neither.

If you should ask them why they came, what was the compelling force that drew them, I believe many would say, in one form or another, "He understood me; nobody understood me so well." This was true; in anything which he apprehended directly he had the most uncanny powers of perception. Not only had he developed his hearing to an extraordinary degree (he often guessed the height of a newcomer from the position of a voice), but he seemed to have developed other senses of apprehension unknown to the normally endowed individual. The minute you walked into his room he knew all about you, inwardly and outwardly. He saw you whole, and in his presence you felt whole. The beautiful prayer from the *Phaedrus* was answered: "The outward and the inward man were at one."

This is not to say there was for him no "outward man." For Edward Sheldon did not belittle the material world. He was alive to its beauties and its richness. He delighted in any descriptions you gave him of the changing seasons. The last golden wasps of autumn and the first purple heads of the skunk cabbages were important items of news to him. Once, in answer to a letter of mine describing a spring day in the country, he wired back enthusiastically:

SO GLAD YOU COULD LIE UNDER A TREE!

And if he was still aware of the beauty of the outward world, he did not overlook its ugliness, its complications, and its troubles. If one went to him with problems, spoken or unspoken, one left with many solved —or, rather, dissolved in his presence. For it was not necessary always to mention them. In front of him they were likely to fall into proper proportion. False worries he might prick with his dry humor; actual problems, though so much less than his own, he never belittled. Sometimes, with his acute perception, he would put his finger—very gently —on the sensitive point, as if to say, like the doctor, "It is here that it hurts the most." And he would be quite wise and practical about the cure. He could be stern, too, in his admonitions. "That's your Puritan conscience again," he would chide me sometimes. "A conscience is fine if it stimulates you to action; terrible, if it keeps you from your true work. Like worry: worry is wonderful if it moves you to do things; corroding, if it doesn't. The wonderful thing about the Puritans was their energy."

No, he saw the outward active man, in his outward activities.

"But he saw us in too beautiful a light," someone once protested. "Suppose his eyes had been opened and he had really seen us for what we were—would he not have been terribly disillusioned?"

I do not believe so; his genius was for seeing *through* the outer man to the inner one. It was his understanding of the inner man that was the most miraculous and for which one was most grateful. After all, as Saint-Exupéry's *Little Prince* says, "The eyes are blind; one can only see with the heart." Edward Sheldon saw with the heart. He saw people with love, all of them, even the newcomers like myself. He saw them, therefore, creatively; not only as they were, but as they strove to be, as they were meant to be. He became for many people the creative observer in their lives.

The creative observer is a familiar but usually undervalued character in life. We have all known him and been grateful to him, but we are inclined to take him for granted. There is usually one, sometimes more, in the circle of one's friends. He stands a little removed from the daily round, but near enough to watch. He never interferes; he observes. He is perceptive, kind, appreciative, sometimes critical, but always detached. Even though he is not actively involved in one's life, he has a direct effect on it. When he is on the side lines, one's task immediately takes on new meaning and dignity. It is easier to go on when he is standing there.

A creative observer mirrors back your own life—yes—but your life seen in order, in form, in pattern, even—actually—in beauty. In this capacity, he attains the stature of a creative artist. He performs the function of an artist as analyzed once by the poet Auden. He "finds the order latent in the apparent chaos" of your life. He finds the pattern already there but unaccented. He reveals the beauty existing but unrecognized. This is not a process of deception but of discovery. It is also a process of creation. Edward Sheldon, who had been forced to abandon being a creative artist with stage figures, became one with living people. The brilliant career he left behind in the medium of drama was fulfilled in the medium of life itself.

Have I come back then to the oversimplified conclusion that Edward Sheldon was a saint? Many of us shrink before a word so dazzlingly bright in its connotations of perfection; an image, so lacking in shadows that it is almost invisible to the human eye; a term, too abstract to fit an ordinary mortal in the world today. But if the word *saint* be taken as a symbol for an ordinary man who had overcome superhuman difficulties in his own life; who, after overcoming them, still had ardor enough left to give to those he came in contact with; whose vision was so sharpened by suffering and illuminated by love that he saw everyone as they were meant to be; and, finally, a man who lived a large proportion of his life in a world of eternal values, free of the pressures of time and fear, greed and passion—yes, then it might be said that Edward Sheldon filled the symbol of sainthood.

The last time I went to see him I read to him from T. S. Eliot's *Four Quartets.* "Read that again," I can hear his breathless whisper. I think I read him three times the stanzas from Eliot's poem, *East Coker,* so concerned with eternity and eternal living:

> *Home is where one starts from. As we grow older*
> *The world becomes stranger, the pattern more complicated*
> *Of dead and living. Not the intense moment*
> *Isolated, with no before and after,*
> *But a lifetime burning in every moment. . . .*
>
> *Love is most nearly itself*
> *When here and now cease to matter.*
> *Old men ought to be explorers*
> *Here and there does not matter*
> *We must be still and still moving*
> *Into another intensity*
> *For a further union, a deeper communion*
> *Through the dark cold and the empty desolation,*
> *The wave cry, the wind cry, the vast waters*
> *Of the petrel and the porpoise. In my end is my beginning.*

On this note I left him, promising, as always, to come back very soon. But I was not to see him again.

Those of us who knew him—even I who had known him for so short a time—had mixed emotions when we heard of his sudden and peaceful death. First, the instinctive selfish wrench of pain to lose such a friend and companion. (Hereafter we would have to be the creative observer for ourselves.) And then, perhaps, a sense of wonder at the personality of the man we had known, the image illuminated more sharply, as always, at the moment of loss. And consequently a feeling of responsibility at having known such a person. Public responsibility to let more people know about him, to let more of the world into his quiet room. Private responsibility, which is more difficult for it involves trying to remain the person one was in that room. And this means living in that timeless atmosphere which Edward Sheldon created around him. It demands from one that nearly impossible task of living in the present moment as if it were eternity.

For "eternity," according to Boethius, "is the complete and perfect possession of unlimited life all at once." Paradoxically, this "unlimited life all at once" is what one felt in the presence of this man who had almost no life at all in the worldly or physical meaning of the word. Seated beside him, in the heart of the world's most hurried and high-pressured city, no one ever had a feeling of hurry or pressure. The sense of eternity in which he lived was passed over to the people who sat with him. There, one was able to live for a few minutes—as he lived always.

For Edward Sheldon himself, so far advanced in this difficult task of living eternally, one had no fear, only the certainty that for him the Eliot lines were now being enacted, were coming true. The flesh had become word:

> *We must be still and still moving*
> *Into another intensity*
> *For further union, a deeper communion. . . .*
> *In my end is my beginning.*

VAN WYCK BROOKS

A Season in Hell

TIMES HAVE always been like these. We were born in an off period, 1880–1914, and we can fool ourselves into believing that that was a 'normal era.' It was not. It was a short and pleasant breathing space. Now we are experiencing normal times." So, in 1938, Hendrik van Loon wrote to me, long after the decade I have been recollecting, when there had been a total change in the climate of opinion and feeling that sways the minds of writers and colours their books. In 1920, in the United States, Utopia had still seemed at hand, as it seemed also in Russia after 1917, although it was a lost cause in the rest of Europe, while the ideas of the Enlightenment were active still in American minds and in the minds especially of American writers. But the time had come when these ideas, as a younger writer was to say, "evoke our doubt or mistrust" and "cause us anguish." I am sure that in these words Jacques Barzun was expressing a widespread point of view of the new generation.

Many have attempted to define the change from the "infra-red" epoch of the past to the "ultra-violet" epoch of the thirties and after,— to follow Arthur Koestler's diagnosis,—when humanity seemed to pass into a dark night of the soul. Nothing could have been more marked than the transformation of the literary world from the state of mind of a dozen years before when, as Waldo Frank had said, at the time of *The Seven Arts,* "There is a murmur of suppressed excitement in the air." It was, he added, "like that which hovers over a silent crowd before the appearance of a great procession." Had this procession come and gone? Certainly no one in 1930 looked for any such thing to appear in the future, for "a dreadful apathy, unsureness and discouragement is felt to have fallen upon us," Edmund Wilson wrote in the following year. Gertrude Stein said, in fact, that there was no future,—there was "no future any more"; while Paul Rosenfeld, editing *The American Caravan,* noted that after 1930 every contribution to this yearbook was tragic. In the great number of papers that were submitted to it, he said, there was not one cheerful composition. Paul was dismayed by this uniform note, so different from that of the time when he, like all our contemporaries, had begun to write and when he had half expected to see "ideas at every street corner and rivers of living water in the street." Over the gate of the thirties one seemed to see the words, "Abandon hope, all ye who enter here."

The writers were generally prepared at least to abandon all interest in the future of the world unless they were Marxists who did not believe in the will and who thought that Utopia was coming by an automatic process; while a series of anti-Utopias in the years to come were to present the future as inevitably dismal. Feeling that they could do nothing whatever to change this unpromising picture, the writers quite naturally looked in the other direction and many began to idealize the Middle Ages and fixed the mind on another world and life. Nor were they more disposed to contemplate the future when the menace of atomic destruction rose over the world and when, like old men who fear that tomorrow they are going to develop some fatal disease, they buried all thoughts of the future in thoughts of the past. Constantly more insecure, they were obsessed with security and the orthodoxy that gave them a feeling of this, and, in their dream of authority and unity, they seemed to wish to avoid the paths that had led to so many developments of the livelier twenties. Adventurousness, curiosity and independence had lost their charm in a world that was full of snares and pitfalls, and they were inclined to share Cardinal Newman's "fierce thoughts against the Liberals" whose gullibility, they felt, had deceived and betrayed them. Nor could they continue to trust themselves when all humanity, as it seemed to them, had revealed such fathomless depths of depravity and evil.

For, with the new generation, the moral effects of the first world war spread to the remotest corner of the realm of writers, and this reproduced the symptoms of the Hellenistic age, as we have been taught by eminent scholars to see it. The sense of failure in that age, the loss of hope in the present world and in organized effort and human calculation, together with the lapse of self-confidence that accompanied this, had developed in the Greeks to a pessimistic mysticism that was focussed on a dream-world far away. Humanism, as the thirties advanced, became more and more a byword, and art, as Ortega said, was dehumanized also, while the mind of the present ransacked the past for earlier minds, both small and great, that confirmed its own disillusion and despair.

Meanwhile, I experienced my own season in hell.

One day during these later years of which I have been writing I happened to visit a certain refugee author, an Austrian, known the world over, with only a few months to live, who had settled in a college town not far away. I found him in a cluttered shabby room in a dreary students' lodging-house, looking out on a back yard full of mud and rubbish, where a closet door stood open revealing his wardrobe, a battered old hat and a threadbare coat or two. In one corner was a kerosene stove on which he evidently cooked the meals that he drew from bottles and cans piled beside it, and various noxious smells and sounds drifted, as the talk went on, through the dingy golden-oak woodwork of the windows and the walls. He remarked that he was sixty-five and it struck me how easy it would be to take all this for granted if one were twenty,—when anything will pass for picturesqueness,—while many another at his age, obliged to exist in a similar way, would have hanged themselves forthwith from the door of the closet. But he was obviously living in quite another world. Apropos of nothing, he suddenly exclaimed, "The Engadine is beautiful. It is really beautiful! I know because I have just been rereading the novel I wrote about it fifteen years ago."

This great man was living in a dream of his own imagination, and all writers, in fact, exist under a sort of spell or, one might say, within a magic circle. They live under a dome of many-coloured glass, and they see the world, including themselves, as this many-coloured glass iridescently stains it. If the dome is broken, if the bubble bursts, as one might otherwise put it, and they see life in its nakedness, or see themselves so,—as mere old men in sordid lodging-houses,—they are apt to fall into the melancholy leading to despair which the monks called acedia in the Middle Ages. Most of the recorded instances of mediæval suicide were occasioned by acedia in the monasteries, I have been told, and something similar surely accounts for the catastrophic endings that have so often marked the lives of writers.

There came a time in the middle twenties when my own bubble burst, when the dome under which I had lived crumbled into ruin, when I was consumed with a sense of failure, a feeling that my work had all gone wrong and that I was mistaken in all I had said or thought. What had I been doing? I had only ploughed the sea, as a certain great man once remarked, and I thought of my writing "with rage and shame," E. M. Forster's phrase for his own feeling about his early work. I was pursued especially with nightmares in which Henry James turned great luminous menacing eyes upon me. I was half aware, in connection with him, of the division within myself, and with all the bad conscience of a criminal I felt I had viewed him with something of Plato's "hard little eye of detraction." In short, in this middle of my life, I was thoroughly bedevilled. I saw myself as a capsized ship at night with the passengers drowned underneath and the keel in the air. I could no longer sleep, I scarcely sat down for a year, I lived in a Plutonian psychical twilight. Even the sun was off-colour to me, I was a prey to vertigo, at moments my brain seemed to be deranged, and when I napped for an hour or so I dreamed that I was about to be hanged or that something had occurred in my blood-stream that was evidently fatal. All my affections and interests fell into abeyance, and it seemed to me that, where normal depressions occasionally sank to zero, mine sank from zero indefinitely down. The nadir of common depressions was the peak of mine. Nine-tenths of all my energy was involved in a neurosis and barely one-tenth was left for living.

I had always been possessed by this idea or that, usually the notion of the book I happened to be writing, which I pursued like a beagle with his nose to the ground; and I was possessed now with a fantasy of suicide that filled my mind as the full moon fills the sky. It was a fixed idea. I could not expel this fantasy that shimmered in my brain, and I saw every knife as something with which to cut one's throat and every high building as something to jump from. A belt was a garotte for me, a rope existed to hang oneself with, the top of a door was merely a bracket for the rope, every rusty musket had its predestined use for me and every tomb in a graveyard was a place to starve in. I could see an axe only as lethal and every bottle meant for me something to be swallowed in splinters or to slash one's wrists with, while even the winter snow fell in order to give one pneumonia if one spent a night lying on the ground. Meanwhile, every morning, when I began to sleep again, I awoke with my arms folded over my breast. I had been dreaming that I was dead at last and unconsciously arranged my limbs in the posture of a mummy.

In my *crise à quarante ans* I shrank from all human relations, and this explained the image Paul Rosenfeld happened upon in the fine essay he wrote about me. He spoke of a house with the shades drawn and a man sitting within, a man who could not hear the knock when life drove up to the door with her merry summons. How could Paul ever have guessed what was happening in that house? Nor did Sherwood Anderson know why it was that we drifted apart when he wrote, "I did not put Brooks aside. He put me aside." But, calling me a New Englander, though he knew well I was not one, he pictured in a striking phrase my mental condition. Observing that I had the "beauty" of the New England mind, he said I suffered from its "cold inner fright."

One of the doctors whom I saw and who had read *The Ordeal of Mark Twain* asked me if I considered that "reason" or "emotion" had been the determining element in my mind and work. The question had never occurred to me, but, recalling my struggles to make this book logical and clear, I replied, "Reason, I suppose," and the doctor smiled. He shook his head and walked away, and I saw at once that he was right. I had always worked by following my nose, I had never been able to think anything out but rather *felt* things out in a cumbersome fashion, and, writing always intuitively, I was emotionally paralyzed now or, as Dr. Brill said, "too disturbed for treatment." My wife had written to Dr. Jung, whom Joel Spingarn knew well and who replied sympathetically and kindly from Zurich. The psychology of my illness, he wrote, was transparent enough: what I had was "chronic melancholia" and "a terribly hard case for treatment, if possible at all." He added, "Things seem to have gone very far," saying that even to attempt a cure would be hazardous under the circumstances. He then suggested the old expedient of a year on a Western ranch, for, in primitive surroundings, complicated situations often dissolved, as he put it, or were eased at least.

The upshot was that, like Peer Gynt, I went back to the buttonmoulder. I was to spend four years in houses of the dead, or, as one might say, the wounded, or the about-to-be-reborn, at Stockbridge, at Katonah, at White Plains and in England. It struck me at once that my fellow-inmates all had queer eyes, which I took for a sign of the clan I now belonged to, the clan of those to whom they said, "What *were* you?" as if you had actually arrived in the land of shades. All I remember of Stockbridge now was a drive one day to Pittsfield and Herman Melville's farm on a lonely road, where one still saw the name "Arrowhead" boldly carved on the carriage-block and a house all in sagging disrepair. It was a dirtyish yellow and some windows were broken. But there was the big chimney of which Melville had written and the famous piazza he had built, to remind himself in the country of the deck of a ship, with its straw-coloured planks rotting away. Peeping through the boards that covered the windows, I saw some of his old folios within, together with a big ship's model on a bracket on the wall, which took me seventy years back to the day when this *exalté* had also undergone a season in hell.

I was to find myself presently in an English sanitarium where I spent eight months at Harrow-on-the-Hill in a long low Queen Anne manor-house that was later to become the infirmary of the neighbouring Harrow school. There I conceived the delusion that I was about to be buried alive, not in the earth but walled in a small chamber; and I believed that "they" were coming for me. For many mornings, waking early from an artificial sleep, I heard them putting together a large box for me below, a box that, in my fantasy, had arrived in sections to be hammered together in the house with nails or pegs. To me this accounted for the resonant clatter of the housemaids who were merely pulling up the Venetian blinds. If I was not to be buried alive why should people have talked to me about the crypt of St. Paul's or the wax funeral figures,—the Effigies,—in their glass cases in Westminster Abbey? I was persuaded that the doctor had induced Parliament to pass a bill enabling him to bury me alive, a notion that later suggested to me how large was the ego in my cosmos (in the phrase of the elderly German in Kipling's tale). There was even a day when I stood by the table in my circular room in the tower,—it was a sunny spring day, the curtains were flapping, and the daffodils were all out in the grass below,—when I had a sudden vision of the end of the world, a catastrophe caused solely by my fate. For this had occasioned a breakdown of all who were attached to me and who were also, in consequence, buried alive, while those who were attached to them came to the same end, and so on, and on, *ad infinitum*. As in some monstrous cosmic general strike, all mankind was engulfed, all movement ceased. I could see the steamships stopping in the middle of the ocean, while invisible waves of horror encircled the world.

There were other trances, like opium dreams, illusions of infinite time and space, into which I fell abruptly during these four years. I remember, at home again, looking up at windows that had meant much to me not long before, and wondering how it was possible for me, in 1929, to have bridged the vast chasm of years since 1906. That year seemed more remote than the great days of Egypt. Meanwhile, I found myself in the rose-embosomed hospital that William Seabrook described in his book *Asylum* where the ornamental iron-work over the windows disguised the actuality of bars. The long corridor was hung with steel-engravings of William Tell, the Parthenon, King Lear and his daughters, and the guards, patrolling the red carpet, kept under constant surveillance the doorless rooms in which anything might happen. A rattling of the main door, at nine o'clock sharp in the morning, proclaimed the official entrance of the froglike doctor, the bearded panjandrum with the long chain of keys and his retinue of assistants, orderlies and nurses. Passing from patient to patient, scattering insults and ironies,—a sort of cold-shock treatment that was then in vogue,—he would order the hydropathic hose for the man who had jumped off Brooklyn Bridge and the pack for the young man who presently drowned himself (when he was permitted to go home for a

Sunday). Then, with carpentry, basketry, weaving, one went back to the kindergarten, with the hope, supposedly, that a new man would grow from the little child one had become again.

Out of the purgatorial mist that now envelops the scene for me more than one tragic and shadowy character emerges. There was the famous doctor who had become a destructive child and who tried to smash his bedstead in the middle of the night. Then there was the old gentleman whom I saw standing on a chair in his room attaching his suspenders to the chandelier, in a patient methodical effort to encircle his neck, and there was the florist whose name was emblazoned on many a New York street, a religious maniac who was also homicidal. He fell to his knees and prayed one day when four of us were playing bridge, then suddenly sprang up and tried to strangle my partner. There was the newspaper publisher who said he must see the doctor at once about an affair involving ten million dollars, whose aeroplane was ticking outside waiting to take him to Africa where he was going for a spell of big-game hunting. He hadn't a minute to spare, he said, then, seizing a large flower-pot, he threw it through the window and sat down on the floor with a wild laugh. There was a charming old man, besides, who one saw strolling about the grounds in white flannel trousers and a parti-coloured blazer,—General A., I was told he was, and I knew this could not be true because I had read his obituary ten years before. I had read this because he was the uncle of one of my friends and I had met him when I was a boy; but, dead as he was supposed to be, this really was General A., whose family had announced that he was dead when they shut him up. He had even escaped once and appeared at his club in New York, where the attendants who had known him took him for a ghost and whence he had been spirited back to the hospital again. There, I was told, whenever he could, this beautifully groomed old gentleman rubbed in his hair the poached eggs from his breakfast tray. Dreadful to me was the daily exit of the inmates of the so-called violent ward who appeared, in a long queue, for exercise just before noon, marching in single file, with white-coated orderlies flanking them, and winding through the grounds to the cracking of invisible whips. It was a Doré picture, in real life, from the Inferno. The queue was led by a grey-haired giant, an ex-Presbyterian clergyman, who shouted obscenities and oaths as he capered on the path.

Such are my memories of those years when my existence seemed to me a "lost traveller's dream under the hill"; and even after I came back to life and sailed out clear and free I remained conscious at moments of an abyss beside me. I seemed to catch out of the tail of my eye a cold black draughty void, with a feeling that I stood on the brink of it in peril of my reason; but it was only rarely now that I had this glimpse of the *néant,* and in the end my crisis was invaluable for me. I felt as one of my friends felt after he too struck bottom and had "come up more and more ever since," finding his own grave break-down a "complete purgation." To me he wrote, "I predict you'll find new springs of energy that you had never suspected"; and so, in fact, it proved to be when I returned to love and work with a feeling that my best years still lay before me. Hawthorne had spoken of the dark caverns into which all men must descend if they are to know anything beneath the surface, or what he called the illusive pleasures of existence. It seemed to me now that I understood him, and I wondered if this did not justify the later phase of the world's mind too and the literary mind that reflected its darkness.

ANNE FRANK

The diary kept by Anne Frank in her early teens has been received as one of the most remarkable and moving personal documents of our time. Born in Germany in 1929, three years before Hitler's accession to power, she lived there with her family into the early Thirties. They were Jews, and soon after the beginning of the Nazi regime, they migrated to Holland. Up to the time of the Nazi occupation of Holland, they were able to live normal lives, but with the coming of the Nazis, they were forced into hiding, and took refuge in the abandoned half of an office building. There they were joined by another refugee family. The diary, which Anne began at the age of thirteen, records their life, with its increasing privations and dangers. She continued it for two years, until they were discovered by the Gestapo in 1944. Friends of the Frank family found the diary after the raid, in which the entire group were arrested and sent to concentration camps. Two months before the liberation of Holland, in March, 1945, Anne died in the camp at Bergen-Belsen. Her diary was first published in Holland, in 1947. Following its publication in this country, it was successfully adapted for the stage.

There are those who are skeptical as to its complete authenticity, and who think it may have been doctored for publication. There is, however, no proven ground for this belief. The only basis for it is the amazingly mature quality of the writing, and the depth of its insights, for Anne set down not only her own thoughts, but her observations regarding the other members of the two families and their behavior under the stress of the difficult situation in which they all lived. She was a child of great sensitivity and intelligence, and her exposure to some of the most shocking events of our century resulted in one more valuable record of man's double-barreled capacity for depravity and nobility of spirit. I have chosen a few of the diary's most revealing pages.

The Diary of a Young Girl

Saturday, 20 June, 1942

I HAVEN'T written for a few days, because I wanted first of all to think about my diary. It's an odd idea for someone like me to keep a diary; not only because I have never done so before, but because it seems to me that neither I—nor for that matter anyone else—will be interested in the unbosomings of a thirteen-year-old schoolgirl. Still, what does that matter? I want to write, but more than that, I want to bring out all kinds of things that lie buried deep in my heart.

There is a saying that "paper is more patient than man"; it came back to me on one of my slightly melancholy days, while I sat chin in hand, feeling too bored and limp even to make up my mind whether to go out or stay at home. Yes, there is no doubt that paper is patient and as I don't intend to show this cardboard-covered notebook, bearing the proud name of "diary," to anyone, unless I find a real friend, boy or girl, probably nobody cares. And now I come to the root of the matter, the reason for my starting a diary: it is that I have no such real friend.

Let me put it more clearly, since no one will believe that a girl of thirteen feels herself quite alone in the world, nor is it so. I have darling parents and a sister of sixteen. I know about thirty people whom one might call friends—I have strings of boy friends, anxious to catch a glimpse of me and who, failing that, peep at me through mirrors in class. I have relations, aunts and uncles, who are darlings too, a good home, no—I don't seem to lack anything. But it's the same with all my friends, just fun and joking, nothing more. I can never bring myself to talk of anything outside the common round. We don't seem to be able to get any closer, that is the root of the trouble. Perhaps I lack confidence, but anyway, there it is, a stubborn fact and I don't seem to be able to do anything about it.

Hence, this diary. In order to enhance in my mind's eye the picture of the friend for whom I have waited so long, I don't want to set down a series of bald facts in a diary like most people do, but I want this diary itself to be my friend, and I shall call my friend Kitty. No one will grasp what I'm talking about if I begin my letters to Kitty just out of the blue, so, albeit unwillingly, I will start by sketching in brief the story of my life.

My father was thirty-six when he married my mother, who was then twenty-five. My sister Margot was born in 1926 in Frankfort-on-Main,

I followed on June 12, 1929, and, as we are Jewish, we emigrated to Holland in 1933, where my father was appointed Managing Director of Travies N.V. This firm is in close relationship with the firm of Kolen & Co. in the same building, of which my father is a partner.

The rest of our family, however, felt the full impact of Hitler's anti-Jewish laws, so life was filled with anxiety. In 1938 after the pogroms, my two uncles (my mother's brothers) escaped to the U.S.A. My old grandmother came to us, she was then seventy-three. After May 1940 good times rapidly fled: first the war, then the capitulation, followed by the arrival of the Germans, which is when the sufferings of us Jews really began. Anti-Jewish decrees followed each other in quick succession. Jews must wear a yellow star,[1] Jews must hand in their bicycles, Jews are banned from trams and are forbidden to drive. Jews are only allowed to do their shopping between three and five o'clock and then only in shops which bear the placard "Jewish shop." Jews must be indoors by eight o'clock and cannot even sit in their own gardens after that hour. Jews are forbidden to visit theaters, cinemas, and other places of entertainment. Jews may not take part in public sports. Swimming baths, tennis courts, hockey fields, and other sports grounds are all prohibited to them. Jews may not visit Christians. Jews must go to Jewish schools, and many more restrictions of a similar kind.

So we could not do this and were forbidden to do that. But life went on in spite of it all. Jopie used to say to me, "You're scared to do anything because it may be forbidden." Our freedom was strictly limited. Yet things were still bearable.

Granny died in January 1942; no one will ever know how much she is present in my thoughts and how much I love her still.

In 1934 I went to school at the Montessori Kindergarten and continued there. It was at the end of the school year, I was in form 6B, when I had to say good-by to Mrs. K. We both wept, it was very sad. In 1941 I went, with my sister Margot, to the Jewish Secondary School, she into the fourth form and I into the first.

So far everything is all right with four of us and here I come to the present day.

Friday, 9 October, 1942

Dear Kitty,

I've only got dismal and depressing news for you today. Our many Jewish friends are being taken away by the dozen. These people are treated by the Gestapo without a shred of decency, being loaded into cattle trucks and sent to Westerbork, the big Jewish camp in Drente.

---

[1] To distinguish them from others, all Jews were forced by the Germans to wear, prominently displayed, a yellow six-pointed star.

Westerbork sounds terrible: only one washing cubicle for a hundred people and not nearly enough lavatories. There is no separate accommodation. Men, women, and children all sleep together. One hears of frightful immorality because of this; and a lot of the women, and even girls, who stay there any length of time are expecting babies.

It is impossible to escape; most of the people in the camp are branded as inmates by their shaven heads and many also by their Jewish appearance.

If it is as bad as this in Holland whatever will it be like in the distant and barbarous regions they are sent to? We assume that most of them are murdered. The English radio speaks of their being gassed.

Perhaps that is the quickest way to die. I feel terribly upset. I couldn't tear myself away while Miep told these dreadful stories; and she herself was equally wound up for that matter. Just recently for instance, a poor old crippled Jewess was sitting on her doorstep; she had been told to wait there by the Gestapo, who had gone to fetch a car to take her away. The poor old thing was terrified by the guns that were shooting at English planes overhead, and by the glaring beams of the searchlights. But Miep did not dare take her in; no one would undergo such a risk. The Germans strike without the slightest mercy. Elli too is very quiet: her boy friend has got to go to Germany. She is afraid that the airmen who fly over our homes will drop their bombs, often weighing a million kilos, on Dirk's head. Jokes such as "he's not likely to get a million" and "it only takes one bomb" are in rather bad taste. Dirk is certainly not the only one who has to go: trainloads of boys leave daily. If they stop at a small station en route, sometimes some of them manage to get out unnoticed and escape; perhaps a few manage it. This, however, is not the end of my bad news. Have you ever heard of hostages? That's the latest thing in penalties for sabotage. Can you imagine anything so dreadful?

Prominent citizens—innocent people—are thrown into prison to await their fate. If the saboteur can't be traced, the Gestapo simply put about five hostages against the wall. Announcements of their deaths appear in the papers frequently. These outrages are described as "fatal accidents." Nice people, the Germans! To think that I was once one of them too! No, Hitler took away our nationality long ago. In fact, Germans and Jews are the greatest enemies in the world.

Yours, Anne

Thursday, 19 November, 1942

Dear Kitty,

Dussel is a very nice man, just as we had all imagined. Of course he thought it was all right to share my little room.

Quite honestly I'm not so keen that a stranger should use my things, but one must be prepared to make some sacrifices for a good cause, so I shall make my little offering with a good will. "If we can save someone, then everything else is of secondary importance," says Daddy, and he's absolutely right.

The first day that Dussel was here, he immediately asked me all sorts of questions: When does the charwoman come? When can one use the bathroom? When is one allowed to use the lavatory? You may laugh, but these things are not so simple in a hiding place. During the day we mustn't make any noise that might be heard downstairs; and if there is some stranger—such as the charwoman for example—then we have to be extra careful. I explained all this carefully to Dussel. But one thing amazed me: he is very slow on the uptake. He asks everything twice over and still doesn't seem to remember. Perhaps that will wear off in time, and it's only that he's thoroughly upset by the sudden change.

Apart from that, all goes well. Dussel has told us a lot about the outside world, which we have missed for so long now. He had very sad news. Countless friends and acquaintances have gone to a terrible fate. Evening after evening the green and gray army lorries trundle past. The Germans ring at every front door to inquire if there are any Jews living in the house. If there are, then the whole family has to go at once. If they don't find any, they go on to the next house. No one has a chance of evading them unless one goes into hiding. Often they go around with lists, and only ring when they know they can get a good haul. Sometimes they let them off for cash—so much per head. It seems like the slave hunts of olden times. But it's certainly no joke; it's much too tragic for that. In the evenings when it's dark, I often see rows of good, innocent people accompanied by crying children, walking on and on, in charge of a couple of these chaps, bullied and knocked about until they almost drop. No one is spared—old people, babies, expectant mothers, the sick—each and all join in the march of death.

How fortunate we are here, so well cared for and undisturbed. We wouldn't have to worry about all this misery were it not that we are so anxious about all those dear to us whom we can no longer help.

I feel wicked sleeping in a warm bed, while my dearest friends have been knocked down or have fallen into a gutter somewhere out in the cold night. I get frightened when I think of close friends who have now been delivered into the hands of the cruelest brutes that walk the earth. And all because they are Jews!

Yours, Anne

Monday, 3 April, 1944

Dear Kitty,

Contrary to my usual custom, I will for once write more fully about food because it has become a very difficult and important matter, not only here in the "Secret Annexe" but in the whole of Holland, all Europe, and even beyond.

In the twenty-one months that we've spent here we have been through a good many "food cycles"—you'll understand what that means in a minute. When I talk of "food cycles" I mean periods in which one has nothing else to eat but one particular dish or kind of vegetable. We had nothing but endive for a long time, day in, day out, endive with sand, endive without sand, stew with endive, boiled or *en casserole;* then it was spinach, and after that followed kohlrabi, salsify, cucumbers, tomatoes, sauerkraut, etc., etc.

For instance, it's really disagreeable to eat a lot of sauerkraut for lunch and supper every day, but you do it if you're hungry. However, we have the most delightful period of all now, because we don't get any fresh vegetables at all. Our weekly menu for supper consists of kidney beans, pea soup, potatoes with dumplings, potato-chalet and, by the grace of God, occasionally turnip tops or rotten carrots, and then the kidney beans once again. We eat potatoes at every meal, beginning with breakfast, because of the bread shortage. We make our soup from kidney or haricot beans, potatoes, Julienne soup in packets, French beans in packets, kidney beans in packets. Everything contains beans, not to mention the bread!

In the evening we always have potatoes with gravy substitute and— thank goodness we've still got it—beetroot salad. I must still tell you about the dumplings, which we make out of government flour, water, and yeast. They are so sticky and tough, they lie like stones in one's stomach—ah, well!

The great attraction each week is a slice of liver sausage, and jam on dry bread. But we're still alive, and quite often we even enjoy our poor meals.

Yours, Anne

Sunday morning, just before eleven o'clock,

16 April, 1944

Darlingest Kitty,

Remember yesterday's date, for it is a very important day in my life. Surely it is a great day for every girl when she receives her first kiss? Well, then, it is just as important for me too! Bram's kiss on my right cheek doesn't count any more, likewise the one from Mr. Walker on my right hand.

How did I suddenly come by this kiss? Well, I will tell you.

Yesterday evening at eight o'clock I was sitting with Peter on his divan, it wasn't long before his arm went round me. "Let's move up a bit," I said, "then I don't bump my head against the cupboard." He moved up, almost into the corner, I laid my arm under his and across his back, and he just about buried me, because his arm was hanging on my shoulder.

Now we've sat like this on other occasions, but never so close together as yesterday. He held me firmly against him, my left shoulder against his chest; already my heart began to beat faster, but we had not finished yet. He didn't rest until my head was on his shoulder and his against it. When I sat upright again after about five minutes, he soon took my head in his hands and laid it against him once more. Oh, it was so lovely, I couldn't talk much, the joy was too great. He stroked my cheek and arm a bit awkwardly, played with my curls and our heads lay touching most of the time. I can't tell you, Kitty, the feeling that ran through me all the while. I was too happy for words, and I believe he was as well.

We got up at half past eight. Peter put on his gym shoes, so that when he toured the house he wouldn't make a noise, and I stood beside him. How it came about so suddenly, I don't know, but before we went downstairs he kissed me, through my hair, half on my left cheek, half on my ear; I tore downstairs without looking round, and am simply longing for today!

Yours, Anne

Monday, 17 April, 1944

Dear Kitty,

Do you think that Daddy and Mummy would approve of my sitting and kissing a boy on a divan—a boy of seventeen and a half and a girl of just under fifteen? I don't really think they would, but I must rely on myself over this. It is so quiet and peaceful to lie in his arms and to dream, it is so thrilling to feel his cheek against mine, it is so lovely to know that there is someone waiting for me. But there is indeed a big "but," because will Peter be content to leave it at this? I haven't forgotten his promise already, but...he *is* a boy!

I know myself that I'm starting very soon, not even fifteen, and so independent already! It's certainly hard for other people to understand, I know almost for certain that Margot would never kiss a boy unless there had been some talk of an engagement or marriage, but neither Peter nor I have anything like that in mind. I'm sure too that Mummy never touched a man before Daddy. What would my girl friends say about it if they knew that I lay in Peter's arms, my heart against his chest, my head on his shoulder and with his head against mine!

Oh, Anne, how scandalous! But honestly, I don't think it is; we are shut up here, shut away from the world, in fear and anxiety, especially just lately. Why, then, should we who love each other remain apart? Why should we wait until we've reached a suitable age? Why should we bother?

I have taken it upon myself to look after myself; he would never want to cause me sorrow or pain. Why shouldn't I follow the way my heart leads me, if it makes us both happy? All the same, Kitty, I believe you can sense that I'm in doubt, I think it must be my honesty which rebels against doing anything on the sly! Do you think it's my duty to tell Daddy what I'm doing? Do you think we should share our secret with a third person? A lot of the beauty would be lost, but would my conscience feel happier? I will discuss it with "him."

Oh, yes, there's still so much I want to talk to him about, for I don't see the use of only just cuddling each other. To exchange our thoughts, that shows confidence and faith in each other, we would both be sure to profit by it!

Yours, Anne

Monday, 22 May, 1944

Dear Kitty,

On May 20th Daddy lost five bottles of yoghourt on a bet with Mrs. Van Daan. The invasion still hasn't come yet; it's no exaggeration to say that all Amsterdam, all Holland, yes, the whole west coast of Europe, right down to Spain, talks about the invasion day and night, debates about it, and makes bets on it and ... hopes.

The suspense is rising to a climax. By no means everyone we had regarded as "good" Dutch have stuck to their faith in the English; by no means everyone thinks the English bluff a masterly piece of strategy, oh no, the people want to see deeds at last, great, heroic deeds. Nobody sees beyond his own nose, no one thinks that the English are fighting for their own land and their own people, everyone thinks that it's their duty to save Holland, as quickly and as well as they can.

What obligations have the English towards us? How have the Dutch earned the generous help that they seem so explicitly to expect? Oh no, the Dutch will have made a big mistake, the English, in spite of all their bluff, are certainly no more to blame than all the other countries, great and small, which are not under occupation. The English really won't offer us their apologies, for even if we do reproach them for being asleep during the years when Germany was rearming, we cannot deny that all the other countries, especially those bordering Germany, also slept. We shan't get anywhere by following an ostrich policy. England and the whole world have seen that only too well now, and that is why, one by one, England, no less than the rest, will have to make heavy sacrifices.

No country is going to sacrifice its men for nothing and certainly not in the interests of another. England is not going to do that either. The invasion, with liberation and freedom, will come sometime, but England and America will appoint the day, not all the occupied countries put together.

To our great horror and regret we hear that the attitude of a great many people towards us Jews has changed. We hear that there is anti-Semitism now in circles that never thought of it before. This news has affected us all very, very deeply. The cause of this hatred of the Jews is understandable, even human sometimes, but not good. The Christians blame the Jews for giving secrets away to the Germans, for betraying their helpers and for the fact that, through the Jews, a great many Christians have gone the way of so many others before them, and suffered terrible punishments and a dreadful fate.

This is all true, but one must always look at these things from both sides. Would Christians behave differently in our place? The Germans have means of making people talk. Can a person, entirely at their mercy, whether Jew or Christian, always remain silent? Everyone knows that is practically impossible. Why, then, should people demand the impossible of the Jews?

It's being murmured in underground circles that the German Jews who emigrated to Holland and who are now in Poland may not be allowed to return here; they once had the right of asylum in Holland, but when Hitler has gone they will have to go back to Germany again.

When one hears this one naturally wonders why we are carrying on with this long and difficult war. We always hear that we're all fighting together for freedom, truth, and right! Is discord going to show itself while we are still fighting, is the Jew once again worth less than another? Oh, it is sad, very sad, that once more, for the umpteenth time, the old truth is confirmed: "What *one* Christian does is his own responsibility, what *one* Jew does is thrown back at all Jews."

Quite honestly, I can't understand that the Dutch, who are such a good, honest, upright people, should judge us like this, we, the most oppressed, the unhappiest, perhaps the most pitiful of all peoples of the whole world.

I hope *one* thing only, and that is that this hatred of the Jews will be a passing thing, that the Dutch will show what they are after all, and that they will never totter and lose their sense of right. For anti-Semitism is unjust!

And if this terrible threat should actually come true, then the pitiful little collection of Jews that remain will have to leave Holland. We, too, shall have to move on again with our little bundles, and leave this beautiful country, which offered us such a warm welcome and which now turns its back on us.

I love Holland. I who, having no native country, had hoped that it might become my fatherland, and I still hope it will!

Yours, Anne

Anne's diary ends here. On August 4, 1944, the Grüne Polizei made a raid on the "Secret Annexe." All the occupants, together with Kraler and Koophuis, were arrested and sent to German and Dutch concentration camps.

The "Secret Annexe" was plundered by the Gestapo. Among a pile of old books, magazines, and newspapers which were left lying on the floor, Miep and Elli found Anne's diary. Apart from a very few passages, which are of little interest to the reader, the original text has been printed.

Of all the occupants of the "Secret Annexe," Anne's father alone returned. Kraler and Koophuis, who withstood the hardships of the Dutch camp, were able to go home to their families.

In March 1945, two months before the liberation of Holland, Anne died in the concentration camp at Bergen-Belsen.

IULIA DE BEAUSOBRE

Mme. de Beausobre had been a member of the old Russian intelligent-sia, and at the outbreak of the Bolshevik revolution was living in Paris with her French husband. Although they could have remained in France and in safety, they felt impelled to participate in the momentous events which were, in John Reed's words, to shake the world. Their troubles began soon after their return to Russia. Their child died in infancy, M. de Beausobre fell ill of typhus, but recovered. Then, for more than ten years, he worked in the State Bank and the State Publishing Department, while Mme. de Beausobre taught French and English, translated, and did other literary work. But as for so many others of their class, the day came when they were arrested and thrown into prison.

The Woman Who Could Not Die, a few pages from which are reprinted here, is the story, and an eloquent one, of Mme. de Beausobre's experience in prison. The world knows what the victims of the Soviet terror have endured; what it meant to a sensitive and cultivated woman has perhaps never been more graphically described than in the pages of Mme. de Beausobre's book. It is notable not merely for its picture of prison life, but as a record as well of the courage and compassion with which she faced up to a ruthless, ugly, and degraded world.

The Woman Who Could Not Die

I HAVE not been too well lately, so Nicolay's councillors insist on our going into the high hills of Persia for the summer.

On a still night, as clear as dark blue crystal, our caravan leaves the tall clay walls and the gigantic shady trees of Samarkand. My camel lunges and sways to a rhythm that I love because of early childhood's memories. The silk hangings of the canopy that surround me flutter lightly in the night wind. This awakens in their folds a hundred lurking scents of improbable Eastern spices. If I raise the silk swaying gently on my left, I can see the back and neck of a tall dun-coloured camel—the twin of mine. On its hump sways the sky-blue palanquin that protects our children and their nurse from wind and dust; also from the scorching sun in the day-time. If I raise the silk swaying gently on my right, I can see Nicolay on his horse. Even when I do not raise the hangings I can hear the soft munch-munch and the gentle cling-clang that tell me he is there, on his mount.

When we have passed the last outposts, and the unfathomable desert closes round us, a horseman breaks the silence with a low and sadly rippling chant. Another joins in with a high treble. And soon all the men are singing the centuries-old legends of life and death, of love and hate, of hope and of despair, of coming and of going. Of the coming of the child and the killing of the man. And of woman's bliss and sorrow.

Lulled by the chant, the scent, and the swaying movement, I drop off to sleep thinking of the oasis we shall come to at dawn. The silver freshet will be trickling cool and clear. The tall palms will be swaying their enormous green hands high above us in an ever-brightening sky of tenderest sunrise-blue. The children will dip their hands in the icy water. The women will gather dates. The men will lay the fire, un-harness and tether the horses and camels. The gentle moon will be setting on my left, and on my right the immense ball of ruddy flame will come rushing out of the awakening earth. I can hear the quick-ening rhythm of its song, the clangour of its all-devouring, all-engender-ing onslaught.... But why is this delicate boy, with flaxen hair and the sad eyes of a Byzantine Madonna, staring at me in awe? What does he want? Why is he so persistent? Oh, Boy, Boy, why must you break into the reality of my colourful life with the dried-up unreal phan-tasmagoria of yours?

But he does not go away. He is leaning forward with a look that has a shade of horror in it. Appealingly he says:

"It is morning, the day is here again, Citizen. Get up. You must get up. We must take you to the wash-place. Do get up. Wake up, it is morning."

The growing, wondering horror in his eyes causes me to bound over the chasm that yawns between us. The mental effort of the leap is so overpowering that it makes the muscles of my body contract. I sit up with a jerk. Bolt upright. My head swims. My breath comes in snatches. But the sad and frightened child must be reassured imme-diately. I strive desperately to look ordinary, to sound quite ordinary too.

"Yes. I thank you. I shall get dressed now. I shan't take long."

His eyes shudder all over my face once more. Then he goes. Is this madness?

I try to look life squarely in the face.

They say they will kill us both. If they do—so much the better after all—one gets so weary! But what if they do not? Nicolay is not the man to get unhinged under any circumstances. He is also not the man to die easily or to be shattered easily by anything. Yet if I let myself die of this, or if I go out of my mind here, that will shatter him profoundly: for life, no matter how long he may live.

So it is clear that I must not die unless they kill me, and above all I must not lose my reason. But if I refrain from dreaming dreams that are speedily becoming my masters instead of remaining my slaves, I shall have to think as *They* want me to. I refuse to do that! I refuse to be forced into self-torture. My mind and spirit are free. Why should they torment themselves or me? Perhaps I could make objective stories of my too vivid subjective dreams. It seems the only thing.

Having come to this resolution, I drowse all day in the hushed grey twilight of my cell.

When evening comes and the light is switched on, anxiety and foreboding awaken in the Inner. Above me, to the right of me, to the left of me, wherever I direct my attention in this immense building men, agonized by what the Russians call *smértnaya toska,* pace their cells. To and fro. To and fro. The hopeless restlessness of caged tigers and lions is upon them.... How could I enjoy going to the zoo? How could I study the movements of caged animals? Sketch them! Some of the pacing men are wearing heavy boots, others creaky shoes. That thud-thud over there is the sound of a heavy man walking in his socks.

Somewhere in this stony maze Nicolay too is pacing...pacing, thinking...thinking. My God, if only— No! I am not going to think in that way. I am going to tell myself a story.

"Your name, Citizen."

"Iulia de Beausobre."

"You will be taken before the examining officer. Get ready."

As we wind our way up and down and through the maze of passages and staircases I am only half awake. A thin but most persistent thread of thought, woven into a semi-circle of vivid pictures, still grips my imagination. The incidents of the story are spread out before me as on an open fan.

We enter a room. With a jerk I come down into earth's realities. The carpet under my feet is dark ruby red. Already I can breathe the smell of incense blending with the typical smell of Father's study, cedar wood and sandal wood. I clench my fists and dig my nails into the palms of my hands to stop myself from drifting away to re-live my brother's christening.

The effort of keeping a clear awareness of my surroundings makes me go cold with a clammy sweat. I set my teeth hard so that they shall not chatter. I tear my eyes away from the red carpet.

This room is large and well lit, but the light is soft. The walls are blue, neither pale nor dark. Deep and low dark brown leather arm-chairs are placed here and there, in groups. Uniformed men are sitting in some of them. Chatting. And drinking tea with piles of cakes—the gaudy kind, no larger than a bite or two. There is a writing-desk at the end of the room. Attila is sitting behind it, facing the door. He signs the chit stating that I have been duly delivered. The other men are the Bison, Neo-Narcissus, the Death's-Head and—the Snake.

I must not shudder. I must force myself not to mind even this one.

Attila looks up at me. "Come here," and he points to a chair by his desk. I sit down with my back to the others.

"Do you ride?"

This is so unexpected that it almost makes me laugh nervously. I try to look as indifferent as he sounds.

"I used to, when I was young."

"You are not too old to do so now. You can get excellent mounts at the Manège. And quite cheap."

"I had not thought of it."

"You should."

The Bison lounges up to us, hands thrust into his pockets, eyes half closed, heavy eyelids and sweeping, silky, jet-black eyelashes.

"Nothing more beautiful than a woman on horseback. The two most lovely things in the world. When they are there, together, life is complete."

Am I dreaming? He blows out his nostrils and smiles a little. Then: "Lovely woman, your friend, my compatriot the Princess Tamara."

My heart sinks as it always does when you hear a name pronounced within these walls.

"Yes, she is extremely beautiful."

"Our Georgian women are all like that, you know? Great friend of yours, is she?"

"Yes. Very great."

"A great friend of your husband's too," he says with a look and intonation that can leave no doubt as to his exact meaning.

This is so primitive that I must make an effort to keep from smiling. It is easy to control one's lips, I find, but not one's eyes. . . . It is hardly worth making the effort, perhaps? So I let myself smile with lips and eyes and say:

"Ever so great. I *hope.*"

At this he grins almost admiringly, owning up to my having scored this time.

The Leonardo whispers hurriedly: He is a bully, so are all of them. Steel yourself. You must be blatantly invulnerable.

But, Leonardo ...

Enough, we can discuss it later.

Attila is saying: "Strange that your house should always be full of men, that you should not know any women. Is Tamara really your only woman friend?"

Oh, my God! ... Fool, says the Leonardo, those are the things they know before they ask them. Come on....

To Attila I say: "No, not quite the only one."

"Who else?"

"Well, Daria ..."

"The *Princess* Daria," breaks in the voice of Neo-Narcissus. "Don't you think it most symptomatic that you should have only two friends, both *Princesses?*"

I look round to answer him.

"Look at *me!* You don't turn round!" thunders Attila.

I do look at him and try to make it clear that I am neither worried, hurt, nor shocked by his rudeness, merely astonished. Coldly astonished. Out of the corner of my eye I can see the Bison looking at him too, trying to convey that *that* is quite the wrong way to deal with *this* one.

"Don't you think it strange?" repeats Neo-Narcissus.

I don't want to say that they are by no means the only women we know, so looking up at the ceiling I say quite airily:

"Why strange? There are heaps of titled people in the world." And with a smile to the Bison—"Particularly in your part of the world."

"Oh, everyone is a prince in Georgia," he says, laughing. But his skin has reddened slightly and he walks away.... Is he one of them, I wonder?

"Blood-red sunsets ..." says the Death's-Head dreamily, walking up and down between the window beyond Attila and the door on my left. "Blood-red sunsets! ... A man who is planning murder is very likely to see even a blue sky spattered with blood! Don't you think?" And he stops right in front of me.

"A man who is devoted to the flag of his country, the Red flag of the U.S.S.R., might see its roseate tinge spread over all things, don't you think?"

I try to sound as dreamy and detached as he does. Laughing loud, the Bison pokes the Death's-Head in the ribs and I know that I shall never be forgiven this petty victory. I feel terribly alone.

The Leonardo whispers: Do try not to tease the brutes. Can't you be invulnerable without being aggressive or stupidly "clever"?

Attila says: "I have been looking at Beausobre's book, *The Moneys of the World;* so useful for a code!"

"A code?"

"Yes. A code. As the English use their Bible in the Personal Column of *The Times.*"

"But how?"

"It is for you to tell us *how*"—from behind me the strangely high-pitched tones of the Snake's voice worm themselves into my heart.

"*You* must give us the key to it," adds the Bison, coming towards us again. His voice is impudently gentle and caressing. "The key, you know? That little thing that leads to vast possibilities." And he fumbles with some object in his right hip pocket.

"Out with it!" exclaims Neo-Narcissus, who must be munching a cake, lolling in a large armchair somewhere behind me. And contemptuously he adds: "Why *do* we waste so much time on her!"

The Snake comes round and stares at the bridge of my nose with glassy white-grey eyes.

"You will tell us sooner or later," he says in his strangely sibilant voice. "But it were better for you to tell us now. Not that we torture people—oh, no! But...they torture themselves, you know....They are all torturing themselves" (he waves his hands in a wide and all-embracing gesture). "Beausobre too is torturing himself!"

The Snake's voice breaks on a squeak. His white-grey eyes shine with devilish mirth, but under the mirth there lurks a glint of reflected horror. The reflected horror of something he wants desperately to forget. What can it be?

"The code of Beausobre's book!" he hisses again, coming even closer.

"There is no code."

"You mean *you* do not know that there is a code," suggests the Bison very kindly.

The Snake signals to Attila that he should write down all my words carefully.

"I mean—I *know* that there is no code."

"How can you know?" says Neo-Narcissus. "You don't know everything about him." And they all laugh noisily.

"I do. What I do not know simply is not there. *I* know of no code—so there *is* no code."

"People have told us that there is. Men who know."

"They must be ... dreaming."

"Mad, you mean, mad!" giggles the Snake with demented delight. "No, they are not mad *yet*. But they will be! They *will*." (He comes up still closer to me.) "... We do *not* apply torture." He hisses in a way that would convince anyone that they did.

Attila's eyes have a strange glint in them too.

"I have been counting up how many prisoners on an average go out of their mind in the Inner," he says.

The Bison takes the thing he has been fumbling with out of his pocket and puts it on the desk.

"Pretty toy," he remarks to Attila. "A fool of a terrorist, a chit of a girl no taller than that" (he snaps his fingers about four feet above the floor) "tried to use it the other day. She'll have to be shot, beauty and youth notwithstanding. Quite a pity really. They are such fools, those women!"

It is a minute revolver inlaid with mother-of-pearl. When we were children, Mother had one just like it. She used to take it with her when Father was not there on our five days' cross-country journeys to Alexandrovka in spring and back to Petersburg in the autumn. ...

Was anyone ever so lonely as I am?

Oh, no! jeers the Leonardo, the rest of the world know only joy. You are a unique case even in Russia.

Russia!—I think—one-sixth of the world! And not only in Russia, in other places too, perhaps, men are being tortured by men. ... Why?

"Do you like music?" asks the Bison.

"Music? Yes."

"I was at the opera last night; Keetege, lovely thing! Idiotic all that about paradise, of course. But what music! You paint?"

"Yes, a bit."

"A very strange bit too," remarks the Neo-Narcissus scathingly. He, the Death's-Head and the Snake have gone back to the soft armchairs behind me. They must be looking at some water-colours of mine that the Death's-Head confiscated when he was searching our rooms.

"Why do you paint as though you were mad?" asks Neo-Narcissus, "Does it look mad?"

"Well, I ask you. ... What is it, anyhow?"

"Just dreams."

"Dreams! You should show them to an alienist."

"I had thought of doing so."

After a moment's pause, filled only with the rustle of paper:

"You must really be quite mad, you know?"

"Perhaps."

"Mad people sometimes reveal quite a lot about what is floating round them in the minds of others," says the Snake. "Quite unwittingly too. Super-sensitive barometers, you know. Most useful!"

He comes round and faces me again.

"I think," he says meditatively, "we shall keep you in the Inner for life. You will be our super-sensitive barometer, yes?"

He stares strangely. My heart flutters wildly. It seems to rise to my throat, then above my throat into my head. It is bursting through the top of my skull.... Oh, do not forsake me, Thou....

.   .   .   .   .   *Peace, Child, Peace*   .   .   .   .   .

The Snake's eyes are popping out of his head. His nostrils are very white, they flutter slightly. There are a few tiny drops of sweat above his upper lip. He looks nonplussed and irritated. My jailer comes into the room. Attila must have telephoned for him while I was talking to the others. The jailer and Attila sign the small piece of paper. I get up. The door opens again. Softly, but firmly.

It is the man with the beautiful voice. His eyes are hidden behind smoked spectacles, all his teeth are quite obviously false. His skin is dead-white ... like the bones of small animals, ploughed up in the soft brown earth of a field. He comes towards me very directly, with long, light strides, and holds out his hand. It is big, well shaped, and warm. The examiners stand up. All except the Snake. Someone closes the door.

The man with the beautiful voice holds my hand lightly, bends over it low without raising it at all, and touches it with his lips, in the old-fashioned way in which my father's contemporaries used to: with an inimitable blend of self-effacement and self-assertion. Then, unbending and facing me, he says very simply, as though the presence of the other examiners were a trifle of no importance:

"If ever you wish to see *me, I* shall always be o-n-l-y t-o-o g-l-a-d."

The beauty of his extraordinary voice is so vivid that it seems to have a life of its own. A life of great significance, quite apart from his life. But it is the voice of a man younger than *I* am, let alone my father. Who is he? What can he be, strange creature?

He goes to the door and holds it open for me. With a slight bow to him, I pass out into the corridor, followed closely by my jailer.

Am I really mad? Are they all mad? Is the whole world mad?

The tramp-tramp of our feet sounds drear and hollow up and down and through the maze of passages and staircases. Some bits of the way are stifling-hot, others icy-cold. Some of it is lit up with astonishing brightness. Sometimes the light is very dim. But invariably within the living silence that throbs beyond the walls of the passages and staircases

I can feel the tremor of *smértnaya toska*. However, as we proceed slowly on the way back to my cell, the Leonardo insulates me from all this, wrapping me up in the mantle of his thoughts:

A great bond is formed, he says, between the man who is tortured day in, day out, and the man who day in, day out, tortures him. Greater than there could possibly be between the tortured man and a blithe free citizen who understands nothing because he does not want to see or know a thing. If you ponder on this you may find the justification for your apparently absurd suffering.

But, Leonardo, surely there is no justification for a crowd of well-fed, reasonably strong men bullying a weary, undernourished, half-demented woman who doesn't even know what it is all about.

Don't you know?

Only in a most sweeping, general way.

I was not alluding to that knowledge. If you want to understand, to know the truth about this sort of thing, you must rise higher and look deeper. If you do, you can transform the ghastly bond into that magic wand which changes horror into beauty.... It is unpardonable that anyone should be tortured, even you—if *you* merely leave it at that. But, surely, when you overcome the pain inflicted on you by them, you make *their* criminal record less villainous? Even more, you bring something new into it—a thing of precious beauty. But when, through weakness, cowardice, lack of balance, lack of serenity, you augment your pain, their crime becomes so much the darker, and it is darkened by you. If you could understand this, your making yourself invulnerable would not be *only* an act of self-preservation; it would be a kindness to *Them*.... Look down right into the depths of your heart and tell me—Is it not right for you to be kind to them? Even to them? Particularly to them, perhaps? Is it not right that those men who have no kindness within them should get a surplus of it flowing towards them from without?

The whole of me responds with a "Yes!" like a throb of thundering music. It is so shattering that it makes me stagger. The jailer steadies me: "Take care!" He looks concerned, he has the gentle eyes of a puppy. "All right?" "Yes," and we move on.

Drowsily I think: Oh, Leonardo, what if we are both only mad after all, my dear?

Lying on my spiky bed in the glare of my cell, I cannot keep sufficiently awake to think, nor can I go to sleep entirely and let myself forget everything. My body is a long, thin object full of burning pain. Within the whole of the flaming width and depth and length of it an ice-cold pattern is gradually forming. It must be the nerves of this body of mine. They quiver incessantly and tingle as with the bite of frost. The contracted iciness of this network of nerves smarting within my expanding, burning body causes a feeling of pain so intolerably acute that with a jerk I fling the whole icy maze out of me.

Strange. With their iciness all heat has left my body, every vestige of warmth. I am a block of ice. But hovering above me is the network of my nerves, transformed into an intricate system of looking-glasses. In these looking-glasses the whole of my life is mirrored. Also the life of the Inner. The life of the examiners. The life of Russia. The life of Man. All is quite clear. All is most perfectly intelligible. And nothing matters. How can anything matter when all is cold and clear?

Then in one of the looking-glasses I catch the reflected image of the memory of Peace. The warm, the glowing memory of Delightful Peace.

This iciness that grips me is not peace, it is despair. Peace does not sting either with frost or flame. Peace may not give clear sight, perhaps, but it bestows profoundest insight. Out of the icy wilderness of utter indifference, out of the shattering, all-embracing, chill understanding that wrecks all feeling of security, one flame calls in a limitless dark universe. One flame that still hovers within my iced body, burning bright and straight as the flame of a taper before the Crucifix. Then all in me dies. All except my hearing. And to my hearing there comes a voice:

Out of the confines of eternity I flow to man as light. From man I flow to man as warmth. When the great sun rises in the heart of man, I flow back to the limits of eternity as love. I am the pivot of the human world. I am security. My breath is Peace. Seek in the miracle of warmth flowing from harrowed man to harrowed man. Seek and you will find me.

BETSEY BARTON

The daughter of Bruce Barton, Betsey Barton is one of that small band of people who, having had life cut from under them by accident or disease, have fought against despair and emerged from the struggle stronger than they had been, and with an undiminished if not even increased love of life and of other human beings. At the age of sixteen, her spine was shattered in an automobile accident, and she has never walked again, and never will. It was a bitter turn of fate for a youngster brimful of vitality, spirit, and intelligence, and for a time it was not only her spine which had been shattered. But with the help of her parents and the professional understanding and assistance she was fortunate enough to find she won through to a deeper understanding of life's values, of herself, and of others. She learned, as so many do who have the capacity to learn, that, in her own words, "we only advance through suffering." This is an ancient truth, but a dangerous one, for many of us have not the capacity to endure suffering beyond the ordinary limits which are the lot of every human being. But Betsey Barton had, and out of the inner hell from which she herself emerged, she found herself able to help others who had undergone a similar experience.

From her hard-won knowledge have come four books: *And Now to Live Again, The Long Walk, Shadow of the Bridge,* and *As Love Is Deep.* What follows here are a few pages from *And Now to Live Again,* in which she tells, out of her own and others' experience, how triumph can be wrested from disaster.

And Now to Live Again

I HAD the privilege last winter of getting to know a young man who had been in an accident which had had the same effects as mine. In the arrogant way which we sometimes have, I had believed I might be of some help to him, and he had come to the Institute.

Five months after he had first entered the place he was walking on braces and getting around independently. He worked hard, with great determination and concentration. He took every scrap of information I was able to give him from my experience and put it to good use. Not only was his advance rapid, but his spirit cheered the place there and made the others happier and more hard-working because of his presence.

I visited him after five months, just to see how he was, and my arrogant wish to help him was knocked off. For I saw what he had done, and this gave me so much faith that I could do the same that I determined to go down and work side by side with him every afternoon. By my reaching out to help him, the tables had been turned, and he began to help me ten thousand times more than I had ever dreamed of helping him.

The example of this young man not only inspired me to try once again to walk, but his attitude cheered and puzzled me. His accident had happened only two years before, and yet he showed none of the painful and hesitant signs which I had shown in becoming used to my new life. He forged right ahead, apparently without regrets, helping us all by his marvelous gaiety. I noticed that when he wore his exercise shirt he had a little medal on a chain around his neck, and one day I asked him about it.

I learned then why he had been able to readjust so quickly to his accident, an accident which had been due to a careless mistake even more meaningless and empty than my own. I learned why he had been able to be of such cheer and help, not only to me, but to the rest of us who came in contact with him. It was because he had faith. He had an utter belief in a spirit more powerful than himself which was taking care of him, and which fed him, and which in its infinite wisdom had decreed this test for him. He could not understand the reason for the test, but the way he was to meet it had been plain. And so he had not despaired, he had lost no time in looking back. He had, in the simple trust which pervades his whole being, gone forward, believing.

The view we take of life, what we believe life and its purpose to be, will etch the lines of our reaction to disaster. It is the greatest single determinant in the success or failure of this rebirth, for we are part of infinite spirit which created us and which, in its nature, requires that we believe in it if we are to find happiness. And only a belief in the spirit and an understanding of it can answer the questions which torture the faithless when disaster strikes.

Thus if reëducation is to be complete, it must make this final contribution to our total being (or perhaps it is better to say, his first contribution). The Center I envisage as a way-station in which this rebirth would come about would be essentially a religious place, where not only the hungers of the mind and body and heart might be fed, but the hunger without which the other three can not be fed: the hunger of the spirit.

For those of us who are without any faith when we are hurt the going must be hard. The little faith I had before my accident was knocked clean out of me by its impact. And because rescue was so long delayed in reaching me, it took many years to build up a faith which could withstand whatever might come. Because the majority of us will be caught without a faith when we are hit, it might be useful to record here some of the thoughts I had then. The pitiful wandering of their quest might find its echo in your heart.

I was concerned at first, most of all, with a sense of sin, of guilt. My religion had taught me that when we sin we are punished for our sin. I was being punished, obviously. Therefore, I concluded that some way, somehow, I had unwittingly committed some terrible sin. What sin it could be that demanded such a drastic expiation I could not imagine. I searched my past for some subtle crime which had been so far-reaching in its hurt of others that it demanded this cruel purgation.

I was reminded of this reaction of mine two years ago, by the last sentence a little friend of ours spoke before she died. This child, barely seventeen, had been the friend of my younger brother. They had been out several times together in Boston and had fun and they were to have had a date one evening in the winter, which she had called off because of a previous engagement. My brother had told her it did not matter, and they had arranged to meet the next day.

The next day we heard she was in the hospital. She had gone to the Cocoanut Grove, been caught in the fire there, and had been severely burned. The child lay in her hospital bed without saying anything. They made her comfortable and waited, almost hoping she would die, for if she lived she would be terribly scarred. She said nothing until the time came. And then she cried a little and spoke the thought that had been holding her there in its grasp so quietly. "Dad always told me not to go to night clubs," she whispered. Then she lay in silence again until she died.

The feeling of guilt comes to those of us who were in an accident which might have been avoided had we been allowed to see ahead a little, had we been a bit more careful. And the whole question of pain and of suffering turns its face to us when we find that we are not guilty, really, that disaster is not punishing us in the way it should for some wrong we had committed, that it seems to fall on good and bad, on the just and the unjust. And so in the beginning the problem of pain tortured me.

The unknown soldier returns to demand why he had to die in what seemed a meaningless explosion of shrapnel after the signing of the Armistice had been agreed upon. His death seems to him to have been useless and devoid of purpose. For those of us who did not die in our particular explosions of accident and disease, the question lies pressingly at hand. It becomes a major concern, greater than the desire for health, for love, for a useful life. It may be that we can not even take up the tools and start to rebuild our lives until the question is answered. For there are times when the hunger of the quest within us tears at us with its starving fingers and we are unable to make any outward effort until its aching void is somehow filled.

Each person finds the answers in different ways within the confines of his own heart. But it may be useful to my contemporaries who are now being shattered in this war to find that another once had as little faith as they perhaps have, and still was able to assemble one from the ruins of her life.

Three years after my accident I was still questioning.

"*May 20, 1937:* Such hurt as this should be a spur to action. Such pain as this should help me achieve my end, for all live things are born out of pain, and surely there is no better thing than life. Renewed vigor, strength, and vitality should come to me now if pain is the creator. But as I look about me and think of others like myself I see that it can not always be so.

"Look at all the invalids who die without recovery and are the more hopeless for their wounds are man-made and not the result of plague. Thousands everywhere, if you but look behind the frail veil of normal people. There must be a reason for this buried life, this stifled life, these myriads of sufferers. Oh, God, there has to be!

"*May 24:* Such a silly fate. To go on and on down life's road with the compliments of all about me and myself in the midst of it, straining my soul to appear what I am not. For you see I have no outlook, no philosophy. I have gained no peace by my hours of idleness. Underneath I am just as puzzled, just as bewildered as you. And the more so when I see those of you who are older, who have lived, and who still have found nothing, nothing at all which you really understand, nothing of the beginning and the machinery and the pattern which make sense to you. That is really why I am bewildered, because there is nothing to look up to in you. For when I do look up I find that you, too, have failed.

"*May 29:* Accident is the unknown quantity. There is no allowance in the universal scheme for survival of the ego and therefore no need to curb accident. Everything has its scheme, its pattern, but accident. That is the lone wolf. It has never been tamed. Because accident is wanton and strikes anywhere and any time, it is, in the end, the master. It has foiled purpose and smudged up the true end and the true beginning. Through it creation has attained perfection only in decay. A world is ours in which decay is governed by accident. It destroys. It kills. It maims. It does all this without reason, without pause for merit or worth.

"If this is not the truth, why then are some of our friends snatched from life before they have yet had the time to prove themselves worthy of life? Accident is the final spendthrift, and our trouble is that we care. There is no reason why our friends or we should survive, except that we want to. We were made to care. If we did not, no matter then whether this friend or that laid down his life. We, poor creatures that we are, only want those we love to remain close to us, so; and closer still. Closer to us so that all this business of being able to think and feel will not seem so purposeless, so alone. We can not stand to be alone; that is why we care.

"So those of us who are left behind, waiting for accident to end our span, wish only for one thing which would lessen our grief, make us feel more necessary to living. For if this one thing becomes clear to us, we will know that we count, that those who have gone count, that there is a reason. We want to know, to feel, somehow, that these terrible deaths of our friends whose lives have just begun, who have walked for so little while upon the earth and rested but a moment here within our ken, we want to know if their dying was for a reason, for some good. If we knew this, then we ourselves would be reassured. And ready to believe...."

The journal goes on endlessly; it became a sort of safety valve for my emotional upheavals; and its wonderings are thrown into greater chaos by the second automobile accident. Here, it seemed, all my forebodings were justified. Accident was indeed the lone wolf. Senseless, hungry, wandering, unreasonable. The first accident might conceivably have been deserved. I might have been punished simply for being careless. But this one in which another car had smashed into us could not have been brought upon me by myself. This one had not been deserved.

Every attempt I made to reason about these new broken bones failed. The first accident I had reconciled myself to at last. It had been my fault; I could see its beginnings in many things; in some ways I had asked for it. But this one had been blank chance. I saw the cause without reason and the effect unreasonable. There was no right in it. The turbulent, meaningless workings of accident engulfed me. I thought of all the upheavals and plagues that daily cut down the lives of all of us. These were uncontrollable. Here the puny efforts of men to seek order out of chaos met their match. The wilful, senseless work of disaster had no harnesser and could not be understood.

My belief in the meaninglessness of life and its purpose was strengthened as I fought with a curious resignation back to health. I came not to care what happened to my body or what they did to it, if they would leave *me* alone. Life was a matter of luck. Each effort, each attempt I made to construct, was always to be swept back with doubled force into the black craw of my luck, which merely happened to be bad.

A couple of years passed then, years in which I went from one man to another, seeking help. Seven years after my original accident, and four years after the second one, years in which I had not ceased to question the universe and to believe that there was no satisfactory answer, I came to my teacher, the man who was to lead me back to health. And as I worked with him and grew stronger, so did the ground within me for belief become fertile. Strength gave me courage, and courage dared to hope that there would be an answer.

A hint of the answer came to me one day in Arizona when Mother and I drove across the desert, through the yellow, dry flatness, into the valley between the hills on the other side of town. There spring had come. The hills with their sharp, rude shrubbery of greasewood and cactus were transformed from ugliness into a glowing tapestry of bright desert colors. The whole dead landscape had come to life. Everywhere the touch of a magic vitalizing force spread deep hues of renewed fertility.

We gazed together, Mother and I, and suddenly the cold dam of bitterness broke within me and the tears rushed to my eyes. The sight of the hills, so alive now after their winter death, so blooming, here forever to flower and fade, to die and come to life through the years, was somehow good. It was as good as the sun had been on my upturned face after the dark hospital room; it reassured me. Here it seemed the giant destructive force I had deplored was sublimated. This was part of the answer to the idiot accident. The force that makes the deserts renew themselves is mightier than death or hurt, and for a while I renewed myself in the sight of that flowering.

A warm feeling swept over me, a love for the surge, the vital, throbbing force that is creativity. I felt instinctively then, and I know now, that to merge with this principle, to accept its ways and workings and purpose without rancor, without rebellion, would be worthy of all the love I could muster for any one or anything, and would finally erase the futile desperation I had felt at the stupidity of what I then called fate.

Through this backward look a pattern becomes apparent to the discerning eye. I was being forced out of myself. The tightness of my-

self as the center of the universe was being worn away. I could only
wonder that it had taken two such blows to even start the process. I
was being carefully led to notice the vastness of the forces at work
around me. I was being asked to awaken to the knowledge of the
creative rather than the destructive spirit. I was being taught.

And so it seemed to me that the bloody wake of accident can be
redeemed and is redeemed in one way: through our reaction to it.
What we have refused to learn by ourselves may be taught in this
harsher way so that finally we accept it and look it in the face. The
forces at work around us seem to hold the seeds of divinity in them as
they patiently bring us to greater understanding. And if we allow ourselves to grow in vision the bitterest suffering can be said to have been
worth while.

The awakening of understanding in one of us was enacted for me last
winter by a young girl who, like myself and the young man mentioned
earlier, was getting used to the loss of her legs. She was dark and
pretty and, I thought, very appealing as she sat beside me in a pair of
cherry colored shorts and a work shirt, with her legs now encased
in braces. She had put a flower in her hair in honor of my coming and
this touched me, too.

She asked me the things she needed to know, and then she turned
to me and shyly laid her hand on my arm. "There is something going
on inside of me that is very strange," she said. "I haven't told any one
about it, yet. Do you mind if I tell you?"

I shook my head and she went on. "You know what it is like," she
said, "because you have felt it, too. But *they* can not. No matter how
hard they try, with their minds, they can not. That's why it is so good
to talk to you. But the funny thing is that I don't mind, that is, losing
my legs this way. Because now I am seeing things I did not see before."
She looked at me questioningly, and when she saw that I had come
with her, she continued.

"Why, do you know I am almost grateful this happened to me. I was
so careless, so spoiled, so blind before. And now I see. Look—it's like
this: The other day I moved my toe for the first time, just a flicker, but
it was something after not having moved it for two years. I was thrilled.
I was in heaven. I have never known such happiness. And I told *them,*
and I showed them. And they looked, but they did not feel it as I did.
They did not know, because you see here is a miracle. I am alive. I
did not die. And now I can take a step, one; and maybe tomorrow, two;
and I will not get so tired."

She had been talking fast, and her eyes were big and very black.

"I see them pass in the halls. Working, walking, going about their
chores. Unconcerned, half-asleep. Dead. And I hold my hands up and

move my fingers and see their beauty. And I know the miracle now, through this, and they do not."

The miracle of the creative spirit. The spirit that we can only partially understand, limited as we are in ourselves, but which we can grow in understanding of throughout our lives. And so in some degree, find more of the answer there must be to what appears to be accident, the answer that lies hidden in the pattern woven by the loving spirit that is too subtle for these eyes to see.

To grow in this sight, to grow in vision of the nature and the purpose of the spirit, this would seem to me to have been what my accidents were teaching me. They were showing me that the law of life is the law of growth: the law which involves the feeling that all of life is a school, an intelligence test, a hatching process, in which we are always being subjected to rebirths, in which we must move ahead from one life to another, from one sphere of realization to another. Moving, breathing, evolving, by coöperating with the universal process, into greater aliveness, deeper intelligence, more acute intuition and insight.

"Growth, order, cultivation, art, these are the proper means by which man displaces accident and subdues the vacant external powers of the universe," wrote Lewis Mumford. "The way of growth is not to become more powerful but to become more human." This then is the task we must believe to be demanded of us by our rebirth: that we quicken ourselves and grow. It is the challenge flung at us by disaster. And if we would be whole, if we would be healed, we must meet it and answer it; not by looking for miracles from without, for the heavenly hand to reach down and caress us into sleep, but by waking to grow in the lawful way, and in so doing to meet the test that is given us in each moment by the love that created us: that we move in the direction which allows the spirit to work through us.

Thus, it has seemed to me from my experience, and from that of my people, that whether we attain to complete wholeness again or not through our reëducation, if we are born again out of disaster with a faith where there was none before, or if the faith we had before is somehow strengthened, then life will be not only bearable, but meaningful, an experience which will expand for the rest of our days in beauty and in richness.

JOHN GUNTHER

Born in Chicago in 1901, John Gunther became one of the most celebrated foreign correspondents of his time—a time in which the world-
ranging newspaper reporter achieved a degree of importance in the
public eye which had never been accorded him before. His career in
foreign correspondence began in London in 1924, and was eventually
to embrace every continent and nearly every country in the world.
There is probably no more widely traveled man alive.

He first won fame with his book *Inside Europe,* which has been
followed by a series of others bearing similar titles—*Inside Asia, Inside
Latin America, Inside U.S.A., Inside Africa*—together with novels,
biography, current history, and a vast amount of writing for periodicals.
A man of great energy and vitality, he has a remarkable mastery of
detail and with it a sure sense of the interesting and significant fact.

Mr. Gunther is represented here by a selection from one of his books
which stands apart from all the others. *Death Be Not Proud* is a
portrait of his son, and an account of the boy's gallant fight against a
tumor of the brain of which he died at the age of seventeen. Every
reader, I think, will find it a deeply moving record, and of all John
Gunther's books, this one, I suspect, is the one in which he takes the
greatest pride—as well he might.

Death Be Not Proud

SMOOTHLY, steadily, ominously, the next two weeks slipped by.
The bulge disappeared entirely for an interval and was replaced
by what we had prayed for for a year, a concavity. Johnny was worried,
though. The bandage was too big for him to feel through. On May 4
he said, "I must ask Connie [Traeger] if Mount got out as much as
Putnam did." He said to a visitor, "I wonder if the bump is still there.
I'm not convinced." Also he began to inquire with great earnestness
why a plate had not been inserted, which must have meant that, finally,

he had given up hope that the bone would grow back of itself. He said indignantly to one friend, "If only they'd put in a plate, one of the new types of plate made of tantalum, at least I'd be able to swim and sail."

Frances, who was holding up wonderfully under a strain that had become unendurable, went off to Florida for a brief rest, and, with my sister standing by, I got away later for a week in Virginia. There came one violent hour in the solarium before I left. Johnny was passionate and stormy. He exploded, "I'm always in a haze! I was in a haze up in school last year! The tumor must have been starting then, only nobody knew it! People kidded me about it, and it was very disagreeable. I talked it over with Steve [one of his classmates] but came to no conclusion. I'm sensitive about being kidded. I didn't like it, and I don't like it now! It wasn't my fault that I was in such a haze!"

He relaxed. "My mother and father think that anything connected with me is remarkable. These strange parents..."

Mount dropped in and he turned to him furiously. "Get me out of here by crack of dawn Thursday, or I'll sneak out by myself! Stop all this persecution!" He asked him to speed up his recovery by giving him electric shock therapy. Mount, with his deadpan face and the grave, warm brown eyes, was so dumfounded by Johnny's outburst that he did not know what to say. He fumbled and tried to joke. "Electricity costs a lot and we save it for our serious cases."

Then Johnny attacked my book. "You step backward to be fair too much. You ought to have more muckracking (sic). You beat around the bush. You should have begun the Dewey chapter with the simple statement, 'Nobody trusts Tom Dewey!' That was what you were trying to say in five thousand words. Libel lawyers? Fire the libel lawyers! You've written three books, they've all sold half a million copies, tell Cass to take it or leave it and fire the lawyers!"

But there were lighter moments. One nurse said, "I'll be just like your mother to you." He answered, "Okay, provided you don't go too far." I was being profiled by Dick Rovere of the *New Yorker*, and I brought Rovere up there one day and Johnny looked him over and said, "So you're the hatchet man." Later he told me, "Well, I hope he digs up a lot of dirt about you." I said Rovere was a fine fellow. Johnny: "Wait till you see what kind of piece he writes."

"Did you sleep well?" the nurse asked one morning.

"Like an octopus."

This is, I believe, the last letter he ever wrote. He had pleaded with his mother to get away for her brief holiday, and while she was in Florida he telephoned her a couple of times and then wrote this:

DEAR MOTHER,

Today is the last day at this——hospital! Thanks for your letters, and be sure to remember the words of wisdom which I tried to impart to you a few minutes before your departure. I feel fine but seem to be struck with a most monstrous attack of lazyness. What a job it is for my poor nurse to get me up in the morning! I've gotten into an awful habit of drinking coffee in the morning, and find it necessary to keep me awake—at least enough so I don't fall asleep and drown in the bathtub!

It made me happy to hear that you will be returning soon. In a week or so I will go back to Deerfield to take the exams, and to say hello and goodbye!

O! How wonderful food is again! Bacon and eggs! salt! steaks! How I eat! mushrooms! last night I played poker with some fellow patients! —great fun! I've almost finished the English anthology which we were reading

lots of love and kisses

JOHNNY

He was cleared to go home on May 15, only two weeks after the operation. So for the last time Johnny checked out of Neurological. He ended the experience with a wry wisecrack. We marched out and I said the hospital knew us so well by this time that they sent the bill by mail. Johnny jibed: "You mean by parcel post."

*   *   *

What a lot goes into a life, into a brain—all that the fragile shell of cranium holds! Usually the size of a skull, and the brain concealed within, is an index of mental capacity. Johnny's brain, we learned later, weighed two thousand grams. The average for a normal, fully-grown male is fifteen hundred. The largest male brain ever known weighed 2,222.

*   *   *

He remained pretty well, but now it became increasingly difficult for him to fix his belt or shoelaces. He was too proud to admit this, and Marie, our admirable housekeeper, helped him to put on his shoes one morning. Johnny said, "I'm only giving way to your maternal instinct." Carl, our old elevator man, wept once when he saw how warped his face was and how difficult it was for him to walk. Johnny said to him coolly, "I haven't had any chance to exercise, and so my foot is tired."

Marie told me of another colloquy. A schoolmate whom he had not seen for years called up.

JOHNNY: "I should warn you that my head is bandaged because I have a brain tumor."

BOY: "I've never known anybody with a brain tumor."

JOHNNY: "You know me."

BOY: "What's it like?"

JOHNNY: "I've been lucky. I have no pain, and there has been no impairment of my faculties."

The boy came over that afternoon, and Johnny cleaned him up in a game of chess.

The effort to pretend that the tumor was nothing cost him dearly; the price of his invincible fight was great fatigue. It took a miserable lot out of him to pretend to ignore what he must have now known to be the truth, that he wasn't getting any better. The faraway look was in his eyes more often now. But it was impossible for us not to support his optimism, because any discouragement would have been a crushing blow. All he had now was his will to live. We had to keep that up at any cost. The cord of life was wearing very thin, and if we took away hope, it would be bound to snap.

After a struggle one morning he gave up trying to tie his tie, and things would drop out of his left hand more frequently. "My left hand is a mess." The hand cupped sharply and he looked frightened. "The nerves are crazy in this left hand. I can't get it open."

He always loved to joke with me about my size. I said one day that I was tired enough to stay asleep until I starved to death. Reply: "That would take quite some time, Father." I had a massage and reported that I had lost some weight. Comment: "How much did the masseur lose?"

He read the papers carefully and with Frances listened to every important broadcast. He said, "The reason why the Republicans don't offend and oppose those Southern Democrats is because they may need their help some day." Some friends talked once about the great vitality of the United States. He asked, "But may not vitality end in smugness? Isn't it possible, too, that vitality could express itself in reaction, in the wrong direction?" He turned to me. "In Volume Two, hit them hard, Father!" I can tell you all right whom he meant by "them"—anybody cheap, anybody shoddy or vulgar, anybody selfish and corrupt, anybody on-the-make or feathering his nest in the name of false principle.

He dropped a pill.

"Is it still all right?" I asked stupidly enough, reaching for it.

"It will be if you pick it up off the floor."

On Sunday mornings Frances read to him from the Hebrew Bible.

the Christian Gospels, the Hindu scriptures, Confucius, and other eastern sages. One of the last things he read was the Psalms. I read to him,
too, though not so much. One of the books he was going through for
English was a poetry anthology; he would look bored or turn away
whenever he chanced on a poem about Death.

One day came an unbearably moving moment when he announced,
as if casually, that perhaps he was having the bump for *us!*

The phone rang on May 25 and Mr. Boyden's cheerful, assured voice
came through. "I've gone through Johnny's papers and examinations,"
he said. "You know he did extra work in his freshman year and has
some surplus credits. He has caught up to his class in everything except
one examination, and we are going to give him a diploma. This
isn't a favor. It is Johnny's right. Come up next week, and he will graduate with his class."

Johnny yawned and tried to look casual, and we all burst into tears.

We drove to Deerfield on May 27, and Johnny graduated on June 4,
though he had not been to school for fourteen months. The days passed
in a proud procession, and I think probably it was the happiest week of
his life.

It seemed chilly when we started, and Johnny, as always extracting
compensation out of any ill fortune, said, "Well, at least we don't have
a heat wave." We passed through Hartford and he asked, "Were you
here when you did your research?—I wouldn't dream of asking how
long you stayed, probably half an hour." I was full of nerves as we
got near Deerfield with its stiff old houses and great fanlike elms, and
impatiently I asked him if I had overshot the side road and did he
recognize any landmarks. He replied gently, "You know I don't see
well out of my left eye."

Then without the slightest self-consciousness he took his place in his
class. He sat between old friends in the dining hall (the instructors had
warned them) and Frances whispered that they should inconspicuously
cut his meat if necessary. The boys stared at him for a second as if he
were a ghost—of course his hair had not grown back fully after the last
operation and he wore a white turban—and then accepted his appearance without question.

Every evening after dinner an informal ceremony takes place at
Deerfield which is one of the distinguishing marks of this magnificent
school; each boy from Freshman to Senior meets with Mr. Boyden,
and the roll of the entire school is called. The boys are heaped together
on the floor. Usually there is a casualty or two—some youngsters hurt
in a football game—for whom there are big leather chairs. Johnny
eased himself into one of these, and his name was called in the roll

exactly as if he had never been absent for a moment. Then he limped slowly and proudly to the Senior Dorm where he would have been living this past year, and looked at what should have been his room with a piercing yearning. Boys were moving back and forth in the orderly bustle that precedes commencement. Johnny had the attitude of one who is both a participant in and a spectator of a great event. Mr. Boyden crept up to us and asked if we were sure he would not get too tired. Then he joined calmly in a bull session.

It was decided that he should sleep in the infirmary—a building he knew only too exasperatingly well. The next morning we came to pick him up at what we thought was a reasonable hour. But he had left the building before eight, alone, and was at that moment taking the final exam in chemistry! He passed it B Minus—though he had never taken a regular chemistry course in his life.

Later that day I bumped into him accidentally on the bright sunlit grass as he dragged himself from behind a hedge in shadow. His left shoulder sagged: his arm hung almost useless; his mouth was twisted with effort; the left side of his lip sank down; his eyes were filmy; he was happy. "Oh, pardon me, sir," Johnny said. He had not recognized me, and thought that I was some master he did not know.

Everybody tried hard to keep him from being too active. But he said, "Walking around this way helps the wound heal." Frances told him to sit around in the sun—how they both loved the sun!—and get brown and he answered, "All you are interested in, Mother, is my color!" When he had trouble with knife and fork one evening, he told her in exquisite parody of what she often said, "Be patient. Believe in calmness and Nirvana." It was a lovely day the next day and Johnny spent an hour learning some calculus from a fellow student. He worked out the equations on the bottom of a paper plate during a picnic lunch in the soft grass. Frances remonstrated that he might be getting tired. He replied briefly, "There's no future to just sitting."

The day before graduation was strenuous, with a lunch for the parents at noon and then a baseball game which Johnny watched with serious interest for about four innings. The dress-up banquet that night, to celebrate among other things Mr. Boyden's forty-fifth year as headmaster, lasted three hours; Johnny did not miss a minute of it. He tramped across the lawn afterward, with his classmate Henry Eisner holding his hand, for the off-the-record talk Mr. Boyden gives each graduating class. Then the class, standing under the trees in a night grown chilly, serenaded the Boydens on the front porch. Johnny, on the outskirts of the massed pack of boys, looked suddenly exhausted, and I slipped away from the adults to join him inconspicuously, standing just behind him. He did not mind, though as a rule he loathed having

us anywhere near him at school. I was afraid he might fall. Then I
heard his light, silvery tenor chime in with the other voices. The song
floated across the lawn and echoed back. We hiked to the infirmary
and Johnny ran into a classmate who had won an award. "Congratulations!" he snapped briskly.

The next morning the boys assembled early for the quarter-mile
walk to the white-frame Deerfield church, arranging themselves four
abreast in order of their height. I did not think Johnny could manage
such a march. He shook us off and disappeared. The procedure is that
the boys, reaching the church, line up behind the pews, and then walk
one by one down the center aisle, as each name is called. Mr. Flynt, the
president of the board of trustees, then shakes hands with each boy,
giving him his diploma in the left hand. We explained that Johnny
might not be able to grasp the smooth roll of diploma with his left
fingers, and asked Mr. Flynt to try to slip it into the right hand instead.
The boys began to march in slowly, and though Johnny should have
been conspicuous with his white bandage, we did not see him and I
was in an agony fearing that he had fallen out. Mr. Boyden, sweeping
the assembly with his all-embracing sharp affectionate glance, caught
Frances's eye and nodded to her reassuringly. One by one the names
were called out, and each boy disassociated himself from the solid group
and marched forward alone. The call was alphabetical, and by the time
the G's were reached we were limp with suspense, since we did not
know for sure that Johnny had even got into the church. As each boy
passed down the aisle, there was applause, perfunctory for some, pronounced for others. Gaines, Gillespie, Goodwin, Griffin, Gunther.
Slowly, very slowly, Johnny stepped out of the mass of his fellows and
trod by us, carefully keeping in the exact center of the long aisle, looking neither to the left nor the right, but straight ahead, fixedly, with
the white bandage flashing in the light through the high windows, his
chin up, carefully, not faltering, steady, but slowly, so very slowly. The
applause began and then rose and the applause became a storm, as every
single person in that old church became whipped up, tight and tense,
to see if he would make it. The applause became a thunder, it rose and
soared and banged, when Johnny finally reached the pulpit. Mr. Flynt
carefully tried to put the diploma in his right hand, as planned. Firmly
Johnny took it from right hand to left, as was proper, and while the
whole audience rocked now with release from tension, and was still
wildly, thunderously applauding, he passed around to the side and,
not seeing us, reached his place among his friends.

That evening we talked of Harvard. Some of the boys were getting
their admission notices, and Johnny, now that he had actually been

graduated, wondered when his would come. He was impatient. He had a great sense of the passage of time.

Everything that Johnny suffered was in a sense repaid by the few heroic moments of that walk down the center aisle of that church. This was his triumph and indomitable summation. Nobody who saw it will ever forget it, or be able to forget the sublime strength of will and character it took.

ELIENA KRYLENKO

Eliena Krylenko (Mrs. Max Eastman), who died in 1956 at the age of sixty-one, was a ballet dancer and a gifted painter, but marked as her achievement was in those fields, it was overshadowed by the rare and vibrant quality of her personality. In common with many of her friends, I have never known a man or woman who exuded so much joy in living. Her smile and laugh were gaiety incarnate; her modesty endearing; her interest in a host of things, unquenchable; her spirit, undying. Less than a year before her physical death she had fallen ill of cancer. I reprint here, because it is such a moving document, the words of greeting and farewell she wrote a few weeks before she died, addressed to those of her friends who summered or lived the year round in the place she loved the best, the island of Martha's Vineyard. Her message was published in the *Vineyard Gazette,* shortly after her death.

Undying Spirit

ONCE more I want to say a word of greeting and of best wishes to my dear friends and fellow-citizens of Gay Head—those whom I have known personally and those whom I knew only by sight. We have shared for fifteen years so many activities, so many gay or disastrous events: the war, the hurricanes, fires, weddings, wedding anniversaries, voting, square-dances (with Adrian calling), red-brown cranberry days, exhilarating mornings scalloping on the pond, and above all the happy hours you let me spend with your children dancing in the town hall.

It moved me deeply today to learn from Amos of your concern about me, which means that you accept me as a part of your lives. I have felt happy and at peace ever since Max agreed that East Pasture is to be the place of my rest, and that he is not going to leave me and our home here. Now I can feel that I am just stepping aside on the shore, joining the others that landed ahead of me—dear Betty Ryan, and friendly Lindus, and Vi, and gay and vibrant Adrian, his lovely wife, and the others we remember—to watch you go scalloping in winter on a bright sunny day.

Another reason your concern makes me happy is that it tells me I am leaving Max among friends. Perhaps you and he, with the help of a few hurricanes, will be able to stave off the onrush of "progress" and preserve some of the simple and quiet beauty of this legendary land. I hope so.

And now my love to you all and good luck.

ELIENA KRYLENKO-EASTMAN

September, 1956